John Wetlispoch
817 Block Road
Joliet, IL
815 722 3724

EDUCATIONAL ADMINISTRATION

CONCEPTS AND PRACTICES

EDUCATIONAL ADMINISTRATION

CONCEPTS AND PRACTICES

FRED C. LUNENBURG
University of Louisville

ALLAN C. ORNSTEIN
Loyola University of Chicago

WADSWORTH PUBLISHING COMPANY

Belmont, California
A Division of Wadsworth, Inc.

To Our Children

Cherie and McNeil
Every day, without knowing it, you add meaning to my life   (FCL)

Jason, Stacey, and Joel
Remember the past, hold on to your memories;
face the future with boldness and vision;
always be generous, wise, and optimistic   (ACO)

EDUCATION EDITOR   Suzanna Brabant
EDITORIAL ASSISTANTS   Laurie Wiegler and Andrea Varni
PRODUCTION   Mary Douglas
PRINT BUYER   Martha Branch
PERMISSIONS EDITOR   Jeanne Bosschart
DESIGNER   Diane Beasley
DEVELOPMENTAL EDITORS   Mary Arbogast and Judith McKibben
COPY EDITOR   Betty Duncan-Todd
TECHNICAL ILLUSTRATOR   John Foster
COMPOSITOR   Omegatype Typography, Inc.
COVER   Adriane Bosworth
SIGNING REPRESENTATIVES   Jonelle Calon, Elizabeth Covello

Printed in the United States of America

1 2 3 4 5 6 7 8 9 10—95 94 93 92 91

Library of Congress Cataloging in Publication Data

Lunenburg, Frederick C.
    Educational administration : concepts and practices / Fred C.
Lunenburg, Allan C. Ornstein.
       p.   cm.
    Includes bibliographical references and indexes.
    ISBN 0-534-14850-6
    1. School management and organization—United States.
I. Ornstein, Allan C.   II. Title.
LB2805.L82   1991
371.2′00973—dc20   90-47183
                                           CIP

CONTENTS

II ADMINISTRATIVE PROCESSES   87

III   THE STRUCTURAL FRAMEWORK FOR EDUCATION   243

IV ADMINISTRATION OF PROGRAMS AND SERVICES   379

ADMINISTRATIVE ADVICE

PRO/CON DEBATES

PREFACE

Educational administrators face a challenging and changing climate in our nation's schools. In the past, textbooks in educational administration have focused mainly on theory and research as a way of providing a knowledge base and preparation for students and professionals. In *Educational Administration: Concepts and Practices*, we have attempted to go beyond this tradition by including, in addition to comprehensive coverage of theory and research, a third component: practical applications that help educational administrators make use of the knowledge base they acquire. This practical, applied component makes our book a unique entry to the literature and a resource that we believe will enhance the abilities of future and current educational administrators to become effective leaders in our changing educational climate.

The practical and applied component of *Educational Administration: Concepts and Practices* can be found in many aspects of this text.

- New and unique coverage of topics such as women and minorities, careers, organizational change, curriculum development, and personnel administration are included.
- Chapter openings begin with five to eight questions designed to focus the reader's attention on the major issues within the chapter.
- "Administrative Advice" sections (three to four per chapter) demonstrate how significant concepts can be applied to administrative practice.
- "Pro/Con Debates" (one per chapter) illustrate opposing perspectives on major issues facing educational administrators.
- Summaries at the ends of chapters highlight critical points and especially salient issues in theory, research, and applications.

- A list of key terms and discussion questions at the end of each chapter stimulate application of concepts and enhance understanding of the chapter.
- Extensive documentation throughout and suggestions for additional readings at the end of each chapter encourage readers to pursue further exploration of significant subject matter.

ORGANIZATION OF THE TEXT

This book contains sixteen chapters in four major parts. The introductory chapter defines the field, looks at how it came into existence, and presents a conceptual model which provides a framework for the remainder of the book. The next chapter focuses on several alternative approaches to organizational structure. The last chapter in this opening part provides a cultural context for the study and application of educational administration.

After this foundation is provided, Part II examines the basic administrative processes with chapters on motivation, leadership, decision making, communication, and organizational change. Part III focuses on the structural framework for education. The chapter on the federal government and education is followed by the state role in education, and the chapter on the local school district is followed by legal considerations in education. Part IV explores the administration of programs and services. Specific chapters deal with curriculum development, school finance, personnel administration, and careers in educational administration.

The four parts and sixteen chapters of the book are relatively self-contained. Thus, an entire part, selected chapters, or even portions of chapters, could be deleted or studied in a different sequence without damaging the flow or content of the book. This book is the result of a team effort of the two authors; however, individual authors assumed responsibility for certain parts of the book as follows: Dr. Lunenburg, Chapters 1 through 8 and 12, 15, and 16; and Dr. Ornstein, Chapters 9, 10, 11, 13, and 14.

ACKNOWLEDGMENTS

This book has been a cooperative effort between scholars and experienced editors and publishers. We wish to thank Linda Tinelli Sheive, Educational Administration Department Chair at SUNY Oswego, for conducting and writing the Pro/Con Debates. We wish to express our appreciation to the reviewers and others whose suggestions led to improvements in this book:

Paul Baker	Illinois State University
Dale L. Bolton	University of Washington
Norman Boyles	Iowa State University
James A. Conway	The State University of New York at Buffalo
Philip A. Cusick	Michigan State University
Andrew E. Dubin	San Francisco State University
Janet Fredericks	Northeastern Illinois University
Lloyd E. Frohreich	University of Wisconsin, Madison
Anita M. Pankake	Kansas State University
Glenn B. Schroeder	University of Northern Colorado
Linda Tinelli Sheive	The State University of New York at Oswego

We also thank a number of people at Wadsworth whose contributions made this a much better book. Among these are Suzanna Brabant, Acquisitions Editor; Laurie Wiegler and Andrea Varni, Editoral Assistants; Mary Arbogast and Judith McKibben, Developmental Editors; Mary Douglas, Production Editor; Betty Duncan-Todd, Copy Editor; Jeanne Bosschart, Permissions Editor; and Hal Humphrey, Production Services Coordinator.

For their help with the numerous critical tasks of manuscript preparation, we would like to thank Sandy Hartz, Linda Moore, and Kim Simpson of the Univeristy of Louisville. We are grateful to Raphael O. Nystrand, Dean of the School of Education at the University of Louisville, for creating an environment and contributing the resources necessary to complete this book. Special thanks is also extended to Loyola University's Research Services, especially Tom Bennett, who provided funds for secretarial assistance. Finally, Dr. Ornstein must thank Valerie, his wife and partner, who has always been understanding and encouraging.

Fred C. Lunenburg
Allan C. Ornstein

FOREWORD

During the past decade, the nation's attention has again been riveted on education. Numerous publications offer a myriad of recommendations focused on what must be done to improve the quality of education in America. This intense desire for a new and restructured education process offers many windows of opportunity for positive change.

When school reform efforts are directed to and given a sense of direction by those local leaders who are responsible for effective change in our nation's schools, the results have been favorable. *Educational Administration: Concepts and Practices*, will serve as a valuable primer for prospective school leaders as they work toward effecting change in an orderly, efficient, and effective manner.

Its authors, Fred Lunenburg and Allan Ornstein, have addressed both the concepts surrounding educational change and the processes they feel are essential for improvement, and they have done it in a forthright and interesting manner. In addition, the authors have discussed the fundamental principles of effective administrative leadership, including the need to effectively manage the process of collaboration and coordinate improvement efforts.

Creative, high quality leadership is essential to the reform and restructuring of American education, as our schools strive to meet the needs and challenges of our society.

Richard D. Miller
Executive Director
American Association of
School Administrators

THE AUTHORS

Fred C. Lunenburg is associate professor of educational administration at the University of Louisville. The author of numerous publications on leadership and organizational climate, he was superintendent of schools for the Elkhorn (Wisconsin) Public Schools and high school principal for the Oshkosh (Wisconsin) Public Schools. Dr. Lunenburg has an extensive research program at the University of Louisville and teaches organizational theory and administrative research. He is a consultant to private- and public-sector organizations and conducts workshops on organizational behavior in the United States and abroad. He has recently been involved in leadership training for the Kentucky Principal Intern Program and the National Association of Secondary School Principals Assessment Center project.

Allan C. Ornstein is professor of education at Loyola University Chicago. He is the author of 25 books and some 350 articles in education, including *Foundations of Education*, the number-one selling text for the last six years for introductory education courses in the United States. He is a feature/departmental writer for the National Association of Secondary School Principals and publishes regularly in the *American School Board Journal*, *Executive Educator*, *School Administrator*, and *Phi Delta Kappan*. Dr. Ornstein has been consultant for more than 50 government and educational agencies, including the Chicago and New York City School districts. He is a former Fulbright-Hayes Scholar and member of the Fulbright-Hayes screening committee.

EDUCATIONAL ADMINISTRATION

CONCEPTS AND PRACTICES

I.

FUNDAMENTAL PRINCIPLES AND CONCEPTS

1

DEVELOPMENT OF ADMINISTRATIVE THEORY

In this chapter, we attempt to answer these questions concerning theoretical and historical developments in administration. We begin our discussion by exploring the nature of theory in administration and discuss six functions of theory in educational administration. Then we identify and explain major developments in the history of administrative thought: classical, human relations, and behavioral science approaches to administration. Finally, we examine contingency theory in educational administration, and we conclude the chapter with a comprehensive, open-systems model.

THEORY

Educational administrators are professionals who have a code of ethics and are licensed by state boards of education.[1] Thus, their behavior is guided by acceptable standards of practice. One of the best criteria of a profession, however, is that it has matured as a science; that is, it has developed a solid theoretical base—a body of organized and tested knowledge. Such is the case with educational administration as a social science.[2] Theory in educational administration has been evolving since the 1950s. To an increasing degree, educational administration is characterized by using theory to explain and predict phenomena in educational organizations.[3]

What are theories? Fred Kerlinger defines *theory* as . . . "a set of interrelated constructs (concepts), definitions, and propositions that present a systematic view of phenomena by specifying relations among variables with the purpose of explaining and predicting phenomena."[4] Daniel Griffiths includes many of the same ideas in his discussion of theory. He adds that a theory is a deductively connected set of empirical laws and that all statements in a theory are generalizations that explain the empirical laws and unify the areas of subject matter.[5]

A theory then is a statement (generalization) that explains some phenomena in a systematic way. Theories may range from a simple generalization to a complex set of laws, from philosophical to scientific. Some theories deal with simple generalizations such as results of educational polls or school surveys undertaken by state accrediting associations. Such studies involve measures of the nature of some condition at a particular time. They explain what is. More sophisticated theories may seek to explain why particular phenomena occur; examples are Einstein's theory of relativity and Newton's theory of the physical universe. Most theories in the social sciences require a process of refinement through revision and extension.[6]

Functions of Theories

Many school administrators feel uncomfortable with theories. They prefer that social scientists provide them with practical prescriptions for administering their schools. Upon closer examination, however, almost every action a school administrator takes is based to some degree on a theory. For example, a school administrator may include subordinates in a decision involving an issue that is relevant to them and that they have the expertise to make, instead of making the decision unilaterally. This choice is made because including subordinates in decisions, which pass the tests of relevance and expertise, will likely increase their commitment to carry out the decision once it is made.[7] Without realizing it, the school administrator made this choice on the basis of a theory.

Educational administrators would most likely flounder without theories to guide them in making choices. Thus, theories provide a guiding framework for understanding, predicting, and

---

[1]American Association of School Administrators, "Code of Ethics for School Administrators" (Arlington, VA: The Association, 1991).

[2]It may be more accurate to refer to educational administration as an "applied science" because generalizations from the fields of psychology, social psychology, sociology, anthropology, economics, and the like are applied to the solution of problems in educational administration.

[3]See, for example, Andrew W. Halpin (ed.), *Administrative Theory in Education* (New York: Macmillan, 1958); Daniel E. Griffiths (ed.), *Behavioral Science and Educational Administration* (Chicago: University of Chicago Press, 1964); and Griffiths, "Administrative Theory," in N.J. Boyan (ed.), *Handbook of Research on Educational Administration* (New York: Longman, 1988), pp. 27–51.

[4]Fred N. Kerlinger, *Foundations of Behavioral Research*, 2nd ed. (New York: Holt, Rinehart & Winston, 1973), p. 9.

[5]Griffiths, "Administrative Theory."

---

[6]William Wiersma, *Research Methods in Education* (Philadelphia: Lippincott, 1969).

[7]Edwin M. Bridges, "A Model of Shared Decision-Making in the School Principalship," *Educational Administration Quarterly*, 3 (1967), pp. 49–61.

controlling behavior in organizations. Theories also contribute to the advancement of knowledge in the field.[8] Deobold Van Dalen has suggested six functions of theories, and we follow his categorization in this discussion.[9]

Identifying Relevant Phenomena   Theories determine the number and kinds of phenomena that are relevant to a study. A theory tells a social scientist what to observe and to ignore. For example, social scientists may study school administration from the open-systems perspective. (Open-systems theory is discussed later in this chapter.) A relevant component in the open-systems approach is the external environment that impacts the organization. Several subsystems exist within this environment. Among the more important are economic, political, productive, distributive, and resource systems. Social scientists may study the external environment from all these frameworks. A multiplicity of phenomena is associated with each subsystem. Social scientists will not know precisely what phenomena to observe until they construct theoretical solutions for each problem area under investigation.

Classifying Phenomena   Scientists rarely work efficiently with masses of phenomena; therefore, they construct theoretical frameworks for classification. The physical sciences have been successful in developing such conceptual schemes. Geologists have developed schemes for classifying rocks, and botanists have devised systems for classifying plants.

An example of a classification scheme in educational administration is the study of organizational climate by Andrew Halpin and Don Croft.[10] Using factor analysis, they developed eight dimensions of organizational climate and classified climates into six categories: open, autonomous, controlled, familiar, paternal, and closed. Another example of a classification system in educational administration is the work of Henry Mintzberg. After extensive, structured observation of five executives (one a school superintendent), Mintzberg classified managerial activities into ten administrative roles: figurehead, leader, liaison (interpersonal); monitor, disseminator, spokesperson (informational); and entrepreneur, disturbance-handler, resource-allocator, negotiator (decisional).[11] If educational administrators fail to develop theoretical frameworks for classifying phenomena, they will limit the advancement of knowledge in the field.

Formulating Constructs   Reliable information can be obtained through direct observation and measurement. Many aspects of behavior cannot be directly observed. Intelligence is not an observable entity; it is inferred from using instruments that sample subject behavior. Affective predispositions such as attitudes, interests, and opinions cannot be observed directly; they are observed indirectly as they manifest themselves in behavior. Consequently, social scientists have developed constructs to explain why certain types of behavior occur. These constructs are often referred to as "hypothetical constructs" to imply that they are a construction of the social scientist's imagination. Kurt Lewin's force-field analysis is an example of a theoretical construct.[12]

Summarizing Phenomena   Theories summarize isolated lists of data into a broader conceptual scheme of wider applicability. These summaries can be stated with varying degrees of comprehensiveness and precision. They may range from simple generalizations to complex theo-

[8]Jack A. Culbertson, "A Century's Quest for a Knowledge Base," in N. J. Boyan (ed.), *Handbook of Research on Educational Administration* (New York: Longman, 1988), pp. 3–26.

[9]Debold B. Van Dalen, *Understanding Educational Research* (New York: McGraw-Hill, 1966).

[10]Halpin and Croft, *The Organizational Climate of Schools* (Chicago: University of Chicago Press, 1963).

[11]Henry Mintzberg, *The Nature of Managerial Work* (New York: Harper & Row, 1973).

[12]Kurt Lewin, *Field Theory in Social Science* (New York: Harper & Row, 1951).

retical relationships. A school superintendent making a generalization about the practice of granting certificates of achievement to outstanding teachers in the school district is an example of low-level summarizing. This type of summary is not usually referred to as a "theory." But the superintendent might construct a more complex generalization, one that describes the relationship between phenomena. For example, after observing such phenomena as granting certificates of achievement to deserving teachers, the superintendent may note a relationship: Public recognition is a means of motivating teachers. Summarizing and explaining phenomena permit deeper understanding of data and translate empirical findings into a more comprehensive, theoretical framework.

In the natural sciences, for instance, the theory of oxidation places many of the chemical reactions common to everyday life into focus. The more comprehensive the theory, which is supported by verified observations, the more mature the science becomes.

Predicting Phenomena   Theories permit the social scientist to predict the existence of unobserved instances conforming to it. For example, Abraham Maslow has made the following generalization: People at work seek to satisfy sequentially five levels of needs arranged in a prepotency hierarchy.[13] A deprived need dominates the person's attention and determines behavior. Once this deficit is satisfied, the next higher-level need is activated, and the individual progresses up the hierarchy. When the level of self-actualization is reached, progression ceases to operate. The more this need is satisfied, the stronger it grows. On the basis of this theory, one can expect to find a similar pattern of behavior in a variety of work settings where no statistics have been generated. That is, theory enables one to predict what should be observable where no data are available.

Revealing Needed Research   Theories generalize about phenomena and predict phenomena. They also pinpoint crucial areas to be investigated and crucial questions to be answered. Earlier we noted that theories in the social sciences may lack supporting evidence and therefore require a refining process. Such refinement through revision and extension is necessary to provide the maturity required for continually expanding the knowledge base in educational administration.

CLASSICAL ORGANIZATIONAL THEORY

Classical organizational theory emerged during the early years of this century. It includes two different **management perspectives**: scientific management and administrative management. Historically, scientific management focused on the management of work and workers. Administrative management addressed issues concerning how the overall organization should be structured.

Scientific Management

Prior to the turn of the century, there was almost no systematic study of management. The practice of management was based on experience and common sense. Frederick W. Taylor tried to change that view. His basic theme was that managers should study work scientifically to identify the "one best way" to perform a task. An engineer, Taylor pursued the idea that through careful scientific analysis the efficiency of work could be improved.

Taylor's **scientific management** can be summarized as consisting of four principles:[14]

1. *Scientific Job Analysis*. Through observation, data gathering, and careful measurement,

---

[13]Abraham Maslow, *Eupsychian Management* (Homewood, IL: Irwin, 1965).

[14]Frederick W. Taylor, *Principles of Scientific Management* (New York: Harper, 1911).

management determines the "one best way" of performing each job. Such job analysis would replace the old rule-of-thumb method of doing things.

2. *Selection of Personnel*. Once the job was analyzed, the next step was to scientifically select and then train, teach, and develop workers. In the past, workers chose their own work and trained themselves.

3. *Management Cooperation*. Taylor suggested that managers should cooperate with workers, to ensure that all work being done was in accordance with the principles of the science that had been developed.

4. *Functional Supervising*. Taylor recognized a division of work between managers and workers. Managers assumed planning, organizing, and decision-making activities, whereas workers performed their jobs. In the past, almost all work and the greater part of the responsibility were thrust on workers.

The four principles of scientific management were designed to maximize worker productivity. In his early career as a laborer in the steel industry, Taylor observed firsthand how workers performed well below their capacities. He referred to this activity as "soldiering." Taylor felt that scientific management—time study for setting standards, separation of managerial and employee duties, and incentive systems—would correct the problem. Rather than relying on past practice or rules of thumb, he provided managers with explicit guidelines for improving production management, based on proven research and experimentation.

Administrative Management

The second perspective on classical organizational theory is **administrative management**. Whereas scientific management focused on jobs of individual workers, administrative management concentrated on the management of an entire organization. The primary contributors to administrative management were Henri Fayol, Luther Gulick, and Max Weber.

Henri Fayol was an engineer and French industrialist. For many years, he served as managing director of a large coal-mining firm in France. He attributed his success as a manager not to any personal qualities he may have possessed but, rather, to a set of management principles that he used. Fayol claimed that all managers perform five basic functions: planning, organizing, commanding, coordinating, and controlling.

Besides the five basic management functions, Fayol identified fourteen principles that he felt should guide the management of organizations and that he found useful during his experience as a manager (Table 1-1).

Fayol's fourteen principles of management emphasize chain of command, allocation of authority, order, efficiency, equity, and stability. Max Weber also recognized the importance of these factors. But Fayol was the first to recognize management as a continuous process.

Luther Gulick, another classical theorist, augmented Fayol's five basic management functions while serving on Franklin D. Roosevelt's Committee on Government Administration. He coined the acronym POSDCoRB, which identified seven functions of management: planning, organizing, staffing, directing, coordinating, reporting, and budgeting.[15]

1. *Planning* involves developing an outline of the things that must be accomplished and the methods for accomplishing them. The activity attempts to forecast future actions and directions of the organization.

2. *Organizing* establishes the formal structure of authority through which work subdivisions are arranged, defined, and coordinated to implement the plan.

3. *Staffing* involves the whole personnel function of selecting, training, and developing the

[15]Luther Gulick and Lyndall Urwick (eds.), *Papers on the Science of Administration* (New York: Columbia University Press, 1937).

TABLE 1 ■ 1	Fayol's Fourteen Principles of Management

COMPONENT	DESCRIPTION
Division of work	The object of division of work is improved efficiency through a reduction of waste, increased output, and a simplification of job training.
Authority	Authority is the right to give orders and the power to extract obedience. Responsibility, a corollary of authority, is the obligation to carry out assigned duties.
Discipline	Discipline implies respect for the rules that govern the organization. Clear statements of agreements between the organization and its employees are necessary, and the state of discipline of any group depends on the quality of leadership.
Unity of command	An employee should receive orders from only one superior. Adherence to this principle avoids breakdowns in authority and discipline.
Unity of direction	Similar activities that are directed toward a singular goal should be grouped together under one manager.
Subordination of individual interest	The interests of individuals and groups within an organization should not take precedence over the interests of the organization as a whole.
Remuneration	Compensation should be fair and satisfactory to both employees and the organization.
Centralization	Managers must retain final responsibility, but they should give subordinates enough authority to do the task successfully. The appropriate degree of centralization will vary depending on circumstances. It becomes a question of the proper amount of centralizing to use in each case.
Scalar chain	The scalar chain, or chain of command, is the chain of superiors ranging from the ultimate authority to the lowest ranks. The exact lines of authority should be clear and followed at all times.
Order	Human and material resources should be coordinated to be in the right place at the right time.
Equity	A desire for equity and equality of treatment are aspirations managers should take into account in dealing with employees.
Stability of personnel	Successful organizations need a stable workforce. Managerial practices should encourage long-term commitment of employees to the organization.
Initiative	Employees should be encouraged to develop and carry out plans for improvement.
Esprit de corps	Managers should foster and maintain teamwork, team spirit, and a sense of unity and togetherness among employees.

SOURCE: Adapted from Henri Fayol, *General and Industrial Administration* (New York: Pitman, 1949), pp. 20–41 (originally published in French in 1916 with the title *Administratim Industrielle et Generale*).

staff and maintaining favorable working conditions.

4. *Directing*, closely related to leading, includes the continuous task of making decisions, communicating and implementing decisions, and evaluating subordinates properly.

5. *Coordinating* involves all activities and efforts needed to bind together the organization in order to achieve a common goal.

6. *Reporting* verifies progress through records, research, and inspection; ensures that things happen according to plan; takes any corrective action when necessary; and keeps those to whom the chief executive is responsible informed.

7. *Budgeting* concerns all activities that accompany budgeting, including fiscal planning, accounting, and control.

One of the most influential contributors to classical organizational theory was German sociologist Max Weber, who first described the concept of bureaucracy. Weber's contributions were not recognized until years after his death.[16] Weber's concept of bureaucracy is based on a comprehensive set of rational guidelines. Similar in concept to many of Fayol's fourteen principles, Weber's guidelines were believed to constitute an ideal structure for organizational effectiveness. Weber's "ideal" bureaucracy and Fayol's fourteen principles of management laid the foundation for contemporary organizational theory.[17]

Classical organizational theories and their derived principles have many critics. An emphasis on efficiency characterized the classical approach to management. To these theorists, an efficiently designed job and organization were of prime importance. Psychological and social factors in the workplace were ignored. The critics claim that when managers ignore the social

and psychological needs of workers, organizations do not provide adequate motivation to their employees. The classicists assumed that financial incentives would ensure worker motivation. In short, the focus of classical organizational theory was on the task, with little attention given to the individual or group in the workplace. This flaw was primarily responsible for the emergence of the second approach to management thought: the human relations approach.

HUMAN RELATIONS APPROACH

The **human relations approach** is considered to have started with a series of studies conducted at the Hawthorne Plant of Western Electric near Chicago by Elton Mayo and his associates between 1927 and 1933.[18] These studies, widely known as the **Hawthorne studies**, have strongly influenced administrative theory.

The Hawthorne Studies

The Hawthorne studies consisted of several experiments. They included the first Relay Assembly Test Room, the second Relay Assembly Group, the Mica-Splitting Group, the Typewriting Group, and the Bank Wiring Observation Room experiments. In addition, an interview program involving 21,126 employees was conducted to learn what workers liked and disliked about their work environment.

Two experiments in particular are noteworthy. In the Relay Assembly Test Room experiments, the research began with the designation of two groups of female workers. Each group performed the same task and was located in two separate rooms, each of which was equally

---

[16]Max Weber, *The Theory of Social and Economic Organization* (trans., Talcott Parsons), New York: Oxford University Press, 1947).

[17]Peter M. Blau and Marshall W. Meyer, *Bureaucracy in Modern Society*, 3rd ed. (New York: Random House, 1987).

[18]Elton Mayo, *The Human Problems of an Industrial Civilization* (New York: Macmillan, 1933); and Fritz J. Roethlisberger and William J. Dickson, *Management and the Worker* (Cambridge, MA: Harvard University Press, 1939).

lighted. One group, designated the control group, was to have no changes made in lighting or other work-environment factors. The other was the experimental group in which lighting and other environmental factors were varied. Changes in the productivity of the two groups was subsequently measured and analyzed. Regardless of the light level or various changes in rest periods and lengths of workdays and workweeks, productivity in both the control and the experimental groups improved; in fact, the worse things got, the higher the productivity rose.

In the Bank Wiring Observation Room experiments, a group of nine men were paid on a piecework incentives pay system. That is, their pay increased as their productivity increased. Researchers expected that worker productivity would rise over time. As in the Relay Assembly Test Room experiments, researchers found an unexpected pattern of results. They discovered that the group informally established an acceptable level of output for its members. Most workers, the "regulars," ignored the incentive system and voluntarily conformed to the group's standard level of acceptable output, called a *group norm*. Those who did not conform, the "deviants," were disciplined by the group to bring their output in line with the group's standard output. Workers who produced too much were called "rate-busters" and sometimes were physically threatened to make them conform with the rest of the group. On the other hand, employees who underproduced were labeled "chislers" and were pressured by the group to increase their productivity.

To understand the complex and baffling pattern of results, Mayo and his associates interviewed over 20,000 employees who had participated in the experiments during the six-year study. The interviews and observations during the experiments suggested that a human–social element operated in the workplace. Increases in productivity were more of an outgrowth of group dynamics and effective management than any set of employer demands or physical factors. In the lighting experiment,

for example, the results were attributed to the fact that the test group began to be noticed and to feel important. Researchers discovered that the improvement in productivity was due to such human–social factors as morale, a feeling of belongingness, and effective management in which such interpersonal skills as motivating, leading, participative decision making, and effective communications were used. Researchers concluded, from the results of the incentive pay-system experiment, that informal work groups emerged with their own norms for appropriate behavior of group members. In short, the importance of understanding human behavior, especially group behavior, from the perspective of management was firmly established.

Other Contributors to the Human Relations Approach

Mayo and his associates were not the only contributors to the human relations approach. There were several strong intellectual currents, which influenced the human relations movement, during this period. Kurt Lewin emphasized field theory and research known as group dynamics.[19] Noteworthy is his work on "democratic" and "authoritarian" groups. Lewin and his associates generally concluded that democratic groups, in which members actively participate in decisions, are more productive in terms of both human satisfaction and the achievement of group goals than are authoritarian groups.[20] Furthermore, much of the current work on individual and organizational approaches to change through group dynamics (sensitivity training, team building, Alcoholics Anonymous, and Weight Watchers) and the action–research approach to organizational development is based on Lewin's pioneering work.

---

[19]Kurt Lewin, *Field Theory in Social Science*.
[20]Kurt Lewin, Ronald Lippitt, and Robert White, "Patterns of Aggressive Behavior in Experimentally Created 'Social Climates,' " *Journal of Social Psychology*, 10 (1939), pp. 271–299.

Carl Rogers deserves mention here as well. Not only did he develop a procedure for industrial counseling[21] while working with Mayo and his associates at Western Electric, but the meta-psychological assumptions on which his client-centered therapy[22] is based also provides the skeletal framework on which the human relations approach is built. For example, according to Rogers, the best vantage point for understanding behavior is from the internal frame reference of the individual, who exists in a continually changing world of experience, who perceives the field of experience as reality for her; and who strives to actualize, maintain, and enhance her own human condition.[23]

The writings of Jacob Moreno made a substantial contribution to the human relations movement. Like Lewin, Moreno was interested in interpersonal relations within groups. He developed a sociometric technique: People develop selective affinities for other people. Groups composed of individuals with similar affinities for one another will likely perform better than groups lacking such affective preferences.[24]

Additional contributors to the human relations school of thought include William Whyte and George Homans. Using a field-study methodology similar to the one used by Mayo, Whyte studied the nature and functioning of work-group behavior in the restaurant industry. He examined intergroup and intragroup conflict, status within groups, workflow, and the like. Consistent with Moreno's sociometric theory Whyte found that selective preferences among group members are associated with such factors as similarities in age, sex, and outside interests.[25] His study is significant because the findings are based on observations of real-life situations rather than isolated laboratory conditions. George Homans's general theory of small groups was a major landmark. Homans conceptualized the totality of group structure and functioning that has received wide attention among organizational theorists and practitioners alike.[26]

The major assumptions of the human relations approach include the following ideas:

1. Employees are motivated by social and psychological needs and by economic incentives.
2. These needs, including but not limited to recognition, belongingness, and security, are more important in determining worker morale and productivity than the physical conditions of the work environment.
3. An individual's perceptions, beliefs, motivations, cognition, responses to frustration, values, and similar factors may affect behavior in the work setting.
4. People in all types of organizations tend to develop informal social organizations that work along with the formal organization and can help or hinder management.
5. Informal social groups within the workplace create and enforce their own norms and codes of behavior. Team effort, conflict between groups, social conformity, group loyalty, communication patterns, and emergent leadership are important concepts for determining individual and group behavior.
6. Employees have higher morale and work harder under supportive management. The human relationists believe that increased morale results in increased productivity.
7. Communication, power, influence, authority, motivation, and manipulation are all important relationships within an organization, especially between superior and subordinate. Effective communication channels should be developed between the various levels in the hierarchy. The human relationists

[21]Carl R. Rogers, *Counseling and Psychotherapy* (Boston: Houghton Mifflin, 1942).

[22]Carl R. Rogers, *Client-Centered Therapy* (Boston: Houghton Mifflin, 1951).

[23]Ibid., pp. 483–494.

[24]Jacob L. Moreno, *Who Shall Survive?* rev. ed. (New York: Beacon House, 1953).

[25]William F. Whyte, *Human Relations in the Restaurant Industry* (London: Pittman, 1949).

[26]George C. Homans, *The Human Group* (New York: Harcourt, Brace & World, 1950).

emphasize democratic rather than authoritarian leadership.

The human relationists used field-study methods extensively as well as laboratory experiments to study the work environment. These social scientists made important contributions to our understanding of employee behavior in the workplace.

BEHAVIORAL SCIENCE APPROACH

Behavioral scientists considered both the classicists' rational–economic model and the human relationists' social model to be incomplete representations of employees in the work setting. A number of authors attempted to reconcile or show points of conflict between classical and human relations theory; thus, the **behavioral science approach** was born. These behavioral scientists fueled a new interest in the individual and the way in which he relates to the organization.

The Individual and the Organization

Chester Barnard Although a contemporary of many human relationists, Chester Barnard was one of the first authors to take the behavioral science approach. For many years, Barnard served as president of the New Jersey Bell Telephone Company. His executive experience and extensive readings in sociology and organizational psychology resulted in one of management's few classic textbooks.[27]

His best-known idea was the **cooperative system**, an attempt to integrate, in a single framework, human relations and classical management principles. Barnard argues that the executive must meet two conditions if cooperation and financial success are to be attained. First,

the executive must emphasize the importance of *effectiveness*, which is the degree to which the common purpose of the organization is achieved. Second, the executive must be aware of *efficiency*, which is the satisfaction of "individual motives" of employees.[28] His major point is that an organization can operate and survive only when both the organization's goals and the goals of the individuals working for it are kept in equilibrium. Thus, managers must have both human and technical skills.

E. Wight Bakke Another major contributor to the behavioral science approach was E. Wight Bakke of the Yale University Labor and Management Center. He views the organization as embodying a **fusion process**.[29] The individual, he argues, attempts to use the organization to further her own goals, whereas the organization uses the individual to further its goals. In the fusion process, the organization to some degree remakes the individual and the individual to some degree remakes the organization. The fusion of the "personalizing process" of the individual and the "socializing process" of the organization is accomplished through the "bonds of organization," such as the formal organization, the informal organization, the workflow, the task(s) to be completed, and the system of rewards and punishments.

Chris Argyris Having views similar to Bakke's, Chris Argyris argues that there is an inherent conflict between the individual and the organization.[30] This conflict results from the incompatibility between the growth and development of the individual's maturing personality and the repressive nature of the formal organization. Argyris believes that people progress from a state of psychological immaturity and dependence to maturity and independence and that many mod-

---

[27]Chester I. Barnard, *The Functions of the Executive* (Cambridge, MA: Harvard University Press, 1938).

[28]Ibid.

[29]E. Wight Bakke, *The Fusion Process* (New Haven, CT: Yale University Press, 1955).

[30]Chris Argyris, *Personality and Organization* (New York: Harper & Row, 1957).

ern organizations keep their employees in a dependent state, preventing them from achieving their full potential. Further, Argyris believes that some of the basic principles of management are inconsistent with the mature adult personality. The resulting incongruence between individual personality and the organization causes conflict, frustration, and failure for people at work. People learn to adapt to the failure, frustration, and conflict resulting from the incongruency by ascending the organizational hierarchy, by using defense mechanisms, or by developing an apathetic and indifferent orientation toward their work that ultimately leads to the dysfunction of the organization's goals. This trend to conformity has been espoused in such popular books as *The Organization Man*[31] and *Life in the Crystal Palace*.[32]

Jacob Getzels and Egon Guba   A useful theoretical formulation for studying administrative behavior is the social systems analysis developed for educators by Jacob Getzels and Egon Guba.[33] Getzels and Guba conceive of the social system as involving two classes of phenomena that are independent and interactive. First are institutions with certain roles and expectations that together constitute the **nomothetic dimension** of activity in the social system. Second are the individuals with certain personalities and need-dispositions inhabiting the system that together constitute the **idiographic dimension** of activity in the social system. Behavior then in any social system can be seen as a function of the interaction between personal needs and institutional goals. Conformity to the institution, its roles, and its expectations results in organizational effectiveness, whereas conformity to individuals, their personalities, and their need-dispositions results in individual efficiency.

(Note the similarity between Getzels and Guba's framework and those of Barnard, Bakke, and Argyris.)

Abraham Maslow   The behavioral science approach has drawn heavily on the work of Abraham Maslow, who developed a **need hierarchy** that an individual attempts to satisfy.[34] Maslow's theory suggests that an administrator's job is to provide avenues for the satisfaction of employee's needs that also support organizational goals and to remove impediments that block need-satisfaction and cause frustration, negative attitudes, or dysfunctional behavior.

Douglas McGregor   Based on the work of Maslow, Douglas McGregor formulated two contrasting sets of assumptions about people and the management strategies suggested by each. He called these **Theory X** and **Theory Y**.[35] McGregor believed that the classical approach was based on Theory X assumptions about people. He also thought that a modified version of Theory X was consistent with the human relations perspective. That is, human relations concepts did not go far enough in explaining people's needs and management's strategies to achieve them. McGregor viewed Theory Y as a more appropriate foundation for guiding management thinking.

Frederick Herzberg   Extending the work of Maslow, Frederick Herzberg developed a two-factor theory of motivation.[36] Herzberg makes a distinction between factors that cause or prevent job dissatisfaction (**hygiene factors**) and factors that cause job satisfaction (**motivation factors**). Only the latter group of factors can lead to motivation. Herzberg's hygiene factors relate closely to Maslow's lower-level needs: physiolog-

[31]William H. Whyte, *The Organization Man* (New York: Simon & Schuster, 1956).

[32]Allan Harrington, *Life in the Crystal Palace* (London: Jonathan Cape, 1960).

[33]Jacob W. Getzels and Egon G. Guba, "Social Behavior and the Administrative Process," *School Review,* 65 (1957), pp. 423–441.

[34]Abraham Maslow, *Motivation and Personality*, rev. ed. (New York: Harper & Row, 1970).

[35]Douglas McGregor, *The Human Side of Enterprise* (New York: McGraw-Hill, 1960).

[36]Frederick Herzberg, *Work and the Nature of Man* (Cleveland: World, 1966).

ical, safety, and social; his motivation factors relate to the needs at the top of Maslow's hierarchy: esteem and self-actualization. Recognition of motivation factors calls for a different style of management from that proposed by the classical or human relations advocates.

Rensis Likert   Another writer concerned with the way in which the goals of individuals and those of the organization can coincide is Rensis Likert. Likert conducted extensive empirical research at the Institute for Social Research—University of Michigan to examine the effect of management systems on employees' attitudes and behavior. He developed four management systems, ranging from **System 1**—Exploitive Authoritative—to **System 4**—Participative-Group.[37] Each system characterizes an organizational climate based on several key dimensions of effectiveness, including leadership, motivation, communications, interaction/influence, decision making, goal setting, control, and performance goals. Likert posits the participative-group system (System 4) as coming closest to the ideal. The essence of System 4 theory is based on three key propositions: supportive relationships, group decision making in an overlapping group structure, which he calls "linking-pins,"[38] and high-performance goals of the leader. (Note the parallel here to McGregor's Theory X and Theory Y dichotomy.) Likert, however, provides more categories and more specificity. His Systems 1–4 represent four different leadership styles.

Managing Education Like a Business

According to one prominent educator, there is no reason why schools cannot be run like businesses—achieving the objectives of the organi-

zation efficiently while keeping an eye on accountability. One problem is that many superintendents, principals, and teachers are not knowledgeable about the principles of management. We need to look toward business for insights on managing schools. Principals may need to run their schools more like businesses if they are to provide a cost-effective product; they should re-evaluate and combine management and academic skills, and instill pride in their consumers (or students). (See Administrative Advice 1-1.)

Leadership

We will examine the conceptual frameworks of several leadership theorists in Chapter 5. A few deserve brief mention here for their contributions to the behavioral science school of thought.

Robert Blake and Jane Mouton   In the area of leadership, Robert Blake and Jane Mouton assess managerial behavior on two dimensions: concern for production and concern for people. Managers can plot their scores on an eighty-one-celled **managerial grid**.[39] The grid is designed to help managers identify their own leadership styles, to understand how subordinates are affected by their leadership style, and to explore the use of alternative leadership styles consistent with employees' needs.

Fred Fiedler   **Contingency theories** of leadership have come into vogue in recent years. Fred Fiedler developed a contingency theory of leadership effectiveness.[40] The basic premise is that in some situations relationship-motivated leaders perform better, while other conditions make it more likely that task-motivated leaders will be most effective. Three variables determine the

[37]Rensis Likert, "From Production and Employee-Centeredness to Systems 1–4," *Journal of Management*, 5 (1979), pp. 147–156.
[38]Rensis Likert and Jane Gibson Likert, *New Ways of Managing Conflict* (New York: McGraw-Hill, 1976).

[39]Robert R. Blake and Jane S. Mouton, *The Managerial Grid III* (Houston: Gulf, 1985).
[40]Fred E. Fiedler and Martin M. Chemers, *Improving Leadership Effectiveness*, 2nd ed. (New York: Wiley, 1984).

ADMINISTRATIVE ADVICE 1-1

■

A Plan for Urban Schools

By using approaches that have been proven effective in business administration, educators can improve schools. The following is an action plan that can produce positive results in urban schools:

- *Provide Flexibility for Teachers to Adjust Schedules for Students.* Some students require three hours a day to learn how to read, whereas others may require only half that time. Teachers must be able to accommodate varying student needs.
- *Require Preschool Programs for Limited English-Speaking Students and the Culturally Disadvantaged.* Students from these backgrounds who start school in the first grade usually end up two or three years behind other students by the time they reach middle school, and a large percentage usually drops out of school because they cannot compete academically.
- *Apply Emerging Technology to Education.* Public television, computers, and videos used properly can assist teachers as they search for strategies to assist at-risk students.
- *Adjust Class Sizes for the Underachievers.* Underachievers should be assigned to smaller classes, particularly in basic-skills classes until they start functioning at grade level.
- *Assess Student Needs Every Year and Develop Strategies to Remove Student Deficiencies.* Every school district should adopt some technique to measure student achievement and provide an analysis of academic areas where students did not achieve satisfactorily. Then a teacher can determine what a student has not learned and can develop a remedial plan for the next year.
- *Provide for an Annual Evaluation of Student Performance.* Every school must be able to compare the results with the previous year's achievement to determine if a student is working up to

his potential—or if the teacher has achieved curriculum goals.
- *Require Teacher Training on How to Interact with Students and Teach to Different Learning Styles of Students.* Teachers must be able to relate to students of all ethnic or cultural groups and be able and willing to vary their methods of instruction. The teacher's ability to recognize the student's learning style is also critical.
- *Schedule Extracurricular Activities After School, on Saturdays, and During the Summer.* Sports teams, marching bands, and other extracurricular activities have a tendency to dip into part of the already short instructional day. Schools should schedule all extracurricular activities so that they do not take time away from academic instruction.
- *Increase School Accountability with Less Process and Fewer Regulations.* Federal and state regulations mandate so many processes and procedures that they are sometimes more harmful than helpful. Teachers should be given the flexibility to deal with individual differences among students, while being held accountable for results.
- *Increase Accountability for School Boards, Teachers, Parents, and Students.* Accountability is a joint effort involving board members, school administrators, teachers, parents, and students.

Source: Adapted from Linus Wright, "Business and Education: A Symbiotic Match," *Principal*, 69 (1989), pp. 18–19. Copyright 1989, National Association of Elementary School Principals. Used by permission.

situations under which one or the other type of leader will be most effective: leader–member relations (the degree to which the leader feels accepted by her followers), task structure (the degree to which the work to be done is clearly outlined), and position power (the extent to which the leader has control over rewards and punishments the followers receive).

Paul Hersey and Kenneth Blanchard   Another popular leadership theory is situational leadership developed by Paul Hersey and Kenneth Blanchard.[41] **Situational leadership theory** is based primarily on the relationship between follower maturity, leader task behavior, and leader relationship behavior. In general terms, the theory suggests that the style of leadership will be effective only if it is appropriate for the maturity level of the followers.

Other Important Contributors   The great diversity of contingency perspectives in the behavioral science school makes it impossible to discuss all of its contributors here. Social scientists like Victor Vroom,[42] William Reddin,[43] and Amitai Etzioni[44] did much to assist its development. Finally, Warren Bennis, in his best-selling book on leadership, identifies bureaucracy and other classical management principles as the "unconscious conspiracy" that prevents leaders from leading.[45]

A key contribution of the contingency perspective may best be summarized in the observation that there is no one best way to administer an organization. There are no motivation strategies, organizational structures, decision-making patterns, communication techniques, change approaches, or leadership styles that will fit all situations. Rather, school administrators must find different ways that fit different situations.

DEVELOPMENT OF ADMINISTRATIVE THOUGHT

We have attempted to place the development of administrative thought into a loose historical framework. In general, three models emerge: classical organizational theory, the human relations model, and the behavioral science approach. The classical "rational" model evolved around the ideas of scientific and administrative management, including the study of administrative processes and managerial functions. The human relations "social" model was spurred by some early seminal social science research, including experimentation and analysis of the social and psychological aspects of people in the workplace and the study of group behavior. The more recent behavioral science approach was an attempt to reconcile the basic incongruency between the rational–economic model and the social model. Table 1-2 briefly summarizes the major differences among the three approaches to administrative thought.

As shown in Table 1-2, differences in leadership, organization, production, process, power, administration, reward, and structure are important distinguishing characteristics of the three approaches to administrative thought. We can see how the evolution of organization and administrative theory has developed from a concern for efficiency and the basic principles of management to an emphasis on human and psychological factors and, finally, to social systems and contingency theory. While we have not included all people who have made contributions in the evolution of administrative thought, major contributors and basic concepts are noted and primary eras in the evolution are highlighted. Furthermore, no attempt is made to date the eras precisely. In fact, if we view the sequence of developments in organizational and administrative theory, we notice a correlational rather than a compensatory tendency. Traces of the past coexist with modern approaches to administration, with heavy emphasis on contingency and social systems theory today.

[41]Paul Hersey and Kenneth Blanchard, *Management of Organizational Behavior*, 5th ed. (Englewood Cliffs, NJ: Prentice-Hall, 1988).

[42]Victor Vroom and Arthur Jago, *The New Leadership: Managing Participation in Organizations* (Englewood Cliffs, NJ: Prentice-Hall, 1988).

[43]William J. Reddin, *Managerial Effectiveness* (New York: McGraw-Hill, 1970).

[44]Amitai Etzioni, *A Comparative Analysis of Complex Organizations*, rev. ed. (New York: Free Press, 1975).

[45]Warren G. Bennis, *Why Leaders Can't Lead: The Unconscious Conspiracy Continues* (San Francisco: Jossey-Bass, 1989).

TABLE 1 ■ 2   Overview of the Three Major Developments in Administrative Thought

PERIOD	MANAGEMENT ELEMENTS	PROCEDURES	CONTRIBUTORS AND BASIC CONCEPTS
Classical organizational theory	Leadership Organization Production Process Authority Administration Reward Structure	Top to bottom Machine Individual Anticipated consequences Rules; coercive Leader separate Economic Formal	Taylor (time-and-motion study, functional supervisor, piecerate) Fayol (five basic functions, fourteen principles of management) Gulick (POSDCoRB) Weber (ideal bureaucracy)
Human relations approach	Leadership Organization Production Process Authority Administration Reward Structure	All directions Organism Group Unanticipated consequences Group norms Participative Social and psychological Informal	Mayo, Roethlisberger, and Dickson (Hawthorne studies); intellectual undercurrents: Lewin (group dynamics); Lewin, Lippitt, and White (leadership studies); Rogers (client-centered therapy); Moreno (sociometric technique); Whyte (human relations in the restaurant industry); Homans (small groups)
Behavioral science approach	Consideration of all major elements with heavy emphasis on contingency leadership, climate, and social systems theory		Barnard (cooperative systems); Bakke (fusion process); Argyris (optimal actualization—organization and individual); Getzels and Guba (social systems theory—nomothetic and idiographic); Maslow (need hierarchy); Herzberg (hygiene–motivation); McGregor (Theory X and Y); Likert (Systems 1–4); Halpin and Croft (open–closed climates); Blake and Mouton (managerial grid); Fiedler (contingency theory); Vroom (expectancy theory); Reddin (3-D leadership); Etzioni (compliance theory); Mintzberg (structure of organizations); Hersey and Blanchard (situational leadership); Bennis (leadership—unconscious conspiracy)

In analyzing the role of the principal, Marshall Sashkin and Gene Huddle identified thirteen major task dimensions of the principal's job.[46] They divided these task dimensions into two ma-jor categories, similar to those we have discussed in this chapter. One category includes managerial and bureaucratic tasks (classical organizational theory) normally associated with the role of administrator—creating and enforcing policies, rules, procedures, and authority relations. The other category Sashkin and Huddle call "building cultural linkages." This category, which is an extension of the human relations

[46]Marshall Sashkin and Gene Huddle, "A Synthesis of Job Analysis Research on the Job of the School Principal," unpublished manuscript, Washington D.C.: Office of Educational Research and Improvement, U.S. Department of Education, 1986.

ADMINISTRATIVE ADVICE 1-2

■

TASK AND SKILL DIMENSIONS OF THE ADMINISTRATOR'S JOB

Effective school administrators create more effective schools by deliberately designing their actions so that those actions build cultural as well as bureaucratic linkages.
Below are a number of tasks and related skills for effective management of schools (and
school districts).

BUILDING BUREAUCRATIC LINKAGES

- *Task: Building Sound Relations with the Central Office*
  Skills needed: Liaison skills and negotiating skills.
- *Task: Monitoring Organizational Information*
  Skills needed: Scanning and monitoring informa-
  tion and using information networks.
- *Task: Coordinating School Activities*
  Skills needed: Time management, working with
  groups, and interpersonal skills.
- *Task: Managing Financial Resources*
  Skills needed: Developing budgets and mathemati-
  cal skills.
- *Task: Maintaining the School Building*
  Skills needed: Developing maintenance schedules
  and using general management procedures and
  practices.
- *Task: Directing School Support Services*
  Skills needed: Designing policies, procedures, and
  rules and developing and monitoring contracts.
- *Task: Staffing*
  Skills needed: Use of selection methods, assess-
  ment and appraisal skills, and coaching and devel-
  opment skills.

BUILDING CULTURAL LINKAGES

- *Task: Establishing an Atmosphere Conducive to
  Learning*
  Skills needed: Organizational communication, in-
  terpersonal communication, and using symbols.
- *Task: Setting High Expectations*
  Skills needed: Goal setting, interpersonal commu-
  nication, and interpersonal relationship skills.
- *Task: Setting School Goals*
  Skills needed: Goal setting and organizational
  communication.
- *Task: Instructional Leadership*
  Skills needed: Working with groups and commit-
  tees, observational methods for assessment, and
  coaching skills.
- *Task: Organizational Communication*
  Skills needed: Using teams, committees, and task
  forces; using internal communication networks;
  and conflict management skills.
- *Task: Building Parent and Community Support*
  Skills needed: Representing the school to the community, public relations skills, and public communications skills.

Source: Adapted from Marshall Sashkin and Gene Huddle, "Recruit Top Principals." *School Administrator*, 2 (1988), 12–13.
Used by permission.

---

and behavioral science approaches to management, includes establishing behavioral norms,
using symbols, instituting rituals, and telling
stories designed to build the cultural foundations of organizational excellence. (See Administrative Advice 1-2.)

SYSTEMS THEORY

One of the more useful concepts in understanding organizations is the idea that an organization is a system. A system can be defined as "a

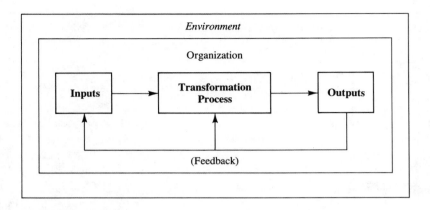

FIGURE 1-1   Basic Systems Model

set of interrelated elements that functions as a unit for a specific purpose."[47] **Systems theory** is presented here not as a separate management approach but as a way of viewing organizations. Systems theorists suggest that an organization must be studied as a whole, taking into consideration the interrelationships among its parts and its relationship with the external environment.[48]

Basic Systems Model

Figure 1-1 depicts the basic systems theory of organizations, which has five parts: inputs, a transformation process, outputs, feedback, and the environment. *Inputs* are the human, material, financial, or information resources used to produce a product or service. Through technology and administrative functions, the inputs undergo a *transformation process*. In schools the interaction between students and teachers is part of the transformation or learning process by which students become educated citizens ca-

pable of contributing to society. *Outputs* include the organization's products and services. An educational organization generates and distributes knowledge. *Feedback* is information concerning the outputs or the process of the organization that influences the selection of inputs during the next cycle. Such information may lead to changes in both the transformation process and future outputs. The *environment* surrounding the organization includes the social, political, and economic forces that impinge on the organization. The conceptualization of the organization as an open system is one of the most important concepts of systems theory. Presumably, all school organizations are open systems.

A Systems View of School Administration

It is useful to analyze the operation of an educational organization and the role of school administrators within that operation from an **open-systems framework**. The dimensions of a school district's operation can be grouped into the three broad categories of inputs, transformation process, and outputs. This framework aids in the analysis of school district operations and, more specifically, in the organization's system of operational management. It contributes

[47]Randall B. Dunham and Jon L. Pierce, *Management* (Glenview, IL: Scott, Foresman, 1989), p. 151.
[48]Peter P. Schoderbek, Charles G. Schoderbek, and Asterios G. Kefalas, *Management Systems: Conceptual Considerations*, 3rd ed. (Plano, TX: Business Publications, 1985).

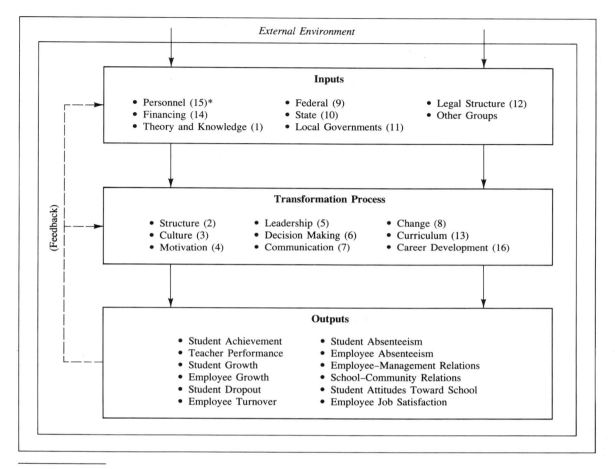

FIGURE 1-2   A Systems View of School Administration   (*The numbers indicate chapters in this book.)

greatly to the quick and accurate diagnosis of problems, and it can focus the school administrator's efforts on the key areas to introduce change in the system.

The basic systems model is expanded to focus on the role of the school administrator in operating a school or school district. Figure 1-2 shows the interrelationships among the dimensions of the operational management system. (Many of the topics will be discussed in subsequent chapters.) This figure, although oversimplifying the relationships, helps make clear the pattern of interrelationships in oper-

ating a school district or other educational institution.

Inputs   The school district's *environment* provides it with personnel, financing, and theory/knowledge. In addition, federal, state, and local governments enact laws that regulate school district operations. Other groups make demands on the school district as well. Students, for example, want relevant and useful curriculum content to prepare them for the world of work or higher education. Teachers want higher salaries, better working conditions, fringe benefits, and job security. School board members want a high return on their investment, that is, quality education within an operating budget. Similarly, the community expects the schools to provide quality education to all the district's clients without an increase in taxes. And special-interest groups have a variety of agendas. Each group has its own goals, which often conflict. The job of the school administrator is to integrate these diverse goals into a viable plan of action.

Transformation Process Organizations convert the inputs from the external environment into some form of output. Work of some kind is done in the system to produce output. The system adds a "value added" to the work in process.[49] This transformation process includes the internal operation of the organization and its system of operational management. Some components of the system of operational management include the technical competence of school administrators, including their decision-making and communication skills, their plans of operation, and their ability to cope with change. Activities performed by school administrators within the organization's structure will affect the school district's outputs.

Outputs The school administrator's job is to secure and use inputs from the external environment, transform them through administrative activities such as providing a structure, developing a culture, motivating, leading, decision making, communicating, implementing change, developing curriculum, administering personnel, and financing the institution to produce outputs. In school organizations, outputs include student achievement, teacher performance, growth levels of students and employees, student dropout, employee turnover, student and employee absenteeism, employee–management relations, school–community relations, student

attitudes toward school, and employee job satisfaction (see Figure 1-2).

Finally, the external environment reacts to these outputs and provides feedback to the system. Feedback is crucial to the success of the school district operation. Negative feedback, for example, can be used to correct deficiencies in the school administrator's operational plan of action, which in turn will have an effect on the school district's outputs.

Our nation's future will depend on how well our citizens perform and produce in the world marketplace. Responsibility for preparing people to perform falls on our nation's schools. School administrators are at the vortex of this responsibility. What then are the components of leadership in high-performing school organizations? (See Administrative Advice 1-3.)

SUMMARY

1. The practice of educational administration has changed in response to historical conditions and theoretical developments.
2. To an increasing degree, educational administration is characterized by using theory to explain and predict phenomena in educational organizations.
3. The functions of theories include the following: identification of relevant phenomena, classification of phenomena, formulation of constructs, summarization of phenomena, prediction of phenomena, and revelation of needed research.
4. Since the early 1900s, three major perspectives on administration have evolved: the classical perspective, the human relations perspective, and the behavioral science perspective.
5. Two contemporary extensions of administrative perspectives are contingency theory and systems theory. Contingency theories suggest that numerous factors or situations affect leadership, many of which cannot be predetermined or perfectly controlled. Systems theory is usually discussed in terms of inputs, a transformation process, outputs, feedback, and environment.
6. The major dimensions of leadership may be divided into two categories—task dimensions and human relations skills.

---

[49]Thomas J. Sergiovanni, *Value Added Leadership* (New York: Harcourt Brace Jovanovich, 1990).

ADMINISTRATIVE ADVICE 1-3

■

LEADERSHIP IN HIGH-PERFORMANCE ORGANIZATIONS

The following are the major components of leadership in high-performance organizations:

- *Organize for Outcomes*. When high-performance leaders take a systematic look at instruction, they have results in mind. The bottom line is student learning. For high-performance leaders, the instructional delivery system operates on a foundation of well-defined objectives, strategies, and outcomes.
- *Share Leadership and Decision Making*. A truly effective leader involves people in decisions that affect them and what they do. Site-based management is alive and well in peak-performance organizations.
- *Effect Staff and Career Development*. Leaders of high-performance organizations are the first to admit that they must get things done through people. Casey Stengel, former manager of the New York Yankees, perhaps said it best, "Managing is getting paid for home runs someone else hits." Our challenge is to be sure every person on the school staff has the knowledge and skills to hit home runs.
- *Assess Student Progress and Accountability*. Why are schools so intent on charting student progress? Leaders of high-performance organizations need to know how students are doing. Standardized and criterion-referenced tests, for example, can guide us in providing both reinforcement and course corrections. This type of attention to results can lead to an even better education for each student and a more finely tuned organization.
- *Apply the Components of Restructuring*. Restructuring schooling means different things to different people. Some welcome it; some fear it. However, the process of restructuring can ener-

gize an organization, especially when it is primarily defined as "renewal."
- *Involve the Parents and Community*. When we involve parents in their child's education, they feel a greater sense of ownership for the schools. The same is true for others in the community. If we want community support, then we need to communicate effectively.
- *Encourage School Partnerships*. Schools cannot operate in isolation. They need to work effectively with partners. Who are those partners? Business leaders, community youth-serving agencies, religious groups, governors and state legislators, and the news media.
- *Provide Special Programs for Students Who Need Them*. One thing is certain—no two students are alike. Each is unique, and each brings to school a set of talents, experiences, learning styles, and, sometimes, problems. Of course, some of our students require specialized help.
- *Collaborate with Community Agencies*. Schools and other human service organizations need to work together as they serve their clients. Parents and community members are school partners, as are community agencies.
- *Commit to Funding*. While a commitment to excellent and sound planning can help an organization, adequate funding is still necessary for high performance.

Source: Adapted from Dean Speicher, "Leadership in High-Performance Organizations," *School Administrator*, 46 (1989) (four-part series on leadership (four issues)), p. 6. Used by permission.

TRAINING SCHOOL LEADERS

Xerox's CEO David Kearns said that schools "are admirably suited to the economy and culture of the 1950s and spectacularly unsuited to the high-tech future of the next century." He believes that education is big business and the same theories that guide industrial executives are the ones school leaders need to solve education's problems.

QUESTION Is the management training provided by business and industry for their leaders the best source of information and skill development for principals and superintendents?

ARGUMENTS PRO

1 Organizational theory is generic. Its essential concepts are applicable in all organizations.

2 Most organizational theory taught in educational administration courses was generated by researchers in the industrial setting. Industrial management thought leads the way. Why not do away with intermediaries?

3 Business and school leaders need to work more closely together. If they share the same training, think about the same ideas, and speak the same language, it will improve the collegial relationship between schools and the communities they serve.

4 Management training is current and tested. Industry has invested heavily in the development of management-training programs. If that resource is being offered to schools, it would be foolish not to take advantage of the offer.

5 Management trainers understand organizational theory well and can teach adult learners in all types of organizations to apply theory to their settings.

ARGUMENTS CON

1 Business is private enterprise; schools are public service agencies. It would be a dangerous mistake to borrow management theory wholesale.

2 Many aspects of management theory do not apply in educational settings. It takes several years to adapt management theory into educational administrative theory. Educational researchers play an important role in sifting and applying organizational theory.

3 The scions of industry are one consumer group for schools. Educators' relationship to them is important but no more important than the relationship with the leaders of other consumer groups such as parents, colleges, and civic agencies. While educators should be open to feedback from clients, they should not be coopted by them.

4 Management training is behaviorist and outcome-driven. It does not consider the social and psychological needs of the teacher as much as the profits of the organization.

5 Management trainers understand profit-driven organizations but do not understand the norms and values of educators.

KEY TERMS

classical management perspective

scientific management

administrative management

human relations approach

Hawthorne studies

behavioral science approach

cooperative system

fusion process

nomothetic–idiographic dimensions

need hierarchy

Theory X and Y

motivation–hygiene factors

Systems 1–4 theories

managerial grid

situational leadership theory

contingency theory

systems theory

open-systems framework

DISCUSSION QUESTIONS

1. What are the functions of theories in educational administration?
2. Why is it important to understand the different approaches to administrative theory that have evolved throughout the history of organizations?
3. What is the behavioral science approach? How does it differ from earlier approaches to administration?
4. Discuss the basic concepts underlying contingency theory.
5. What are the major components of systems theory?

SUGGESTED READINGS

Norman J. Boyan (ed.), *Handbook of Research on Educational Administration* (New York: Longman, 1988). An assessment and evaluation of the major areas of thought and inquiry prevalent in the field of educational administration over the past thirty years.

Roald Campbell et al., *History of Thought and Practice in Educational Administration* (New York: Teachers College Press, 1987). A comprehensive discussion of the history of thought in educational administration.

Richard L. Daft, *Organization Theory and Design*, 3rd ed. (St. Paul: West, 1989). A comprehensive and current synthesis of management theory with application to school administration.

Randall B. Dunham and Jon L. Pierce, *Management* (Glenview, IL: Scott, Foresman, 1989). A comprehensive discussion of the principles of management with application to organizations, including schools.

Robert C. Ford, Barry M. Armandi, and Cherrill P. Heaton, *Organization Theory: An Integrative Approach* (New York: Harper & Row, 1988). A scholarly treatment of social science theory as applied to organizations.

Fred Luthans, Richard M. Hodgetts, and Stuart A. Rosenkrantz, *Real Managers* (Cambridge, MA: Ballinger, 1988). A study of the impact of leadership on organizational performance.

Leon C. Megginson, Donald C. Mosley, and Paul H. Pietri, Jr., *Management*, 3rd ed. (New York: Harper & Row, 1989). A very comprehensive treatment of the principles of management including the evolution of management thought.

2

ORGANIZATIONAL STRUCTURE

In this chapter, we attempt to answer these questions concerning organizational structure in schools. Our primary emphasis is on formal rather than informal relationships concerning organizational structure. We begin our discussion by examining the basic concepts of organizational structure. We then discuss the bureaucratic model of organizational structure. Next, we present the participatory management model and compare the two approaches to organizing schools. We then describe three alternative models of organizational structure: organic and mechanistic organizations, compliance theory, and strategy–structure typology. Finally, we discuss the school as a social system using several of Getzels's models.

BASIC CONCEPTS OF ORGANIZATIONAL STRUCTURE

Basic concepts of organizational structure provide a framework for vertical control and horizontal coordination of the organization. We discuss some of these concepts to provide the background for a more thorough analysis of the bureaucratic, participatory management, and alternative models of organizational structure. These important dimensions include job specialization, departmentalization, chain of command, authority and responsibility, centralization/decentralization, line and staff authority, and span of management.

Job Specialization

A basic concept of organizational structure is to divide the work to be accomplished into specialized tasks and to organize them into distinct units. Examples of **job specialization** are the division of the school into elementary, middle, and high school units; the distinction between administrative and teaching functions; and the variety of position certificates required by the fifty state departments of education, including superintendent, business manager, principal, supervisor, various teaching specialties, and the like.

Departmentalization

Departmentalization, the organizationwide division of work, permits the organization to realize the benefits of job specialization and to coordinate the activities of the component parts. School districts may be broadly divided into divisions of instruction, business, personnel, and research and development. Further subdividing of a division such as instruction may produce departments responsible for specific subjects, for example, English, social studies, mathematics, and science. Departments, frequently labeled divisions, building units, departments, or teams, often indicate hierarchical relationships. Thus, an assistant superintendent may lead a division; a principal, a building unit; a department head, an academic department within a building unit; and a teacher, a grade-level team in a school.

Chain of Command

Chain of command, concerned with the flow of authority and responsibility within an organization, is associated with two underlying principles. *Unity of command* means that a subordinate is accountable to only one person—the person from whom he receives authority and responsibility. The *scalar principle* means that authority and responsibility should flow in a direct line vertically from top management to the lowest level. It establishes the division of work in the organization in hierarchical form.

Although organizations differ in the degree of their vertical divisions of work and the extent to which it is formalized, they all exhibit aspects of this characteristic. For example, in the military, the vertical specialization is established by specific definitions of roles for the various positions, and there are definite status differences among levels. Within the officer ranks in the Navy, there is a distinct difference of role and status in the hierarchy from ensign to admiral. In the university, there is a hierarchy within the professional ranks: instructor, assistant, associate, and full professor. In the school district organization, there are vertical differentiations of positions ranging from teachers to department heads, principals, directors, and superintendents. These levels are typically well defined, with differences in role and status for the various positions.

Authority and Responsibility

Authority is the right to make decisions and direct the work of others. It is an important concept in organizational structure because administrators and other personnel must be authorized to carry out jobs to which they are assigned. Furthermore, authority and responsibility should be linked; that is, **responsibility** for the execution of work must be accompanied by the authority to accomplish the job.

In a school district, authority stems from the board of education. This body then delegates to the superintendent of schools the authority necessary to administer the district. As authority is delegated further, it becomes narrower in scope. Each succeedingly lower-level occupant has narrower limits on her areas of legitimate authority. This view of authority and responsibility provides the framework for legitimizing organizational hierarchy and provides the basis for direction and control.

Centralization/Decentralization

Delegation of authority between a superior and a subordinate is a way of sharing power. The cumulative effect of all these superordinate–subordinate empowerment practices can have a dramatic impact on the overall organization. If administrators in a school district tend to delegate considerable authority and responsibility, more decisions are made at lower levels in the organization. Subordinates in such districts possess considerable influence in the overall operation of the school district. In these cases, the organization follows an administrative philosophy of **decentralization**. On the other hand, when school administrators retain most of the authority, depending on subordinates to implement decisions only, the organization is practicing **centralization**. Centralization and decentralization represent opposite ends of a continuum. That is, authority is delegated to a relatively small or large degree in the organization.

Should organizations centralize or decentralize? In the United States and Canada, the trend over the last thirty years has been toward greater decentralization of organizations.[1] Decentralization is said to have the following advantages: It makes greater use of human resources, unburdens top-level administrators, ensures that decisions are made close to the firing line by personnel with technical knowledge, and permits more rapid response to external changes.[2]

Line and Staff Authority

Another way to view organizational structure is as line and staff authority. **Line authority** is that relationship in which a superior exercises direct supervision over a subordinate—an authority relationship in a direct line in the chain of command. Line authority relates specifically to the unity of command principle and the scalar principle. For example, line administrators such as the superintendent, assistant superintendent, directors of elementary and secondary education, and principals have authority to issue orders to their subordinates. Thus, the superintendent can order the assistant superintendent of instruction to implement a curriculum change, and the assistant superintendent in turn can order the directors of elementary and secondary education to do the same, and so on down the chain of command.

Staff authority is advisory in nature. The function of personnel in a staff position is to create, develop, collect, and analyze information, which flows to line personnel in the form of advice. Staff personnel do not possess the legitimate authority to implement this advice. One familiar example of staff is the "assistant to" in which the person assists the superintendent or other superior in a variety of ways. Another example is the legal counsel who advises the su-

---

[1]Richard L. Daft, *Management* (New York: Dryden Press, 1988).
[2]Samuel C. Certo, *Principles of Modern Management* (Needham Heights, MA: Allyn and Bacon, 1989).

perintendent in legal matters affecting the schools.

Span of Management

Span of management refers to the number of subordinates reporting directly to a supervisor. Is there an ideal span of management? There is no agreement regarding what is the best span of management. The most widely used criteria on this point suggest that spans can be larger at lower levels in an organization than at higher levels.[3] Because subordinates in lower-level positions typically perform much more routine activities, subordinates can be effectively supervised at lower levels. In practice, larger spans are often found at lower levels in organizations. Elementary schools, for example, are characterized by very large spans, as many as fifty or more teachers reporting to one principal. In such organizations, there is a tendency to assign team leaders within a school. These team leaders (teachers) report to the school principal. They may not be officially legitimized as a layer of administration within the school. The "informal" team-leader approach permits a principal to expand the number of teachers he can effectively supervise. At the same time, this unofficial position does not result in another cumbersome layer of administration.

Figure 2-1, highlighting each basic concept of organizational structure, illustrates how these key concepts function in a school setting and are the foundation for most structure decisions. In practice, one can observe these structural dimensions in most organizations.

THE BUREAUCRATIC MODEL

Today the term **bureaucracy** has a negative connotation. We tend to associate bureaucracy with rigidity, meaningless rules, red tape, paperwork, and inefficiency. In fact, there is almost no evil that has not, at some point, been attributed to bureaucracy.

The pioneering work on bureaucracy is credited to the famous German sociologist Max Weber, who made a comparative study of many organizations existing at the turn of the twentieth century. From his study, Weber evolved the concept of bureaucracy as an ideal form of organizational structure.

Bureaucratic Characteristics

According to Weber, the ideal bureaucracy possesses the following characteristics:[4]

- *Division of Labor*. Divide all tasks into highly specialized jobs. Give each jobholder the authority necessary to perform these duties.
- *Rules*. Perform each task according to a consistent system of abstract rules. This practice helps ensure that task performance is uniform.
- *Hierarchy of Authority*. Arrange all positions according to the principle of hierarchy. Each lower office is under the control of a higher one, and there is a clear chain of command from the top of the organization to the bottom.
- *Impersonality*. Maintain an impersonal attitude toward subordinates. This social distance between managers and subordinates helps ensure that rational considerations are the basis for decision making, rather than favoritism or prejudices.
- *Competence*. Base employment on qualifications and give promotions based on job-related performance. As a corollary, protect employees from arbitrary dismissal, which should result in a high level of loyalty.

---

[3]Robert P. Vecchio, *Organizational Behavior* (New York: Dryden Press, 1988).

[4]Max Weber, *The Theory of Social and Economic Organization*, trans. T. Parsons (New York: Oxford University Press, 1947).

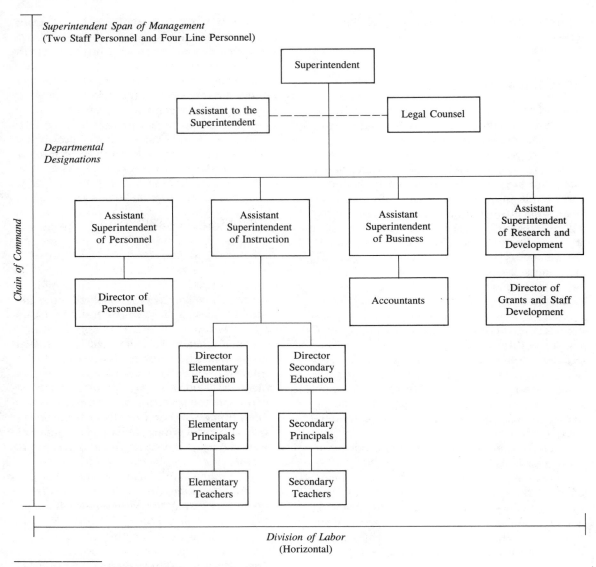

FIGURE 2-1   An Organizational Structure for a Hypothetical School District

Weber's characteristics of bureaucracy apply to many large-size organizations today. General Motors, Xerox, the U.S. military system, the Vatican, most universities, and boards of education are bureaucracies. However, not all characteristics outlined by Weber appear in practice as they were originally intended.[5] Numerous misconceptions in the literature exist regarding Weber's concept of the ideal bureaucracy. Although

[5]Guy Benveniste, *Professionalizing the Organization: Reducing Bureaucracy to Enhance Effectiveness* (San Francisco: Jossey-Bass, 1987).

few "pure" bureaucracies exist today, almost all organizations have some elements of bureaucracy within their structure.

Bureaucratic Dysfunctions

Although Weber's intention was based on rational behavior, the bureaucratic characteristics he formulated have some built-in dysfunctions. First, a high degree of division of labor may reduce the challenge and novelty of many jobs, which can eventually result in reduced performance, absenteeism, or turnover. Second, heavy reliance on bureaucratic rules can cause inefficiency or inertia. For example, rules often become ends in themselves rather than the means toward an end. Rules can also lead to excessive red tape and rigidity. Third, Weber advocated that hierarchy of authority helps coordinate activities, maintains authority, and serves a communication function. In theory the hierarchy has a downward and an upward communication flow. In practice, however, it typically has only a downward orientation. Many subordinates withhold information from superiors and are frustrated because they do not have an opportunity to participate in decision making. Fourth, Weber proposed that employment and promotion be based on qualifications and performance. This he felt would reduce favoritism and personal prejudices. Because performance is difficult to measure in many professional jobs, the tendency is to base promotions more on seniority and loyalty than on competence and merit. Finally, the impersonal nature of bureaucracy is probably its most serious shortcoming. Recent critics of bureaucracy attack it as emphasizing rigid, control-oriented structures over people.

New viewpoints are leading to a decline in the use of bureaucratic structure in modern organizations.[6] School administrators in the 1990s will see a change in some of their duties. One change will be a shift away from simply supervising the work of others to that of contributing directly to the school district's objectives. Instead of shuffling papers and writing reports, the modern administrator may be practicing a craft.[7]

The renowned organization theorist Warren Bennis represents one of the extreme critics of bureaucratic structuring in organizations. Over two decades ago, he forecasted the demise of bureaucracy.[8] In his latest book *Why Leaders Can't Lead*,[9] he exposes the hidden obstacles in our organizations—and in society at large—that conspire against good leadership. According to Bennis, within any organization an entrenched bureaucracy with a commitment to the status quo undermines the unwary leader. This creates an unconscious conspiracy in contemporary society, one that prevents leaders—no matter what their original vision—from taking charge and making changes.

In recent years, popular writers have expressed increasing dissatisfaction with bureaucratic structures. This is reflected in the phenomenal appeal of numerous best-selling books such as *In Search of Excellence*, *The Renewal Factor*, *Thriving on Chaos*, *Reinventing the Corporation*, and *The One Minute Manager*.[10] The basic theme permeating these books is that there are viable alternatives to the bureaucratic model. There is a strong implication that warm, nurturing, caring, trusting, challenging organizations produce high productivity in people.

[6]Peter Nulty, "The Economy of the 1990s: How Managers Will Manage," *Fortune*, 115 (1987), pp. 47–50.

[7]Arthur Blumberg, *School Administration as a Craft* (Needham Heights, MA: Allyn and Bacon, 1989).

[8]Warren G. Bennis, *Changing Organizations* (New York: McGraw-Hill, 1966).

[9]Warren G. Bennis, *Why Leaders Can't Lead: The Unconscious Conspiracy Continues* (San Francisco: Jossey-Bass, 1989).

[10]Thomas J. Peters and Robert H. Waterman, *In Search of Excellence* (New York: Harper & Row, 1982); Robert Waterman, *The Renewal Factor* (New York: Bantam Books, 1987); Tom Peters, *Thriving on Chaos* (New York: Harper & Row, 1988); John Naisbitt and Patricia Aburdene, *Reinventing the Corporation* (New York: Warner Books, 1985); and Kenneth Blanchard and Spencer Johnson, *The One Minute Manager* (New York: Morrow, 1982).

ADMINISTRATIVE ADVICE 2-1

■

RESTRUCTURING SCHOOLS: CHANGING HOW THE BUREAUCRACY WORKS

The wholesale change involved in restructuring the bureaucracy of a school raises a number of questions:

- Can union contracts, board policies, administrative procedures, state mandates, and federal regulations be waived if necessary to support restructuring?
- Will there still be school system goals, standards, and expectations?
- What will change mean for the least—and most—successful students?
- What is the role of the school principal, as well as the central office administrators and staff?
- Who will be held accountable for the students' learning, and how will the results be assessed?

- How will the reward and incentive system be changed?
- Will each school develop its own budget?
- Is there a danger that teachers and students in every school will be tempted to be different simply for the sake of being different?
- Are these changes really for the best, and do teachers and parents want them?

Source: Adapted from Thomas W. Payzant, "To Restructure Schools, We've Changed the Way the Bureaucracy Works," *American School Board Journal*, 176 (1989), pp. 19–20. Copyright 1989, the National School Boards Association. Used by permission.

On the surface, school restructuring appears to be worthwhile. It makes good sense to give teachers the power to make important decisions about how their school is run and how teaching occurs—and then hold them accountable for the results. But in practice, giving teachers greater authority is not a simple matter. Most educators embrace stability and accept change cautiously. When we talk about restructuring schools, we're really talking about changing the way the present bureaucracy works—the way we organize, structure, and allocate resources in the schools. (See Administrative Advice 2-1.)

There may be, however, disadvantages to restructuring, as the PRO/CON Debate indicates.

THE PARTICIPATORY MANAGEMENT MODEL

Participatory management represents an extension of the bureaucratic model. The excessive rigidity and inherent impersonality of the bureaucratic approach stimulated interest in participatory management. These new theories of organization place greater emphasis on employee morale and job satisfaction. Participatory management stresses the importance of motivating employees and building an organization for that purpose. The organization is structured to satisfy employees' needs, which will in turn result in high worker productivity.

Theory X and Theory Y

In 1960 Douglas McGregor presented a convincing argument that most managerial actions flow directly from the assumptions managers hold about their subordinates.[11] The idea is that man-

---

[11]Douglas McGregor, *The Human Side of Enterprise* (New York: McGraw-Hill, 1960).

PRO/CON DEBATE

■

SCHOOL RESTRUCTURING

The educational reform literature of the 1980s emphasizes that the bureaucratic organizational pattern has not produced the desired results in U.S. schooling. In the last decade, many business and industrial organizations restructured by allowing employees more authority to participate in decision making. The result? Higher-quality products and more competitiveness in the marketplace.

QUESTION If schools are restructured to be less bureaucratic, will students receive a better education?

ARGUMENTS PRO

1 Bureaucratic restraints impede teachers. In a bureaucracy, teachers' decisions are limited to those they make in the classroom. They cannot make decisions about curriculum or resource and personnel allocation quickly and easily. This difficulty negatively affects classroom instruction and student learning.

2 Teachers must be held more accountable for outcomes. We are increasing teacher certification requirements and teacher salaries in order to secure a more professional work force. Professionals need a wider sphere of influence. They must have the authority to change whatever needs to be changed in order to improve the outcome.

3 Serious problems require drastic solutions. Too many children are ill served by their schools. If we don't restructure schools, another generation of these children will be lost.

4 The bureaucratic model is obsolete in an information age. Business is abandoning it because it no longer works. Schools will become more alienated from society if they cling to old ways of operating while the rest of the world is changing.

5 The notion of bureaucracy is less and less relevant in the postindustrial society. Futurists indicate that a high-tech world demands a high-tech work place. Bureaucracy is the essence of low-technology.

ARGUMENTS CON

1 The educational bureaucracy protects teachers. Administrators assume the burden of making decisions that affect the school so that teachers are free to concentrate their energies on teaching and learning in the classroom.

2 Teachers don't want to participate in school decision making; their expertise is teaching and learning. Teachers expect administrators to make school-based decisions. If teachers wished to engage in a wider area of decision making, they would become administrators.

3 Drastic restructuring is too risky. We should proceed with caution, engage in research, learn from our experience, and carefully plan the future. Children are not well served when they are guinea pigs in an experimental setting.

4 Schools are highly complex organizations. Efficiency demands a clear division of labor. All teachers should follow the same rules to ensure that all children are served uniformly. To ensure that everyone is treated equally, we need administrators who are impartial judges.

5 Teacher unions are attempting to gain control of schools. School restructuring is the union's strategy to eliminate school administrators.

agement's views of people control operating practices as well as organizational structure. McGregor referred to these contrasting sets of assumptions as **Theory X** and **Theory Y**.

Managers with Theory X assumptions have the following views of people:

- The average person dislikes work and will avoid it if possible.
- Because people dislike work, they must be coerced, controlled, directed, and threatened.
- The average person prefers to be directed and controlled by someone in authority.

The opposite assumptions characterize the Theory Y manager:

- Work is as natural as play or rest.
- Commitment to objectives is a function of rewards for achievement.
- Under proper conditions, people accept and seek responsibility.

McGregor considers Theory X to be incompatible with democratic or participatory organizations because it conflicts with human/individual need-fullfillment on the job. Therefore, McGregor espouses Theory Y because people's behavior in modern organizations more nearly matches its set of assumptions.

Theory Y does not concentrate on organizational structure as much as it argues for a general management philosophy that would force reconsideration of structural dimensions. For example, job enrichment would replace highly specialized jobs and departments. Span of control would be wide, not narrow, in order to provide greater freedom and opportunities for growth and fulfillment of employees' needs. Emphasis on hierarchy would be replaced by emphasis on decentralization and delegation of decisions. Formal, rational authority would give way to "empowerment" of subordinates.

Individual Versus Organization

The school administrator's job is to contribute to the achievement of organizational effectiveness.

An important part of this effort is to enlist the support of subordinates to this same end. In a school setting, this includes teachers and all other professionals who work with students. Chris Argyris suggests that rigid, impersonal organizations such as those prescribed by the bureaucratic perspective hinder employees from using their full potential. He describes the growth or development of human personality and advocates the premise that organizational structure is often incongruent with the fulfillment of human needs. This basic philosophy is stated succinctly by Argyris: "An analysis of the basic properties of relatively mature human beings and the formal organization leads to the conclusion that there is an inherent incongruency between the self-actualization of the two."[12] This basic incongruency creates conflict and frustration for the participants.

Argyris proposes that the human personality progresses along an **immaturity–maturity continuum**—from immaturity as an infant to maturity as an adult. He views this progression in psychological rather than in purely physiological terms. That is, at any age, people can have their degree of growth or development plotted according to seven dimensions. (Table 2-1).

According to Argyris's continuum, as individuals mature, they have increasing needs for more activity, a state of relative independence, behaving in many different ways, deeper interests, a long-time perspective, occupying a superordinate position in reference to their peers, and more awareness of and control over themselves.

Argyris believes that teachers and other professionals want to be treated as mature people, but modern bureaucratic organizations often treat people as if they fit the immature personality type. Teachers and other profession-

---

[12]Chris Argyris, *Personality and Organization* (New York: Harper & Row, 1957), p. 175; see also Chris Argyris, "Personality and Organization Theory Revisited," *Administrative Science Quarterly*, 18 (1973), pp. 141–167.

TABLE 2■1   The Immaturity–Maturity Continuum

IMMATURITY CHARACTERISTICS	MATURITY CHARACTERISTICS
Passivity	Activity
Dependence	Independence
Few ways of behaving	Many ways of behaving
Shallow interests	Deeper interests
Short-time perspective	Long-time perspective
Subordinate position	Superordinate position
Lack of self-awareness	Self-awareness and control

SOURCE: Adapted from Chris Argyris, *Personality and Organization* (New York: Harper & Row, 1957), p. 50.

als react to this treatment by becoming either aggressive or apathetic, which starts a chain reaction. School administrators then impose further restrictions, which turn out to be counterproductive. This hinders optimum organizational effectiveness.

The restraining effects of bureaucratic organizational structure can be alleviated by less rigid rules and operating procedures, a decrease in the division of labor, greater delegation of authority, more participation in decision making, and a more fluid structure throughout the organization. Argyris believes that a more participatory management structure can result in the growth and development of human personality and hence eliminate the incongruency between the individual and the organization.[13]

System 4 Organization

Like McGregor and Argyris, Rensis Likert opposes the kinds of organizations that hew to the bureaucratic model. Likert's theory treats the structural prescriptions for organizational ef-

fectiveness more explicitly and completely. He builds his structural recommendations around three key elements that undergird four systems of organization.

Based on many years of research conducted in various organizational settings—industrial, government, health-care, and educational— Likert proposed four basic systems of organization.[14] System 1, which Likert originally labeled exploitive authoritative, follows the bureaucratic or classical structure of organization. Characteristics of the classical structure include limited supportive leadership, motivation based on fear and superordinate status, one-way downward communication, centralized decision making, close over-the-shoulder supervision, no cooperative teamwork, and low performance goals of managers.

The **System 4 organization**, which Likert calls participative group, is more team-oriented. There is a high level of trust and confidence in the superior; communication flows freely in all directions; decision making occurs throughout the organization; cooperative teamwork is encouraged; and managers actively seek high performance goals. System 2 is less classical than System 1, and System 3 is less supportive than System 4 while coming closer to Likert's ideal model of organization. Table 2-2 shows the characteristics of System 1 and System 4, the extreme ends of Likert's systems continuum.

Key Elements of System 4   According to Likert, System 4 has three key elements: the manager's use of the principle of supportive relationships, the use of group decision making in an overlapping group structure, and the manager's high-performance goals for the organization.[15] The underlying theory is that if an organization is to be highly effective, the leadership and other processes of the organization must ensure that, in

---

[13]Chris Argyris, *Integrating the Individual and the Organization* (New York: Wiley, 1964).

[14]Rensis Likert, "From Production—and Employee Centeredness to Systems 1–4," *Journal of Management*, 5 (1979), pp. 147–156.

[15]Rensis Likert, *The Human Organization* (New York: McGraw-Hill, 1967).

TABLE 2 ▪ 2   Characteristics of System 1 and System 4

ORGANIZATIONAL CHARACTERISTICS	SYSTEM 1 ORGANIZATION	SYSTEM 4 ORGANIZATION
Leadership	Little confidence and trust between administrators and subordinates	Subordinate ideas are solicited and used by administrators
Motivation	Taps fear, status, and economic motives exclusively	Taps all major motives except fear
Communication	One-way, downward communication	Communication flows freely in all directions
Interaction–influence	Little upward influence; downward influence overestimated	Substantial influence upward, downward, and horizontally
Decision making	Centralized; decisions made at the top	Decentralized; decisions made throughout the organization
Goal setting	Established by top-level administrators and communicated downward	Established by group participation
Control	Close over-the-shoulder supervision	Emphasis on self-control
Performance goals	Low and passively sought by administrators; little commitment to developing human resources	High and actively sought by administrators; full commitment to developing human resources

SOURCE: Adapted from Rensis Likert, *The Human Organization* (New York: McGraw–Hill, 1967), pp. 197–211.

all interactions between the superordinate and subordinate, the subordinate will perceive the relationship as enhancing her own sense of personal worth and importance in the organization. Furthermore, Likert argues that "an organization will function best when its personnel function not as individuals but as members of highly effective work groups with high performance goals."[16] In this way, decisions are group decisions, not simply orders from above. And the manager is seen as a "linking-pin"; that is, he is the head of one group but a member of another group at the next higher level. For example, the high school principal is the manager of school staff but also a subordinate to an administrator at the central office in another group at the next

level in the organization. Thus, the principal serves as an important communication link between two levels of organization—school and school district.

System 4 Variables   Likert identifies System 4 as the ideal model of organization. The object of Likert's organizational approach is to move an organization as far as possible toward System 4. To analyze an organization's present system and move it toward System 4, Likert uses an organizational paradigm consisting of three broad classes of variables.

Causal variables are independent variables that affect both the intervening and end-result variables. They include the administrator's assumptions about subordinates, the organization's objectives and how they emerge, administrative behavior and practices, the na-

---

[16]Rensis Likert, *New Patterns of Management* (New York: McGraw-Hill, 1961), p. 105.

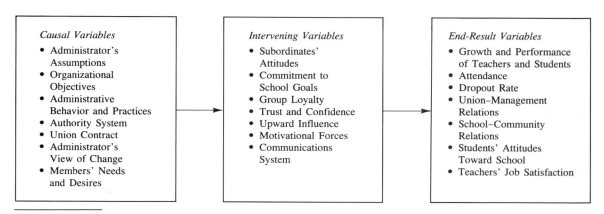

FIGURE 2-2   Relationships Among Causal, Intervening, and End-Result Variables in a System 4 Organization

ture of the authority system that prevails, the union contract, the administrator's view of change, and the needs and desires of members of the organization. Causal variables are within the control of administration, and the value that administration places on these variables will determine the organization's management system. Causal variables then are the ones administrators should attempt to change in order to move the organization to System 4.

Intervening variables, representing the internal state and health of the organization, are those variables that are subsequently affected by causal variables. They include the attitudes that subordinates have toward their jobs, their superiors, peers, and subordinates; their commitment to organizational goals; their levels of performance goals; their levels of group loyalty and group commitment to the organization; their confidence and trust in themselves and their superiors; their feeling of upward influence in the organization; their motivational forces; and the extent to which communications flow freely and in all directions within the organization.

End-result variables are dependent variables that represent the achievements of the organization. In schools they include performance and growth levels of teachers and students, absence and turnover or dropout rates of employees and

students, union–management relations, school–community relations, students' attitudes toward school, and levels of intrinsic job satisfaction of school employees. Figure 2-2 shows the relationship among the variables.

To move an organization to System 4, Likert recommends using the survey-feedback method and leadership training. Using his Profile of Organizational Characteristics instrument, the organization can determine the management system that it is currently using.[17] The survey instrument measures the eight characteristics of organizational systems (see Table 2-2). Respondents are given a continuum of choices for each item on the questionnaire in which they indicate whether the organization tends to be exploitive authoritative (System 1), benevolent authoritative (System 2), consultative (System 3), or participative group (System 4). Respondents are also asked to determine their perception of where they would like the organization to be on the continuum. An organization–systems profile chart, which provides visual evidence of the organization's present management system and the desired system, is then plotted for the institution. Another instrument, the Profile of a School, also measures the organizational sys-

[17]Rensis Likert and Jane Gibson Likert, *New Ways of Managing Conflict* (New York: McGraw-Hill, 1976).

tems of schools.[18] It has several versions that can be used with students, teachers, counselors, principals, superintendents, central office administrators, school board members, and parents. By comparing the perceptions of several subgroups within the organization, it is now possible to measure the management system of a school or an entire school district.

The profile charts become a basis for discussing and analyzing an organization's management system so that plans for improving it can be made. Because effectiveness and System 4 go together in Likert's theory, the implications for organizational improvement are straightforward: Move the present management style of the organization to System 4 and keep it there. This is accomplished by training all administrators throughout the organization to acquire the skills needed for achieving a System 4 structure: manifesting supportive leadership, focusing on high performance goals, and building intact work groups into more effective teams.

Transformation Leadership

Terrence Deal contends that the movement toward participatory management involves transforming the basic character of schools.[19] He focuses on the word *culture*. Deal contends that culture is concerned with shared values, rituals, and symbols. Deal suggests that the core problems of schools, for the most part, are not technical but social.

Previous efforts to improve schools have concentrated on correcting visible structural flaws such as the organizational hierarchy, centralization/decentralization, or decision-making authority. Such changes overlook more durable cultural values and mindscapes that underlie everyday behavior. These deeper patterns provide meaning and continuity. Modifying them involves another level of changes that most reform efforts have ignored.

Deal contends that symbolic structures and patterns cannot be reformed; they must be transformed. To transform an organization is to change its basic character. Examples are Lee Iaccoca's transformation of Chrysler or AT&T's struggle to compete in a deregulated communications industry. Such basic structural changes, however, are the exception rather than the rule.

Value-Added Leadership

In a ground-breaking examination of **value-added leadership**, Amitai Etzioni provides a case for moral authority as a basis for management.[20] Etzioni acknowledges the importance of basic, extrinsic motivation and higher-order, intrinsic motivation (see Maslow and Herzberg, Chapter 4). But Etzioni goes further. He contends that what means most to people is what they believe, how they feel, and the shared norms, values, and cultural symbols that emerge from the groups with which they identify. He maintains that morality and shared values and commitments are far more important motivators than the basic, extrinsic needs and motives and even some intrinsic concerns. (Note the similarity between Etzioni and Deal's concept of culture.)

Thomas Sergiovanni has further specified the concept of value-added leadership.[21] He contends that when moral authority transcends bureaucratic leadership in a school, the outcomes in terms of commitment and performance far exceed expectations. His four stages of value-added leadership are:

1. *Leadership by Bartering*. The leader and led strike a bargain within which the leader

---

[18]Additional information on the Profile of a School instrument can be obtained from Rensis Likert Associates, 630 City Center Building, Ann Arbor, Michigan.
[19]Terrence E. Deal, "Reframing Reform," *Educational Leadership*, 47 (1990), pp. 6–12.

[20]Amitai Etzioni, *The Moral Dimension: Toward a New Theory of Economics* (New York: Free Press, 1988).
[21]Thomas J. Sergiovanni, *Value-Added Leadership: How to Get Extraordinary Performance in Schools* (New York: Harcourt Brace Jovanovich, 1990).

gives to the led something they want in exchange for something the leader wants.
2. *Leadership by Building*. The leader provides the climate and interpersonal support that enhances the led's opportunities for fulfillment of needs for achievement, responsibility, competence, and esteem.
3. *Leadership by Bonding*. The leader and led develop a set of shared values and commitments that bond them together in a common cause.
4. *Leadership by Banking*. The leader institutionalizes the improvement initiatives as part of the everyday life of the school. This conserves human energy and effort for new projects and initiatives.[22]

A new kind of hierarchy then emerges in the school—one that places purposes, values, and commitments at the apex and teachers, principals, parents, and students below, in service to these purposes. According to Sergiovanni, moral authority is a means to add value to an administrator's leadership practice, and this added value results in extraordinary commitment and performance in schools.

To implement this new kind of hierarchy, Roland Barth views restructuring as improving schools from within.[23] In his best-selling book, he examines the adults—parents, teachers, principals, and central office administrators—who help children learn. He describes how these stakeholders can assume responsibility for shaping their own school system. He stresses the importance of collaboration among these stakeholders in promoting learning and promoting schools. He sees transformation as focusing on the fact that the different roles of the major stakeholders serve a common purpose—to improve the education of all children in the school system. According to Barth, change in the classroom is the only change that really matters.

Participatory management proponents have high concern for people in structuring organizations. They view people as the most important resource of the organization. Supportiveness, participation, shared decision making, "empowerment," flexibility, and employee growth and development are the keys to participatory management.

Site-Based Management

Site-based management represents a change in how a school district is structured, that is, how authority and responsibility are shared between the district and its schools. It changes roles and responsibilities of staff within schools and how the school district's central office staff is organized with respect to its size, roles, and responsibilities.[24] Professional responsibility replaces bureaucratic regulation. School districts accomplish this new structure in two ways: (1) increasing autonomy through some type of relief from constraining rules and regulations and (2) sharing the authority to make decisions with the school's major stakeholder groups, including teachers, parents, students, and other community members.[25]

In practice, authority to make changes at the building level is typically granted by some type of waiver process. Usually, a waiver process is the result of agreements between the school district and teachers' union that expand the scope of authority granted individual school sites. In a few cases, districts may also have agreements with their states that permit waivers from state regulations or laws that mandate school-based decision making.[26] For example, in

---

[22]Ibid, pp. 39–40
[23]Roland Barth, *Improving Schools from Within* (San Francisco: Jossey-Bass, 1990).

[24]Richard F. Elmore, *Early Experiences in Restructuring Schools: Voices from the Field* (Washington, D.C.: National Governor's Association, 1988).
[25]Jane L. David, "Synthesis of Research on School-Based Management," *Educational Leadership*, 46 (1989), pp. 45–53.
[26]Jane L. David, *Restructuring in Progress: Lessons from Pioneering Districts* (Washington, D.C.: National Governors' Association, 1989).

Kentucky school principals can hire, transfer, and fire teachers without school board approval according to a new state law.[27]

To increase shared decision making, a school typically forms a school-site council with representatives from the school's major stakeholder groups. The composition of this council, how members are selected, and what their responsibilities are vary considerably between and within school districts. Some councils are composed of teachers elected from the entire faculty or by grade level or department. Others are composed of members from pre-existing committees such as the curriculum, staffing, or budget committees. In some schools, the entire faculty constitutes the council.[28]

Before site-based management can work, the local school board must firmly commit to support shared decision making. In fact, unless school board members are behind it, any attempt to move the decision-making process closer to the school site will fail. (See Administrative Advice 2-2.)

ALTERNATIVE MODELS OF ORGANIZATIONAL STRUCTURE

The bureaucratic and participatory management models laid the groundwork for more complex approaches to organizational structure. Top-level school administrators must consider the relative suitability of alternative approaches to organizational structure, based on the problems they face and the environment in which they work. We describe some alternative approaches to organizational structure, including Etzioni's compliance theory, Hage's mechanistic–organic organizations, and Mintzberg's strategy–structure typology.

Compliance Theory

Etzioni has developed an innovative approach to the structure of organizations.[29] He classifies organizations by the type of power they use to direct the behavior of their members and the type of involvement of the participants. Etzioni identifies three types of organizational power: coercive, utilitarian, and normative, and relates these to three types of involvement: alienative, calculative, and moral (Figure 2-3, page 40). This figure, while grossly oversimplifying the relationships, helps to make clear the pattern among the components. It should be noted that life in organizations is much more complicated.

Coercive power uses force and fear to control lower-level participants. Examples of organizations that rely on coercive power include prisons, custodial mental hospitals, and basic training in the military.

Utilitarian power uses remuneration or extrinsic rewards to control lower-level participants. Most business firms emphasize such extrinsic rewards. These rewards include salary, merit pay, fringe benefits, working conditions, and job security. Besides many business firms, utilitarian organizations include unions, farmers' co-ops, and various government agencies.

Normative power controls through allocation of intrinsic rewards, for example, interesting work, identification with goals, and making a contribution to society. Management's power in this case rests on its ability to manipulate symbolic rewards, allocate esteem and prestige symbols, administer ritual, and influence the distribution of acceptance and positive response in the organization.

Many professional people work in normative organizations. Examples of such organizations are churches, political organizations, hospitals, universities, and professional associations (such as the American Association of School Admin-

---

[27]Kentucky Education Reform Act of 1990 (House Bill 940).

[28]David, *Restructuring in Progress.*

[29]Amitai Etzioni, *A Comparative Analysis of Complex Organizations*, rev. ed. (New York: Free Press, 1975).

ADMINISTRATIVE ADVICE 2-2

■

SITE-BASED MANAGEMENT

If you are interested in site-based management but are unsure where to begin or what role the school board should play, the following suggestions are offered:

■ *Commit Your Board to Action.* Many school systems have experimented with site-based management on a small scale, only to have board members hesitate and question further support of decentralization. Such second thoughts often stem from a fear of losing control or a lack of trust in employees' ability to make decisions.

■ *Involve Administrators Early.* Efforts at site-based management have faltered in many school systems because of the resistance of administrators who are fearful of losing authority and control. These people, who have held the purse strings and made the decisions for years, aren't easily convinced that involving others in what has always been their purview is necessary, helpful, or efficient.

■ *Seek Outside Expertise.* Inviting consultants to help develop your site-based management plan can be beneficial. Few school systems have experts on staff who can train others in consensus building, group-process skills, and shared decision making. An outside consultant can provide this expertise—plus knowledge of progressive management concepts and experience in the problems surrounding site-based management.

■ *Visit Other School Systems.* You can learn from the experiences of others involved in site-based management. Send teachers, administrators, and board members across the United States to visit school districts and attend conferences where they can discover how others are implementing shared decision making.

■ *Work Closely with Unions.* In some school systems, employees are suspicious of site-based management. The promise of shared decision making might appear to be only a lure to win teachers' acceptance of an increased workload. Involve union leaders in the early stages of planning.

■ *Be Aware of Time Commitments.* There's no way around it: Involving employees in administrative decisions is time-consuming, which can be frustrating. Administrators become irritated at the delays involved in making decisions by committee, and teachers feel pressured by the additional work outside the classroom. Sooner or later, people are bound to question the value of site-based management.

■ *Adopt Appropriate Policies.* For site-based management to succeed, your board must work in collaboration with teachers to develop district policies that formalize the new management system.

■ *Start with a Pilot Program.* Start small and move slowly. Don't make the mistake of moving some schools into site-based management before they are ready. Some staffs are more receptive to shared decision making than others, and you shouldn't force people into a process that's time-consuming and demands that they take on added responsibilities.

Source: Adapted from James E. Mitchell, "Share the Power," *American School Board Journal*, 177 (1990), pp. 42–43. Copyright 1990, the National School Boards Association. Used by permission.

Types of Power

	Coercive	Utilitarian	Normative
Alienative	X		
Calculative		X	
Moral			X

Types of Involvement

FIGURE 2-3   Etzioni's Compliance Types

istrators, National Association of Secondary School Principals, and National Education Association). Public schools probably fit this category for the most part, although there are vast differences in their use of power to gain member compliance, particularly the control of pupils.

Types of Involvement   All three types of power can be useful in obtaining subordinates' cooperation in organizations. However, the relative effectiveness of each approach depends on the organizational participant's involvement. Involvement refers to the orientation of a person to an object, characterized in terms of intensity and direction. Accordingly, people can be placed on an involvement continuum that ranges from highly negative to highly positive. Etzioni suggests that participants' involvement can be broadly categorized as alienative, calculative, or moral.

Alienative involvement designates an intense, negative orientation. Inmates in prisons, patients in custodial mental hospitals, and enlisted personnel in basic training all tend to be alienated from their respective organizations.

Calculative involvement designates either a negative or a positive orientation of low intensity. Calculative orientations are predominant in relationships of merchants who have permanent customers in various types of business associations. Similarly, inmates in prisons ("rats") who have established contact with prison authorities often have predominantly calculative attitudes toward those in power.

Moral involvement designates a positive orientation of high intensity. The involvement of the parishioner in her church or synagogue, the devoted member of his political party, and the loyal follower of her leader are all moral.

Relationship of Power to Involvement   According to Etzioni, when an organization employs coercive power, participants usually react to the organization with hostility, which is alienative involvement. Utilitarian power usually results in calculative involvement; that is, participants desire to maximize personal gain. Finally, normative power frequently creates moral involvement; for instance, participants are committed to the socially beneficial features of their organizations.

Some organizations employ all three powers, but most tend to emphasize only one, relying less on the other two. Power specialization occurs because, when two types of power are emphasized simultaneously with the same participant group, they tend to neutralize each other.

Applying force, fear, or other coercive measures, for example, usually creates such high-degree alienation that it becomes impossible to apply normative power successfully. This may be one reason why using coercive control in gaining student compliance in schools often leads to a displacement of educational goals.[30] Similarly, it may be why teachers in progressive schools tend to oppose corporal punishment.

---

[30]William Glasser, *The Quality School* (New York: Harper & Row, 1990).

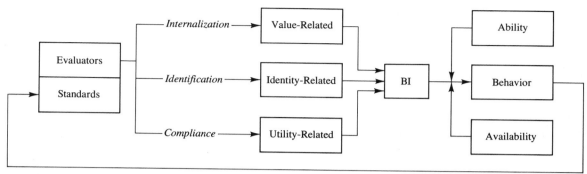

NOTE: BI stands for Behavioral Intentions

FIGURE 2-4   A Social Influence Model (SOURCE: Adapted from M. Sussman and Robert P. Vecchio, "A Social Influence Interpretation of Worker Motivation," *Academy of Management Review*, 7 (1982), p. 184. Used by permisison.)

In most organizations, types of power and involvement are related in the three combinations depicted in Figure 2-3. Of course, a few organizations combine two or even all three types. For instance, some teachers' unions use both utilitarian and normative power to gain compliance from their members. Nevertheless, school officials who attempt to use types of power that are not appropriate for the environment can reduce organizational effectiveness. Schools tend to be normative organizations. According to this logic, oppressive use of coercive and utilitarian power with teachers and students can be dysfunctional.

Inducement Approaches to Gaining Compliance

Two well-known researchers, M. Sussman and Robert Vecchio propose a social-influence model consisting of several inducement approaches to gaining subordinate compliance.[31] Using Etzioni's compliance typology, Sussman and Vecchio suggest that an administrator's attempts to exert influence over a subordinate follow a cycle in which he tries one of three influence approaches in accordance with three need levels (see Chapter 4) and three types of power. Figure 2-4 depicts a form of the model in which an administrator will attempt to use compliance, identification, or internalization to influence a subordinate. He may try threats, appeals to a subordinate's sense of organizational affiliation, or appeals to the subordinate's value system.

Such attempts will succeed or fail to the extent that the subordinate is inclined to accept utility-related, identity-related, or value-related incentives. For certain types of subordinates, a particular type of appeal may be more prevalent, as outlined in Etzioni's types of involvement. Acceptance of the administrator's attempt leads to behavioral intentions, which are constrained by ability and availability, of the subordinate to behave in the prescribed manner. That is, a subordinate may lack the ability to perform the task in the desired manner or may not have the resources to perform the task. The subordinate's behavior is then compared to the standards the administrator has established. If the influence attempt has failed, the administrator will make other attempts using different types of influence. The model suggests that subordinates may require different influence approaches to obtain desired behavior. According to Sussman and Vecchio, administrators who learn to use a variety of inducement approaches are relatively more effective than other administrators.

[31]M. Sussman and Robert P. Vecchio, "A Social Influence Interpretation of Worker Motivation," *Academy of Management Review*, 7 (1982), pp. 177–186.

Mechanistic–Organic Organizations

A number of writers have called attention to the incongruency between bureaucratic and professional norms. Specifically, they argue that occupants of hierarchical positions frequently do not have the technical competence to make decisions about issues that involve professional knowledge. For example, one study found that there was a basic conflict in educational organizations between authority based on bureaucracy and authority based on professional norms.[32] Another study came to a similar conclusion: "The central notions of bureaucratization and professionalization are logically incompatible."[33] A study of teachers' roles in the authority structure of the schools found that there was a need for separating spheres of authority in schools: that is, delegating strictly administrative decisions to those in hierarchical positions, while allowing teachers to make decisions requiring professional knowledge.[34] Other research supports the notion that bureaucratic orientations and professional attitudes need not conflict if teachers are provided with sufficient autonomy to carry out their jobs.[35]

We can conclude from this research that most schools have both bureaucratic and professional characteristics that are often incompatible but need not be. Jerald Hage suggests an axiomatic theory of organizations that provides a framework for defining two ideal types of organizations: **mechanistic** (bureaucratic) and **organic** (professional).[36] His theory identifies eight key variables found in schools and other organizations. These key variables are arranged in a means–ends relationship and are interrelated in seven basic propositions.

Eight Organizational Variables   Complexity, centralization, formalization, and stratification are the four variables that constitute the organizational *means* by which schools are structured to achieve objectives. Adaptiveness, production, efficiency, and job satisfaction are the four variables that represent categories for sorting organizational *ends*. We describe each in turn.

1. **Complexity**, or specialization, refers to the number of occupational specialities included in an organization and the length of training required of each. Person specialization and task specialization distinguish the degree of specialization. A teacher who is an expert in English literature is a person specialist, whereas one who teaches eleventh-grade English is a task specialist. The greater the number of person specialists and the longer the period of training required to achieve person specialization (or degree held), the more complex the organization.

2. **Centralization**, or hierarchy of authority, refers to the number of role incumbents who participate in decision making and the number of areas in which they participate. The lower the proportion of role incumbents who participate and the fewer the decision areas in which they participate, the more centralized the organization.

[32]Ronald G. Corwin, "Militant Professionalism, Initiative, and Compliance in Public Education," *Sociology of Education*, 38 (1965), pp. 310–331.

[33]Keith F. Punch, "Bureaucratic Structure in Schools: Towards Redefinition and Measurement," *Educational Administration Quarterly*, 5 (1969), p. 54.

[34]Norman J. Boyan, "The Emergent Role of the Teacher and the Authority Structure of the School," in R. Allen and J. Schmid (eds.), *Collective Negotiations and Educational Administration* (Fayetteville: University of Arkansas Press, 1966).

[35]James H. Balderson, "The Bureaucratization of Teacher Behavior Scale and the Measurement of School Organization Structure." Paper presented at the annual meeting of the American Educational Research Association, New York, 1977; Kevin Marjoribanks, "Bureaucratic Orientations, Autonomy, and the Professional Attitudes of Teachers," *Journal of Educational Administration*, 15 (1977), pp. 108–113.

[36]Jerald Hage, "An Axiomatic Theory of Organizations," *Administrative Science Quarterly*, 10 (1955), pp. 289–320.

3. **Formalization**, or standardization, refers to the proportion of codified jobs and the range of variation that is tolerated within the parameters defining the jobs. The higher the proportion of codified jobs in schools and the less the range of variation allowed, the more formalized the organization.

4. **Stratification**, or status system, refers to the difference in status between higher and lower levels in the school's hierarchy. Differentials in salary, prestige, privileges, and mobility among position occupants in the school's hierarchy usually measure this status difference. The greater the disparity in rewards between the top and bottom status levels and the lower the rates of mobility between them, the more stratified the organization.

5. **Adaptiveness**, or flexibility, refers to the use of professional knowledge and techniques in the instruction of students and the ability of a school to respond to environmental demands. The more advanced the knowledge base, instructional techniques, and environmental response, the more adaptive the organization.

6. **Production** refers to the quantity and quality of output. A distinction can be made between quantity and quality of output. Some schools are more concerned with quantity and less concerned with quality, and vice versa. This variable is difficult to measure because of the dichotomy between quantity and quality. For example, some universities are "degree mills," that is, they award a large number of degrees each year with little concern for quality. Other institutions are less concerned about increasing the quantity of degrees awarded and more concerned about the quality of the product (the degree recipient). The greater the emphasis on quantity, not quality, of output, the more productive the organization.

7. **Efficiency**, or cost, refers to financial as well as human resources and the amount of idle resources. For example, class-size ratios of one teacher to thirty students are more efficient than a one-to-ten ratio. The lower the cost per unit of production, the more efficient the organization.

8. **Job satisfaction**, or morale, refers to the amount of importance a school places on its human resources. Measures of job satisfaction include feelings of well-being, absenteeism, turnover, and the like. The higher the morale and the lower the absenteeism and turnover, the higher the job satisfaction in the organization.[37]

Seven Organizational Propositions Central to Hage's axiomatic theory are seven propositions, which have been drawn from the classic works of Weber,[38] Barnard,[39] and Thompson.[40] The major theme permeating Hage's theory is the concept of functional strains, that is, the maximization of one organizational-means variable results in the minimization of another. The eight key variables are related in fairly predictable ways. For instance, high centralization results in high production and formalization, high formalization in turn results in high efficiency, high stratification results in low job satisfaction and adaptiveness and high production, and high complexity results in low centralization. These ideas are expressed in seven propositions:

- The higher the centralization, the higher the production
- The higher the formalization, the higher the efficiency
- The higher the centralization, the higher the formalization
- The higher the stratification, the higher the production

[37]Ibid.

[38]Max Weber, *The Theory of Social and Economic Organization*.

[39]Chester Barnard, "Functions and Pathology of Status Systems in Formal Organizations," in William F. Whyte (ed.), *Industry and Society* (New York: McGraw-Hill, 1964), pp. 46–83.

[40]Victor Thompson, *Modern Organization* (New York: Knopf, 1961).

TABLE 2-3   Characteristics of Mechanistic and Organic Organizational Forms

MECHANISTIC ORGANIZATION (BUREAUCRATIC)	ORGANIC ORGANIZATION (PROFESSIONAL)
Low complexity	High complexity
High centralization	Low centralization
High formalization	Low formalization
High stratification	Low stratification
Low adaptiveness	High adaptiveness
High production	Low production
High efficiency	Low efficiency
Low job satisfaction	High job satisfaction

SOURCE: Adapted from Jerald Hage, "An Axiomatic Theory of Organizations," *Administrative Science Quarterly,* 10 (1965), p. 305. Used by permission.

- The higher the stratification, the lower the job satisfaction
- The higher the stratification, the lower the adaptiveness
- The higher the complexity, the lower the centralization[41]

Two Ideal Types   The interrelationship of the eight key variables in seven basic propositions was used to define two ideal types of organizations, as Table 2-3 shows. Mechanistic and organic concepts are organizational extremes that represent "ideal" types; that is, they are pure types not necessarily found in real life. No school is completely mechanistic (bureaucratic) nor completely organic (professional). Most schools fall somewhere between these two extremes.

Bureaucratic-type schools tend to have a hierarchical structure of control, authority, and communication with little shared decision making (high centralization); each functional role requires precise definitions of rights and obligations and technical methods (high formalization); emphasis on status differences between hierarchical levels in the organization exists (high stratification); emphasis on quantity, not quality, of output at least cost is prevalent (high production, high efficiency); little emphasis on professional expertise in both subject-matter knowledge and instructional methodology exists (low complexity); there is little responsiveness to changing needs of students, society, and subject matter (low adaptiveness); and human resources are of little importance (low job satisfaction).

High complexity, adaptiveness, and job satisfaction characterize the model of the ideal professional-type school. That is, school administrators respect the professional knowledge of teachers, respond readily to the changing needs of the school and society, and consider the intrinsic satisfaction of teachers to be an important school outcome. Furthermore, centralization is low because administrators encourage teacher participation in decision making and delegate considerable authority and responsibility to teachers in the operation of the school. A network structure of control, authority, and communication prevails. School administrators adjust and continually redefine tasks and avoid always "going by the book." The organization de-emphasizes status differences among the occupants of the many positions in the hierarchy and adopts a collegial, egalitarian orientation. Low efficiency and productivity also characterize the ideal professional school. School administrators in the professional-type school are not as concerned with the quantity of output as they are with the quality of outcomes. Professional-type schools are probably more expensive to operate than bureaucratic-type schools because professional-school administrators tend to de-emphasize quantity of output at least cost. Such schools tend to be less efficient but more effective.

Each ideal type of school has advantages and disadvantages. Moreover, there are limits on how much a school administrator can emphasize one

---

[41]Hage, "An Axiomatic Theory of Organizations."

organizational-end variable over another. For example, if there is no codification of jobs (formalization), then a condition of normlessness prevails, which will likely result in low job satisfaction of faculty members. If schools do not respond to the knowledge explosion, technological innovations, and the changing needs of students and society, schools are apt to fail in the face of an everchanging environment. Conversely, too high a change rate is likely to result in increased costs involved in implementing new programs and techniques. Limits exist on each of the eight variables beyond which a school dare not move. Hage expresses it this way: "Production imposes limits on complexity, centralization, formalization, stratification, adaptiveness, efficiency, and job satisfaction."[42] That is, extremes in any variable result in the loss of production, even in a school that has the means to maximize this end.

All the relationships specified in the seven propositions are curvilinear. For instance, if centralization becomes too high, production drops; if stratification becomes too low, job satisfaction falls. Therefore, exceeding the limits on any variable results in a reversal of the hypothesized relationships specified in the seven propositions. According to Hage, "These represent important qualifications to the axiomatic theory."[43]

The tension between the mechanistic (bureaucratic) and organic (professional) models is constantly negotiated between teachers and administrators. Sometimes it is resolved in favor of professionals, and sometimes it is resolved in favor of administrators.[44]

Because schools are fragile political coalitions, each decision must be considered strategically, examining its implications for all the major stakeholders.[45] Thus, school administrators must examine several strategic questions before a professional-school orientation can be effectively implemented. (See Administrative Advice 2-3.)

Two writers contend that administrators have a choice in how they lead their schools. Traditionally, they have chosen bureaucratic leadership behaviors. These authors note how sharply the ideals of long-standing bureaucracy differ from the more innovative concepts of a professional structure.[46] They propose seven bureaucratic–professional continua (Figure 2-5).

- *Stability Versus Activity*. Stability gives focus to predictability, consistency, and regularity. Activity allows teachers more trials at innovation, and teachers who innovate become better at innovation.
- *Intention Versus Distinction*. Intention is a goal-based behavior that places intent ahead of action. Distinction is the retrospective interpretation of what works. Administrators who foster distinction are conscious of working with culture building; that is, they provide a shared meaning of "what is going on," using individual and group sense making, and creating underlying assumptions.
- *Accountability Versus Efficacy*. Administrators who formally hold teachers accountable are asking for compliance through control mechanisms. The professional option to accountability is efficacy. When administrators pay attention to making teachers feel good about themselves, the self-efficacy of teachers is being promoted.
- *Regularity Versus Variability*. When administrators use a behavior of regularity, they are pro-

[42]Ibid., p. 307.

[43]Ibid.

[44]Samuel B. Bacharach, Peter Bamberger, and Sharon C. Conley, "The See-Saw Metaphor and Managing Professionals," unpublished paper, Cornell University, 1988.

[45]Jeffrey Pfeffer and Gerald R. Salanik, "Organization Design: The Case for a Coalitional Model of Organizations," in J. R. Hackman, E. E. Lawler, and L. W. Porter (eds.), *Perspectives on Behavior in Organizations* (New York: McGraw-Hill, 1983), pp. 102–111.

[46]Gerald D. Bailey and William F. Adams," Leadership Strategies for Nonbureaucratic Leadership," *NASSP Bulletin*, 74 (1990), pp. 21–28.

ADMINISTRATIVE ADVICE 2-3

■

STRATEGIC QUESTIONS

In structuring a professional-school orientation, school administrators must answer the following strategic questions:

■ *In which decisions will professional teachers become involved?* There appears to be general agreement among the major stakeholders that teachers should be more involved in making decisions. However, we need to specify the areas in which teachers will play larger roles in decision making.

■ *Who will make what decisions in the school?* How much influence should teachers have with respect to decisions affecting other parties in the school—students, teachers, support staff, principals, central office administrators, school board members? The roles of these stakeholders may need to be clarified or redefined in a professional-school structure.

■ *What are the basic tasks of administrators and teachers in the context of a professional-school*

structure? Put another way, what is the basis of teachers' expertise and professional identity? That is, the amount of participation in decision making probably should be contingent on whether the issue is relevant to teachers and whether teachers have the expertise to make the decision.

■ *What is the role of teacher unions in a professional-school structure?* The involvement of teacher unions is a key strategic issue in structuring a professional-school orientation.

Source: Adapted from Sharon C. Conley and Samuel B. Bacharach, "From School-Site Management to Participatory School-Site Management," *Phi Delta Kappan*, 71 (1990), pp. 539–544.

Bureaucratic Leadership: Behaviors of Administrators	*Professional Leadership: Behaviors of Administrators*
Stability ← - - - - - - -	- - - - - - → Activity
Intention ← - - - - - - -	- - - - - - → Distinction
Accountability ← - - - - - -	- - - - - - → Efficacy
Regularity ← - - - - - - -	- - - - - - → Variability
Intervention ← - - - - - -	- - - - - - → Facilitation
Control ← - - - - - - -	- - - - - - → Empowerment
Holism ← - - - - - - -	- - - - - - → Disaggregation

FIGURE 2-5   Bureaucratic Versus Professional Structure (SOURCE: Adapted from Gerald D. Bailey and William F. Adams, "Leadership Strategies for Nonbureaucratic Leadership," *NASSP Bulletin*, 74 (1990), pp. 21–28. Used by permission.)

viding reliability through rules, policies, job descriptions, and standard operating procedures. Variability encourages cooperative decision making and "product champions" through supporting primary work groups.

■ *Intervention Versus Facilitation.* An intervention leadership behavior reflects the hierarchical constructs of bureaucratic functioning. Administrators establish goals for teachers, monitor operations, and evaluate for outcomes. Facilitation presumes that the school is populated with skilled, committed teachers and that decision making, problem solving, and innovation are best handled closest to the point of action.

■ *Control Versus Empowerment.* A leadership behavior of control "keeps the administrator in charge." By empowering teachers, administrators are multiplying the points at which action can be initiated.

■ *Holism Versus Disaggregation.* Holism is characterized by tightening control, intervention, accountability, and regularity. Disaggregation means that administrators promote loose coupling, which leads to novelty and flexibility.

Strategy–Structure Typology

Another alternative approach to organizational structure concerns the relationship between organizational strategy and structure. This approach began with the landmark work of Alfred Chandler, who traced the historical development of such large American corporations as DuPont, Sears, and General Motors.[47] He concluded from his study that an organization's strategy tends to influence its structure. He suggests that strategy indirectly determines such variables as the organization's tasks, technology, and environ-

ments, and each of these influences the structure of the organization.

More recently, social scientists have augmented Chandler's thesis by contending that an organization's strategy determines its environment, technology, and tasks. These variables coupled with growth rates and power distribution affect organizational structure. Henry Mintzberg suggests that organizations can be differentiated along three basic dimensions: (1) the key part of the organization, that is, the part of the organization that plays the major role in determining its success or failure; (2) the prime coordinating mechanism, that is, the major method the organization uses to coordinate its activities; and (3) the type of decentralization used, that is, the extent to which the organization involves subordinates in the decision-making process.[48] The key parts of an organization are shown in Figure 2-6 and include the following:

■ *The strategic apex* is top management and its support staff. In school districts, this is the superintendent of schools and his administrative cabinet.

■ *The operative core* are the workers who actually carry out the organization's tasks. Teachers constitute the operative core in school districts.

■ *The middle line* is middle- and lower-level management. Principals are the middle-level managers in school districts.

■ *The technostructure* are analysts such as engineers, accountants, planners, researchers, and personnel managers. In school districts, divisions such as instruction, business, personnel, research and development, and the like constitute the technostructure.

■ *The support staff* are the people who provide indirect services. In school districts, similar services include maintenance, clerical, food service, legal counsel, and consulting to provide support.[49]

---

[47]Alfred D. Chandler, *Strategy and Structure* (Cambridge, MA: MIT Press, 1962); see also Chandler, *The Visible Hand: The Managerial Revolution in America* (Cambridge, MA: Belknap Press, 1977).

[48]Henry Mintzberg, *The Structuring of Organizations* (Englewood Cliffs, NJ: Prentice-Hall, 1979).
[49]Ibid.

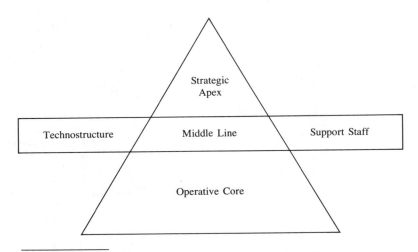

FIGURE 2-6   The Key Parts of an Organization (SOURCE: Adapted from Henry Mintzberg, "Organization Design: Fashion or Fit?" *Harvard Business Review*, 59 (1981), p. 105. Copyright © by the President and Fellows of Harvard College. Used by permission.

The second basic dimension of an organization is its prime coordinating mechanism. These include the following:

- *Direct supervision* means that one individual is responsible for the work of others. This concept refers to the unity of command and scalar principles discussed earlier.
- *Standardization of work process* exists when the content of work is specified or programmed. In school districts, this refers to job descriptions that govern the work performance of educators.
- *Standardization of skills* exists when the kind of training necessary to do the work is specified. In school systems, this refers to state certificates required for the various occupants of a school district's hierarchy.
- *Standardization of output* exists when the results of the work are specified. Because the "raw material" that is processed by the operative core (teachers) consists of people (students), not things, standardization of output is more difficult to measure in schools than in other nonservice organizations. Neverthe-

less, a movement toward the standardization of output in schools in recent years has occurred. Examples include competency testing of teachers, state-mandated testing of students, state-mandated curriculum, prescriptive learning objectives, and other efforts toward legislated learning.
- *Mutual adjustment* exists when work is coordinated through informal communication. Mutual adjustment or coordination is the major thrust of Likert's "linking-pin" concept discussed earlier.[50]

The third basic dimension of an organization is the type of decentralization it employs. The three types of decentralization are the following:

- *Vertical decentralization* is the distribution of power down the chain of command, or shared authority between superordinates and subordinates in any organization.
- *Horizontal decentralization* is the extent to which nonadministrators (including staff)

---

[50]Ibid.

TABLE 2 ▪ 4   Mintzberg's Five Organizational Structures

STRUCTURAL CONFIGURATION	PRIME COORDINATING MECHANISM	KEY PART OF ORGANIZATION	TYPE OF DECENTRALIZATION
Simple structure	Direct supervision	Strategic apex	Vertical and horizontal centralization
Machine bureaucracy	Standardization of work processes	Technostructure	Limited horizontal decentralization
Professional bureaucracy	Standardization of skills	Operating core	Vertical and horizontal decentralization
Divisionalized form	Standardization of outputs	Middle line	Limited vertical decentralization
Adhocracy	Mutual adjustment	Support staff	Selective decentralization

SOURCE: Adapted from Henry Mintzberg, *The Structuring of Organizations* (Englewood Cliffs, NJ: Prentice-Hall, 1979), p. 301. Used by permission of the publisher.

---

make decisions, or shared authority between line and staff.

- *Selective decentralization* is the extent to which decision-making power is delegated to different units within the organization. In school districts, these units might include instruction, business, personnel, and research and development divisions.[51]

Using the three basic dimensions—key part of the organization, prime coordinating mechanism, and type of decentralization—Mintzberg suggests that the strategy an organization adopts and the extent to which it practices that strategy result in five structural configurations: simple structure, machine bureaucracy, professional bureaucracy, divisionalized form, and adhocracy. Table 2-4 summarizes the three basic dimensions associated with each of the five structural configurations. Each organizational form is discussed in turn.[52]

Simple Structure   The **simple structure** has as its key part the strategic apex, uses direct su-

pervision, and employs vertical and horizontal centralization. Examples of simple structures are relatively small corporations, new government departments, medium-sized retail stores, and small elementary school districts. The organization consists of the top manager and a few workers in the operative core. There is no technostructure, and the support staff is small; workers perform overlapping tasks. For example, teachers and administrators in small elementary school districts must assume many of the duties that the technostructure and support staff performed. Frequently, however, small elementary school districts are members of cooperatives that provide many services (i.e. counselors, social workers) to a number of small school districts in one region of the county or state.

In small school districts, for example, the superintendent may function as both superintendent of the district and principal of a single school. Superintendents in such school districts must be entrepreneurs. Because the organization is small, coordination is informal and maintained through direct supervision. Moreover, this organization can adapt to environmental changes rapidly. Goals stress innovation and long-term survival, although innovation may be

---

[51]Ibid.
[52]Ibid.

difficult for very small rural school districts because of the lack of resources.

Machine Bureaucracy   **Machine bureaucracy** has the technostructure as its key part, uses standardization of work processes as its prime coordinating mechanism, and employs limited horizontal decentralization. Machine bureaucracy has many of the characteristics of Weber's ideal bureaucracy and resembles Hage's mechanistic organization. It has a high degree of formalization and work specialization. Decisions are centralized. The span of management is narrow, and the organization is tall—that is, many levels exist in the chain of command from top management to the bottom of the organization. Little horizontal or lateral coordination is needed. Furthermore, machine bureaucracy has a large technostructure and support staff.

Examples of machine bureaucracy are automobile manufacturers, steel companies, and large government organizations. The environment for a machine bureaucracy is typically stable, and the goal is to achieve internal efficiency. Public schools possess many characteristics of machine bureaucracy, but most schools are not machine bureaucracies in the pure sense. However, large urban school districts (New York, Los Angeles, and Chicago) are closer to machine bureaucracies than other medium-sized or small school districts.

Professional Bureaucracy   **Professional bureaucracy** has the operating core as its key part, uses standardization of skills as its prime coordinating mechanism, and employs vertical and horizontal decentralization. The organization is relatively formalized but decentralized to provide autonomy to professionals. Highly trained professionals provide nonroutine services to clients. Top management is small; there are few middle managers; and the technostructure is generally small. However, the support staff is typically large to provide clerical and maintenance support for the professional operating core. The goals of professional bureaucracies are to innovate and provide high-quality services.

Existing in complex but stable environments, they are generally moderate to large in size. Coordination problems are common. Examples of this form of organization include universities, hospitals, and large law firms.

Some public school districts have many characteristics of the professional bureaucracy, particularly its aspects of professionalism, teacher autonomy, and structural looseness. For example, schools are formal organizations, which provide complex services through highly trained professionals in an atmosphere of structural looseness.[53] These characteristics tend to broaden the limits of individual discretion and performance. Like attorneys, physicians, and university professors, teachers perform in classroom settings in relative isolation from colleagues and superiors, while remaining in close contact with their students. Furthermore, teachers are highly trained professionals who provide information to their students in accordance with their own style, and they are usually flexibile in the delivery of content even within the constraints of the state- and district-mandated curriculum. Moreover, like some staff administrators, teachers tend to identify more with their professions than with the organization.

Divisionalized Form   The **divisionalized form** has the middle line as its key part, uses standardization of output as its prime coordinating mechanism, and employs limited vertical decentralization. Decision making is decentralized at the divisional level. There is little coordination among the separate divisions. Corporate-level personnel provide some coordination. Thus, each division itself is relatively centralized and tends to resemble a machine bureaucracy. The technostructure is located at corporate headquarters to provide services to all divisions; support staff is located within each

---

[53]Charles E. Bidwell, "The School as a Formal Organization," in J. G. March (ed.), *Handbook of Organizations* (Chicago: Rand McNally, 1965), pp. 972–1022; and Karl E. Weick, "Educational Organizations as Loosely Coupled Systems," *Administrative Science Quarterly*, 21 (1976), pp. 1–19.

division. Large corporations are likely to adopt the divisionalized form.

Most school districts typically do not fit the divisionalized form. The exceptions are those very large school districts that have diversified service divisions distinctly separated into individual units or schools. For example, a school district may resemble the divisionalized form when it has separate schools for the physically handicapped, emotionally disturbed, and learning disabled; a skills center for the potential dropout; a special school for art and music students; and so on. The identifying feature of these school districts is that they have separate schools within a single school district, which have separate administrative staffs, budgets, and so on. Elementary and secondary school districts that have consolidated but retained separate administrative structures with one school board are also examples of the divisionalized form. As might be expected, the primary reason for a school district to adopt this form of structure is service diversity while retaining separate administrative structures.

Adhocracy The **adhocracy** has the support staff as its key part, uses mutual adjustment as a means of coordination, and maintains selective patterns of decentralization. The structure tends to be low in formalization and decentralization. The technostructure is small because technical specialists are involved in the organization's operative core. The support staff is large to support the complex structure. Adhocracies engage in nonroutine tasks and use sophisticated technology. The primary goal is innovation and rapid adaptation to changing environments. Adhocracies typically are medium-sized, must be adaptable, and use resources efficiently. Examples of adhocracies include aerospace and electronic industries, research and development firms, and very innovative school districts. No school districts are pure adhocracies, but medium-sized school districts in very wealthy communities may have some of the characteristics of an adhocracy. The adhocracy is somewhat similar to Hage's organic organization.

Strategy and Structure The work begun by Chandler and extended by Mintzberg has laid the groundwork for an understanding of the relationship between an organization's strategy and its structure. The link between strategy and structure is still in its infancy stage. Further research in this area, particularly in service organizations like schools, will enhance school administrators' understanding of school organizations. In the meantime, school leaders must recognize that organization strategy and structure are related.

THE SCHOOL AS A SOCIAL SYSTEM

We can view the school as a social system. A **social system** refers to activities and interactions of group members brought together for a common purpose.[54] Thus, a school district, a school, and a classroom can all be viewed as social systems. A useful framework for understanding the administrative process within social systems is the Getzels–Guba model (Figure 2-7).[55]

Dimensions of a Social System

Jacob Getzels and Egon Guba conceive of the social system as involving two dimensions that are independent and interactive. First are institutions with certain roles and expectations that will fulfill the goals of the system. Second are individuals with certain personalities and need–dispositions inhabiting the system, whose interactions comprise observed behavior. Thus, ob-

[54]George C. Homans, *The Human Group* (New York: Harcourt, Brace, and World, 1950).
[55]Jacob W. Getzels and Egon G. Guba, "Social Behavior and the Administrative Process," *School Review*, 65 (1957), pp. 423–441; see also James M. Lipham, "Getzels's Models in Educational Administration," in N. J. Boyan (ed.), *Handbook of Research on Educational Administration* (New York: Longman, 1988), pp. 171–184.

Nomothetic Dimension

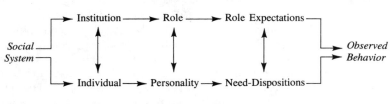

FIGURE 2-7   The Getzels–Guba Model (SOURCE: From Jacob W. Getzels and Egon G. Guba, "Social Behavior and the Administrative Process," *School Review*, 65 (1957), p. 429. Used by permission of the University of Chicago Press.)

served behavior can be understood as a function of these major elements: institution, role, and expectations, which together constitute the *nomothetic*, or normative, dimension of activity in a social system; and individual, personality, and need-dispositions, which together constitute the *idiographic*, or personal, dimension of activity in a social system.

Translated into the school setting, this means that an organization is designed to serve one of society's needs—to educate. In this organization, there are positions, or roles, such as the roles of the student, teacher, principal, superintendent, and the like. For each individual who occupies a given role, there are role expectations. Role expectations represent not only the duties and actions expected from each role player but also the expectations concerning the quality of performance. The various roles and role expectations constitute the nomothetic dimension of the social system.

The idiographic dimension includes individuals who occupy the roles and their personal needs. Schools as social systems must be "peopled," and all kinds of individuals who have their own idiosyncrasies "people" them. Thus, individuals chosen to occupy roles are different from one another in action and in reaction, and we can analyze these differences in terms of personality. Personality is determined in part by needs, which predispose a person to behave in a

certain way in a given situation. In other words, the individual who occupies a given role has needs she tries to fulfill. These are personalized needs and may not be associated with the needs of the school system.

Behavior can be stated in the form of the equation $B = f(R \times P)$, where B is observed behavior, f is function, R is a given institutional role defined by the expectations attached to it, and P is the personality of the role player defined by his need-dispositions.[56] The proportion of role and personality factors determining behavior varies with the specific act, the specific role, and the specific personality involved.

It is presumed in the military that behavior is influenced more by role than personality, whereas with the free-lance artist, behavior is influenced more by personality than by role. Many other examples can illustrate this variation in the influence exerted by role or personality on behavior. In educational organizations, we could hypothesize that the proportion of role and personality might be balanced somewhere between the two. But different educational systems are characterized by different proportions of role and personality.[57]

---

[56]Jacob W. Getzels, "Administration as a Social Process," in A. W. Halpin (ed.), *Administrative Theory in Education* (New York: Macmillan, 1958), pp. 150–165.
[57]Ibid.

Expanded Model: Cultural Dimensions

The developers of this early model recognized its oversimplification. In focusing on the sociological dimension with "role" as the central concept and on the psychological dimension with "personality" as the central concept, other dimensions had been omitted, thus giving the model a closed-systems orientation. To overcome this deficiency, Getzels and Herbert Thelen expanded the basic model to describe the classroom as a unique social system.[58] According to these social system theorists, the sociological aspects of an institution are mediated by cultural factors—the ethos, mores, and values—in which the institution is embedded. The expectations of the roles must, it seems, be somehow related to the ethos or cultural values. Similarly, the individual's personality functions in a biological organism with certain potentialities and abilities, with the need-dispositions of the personality mediated in some way by these constitutional conditions.

Getzels, James Lipham, and Roald Campbell further extended the model for school administrators. They added a second cultural dimension to interact with the psychological aspects of the individual.[59] The composite model of the school as a social system depicts educational administration as a social process (Figure 2-8). The bottom line in their model indicates that the culture, ethos, and values held by individuals in schools and school systems explain much social behavior. The model also clearly indicates that any social system (classroom, school, or school district) must operate within a larger environment. The addition of these dimensions gives Getzel's composite model a more open-systems orientation.

Some Derivations Getzels's models suggest three sources of potential conflicts: role conflicts, personality conflicts, and role–personality conflicts.[60] *Role conflicts* refer to situations where a role player is required to conform simultaneously to expectations that are contradictory or inconsistent. Adjustment to one set of expectations makes adjustment to the other difficult or impossible. For example, a teacher may attempt to be a devoted mother and simultaneously a successful career woman. A university professor may be expected by her department head to emphasize teaching and service to students and the community, respectively, while the academic dean expects her to emphasize research and publication. Role conflicts represent incongruencies in the nomothetic dimension (see Figure 2-7).

Personality conflicts occur as a result of opposing need-dispositions within the personality of the individual role players. For example, a teacher may be expected, as a social norm, to maintain adequate social distance between herself and the students. However, she may feel the need for more extensive interactions. Personality conflicts represent incongruencies in the idiographic dimension of the social systems model.

Role–personality conflicts occur as a result of discrepancies between the institution's role expectations and the individual's need-dispositions. For example, suppose an introverted personality–type school administrator were placed in the role of superintendent in a small- to medium-sized school district. The board of education makes clear its expectation that the newly appointed administrator maintain high visibility and extensive contact with the community. The superintendent, however, has a high need for privacy and anonymity. The superintendent in this school district would experience a role–personality conflict. As shown in Figure 2-7, role–personality conflicts represent incongruencies between the nomothetic and idiographic dimensions of the social systems model.

---

[58]Jacob W. Getzels and Herbert A. Thelen, "The Classroom as a Social System," in N. B. Henry (ed.), *The Dynamics of Instructional Groups*, 59th Yearbook of the National Society for the Study of Education, Part II (Chicago: University of Chicago Press, 1960), pp. 53–83.

[59]Jacob W. Getzels, James M. Lipham, and Roald F. Campbell, *Educational Administration as a Social Process* (New York: Harper & Row, 1968).

---

[60]Getzels, "Administration as a Social Process."

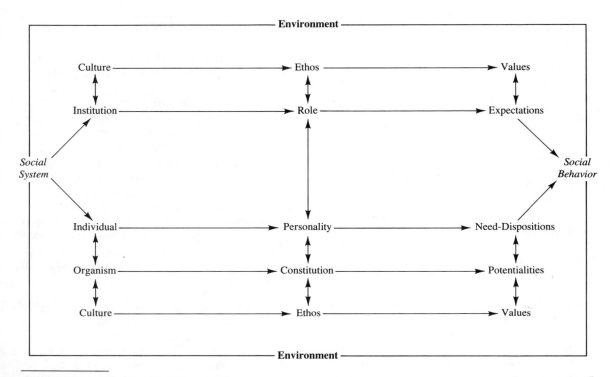

FIGURE 2-8   Composite Model of Behavior in Social Systems (SOURCE: Adapted from Jacob W. Getzels, James M. Lipham, and Roald F. Campbell, *Educational Administration as a Social Process* (New York: Harper & Row, 1968), p. 105.)

According to Getzels, incongruencies in the nomothetic and idiographic dimensions, or in their interaction, are symptomatic of administrative failure and lead to a loss in individual and institutional productivity.[61]

Furthermore, Getzels's models suggest three leader–followership styles: normative (nomothetic), personal (idiographic), and transactional.[62] The *normative style* emphasizes the fulfillment of institutional role requirements and obligations rather than the personal needs of individuals. Role definition, authority vested in roles, and organizational goal achievement are stressed. The *personal style* emphasizes the

personal activities and propensities of individuals. Minimum role definition, a diffusion of authority, and efforts to maximize each individual's meaningful contribution to the organization are stressed. The *transactional style* represents a balance of emphasis on the performance of the role requirements of the organization and the expression of personal needs of individuals. The school administrator moves alternately toward the normative style or the personal style depending on the situation.

Getzels's Latest Model: Communities Dimension

In the late 1970s, Getzels expanded his social systems model still further by including a com-

----
[61]Ibid.

[62]Getzels, Lipham, and Campbell, *Educational Administration as a Social Process*.

munities dimension.[63] Here Getzels makes much more manifest the cultural setting of the school as a social system and extends its usefulness as an open-systems model. He identifies six communities of education and defines communities as groups of people conscious of a collective identity through common cognitive and affective norms, values, and patterns of social relationships. He defines each type of community as follows:

- **Local community** is established in a particular neighborhood or region. Examples include a local neighborhood or school community.
- **Administrative community** is established in a specific, politically determined identity. A country, a city, or a school district are examples.
- **Social community** is established in a particular set of interpersonal relationships not restrained by local or administrative boundaries. An example would be all the people in one's community of friends.
- **Instrumental community** is established through direct or indirect activities and interactions with others who are brought together for a common purpose. Examples include a professional group such as teachers or professors who make up an educational community, a teacher's union, or a philanthropic community.
- **Ethnic community** is established through affinity with a particular national, racial, or socioeconomic group. Italian, black, or upper-class communities are examples.
- **Ideological community** is established in a particular historic, conceptual, or sociopolitical community that stretches across the local, administrative, social, instrumental, and ethnic communities. Examples include Christian, scholarly, or communist communities.[64]

Getzels's revised and latest models make much more explicit the cultural setting of the school as a social system. The concept of culture, long the mainstay of anthropology since its beginnings, is not new. Recently, the concept of organizational culture has enjoyed tremendous appeal in both the popular and professional management literature.

Getzels's models of the school as a social system are widely treated in introductory textbooks in educational administration, textbooks that deal specifically with the school principalship, textbooks on supervision, and references on organizational behavior and theory in educational administration. In addition, the *Handbook of Research on Educational Administration*, a project of the American Educational Research Association, devotes an entire chapter to Getzels's models in educational administration.[65]

Summary

1. Basic concepts of organizational structure provide a framework for vertical control and horizontal coordination of schools. These important dimensions include job specialization, departmentalization, chain of command, authority and responsibility, centralization/decentralization, line and staff authority, and span of management.
2. According to this view, division of labor, abstract rules, vertical hierarchy of authority, impersonality in interpersonal relations, and advancement based on competence characterize the ideal bureaucratic structure.
3. The participatory management model is the antithesis of the ideal bureaucracy. Supportiveness, shared leadership, flexibility, and employee growth and development are the keys to participatory management.
4. Compliance theory, mechanistic and organic organizations, and strategy–structure typology are alternative approaches to organizational structure. These approaches integrate several ideas from the

[63]Jacob W. Getzels, "The Communities of Education," *Teachers College Record*, 79 (1978), pp. 659–682.
[64]Ibid.

[65]Lipham, "Getzels's Models in Educational Administration," pp. 171–184.

classical and participatory management models and the fundamentals of organizational structure.

5. Getzels's models of the school as a social system have proven to have enduring appeal and widespread application in the administration of schools.

5. Describe the mechanistic or organic characteristics of a school with which you are familiar.

KEY TERMS

job specialization	transformation leadership
departmentalization	
chain of command	value-added leadership
authority and responsibility	site-based management
centralization/ decentralization	compliance theory
	mechanistic organization
line and staff authority	organic organization
span of management	simple structure
bureaucracy	machine bureaucracy
Theory X and Theory Y	professional bureaucracy
immaturity–maturity continuum	divisionalized form
	adhocracy
System 4 organization	social system

DISCUSSION QUESTIONS

1. Which fundamentals of structuring are associated with the following organizational forms: (a) simple structure, (b) machine bureaucracy, (c) professional bureaucracy, (d) divisionalized form, and (e) adhocracy?

2. Why are many of the characteristics of Weber's ideal bureaucracy still used in schools today?

3. Likert developed a paradigm consisting of three sets of variables: causal, intervening, and end-result variables. Do you think that Likert's paradigm is useful in assessing the effectiveness of a school or school district? Why?

4. Using Etzioni's typology, is it possible to analyze a particular type of organization, such as a school, as representing more than one kind of organization? Explain.

SUGGESTED READINGS

Samuel B. Bacharach (ed.), *Education Reform: Making Sense of It All* (Needham Heights, MA: Allyn and Bacon, 1990). Authoritative, thought-provoking articles that speak out on topics ranging from the history of educational reform to reforming the reform movement that gives the reader valuable suggestions for restructuring schools.

Roland Barth, *Improving Schools from Within* (San Francisco: Jossey-Bass, 1990). A fresh outlook at restructuring that stresses the importance of collegiality in promoting learning and improving schools.

Warren G. Bennis, *Why Leaders Can't Lead: The Unconscious Conspiracy Continues* (San Francisco: Jossey-Bass, 1989). A discussion of how bureaucracy and other classical management principles prevent leaders from leading.

Richard F. Elmore and Associates, *Restructuring Schools: The Next Generation of Educational Reform* (San Francisco: Jossey-Bass, 1990). An important contribution to the growing body of knowledge on school reform that weaves together the major issues surrounding contemporary school restructuring including political and policy considerations.

Phillip S. Schlechty, *Schools for the 21st Century: Leadership Imperatives for Educational Reform* (San Francisco: Jossey-Bass, 1990). A compelling action plan for educators, public policymakers, and citizens who care about improving schools.

Thomas J. Sergiovanni, *Value-Added Leadership: How to Get Extraordinary Performance in Schools* (New York: Harcourt Brace Jovanovich, 1990). A scholarly treatment of moral authority as a means to add value to leadership practice resulting in extraordinary performance in schools.

Paul W. Thurston (ed.), *Advances in Educational Administration, Vol. 1, Perspectives on Educational Reform* (Greenwich, Conn.: JAI Press, 1990). A collection of articles written by prominent scholars from a variety of disciplines exploring topics dealing with school restructuring.

3.

ORGANIZATIONAL CULTURE

In this chapter, we attempt to answer these questions concerning organizational culture in school settings. We begin our discussion by exploring the nature and characteristics of organizational culture. Next we discuss how organizational cultures are created, maintained, and changed. Then we discuss the features of corporate cultures of excellent firms and their relationship to school organizations. We examine differences between Japanese and American management styles and their implications for administering schools. We discuss the similarities between organizational culture and organizational climate. Finally, we present and analyze four well-known organizational climate constructs with implications for improving school effectiveness.

THE NATURE OF ORGANIZATIONAL CULTURE

In recent years, organizational culture has been popularized by best-selling books such as *In Search of Excellence*,[1] *A Passion for Excellence*,[2] and *Corporate Cultures*.[3] Although much has been written about organizational culture, little research supports the concept. For example, two academic journals devoted entire issues to organizational culture, but most articles were speculative in nature.[4]

Definition and Characteristics

The culture of an organization is all the beliefs, feelings, behaviors, and symbols that are characteristic of an organization. More specifically, **organizational culture** is defined as shared philosophies, ideologies, beliefs, feelings, assumptions, expectations, attitudes, norms, and values.[5]

While there is considerable variation in the definitions of organizational culture, it appears that most contain the following characteristics:

- *Observed Behavioral Regularities*. When organizational members interact, they use common language, terminology, and rituals and ceremonies related to deference and demeanor.
- *Norms*. Standards of behavior evolve in work groups, such as "a fair day's work for a fair day's pay." The impact of work-group behavior, sanctioned by group norms, results in standards and yardsticks.
- *Dominant Values*. An organization espouses and expects its members to share major values. Typical examples in schools are high performance levels of faculty and students, low absence and dropout rates, and high efficiency.
- *Philosophy*. Policies guide an organization's beliefs about how employees and clients are to be treated. For example, most school districts have statements of philosophy or mission statements.
- *Rules*. Guidelines exist for getting along in the organization, or the "ropes" that a newcomer must learn in order to become an accepted member.
- *Feelings*. This is an overall atmosphere that is conveyed in an organization by the physical layout and the way in which members interact with clients or other outsiders.[6]

None of the aforementioned characteristics by itself represents the essence of organizational culture. However, the characteristics taken collectively reflect and give meaning to the concept of organizational culture.

The culture of an organization is interrelated with most other concepts in educational administration, including organizational structures, motivation, leadership, decision making, communications, and change. To better understand this concept, Figure 3-1 depicts organizational culture within the context of social systems theory and more specifically open-systems theory, being characterized by inputs, a transformation process, outputs, external environment, and feedback.

[1]Thomas J. Peters and Robert H. Waterman, *In Search of Excellence: Lessons from America's Best Run Companies* (New York: Harper & Row, 1982).

[2]Thomas J. Peters and Nancy Austin, *A Passion for Excellence: The Leadership Difference* (New York: Random House, 1985).

[3]Terrence E. Deal and Allan A. Kennedy, *Corporate Cultures: The Rites and Rituals of Corporate Life* (Reading, MA: Addison-Wesley, 1984).

[4]Philip A. Cusick (ed.), "Organizational Culture and Schools," *Educational Administration Quarterly*, 11 (1987), whole issue; Mariann Jelinek, Linda Smircich, and Paul Hirsch (eds.), "Organizational Culture," *Administrative Science Quarterly*, 28 (1983), whole issue.

[5]Ralph H. Kilmann, Mary L. Saxton, and Ray Serpa (eds.), *Gaining Control of the Corporate Culture* (San Francisco: Jossey-Bass, 1985).

[6]Edgar H. Schein, *Organizational Culture and Leadership* (San Francisco: Jossey-Bass, 1985).

Organizations import energy from the environment in the form of information, people, and materials. The imported energy undergoes a transformation designed to channel behavior toward organizational goals and fulfill members' needs. Administrative processes (e.g., motivation, leadership, decision making, communication, and change) and organizational structures (i.e., job descriptions, selection systems, evaluation systems, control systems, and reward systems) have a significant impact on organizational culture and vice versa. In turn, these administrative processes and organizational structures export a product into the external environment. In a school, the output may be students' knowledge, skills, and attitudes or attendance, dropout rates, and more precise performance criteria such as scholastic awards. Figure 3-1 also shows that the organization not only influences but is also influenced by the external environment. And the social system uses feedback in an attempt to examine its present culture or to create a new culture.

Uniformity of Culture

Figure 3-1 shows the interrelationship of organizational culture with most other concepts in educational administration. Thus, culture represents the organization's cumulative learning, as reflected in organizational structures, people, administrative processes, and the external environment. This tends to perpetuate beliefs and behavior and specifies the goals, values, and mission of the organization and the criteria by which to measure the organization's success.

Subcultures   Large and complex organizations do not typically manifest single homogeneous beliefs, values, and behavior patterns. In other words, there may be more than one culture in an organization. First, there are differences between the formal culture, which consists of the ideal philosophy of the organization and how organizational members should behave, and the informal culture, which consists of the actual manifestations of the ideal philosophy in the day-

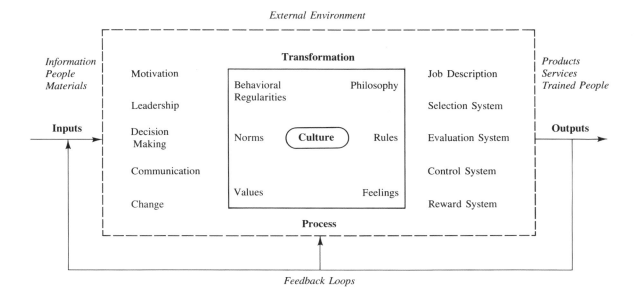

FIGURE 3-1   Dimensions of Organizational Culture

to-day behavior of organizational members. Second, there are likely to be different cultures in various functional groups in the organization, such as the divisions of instruction, business, personnel, and research and development in a large school district; differences between student, teacher, and administrator groups; and differences between elementary, middle school, and high school levels. Put another way, whenever the task requirements have resulted in a unique combination of people, structures, and function, the requirement to fulfill the group's goals will result in a unique culture.[7]

Dominant Culture   Besides the subcultures that exist in an organization, the larger organization may also have a culture that distinguishes it from other large systems. For example, one large school district highly favored innovation. This philosophy translated itself into a variety of practices including team teaching, flexible scheduling, teacher–advisor programs, report-card conferences, use of speakers' bureaus, collaboration with business firms, and internships. It resulted in values that emphasized good interpersonal relations between students and teachers, teachers and administrators, teachers and parents, and school and community.

Thus, central office administrators created policies and made decisions that perpetuated the overall school district's philosophy of innovation. Most key administrators portrayed the same image. They demonstrated excellent interpersonal and verbal skills and strived to be accessible to students, teachers, parents, and the community. They spent a portion of their time cultivating relations with the business community through membership in the Rotary, Kiwanis, Lions Club, Chamber of Commerce, and so on. This example shows that even large and relatively heterogeneous school districts that are known to have

dominant cultures can improve their educational goals. (See Administrative Advice 3-1.)

DEVELOPING, MAINTAINING, AND CHANGING ORGANIZATIONAL CULTURE

Organizational cultures are created, maintained, and changed through similar processes. But the following questions arise: How does an organizational culture develop? How is the culture of an organization maintained? Can organizational culture be changed by administrative action? In this section, we explore the answers to these questions.

Creating Organizational Culture

The process of creating an organizational culture is complex. Organizational heroes, rites and rituals, and communication networks play key roles in creating organizational cultures.[8]

Heroes   Most successful organizations have their **heroes**. Heroes are born and created. The born hero is the visionary institution-builder like Henry Ford, founder of Ford Motor company, and Mary Kay Ash, founder of Mary Kay Cosmetics. Created heroes, on the other hand, are those the institution has made by noticing and celebrating memorable moments that occur in the day-to-day situational life of the organization. Thomas Watson, head of IBM, is an example of a situation hero. Other well-known heroes include Lee Iacocca at Chrysler, Sam Walton at Wal-Mart, and Vince Lombardi, the legendary coach of the Green Bay Packers. Heroes perpetuate the organization's underlying values, provide role models, symbolize the organization to others,

---

[7]Robert F. Allen et al., *The Organizational Unconscious: How to Create the Corporate Culture You Want and Need*, 2nd ed. (Burlington, VT: Human Resource Institute, 1987).

[8]Much of this discussion is based on Deal and Kennedy, *Corporate Cultures.*

ADMINISTRATIVE ADVICE 3-1

START WITH CULTURE TO IMPROVE YOUR SCHOOLS

Every school and school district has a culture that gives meaning to its educational program. Culture is the shared goals, values, and mission of the organization. Some schools and school districts have strong and cohesive cultures; others have weak and fragmented cultures. Below are characteristics of strong cultures that provide support for school improvement. Administrators should heed these characteristics when attempting to understand a school or school district's organizational culture.

- *Shared Beliefs*. Organizations with strong cultures have a system of shared beliefs that provides a sense of common direction for employees' behavior.
- *What Tomorrow Can Be*. Vision imbues the culture of the organization with a purpose of what is important. It is a mental picture of what tomorrow can be—an image of the future.
- *Personified Values*. Significant events and the heroes who shaped them—that is, those persons who personify the values of the school—are im-

portant. Research your school's past and write histories about them.
- *Heart of Beliefs*. Guiding beliefs form the heart of an organization. They set the tone for a school or district and influence how administrators involve people, listen to them, and respond to their needs.

Source: Adapted from Jack Blendinger and Linda T. Jones, "Start with Culture to Improve Your Schools." *School Administrator*, 46 (1989), pp. 22–25. Used by permission.

and set performance standards that motivate participant achievement.

Rites and Rituals   Another key aspect in creating organizational cultures are the everyday activities and celebrations that characterize the organization. Most successful organizations feel that these rituals and symbolic actions should be managed. Through **rites** and **rituals**, recognition of achievement is possible.[9] The Teacher of the Year Award and National Merit Schools initiated by President George Bush are examples.[10]

(However, debate arises over the public honoring of schools; see the PRO/CON Debate.) Similarly, a number of ceremonial rituals may accompany the appointment of a new superintendent of schools, including press and other announcements, banquets, meetings, and speeches.

Some organizations have even created their own reward rituals. Several years ago, James Councilman, then Indiana University swimming coach, awarded jelly beans to the swimmer doing his best set of repeats in practice or achieving some goal set by the coach. The ceremony became known as "jelly bean day" and served as a symbol of a job well done.

Communication Networks   Stories or myths of heroes are transmitted by means of the **communications network**. This network is characterized by various individuals who play a role in the culture of the organization. Each institution has storytellers who interpret what is going

[9]Harrison M. Trice and Janice M. Beyer, "Studying Organizational Culture through Rites and Ceremonials," *Academy of Management Review*, 9 (1984), pp. 653–669; Trice and Beyer, "Using Six Organizational Rites to Change Culture," in R. H. Kilman, M. L. Saxton, and R. Serpa, (eds.), *Gaining Control of the Corporate Culture* (San Francisco: Jossey-Bass, 1985).
[10]George Bush, "Excellence in Education: President George Bush's Strategy," *Education Digest*, 54 (1989), pp. 3–6.

PRO/CON DEBATE

■

RECOGNIZING EXCELLENT SCHOOLS

Excellence is an appropriate goal for all schools, but too often the culture of schools encourages mediocrity. Teachers are hesitant to criticize their peers in public settings. Bureaucratic regulations emphasize conformity to established conventions rather than risk taking. Salaries are awarded on the basis of seniority, not merit. What can be done to change these cultural indicators in schools?

QUESTION When excellent schools are recognized through such awards as President Bush's National Merit Schools, is it an incentive for those schools to maintain excellence and for other schools to strive for excellence?

ARGUMENTS PRO

1 When an outstanding school is recognized by the president of the United States, it receives the recognition it deserves. Communities, parents, children, and educators are proud. Everyone wins.

2 The possibility of national recognition for excellence will spur mediocre schools to positive action.

3 Competition is part of the U.S. culture. We recognize outstanding athletes, actors, musicians, poets, car salespersons, and school superintendents. Why not excellent schools?

4 Although we know excellence when we see it, we have not developed yet a national image of excellent public schooling. An award will force us to identify more and better indicators of excellence. Excellence will be pursued more easily by all schools when a clearer picture of it emerges.

5 Principals are key figures in school effectiveness. Excellent schools do not happen by accident. They are led by strong symbolic leaders with clear vision. Such principals deserve rewards and career advancement.

ARGUMENTS CON

1 Those who are recognized as excellent are not necessarily the best. The application process is so demanding and redundant that many have chosen to put their energies into other efforts.

2 The majority of schools do not have the resources to achieve excellence. The recognition that a few receive will be a disincentive for the many.

3 Competition among schools can have negative effects. People in the winning schools develop an unrealistic sense of worth; once they are recognized, some people will rest on their laurels.

4 Principals and teachers will put their energies into meeting the criteria identified by the award rather than dealing with other areas that need improvement. The arbitrary parameters established by the award rather than the clear pursuit of excellence will guide action.

5 Superintendents will expect principals to apply for awards and receive them. Principals whose school won an award will have an advantage when they apply for new principalships. Principals, rather than schools, will be the real winners.

on in the organization. Their interpretation of the information influences the perceptions of others. "Priests" are the worriers of the organization and the guardians of the culture's values.

These individuals always have time to listen and provide alternative solutions to problems. "Whisperers" are the powers behind the throne because they have the boss' ear. Anyone who wants something done will go to the whisperer. "Gossips" carry the trivial day-to-day activities of the organization through the communications network. Gossips are very important in building and maintaining heroes. They embellish the heroes past feats and exaggerate their latest accomplishments. And, finally, "spies" are buddies in the woodwork. They keep everyone well informed about what is going on in the organization. Each of these individuals plays a key role in building and maintaining an organization's culture. It should be noted that the names used here are those ascribed by Deal and Kennedy to emphasize the importance of communication networks in creating an institution's organizational culture.

Maintaining Organizational Culture

Once an organizational culture is created, a number of mechanisms help solidify the acceptance of the values and ensure that the culture is maintained or reinforced (**organizational socialization**). These mechanisms, illustrated in Figure 3-2, are the following steps for socializing employees:[11]

Step 1: *Selection of Entry-Level Candidates*. The socialization process starts with the careful selection of entry-level candidates. Trained recruiters use standardized procedures and focus on values that are important in the culture. Those candidates whose personal values do not fit with the underlying values of the organization are given ample opportunity to opt out (deselect).

Step 2: *Humility-Inducing Experiences*. After the chosen candidate is hired, considerable training ensues to expose the person to the culture. Humility-inducing experiences, which cause employees to question prior beliefs and values, are assigned, thereby making new employees more receptive to the values of the new culture. Many organizations give newly hired employees more work than they can reasonably handle and assign work for which the individual is overqualified. For example, a new faculty member of a university may be assigned undesirable tasks, which senior professors of the department do not wish to perform: teaching the basic courses, off-campus assignments, assignment to several committees, heavy advisement loads, field work, and assignment to an inequitable number of doctoral committees. The message conveyed to the newcomer is, "You must pay your dues."

Step 3: *Job Mastery*. Whereas Step 2 is intended to foster cultural learning, Step 3 is designed to develop the employee's technological knowledge. As employees move along a career path, the organization assesses their performance and assigns other responsibilities on the basis of their progress. Frequently, organizations establish a step-by-step approach to this career plan. For example, the Holmes Group recommends a three-step career-ladder process for teachers: (1) instructors, (2) professional teachers, and (3) career professionals.[12] The Carnegie Task Force on Teaching as a Profession proposes another approach consisting of four steps: (1) licensed teachers, (2) certified teachers, (3) advanced certified teachers, and (4) lead teachers.[13]

Step 4. *Reward and Control Systems*. The organization pays meticulous attention to measuring operational results and to rewarding individual performance. Reward systems are comprehensive, consistent, and focus on those aspects of the organization that are tied to success and the values of the culture. For example, a school district will specify the

---

[11]Richard T. Pascale, "The Paradox of 'Corporate Culture': Reconciling Ourselves to Socialization," *California Management Review*, 27 (1985), pp. 26–41.

[12]Holmes Group, *Tomorrow's Teachers: A Report of the Holmes Group* (East Lansing, MI: The Holmes Group, 1986).

[13]Carnegie Task Force on Teaching as a Profession, *A Nation Prepared: Teachers for the Twenty-First Century* (New York: Carnegie Corporation, 1986).

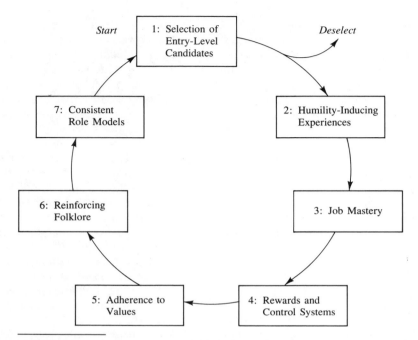

FIGURE 3-2   The Process of Organizational Socialization (SOURCE: Adapted from
Richard T. Pascale, "Paradox of 'Corporate Culture': Reconciling Ourselves to
Socialization," *California Management Review*, 27 (1985), p. 38. Copyright
1985 by the Regents of the University of California. Used by permission of the
Regents.)

factors that are considered important for
success. Operational measures are used to
assess these factors, and performance appraisals of employees are tied to the accomplishment of these factors. Promotions and
merit pay are determined by success on each
of the predetermined critical factors. For instance, those school administrators who violate the culture are often transferred or given
a relatively innocuous staff position at central
office. These administrators are now "off
their career tracks," which can inhibit their
promotion in the organization. This is the
typical pattern used in large bureaucratic
school districts as an alternative to firing the
administrator.

Step 5: *Adherence to Values*. As personnel continue to work for the organization, their be-

havior closely matches the underlying values
of the culture. Identification with underlying
values helps employees reconcile personal
sacrifices caused by their membership in the
organization. Personnel learn to accept the
organization's values and place their trust in
the organization not to hurt them. For instance, school administrators work long
hours on a multiplicity of fragmented tasks
for which they sometimes receive little recognition from their superiors, subordinates,
and the community. They sometimes endure
ineffective school board members and supervisors and job assignments that are undesirable and inconvenient. Identification with the
common values of the organization allows
these administrators to justify such personal
sacrifices.

Step 6: *Reinforcing Folklore*. Throughout the socialization process, the organization exposes its members to rites and rituals, stories or myths, and heroes that portray and reinforce the culture. For example, in one educational institution, the story is told of an administrator who was fired because of his harsh handling of subordinates. The administrator had incorrectly believed a myth that being "tough" with his subordinates would enhance himself in the eyes of his superiors. The organization deemed such managerial behavior to be inconsistent with its organizational philosophy of cultivating good interpersonal relationships and high levels of morale and job satisfaction among all its employees.

Step 7: *Consistent Role Models*. Those individuals who have performed well in the organization serve as role models to newcomers to the organization. By identifying these employees as symbolizing success, the organization encourages others to do likewise. Role models in strong-culture institutions can be thought of as one type of ongoing staff development for all organizational members.

Changing Organizational Culture

To this point, we have discussed how organizational culture is created and maintained. Sometimes an organization determines that its culture needs to be changed. The **change cycle** (Figure 3-3) has the following components:[14]

- *External Enabling Conditions*. Enabling conditions, if they exist, indicate that the environment will be supportive of culture change. Such conditions are in the external environment and impact the organization. In a school setting, examples include scarcity or abundance of students, stability or instability of the external environment, and resource

concentration or dispersion. In combination these external enabling conditions determine the degree of threat to the organization's input sources (information, people, and materials) (see Figure 3-1).

- *Internal Permitting Conditions*. To increase the likelihood of organizational culture change, four internal permitting conditions must exist: (1) a surplus of change resources (managerial time and energy, financial resources, and the like that are available to the system beyond those needed for normal operating); (2) system readiness (willingness of most members to live with the anxiety that comes with anticipated uncertainty that is characteristic of change); (3) minimal coupling (coordination and integration of system components); and (4) change-agent power and leadership (the ability of administrators to envision alternative organizational futures).

- *Precipitating Pressures*. Four factors that precipitate organizational culture change include (1) atypical performance; (2) pressure exerted by stakeholders; (3) organizational growth or decrement in size, membership heterogeneity, or structural complexity; and (4) real or perceived crises associated with environmental uncertainty.

- *Triggering Events*. Culture change usually begins in response to one or more triggering events. Examples include (1) environmental calamities or opportunities such as natural disasters, economic recession, innovations, or the discovery of new markets; (2) managerial crises such as a major shakeup of top administration, an inappropriate strategic decision, or a foolish expenditure; (3) external revolution such as mandated desegregation, PL94–142, or Title IX; and (4) internal revolution such as the installation of a new administrative team within the organization.

- *Cultural Visioning*. Creating a vision of a new, more preferred organizational culture is a necessary step toward that culture's formation. Leaders survey the beliefs, values, assumptions, and behaviors of the organi-

---

[14]Peter J. Frost et al., *Organizational Culture* (Beverly Hills, CA: Sage, 1985).

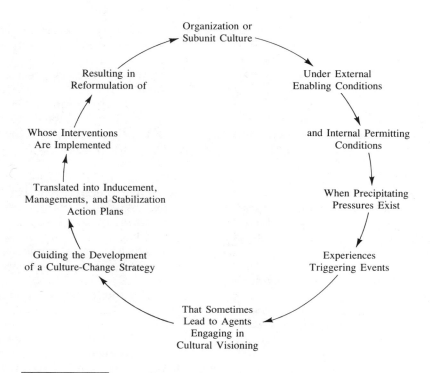

FIGURE 3-3   The Change Cycle of Organizational Culture (SOURCE: Adapted from
Peter Frost et al., *Organizational Culture* (Beverly Hills, CA: Sage, 1985), p. 182.
Copyright 1985 by Sage Publications, Inc. Used by permission of the publisher.)

zation's existing culture. Then they seek
to anticipate future conditions and create
an image of the organization within that
future.
- **Culture-Change Strategy**. Once a new cultural
vision exists, an organization needs a strategy to achieve that culture. Such a strategy
outlines the general process of transforming
the present culture into the new one.
- **Culture-Change Action Plans**. A series of explicit
action plans for the inducement, manage-
ment, and stabilization of change make a
change strategy known. Inducement action
planning involves stimulating organizational
members to a change or countering resistance to change. Management action planning involves outlining interventions and
mobilizing change agents. Stabilization ac-

tion planning focuses on the institutionalization of culture change, that is, establishing
the existence of the new culture as an accepted fact.
- **Implementation of Interventions**. An organization selects culture-change interventions
based on the ecology of a particular organization for each action-plan phase and the
change agent's competencies in implementing them.
- **Reformulation of Culture**. When implemented,
the intervention plans result in a reformu-
lated culture.

Any comprehensive program of organizational change involves an attempt to change the
culture of the organization. (See Administrative
Advice 3-2.)

EFFECTS OF ORGANIZATIONAL CULTURE

As noted earlier, the culture of an organization affects many administrative processes. Among these are motivation, leadership, decision making, communication, and change. Culture also affects an organization's structural processes. The selection process, evaluation system, control system, and reward system must fit with the organization's culture. In addition, culture has an influence on employee performance and organizational effectiveness. Administrators are evaluated on the basis of the results they achieve; therefore, the organization's culture is an important concept because of the results it produces. (See Administrative Advice 3.3)

Views of Excellence

Thomas Peters and Robert Waterman and later Peters and Nancy Austin, in their search for ex-

cellence in America's best-run companies, found culture to be closely tied to the success of those firms.[15] From their research, they identified the following attributes that characterize excellent companies:

- *A Bias Toward Action*. The company continually does, experiments, and tries. An example in a school setting might be implementing management by objectives to guide a school district's mission and measure its results.
- *Close to the Customer*. The company looks to the customer for direction in the formation of new products, quality, and service. School districts that remain tuned-in to their clients' (students') needs while maintaining a close professional relationship with parents remain "close to the customer." One comprehensive study of schools found that high parental involvement was a major factor distinguishing

[15]Peters and Waterman, *In Search of Excellence*; Peters and Austin, *A Passion for Excellence*.

ADMINISTRATIVE ADVICE 3-3

■

BUSINESS RULES FOR SCHOOLS

Education is not like a proprietary business. Nevertheless, school administrators should reamin receptive to using some relevant ideas from the business world. The following nine goals from the corporate world can be adapted easily to an educational setting:

CUSTOMER SERVICE

- *Corporate Goal*. Review the emphasis on customer service throughout the corporation.
- *Adapted Goal*. Review the emphasis on serving students.

Teachers and administrators continually should communicate to students the idea that "We are here to serve you! You are important."

EMPLOYEE SALES SKILLS

- *Corporate Goal*. Emphasize the role of sales skills with employees.
- *Adapted Goal*. Emphasize sales skills with all teachers and other staff.

Make an ongoing effort to sell the vision of where the school is going. Each time an accomplishment moves the school closer to a new image, communicate it to parents, teachers, students, and the community.

EMPLOYEE COMMUNICATIONS

- *Corporate Goal*. Enhance intracompany communications.
- *Adapted Goal*. Enhance communications among teachers and staff.

Make sure teachers and staff have as much information as possible about local school and district achievement, new policies and procedures, programs, and anything that might affect them.

COMPANY DEDICATION

- *Corporate Goal*. Be dedicated to the principles of the enterprise.
- *Adapted Goal*. Be dedicated to the principles of the school district.

A negative attitude toward the central office is quickly noticed and implies division. Stress team effort.

---

high-achieving schools from low-achieving schools.[16]

- *Autonomy and Entrepreneurship*. The company values and fosters risk taking and innovation. School districts that encourage innovation and risk taking, while permitting some failure, have a philosophy of "autonomy and entrepreneurship." Such systems can be characterized as dynamic in that they are

constantly attempting new ways of accomplishing school district objectives.

- *Productivity Through People*. The company demonstrates a belief in the organization's employees through shared decision making and encouragement of new ideas. This is reflected in the language used by the company. The company views the employee as extended family, and there is an absence of rigidity of command. Schools that manifest high levels of trust in subordinates, use participatory decision making, listen to and use members' ideas, and show concern for the

---

[16]James S. Coleman and Thomas Hoffer, *Public and Private High Schools: The Impact of Communities* (New York: Basic Books, 1987).

Administrative Advice 3-3 (continued)

STAFF RECOGNITION

- *Corporate Goal*. Recognize employees.
- *Adapted Goal*. Use the ideas of school employees in developing peer-recognition activities.

Allow teachers and staff to help determine criteria for recognition and the type of any awards such as certificates, gifts, receptions, or other activities.

MARKET LEADER

- *Corporate Goal*. Position the corporation so it is recognized as a leader in the chosen market.
- *Adapted Goal*. Position the school so teachers are recognized as leaders in targeted academic areas.

Provide opportunities for teachers with special abilities to lead in staff-development sessions, serve on districtwide committees, and attend professional workshops.

RULES AND REGULATIONS

- *Corporate Goal*. Ensure companywide compliance with regulations and procedures.

- *Adapted Goal*. Ensure schoolwide compliance with district and state policies and procedures.

Use an in-house monitoring team to compare what is happening to what should be happening according to accepted procedures.

GENERATE PROFITS

- *Corporate Goal*. Achieve profitable level of earnings for the current year.
- *Adapted Goal*. Achieve the targeted level of student performance for the current year.

The bottom line is student academic progress.

MAINTAIN CAPITAL LEVELS

- *Corporate Goal*. Maintain primary capital levels consistent with the approved plan.
- *Adapted Goal*. Maintain the acceptable level of student performance consistent with the school-improvement plan.

Put strategies in place to maintain strong academic performance and overcome academic weaknesses.

Source: Adapted from Henry L. Roddy, "Nine Business Rules for Schools," *School Administrator*, 47 (1990), p. 31. Used by permission.

---

welfare of all employees are practicing "productivity through people."

- *Hands–On, Value–Driven Effort*. The company pays explicit attention to cultural values and devotes substantial effort to promoting and clarifying core values to employees. Strong-culture schools that emphasize high achievement levels of students and high performance and growth of faculty are practicing "hands-on, value-driven effort."
- *"Sticking to the Knitting."* The company stays in businesses they know how to run. This success attribute can be applied to public

schools. The public has thrust upon educators the myth that schools can correct all of society's ills: the breakdown of the family, crime, racial strife, poverty, unemployment, drug abuse, child abuse, teenage pregnancy, and the like. It may be more accurate to say that "more responsibility has been thrust upon the schools than they should accept; more results have been expected than they could possible produce; and in too many

---

[17]William H. Roe and Thelbert L. Drake, *The Principalship*, 3rd ed. (New York: Macmillan, 1986), p. 7.

cases, schools have assumed more than they should."[17] Put another way, schools have been programmed for failure, just as companies have failed who have expanded beyond their ability to compete in the marketplace.

- *Simple Form, Lean Staff*. The company does not use complex matrix structures, and they keep corporate staffs small. In the educational setting, this approach resembles somewhat the concept of site-based management.[18]
- *Simultaneous Loose–Tight Properties*. The company exhibits both tight and loose couplings.[19] It is tight about cultural values and loose or decentralized about autonomy, providing individuals throughout the organization room to perform. By following corporate-world goals, schools can promote strong cultural values while providing people with the opportunity to grow and the flexibility to function within the school district's belief system. (See Administrative Advice 3-3.)

Warren Bennis and Burt Nanus found that many organizations are overmanaged and underled. They ascertain that the leader should be concerned with the organization's basic purpose and general direction.[20] Time should be spent on doing the right thing: creating new ideas, new policies, and new methodologies. From the ninety leaders interviewed, they found the following leadership strategies: (1) attention through vision, (2) meaning through communication, (3) trust through positioning, and (4) deployment of self through positive self-regard and positive thinking. In short, effective

leaders communicate their vision for the company and embody this vision by being reliable, persistent, relentless, and dedicated to the implementation of the vision. Effective leaders know their strengths and weaknesses. They build on their strengths and compensate for their weaknesses. Their focus is on success. The word *failure* is rarely used; unsuccessful attempts are considered learning experiences.

Japanese Management: Theory Z

In recent years, much has been written about the alleged superiority of Japanese management techniques. William Ouchi, an American researcher and theorist, examined and compared high-producing companies in the United States and Japan in order to discover what, if anything, these firms had in common. To explain the success of these companies, Ouchi developed **Theory Z**.[21] Theory Z is an extension of McGregor's Theory X and Theory Y concepts (see Chapter 2). The principal difference is that McGregor's Theory X and Theory Y formulation is an attempt to distinguish between the personal leadership styles of an individual supervisor, whereas Theory Z is concerned with the "culture of the whole organization." That is, Theory Z is not concerned with the attitudes or behavior patterns of an individual supervisor but rather with the difference the organizational culture makes in the way the whole organization is put together and managed. Theory Z culture involves long-term employment, consensual decision making, individual responsibility, slow evaluation and promotion, an informal control system with explicit measures of performance, moderately specialized career paths, and extensive commitment to all aspects of the employee's life, including family.[22]

[18]John I. Goodlad, *A Place Called School* (New York: McGraw-Hill, 1984); Kenneth A. Sirotnik, "The School as the Center of Change," in T. J. Sergiovanni and J. H. Moore (eds.), *Schooling for Tomorrow* (Needham Heights, MA: Allyn and Bacon, 1989), pp. 89–113.

[19]Karl E. Weick, "Educational Organizations as Loosely Coupled Systems," *Administrative Science Quarterly*, 21 (1976), pp. 1–19.

[20]Warren Bennis and Burt Nanus, *Leaders: The Strategies for Taking Charge* (New York: Harper & Row, 1985).

[21]William G. Ouchi, *Theory Z: How American Business Can Meet the Japanese Challenge* (Reading, MA: Addison-Wesley, 1981).

[22]Ibid.

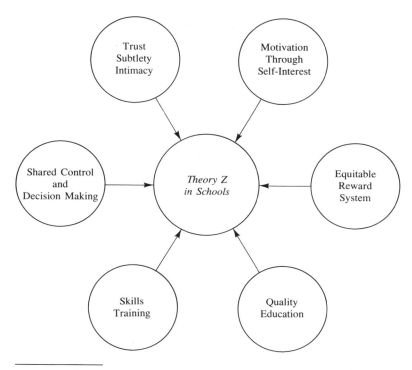

FIGURE 3-4   Major Components of Theory Z as Applied to Schools

The features of Theory Z applied to schools include trust, subtlety, and intimacy; shared control and decision making; training in planning, organizational processes, budgeting systems, and interpersonal skills; motivation through self-interest; rewards over the long run; and the importance of high-quality education.[23] Figure 3-4 depicts these concepts.

Trust, Subtlety, and Intimacy   According to Ouchi, no institution can exist without trust, subtlety, and intimacy. Trust in a school can only exist among people who understand that their objectives are compatible in the long run. The

concept is based on the assumption that if you don't understand what someone else does, if you don't understand their language, their technology, and their problems, then you can't possibly trust them. Trust can be developed only through intimate, professional experience with someone else, including close interpersonal relations between students and students, teachers and students, teachers and teachers, administrators and teachers, and administrators and students.

Shared Control and Decision Making   School administrators must spend adequate time discussing with students, teachers, parents, and the community the objectives of the schools and how the schools are run. School leaders must understand the incentive system available to personnel in their careers and help them to ra-

[23]William Ouchi, "Theory Z and the Schools," *School Administrator*, 39 (1982), pp. 12–19.

tionalize these incentives so that they can trust them. Then, administrators can invite subordinates to share control, which provides stakeholders with input into decisions that will affect the way they perform their responsibilities.

Training   The concept of *quality circles* is advocated. Quality circles consist of small groups of employees who meet regularly to discuss the way they do their jobs and to recommend changes. The purpose is to yield a group-based suggestion system for solving problems and improving the quality of the system.[24] This requires a period of training to increase participation, consensus in decisions, and shared control. The training is directed toward getting to know the organization: its objectives, problems, and overall resources. Specifically, teachers and other nonadministrative personnel are trained in planning, organizational processes (motivation, leadership, decision making, communication, and change), the system's budgetary process, group dynamics, and many of the school administrator's day-to-day activities to which teachers are rarely exposed. The training is designed to create a culture that lends itself to openness, trust, and employee involvement.

Motivation Through Self-Interest   Ouchi believes that there is only one form of interest—self-interest. If you cannot create a setting in which people are permitted to naturally do what seems desirable to them—to satisfy their self-interest—then you are always fighting, constraining, holding back, and can never have high commitment nor high productivity. In the Theory Z organization, because people have participated in shaping the goals and objectives of the system, you can say to people, "Do what comes naturally; do what you prefer to do, because we have agreed that those things you choose to do are simultaneously good for the institution."[25]

Rewards   An organizational memory is essential. Some key person must remember who has gone the extra mile, who is committed, and who has put in extra time; this person must ensure that those efforts are recognized and rewarded. According to Ouchi, if there is that kind of organizational memory, then people will have confidence that as long as they do what is right, there will be equity in the end. They therefore lose whatever incentives they might have to be selfish, narrow-minded, or short-sighted. What does Ouchi say about the lock-step salary schedules prevalent in most school districts? Ouchi responds by saying that it is necessary that schools disassemble the currently bureaucratical approach to evaluation, promotion, and pay.

Importance of High-Quality Education   One of the greatest assets any country has in developing its social health and its economic health is its school systems. High-quality education leads to an educated work force, thereby increasing economic capital in the improved country. An enlightened citizenry is important to the welfare of a nation.

A Typology of Organizational Culture

Carl Steinhoff and Robert Owens developed a framework that suggests four distinctive **culture phenotypes** likely to be found in public schools.[26] These phenotypes are clearly describable and differentiated from one another in terms of the metaphorical language elicited from school participants.

Unlike most students of organizational culture, the researchers examined the culture of schools by survey methods rather than by using the more typical ethnographic approach. To sup-

---

[24]Philip C. Thompson, *Quality Circles: How to Make Them Work in America* (New York: American Management Associations, 1982).

[25]Ouchi, "Theory Z and the Schools," p. 14.

[26]Carl R. Steinhoff and Robert G. Owens, "The Organizational Culture Assessment Inventory: A Metaphorical Analysis of Organizational Culture in Educational Settings." Paper presented at the annual meeting of the American Educational Research Association, New Orleans, April 1988.

port this methodologic approach, Owens found in conducting a long-term ethnographic study of a senior high school that a culture assessment instrument could have been valuable in that study.[27]

Consistent with survey research methods, the researchers drew upon the literature to develop a theory of organizational culture.[28] As discussed earlier, the theory posits that organizational culture is the *root metaphor* of an organization.[29] That is, "the culture of an organization does not merely describe what an organization is like, it describes the essence of the organization itself."[30] With this concept as an organizer, the researchers developed a taxonomic structure of organizational culture. The resulting taxonomy has six interlocking dimensions that define the culture of a school: (1) the history of the organization; (2) values and beliefs of the organization; (3) myths and stories that explain the organization; (4) cultural norms of the organization; (5) traditions, rituals, and ceremonies characteristic of the organization; and (6) heroes and heroines of the organization.

Based on the taxonomy of organizational culture, Steinhoff and Owens constructed the Organizational Culture Assessment Inventory (OCAI) that, when taken as a whole, represents the consensual press, that is, the root metaphor perceived by organizational participants. "Culture as root metaphor promotes a view of organizations as expressive forms, manifestations of

human consciousness."[31] These metaphors serve to illuminate the perceptual reality of the respondents and therefore serve as the basis on which they set goals, make commitments, and execute plans.[32]

School Culture Phenotypes   After several revisions of the initial form of the OCAI, the final version was validated in pilot studies of teachers, principals, and central office administrators in forty-seven elementary and secondary schools. The responses were sorted on the basis of school metaphor to establish metaphorical themes prevalent among the three groups. Data analysis produced four distinctive phenotypes of school culture, each of which can be described in terms of its metaphorical content.[33]

Family Culture. This school can be described using metaphors such as *family*, *home*, or *team*. The principal in this school can be described as a *parent* (strong or weak), *nurturer*, *friend*, *sibling*, or *coach*. In this school, "concern for each other is important as well as having a commitment to students above and beyond the call of duty." Everyone should be willing to be a part of the family and pull their own weight. The school as family then is nurturent and friendly, often cooperative and protective, to which members are alternately submissive and rebellious—leaning on the shoulders, or bosom, of someone who has their best interests at heart.

Machine Culture. This school can be described using the metaphor of the machine. Metaphors for the school include *well-oiled machines*, *political machines*, *beehives of activity*, or *rusty ma-*

[27]Robert G. Owens, "The Leadership of Educational Clans," in L. T. Sheive and M. B. Schoenheit (eds.), *Leadership: Examining the Elusive* (Alexandria, VA: Association for Supervision and Curriculum Development. 1987).

[28]Robert G. Owens and Carl R. Steinhoff, "Toward a Theory of Organizational Culture," Paper presented at the annual meeting of the American Educational Research Association, New Orleans, April 1988.

[29]Linda Smircich, "Concepts of Culture and Organizational Analysis," *Administrative Science Quarterly*, 28 (1983), pp. 339–358.

[30]Steinhoff and Owens, "The Organizational Culture Assessment Inventory: A Metaphorical Analysis of Organizational Culture in Educational Settings," p. 2.

[31]Smircich, "Concepts of Culture and Organizational Analysis," p. 347.

[32]Gareth Morgan, *Images of Organization* (Beverly Hills, CA: Sage, 1986).

[33]To preserve the metaphorical content used to describe the four culture phenotypes, we have quoted liberally from Steinhoff and Owens, "The Organizational Culture Assessment Inventory: A Metaphorical Analysis of Organizational Culture in Educational Settings."

chines. Metaphors for the principal range from *workaholic*, *Paul Bunyan*, and *The General* to *Charlie Brown* and the *slug*. The school as machine then is viewed purely in instrumental terms. The driving force appears to come from the structure of the organization itself, and administrators are described in terms of their varying ability to provide maintenance inputs. The social structure of these schools is tightly woven; however, unlike those of the family culture, its mission is protection rather than warmth. The school *is* a machine teachers *use* to accomplish work.

Cabaret Culture. Metaphors such as a *circus*, a *Broadway show*, a *banquet*, or a *well-choreographed ballet* performed by well-appreciated *artists* describe this school. The principal is seen as a *master of ceremonies*, a *tightrope walker*, and a *ring master*. Teachers in these schools experience many of the same group-binding social activities as do their colleagues in the family culture school. The essential difference is that, in this culture, relationships center on performances and the reactions of the audience. There is great pride in the artistic and intellectual quality of one's teaching, which is carried out under the watchful eye of the maestro. At the cabaret the show must go on!

Little Shop of Horrors Culture. This school can be described as unpredictable, tension-filled *nightmares* having the characteristics of a war zone or revolution. "One never knows whose head will roll next." Teachers report their schools as *closed-boxes* or *prisons*. The principal is a *self-cleaning statue* ready to offer up a sacrifice if it will maintain his position. In general, administrators in this school are seen as individuals whose main function is to keep things smoothed-over. Others have a Napoleon complex that promotes dominance and control or Jekyll–Hyde personalities that promote a *walking-on-eggs* style of adaptive behavior among faculty. Unlike the family and cabaret cultures, teachers in this school lead isolated lives; there is little social activity. For example, written requests are

often needed to hold any social activity—even for special occasions like Thanksgiving. One is expected to conform and to smile when appropriate. Verbal abuse among faculty is common, and closeness seems to be melting away. This culture is cold, hostile, and paranoid. "Almost anything can get you—and it often does."

Steinhoff and Owens's school culture phenotypes resemble somewhat the cultures delineated by Peters and Waterman[34] and the human resource-orientation typology suggested by Nirmal Sethia and Mary Ann Von Glinow.[35] With increasing emphasis in the literature for school administrators to become managers of culture, typologies such as these can be useful in examining the culture of school organizations. Moreover, Steinhoff and Owens's OCAI appears to be a valid and reliable device to provide researchers and practitioners with a rich source of imagery not found in conventional instruments designed to measure organizational environments.

ORGANIZATIONAL CLIMATE

Organizational climate is the total environmental quality within an organization. It may refer to the environment within a school department, a school building, or a school district. Organizational climate can be expressed by such adjectives as *open*, *bustling*, *warm*, *easy going*, *informal*, *cold*, *impersonal*, *hostile*, *rigid*, and *closed*.

Theorists refer to organizational culture and climate as overlapping concepts.[36] Organizational culture has its roots in sociology and anthropology, whereas organizational climate is rooted in psychology. Recent attention to school

---

[34]Peters and Waterman, *In Search of Excellence*.
[35]Nirmal K. Sethia and Mary Ann Von Glinow "Arriving at Four Cultures by Managing the Reward System," in R. Kilmann et al. (eds.), *Gaining Control of the Corporate Culture* (San Francisco: Jossey-Bass, 1985), pp. 400–420.
[36]John B. Miner, *Organizational Behavior: Performance and Productivity* (New York: Random House, 1988).

effectiveness and organizational cultures has re-emphasized the importance of organizational climate. As noted earlier, a great deal has been written about organizational culture in the popular literature, but our research-based knowledge of the concept is very limited. In contrast, organizational climate has been studied with a multitude of variables, methodologies, theories, and models. resulting in a substantial body of research.[37] Studies of organizational climate have been shown to contain elements of leadership, motivation, and job satisfaction. For example, in one comprehensive review of organizational climate studies, these elements have been linked with climate.[38]

We discuss four well-known constructs for conceptualizing organizational climate in schools: Halpin and Croft's concept of open and closed climates; NASSP's Comprehensive Assessment of School Environments; Brookover's School Learning Climate Assessment; and Willower, Eidell, and Hoy's concepts of pupil-control ideology.

Open–Closed Climates

Andrew Halpin and Don Croft postulate a conceptual continuum that extends from **open** to **closed climates**. Their observations of how schools differ provided the major impetus for their research into organizational climate.[39] Halpin notes: "Anyone who visits more than a few schools notes quickly how schools differ from each other in their 'feel.'" And as one moves from school to school, "one finds that each appears to have a 'personality' that we describe here as the 'organizational climate' of the school.

Analogously, personality is to the individual what organizational climate is to the organization."[40]

The instrument that Halpin and Croft constructed is the Organizational Climate Description Questionnaire (OCDQ). It contains sixty-four Likert-type items that are assigned to eight subtests delineated by factor–analytic methods. Four subtests pertain primarily to characteristics of the group, as a group, and the other four to characteristics of the principal as a leader. From the scores of these eight subtests, they then constructed for each school a profile, which determines the relative position of the school on the open-to-closed continuum.[41] Table 3-1 presents the eight subtests together with the open-to-closed intensity scale.

As Table 3-1 shows, the open-climate school is low in disengagement, low in hindrance, very high in esprit, high in intimacy, low in aloofness, low in production emphasis, very high in thrust, and high in consideration. The closed-school climate is depicted as very high in disengagement, high in hindrance, very low in esprit, high in intimacy, high in aloofness, high in production emphasis, low in thrust, and low in consideration.

Using this information, we can sketch a behavioral picture of each climate. Composites for the two extremes of the climate continuum, the open and closed climates, are described next.

Open Climate   An energetic, lively organization that is moving toward its goals and that provides satisfaction for group members' social needs describes the open climate. Leadership acts emerge easily and appropriately from both the group and the leader. Members are preoccupied disproportionately with neither task achievement nor social-needs satisfaction; satisfaction on both counts seems to be obtained easily and almost effortlessly. The main characteristic of this climate is the "authenticity" of the behavior that occurs among all members.

[37]Carolyn S. Anderson, "The Search for School Climate: A Review of the Research," *Review of Educational Research*, 52 (1982), pp. 368–420.

[38]Cecil Miskel and Rodney Ogawa, "Work Motivation, Job Satisfaction, and Climate," in N. J. Boyan (ed.) *Handbook of Research on Educational Administration* (New York: Longman, 1988), pp. 279–304.

[39]Andrew W. Halpin and Don B. Croft, *The Organizational Climate of Schools* (Chicago: University of Chicago Press, 1963).

[40]Andrew W. Halpin, *Theory and Research in Administration* (New York: Macmillan, 1966), p. 131.

[41]Ibid.; Halpin and Croft, *The Organizational Climate of Schools*.

TABLE 3 ▪ 1   The OCDQ Subtests

CHARACTERISTICS	INTENSITY SCALE*	
	Open	Closed
Teacher's Behavior		
Disengagement indicates that teachers do not work well together. They pull in different directions with respect to the task; they gripe and bicker among themselves.	−	+ +
Hindrance refers to teachers' feelings that the principal burdens them with routine duties, committee demands, and other requirements, which teachers construe as unnecessary busy-work.	−	+
Esprit refers to "morale." Teachers feel that their social needs are being satisfied while enjoying a sense of accomplishment in their job.	+ +	− −
Intimacy refers to teachers' enjoyment of friendly social relations with each other.	+	+
Principal's Behavior		
Aloofness refers to formal and impersonal principal behavior; the principal goes by the "book" and maintains social distance from her teachers.	−	+
Production emphasis refers to behavior that is characterized by close supervision of the staff. He is highly directive and task-oriented.	−	+
Thrust refers to behavior in which an attempt "to move the school" is made through the example that the principal sets for teachers.	+ +	−
Consideration refers to behavior that is characterized by an inclination to treat teachers "humanly," to try to do a little something extra for them in human terms.	+	−

SOURCE: Adapted from Andrew W. Halpin, *Theory and Research in Administration* (New York: Macmillan, 1966), pp. 150–151.
* + + Very high emphasis; + high emphasis; − low emphasis; − − very low emphasis.

Closed Climate   A high degree of apathy on the part of all members of the organization characterizes the closed climate. The organization is not "moving"; esprit is low because group members secure neither social-needs satisfaction nor task-achievement satisfaction. Members' behavior can be construed as "inauthentic"; indeed, the organization seems to be stagnant.

The OCDQ has had tremendous heuristic value and has promoted a broad-based interest in school climate within elementary and secondary schools.[42] Two revised versions of the OCDQ were developed recently: one for elementary schools—the OCDQ-RE—and one for secondary schools—the OCDQ-RS.[43]

---

[42]Anderson, "The Search for School Climate: A Review of the Research."

[43]Wayne K. Hoy and Sharon I. Clover, "Elementary School Climate: A Revision of the OCDQ," *Educational Administration Quarterly*, 22 (1986), pp. 93–110; Robert B. Kottkamp, John A. Mulhern, and Wayne K. Hoy, "Secondary School Climate: A Revision of the OCDQ," *Educational Administration Quarterly*, 23 (1987), pp. 31–48.

The overwhelming majority of studies on school climate focus on *adults* in the form of teachers and principal–teacher relations. In fact, school climate has rarely been studied in relation to its effect on student achievement.[44] In recent years, the emphasis in climate has shifted from a management orientation to a focus on students.[45] The three school climate constructs, which we now discuss, are examples of avenues of research in this tradition.

Comprehensive Assessment of School Environments (CASE)

The National Association of Secondary School Principals (NASSP) named a task force to investigate the current literature and measures of school climate. After an extensive review of the literature, the task force found that most existing definitions of climate were unclear, that many climate studies were based on one stakeholder group (usually teachers), that climate and satisfaction measures were frequently confused, and that measures with good psychometric properties were scarce and rarely used by practitioners.

The task force formulated a general model depicting the contextual, input, mediating, and outcome variables of school environments (Figure 3-5). Assumptions accepted in the formulation of the model were

- Climate and satisfaction are distinct but related concepts.
- Climate does not define effectiveness; it only predicts it.
- Student outcomes (cognitive, affective, and psychomotor) and efficiency data (cost) are

the most appropriate measures of school effectiveness.[46]

The model of the school environment developed by the NASSP task force goes beyond a simple consideration of school climate to encompass a full range of inputs and outputs to the process of school improvement. As Figure 3-5 shows, perceptions of climate held by stakeholder groups (students, teachers, parents) are mediating variables—influencing factors—not outcome measures. Teacher and parent satisfaction are input variables. Student satisfaction is both a mediating variable and an outcome measure; it both influences school success and corroborates it.

The Instruments   The **Comprehensive Assessment of School Environments** (**CASE**) battery consists of four survey instruments: the NASSP School Climate Survey, which is designed to elicit responses from all major stakeholder groups (students, teachers, parents), and three separate NASSP Satisfaction Surveys, one for each of the three major stakeholder groups.

The NASSP survey instruments were validated in national pilot and normative studies of 1500 teachers, 14,600 students, and 4400 parents. Each survey has eight to ten subscales touching on all important aspects of the school environment. Computer scoring programs provide separate climate and satisfaction profiles for each school.[47]

The NASSP School Climate Survey collects and measures data about perceptions on the following subscales:

- *Teacher–Student Relationships*. The quality of the interpersonal and professional relationships between teachers and students

[44]Stephen K. Miller, "Thinking About School Climate: Past and Present." Paper presented at the annual meeting of the National Association of Secondary School Principals, Dallas, February 1983.

[45]Thomas J. Sergiovanni and Robert J. Starratt, *Supervision: Human Perspectives*, 4th ed. (New York: McGraw-Hill, 1987).

[46]James W. Keefe, Edgar A. Kelley, and Stephen K. Miller, "School Climate: Clear Definitions and a Model for a Larger Setting," *NASSP Bulletin*, 69 (1985), pp. 70–77.

[47]NASSP Task Force, *Comprehensive Assessment of School Environments: Examiner's Manual* (Reston, VA: National Association of Secondary School Principals, 1987).

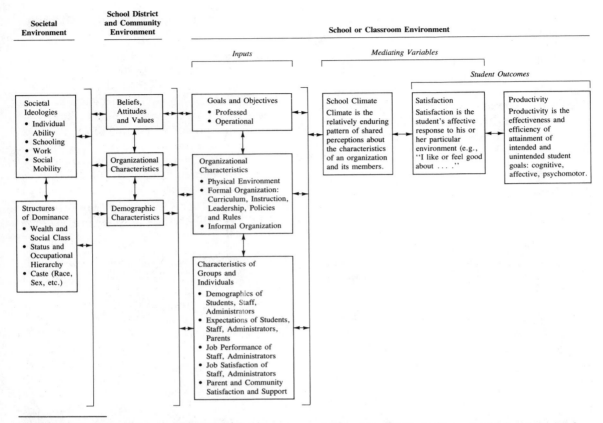

FIGURE 3-5   An Interactive Model of the School Environment (SOURCE: James W. Keefe, "Assessing the Environment of Your School: NASSP Case Model," *NASSP Bulletin*, 73 (1989), p. 36. Used by permission.)

- **Security and Maintenance.** The quality of maintenance and the degree of security people feel at the school
- **Administration.** The degree to which school administrators are effective in communicating with different role groups and in setting high performance expectations for teachers and students
- **Student Academic Orientation.** Student attention to task and concern for achievement at school
- **Student Behavioral Values.** Student self-discipline and tolerance for others
- **Guidance.** The quality of academic and career guidance and personal counseling services available to students

- **Student–Peer Relationships.** Students' care and respect for one another and their mutual cooperation
- **Parent and Community–School Relationships.** The amount and quality of involvement in the school of parents and other community members
- **Instructional Management.** The efficiency and effectiveness of teacher classroom organization and use of classroom time
- **Student Activities.** Opportunities for and actual participation of students in school-sponsored activities

The NASSP survey instruments have been developed as measures within a Comprehensive

Assessment of School Environments (CASE) battery based on the task-force model (see Figure 3-5). The instruments can be used singly or in any combination but the task force encourages their use within the context of the entire model. The principal aim of the measures and procedures of the CASE model is to foster school improvement. CASE data may also be useful in preparing school reports required by state or regional accrediting agencies. Outcomes-based evaluation for school accreditation is gaining support and acceptance from several accrediting bodies.[48] The CASE battery permits the organization and monitoring of outcomes-based data.

School Learning Climate Assessment

An increasing body of literature has identified a series of school factors that distinguish between effective and ineffective schools as measured by student achievement. Wilbur Brookover and his associates developed the **School Learning Climate Assessment** instrument to measure some aspects of the school environment that are known to be related to student learning.[49] Like NASSP's CASE battery, it is designed for practitioners and researchers to use in assessing the school learning climate.

The School Learning Climate Assessment instrument has been validated to distinguish between high-achieving and low-achieving schools. The factors identified are based on an analysis of several sets of data from samples of Michigan and Tennessee elementary schools, derived from student, teacher, and principal responses. The sixty Likert-type items are clustered in seven factors delineated through factor–analytic methods.[50]

---

[48]Ibid.

[49]Wilbur Brookover et al., *A School Learning Assessment Instrument* (East Lansing: Urban Affairs Programs, Michigan State University, 1984).

[50]Wilbur B. Brookover, *A School Learning Climate Assessment Instrument: Factor Identification and Scoring Manual* (East Lansing: Urban Affairs Programs, Michigan State University, 1984).

The seven school learning climate/effectiveness factors are as follows:

- *Administrative Instructional Leadership*. The focus of the school is on instructional-related behavior as opposed to management-oriented activities. Role expectations for appropriate behavior are defined in terms of instructional rather than managerial criteria. Indicators include the following: The "effective teacher" instructs all students to mastery; the "good student" is a high achiever; and the "effective principal" is an instructional leader who promotes high achievement for all students. Specific functions of the principal as instructional leader are to (1) motivate faculty to maximum performance, (2) develop with faculty an objective system of accountability for learning, (3) develop cooperatively procedures for the assessment of curriculum, (4) formulate plans for evaluating and reporting pupil progress, and (5) stimulate continuous study of curricular and instructional innovations.

- *Emphasis on Achievement*. This factor is related to the school's mission and goal consensus among faculty, including a commitment that all students will learn well. Schools are asked to perform many different tasks ranging across core instruction, health and hygiene, providing meals, sex education, and teaching morality. Because schools' efforts are spread across so many areas, the attention paid to any one task often slips. Not surprisingly, evidence suggests that schools that focus their attention on the priority goal of learning basic skills, with faculty consensus on that decision, effect higher student achievement. Ranking and consensus on five common goals are given: (1) preparing students for future change, (2) having students master basic skills, (3) emphasizing different ability levels among students, (4) producing good citizens, and (5) developing students' critical thinking skills.

- *Expectations and Evaluations of Students*. These two variables tap both present and future dimensions of the extent to which teachers

(1) actually expect their students to learn and (2) believe their students have the ability to learn (i.e., evaluations of student learning capacity). This factor is reflected in the ideology of the school concerning the beliefs and attitudes of the faculty. Indicators include the following: (1) all students can learn the school's objectives; (2) all students are expected to reach high standards of achievement; (3) teachers can successfully instruct all students; (4) test performance is an appropriate measure of school success; (5) staff norms promote high performance and achievement; and (6) the staff is committed to producing high achievement for all students, no matter what it takes.

■ *Using Test Data to Evaluate Programs*. Effective use of assessment data include (1) continuing diagnosis, feedback, and monitoring of student progress; (2) accurate records of instructional mastery for all students; (3) corrective instruction based on diagnostic information; and (4) schoolwide data used for evaluating and improving the school's instructional program.

■ *Safe and Orderly Environment*. For the most part, this factor is self-explanatory. It refers to the maintenance of an orderly, work-oriented school environment and classroom discipline. It is based on the premise that a school cannot function effectively unless all students, teachers, and administrators work together. Disruptions of learning cannot be condoned. Students have a responsibility to behave so that they will not interfere with the rights and civil liberties of others to learn. Students behavior must be governed by obligations to parents and guardians, other students, and the community.

■ *Grouping for Instruction*. This refers to the extent to which students are grouped and tracked between and within classes. The scale is scored so that more grouping and tracking (i.e., greater differentiation among students) is negative in effect. This is consistent with findings that overall student achievement in a school tends to be lower when grouping and tracking is more pro-

nounced, a result that has disproportionately negative effects on students in the average and low groups.

■ *Time for Instruction*. The final factor refers to the relationship of time-on-task and learning. The higher the percentage of academic engaged time, the higher the student learning.

The concept of effective schools implies that most schools are not as effective as they might be. Because effectiveness is a continuum, schools can always improve their performance. Unfortunately, schools are not easy to change. Schools that somehow manage to produce achievement levels higher than that predicted by the socioeconomic composition of the school and community are by definition exceptions. If becoming an effective school were easy, effective schools would be the rule rather than the atypical extreme. Nevertheless, there are a number of identifiable characteristics that can be used to measure school quality. (See Administrative Advice 3-4.)

Pupil-Control Ideology

Another method of conceptualizing organizational climate is in terms of the attitudes toward and behavior faculty use to control students. William Glasser has underscored the saliency of pupil control in the organizational life of public schools.[51] Moreover, according to nearly two decades of annual Gallup polls, pupil control remains a key concern of teachers, administrators, and citizens. In fact, a teacher's inability to control students effectively is a major source of dissatisfaction for many of today's teachers.

The importance of pupil control in schools is not surprising. Schools are people-developing or people-changing institutions. The objective of the school as a social institution is to achieve major changes in the child. These changes are not restricted to cognitive behavior (learning)

---

[51]William Glasser, *The Quality School* (New York: Harper & Row, 1990).

ADMINISTRATIVE ADVICE 3-4

■

Characteristics to Measure School Quality

The quality of a school is the result of a number of factors, many of which are listed below. Any school possessing a majority of these characteristics can be called a high-quality school.

■ *Planned Curriculum*. In a high-quality school, the curriculum is well-planned and sequentially organized. All basic subjects are offered regularly—including English, science, mathematics, social studies, and foreign language.

■ *School Board–Approved Curriculum*. If the school board does not approve a curriculum—and if curriculum decisions are not intentional—any consistency of high achievement among students will be incidental. Board members must be able to understand and approve courses in vocational education, special education, and gifted education, as well as the traditional subjects.

■ *Strong Graduation Requirements*. Good schools have graduation requirements that push students beyond minimal expectations. Schools that do so also have a well-organized, sequentially planned curriculum that requires basic courses and stringent academic electives.

■ *Academic Offerings That Go Beyond the Basics*. Basic courses must be augmented by challenging classes in the arts, humanities, physical education, and job training.

■ *Positive Learning Climate*. Seriousness of purpose among students is one way to define a learning climate. It means that students work steadily toward clear goals. For some students, the goal is being admitted to college; for others, it is mastering the skills needed for entry-level jobs.

■ *Good Attendance and Low Dropout Rates*. Evidence of a low dropout rate and high daily attendance (among students and faculty) are important measures of high-quality schools.

■ *High Per-Pupil Expenditure*. A high per-pupil expenditure is an important factor in high-quality schools. Of greater significance, however, is a set of more limited financial indicators: the percentage of the school budget spent on textbooks, field trips, instructional supplies, and

the like. The amounts spent on such items is a good indication of a community's commitment to quality education.

■ *Low Pupil–Teacher Ratio*. Small classes generally promote good discipline and encourage student interaction with teachers.

■ *Superior Library and Media Program*. A well-equipped library says the school board cares about providing students with up-to-date information; and a well-used library indicates teachers are committed to helping students understand the value of research.

■ *Attractive Campus*. Nicely kept buildings say something important about the attitude of students and community toward the schools.

■ *"Solid Gold" Faculty*. The scores teachers receive on the National Teacher Examination (NTE) and their grade-point averages (GPA) in college are one measure of quality. There may be little connection between either NTE scores and GPAs and the ability to teach, but, at least, these scores indicate that teachers know their subjects.

■ *Principal Who Cares*. Outstanding principals hold high expectations for teachers and pupils, require teachers to be punctual and prepare complete lesson plans, make sure teachers assign appropriate amounts of homework, and support teachers in their efforts to maintain a well-run school.

■ *Record of Student Achievement*. Student aptitude and student achievement both must be measured. If students achieve significantly higher than their aptitude, the school is high-quality. High-quality schools help *all* students outperform their abilities.

Source: Adapted from John Goodspeed Stuart, "Use These 13 Characteristics to Measure the Quality of a School," *American School Board Journal*, 170 (1983), pp. 27–28. Used by permission.

but include a wide range of social, emotional, physical, and, in some cases, moral behavior.[52] Organizations that achieve or attempt to achieve the most thoroughgoing change are performing functions crucial to the maintenance of social control.

Furthermore, schools accept as conscripted clients all those who legally must attend. That is, neither the organization (school) nor the client (student) exercises choice concerning participation in the relationship.[53] The mandatory nature of the pupil's participation suggests that schools are dealing with clients whose motivations and desires for the school's services cannot be assumed. It seems reasonable that pupil control would be a major concern.

Evidence to support the prominence of pupil control in schools is provided by a field study of a junior high school in which the researchers indicated that pupil control was the "integrative theme" that pervaded the culture of the school.[54] This study eventually led to the development of the construct of **pupil-control ideology** as a school-climate descriptor. The conceptualization of pupil control and the research initiated by Donald Willower, Terry Eidell, and Wayne Hoy at Pennsylvania State University have permitted some of the first steps toward a systematic analysis of pupil control in the school.[55]

Willower and his colleagues postulate pupil control along a humanistic to custodial contin-

uum. These terms refer to contrasting types of individual ideology and the types of school organization that they seek to rationalize and justify. Prototypes of humanistic and custodial schools are presented next.[56]

The Humanistic School   The model for humanistic control orientation is an educational community in which students learn through cooperative interaction and experience. In this model, learning and behavior are viewed in psychological and sociological terms rather than moralistic ones. Self-discipline is substituted for strict teacher control. The humanistic orientation leads teachers to desire a democratic atmosphere with its attendant flexibility in status and rules, sensitivity to others, open communication, and increased student self-determination. Both teachers and pupils are willing to act on their own volition and to accept responsibility for their actions.

The Custodial School   The prototype of custodial control orientation is the traditional school that often provides a rigid and highly controlled setting concerned with the maintenance of order. Students are generally stereotyped in terms of their appearance, their behavior, and their parents' social status. Teachers who have a custodial orientation tend to conceive of the school as an autocratic organization with a well-defined pupil–teacher status hierarchy. Furthermore, teachers are predisposed to view the flow of power and communication as unilateral and as downward where students must accept the decisions of teachers without question. Teachers do not attempt to understand student behavior but, instead, view it in moralistic terms. Student misbehavior is taken as a personal affront; students are perceived as irresponsible and undisciplined persons who must be controlled through punitive sanctions. Impersonality, pes-

---

[52]Charles E. Bidwell, "The School as a Formal Organization," in J. G. March (ed.), *Handbook of Organizations* (Chicago: Rand McNally, 1965), pp. 972–1022.

[53]Richard O. Carlson, "Environmental Constraints and Organizational Consequences: The Public School and Its Clients," in D. E. Griffiths (ed.), *Behavioral Science and Educational Administration* (Chicago: University of Chicago Press, 1964), pp. 262–276.

[54]Donald Willower and Ronald Jones, "Control in an Educational Organization," in J. Raths, J. Pancella, and J. Van Ness (eds.), *Studying Teaching* (Englewood Cliffs, NJ: Prentice-Hall, 1967), pp. 424–428.

[55]Donald J. Willower, Terry L. Eidell, and Wayne K. Hoy, *The School and Pupil Control Ideology*, rev. ed. (University Park: Pennsylvania State University Studies Monograph No. 24, 1973).

[56]Wayne K. Hoy and Cecil G. Miskel, *Educational Administration: Theory, Research and Practice*, 4th ed. (New York: McGraw-Hill, 1991).

simism, and "watchful mistrust" imbue the atmosphere of the custodial school.

The Pupil-Control Ideology Form

To operationalize pupil-control ideology along a humanistic–custodial continuum, the Pupil Control Ideology form (PCI) was developed and field-tested.[57] The PCI consists of twenty Likert-type items. Examples of items are: "beginning teachers are not likely to maintain strict enough control over their pupils," "pupils can be trusted to work together without supervision," and "it is often necessary to remind pupils that their status in school differs from that of teachers." Responses are made on a 5-point scale in a strongly agree to strongly disagree format. The scoring range is 20 to 100, the higher the score the more custodial the ideology of the respondent. Pooled scores represent the pupil-control ideology of the school. Reliability and validity of the instrument have been reported in numerous studies.[58]

Pupil-Control Ideology: A School-Climate Descriptor

Each school appears to have a prevailing pupil-control ideology that influences its members. For instance, pupil-control ideology is a school characteristic that affects the values of new teachers coming into a school. They are heavily influenced by the prevailing climate. Studies show how student teachers and neophyte teachers gradually shift from very humanistic values proselytized by teacher education staffs to more prevalent values held by teachers in the schools.[59]

One study found that pupil-control ideology was a fruitful measure of the climate of the school; humanism in school pupil-control ideology was associated with openness in organizational climate.[60] Another study tested further the utility of the humanistic–custodial construct as a predictor of school climate. To determine the openness of the climate of the fifty-three-school sample, Fred Lunenberg used three organizational climate subtests of the OCDQ (esprit, thrust, and disengagement) to compare the most humanistic schools and the most custodial schools in terms of their climate-openness scores.[61] There were no surprises. Schools with custodial pupil-control ideologies had significantly lower esprit and thrust scores and significantly higher disengagement scores. That is, custodial schools as compared to humanistic schools appear to have (1) teachers who have low morale, reflecting low job satisfaction with respect to both task-achievement and social-needs satisfaction; (2) principals who are ineffective in directing the activities of teachers through personal example; and (3) teachers who do not work well together, resulting in minimal group achievement.

Two researchers developed and tested hypotheses concerning relationships between pupil-control ideology, pupil-control behavior, and the quality of school life. The hypotheses, tested in 239 elementary and secondary school classrooms in five school districts, were confirmed.[62] Custodialism in pupil-control ideology and in pupil-control behavior (another climate construct) were associated with students' negative reactions to the quality of school life. In addition, differences in pupil-control ideology, pupil-control behavior, and the quality of school life were

[57]Willower, Eidell, and Hoy, *The School and Pupil Control Ideology*.

[58]John S. Packard, "The Pupil Control Studies," in N. J. Boyan (ed.), *Handbook of Research on Educational Administration* (New York: Longman, 1988), pp. 185–207.

[59]Fred C. Lunenburg, "The Influence of Experience on the Student Teacher," *High School Journal*, 69 (1986), pp. 214–217; Wayne K. Hoy and Richard Rees, "The Bureaucratic Socialization of Student Teachers," *Journal of Teacher Education*, 28 (1977), pp. 23–26.

[60]Fred C. Lunenburg and Robert R. O'Reilly, "Personal and Organizational Influence on Pupil Control Ideology," *Journal of Experimental Education*, 42 (1974), pp. 31–35.

[61]Fred C. Lunenburg, *Pupil Control in Schools: Individual and Organizational Correlates* (Lexington, MA: Ginn, 1984).

[62]Fred C. Lunenburg and Linda J. Schmidt, "Pupil Control Ideology, Pupil Control Behavior, and the Quality of School Life," *Journal of Research and Development in Education*, 22 (1989), pp. 36–44.

found among urban, suburban, and rural schools. Urban schools were significantly more custodial in both pupil-control ideology and behavior and had lower quality of school life scores than did either suburban or rural schools.

In a comprehensive study of school climate and alienation of high school students, one study reported that the more custodial and closed the school climate, the greater the students' sense of alienation.[63] Another inquiry involving high school students found a relationship between a humanistic school climate and high levels of self-actualization among the student body.[64]

Yet another study, involving nearly 3000 students in thirty-five elementary schools, found that the humanistic school, not the custodial one, was associated with high student self-concept as a learner. In addition, students' perceptions of a humanistic school climate were positively related to their motivation, task orientation, problem solving, and seriousness about learning.[65]

Do teachers' pupil-control ideologies influence students' feelings toward teachers? Researchers explored this question in a comprehensive study involving nearly 3000 students and teachers in 131 elementary school classrooms. As predicted, custodialism in teacher pupil-control ideology was directly related to students' projections of rejection and hostility toward teachers. The hypothesis was supported in the overall sample of 131 teachers ($r = .60$) and in subsamples of male ($r = .71$) and female ($r = .54$) teachers.[66]

In his recent book, William Glasser verifies the aforementioned research dealing with the relationship between pupil-control styles and organizational climate. Glasser makes a distinction in his book between boss-management (coercive control) and lead-management (noncoercive control).[67] He contends that boss-management results in an adversarial relationship between teachers and students and hinders the quality of learning. The personal power struggle between teacher and pupil becomes a vicious cycle: The student learns less and resists more; the teacher coerces more and teaches less. That is, teachers who use boss-management exclusively will limit the learning in their classes. And a principal who embraces boss-management will make it so hard for her teachers to use lead-management that the whole school will be negatively affected.

Glasser proposes a philosophy of lead-management that is based on the use of persuasion and problem solving to control students. The lead-manager spends all of his time and energy determining how to run the system so that the students will see that it is to their benefit to produce high-quality work. Once quality becomes central to a school's coursework, students will be proud of what they do, and this pride will become as contagious as pride elsewhere. In fact, Glasser believes that schools can make quality as much a part of academics as it is now part of athletics. (Note the similarity between Glasser's boss-management and custodial schools and his lead-management and humanistic schools.)

SUMMARY

1. Organizational culture is the pattern of beliefs and assumptions shared by organizational members. Some important characteristics of organizational culture include observed behavioral regularities, norms, dominant values, philosophy, rules, and feelings.

2. Organizational heroes, rites and rituals, and communication networks play key roles in creating organizational cultures.

3. In maintaining a culture, institutions carry out several steps including careful selection of entry-level

[63]Wayne K. Hoy, "Dimensions of Student Alienation and Pupil Control Orientations of High Schools," *Interchange*, 3 (1972), pp. 38–52.

[64]John Deibert and Wayne Hoy, "Custodial High Schools and Self-Actualization of Students," *Educational Research Quarterly*, 2 (1977), pp. 24–31.

[65]Fred C. Lunenburg, "Pupil Control Ideology and Self Concept as a Learner," *Educational Research Quarterly*, 8 (1983), pp. 33–39.

[66]Fred C. Lunenburg and Jack W. Stouten, "Teacher Pupil Control Ideology and Pupils Projected Feelings Toward Teachers," *Psychology in the Schools*, 20 (1983), pp. 528–533.

[67]Glasser, *The Quality School*.

candidates, humility-inducing experiences, mastery of one's job, implementation of reward and control systems, careful adherence to values, reinforcing folklore, and the use of role models.

4. Changing organizational culture involves the following steps: external enabling conditions; internal permitting conditions; precipitating pressures; triggering events; cultural visioning; culture-change strategy; culture-change action plans; implementation of interventions; and reformulation of the culture.

5. Organizational culture has effects on administrative processes (e.g., motivation, leadership, decision making, communication, and change and organizational structures—(i.e., the selection process, evaluation system, control system, and reward system).

6. Certain types of cultures characterize excellent enterprises. Peters and Waterman offer a generalized concept of excellence. Ouchi postulates Theory Z as an approach to excellence, with specific application to schools.

7. Organizational climate is the total environmental quality within an organization. Four climate constructs were discussed: the open–closed model, CASE, the school learning climate assessment, and the humanistic–custodial model.

KEY TERMS

organizational culture

heroes

rites and rituals

communications network

organizational socialization

change cycle

Theory Z

culture phenotype

family culture

machine culture

cabaret culture

little shop of horrors culture

organizational climate

open–closed climates

Comprehensive Assessment of School Environments (CASE)

School Learning Climate Assessment

pupil-control ideology

DISCUSSION QUESTIONS

1. What is organizational culture? Describe several important characteristics of organizational culture and give some examples of each.

2. How are organizational cultures developed, maintained, and changed?

3. Describe some of the features of the cultures of excellent firms as elaborated by Thomas Peters and Robert Waterman.

4. Discuss the tenets of Theory Z as described by William Ouchi. What are its applications to schools?

5. How do each of the four organizational climate constructs relate to school effectiveness?

SUGGESTED READINGS

Robert F. Allen et al., *The Organizational Unconscious: How to Create the Corporate Culture You Want and Need*, 2nd ed. (Burlington, VT: Human Resource Institute, 1987). A complete guide to strategies that can be used to create a culture within most organizations.

Terrence E. Deal and Allan A. Kennedy, *Corporate Cultures: The Rites and Rituals of Corporate Life* (Reading, MA: Addison-Wesley, 1984). A comprehensive discussion of the development and maintenance of organizational culture.

Ralph H. Kilmann and Teresa J. Covin, *Corporate Transformation: Revitalizing Organizations for a Competitive World* (San Francisco: Jossey-Bass, 1987). A comprehensive discussion of how leaders go about changing an organization's culture.

Ralph H. Kilmann, Mary L. Saxton, and Ray Serpa (eds.), *Gaining Control of the Corporate Culture* (San Francisco: Jossey-Bass, 1985). A discussion of how to accurately assess an organization's culture.

Cecil Miskel and Rodney Ogawa, "Work Motivation, Job Satisfaction, and Climate," in N. J. Boyan (ed.), *Handbook of Research on Educational Administration* (New York: Longman, 1988) pp. 279–304. A comprehensive and current synthesis of the research on organizational climate.

John S. Packard, "The Pupil Control Studies," in N. J. Boyan (ed.), *Handbook of Research on Educational Administration* (New York: Longman, 1988), pp. 185–207. A scientific and scholarly treatment of the more than 300 pupil-control studies that have used the PCI instrument.

Edgar H. Schein, *Organizational Culture and Leadership* (San Francisco: Jossey-Bass, 1985). A definitive guide to issues related to the leader's role in creating, maintaining, or changing an organization's culture.

II

ADMINISTRATIVE PROCESSES

4

MOTIVATION

In this chapter, we attempt to answer these questions concerning work motivation in school organizations. We begin our discussion with some brief definitions of motivation, and we examine the concepts of effort, persistence, and direction of employee motives as a foundation of work motivation. Then we describe and contrast several popular content theories of motivation: need hierarchy, motivation–hygiene, and existence relatedness growth approaches. Next, we examine three of the more applied areas of motivation: expectancy, equity, and goal setting. We conclude the chapter with a discussion of management by objectives.

DEFINING MOTIVATION

School administrators widely agree that **motivation** is a critical determinant of performance in organizations, but there is less agreement on the definition of the word *motivation*. Derived from the Latin word *movere* (which means "to move"), this definition is far too narrow in scope, from an organizational perspective. Motivation has been defined as "those processes within an individual that stimulate behavior and channel it in ways that should benefit the organization as a whole";[1] "the forces acting on and coming from within a person that account, in part, for the willful direction of one's efforts toward the achievement of specific goals";[2] and "motivation means three things: The person works hard; the person keeps at his or her work; and the person directs his or her behavior toward appropriate goals."[3] In general, these definitions seem to contain three common aspects of motivation: effort, persistence, and direction.[4]

Effort   **Effort** concerns the magnitude, or intensity, of the employee's work-related behavior. For example, a superintendent of schools might manifest greater effort by implementing a districtwide program to decrease school dropouts in his school district. A building principal might exhibit greater effort by examining several strategies to increase student attendance in her school building. And a teacher might show greater effort by developing various types of media and other supplementary materials to accompany the text used in a social studies course. All are exerting effort in a manner appropriate to their specific jobs.

Persistence   **Persistence** concerns the sustained effort employees manifest in their work-related activities. For example, the school superintendent who makes many important contributions to the district early in his tenure and then

rests on his laurels for several years prior to retirement would not be considered highly motivated. Likewise, the building principal who works very hard in the morning each day and then leaves the job to play golf in the afternoon would not be considered highly motivated. Neither school employee has been persistent in applying effort on the job.

Direction   Whereas effort and persistence concern the quantity of work performed, **direction** refers to the quality of an employee's work—that is, the investment of sustained effort in a direction that benefits the employer. From an employer's perspective, a high school counselor is expected to provide sound advice, concerning available and suitable career opportunities or appropriate college placements, to her group of graduating seniors. To the extent that correct decisions are made by the counselor, persistent effort is translated into desired school outcomes.

These three aspects of motivation serve as the basis for our discussion of the most prominent theories of motivation. Most theories can be separated into two major categories, according to whether they are concerned with the content or process of motivation. Table 4-1 summarizes these approaches.

CONTENT THEORIES

Content theories of motivation focus on the question, What energizes human behavior? The three most popular content theories of motivation are Maslow's need hierarchy theory, Herzberg's motivation–hygiene theory, and Alderfer's existence relatedness growth theory. These theories have received considerable attention both in research exploration and organizational application.

Need Hierarchy Theory

Abraham Maslow's **need hierarchy theory** is probably one of the best known and most widely

[1]John B. Miner, *Organizational Behavior: Performance and Productivity* (New York: Random House, 1988), p. 158.
[2]R. Dennis Middlemist and Michael A. Hitt, *Organizational Behavior: Managerial Strategies for Performance* (St. Paul: West, 1988), p. 144.
[3]Gary Johns, *Organizational Behavior: Understanding Life at Work* (Glenview, IL: Scott, Foresman, 1983), p. 173.
[4]Ibid.

TABLE 4 ▪ 1   Types of Motivation Theories

TYPE	CHARACTERISTICS	THEORIES	EXAMPLES
Content	Concerned with identifying specific factors that motivate people	Need hierarchy Motivation–hygiene Existence relatedness growth	Satisfying people's needs for pay, promotion, recognition
Process	Concerned with the process by which motivational factors interact to produce motivation	Expectancy Equity Goal setting	Clarifying the person's perception of work inputs, performance requirements, and rewards

used theories for the study of motivation in organizations.[5] Maslow identified five basic groups of human needs that emerge in a specific sequence or pattern—that is, in a hierarchy of importance. In this scheme, once one need is satisfied, another emerges and demands satisfaction, and so on through the hierarchy. The five levels of needs, which represent the order of importance to the individual, are physiological, safety, social, esteem, and self-actualization (Table 4-2).

1. *Physiological needs* include the need for food, water, and shelter. Once these needs are sufficiently satisfied, other levels of needs become prominent and provide motivation for an individual's behavior. Organizations might satisfy these needs by providing a base salary and basic working conditions such as heat, air-conditioning, and cafeteria services.
2. *Safety needs* include protection against danger, threat, and deprivation, including avoidance of anxiety. Organizations can provide these needs with safe working conditions, fair rules and regulations, job security, pension and insurance plans, salary increases, and freedom to unionize.

3. *Social needs* include affection, affiliation, friendship, and love. People who reach this third level in the hierarchy have primarily satisfied physiological and safety needs. Organizations might meet these needs by including employee-centered supervision, providing opportunities for teamwork, following group norms, and sponsoring group activities such as organized sports programs and school or districtwide picnics.
4. *Esteem needs* focus on self-respect and includes recognition and respect from others. Fulfilling esteem needs produces feelings of self-confidence, prestige, power, and control. Organizations can satisfy this need through recognition and award programs, articles in the district newsletter, promotions, and prestigious job titles (e.g., Team Leader, Director of Computer Services, or Senior Researcher).
5. *Self-actualization needs* focus on the attainment of one's full potential for continued self-development; in Maslow's words, the desire to become, "more and more what one idiosyncratically is, to become everything one is capable of becoming."[6] Unlike the other needs, self-actualization is manifested differently in different people. For example,

---

[5]Abraham H. Maslow, *Motivation and Personality*, rev. ed. (New York: Harper & Row, 1970).

[6]Ibid., p. 46.

TABLE 4 ■ 2   Maslow's Need Hierarchy

	GENERAL FACTORS	NEED LEVELS	ORGANIZATIONAL FACTORS
Complex Needs ↑	Growth Achievement Advancement	Self-actualization (5)	Challenging job Advancement in organization Achievement in work
	Self-esteem Esteem from others Recognition	Esteem (4)	Titles Status symbols Promotions
	Affection Acceptance Friendship	Social (3)	Quality of supervision Compatible work group Professional friendships
↓	Safety Security Stability	Safety (2)	Safe working conditions Fringe benefits Job security
Basic Needs	Water Food Shelter	Physiological (1)	Heat and air conditioning Base salary Working conditions

to achieve ultimate satisfaction, a musician must create music, an artist must paint, a teacher must teach students, and an administrator must lead people. Organizations might provide self-actualization by involving employees in planning job designs, making assignments that capitalize on employees' unique skills, and relaxing structure to permit employees' personal growth and self-development.

Research on the Need Hierarchy Theory   One of the first and most widely used measures of Maslow's need hierarchy theory, the Need Satisfaction Questionnaire (NSQ), was developed by Lyman Porter.[7] Porter modified Maslow's hierarchy by eliminating physiological needs on grounds that they are widely satisfied and thus of relatively little importance in organizational settings in North America. In addition, Porter

added autonomy needs, which he inserted between Maslow's esteem and self-actualization needs.

There have been many research studies of the need hierarchy theory in educational organizations. Studies of 233 educators from a suburban Rochester, New York, school district and of 1593 secondary school teachers in thirty-six Illinois high schools reported large need deficiencies for the higher-level needs (esteem, autonomy, and self-actualization) with esteem showing the greatest need deficiency.[8] A later study of teacher need deficiencies was somewhat similar to those of the two earlier ones. The three higher-level needs were still the dominant areas of perceived need deficiency. There was, however, a significant increase in the security need

[7]Lyman W. Porter, *Organizational Patterns of Managerial Job Attitudes* (New York: American Foundation for Management Research, 1964).

[8]Francis M. Trusty and Thomas J. Sergiovanni, "Perceived Need Deficiencies of Teachers and Administrators: A Proposal for Restructuring Teacher Roles," *Educational Administration Quarterly*, 2 (1966), pp. 168–180; Fred D. Carver and Thomas J. Sergiovanni, "Complexity, Adaptability and Job Satisfaction in High Schools: An Axiomatic Theory Applied," *Journal of Educational Administration*, 9 (1971), pp. 15–30.

in the later study. The authors attributed this increase in the security needs of teachers as a reflection of a tightening job market and pressures of reduction in force.[9] Other researchers examined the need deficiencies of teachers and administrators. The findings revealed that school administrators had fewer need deficiencies than did teachers on all five subscales of Porter's NSQ—security, social, esteem, autonomy, and self-actualization.[10] In a study comparing female homemakers and women working in professional and managerial positions, safety and social needs emerged as more important among homemakers; esteem and autonomy needs did not differ markedly between the two groups; and self-actualization was of highest importance in both instances.[11]

Outstanding schools require leaders who have the ability to motivate people to maximize their performances, to grow professionally, and to change. To achieve these goals, school administrators must know and be able to apply the basic theories of motivation. (See Administrative Advice 4-1.)

Maslow's need hierarchy theory has a commonsense appeal that has resulted in wide discussion and application of the theory among practitioners. Despite this appeal, limited research has been done to validate the theory. The findings are mixed. A review of relevant research found little support for Maslow's framework.[12]

Evidence that supports the five distinct need categories is scant, but a two-level hierarchy of lower-order and higher-order needs may exist. In addition, the idea of prepotency has been questioned.[13] In this regard, evidence—particularly at the higher-order needs level—supports the view that unless physiological needs and safety needs are satisfied, employees will not be concerned with higher-order needs. Little evidence, however, supports the view that a hierarchy exists once one moves above the security level.[14] For example, an individual can have strong social, esteem, and self-actualization needs simultaneously. In fact, Maslow's clinical studies showed that the idea of prepotency may not be relevant for all individuals.[15] Nevertheless, Maslow's theory has not been completely disproved. There is evidence that people do tend to think of their own needs in terms of the five categories that Maslow defined.[16] Another study empirically demonstrated the viability of both five- and two-level need categories, suggesting that the two perspectives need not be mutually exclusive.[17]

Motivation–Hygiene Theory

Frederick Herzberg developed a unique and exciting motivation theory that builds on Maslow's earlier work. The theory has been called the motivation-hygiene theory, the **two-factor the-**

[9]Mary Beth Anderson and Edward F. Iwanicki, "Teacher Motivation and Its Relationship to Burnout," *Educational Administration Quarterly*, 20 (1984), pp. 109–132.

[10]Grace B. Chisolm, Roosevelt Washington, and Mary Thibodeaux, "Job Motivation and the Need Fulfillment Deficiencies of Educators." Paper presented at the annual meeting of the American Educational Research Association, Boston, 1980.

[11]Ellen L. Betz, "Need Fulfillment in the Career Development of Women," *Journal of Vocational Behavior*, 20 (1982), pp. 60–61.

[12]Mahmoud A. Wahba and Lawrence G. Bridwell, "Maslow Reconsidered: A Review of the Research on the Need Hierarchy Theory," *Organizational Behavior and Human Performance*, 15 (1976), pp. 212–240.

[13]Ibid.

[14]Lyman W. Porter, Edward E. Lawler, and J. Richard Hackman, *Behavior in Organizations* (New York: McGraw-Hill, 1975).

[15]John B. Miner, *Theories of Organizational Behavior* (Hinsdale, IL: Dryden Press, 1980).

[16]Simcha Ronen and Allen I. Kraut, "An Experimental Examination of Work Motivation Taxonomies," *Human Relations*, 33 (1980), pp. 505–516.

[17]Vance F. Mitchell and Pravin Moudgill, "Measurement of Maslow's Need Hierarchy," *Organizational Behavior and Human Performance,* 16 (1976), pp. 334–339.

ADMINISTRATIVE ADVICE 4-1

■

PRACTICAL MOTIVATIONAL STRATEGIES

Applying the concepts of motivation theory is sometimes difficult to achieve. However, if this is done effectively, school administrators can help teachers become more effective and more fulfilled instructors. Below are some practical motivational strategies to enhance teacher performance and growth.

■ *Personal Regard*. To show personal regard, personally follow up on all faculty concerns, affirm the inquiry, and appropriately question to determine a common understanding; each day, discuss informally—with a set number of faculty members—what can be done to assist them; and be sensitive to faculty members' feelings when implementing new policies and procedures.

■ *Communication*. To enhance communication, develop, publish, and model clear and consistent educational goals; seek opinions and viewpoints on changes that affect the faculty; listen to understand, not to respond or to defend; and listen, listen, listen.

■ *Recognition*. To recognize teachers, start each faculty meeting or memo with words of appre-

ciation for a job well done; promote teacher successes when talking to students, parents, central office personnel, the community, and other teachers; inform teachers of professional opportunities that might appeal to them; and give teachers specific praise face to face frequently.

■ *Participation*. To allow participation in the decision-making process, use cooperative goal setting in formative evaluation; elect an administrative advisory committee; allow faculty to have a major voice in staff development, evaluation, and in-service programs; and create ad hoc, small groups to brainstorm problems.

Source: Adapted from Lynn E. Lehman, "Practical Motivational Strategies for Teacher Performance and Growth," *NASSP Bulletin*, 73 (1989), pp. 76–80. Used by permission.

---

ory, and the dual-factor theory.[18] Like Maslow's need hierarchy theory, the motivation–hygiene theory seeks to determine factors that cause motivation. Rather than looking for needs energized within the individual, Herzberg focused attention on the work environment to identify factors that arouse in people either positive or negative attitudes toward their work.

The original research used to develop the theory was conducted with 203 accountants and engineers employed in nine manufacturing

firms in the Pittsburgh area. Herzberg used the critical-incident technique to obtain data for analysis. The subjects in the study were asked to think of times when they felt good about their jobs. Each subject was then asked to describe the conditions that led to those feelings. Herzberg repeated this same approach with a wide variety of other employees. Results obtained from the critical-incident method were fairly consistent across the various subjects. Reported good feelings were generally associated with the job itself—content, intrinsic, or psychological factors. These included achievement, recognition, the work itself, responsibility, advancement, and growth. Herzberg named these

---

[18]Frederick Herzberg, Bernard Mausner, and Barbara S. Snyderman, *The Motivation to Work* (New York: Wiley, 1959).

content factors "job satisfiers," or *motivators*, because they fulfill an individual's need for psychological growth. Reported bad feelings, on the other hand, were generally associated with the environment surrounding the job—context, extrinsic, or physical factors. These included company policies, supervision, interpersonal relations, working conditions, and salary. Herzberg named these context factors "job dissatisfiers," or *hygiene factors* because they are preventative and environmental. Figure 4-1 illustrates these findings.

The motivation–hygiene theory is related to the need hierarchy theory. Herzberg has re-

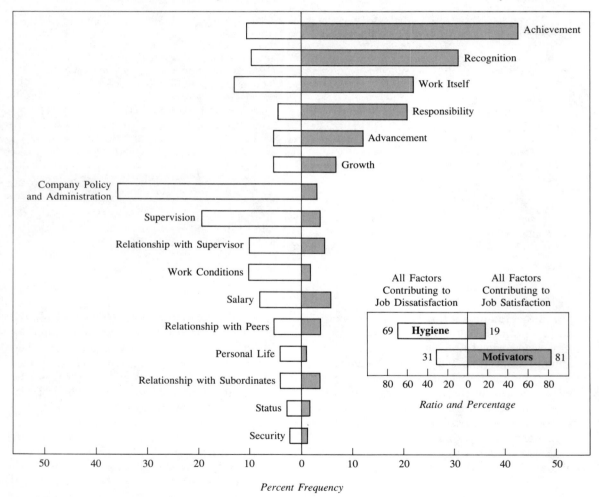

Factors Characterizing 1844 Events on the Job That Lead to Extreme Dissatisfaction

Factors Characterizing 1753 Events on the Job That Lead to Extreme Satisfaction

Percent Frequency

FIGURE 4-1   Comparison of Satisfiers and Dissatisfiers (Source: Adapted from Frederick Herzberg, "One More Time: How Do You Motivate Employees?" *Harvard Business Review,* 65 (1987), p. 112. Copyright © 1987 by the President and Fellows of Harvard College. Used by permission.)

duced Maslow's five-level need system into a two-level system—hygiene needs and motivation needs. Hygiene factors (dissatisfiers) are roughly equivalent to Maslow's lower-level needs, because they serve to reduce dissatisfaction but do not lead to satisfaction. Motivators (satisfiers) are roughly equivalent to Maslow's higher-level needs. According to Herzberg, dissatisfiers may ensure that employees will perform at minimum levels, but motivation, which contributes to superior performance, is possible only through satisfiers. That is, only the work itself and recognition, advancement, personal growth, and development stemming from this work will provide a situation for motivated behavior in the workplace.

Research on the Motivation–Hygiene Theory   The motivation–hygiene theory has been subjected to extensive research, but little research on the theory has been done in the past fifteen years. Thomas Sergiovanni replicated Herzberg's study with teachers. His study suggests that achievement, recognition, and responsibility contribute to teacher motivation. Dissatisfaction seems to result from poor interpersonal relations with students, inadequate styles of supervision, rigid and inflexible school policies and administrative practices, and poor interpersonal relations with colleagues and parents.[19]

Sergiovanni's study deviated in at least two important ways from Herzberg's study, which was conducted in an industrial setting. First, the work itself accounted for both satisfaction and dissatisfaction among teachers. In explaining this finding, Sergiovanni noted "elements of the job of teaching as we presently know it are inherently less satisfying."[20] First, routine housekeeping, attendance taking, procuring milk money, paperwork, study hall supervision,

lunch duty, and so on seem to neutralize the more satisfying aspects of teaching. Second, whereas "advancement" was an important motivator for Herzberg's accountants and engineers, it was conspicuously missing from Sergiovanni's teachers. According to Sergiovanni, teaching as an occupation offers little opportunity for advancement as it is currently structured.[21]

Two other researchers using a sample of teachers in Georgia and a sample of teachers in Saskatchewan, Canada, provided additional support for the two-factor theory.[22] Each used methods similar to Herzberg's. Using the critical-incident method in a mail questionnaire format, another study found support for Herzberg's theory with a sample of college and university faculty.[23] Cecil Miskel compared teachers, principals, and central office administrators' responses using a questionnaire variation of the Herzberg method. He found that teachers have a lower tolerance for work pressure than do principals. In addition, teachers have a greater desire for security than do central office administrators, except those teachers who aspired to administrative positions. The aspiring administrators also expressed a greater desire for the motivators.[24]

In another study, Miskel found that a different conceptual framework concerning motivation, hygiene, and risk factors existed for teachers, school administrators, and industrial managers. Teachers exhibited high concern for hygiene fac-

---

[19]Thomas J. Sergiovanni, "Factors Which Affect Satisfaction and Dissatisfaction of Teachers," *Journal of Educational Administration*, 5 (1967), pp. 66–82.
[20]Thomas J. Sergiovanni and Fred D. Carver, *The New School Executive* (New York: Harper & Row, 1980), p. 108.

[21]Ibid.
[22]Ralph M. Savage, "A Study of Teacher Satisfaction and Attitudes: Causes and Effects," doctoral dissertation, Auburn University, 1967; Rodney A. Wickstrom, "An Investigation into Job Satisfaction Among Teachers," doctoral dissertation, University of Oregon, 1971.
[23]L. Moxley, "Job Satisfaction of Faculty Teaching Higher Education: An Examination of Herzberg's Dual Factor Theory and Porter's Need Satisfaction Research," ERIC Document No. ED 139–349, 1977.
[24]Cecil G. Miskel, "The Motivation of Educators to Work," *Educational Administration Quarterly*, 9 (1973), pp. 42–53.

tors with low-risk propensity; managers showed low concern for hygiene factors with high-risk propensity; and educational administrators, appearing in the middle of the continuum, were similar to teachers in their high concern for hygiene factors but resembled managers in their risk propensity.[25]

School administrators may neglect to consider that dissatisfied teachers may weaken the educational program. Basic motivational principles and techniques can help them meet teacher needs. (See Administrative Advice 4-2.)

Critique of the Motivation–Hygiene Theory   Three consistent criticisms have been leveled against Herzberg's theory. First, Herzberg's theory is regarded as *methodologically bound*; that is, the method he used to measure motivation–hygiene factors determined the results. The subjects in Herzberg's studies were given the following directions by an interviewer: "Think of a time when you felt exceptionally good or exceptionally bad about your job, either your present job or any other job you have had. This can be either the 'long-range or the short-range' kind of situation, as I have just described it. Tell me what happened."[26] In response to such questions, people tend to give socially acceptable answers, that is, what they think the interviewer wants to hear. In reviewing more than twenty studies that used a different method from Herzberg's critical-incident technique, one researcher found only 3 percent that supported the theory.[27]

Second, some critics have questioned the mutual exclusiveness of the satisfaction and dissatisfaction dimensions (i.e., whether there are really two separate dimensions). For example, some researchers have found that motivators appear frequently as satisfiers as well as dissatisfiers.[28] This tendency to appear in the wrong context is also characteristic of the hygienes.[29]

Third, little research has focused on the link between satisfying job experiences and favorable performance effects and on the association between dissatisfying experiences and unfavorable performance effects.[30] The implications of such findings for motivational rather than merely attitudinal hypotheses of the theory are evident. Herzberg's work focused on employee satisfaction, not the actual motivation and performance of the employee.

Despite these criticisms, Herzberg has contributed substantially to school administrators' thinking about what motivates employees. He extended Maslow's need hierarchy theory and made it more applicable to the work environment. Herzberg's theory is useful because it distinguishes between extrinsic job factors and intrinsic job factors such as opportunities for achievement, responsibility, growth, and personal development. This two-factor approach concept altered school administrators' thinking about job motivation. For many years schools, which tended to focus on "hygiene" factors such as salary, job security, and working conditions, ignored intrinsic job factors. Herzberg's theory drew attention to the intrinsic job factors, and these "motivators" have been introduced in school settings. Important developments from the two-factor idea are job enrichment, or quality of work life and shared leadership, which are designed to increase job satisfaction and performance.

[25]Cecil G. Miskel, "Intrinsic, Extrinsic, and Risk Propensity Factors in the Work Attitudes of Teachers, Educational Administrators, and Business Managers," *Journal of Applied Psychology*, 59 (1974), pp. 339–343.

[26]Herzberg, Mausner, and Snyderman, *The Motivation to Work*, p. 141.

[27]Hanafi M. Solimon, "Motivator–Hygiene Theory of Job Attitudes: An Empirical Investigation and Attempt to Reconcile Both the One- and the Two-Factor Theories of Job Attitudes," *Journal of Applied Psychology*, 54 (1970), pp. 452–461.

[28]Robert J. House and Lawrence A. Wigdor, "Herzberg's Dual-Factor Theory of Job Satisfaction and Motivation: A Review of the Evidence and a Criticism," *Personnel Psychology*, 20 (1967), pp. 369–389.

[29]Valerie M. Bockman, "The Herzberg Controversy," *Personnel Psychology*, 24 (1971), pp. 155–189.

[30]John P. Campbell et al., *Managerial Behavior, Performance, and Effectiveness* (New York: McGraw-Hill, 1970).

ADMINISTRATIVE ADVICE 4-2

■

Improving Teacher–Job Satisfaction

The following are some tips that can help school administrators improve teacher–job satisfaction.

■ *Use Praise to Recognize Exemplary Behavior.* Catch your faculty members doing something right and tell them. Often, the only contact teachers have with administrators is when they do something wrong, and then they are "zapped"! Moreover, tell parents about staff accomplishments through the school newsletter.

■ *Rotate Faculty Meeting Locations.* Conduct faculty meetings in different classrooms to give your teachers an opportunity to tell their colleagues about the things they are doing.

■ *Institute a "5–10 Report" from Teachers.* Promote "quick and easy" communication. A 5–10 report takes no more than five minutes to read and ten to write. Each report is divided into three parts: a quick update of job-related activities; a description of the teacher's morale; and an idea for improving the efficiency or effectiveness of the school.

■ *Empower Teachers.* Establish a school leadership team consisting of yourself, teachers you select, and teachers selected by faculty members. Have the team participate in decisions concerning budget preparations, school improvement projects, and the like.

■ *Recognize Group Accomplishments.* Work with your PTA or other support groups to recognize schoolwide accomplishments, perhaps over morning doughnuts or with a staff-appreciation banquet or afternoon cake and ice cream.

■ *Don't Overlook the Little Things.* Design inexpensive birthday or holiday cards that can be produced on duplicating machines or by computer. Before the school year begins, have the school secretary preaddress and stamp each card and arrange for them to be mailed at the appropriate times.

■ *Create a "Bragging Wall" in the Faculty Lounge.* Use an area of the faculty lounge to post "smile-a-grams," articles faculty members have published, newspaper clippings, letters from parents, and other examples of good things that are going on in your school.

■ *Follow Up on Requests.* Get back quickly to faculty members who make requests for a decision or status report. Such behavior demonstrates that you are concerned about their needs.

■ *Select a Faculty Member of the Month.* Make the selection yourself or ask the staff leadership team to help with the decision.

■ *Institute a Teacher-for-a-Day Program.* Select one day a year and recruit key community members to come to your school to teach for the entire day or for a period. Teachers will benefit from a new sense of community participation (especially if the local press covers the story).

Source: Adapted from Terry B. Grier, "15 Ways to Keep Staff Members Happy and Productive," *Executive Educator*, 10 (1988), pp. 26–27. Copyright 1988, the National School Boards Association. Used by permission.

Motivating Midcareer Teachers   The teaching profession is experiencing a profound demographic change. The majority of teachers today are middle-aged and immobile according to a national study. Many have been teaching in one school for most of their professional careers, and their average age is forty-six. Seventy-five percent have been teaching for at least ten years; 50 percent, for over fifteen years. Fifty percent have taught in only one or two schools.[31]

---

[31]C. Emily Feistritzer, *Profile of Teachers in the United States* (Washington, D.C.: National Center for Education Information, 1990).

The first wave of school reform, following the release of *A Nation at Risk*,[32] dealt with broad philosophical questions concerning the structure, mission, curriculum, and methods of schooling. It focused particular attention on the principal as leader in directing school-improvement efforts. Frequently missing from these proposals was recognition of the current demography of the teaching force. Consequently, the second wave of reform, particularly the Carnegie Task Force on Teaching as a Profession[33] and the Holmes Group,[34] expanded the focus to include teachers, emphasizing the need to enhance their motivation and participation. This approach to school improvement represents efforts to restructure schools through shared governance, participatory management, and site-based management, whereby teachers play an active role in the operation of the school.

Although the second wave of reform efforts is based on sound theories of organizational behavior and factors that foster competence, few reports have noted the importance of regarding teachers as developing adults. Any restructuring of school governance and management must include the role of the principal as a developer of professionals.

Sarah Levine has applied career-development research to teachers, emphasizing the school as a context for adult growth and the principal's role as adult developer.[35] She suggests that midcareer teachers are prone to demotivation (boredom, complacency, and loss of challenge), which often results in a leveling off of performance.

Typically, organizations respond to this mid-career syndrome by imposing the following measures: greater central office control over planning, policy, and curriculum to compensate for a lack of initiative on the part of teachers; rigorous evaluation and clinical supervision to motivate veteran teachers; defect-based in-service retraining designed to correct performance deficiencies; and career ladders or other financial rewards to increase incentives to senior faculty members. These measures offer little stimulus to veteran teachers' performance.[36] Moreover, as Herzberg notes, they play a secondary role in motivating employees because they are (hygiene factors), extrinsic to the job itself.[37]

To enhance teachers' motivation and participation, principals will need to focus on ongoing development of their human resources: match the changing needs of teachers over the course of their careers with those of the school or school district. (See Administrative Advice 4-3.)

Existence Relatedness Growth Theory

Clayton Alderfer's existence relatedness growth theory is an extension of Herzberg's and Maslow's content theories of employee motivation.[38] Like Maslow and Herzberg, Alderfer feels that people do have needs, that these needs can be arranged in a hierarchy, that there is a basic distinction between lower-level needs and higher-level needs, and that needs are important determinants of employee motivation in organizations. Alderfer suggests three broad categories of needs: existence (E), relatedness (R), and growth (G)—hence, the **ERG theory**:

1. *Existence needs* comprise all forms of physiological and material desires such as food,

[32]National Commission on Excellence in Education, *A Nation at Risk* (Washington, D.C.: U.S. Department of Education, 1983).

[33]Carnegie Task Force on Teaching as a Profession, *A Nation Prepared: Teachers for the 21st Century* (Washington, D.C.: Carnegie Task Force, 1986).

[34]Holmes Group, *Tomorrow's Teachers: A Report of the Holmes Group* (East Lansing, MI: The Holmes Group, 1986).

[35]Sarah L. Levine, *Promoting Adult Growth in Schools: The Promise of Professional Development* (Needham Heights, MA: Allyn and Bacon, 1989).

[36]Robert Evans, "The Faculty in Midcareer: Implications for School Improvement, *Educational Leadership*, 46 (1989), pp. 10–15.

[37]Frederick Herzberg, "One More Time: How Do You Motivate Employees? *Harvard Business Review*, 65 (1987), pp. 109–120.

[38]Clayton P. Alderfer, *Existence, Relatedness, and Growth* (New York: Free Press, 1972).

ADMINISTRATIVE ADVICE 4-3

■

MOTIVATING MIDCAREER TEACHERS

To combat boredom, loss of enthusiasm, and diminished job interest characteristic of some midcareer teachers, principals must redesign both jobs and organizational structures to provide experience-enhancing roles for teachers. Here are some strategies principals can use to develop and motivate teachers:

■ *Revitalize Careers*. Measures that increase the variety of a teacher's total career experiences include job sharing, voluntary transfers to new jobs within the district, temporary released-time assignments to special projects, developing multiple specialties (becoming adept at two disciplines or two grade levels) so a teacher can move between assignments, and traditional methods that enhance job variety (team teaching, peer-study and supervision groups, intra-school and interschool visiting, curriculum-development workshops, attending conferences, minisabbaticals).

■ *Enrich Jobs*. Measures that improve the quality of experience a given job provides include increasing teachers' control over budget, curriculum, schedule, class size, and so on; providing opportunities for teachers to study and develop new models of school structure and pedagogy; requiring and permitting teachers to take greater responsibility for colleagues with per-

formance problems; and limiting the imposition of externally imposed competency requirements and substantially increasing the role of teachers in determining appropriate outcomes to measure.

■ *Provide Supportive Leadership*. Because many midcareer performance problems are rooted in the loss of motivation, principals must emphasize recognition, exploration, and awareness of choice among teachers whenever possible. Principals can seek ways to maximize teachers' success and experimentation and to reward faculty for their accomplishments and for willingness to explore new interests or experiment with new approaches to problems, even when they fail. Teachers need recognition not only for achievement but also for effort.

Source: Adapted from Robert Evans, "The Faculty in Midcareer: Implications for School Improvement," *Educational Leadership*, 46 (1989), pp. 10–15.

---

clothing, and shelter. In organizational settings, specific examples include salary, fringe benefits, job security, and work conditions. This category corresponds roughly to Maslow's physiological and safety needs.

2. *Relatedness needs* include all those that involve interpersonal relationships with others—supervisors, colleagues, subordinates, family, friends, and so on. Alderfer stresses that relatedness needs can be satisfied by expressing anger and hostility as well as by developing close, warm, and personal relationships with others. This need category

corresponds approximately to Maslow's social needs and to those esteem needs involving feedback from others.

3. *Growth needs* concern the individual's intrinsic desire to grow, develop, and fulfill one's potential. In the workplace, satisfaction of growth needs results when an employee engages in tasks that involve not only the full use of her skills and abilities but also tasks that may require the creative development of new skills and abilities. This category of ERG needs corresponds to Maslow's self-actualization needs and certain aspects

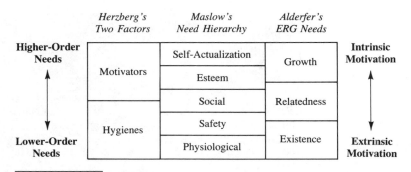

FIGURE 4-2   Relationships Among Content Motivation Theories

of his esteem needs. Figure 4-2 depicts how Alderfer's need categories are related to the Maslow and Herzberg categories.

ERG theory differs from Maslow's need hierarchy theory in two important ways. First, Maslow's theory proposes that a lower-level need must be gratified before other needs become operative. ERG theory, on the other hand, proposes that people may experience several needs simultaneously. Existence needs do not necessarily have to be satisfied before a person can become concerned about the satisfaction of his relatedness or growth needs. Hence, ERG theory is more flexible than is need hierarchy theory and accounts for a wide variety of individual differences in need structure. Second, Maslow's theory proposes that a satisfied need is no longer a motivator. According to Alderfer, however, the continual frustration of higher-order needs will lead employees to regress to a lower-need category. For example, the principal who is unable to secure a position as a superintendent (growth needs) may increase her interest in fulfilling her relatedness needs in order to demonstrate to the higher administration her capabilities for a promotion to superintendent.

Research on ERG Theory   To date, there has not been much research on ERG theory. Most research tends to support Alderfer's theory over

Maslow's and Herzberg's theories.[39] For example, some evidence supports the three classifications of needs.[40] Moreover, some researchers recommend ERG theory over Maslow's theory because the latter was not aimed specifically toward the study of employee motivation in the workplace.[41] Also, there is support for several of Alderfer's basic propositions such as the idea that a satisfied need may remain a motivator—that is, the confirmation that the frustration of relatedness needs increases the strength of existence needs.[42] Overall, "many behavioral scientists tend to view ERG theory as the most current, valid, and researchable theory based on the need concept."[43]

[39]Bronston T. Mayes, "Some Boundary Considerations in the Application of Motivation Models," *Academy of Management Review*, 3 (1978), pp. 51–52.

[40]John P. Wanous and Abram Zwany, "A Cross-Sectional Test of Need Hierarchy Theory," *Organizational Behavior and Human Performance*, 18 (1977), pp. 78–97.

[41]Benjamin Schneider and Clayton P. Alderfer, "Three Studies of Measures of Need Satisfaction in Organizations," *Administrative Science Quarterly*, 18 (1973), pp. 489–505.

[42]Clayton P. Alderfer, Robert E. Kaplan, and Ken K. Smith, "The Effect of Relatedness Need Satisfaction on Relatedness Desires," *Administrative Science Quarterly*, 19 (1974), pp. 507–532.

[43]Clayton P. Alderfer, "A Critique of Salancik and Pfeffer's Examination of Need Satisfaction Theories," *Administrative Science Quarterly*, 22 (1977), pp. 658–659.

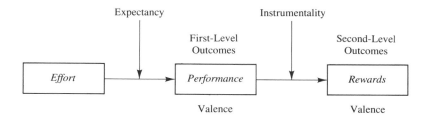

FIGURE 4-3   Basic Expectancy Model

PROCESS THEORIES

The content theories of motivation attempt to identify *what* motivates employees in the workplace (e.g., advancement, self-actualization, and growth). The **process theories**, on the other hand, are more concerned with *how* motivation occurs—in other words, they explain the process of motivation. Expectancy theory, equity theory, and goal-setting theory are the three major process theories that concern this approach to motivation in organizational settings.

Expectancy Theory

Victor Vroom is usually credited with developing the first complete version of the **expectancy theory** with application to organizational settings.[44] More recently, expectancy theory has been expanded and refined by John Naylor and his associates.[45]

Expectancy theory is based on four assumptions. One assumption is that people join organizations with expectations about their needs, motivations, and past experiences. These influence how individuals react to the organization. A second assumption is that an individual's be-

havior is a result of conscious choice. That is, people are free to choose those behaviors suggested by their own expectancy calculations. Another assumption is that people want different things from the organization (e.g., good salary, job security, advancement, and challenge). A fourth assumption is that people will choose among alternatives so as to optimize outcomes for them personally.

Basic Expectancy Model   The expectancy theory based on these assumptions has four key elements: outcomes, expectancy, instrumentality, and valence (Figure 4-3).

Outcomes, classified as first or second level, are the end results of certain work behaviors. First-level outcomes refer to some aspect of performance and are the direct result of expending some effort on the job. Second-level outcomes are viewed as consequences to which first-level outcomes are expected to lead. That is, the end result of performance (first-level outcome) is some type of reward (second-level outcome) for work–goal accomplishment. Examples include salary increases, promotion, peer acceptance, recognition by the supervisor, or a sense of accomplishment.

Expectancy is the strength of belief that job-related effort will result in a certain performance level. Expectancy is based on probabilities and ranges from 0 to 1. If an employee sees no chance that effort will lead to the desired performance level, the expectancy is 0. On the other hand, if the employee is completely certain that the task will be completed, the expectancy has a value of

[44]Victor H. Vroom, *Work and Motivation* (New York: Wiley, 1964).

[45]John Naylor, Robert Pritchard, and Daniel Ilgen, *A Theory of Behavior in Organizations* (New York: Academic Press, 1980).

1. Generally, employee estimates of expectancy lie somewhere between these two extremes.

Instrumentality is the relationship between performance (first-level outcomes) and rewards (second-level outcomes). As with expectancy, instrumentality ranges from 0 to 1. If an employee sees that a good performance rating will always result in a salary increase, the instrumentality has a value of 1. If there is no perceived relationship between the first-level outcome (good performance rating) and the second-level outcome (salary increase), then the instrumentality is 0.

Valence is the strength of an employee's preference for a particular outcome or reward. Thus, salary increases, promotion, peer acceptance, recognition by supervisors, or any other second-level outcome might have more or less value to individual employees. The valence of first-level outcomes is the sum of the product of the associated second-level outcomes and their instrumentalities. That is, the valence of a first-level outcome depends on the extent to which it results in valuable second-level outcomes. Unlike expectancy and instrumentality, valences can be either positive or negative. If an employee has a strong preference for attaining an outcome, valence is positive. At the other extreme, if an employee prefers not attaining an outcome, valence is negative. And if an employee is indifferent to an outcome, valence is 0. The total range is from -1 to $+1$. Theoretically, an outcome has a valence because it is related to an employee's needs. Valence, then, provides a link to the content theories of motivation.

In sum, the basic expectancy model shows that the motivational force that an employee exerts on the job is a function of (1) the perceived expectancy that a certain level of performance will result from expending effort and (2) the perceived instrumentality that rewards will result from a certain level of performance, both of which are moderated by the valences attached to these outcomes by the employee. The combination of these three factors that produces the strongest motivation is high positive valence, high expectancy, and high instrumentality. If any key element is low, then motivation will be moderate. If all three elements are low, weak motivation will result.

Porter–Lawler Model   Lyman Porter and Edward Lawler have extended the concepts of the basic expectancy theory of motivation to examine the factors that influence an employee's performance and satisfaction.[46] For many years, behavioral scientists believed that satisfaction led to performance. This causal relationship can be traced to the human relations era. In recent years, Porter and Lawler have turned the human relationists' proposition around and contend that performance leads to satisfaction. They argue that the intervening variable between these two is rewards. Thus, if employees do a good job and are rewarded for doing so, satisfaction will result. In contrast to human relationists' thinking, performance is viewed as the independent variable and satisfaction as the dependent variable in a causal relationship.

Figure 4-4 depicts the complex relationship that exists between motivation, performance, and satisfaction. As shown in the model, Boxes 1–3 are simply a restatement of the basic expectancy theory of motivation. Value of reward (Box 1) refers to the valence of second-level outcomes. Perceived effort → reward probability (Box 2) refers to perceptions of expectancy and instrumentality. Note that Porter and Lawler recognize that it takes more than effort (Box 3) to produce high performance. They indicate that employees' abilities and traits (Box 4) and their role perceptions (Box 5) will have an effect on performance (Box 6). For example, consider a school principal who manifests high effort but lacks human relations skills, has no knowledge of management techniques, and is confused about the respective roles that teachers, principals, and superintendents play in the school organization. Such a person will perform poorly despite high effort. It is at the point where effort

[46]Lyman W. Porter, Edward E. Lawler, and J. Richard Hackman, *Behavior in Organizations* (New York: McGraw-Hill, 1975).

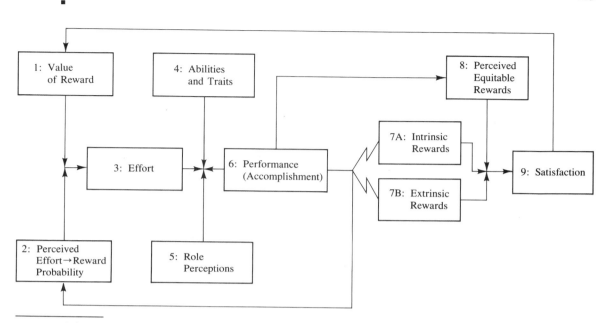

FIGURE 4-4   The Porter–Lawler Model (SOURCE: Adapted from Lyman W. Porter and Edward E. Lawler, *Managerial Attitudes and Performance*, © 1968, p. 37. Used by permission of Irwin, Homewood, IL.)

and performance intersect that supervisors make judgments about the motivation of employees. Hence, our principal might be judged by the superintendent or other direct supervisor as having high but misdirected motivation because he is directing persistent effort that does not help the school achieve its goals.

Performance, then, is the result of effort, abilities and traits, and role perceptions. The resulting level of performance leads to intrinsic rewards (Box 7A). Intrinsic rewards are inherent in the job itself, much like the satisfiers and motivators in Herzberg's two-factor theory. For example, the school principal who assists several teachers needing help will likely feel a sense of accomplishment. Or performance may lead to extrinsic rewards (Box 7B), which are external to the task. Extrinsic rewards are not guaranteed because they are dependent on evaluations of the employee's performance by supervisors and on the willingness of the organization to reward that performance. For example, the school superintendent may or may not recom-

mend attendance at a state or national principal's conference (an extrinsic reward) for good performance by the principal. Furthermore, employees have their own perception of the equitableness of the total reward received. The individual measures the perceived equitable rewards (Box 8) against the rewards she actually receives, which result in the level of satisfaction (Box 9) experienced by the employee.

The Porter–Lawler framework resembles an open-systems model through its two feedback loops. The feedback loop in the lower part of the model runs from the performance–rewards connection to the perceived effort → reward probability. This suggests that if performance is rewarded, the perceived effort → reward probability is strengthened. The feedback loop in the upper part of the model runs from satisfaction to the value of the reward. Porter and Lawler argue that rewards associated with higher-order needs become more attractive, the more the person is rewarded. Thus, intrinsic rewards for performance tend to result in an increased value of these rewards to employees. This is consistent with Maslow's self-actualization needs. Earlier, Maslow suggested that as a self-actualization need is satisfied, it should increase the strength of this need to the individual.[47]

Research on Expectancy Theory   Generally, research supports expectancy theory. It has been able to explain the relationship between salary and managerial performance.[48] Research also shows that expectancy theory is effective for predicting the occupational choices of individuals.[49] Earlier, another study supported Porter and Lawler's predictions that differential performance determines rewards and that rewards produce valence in satisfaction.[50]

The number of research efforts investigating the expectancy theory in educational organizations has grown significantly since the mid-1970s, and studies have reported the following: (1) School principals with higher expectancy motivation are more active in attempting to influence district policy than are those lower in expectancy motivation.[51] (2) Schools high in centralization and stratification are staffed with teachers having low expectancy motivation.[52] (3) A significant relationship exists between principal consideration and high expectancy motivation of teachers.[53] (4) A significant relationship exists between motivation and job satisfaction and performance for a sample of secondary and higher education teachers.[54] Similar results were reported by others.[55] Expectancy motivation is positively related to student achievement, student and teacher attitudes, and communication among educators.[56]

Research evidence validates expectancy theory. Major components of the theory have been measured, and research related to the theory has been done in different organizational settings including schools. However, three major problems associated with expectancy theory have been highlighted. First, expectancy theory has become so complex that it has exceeded the measures to adequately test it.[57] More recently, however, there have been major improvements in measures.[58] Second, research does not sup-

[47]Maslow, *Motivation and Personality*.

[48]Edward E. Lawler, *Pay and Organization Development* (Reading, MA: Addison-Wesley, 1981).

[49]John P. Wanous, Thomas L. Keon, and Janina C. Latack, "Expectancy Theory and Occupational/Organizational Choices: A Review and Test," *Organizational Behavior and Human Performance*, 29 (1983), pp. 66–86.

[50]Anthony Pecotich and Gilbert A. Churchill, "An Examination of the Anticipated Satisfaction Importance Valence Controversy," *Organizational Behavior and Human Performance*, 27 (1981), pp. 213–226.

[51]Richard T. Mowday, "The Exercise of Upward Influence in Organizations," *Administrative Science Quarterly*, 23 (1978), pp. 137–156.

[52]H. Scott Herrick, "The Relationship of Organizational Structure to Teacher Motivation in Multiunit and Non-Multiunit Elementary Schools" (Technical Report No. 322), Madison: Wisconsin Research and Development Center for Cognitive Learning, University of Wisconsin, 1973.

[53]C. A. F. Pulvino, "Relationship of Principal Leadership Behavior to Teacher Motivation and Innovation," doctoral dissertation, University of Wisconsin, 1979.

[54]Cecil Miskel, JoAnn DeFrain, and Kay Wilcox, "A Test of Expectancy Motivation Theory in Educational Organizations," *Educational Administration Quarterly*, 16 (1980), pp. 70–92.

[55]S. Lincoln, L. L. Graham, and E. P. Lane, "Expectancy Theory as a Predictor of Grade-Point Averages, Satisfaction, and Participation in the College Environment." Paper presented at the annual meeting of the Association of the Study of Higher Education, Washington, D.C., 1983; C. D. Oades, "Relationship of Teacher Motivation and Job Satisfaction," doctoral dissertation, University of Manitoba, 1983; J. P. Zaremba, "Relationship of Teacher Motivation to Innovativeness and Job Satisfaction," doctoral dissertation, University of Wisconsin, 1978.

[56]Cecil Miskel, David McDonald, and Susan Bloom, "Structural and Expectancy Linkages Within Schools and Organizational Effectiveness," *Educational Administration Quarterly*, 19 (1983), pp. 49–82.

[57]John P. Campbell and Robert D. Pritchard, "Motivation Theory in Industrial and Organizational Psychology," in M. D. Dunnette (ed.), *Handbook of Industrial and Organizational Psychology* (Chicago: Rand McNally, 1976), pp. 63–130.

[58]Daniel R. Ilgen, Delbert M. Nebeker, and Robert D. Pritchard, "Expectancy Theory Measures: An Empirical Comparison in an Experimental Simulation," *Organizational Behavior and Human Performance*, 28 (1981), pp. 189–223.

port the notion that individuals actually engage in detailed cognitive arithmetic before deciding at what level to perform. For example, researchers report that "upwardly mobile employees tend to engage in the complex multiplicative calculations required by the model, whereas less ambitious employees simply make impulsive decisions before effort is exerted."[59] Finally, some researchers question whether the model is complete in its present form. For example, organizational commitment, identification with the employer, loyalty to the organization itself, and lack of job alternatives may be a function of worker beliefs in outcomes or organizational rewards.[60] Others suggest that some factors such as high energy levels of employees or strong beliefs in the work ethic may override expectancy considerations alone.[61] And still others have examined behavioral–decisions theory approaches to motivation beyond what is inherent in the expectancy formulations.[62]

It appears that expectancy theory can accurately predict an employee's work effort, satisfaction, and performance.[63] Moreover, expectancy theory has been shown to be related to a number of important managerial practices[64] including goal setting and management by objectives, which will be discussed later in this chapter.

Equity Theory

Equity concepts are inherent in the Porter–Lawler model discussed earlier. According to Porter and Lawler, perceived equitable rewards are a major input into employee satisfaction. Earlier, Herzberg found that feelings of inequity was a frequently reported source of dissatisfaction among employees. Although Herzberg did not pay much attention to this finding, a number of theorists have examined the concept of equity to explain employee motivation.[65] Among them, Stacy Adams has developed the most detailed and organizationally relevant equity theory.[66]

Equity theory asserts that employees hold certain beliefs about the outputs they receive from their work and the inputs they invest to obtain these outcomes. The outcomes of employment refer to all things the employee receives as a result of performing the job, such as salary, promotions, fringe benefits, job security, working conditions, job prerequisites, recognition, responsibility, and so on. **Inputs** cover all things that the employee contributes to performing the job and include education, experience, ability, training, personality traits, job efforts, attitude, and so on. Employees expect that the ratio of their outcomes to inputs will be fair or equitable. But how do employees judge fairness?

General Model   Simply put, equity theory argues that employees evaluate the equity, or fairness, of their outcomes by a process of social comparison. Employees compare the ratio of their outcomes to inputs with the ratio of outcomes to inputs for some **comparison other**. The comparison other may be a colleague or a group average (such as prevailing standards in a school, school district, or job role). For example,

[59]Barry M. Staw and Gerald R. Salancik (eds.), *New Directions in Organizational Behavior* (Chicago: St. Clair Press, 1977), p. 77.

[60]Richard W. Scholl, "Differentiating Organizational Commitment from Expectancy as a Motivating Force," *Academy of Management Review*, 6 (1981), pp. 589–599.

[61]Lawrence R. Walker and Kenneth W. Thomas, "Beyond Expectancy Theory: An Integrative Motivational Model from Health Care," *Academy of Management Review*, 7 (1982), pp. 187–194.

[62]Naylor, Pritchard, and Ilgen, *A Theory of Behavior in Organizations.*

[63]Miner, *Organizational Behavior: Performance and Productivity.*

[64]Terence R. Mitchell, "Motivation: New Directions for Theory, Research, and Practice," *Academy of Management Review*, 7 (1982), pp. 86–88.

[65]Karen S. Cook and Karen A. Hegtvedt, "Distributive Justice, Equity, and Equality," *Annual Review of Sociology*, 9 (1983), pp. 217–241.

[66]J. Stacy Adams, "Inequity in Social Exchange," in L. Berkowitz (ed.), *Advances in Experimental Social Psychology*, Vol. 2 (New York: Academic Press, 1965), pp. 267–299.

superintendents often use other superintendents as the comparison others rather than corporate executives. The equity relationship can be diagrammed as follows:

$$\frac{\text{Outcomes (employee)}}{\text{Inputs (employee)}} \quad \text{Versus} \quad \frac{\text{Outcomes (comparison others)}}{\text{Inputs (comparison others)}}$$

When these ratios are equal, the employee should feel that a fair and equitable exchange exists with the employer. Such equitable exchange should contribute to employee–job satisfaction. Conversely, when ratios are unequal, inequity is perceived by the employee, which should contribute to job dissatisfaction. Obviously, the ideal ratio between outcomes and inputs is perfect equity. Schematically, perfect equity is

$$\frac{\text{Outcomes (employee)}}{\text{Inputs (employee)}} \quad = \quad \frac{\text{Outcomes (comparison others)}}{\text{Inputs (comparison others)}}$$

Inequity can occur in either direction: (1) when employees feel their ratio of outcomes to inputs is less than that of the comparison other and (2) when employees feel their ratio of outcomes to inputs is greater than that of the comparison other. The first situation, in which the employee's perceived outcomes-to-inputs ratio is less than the comparison other, can be diagrammed as follows:

$$\frac{\text{Outcomes (employee)}}{\text{Inputs (employee)}} \quad < \quad \frac{\text{Outcomes (comparison others)}}{\text{Inputs (comparison others)}}$$

The second situation, in which the employee's perceived ratio of outcomes to inputs is greater than that of the comparison other, can be diagrammed as follows:

$$\frac{\text{Outcomes (employee)}}{\text{Inputs (employee)}} \quad > \quad \frac{\text{Outcomes (comparison others)}}{\text{Inputs (comparison others)}}$$

This prediction is less straightforward than the former because the employee is at an advantage vis-á-vis the comparison other. Nevertheless, the theory argues that employees will feel uncomfortable about the inequity of their outcome-to-input ratio compared to the outcome-to-input ratio of their comparison other.

Comparisons of the inputs and outputs of the employee and comparison other are similar to those judgments made by employees according to expectancy theory. They are based on the employee's perceptions, which may or may not be valid. Inequity in either direction creates discomfort and tension, and the employee is motivated to reduce the tension and restore equity.

Methods of Restoring Equity   An employee may engage in any of the following behaviors to restore equity:[67]

1. *Alter Inputs*. An employee who feels underpaid may contribute less time and effort to the job or demand a salary increase. An employee who feels overpaid may increase the quantity and quality of his work, expend extra hours without pay, and so on.
2. *Alter Outcomes*. Unions attract members by pledging to improve salary, working conditions, and hours without any increase in employee effort or input. For example, many teacher unions have managed to negotiate a decrease in calendar days while increasing teacher salaries, fringe benefits, and working conditions.
3. *Cognitively Distort Inputs or Outcomes*. According to the theory of cognitive dissonance, the individual tries to modify one of the incompatible perceptions so as to reduce the tension or dissonance. In a sense, that person engages in coping behavior to regain a condition of consonance or equilibrium. For exam-

---

[67]Richard M. Steers and Lyman W. Porter (eds.), *Motivation and Work Behavior*, 3rd ed. (New York: McGraw-Hill, 1983).

ple, if a colleague (comparison other) were receiving disproportionately high outcomes in comparison with another employee, that fact could make the employee tense. As a coping strategy, the employee could distort her perception by reasoning that the comparison other possesses more job knowledge or intelligence than the employee does. Conversely, an employee can justify the disproportionately high outcomes he receives by convincing himself that he possesses more experience or ability than the comparison other does.

4. *Change the Inputs or Outcomes of the Comparison Other.* Behaviors designed to change the actual or perceived inputs or outcomes of the comparison other can take many forms. A colleague (comparison other) may be forced to reduce her inputs, or a colleague may be pressured into leaving the organization. Or the comparison other's inputs or outputs may come to be viewed differently. For example, an employee may come to believe that the comparison other actually works harder than he does and therefore deserves greater outcomes or rewards.

5. *Change the Comparison Other.* If the input-to-outcome ratio of an employee to a comparison other results in feelings of inequity, the employee can switch her comparison other to restore equity. For example, a very ambitious superintendent, who has been comparing herself to the state's top superintendents, may decide instead to use her colleagues in smaller school districts who are paid less than she is as her comparison others.

6. *Leave the Organization.* An employee can request a transfer or leave the organization entirely.

Research on Equity Theory   The limited research to date generally supports the theory and provides some important insights into the concept. First, overpayment (positive inequity) may motivate people to increase their performance.[68] Moreover, overpayment inequity appears to work best with those who have a strong conscience and a sense of what is ethically appropriate.[69] In contrast, underpayment (negative inequity) seems to lead to absenteeism and turnover.[70] Second, some employees seek to establish competitive edges for their supervisor's favor. When these competitive edges are created so that an employee's input-to-output ratio exceeds another's, the employee with the competitive edge may tolerate inequity for a longer period of time.[71] Some employees are more sensitive to inequity than others; consequently, equity theory becomes much more relevant to these individuals. Other employees tend to respond to performance–reward incongruencies more in terms of expectancy theory.[72] The major criticism of equity theory is the inability to predict which method(s) employees will use to restore equity.[73] Research will need to address this issue in order to increase the applicability of equity theory in the motivation of employees in schools.

[68]Jerald Greenberg and Gerald Leventhal, "Equity and the Use of Overreward to Motivate Performance," *Journal of Personality and Social Psychology*, 34 (1976), pp. 179–190.

[69]Robert P. Vecchio, "An Individual-Differences Interpretation of the Conflict Predictions Generated by Equity Theory and Expectancy Theory," *Journal of Applied Psychology*, 66 (1981), pp. 470–481.

[70]Michael R. Carrell and John E. Dettrich, "Employee Perceptions of Fair Treatment," *Personnel Journal*, 55 (1976), pp. 523–524.

[71]R. Dennis Middlemist and Richard B. Peterson, "Test of Equity Theory by Controlling for Comparison Coworkers Efforts," *Organizational Behavior and Human Performance*, 15 (1976), pp. 335–354.

[72]Richard C. Huseman, John D. Hatfield, and Edward W. Miles, "Test for Individual Perceptions of Job Equity: Some Preliminary Findings," *Perceptual and Motor Skills*, 61 (1985), pp. 1055–1064.

[73]Richard T. Mowday, "Equity Theory Predictions of Behavior in Organizations," in Steers and Porter, *Motivation and Work Behavior*.

Satisfaction and Further Motivation

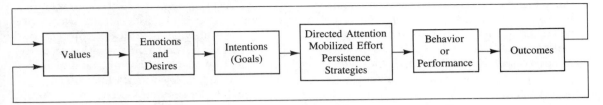

Frustration and Lower Motivation

FIGURE 4-5   General Model of Goal-Setting Theory

Goal-Setting Theory

Goals have a pervasive influence on behavior in school organizations and administrative practice. Nearly every modern school organization has some form of goal setting in operation. Programs such as management by objectives (MBO), planning programming budgeting systems (PPBS), management information systems (MIS), as well as systems analysis and strategic planning, include the development of specific goals.

There has been considerable development of **goal-setting theory** initiated primarily by the work of Edwin Locke. Locke's contributions to goal-setting theory are the following:[74]

1. Difficult goals lead to higher task performance than do easier goals.
2. Specific goals lead to higher performance than do vague goals such as "do your best."
3. The mechanisms by which goals affect performance are directing attention and action, mobilizing effort, increasing persistence, and motivating a search for appropriate performance strategies.

_____

[74]Edwin A. Locke and Douglas Henne, "Work Motivation Theories," in C. L. Cooper and I. Robertson (eds.), *Review of Industrial and Organizational Psychology* (Chichester, England: Wiley, 1986).

4. Feedback appears necessary for goal setting to work because it allows people to compare their performance against their goals.
5. Goal commitment is necessary if goals are to affect performance, and expectation of success and degree of success affect goal commitment.
6. Individual differences in factors like personality and education are not generally related to goal-setting performance.

General Model   Figure 4-5 depicts a simplified view of goal-setting theory. According to the theory, there appear to be two cognitive determinants of behavior: values and intentions (goals). A goal is defined simply as what the individual is consciously trying to do. Locke postulates that the form in which one experiences one's value judgments is emotional. That is, one's values create a desire to do things consistent with them. Goals also affect behavior (job performance) through other mechanisms. For Locke, goals therefore direct attention and action. Furthermore, challenging goals mobilize energy, lead to higher effort, and increase persistent effort. Goals motivate people to develop strategies that will enable them to perform at the required goal levels. Finally, accomplishing the goal can lead to satisfaction and further motivation, or frustration and lower motivation if the goal is not accomplished.[75]

Research on Goal-Setting Theory   One researcher claims that goal setting improves performance about 90 percent of the time.[76] Furthermore, Locke and his associates report that goal setting resulted in a median-performance improvement of 16 percent. And when goal setting was combined with monetary rewards, the median performance increase was over 40 percent.[77] The early evidence came primarily from laboratory investigations; now there is evidence that goal setting works in organizational settings as well.[78]

Several important issues remain unanswered. First, according to Locke, individual differences in factors like personality are not generally related to goal-setting effectiveness. However, employees with strong achievement motivation appear to be more responsive to goal setting than do others.[79] Another unanswered question is the effect that subordinate participation in goal setting has on employee performance. Early research indicated that employee participation in goal setting led to job satisfaction but not increased performance.[80] But employee participation in goal setting can also

improve performance.[81] Finally, evidence indicates that a supportive management style has a moderating effect between goal setting and performance.[82] Despite these unanswered questions, ample evidence shows that goal setting has a significant impact on the motivation and performance of employees (see PRO/CON Debate).

Management by Objectives: An Application of Goal-Setting Theory

Management by objectives (MBO) is a logical extension of goal setting. However, much of the research supportive of MBO came after years of implementation of the MBO process by hundreds of organizations. MBO is usually credited to Peter Drucker who coined the phrase *management by objectives* and stressed the importance of setting measurable performance goals and appraising by results, which he argued should have a positive impact on employee motivation and performance.[83] Credit is also given to Anthony Raia and later to George Odiorne for popularizing an objective-oriented approach to managing.[84] Since its inception two decades ago, MBO has achieved growing acceptance not only in business organizations but also in hospitals, government agencies, and school systems.

While no definitive prototype for MBO programs exists, all involve setting objectives in terms of expected results, working toward these

[75]Edwin A. Locke and Gary P. Latham, *A Theory of Goal Setting and Task Performance* (Englewood Cliffs, NJ: Prentice-Hall, 1989).

[76]Thomas R. Chidester and W. Charles Grigsby, "A Meta-Analysis of the Goal Setting-Performance Literature," *Academy of Management Proceedings,* 44 (1984), pp. 202–206.

[77]Edwin A. Locke et al., "The Relative Effectiveness of Four Methods of Motivating Employee Performance," in K. Duncan, M. Gruneberg, and D. Wallis (eds.), *Changes in Work Life* (New York: Wiley, 1980).

[78]Locke and Latham, *A Theory of Goal Setting and Task Performance.*

[79]Donald J. Campbell, "Determinants of Choice of Goal Difficulty Level: A Review of Situational and Personality Influences," *Journal of Occupational Psychology,* 55 (1982), pp. 79–95.

[80]Locke and Henne, "Work Motivation Theories."

[81]Miriam Erez, P. Christopher Earley, and Charles L. Hulin, "The Impact of Participation on Goal Acceptance: A Two-Step Model," *Academy of Management Journal,* 28 (1985), pp. 50–66.

[82]Gary P. Latham and Lise M. Saari, "Importance of Supportive Relationships in Goal Setting," *Journal of Applied Psychology,* 64 (1979), pp. 151–156.

[83]Peter F. Drucker, *Management: Tasks, Responsibilities, Practices* (New York: Harper & Row, 1973).

[84]George S. Odiorne, *MBO II: A System of Managerial Leadership for the 80s* (Belmont, CA: Fearon Pitman, 1979); Anthony P. Raia, *Managing by Objectives* (Glenview, IL: Scott, Foresman, 1974).

PRO/CON DEBATE

■

GOAL SETTING

Goal-setting theory encourages employees to focus their energies on the organization's goals, which are set by the board of education. The degree of latitude an employee has in setting goals is dependent on the degree of centralization or decentralization of the school district's planning philosophy. Although there are a variety of goal-setting models, in most models school personnel work on goals established by their immediate supervisors, and they also have the latitude to identify their own goals and means to accomplish them.

QUESTION Are teachers more motivated under a system of decentralized planning?

ARGUMENTS PRO

1   Teachers, like other workers, cease to thrive under conditions where others dictate to them. Adults are self-directed, and the greater the role they play in goal setting, the greater will be their investment in the outcome.

2   Decentralized planning, whereby teachers have great latitude in setting goals and the means to accomplish them, will increase their commitment to the goals set.

3   Studies of excellent schools demonstrate that the desired environment for professional work is one that allows for autonomy. Teachers enjoy and appreciate decentralized goal setting when the responsibility is tied to reasonable work loads and adequate time for professional activities.

4   Teachers' work in the classroom is performed in isolation, whereas team goal setting is done in groups. Group work increases collegiality and fosters interdependent rather than dependent or independent action. It meets many of the teachers' motivational needs.

5   Teachers are satisfied when they are engaged in learning. Team goal setting is motivational because it presents a new learning situation for teachers.

ARGUMENTS CON

1   Teachers are motivated by their work in the classroom. They expect administrators to create school conditions that allow them to teach. They have little interest in board of education goals unless the goals relate specifically to their own classroom needs.

2   Decentralized goal setting will not motivate teachers because it is an incentive approach. Teachers neither want nor need incentives to work harder.

3   Case studies show that teachers become quickly disillusioned with their work on committees and content councils designed to formulate school goals. They consider the work "routine," "trivial," or "peripheral."

4   Team goal setting inserts another layer of bureaucracy into the school. It sets some teachers apart as decision makers. It may motivate those on the goal-setting team, but the majority of teachers are not consulted. It causes conflict among teachers.

5   Participation in goal-setting teams distracts teachers from learning about their professional areas—curriculum and instruction. Those who are energized by learning about the organization separate from those actively learning about their craft.

objectives, and reviewing progress toward the objectives. The process, which starts at the top-management level, is an important part of the organization's strategic planning process.

Hierarchy for Setting Objectives The starting point in the task of managing a school system, for example, is a definition of the overall goals of the school district. This definition is the first critical activity of strategic planning. All other planning, organizing, leading, and controlling that is done should implement the school district's goals for the school year. Long-range goals can be set for multiple school years as well. Unless objectives are set, agreed on, and performed on all levels of operating the school district, there will be little basis for measuring the effectiveness of the school district operation.

The process of translating school system goals into contributing subsidiary objectives for central office administrators, principals, and teachers within the school district is accomplished by a process described as means-ends analysis, or developing a hierarchy of objectives.[85] Figure 4-6 depicts how school system and various central office, building, and classroom objectives form a hierarchy. The hierarchy of objectives can be viewed as means that contribute to a single end—the school system goals.

As Figure 4-6 shows, each school building is an end for that building; it is also a means to achieve the school district's goals. The school system goals suggest a framework within which the hierarchy of contributing subsidiary objectives can be set. The responsibility for setting goals rests with the board of education and superintendent of schools. Objectives in turn are generated by assistant superintendents. School principals and directors of support services have responsibility for identifying the performance objectives for their units. Finally, targeted per-formance objectives are produced by department heads and teachers in school buildings.

Applying the concept at all levels of the school district achieves the benefits derived from MBO. For example, if the board of education and the superintendent set a goal "to increase the number of students reading on grade level," all efforts of district personnel will be exerted in that direction. Assistant superintendents, directors, building principals, assistant principals, library media specialists, department heads, and teachers will set and synchronize individual objectives with those of the board of education.

The MBO Process Although there are many variations of MBO programs, the process consists of three phases:

1. *Setting Objectives.* Superiors and subordinates establish, agree on, and state very precisely, preferably in writing, the specific results that are to be achieved within specified time lines.
2. *Developing Delivery Systems.* Strategies, activities, and processes are established to achieve the objectives. The end result is a delivery system that details precisely how individuals or building units will achieve the objectives.
3. *Examining Results.* At periodic times during the school year, results achieved by individuals or building units are compared to the objectives that were set.

Figure 4-7 depicts the three phases. We examine each phase in turn.

Setting Objectives. Statements of school district goals, guide the direction for the school system. But to become useful in managing the district, goals must be translated into what scientists call operational definitions.[86] In other words, they must be expressed as specific, concrete, measurable activities and desired results. Hence,

[85]James G. March and Herbert Simon, *Organizations* (New York: Wiley, 1958).

[86]W. James Popham, *Educational Evaluation*, 2nd ed. (Englewood Cliffs, NJ: Prentice-Hall, 1988).

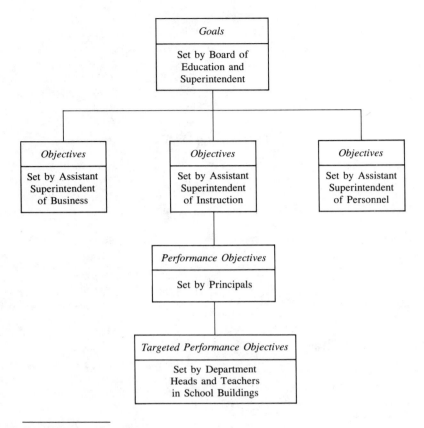

FIGURE 4-6   Hierarchy for Setting Objectives

translated goals become what school administrators call objectives.

Objectives are distinguished from school district philosophies in that they are concrete commitments. In general, objectives have the following characteristics:

1. They are specific.
2. They are challenging but realistic and attainable.
3. They are measurable.
4. They specify a time line for accomplishment.
5. They are accepted by district personnel.

What are the sources of management objectives? There are many sources that provide input into the objective-development process, such as the community, teaching staff, superordinate–subordinate interactions, student-performance data, and program-evaluation information. All the aforementioned sources can be referenced to two primary sources for management objectives: *goals* and *needs*. Figure 4-8 shows this relationship schematically.

A few examples clarify this point.

1. Suppose a group of parents have expressed a concern regarding a specific instructional program. This information, whether gathered through a parent meeting or through a survey, would be considered as **needs assessment**—more accurately, a perceived needs assessment.

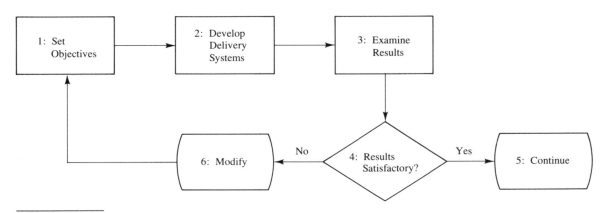

FIGURE 4-7   The MBO Process

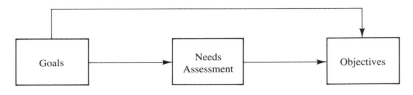

FIGURE 4-8   Relationship of Goals and Objectives in a Needs Assessment

2. Your immediate supervisor suggests that you write an objective in a particular area. This suggestion may stem from a goal that has developed at the board of education level.

3. The annual performance review indicates that you need to continue working on an objective that has not been fully attained. This would be considered as a needs assessment.

4. Performance data demonstrate that students are not attaining skills at a desirable level. This information indicates a need that might reference a goal such as basic-skills development.

What is a needs assessment? One definition is the following:

A needs assessment study is an activity by which the school personnel, students and community members appraise the effectiveness of the school system in terms of existing philosophy and education, goals, strengths and weaknesses. From this study, educational goals, long-range objectives, short-range objectives, and action plans are developed to correct the weaknesses of the school system.[87]

A needs assessment, then, concerns (1) strengths of the school district's program, (2) weaknesses of the district's program, and (3) strategic plans for the future—that is, how district personnel and others plan to alleviate the district's weakness in order to meet its needs.

Each of these three components of the needs assessment should be examined in relation to the following broad general areas of managing the

[87]New Jersey State Department of Education, *District-Wide Improvement Plan* (Trenton: New Jersey State Department of Education, 1989),p. 3.

school system: (1) school–community relations, (2) pupil–personnel services, (3) curriculum and instruction, (4) personnel administration, (5) physical–plant management, (6) business management, (7) staff development, (8) personnel evaluation, (9) program evaluation, and the like.

In short, needs assessment can be identified as discrepancies between what exists and what is desired, which represents a gap in performance of the school district. When these discrepancies are determined, solutions through the fulfillment of management objectives can be developed for closing the gap. An analysis of needs in this manner may result in uncovering additional school district needs that may necessitate revision in the school district's present philosophy and educational goals.

Developing Delivery Systems. The second phase of the MBO process, is a key step in achieving the objectives previously set. The following guidelines will assist educators in the development of delivery systems designed to accomplish performance objectives: Delivery systems should

1. Indicate exactly what is to be accomplished.
2. Describe activities leading to the achievement of objectives.
3. Contain specific target dates.
4. List activities in sequential order leading to the achievement of the objectives.

Figure 4-9 presents a sample performance objective with an accompanying delivery system. Delivery systems have been developed successfully when the performance objective has been achieved.

OBJECTIVE

Using the services of Mr. John Doe, reading consultant, I (Principal), will implement the Houghton Mifflin Reading Program in my building during the next school year and increase the percentage of students on grade level in reading from 25 to 50 percent, as measured by the Metropolitan Reading Test (MRT).

Delivery System (Strategies/Activities/Processes)

1. Complete the training of all teachers in the Houghton Mifflin Reading Program by the first week of the school year.
2. Assist teachers in the development and completion of all materials and institutional tasks for use in the Houghton Mifflin Reading Program by the first week of the school year.
3. Assist teachers in administrating and scoring pretest MRT–Series A by the third week of the school year.

4. Conduct daily tour of classes to assist individual teachers with the Houghton Mifflin Reading Program.
5. Assisted by Mr. Doe, conduct problem-solving conferences on the Houghton Mifflin Reading Program every other Monday at 2:45 PM.
6. Check each class-profile sheet by the last day of each month.
7. Assisted by the teacher, administer and score the MRT by midyear.
8. Using the results from the MRT, the teacher will diagnose and prescribe additional work for students not on grade level.
9. Assist teachers in administering and scoring the MRT–Series B by the seventh month of the school year.
10. Report the results of pretests and posttests to the superintendent of schools by the eighth month of the school year.

FIGURE 4-9   A Performance Objective with an Accompanying Delivery System

Examining Results. The third phase in an MBO program, is the primary basis by which school administrators can determine whether the objectives set have been met. Performance monitoring is considered as an ongoing activity throughout the school year. Figure 4-10 depicts a typical MBO appraisal form. The form provides space for a statement of the objective, a delivery system to achieve the objective, and a performance review to determine if the objective has been met. Note that the form contains all three phases of the MBO process depicted previously in Figure 4-7.

At Step 4 in the MBO process (see Figure 4-7), the evaluator asks whether the results are satisfactory. In the example in Figure 4-9, the principal asks whether the percentage of students reading on grade level has increased from 25 to 50 percent. Two possible sources of difficulty can be identified if the objective has not been achieved: the objective itself or the delivery system used to implement the objective. If one or a combination of these steps is causing unsatisfactory results, possible causes must be eliminated by modifying one or both items and going through the process of recycling.

In sum, MBO allows a school system to determine whether a specific goal produces desired results, to determine whether unsatisfactory results are due to inappropriate goals or inadequate delivery systems, and to recycle events quickly to rectify problems. The end of one MBO cycle

| Goal Statement _____ | School or District _____ |
| Need _____ Source _____ | Administrator _____ Date _____ |

(Only One Goal per Sheet)

Objective (WHAT) (Outcome Statement)	**Delivery System** (HOW) (Strategy, Activity, Process)	**Results** (HOW WILL YOU KNOW) (Periodic Monitoring)

Unplanned Achievements

List Other Achievements Not Recorded Above:

FIGURE 4-10   **Sample MBO Review Form**

is also the beginning of another. The final performance review between superordinate and subordinate leads directly into setting objectives for the next period. School system goals are developed and central office, building, department, and teaching objectives are established from the goals; superordinate–subordinate objective-setting meetings are conducted; and the MBO process recycles, as outlined in Figure 4-7.

SUMMARY

1. Motivation is the extent to which persistent effort is directed toward organizational objectives.
2. Content theories of motivation are concerned with identifying the specific factors that motivate employees. The three content theories discussed were Maslow's need hierarchy theory, Herzberg's motivation–hygiene theory, and Alderfer's ERG theory.
3. Maslow's need hierarchy theory proposes five levels of needs (physiological, safety, social, esteem, and self-actualization). These needs are arranged in a prepotency hierarchy. School administrators often use it when analyzing motivational problems in schools.
4. Herzberg's motivation–hygiene theory proposes that two distinct factors influence motivation—hygienes, which merely prevent dissatisfaction, and motivators, which are the source of satisfaction and motivation for the employee. One important application of this theory, job enrichment, is recommended by the Holmes Group, Carnegie Task Force, and the National Commission on Excellence in Educational Administration for restructuring schools.
5. Alderfer's ERG theory is similar to Maslow's need hierarchy theory, but it is not as rigid concerning prepotency of needs. Like Herzberg's motivation–hygiene theory, ERG theory makes a distinction between intrinsic and extrinsic motivation. The theory is easily understood and useful to school administrators.
6. Process theories of motivation focus on how various factors interact to affect employee motivation. The three process theories discussed were expectancy theory, equity theory, and goal-setting theory.

7. Expectancy theory helps school administrators explain how behavior is directed. It is concerned with why employees choose certain paths toward obtaining outcomes that will satisfy their needs.
8. Equity theory helps school administrators understand how employees calculate what they put into the job with what they receive for their performance and compare that with what they perceive others are contributing and receiving as rewards for performance. Inequitable relationships resulting from such calculations cause the equity-sensitive employee to restore equity.
9. Goal setting helps channel an employee's persistent effort toward organizationally relevant outcomes. Goals can be a powerful motivational device, providing they are accepted by the employee.
10. Management by objectives, or MBO, is a logical extension of goal setting. The MBO process involves three basic stages: (a) superordinates and subordinates in collaboration set objectives; (b) delivery systems are developed to achieve the agreed-on objectives; (c) results are measured against the objectives previously established.

KEY TERMS

motivation	expectancy
effort	instrumentality
persistence	valence
direction	Porter–Lawler model
content theories	equity theory
need hierarchy theory	inputs
two-factor theory	comparison others
ERG theory	goal-setting theory
process theories	management by
expectancy theory	objectives
outcomes	needs assessment

DISCUSSION QUESTIONS

1. Describe how a school administrator would assess the individual needs of employees. Once needs are assessed, discuss how the school administrator

could use the needs hierarchy, the motivation–hygiene theory, and ERG concepts to motivate employees.

2. Of what practical value is the expectancy theory for school administrators? What can school administrators learn from the theory to improve their effectiveness in motivating employees at work?

3. How might a school employee's perceived inequity be dysfunctional to the school system?

4. What are the four key elements of goal-setting theory, and how do they pertain to employee motivation?

5. Outline the three phases of an MBO program. Could this approach be used by your school district? Explain.

SUGGESTED READINGS

Carole Ames and Russell Ames (eds.), *Research on Motivation in Education, Vol. 3: Goals and Cognitions* (San Diego: Academic Press, 1989). A comprehensive discussion of the research in the area of motivation, including theories and critique of the research, specifically related to education.

Earnest R. Archer, *Influence and Motivation: A Managerial Perspective* (Duluth, GA: Wesley, Cabot, and Keith, 1987). A comprehensive discussion of motivation from the perspective of management, that is, what a manager can do to maximize organizational productivity.

Ross Buck, *Human Motivation and Emotion*, 2nd ed. (New York: Wiley, 1988). A discussion of the needs and motives that drive people to high performance or inhibit productivity in organizations.

John P. Houston, *Motivation* (New York: Macmillan, 1985). A solid treatment of motivation from theory to practice.

Lewis Losoncy, *The Motivating Leader* (Englewood Cliffs, NJ: Prentice-Hall, 1985). A complete guide to the leader who is interested in maximizing productivity in organizations.

David C. McClelland, *Human Motivation* (New York: Cambridge University Press, 1988). A scholarly treatment of the needs that motivate people to high levels of productivity both in everyday life and within organizations.

Thomas J. Sergiovanni and John H. Moore (eds.), *Schooling for Tomorrow: Directing Reforms to Issues That Count* (Needham Heights, MA: Allyn and Bacon, 1989). Contains numerous articles written by well-known scholars with implications for motivating school personnel to improve education.

5

LEADERSHIP

We begin our discussion by exploring the nature of leadership in organizations. We examine the concept of influence or power as one of the foundations of leadership. Then we discuss the trait, behavioral, and contingency approaches to leadership. Finally, we present and analyze various styles of leadership. A summary of supporting research on these approaches is included.

THE NATURE OF LEADERSHIP

Since the beginning of this century, the topic of **leadership** has been the object of extensive study. During this time, both researchers and practitioners have sought to analyze and define leadership. Today there are almost as many different definitions of effective leadership as there are researchers who have studied the concept. More than 3000 empirical investigations have examined leadership.[1] Nevertheless, there is sufficient similarity among definitions to permit a rough schema of classification. A sampling of some representative definitions of leadership follows:

- Leadership is "the process of influencing group activities toward the achievement of goals."[2]
- Leadership is "influencing, guiding in direction, course, action, and opinion."[3]
- Leadership is "a dyadic interaction between a leader and each of his or her subordinates."[4]
- Leadership is "the influential increment over and above the mechanical compliance with routine directives of the organization."[5]
- Leadership is "effective influence."[6]
- Leadership "inevitably requires using power to influence the thoughts and actions of other people."[7]

In their review of more than 1000 studies, Warren Bennis and Burt Nanus point out that the research has produced more than 350 definitions of effective leadership with no "clear and unequivocal understanding as to what distinguishes leaders from nonleaders." They offer a clever distinction, however, between a **manager** and **leader**: "A manager does the *thing right*; a leader does the *right thing*."[8] The first person is concerned about carrying out policy; the second person formulates policy. The first person thinks in terms of trees; the second person has a larger view of life and deals with the forest.

To be sure, an organization needs good management, not necessarily good leadership to survive, people who can deal with the day-to-day functions, activities, and routines; otherwise, the organization falls apart from the bottom-up. Very quickly, poor management catches up to the organization. But the person on top need not always be a leader in the sense that she has vision or direction or can cope with the future. It's only after many years that poor leadership takes a toll on the organization, that is, when trends or events catch up to the organization.

Effective leaders, according to Peter Drucker, do not make many decisions. They focus on important ones and ones that have impact on the larger aspects of the organization. They try to think through what is generic and strategic, rather than solve daily problems or "put out fires." They try to make few important decisions on the highest level of conceptual understanding.[9] Effective leaders in organizations engage in decentralized decision-making—that is, responsibility and authority are given to middle management—and shared decision making—that is, decisions are made in a committee or by a group; thus, effective leaders bring in people inside and outside the organization as part of the team.

Whereas managers are concerned with shaping the structures and processes of the organization to produce desired results, leaders have a commitment or vision (a larger view) and shape people around their commitment or vision. John Kennedy, Martin Luther King, Jr., Lee Iacocca, and Vince Lombardi were successful in influencing people according to their ideas and aspirations. They motivated people and brought others together to support their dreams. School superintendents, by nature of their role are

---

[1]Bernard M. Bass, *Stogdill's Handbook of Leadership* (New York: Free Press, 1981).

[2]Bernard M. Bass, *Leadership and Performance Beyond Expectations* (New York: Free Press, 1985), p. 56.

[3]Warren Bennis and Burt Nanus, *Leaders: The Strategies for Taking Charge* (New York: Harper & Row, 1985), p. 21.

[4]George B. Graen, "Role-Making Processes Within Complex Organizations," in M. D. Dunnette (ed.), *Handbook of Industrial and Organizational Psychology* (Chicago: Rand McNally, 1976), p. 116.

[5]Daniel Katz and Robert L. Kahn, *The Social Psychology of Organizations*, 2nd ed. (New York: Wiley, 1978), p. 528.

[6]Chris Argyris, *Increasing Leadership Effectiveness* (New York: Wiley, 1976), p. 227.

[7]Abraham Zaleznik, "Managers and Leaders: Are They Different?" *Harvard Business Review*, 55 (1977), p. 67.

[8]Bennis and Nanus, *Leaders: The Strategies for Taking Charge*, p. 4.

---

[9]Peter F. Drucker, *The Effective Executive* (New York: Harper & Row, 1967).

forced into managerial roles, that is, to get the job done and abide by board policies. Superintendents are organizational people and are not high-profile, individual media types such as Kennedy, King, Iacocca, or Lombardi. Although the biographies and press statements of these people are interesting, their specific policies and practices are not always germane to the school superintendent's role. However, their generic views of motivation, risk, and reward, their holistic beliefs about people and how they organize them, and their courage and commitment to an idea or set of ideas have some bearing on leadership in education.

Although all foregoing definitions differ slightly, they contain two important concepts. First, leadership is a relationship between two or more people in which influence and power are unevenly distributed. This definition differentiates between being the *formal leader* of a group—the person who has the authority to exert influence on the group—and the *informal leader*—the individual who engages in leadership behavior as a participant of a group. For example, the director of personnel may be the person designated by the board of education (management) to negotiate a teaching contract with the teacher's union; but the head of the teacher's union (employee), who is a member of the negotiating committee, may exert more influence in reaching a settlement that is mutually acceptable to the board (management) and the teachers (employees). Emphasis in this chapter is on the formal leader.

The second concept is that leaders do not exist in isolation. Is someone a leader? One way to respond to this question is to look behind the person and see who is following. In most instances, individuals cannot coerce others into behaving in specified ways. Therefore, leadership implies that followers must consent to being influenced. As Chester Barnard has noted, subordinates must be willing to obey the superordinate's command:

> A person can and will accept a communication as authoritative only when four conditions simultaneously occur: (a) he can and does understand

the communication, (b) at the time of the decision, he believes it is not inconsistent with the purpose of the organization, (c) at the time of the decision, he believes it to be compatible with his personal interest, as a whole, and (d) he is able mentally and physically to comply with it.[10]

A school administrator, to be a true leader, must deal with the attitudes, values, and motivations of various groups and people—especially the school board members and professional staff who have their own view of teaching and learning—to survive. The idea is to blend or bend the views of others to coincide with one's own views—not an easy task when board members and staff members are independent-minded. Superintendents and other school leaders should assert their philosophy, goals, and interests while accommodating the views and needs of others.

It is easy for the superintendent to say, "I'm the boss, and this is how it's going to be done." This may work for a short period, but it is not going to work long in schools where political intrigue, special interest groups, and democratic processes can topple strong administrators. Eventually, the "boss" makes enemies on the school board and in the community, and the professional staff drifts away—at least psychologically—so that the elements of teamwork and cooperative planning diminish.

No leader, including the superintendent of schools, can have it his way all the time, even most of the time. The idea is to win the important issues and let people have it partially their way with the small ones. Many strong leaders have learned this lesson the hard way—including Richard Nixon, Frank Bowman and Frank Lorenzo of Eastern Airlines, Douglas MacArthur (after thirty years of serving his country), Harold Spears (after twelve years of serving as superintendent of the San Francisco schools), and Benjamin Willis (after thirteen years of serving as superintendent of the Chicago schools).

---

[10]Chester I. Barnard, *The Functions of the Executive* (Cambridge, MA: Harvard University Press, 1938), p. 165.

Sources of Leader Influence

As noted, leader influence attempts must be accepted—that is, granted—by those being led. In organizations, various bases exist that enable some persons to lead. In other words, what is the source of the leader's power over subordinates? Five distinct sources of leader power, or **influence**, have been identified.[11]

Legitimate Power   **Legitimate power** is power that is vested in the leader's position, or role, in the organizational hierarchy. Legitimate power is based on a mutually accepted perception that the leader has a right to influence a subordinate. For example, in a school organization, the superintendent has the right to expect specified tasks to be completed by principals. Principals in turn can expect certain tasks of the building unit—that is, teachers—and so on throughout the organizational hierarchy.

Reward Power   Leaders usually hold **reward power** in organizations by virtue of their ability to reward subordinates. The strength of the power differs based on the amount of reward that the leader controls and the strength of the subordinate's desire for the reward. Examples of reward power include pay raises, promotions, good assignments, or praise.

Coercive Power   **Coercive power** is the opposite of reward power. It refers to the leader's ability to control and administer punishment to subordinates for noncompliance with the leader's directives. Examples of coercive power include demotions, withholding pay increases, reprimands, undesirable work assignments, and threats to punish.

Expert Power   **Expert power** is based on the special ability and/or knowledge that the leader has and is needed by the group. The leader is seen as capable of analyzing, implementing, and controlling those tasks that the unit has been assigned. Expert power depends on education, training, and experience, so it is an important type of power in managing all the complexities of modern school organizations.

Referent Power   **Referent power** is the ability of leaders to develop followers from the strength of their own personalities. In a sense, this is a form of charisma that draws respect and attracts others to the leader. Well-known historical leaders include Joan of Arc, Mahatma Gandhi, Golda Meir, and Martin Luther King, Jr. Referent power may also emanate from a person's reference or association with another powerful individual in the organizational hierarchy. For example, the title "Assistant to" has been conferred on employees who work closely with people with titles such as college dean, principal, or superintendent of schools. While the "Assistant to the Superintendent" may have neither legitimate, reward, nor coercive power, other employees may perceive that this individual is acting on behalf of the superintendent of schools, which results in her power to influence others.

Power, Influence, and Leadership   A true leader is able to influence others and modify behavior via legitimate and referent power. President Carter had a noble vision about the United States, as well as the world, but could not coalesce groups or people to achieve his goals; the whole country suffered. Presidents Truman and Johnson used their position (or office or power) effectively and were much better able to manipulate groups and people to achieve their ends. Presidents Kennedy and Reagan relied on personal persuasion and were able to sway the nation as a whole, as well as Congress, business, and labor, by charisma and communication. President Roosevelt effectively used both position and personality. President Bush's leadership tends to coincide with the Truman–Johnson model.

Figure 5-1 summarizes the relationship between power, influence, and leadership. The key

---

[11]John R. French and Bertram Raven, "The Bases of Social Power," in D. Cartwright and A. F. Zander (eds.), *Group Dynamics*, 2nd ed. (Evanston, IL: Row, Peterson 1960).

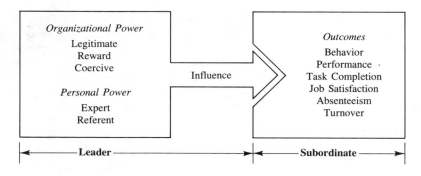

FIGURE 5-1   Sources of a Leader's Influence on Subordinates (SOURCE: Adapted from Gary A. Yukl, *Leadership in Organizations*, © 1981, p. 43. Used by permission of Prentice-Hall, Inc., Englewood Cliffs, NJ.)

to this framework is that leadership as an influence process is a function of the elements of the leader's sources of power and the degree of acceptance with the interests and needs of the subordinates. In the figure, sources of power are divided into personal and organizational. Legitimate, reward, and coercive powers are organizational and are part of the administrator's job. Policies and procedures prescribe them. Expert and referent powers are personal and emanate from a leader's personality.

Research on Sources of Leader Influence

One review of several studies that examined the sources of power concluded the following: [12]

1. Legitimate power can be depended on initially, but continued reliance on it may create dissatisfaction, resistance, and frustration among employees; if legitimate power does not coincide with expert power, there may be negative effects on productivity; and dependence on legitimate power may lead to

only minimum compliance while increasing resistance.
2. Reward power can directly influence the frequency of employee-performance behaviors in the short run. Prolonged use of reward power can lead to a dependent relationship in which subordinates feel manipulated and become dissatisfied.
3. Although coercive power may lead to temporary compliance by subordinates, it produces the undesirable side effects of frustration, fear, revenge, and alienation. This in turn may lead to poor performance, dissatisfaction, and turnover.
4. Expert power is closely related to a climate of trust. A leader's influence can be internalized by subordinates; that is, when a leader uses expert power, attitudinal conformity and internalized motivation on the part of subordinates will result. This in turn requires less surveillance of employees by the leader than does reward or coercive power.
5. Referent power can lead to enthusiastic and unquestioning trust, compliance, loyalty, and commitment from subordinates. Like expert power, considerably less surveillance of employees is required.

One study examined the relationship between the sources of a leader's power, satisfac-

[12]Y. K. Shetty, "Managerial Power and Organizational Effectiveness: A Contingency Analysis," *Journal of Management Studies*, 15 (1978), pp. 178–181.

tion, and performance in five organizational settings (a branch office, a college, an insurance agency, a production facility, and a utility company). Results showed that expert and referent power were positively correlated with subordinate satisfaction and performance, whereas coercive power was negatively related to these two outcome variables.[13] Another study found that expert power is perceived as most effective in inducing employees' acceptance of change, whereas coercive and legitimate power were least effective.[14]

Of more direct relevance to school organizations are two studies that have related the sources of a principal's power to satisfaction and performance. One study was conducted in secondary schools in the United States, and the other study used an elementary school sample from Canada. In the first study, teachers reported greatest satisfaction with their principal and school system when they perceived that the principal's power to influence emanated from their perceiving him as an expert. Conversely, teachers' perceptions of the principal's use of coercive power were associated with dissatisfaction with the principal and school. Moreover, this same principal–teacher relationship was related to a perception of higher student satisfaction with the principal's use of expert power and lower student satisfaction with his use of coercive power.[15] In the second study, elementary schools with principals whose power was perceived to emanate from expertise received higher scores for teacher morale, teacher satisfaction with the principal's performance, and the degree to which the principal favored teachers doing an effective job helping students learn, experimenting with new techniques, and suggesting ideas to improve the school. On the other hand, those schools with principals who were perceived to exercise coercive power to influence teachers received the lowest scores on all measures.[16]

A New Concept of Power

Diane Tracy, a New York management consultant, suggests a new concept of power.[17] The concept has been referred to in the educational literature recently as "empowerment." The new advice is that you can achieve ultimate power by giving it to the people who work for you. Tracy says, that power operates under the same principle as love: The more you give to others, the more you receive in return. Also, she suggests that leaders can maximize their own power and their opportunities for success by enabling the employees they supervise also to achieve their own sense of power and success.

Today, many school districts are recommending a flattening of the pyramid. These administrators are beginning to see the need to involve their faculties in making decisions and solving problems. Real power, according to Tracy, flows from the bottom up, rather than from the top down. . . . If you are successful in giving your people power, they will surely lift you on their shoulders to heights of power and success you never dreamed possible. . . .

Diane Tracy follows up her view of empowerment with practical suggestions on how to achieve a redistribution of power. She recommends ten principles of empowerment:

1. Tell people what their responsibilities are.
2. Give them authority equal to the responsibility assigned them.

[13]Jerald G. Bachman, David G. Bowers, and Philip M. Marcus, "Bases of Supervisory Power: A Comparative Study in Five Organizational Settings," in A. S. Tannenbaum (ed.), *Control in Organizations* (New York: McGraw-Hill, 1968), pp. 224–236.

[14]Robert J. Myers, "Fear, Anger, and Depression in Organizations: A Study of the Functional Consequences of Power," doctoral dissertation, St. John's University, 1977.

[15]Harvey A. Hornstein et al., "Influence and Satisfaction in Organizations: A Replication," *Sociology of Education*, 41 (1968), pp. 380–389.

[16]James H. Balderson, "Principal Power Bases: Some Observations," *Canadian Administrator*, 14 (1975), pp. 3–4.

[17]Diane Tracy, *The Power Pyramid: How to Get Power by Giving It Away* (New York: Morrow, 1990).

3. Set standards of excellence.
4. Provide them with the needed training.
5. Give them knowledge and information.
6. Provide them with feedback on their performance.
7. Recognize them for their achievements.
8. Trust them.
9. Give them permission to fail.
10. Treat them with dignity and respect.

LEADER TRAITS

The popular literature supports the view that leaders are different from other people. If they were not different, neither researchers nor practitioners would have devoted so much attention to the study of leadership. We have noted that leaders can influence their subordinates in accomplishing goals. It seems natural to inquire whether the secret of leadership lies in the characteristics, or traits, of leaders. Are leaders different from nonleaders in terms of personality traits, physical characteristics, motives, and needs? Are there certain **traits** and **skills** that distinguish successful leaders from unsuccessful ones? We will attempt to answer these questions in the following sections.

Traits of Leaders Compared with Nonleaders

Early studies of leadership attempted to isolate traits that would reliably differentiate leaders from nonleaders. Ralph Stogdill reviewed 124 empirical studies conducted between 1904 and 1947.[18] Low-level relationships, ranging between .09 and .26, were found in many different areas. The research suggested that leaders possessed

a number of traits and skills that were not observed in nonleaders. However, the presence of a given trait seemed to vary across situations. Stogdill classified five traits and skills under the following general headings:[19]

1. *Capacity* (intelligence, alertness, verbal facility, originality, judgment)
2. *Achievement* (scholarship, knowledge, athletic accomplishments)
3. *Responsibility* (dependability, initiative, persistence, aggressiveness, self-confidence, desire to excel)
4. *Participation* (activity, sociability, cooperation, adaptability, humor)
5. *Status* (socioeconomic position, popularity)

Several years after Stogdill's widely quoted survey of leadership studies, other research concluded that the numerous studies of personalities of leaders have failed to find any consistent patterns of traits that characterize leaders.[20] Disappointing results such as these are partly attributable to combining leadership studies from varying situations, each of which may have different leadership demands. For example, combining a study assessing the personal traits of basketball coaches with a study examining the personal characteristics of corporate executives will probably result in inconclusive findings. Leadership studies that examine leaders in comparable situations are more likely to reveal traits that differentiate between more effective and less effective leaders.

Traits of Effective Leaders

More recent trait research is being conducted in a different way. Rather than comparing leaders and nonleaders across a number of situations, researchers are comparing effective with inef-

[18]Ralph M. Stogdill, "Personal Factors Associated with Leadership: A Survey of the Literature," *Journal of Psychology*, 25 (1948), pp. 35–71.

[19]Bass, *Stogdill's Handbook of Leadership.*
[20]Cecil A. Gibb, "Leadership," in G. Lindzey (ed.) *Handbook of Social Psychology, Vol. II* (Reading, MA: Addison-Wesley, 1954), pp. 877–920.

fective leaders in the same situation, or they are comparing the relationship between traits and leadership effectiveness. This approach has proved to be a much more difficult problem to research. There is at least one important reason for this difficulty. The term *effectiveness of a leader* is difficult to define. In many instances, one cannot get consensus among observers and group members as to whether a given leader is effective or ineffective. For example, select any college basketball coach or corporate president. The task is to judge each one's effectiveness. Regardless of the objective records of each of these leaders, observers and group members will vary in their assessments of the leaders. Responses may typically range from "she was an outstanding leader" to "she was a very poor leader." Nevertheless, a number of studies have yielded some evidence concerning the predictors of effective leadership. In 1974 Stogdill updated his earlier research by reporting the results of a review of 163 trait studies that had been conducted between 1949 and 1974,[21] and Gary Yukl reviewed and reassessed his findings.[22] The results of these studies are stronger and more consistent than the earlier trait studies. Many of the traits and skills presented in Table 5-1 are representative of those found in other trait studies. However, there is debate over whether a leader's traits and skills, and therefore style, are truly necessary for effective leadership (see PRO/CON Debate).

What are the key traits of superleaders? Good leaders have certain characteristics that make them easy to spot. Although leadership is not absolutely "situation-specific," the leader who is doing an outstanding job in one situation probably can do the same in another. What then are the traits or characteristics that distinguish effective leaders from ineffective ones? (See Administrative Advice 5-1.)

TABLE 5-1   Traits and Skills Associated with Successful Leaders

TRAITS	SKILLS
Adaptable to situations	Intelligent
Alert to social environment	Conceptually skilled
Ambitious and achievement-oriented	Creative
	Diplomatic and tactful
Assertive	Fluent in speaking
Cooperative	Knowledgeable about group task
Decisive	Organized
Dependable	Persuasive
Dominant (desire to influence others)	Socially skilled
Energetic (high activity level)	
Persistent	
Self-confident	
Tolerant of stress	
Willing to assume responsibility	

SOURCE: Adapted from Gary A. Yukl, *Leadership in Organizations,* 2nd ed., © 1989, p. 176. Used by permission of Prentice-Hall, Inc., Englewood Cliffs, NJ.

The trait approach to leadership is still very much alive today. However, most of the current research focuses on job-related skills rather than personality traits of leaders, as exemplified by the work of Warren Bennis and Robert Katz. Katz has identified the technical, conceptual, and human skills needed for effective leadership.[23] Bennis includes skills such as the ability (1) to create and communicate a vision of what the organization should be, (2) to communicate with and gain the support of multiple constituencies, (3) to persist in the desired direction even under bad conditions, and (4) to create the appropriate culture and to obtain the desired results.[24] These leadership skills can be identified and measured in the assessment center approach.

[21]Ralph M. Stogdill, *Handbook of Leadership: A Survey of Theory and Research* (New York: Free Press, 1974).
[22]Gary A. Yukl, *Leadership in Organizations*, 2nd ed. (Englewood Cliffs, NJ.: Prentice-Hall, 1989).

[23]Robert Katz, "Skills of an Effective Administrator," *Harvard Business Review,*" 52 (1974), pp. 90–102.
[24]Warren Bennis, "The Artform of Leadership," *Training and Development Journal*, 36 (1982), pp. 44–46.

PRO/CON DEBATE

■

LEADERSHIP STYLE

The contemporary heroes of education are people like Joe Clark who revitalized an inner-city high school, Jaime Escalante who taught calculus to Hispanic youth, and Madeline Hunter who brought research to classroom teachers. These are people with common characteristics: a vision and the perseverance to actualize it. Their styles of interaction with others as they pursue their visions are relatively constant although different.

QUESTION Is a person's leadership style really important?

ARGUMENTS PRO

1 Leaders have followers. The ways leaders work with their followers is important. In the worst possible scenario, followers rebel or withdraw, and the leader's vision remains a dream.

2 An understanding of leadership style and the ability to flex one's style are important for school administrators. The context of administration changes, and situations differ. Able leaders are always open to new ways of thinking about how to work better with people in a variety of situations.

3 Researchers investigating leadership style have identified several models that practicing administrators find useful. The value of this work is evident: Journal articles on the topic are well read; conference sessions on leadership style are well attended; and books on leadership are on nonfiction best-seller lists.

4 Principals and superintendents lose their jobs because their styles are incompatible with the values and/or norms of organizations. When the loss of high-visibility leaders is analyzed in the popular press, leadership style invariably surfaces as the problem.

ARGUMENTS CON

1 Style is a means to achieve an end. Time spent thinking about style is better invested in the development of good substantial ideas. People will follow leaders with good ideas.

2 School administrators are identified because they have effective styles of working with people to accomplish organizational goals. In most instances, their styles remain the same over their careers.

3 The research on leadership style has not made the impact on education that other areas of inquiry have made. Research-and-development funds are better spent on areas such as effective schools where the impact is clear or ethics where the impact is needed.

4 There is an old adage about success in administration: the right person in the right job at the right time. As contexts change, career administrators change their jobs but not their styles.

Assessment Centers: Using Traits and Skills to Select Leaders

One method that has been used to select leaders is the **assessment center**, a technique that uses a number of traits and skills to assess a person's suitability for being hired or promoted.[25] The exact methods of assessment centers have been somewhat unclear. However, a task force on the development of assessment center standards has established a set of specific

---

[25]George C. Thornton and William C. Byham, *Assessment Centers and Managerial Performance* (New York: Academic Press, 1982).

ADMINISTRATIVE ADVICE 5-1

KEY TRAITS OF SUPERLEADERS

A good leader usually can succeed in most organizations. The following are some specific traits that distinguish outstanding leaders from the rest. These are based on the views of John Gardner, former Secretary of the Department of Health, Education, and Welfare.

- *Physical Vitality and Stamina.*
- *Intelligence and Judgment-in-Action.* Judgment is the ability to combine hard data, questionable data, and intuitive guesses to arrive at a conclusion that events prove to be correct. Judgment-in-action includes effective problem solving, the design of strategies, the setting of priorities, and intuitive and rational judgments. Most important, perhaps, it includes the capacity to appraise the potentialities of co-workers (and opponents).
- *Willingness (Eagerness) to Accept Responsibility.*
- *Task Competence.* Top-level leaders cannot hope to have competence in more than a few of the matters under their jurisdiction, but they must have knowledge of the whole system over which they preside, its mission, and the environment in which it functions.
- *Understanding of Followers/Constituents and Their Needs.*
- *Skill in Dealing with People.*
- *Need to Achieve.*
- *Capacity to Motivate.* More than any other attribute, this is close to the heart of the popular conception of leadership—the capacity to move people to action, to communicate persuasively, and to strengthen the confidence of followers.

- *Courage, Resolution, and Steadiness.* Clearly, a leader needs courage—not just bravery of the moment but courage over time, not just willingness to risk but to risk again and again—to function well under prolonged stress and to survive defeat and keep going.
- *Capacity to Win and Hold Trust.*
- *Capacity to Manage, Decide, and Set Priorities.*
- *Confidence.* To take the risks that leaders take and to handle the criticism and hostility that leaders must absorb requires confidence.
- *Ascendance, Dominance, and Assertiveness.* The individuals who achieve leadership roles are apt to have a fairly strong impulse to take charge. Their assertiveness doesn't necessarily conform to the stereotype of the visibly forceful leader—some are quiet and unspectacular—but whatever their outward style, their inner impulse is to leave their thumbprints on events.
- *Adaptability and Flexibility of Approach.* The attributes required of a leader depend on the kind of leadership being exercised, the context, the nature of followers, and so on.

Source: Adapted from John W. Gardner, Leadership: Attributes and Context," *NASSP Bulletin,* 73 (1989), p. 58. Used by permission.

guidelines concerning exactly what an assessment center is. A brief summary of these standards is as follows:[26]

[26]J. L. Moses et al., "Standard and Ethical Considerations for Assessment Center Operations, Task Force on Development of Assessment Center Standards." Third International Congress on the Assessment Center Method, Quebec, May 1975.

1. Multiple assessment techniques, including at least one simulation exercise, must be used.
2. Multiple assessors with prior training must be used.
3. Selection or development judgments/decisions must be based on pooled information from assessors and techniques.
4. Overall evaluations must be made by asses-

sors at a time other than the time of actual observation.

5. Simulation exercises must be tested prior to use to ensure that they provide reliable, objective, and relevant information for the organization in question.

6. The various dimensions, attributes, characteristics, qualities that are evaluated must be derived from an analysis of relevant job behaviors.

7. The purpose of the technique used must provide information for evaluating the dimensions, attributes, or qualities previously determined.

Defining standards as these should help ensure that using only a test battery, only one simulation exercise, or only panel interviews is not considered an assessment center. Specifically, the most frequently used techniques include leaderless-group exercises, in-basket exercises, oral presentations, case analysis, and letter-writing exercises.

History of the Assessment Center   The assessment center idea is not new. First developed in the early 1900s by German psychologists, it was adopted later by the German military high command in the 1930s for use in choosing officers; subsequently, the British War Office used it for the same purpose. The U.S. Office of Strategic Services (OSS), forerunner of the CIA, was the U.S. pioneer of the assessment method. The OSS specified the personality traits and behavioral skills it thought an effective secret agent needed. To test for them, the renowned Harvard psychologist Henry Murray (and his colleagues) designed a series of simulated situations. One required prospective spies to assume quickly and use convincingly a false identity even under intense interrogation.[27]

For all practical purposes, the assessment method was abandoned at the end of World War II until 1956, when American Telephone and Telegraph (AT&T) launched its ambitious Management Progress Study of the careers of over 400 young executives. AT&T used a factor analysis of the assessment dimensions, which produced the following factors together with the variables loading most highly on each, to select potential managers:[28]

1. *General Effectiveness*. Overall staff prediction, decision making, organization and planning, creativity, need for advancement, resistance to stress, and human relations skills

2. *Administrative Skills*. Organization and planning and decision making

3. *Interpersonal Skills*. Human relations skills, behavior flexibility, and personal impact

4. *Control of Feelings*. Tolerance of uncertainty and resistance to stress

5. *Intellectual Ability*. Scholastic aptitude and range of interests

6. *Work-Oriented Motivation*. Primacy of work and inner work standards

7. *Passivity*. Ability to delay gratification, need for security, and need for advancement (scored negatively)

8. *Dependency*. Need for superior approval, need for peer approval, and goal flexibility

This study has become the basis for most, if not all, of the subsequent development work related to assessment centers.[29] It should be noted that the eight dimensions currently being used at AT&T to identify leadership potential are closely related to the traits and skills found to be predictive of leadership effectiveness in the earlier trait studies of Stogdill and others.

The NASSP Principals Assessment Center   A good example of the assessment center concept in the selection of school administrators is the Principals Assessment Center of the National Association of Secondary School Principals (NASSP).

---

[27]Berkeley Rice, "Measuring Executive Muscle," *Psychology Today*, 12 (1978), p. 99.

[28]Thornton and Byham, *Assessment Centers and Managerial Performance*.

[29]Lloyd E. McCleary and Rodney T. Ogawa, "Locating Principals Who Are Leaders: The Assessment Center Concept," *Educational Considerations*, 12 (1985), p. 8.

The NASSP Principals Assessment Center is aimed at determining the extent to which participants possess skills needed to succeed as a principal. Initiated in 1975, today there are over fifty operating centers in the United States, Canada, Germany, and Australia with others planned for the near future. More than 3000 assessors have been trained and accredited, and 6000 potential school administrators have gone through assessment.[30]

The NASSP Principals Assessment Center comprises six exercises: two leaderless-group exercises, two in-basket simulations, a fact-finding exercise, and a personal interview. A group of assessors (usually six assessors for twelve participants) observes participants while they are completing assessment exercises. Some centers, however, like the University of Louisville's Assessment Center, use a twelve on twelve model. All assessors are trained under rigorous standards before being certified by NASSP. Behavior is recorded on twelve generic skill dimensions. Table 5-2 presents the twelve skill dimensions and their definitions.

After candidates complete two days of simulations and exercises, assessors build a composite picture of the candidate, describing performance in the twelve generic skill areas and offering suggestions for professional development. The final element of an assessment center is an individual debriefing interview with each participant, usually conducted by the center's project director.

A validation study of the assessment center was conducted by Neal Schmitt and associates at Michigan State University. A summary statement from the validation study noted: In conclusion, we see the assessment center as a content-valid procedure for the selection of school administrators. Evidence concerning its criterion-related validity is also positive, especially as it relates to supervisory performance ratings. Further, assessment center ratings are

related to later student perceptions of school climate.[31]

The Assessment Center Process

Figure 5-2 outlines the assessment center process, which is based on the identification of personal traits and job-related skills. As Figure 5-2 shows, basically nine steps are in the assessment center process, from identification of skill dimensions (Step 1) to debriefing interviews with participants for leadership positions (Step 9). In essence, the figure shows the developmental stages required to develop and implement an assessment center project.

LEADERSHIP BEHAVIOR

Another way of understanding leadership is to compare the behaviors of effective and ineffective leaders to see how successful leaders behave. The focus shifts from trying to determine what effective leaders *are* to trying to determine what effective leaders *do*. The issues to be explored include, In what way do leaders lead? How hard do leaders push their subordinates? How much do they listen and use their subordinates' ideas? The dichotomy between the trait and behavioral approach is not as sharp a division as one might suspect. A leader's personal traits and characteristics probably influence his leadership behavior or style. For example, an individual who feels adequate about himself and feels comfortable with people will ordinarily adopt a people-oriented behavior style. On the contrary, a person who feels inadequate about himself and feels threatened by people will probably adopt a production-oriented behavior style.

[30]Paul W. Hersey, *How NASSP Helps Identify, Develop Superior Principals* (Reston, VA: National Association of Secondary School Principals, 1987).

[31]Neal Schmitt et al., *Criterion-Related and Content Validity of the NASSP Assessment Center* (Reston, VA: National Association of Secondary School Principals, 1983).

| TABLE 5 ▪ 2 | Twelve Skill Dimensions of the NASSP Principals Assessment Center |

Administrative Skills

1. *Problem Analysis.* Ability to seek out relevant data and analyze complex information to determine the important elements of a problem situation; searching for information with a purpose
2. *Judgment.* Ability to reach logical conclusions and make high-quality decisions based on available information; skill in identifying educational needs and setting priorities; ability to critically evaluate written communications
3. *Organizational Ability.* Ability to plan, schedule, and control the work of others; skill in using resources in an optimal fashion; ability to deal with a volume of paperwork and heavy demands on one's time
4. *Decisiveness.* Ability to recognize when a decision is required (disregarding the quality of the decision) and to act quickly

Interpersonal Skills

5. *Leadership.* Ability to get others involved in solving problems; ability to recognize when a group requires direction, to effectively interact with a group to guide them to accomplish a task
6. *Sensitivity.* Ability to perceive the needs, concerns and personal problems of others; skill in resolving conflicts; tact in dealing with persons from different backgrounds; ability to deal effectively with people concerning emotional issues; knowing what information to communicate and to whom
7. *Stress Tolerance.* Ability to perform under pressure and during opposition; ability to think on one's feet

Communication

8. *Oral Communication.* Ability to make a clear oral presentation of facts or ideas
9. *Written Communication.* Ability to express ideas clearly in writing; to write appropriately for different audiences—students, teachers, parents, and others

Other Dimensions

10. *Range of Interests.* Competence to discuss a variety of subjects—educational, political, current events, economic, etc.; desire to actively participate in events
11. *Personal Motivation.* Need to achieve in all activities attempted; evidence that work is important in personal satisfaction; ability to be self-policing
12. *Educational Values.* Possession of a well-reasoned educational philosophy; receptiveness to new ideas and change

SOURCE: Adapted from National Association of Secondary School Principals, *Assessor's Manual: NASSP Principals Assessment Center,* rev. ed., © 1990, pp. 11–12. Used by permission of National Association of Secondary School Principals, Reston, VA.

Three widely known studies of classic behavioral theories of leadership were conducted at the University of Iowa, Ohio State University, and the University of Michigan. Each theory is closely identified with the sponsoring university. We examine each theory by describing and classifying the leader behavior constructs developed in each theory. Then we examine some of the subsequent research associated with each theory; that is, the effects of leader behaviors on organizational outcomes such as job satisfaction, morale, and productivity.

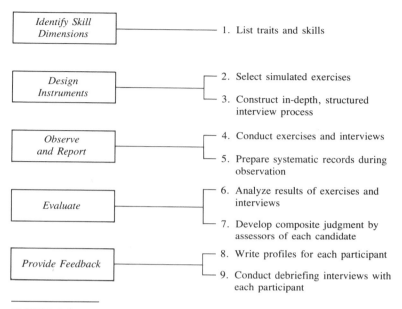

FIGURE 5-2   The Assessment Center Process

The Iowa Studies: Authoritarian, Democratic, and Laissez-Faire Leadership

An early attempt to classify and study the effects of different styles of leader behavior on the group was conducted at the University of Iowa.[32] In a series of experiments, the Iowa researchers manipulated three leadership styles to determine their effects on the attitudes and productivity of subordinates. Leadership was classified into three different types according to the leader's style of handling several decision-making situations during the experiments:

- **Authoritarian leadership**. Leaders were very directive and allowed no participation in decisions. They structured the complete work situation for their subordinates. Leaders took full authority and assumed full responsibility from initiation to task completion.
- **Democratic leadership**. Leaders encouraged group discussion and decision making. Subordinates were informed about conditions affecting their jobs and encouraged to express their ideas and make suggestions.
- **Laissez-faire leadership**. Leaders gave complete freedom to the group and left it up to subordinates to make individual decisions on their own. Essentially, leaders provided no leadership.

Table 5-3 presents a complete description of the three leadership styles. The table summarizes typical behaviors performed by leaders us-

[32]Kurt Lewin, Ronald Lippitt, and Robert K. White, "Patterns of Aggressive Behavior in Experimentally Created 'Social Climates,' " *Journal of Social Psychology*, 10 (1939), pp. 271–299.

TABLE 5-3   Differences in Leader Behavior Style as Identified by the Iowa Researchers

BEHAVIOR	AUTHORITARIAN	DEMOCRATIC	LAISSEZ-FAIRE
Policy determination	Solely by leader	By group's decision	No policy—complete freedom for group or individual decision
Establishment of job techniques and activities	Solely by leader	Leader suggests—group chooses	Up to individual
Planning	Solely by leader	Group receives sufficient information to obtain perspective needed to plan	No systematic planning
Establishment of division of labor and job assignments	Dictated by leader	Left to group decision	Leader uninvolved
Evaluation	Leader personal in praise and criticism	Evaluation against objective standards	No appraisal—spontaneous evaluation by other group members

SOURCE: Adapted from Kurt Lewin, Ronald Lippit, and Robert K. White, "Patterns of Aggressive Behavior in Experimentally Created 'Social Climates,'" *Journal of Social Psychology,* 10 (1939), pp. 271–299. Copyright 1939 by Heldref Publications. Used by permission of the Helen Dwight Reid Educational Foundation.

ing the three different leadership styles in a variety of dimensions of leadership behavior.

Some of the results of the Iowa leadership studies include the following:[33]

1. Of the three styles of leadership, subordinates preferred the democratic style the best, which makes intuitive sense. The general trend today is toward wider use of participatory management practices because they are consistent with the supportive and collegial models of modern organization.
2. Subordinates preferred the laissez-faire leadership style over the authoritarian one. For subordinates, even chaos was preferable to rigidity.

3. Authoritarian leaders elicited either aggressive or apathetic behavior that was deemed to be reactions to the frustration caused by the authoritarian leader.
4. Apathetic behavior changed to aggressive behavior when the leadership style changed from authoritarian to laissez-faire; the laissez-faire leader produced the greatest amount of aggressive behavior.
5. Productivity was slightly higher under the authoritarian leader than under the democratic one, but it was lowest under the laissez-faire leader.

Later studies done at the University of Michigan, however, indicate a sharp increase in productivity initially under authoritarian lead-

[33]Ibid.

ership, but this was followed by drastic decreases in productivity over the long run for authoritarian-led groups; and these groups ultimately reached levels well below democratically led groups in productivity.[34]

Status of the Iowa Studies   Other behavioral science researchers have subjected the Iowa leadership studies to a great deal of criticism. The main concern has been with the methodology: many variables in the Iowa studies were not controlled. Nevertheless, these leadership studies stand as a landmark in their attempt to determine the effects of leader behaviors on a group's attitude and productivity. Like the early trait studies, the Iowa leadership studies are often too quickly dismissed because they were experimentally crude.

In sum, the Iowa studies were important in that they helped focus attention on the investigation of leadership *behavior.* Furthermore, they provided a useful basis for describing and classifying alternative leader behavior styles. In fact, today the three styles identified by the Iowa researchers fifty years ago are commonplace in the popular literature and in parlance among practitioners in the field of educational administration.

The Ohio State Studies: Initiating Structure and Consideration

The research at Ohio State University aimed at identifying leader behaviors that were important for the attainment of group and organizational goals. Specifically, researchers sought to answer the following questions: What types of behavior do leaders display? What effect do these leader behaviors have on work-group performance and satisfaction?

During these studies, researchers from the disciplines of psychology, sociology, and eco-

nomics developed and used the Leader Behavior Description Questionnaire (LBDQ) to study leadership in different types of groups and situations.[35] Studies were made of Air Force commanders and members of bomber crews; officers, noncommissioned personnel, and civilian administrators in the Department of the Navy; executives of regional cooperatives; manufacturing supervisors; leaders of various student and civilian groups; and teachers, principals, and school superintendents.

Group responses to the LBDQ were then subjected to factor analysis, a mathematical technique that permits identification of a smaller set of common dimensions undergirding a large set of questionnaire responses. From the factor analysis came two dimensions that characterized the behavior of leaders in the numerous groups and situations investigated: initiating structure and consideration.

Initiating Structure   **Initiating structure** refers to the extent to which a leader focuses directly on organizational performance goals, organizes and defines tasks, assigns work, establishes channels of communication, delineates relationships with subordinates, and evaluates work-group performance. Leaders who initiate structure assign staff members to particular tasks, maintain definite standards of performance, emphasize meeting deadlines, encourage the use of uniform procedures, let staff members know what is expected of them, and see to it that staff members are working up to capacity.

Consideration   **Consideration** refers to the extent to which a leader exhibits trust, respect, warmth, support, and concern for the welfare of subordinates. Leaders who manifest consideration listen to staff members' ideas, are friendly and approachable, treat all staff members as equals, and frequently use employee ideas. A

---

[34]David G. Bowers, *Systems of Organization: Management of Human Resource* (Ann Arbor: University of Michigan Press, 1977).

[35]Ralph M. Stogdill and Alvin E. Coons (eds.), *Leader Behavior: Its Description and Measurement* (Columbus: Bureau of Business Research, Ohio State University, 1957).

high consideration score indicates psychological closeness between leader and subordinate; a low consideration score indicates a more psychologically distant and impersonal approach on the part of the leader.

The result was a two-dimensional leadership model. These dimensions are seen as being independent, thus resulting in four leadership behaviors as depicted in Figure 5-3.

Studies on Initiating Structure and Consideration

Researchers have conducted numerous studies to determine the effects of these four styles on subordinate performance and satisfaction. It is not within the scope of this text to provide an exhaustive review of these myriad studies. Instead, we will briefly review a few of the more important studies in education: encompassing the roles of superintendents, principals, and teachers.

Superintendents who were rated as effective leaders by both staff and school board members were described as high on both initiating struc-

ture and consideration.[36] Another researcher reported that effective principals had higher scores on initiating structure and consideration than did ineffective principals.[37] Performance evaluations of school principals' leadership were positively related to consideration and negatively related to domination and social distance, which provided support for the theory.[38]

In a study of the relationship of principals' leadership to pupil performance in Canadian public schools, both initiating structure and consideration by the principals, as described by teachers, were significantly and positively related to pupils' examination scores on a provincewide exam.[39] Another Canadian study found that pupil performance was associated with principals' LBDQ scores.[40] And in another large-scale Canadian study, results indicated that initiating structure and consideration by teachers were positively and significantly related to the scores of pupils on tests of school achievement.[41] Using 872 teacher descriptions of fifty-three principals, another researcher found that both initiating structure and consideration were highly correlated with two representative functions: (1) representing interests of teachers to superordinates and (2) representing teachers' interests to the schools' clientele. The report

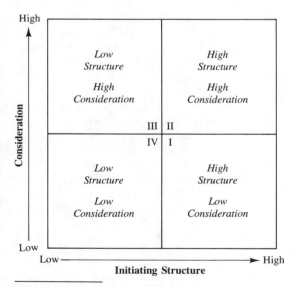

FIGURE 5-3   Ohio State Leadership Grid

[36]Andrew W. Halpin, *The Leader Behavior of School Superintendents*, (Columbus: Ohio State University, 1956).

[37]Alan F. Brown, "Reactions to Leadership," *Educational Administrational Quarterly*, 3 (1967), pp. 62–73.

[38]M. Seeman, "A Comparison of General and Specific Leader Behavior Descriptions," in Stogdill and Coons, *Leader Behavior: Its Description and Measurement*.

[39]Betty T. Keeler and John H. M. Andrews, "Leader Behavior of Principals, Staff Morale, and Productivity," *Alberta Journal of Educational Research*, 9 (1963), pp. 179–191.

[40]Thomas B. Greenfield, "Research on the Behavior of Educational Leaders: Critique of a Tradition," *Alberta Journal of Educational Research*, 14 (1968), pp. 55–76.

[41]Thomas B. Greenfield and John H. M. Andrews, "Teacher Leader Behavior," *Alberta Journal of Educational Research*, 7 (1961), pp. 92–102.

concluded that initiating structure and consideration were not solely concerned with internal leadership but were reflected in the manner leaders dealt with outsiders and higher authority.[42]

In sum, the two-dimensional theory of leader behavior that evolved from the Ohio State leadership studies represents a widely accepted research-based approach to the study and practice of leadership. The major value of this approach is the clear demonstration that these two dimensions of leadership behavior are real and observable and account for a great proportion of actual leader behavior. Research finds that the high initiating structure–high consideration leader behaviors (Quadrant 2, Figure 5-3) result in higher satisfaction and performance among school administrators than do any of the other three leader behaviors. The implications of these findings are that they provide a framework for solving problems in school organizations. That is, we can treat initiating structure and consideration as dependent variables in leadership development and training programs. Our assumption is that we can shift leadership behavior in the desired direction; for example, from low initiating structure to high initiating structure and from low consideration to high consideration.

The Michigan Studies: Production-Centered and Employee-Centered

Around the time that the Ohio State leadership studies were being conducted, a series of leadership studies were in progress at the University of Michigan's Institute for Social Research. The Michigan researchers used an approach to identify leaders who were rated as either effective or ineffective and then studied the behavior of these leaders in an attempt to develop consistent patterns of behavior that differentiated effective from ineffective leaders.

The Michigan studies identified two distinct leadership behaviors that were very similar to the initiating-structure and consideration dimensions, which evolved from the Ohio State studies. The two dimensions identified were called production-centered leadership and employee-centered leadership. A description of each concept and the leader behaviors associated with each are presented next.

Production-centered leader behavior is very similar to high initiating–structure leader behavior. The **production-centered leader** emphasizes employee tasks and the methods used to accomplish them. Leaders who are production-centered set tight work standards, organize tasks carefully, prescribe work methods to be followed, and closely supervise their subordinates' work.

Employee-centered leader behavior is very similar to high consideration leader behavior. An **employee-centered leader** emphasizes the employees' personal needs and the development of interpersonal relationships. Leaders who are employee-centered tend to have supportive relations with their subordinates, use group rather than individual decision making, encourage subordinates to set and achieve high performance goals, and endeavor to treat subordinates in a sensitive, considerate way.

Hundreds of studies in a wide variety of business, hospital, government, and other organizations were conducted. Thousands of employees, performing unskilled to highly professional and scientific tasks, completed a variety of questionnaires developed by the Michigan researchers. The initial research indicated that the most productive work groups tended to have leaders who were employee-centered rather than production-centered.[43] Subsequent research, however, con-

[42]R. Jean Hills, "The Representative Function: Neglected Dimension of Leadership Behavior," *Administrative Science Quarterly*, 8 (1963), pp. 83–101.

[43]Rensis Likert, *New Patterns of Management* (New York: McGraw-Hill, 1961); Likert, *The Human Organization: Its Management and Value* (New York: McGraw-Hill, 1967).

ADMINISTRATIVE ADVICE 5-2

TEN WAYS TO KILL LEADERSHIP

- *Conduct Annual Evaluations Based on Generalities Rather Than Specifics*. Do not let the evaluatee know what is expected of her. Then, when the evaluatee wanders around the school district in a daze, you can deliver a warning notice that performance is not up to par. Remember, the goal is to keep them guessing!

- *Keep Praise at a Low Level*. Watch what you say when the evaluatee performs at a high level of competency. Don't let employees know that the job was well done; they may become motivated.

- *Keep Asking for Detailed Reports*. Demand constant feedback by requiring lengthy reports on issues that could otherwise be handled effectively with a yes or no answer.

- *Make Sure Meetings Last a Long Time*. Drag out meetings with irrelevant questions and ask for more discussion before making decisions. Don't follow the agenda and let anyone speak for as long as they like. The key is to keep having irrelevant meetings.

- *Criticize Performance in Public*. Knock out leadership in a person by embarrassing him in public. Put an employee on the defensive or engage him in a shouting match.

- *Use the Words, "I Have Been Told by Some That Such and Such Happened."* Undermine a person's self-

esteem and help create distrust within the team. When asked to name the "some," don't say who the "some" are. Instead, say that you want to maintain confidentiality.

- *Play Sneak Attack*. Lay traps and use camouflage that can't be easily seen or discovered by the employee. Going behind the backs of employees in an attempt to discredit them will keep many good rising stars in school administration off the highway of success.

- *Expect Perfection*. Don't accept the notion that failure can lead to success. If you do, you will find people succeeding from their failures through words of encouragement.

- *Turn Down Requests for Professional Growth and Development*. Inform employees that the "fires" at home need to be tended and that wandering off to some professional convention will look bad in the eyes of the public.

- *Attempt to Please Everyone*. Hand out unwarranted praise. When a school administrator goes around praising everyone, including those who don't deserve it, those who are deserving become discouraged.

Source: Adapted from Don Fuhr, "Ten Best Ways to Kill Leadership," *School Administrator*, 9 (1988), pp. 50–51. Used by permission.

cluded that leaders with the best production records were both production-centered and employee-centered.[44] However, the Michigan research findings have not been totally consistent. In comparison, the Ohio State leadership studies appear to have become more famous, at least in

the educational setting, because of the number of studies that were generated by the initiating-structure and consideration dimensions. And many of these studies were done in school organizations.

Although much has been written about effective leadership, little has been said about what it takes to effectively destroy leadership and morale. Administrative Advice 5-2 offers some advice on this issue.

---

[44]Bowers, *Systems of Organization: Management of Human Resource.*

TABLE 5 ▪ 4   Overview of Leadership Behavior Theories

SOURCE	LEADERSHIP BEHAVIORS	RESEARCH METHOD	SUMMARY OF RESULTS
University of Iowa studies	Authoritarian Democratic Laissez-faire	Experimental: manipulated several decision-making situations and tested different leadership styles to measure the effects of style on outcomes	Overall, democratic leadership is best Authoritarian leadership created aggression and apathy and lower subordinate satisfaction Laissez–faire leadership produced the most aggression Authoritarian leadership increased productivity initially, but productivity decreased drastically over the long run
Ohio State studies	Initiating structure Consideration	Survey: questionnaires completed by leaders, supervisors, subordinates, and peers	Generally, high initiating structure and consideration increased productivity and satisfaction, but findings were inconsistent
University of Michigan studies	Production-centered Employee-centered	Survey: questionnaires completed by leaders, supervisors, subordinates, and peers	Initial studies found employee-centered leadership best, but later studies found a mix of employee- and production centered leadership increased productivity and satisfaction

Leadership Behavior Theories: Similarities and Conclusions

A review of the leader behavior theories reveals a number of similarities and conclusions. Table 5-4 presents a few of these points. First, the three theories attempted to explain leadership in terms of the behavior of the leader—that is, what the leader *does*, not her personal traits and skills. Once leader behavior was identified, researchers measured the effects of leader behavior on productivity and satisfaction. The Iowa studies un-

covered three leader behaviors, and the Ohio State and Michigan studies isolated two dimensions of leadership behavior that related to task orientation and people orientation. Second, the research we have discussed thus far has not considered the effects of situational factors on leadership—that is, differences in tasks completed, differences in the makeup of the group to be led, and differences in the external environment. All these factors have a bearing on the functions that must be performed by the leader and consequently on the appropriate leadership behavior to use in a given situation.

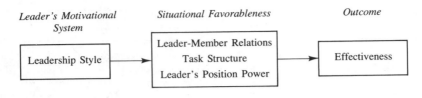

FIGURE 5-4   Major Variables in Fiedler's Contingency Theory

CONTINGENCY LEADERSHIP

Efforts to discover the one best set of leader traits and the one best set of leader behaviors *in all situations* have failed. Contemporary researchers and school administrators are more likely to believe that the practice of leadership is too complex to be represented by a single set of traits or behaviors. Instead, the idea that effective leadership behavior is "contingent" on the situation is more prevalent today.

The contingency approach to leadership is considerably more complex than either the trait or the behavioral approaches. According to **contingency theory**, effective leadership depends on the interaction of the leader's personal traits, the leader's behavior, and factors in the leadership situation. Essentially, the contingency approach is based on the proposition that effective leadership cannot be explained by any one factor. At the same time, the contingency approach does not deny the importance of the leader's traits or behavior. Instead, it proposes that both must be considered in the context of the situation in which the leader must lead. We discuss two contingency theories of leadership that have received a great deal of attention. The questions we ask regarding contingency leadership shift from, Is authoritarian, initiating structure, production-centered leadership more effective than democratic, consideration, employee-centered leadership? to a different question: In what situations will production-centered leadership be effective, and under what set of circumstances will employee-centered leadership be effective?

Fiedler's Contingency Theory

Fred Fiedler and his associates have spent two decades developing and refining a contingency theory of leadership.[45] According to the theory, the effectiveness of a leader in achieving high group performance is contingent on the leader's motivational system and the degree to which the leader controls and influences the situation. The three situational factors include leader–member relations, task structure, and the leader's position power. Figure 5-4 depicts the interrelationship among these variables. We discuss the three components of Fiedler's theory—leadership style, situational favorableness, and the contingency model—and the empirical evidence concerning the validity of the theory.

Leadership Style   Fiedler developed a unique technique to measure leadership style. Measurement is obtained from scores on the *least preferred co-worker* (LPC) scale. Table 5-5 presents an example of an LPC scale. The scale usually contains twenty-four pairs of adjectives, written as a bipolar list, each of which could be used to describe a person. The leader completing the LPC scale is asked to describe the person with whom he worked least well in accomplishing some task, by placing Xs at the appropriate points between each of the adjective pairs. The most positive response for each pair of adjectives

---

[45]Fred E. Fiedler and Martin M. Chemers, *Improving Leadership Effectiveness: The Leader Match Concept*, 2nd ed. (New York: Wiley, 1984).

TABLE 5 ■ 5   Sample of Items from the LPC Scale

		SCORING
Pleasant	Unpleasant	_____
8 7 6 5 4 3 2 1		
Friendly	Unfriendly	_____
8 7 6 5 4 3 2 1		
Rejecting	Accepting	_____
8 7 6 5 4 3 2 1		
Tense	Relaxed	_____
8 7 6 5 4 3 2 1		
Distant	Close	_____
8 7 6 5 4 3 2 1		
Cold	Warm	_____
8 7 6 5 4 3 2 1		
Supportive	Hostile	_____
8 7 6 5 4 3 2 1		
Boring	Interesting	_____
8 7 6 5 4 3 2 1		

SOURCE: Adapted from Fred E. Fiedler and Martin M. Chemers, *Improving Leadership Effectiveness: The Leader Match Concept,* 2nd ed., © 1984, p. 19. Used by permission of John Wiley & Sons, Inc., New York.

is assigned a score of 8 and the least positive response a score of 1. Summing all item scores on the instrument gives a leader's LPC score. A high score indicates that the leader views her least preferred co-worker in relatively favorable terms. A low score means that the least preferred co-worker is described in a very negative, rejecting manner.

How can the leader's LPC score be interpreted? Fiedler interprets a leader's LPC score to be a personality trait that reflects the leader's motivational system or behavioral preferences. High-LPC leaders (those who perceive their least preferred co-workers positively) have as their basic goal the desire to maintain close interpersonal relationships with subordinates and behave in a considerate and supportive manner toward them. If the leader reaches this goal, he will be able to attain such secondary goals as status and esteem. In return, these leaders want their subordinates to admire and recognize them. Low-LPC leaders have a different motiva-

tional structure: task accomplishment is their primary goal. Needs such as esteem and status are fulfilled through the accomplishment of tasks, not directly through relationships with subordinates. Hence, a high-LPC score indicates a relationship-motivated (employee-centered) leader whose interpersonal-relationship needs have first priority, and a low-LPC score indicates a task-motivated (production-centered) leader whose task-achievement needs have first priority.

Situational Favorableness   After classifying leaders according to their LPC scores, Fiedler set out to discover what type of leader is most effective. The basic premise of his contingency theory is that in some situations high-LPC (relationship-motivated) leaders will be more effective, whereas other circumstances make it more likely that low-LPC (task-motivated) leaders will be most effective. Fiedler concludes therefore that the relationship between leadership style and effectiveness depends on several factors in the situation. He identified three: leader–member relations, task structure, and position power.

Leader–member relations refer to the quality of the relationship between the leader and the group. The degree of confidence, trust, and respect subordinates have in the leader assesses it. Good or bad classifies leader–member relations. The assumption is that if subordinates respect and trust the leader, it will be easier for the leader to exercise *influence* in accomplishing tasks. For example, if subordinates are willing to follow a leader because of her referent power, they are following the leader because of her personality, trustworthiness, and so on. On the other hand, when the relationship between the leader and her subordinates is not good, the leader may have to resort to special favors (reward power) to get good performance from subordinates.

Task structure refers to the nature of the subordinate's task—whether it is routine (structured) or complex (unstructured). Task structure can be operationally defined by (1) the extent of goal clarity (i.e., the degree to which the task requirements are known by subordinates), (2) the multiplicity of goal paths (i.e., whether there are many or few procedures for solving the problem), (3) the extent of decision verifiability (i.e., whether performance can be easily evaluated), and (4) the solution specificity (i.e., whether there are one or many correct solutions). When the task to be performed is highly structured, the leader should be able to exert considerable influence on subordinates. Clear goals, clear procedures to achieve goals, and objective performance measures enable the leader to set performance standards and hold subordinates accountable (for example, "type ten error-free manuscript pages per hour"). On the other hand, when the task is unstructured, the leader may be in a poor position to evaluate subordinate performance because the goals are unclear, there are multiple paths to achieve them, and the leader may possess no more knowledge about the task than the subordinates (for example, "devise a plan to improve the quality of life in our school").

Position power refers to the extent to which the leader possesses the ability to influence the behavior of subordinates through legitimate, reward, and coercive powers. Examples are the power to hire and fire, to give pay raises and promotions, and to direct subordinates to task completion. The more position power held by the leader, the more favorable the leadership situation. In general, committee chairpersons and leaders in voluntary organizations have weak position power. School boards, superintendents, and principals of school organizations have strong position power.

Contingency Model   Leader–member relations, task structure, and position power determine the situational favorableness for the leader. To combine these factors in the simplest way, Fiedler simply split each into two categories and thus produced eight possible combinations (Figure 5-5). The eight situations vary in terms of their overall favorableness for the exercise of leadership. As Figure 5-5 shows, the most favorable situation (greater leader influence) is one in which leader–member relations are good, the task is highly structured, and the leader has strong position power. The least favorable situation (least leader influence) is one in which leader–member relations are poor, tasks are unstructured, and leader position power is weak.

Fiedler hypothesized that the favorableness of the situation with the leadership style determines effectiveness. He reviewed studies conducted in over 800 groups to investigate which type of leader was most effective in each situation.[46] Among the groups studied were Air Force bomber crews, combat tank crews, basketball teams, fraternity members, surveying teams, open-hearth steel employees, form-supply service employees, and educational administrators. The general conclusion reached, as shown in Figure 5-6, is that task-motivated leaders were most effective in extreme situations where the leader either had a great deal of influence or very little power and influence. Relationship-moti-

---

[46]Fred E. Fiedler, *A Theory of Leadership Effectiveness*, (New York: McGraw-Hill, 1967).

Leader–Member Relations	Good				Poor			
Task Structure	Structured		Unstructured		Structured		Unstructured	
Position Power	Strong	Weak	Strong	Weak	Strong	Weak	Strong	Weak
Situations	I	II	III	IV	V	VI	VII	VIII

Favorable ◄———————————————————————► Unfavorable

FIGURE 5-5   Fiedler's Contingency Model (SOURCE: Adapted from Fred E. Fiedler, *A Theory of Leadership Effectiveness*, © 1967, p. 37. Used by permission.)

vated (high-LPC) leaders were most effective where the leader had moderate power and influence.

Why is the task-motivated leader successful in very favorable situations? Fiedler provided the following explanation:

> In the very favorable conditions in which the leader has power, informal backing, and a relatively well-structured task, the group is ready to be directed and the group expects to be told what to do. Consider the captain of an airliner in its final landing approach. We would hardly want him to turn to his crew for a discussion on how to land.[47]

To explain why the task-motivated leader is successful in a highly unfavorable situation, Fiedler cites the following example:

> . . . [T]he disliked chairman of a volunteer committee . . . is asked to plan the office picnic on a beautiful Sunday. If the leader asks too many questions about what the group ought to do or how he should proceed, he is likely to be told that "we ought to go home."[48]

As Figure 5-6 shows, the relationship-motivated (high-LPC) leader is effective in the intermediate range of favorableness (octants 4, 5, 6, and 7). An example of such situations is the typical university committee staffed by professionals. In these situations, the leader may not be completely accepted by the group, the task

may be ambiguous, and little power may be vested in the leader. Under such circumstances, Fiedler's theory predicts that relationship-motivated leaders will be most effective.

Research on the Contingency Model   Fiedler's contingency model has stimulated a considerable amount of research; the results are mixed. Most research has been supportive of the theory.[49] However, the model has been criticized on several counts. Critics have argued that Fiedler's preference for a task-motivated style (in four of eight situations) is diametrically opposed to the findings of Likert,[50] and Fiedler fails to explain the effectiveness of high-LPC leaders in the middle four octants. At least one study shows that middle-LPC leaders perform over the entire situational range.[51] The LPC measure itself has been criticized in terms of its practical application in an organizational setting.[52] Other research suggests that the LPC may be a measure of cognitive complexity rather than leadership

---

[47]Ibid., p. 147.
[48]Ibid.

[49]Robert W. Rice, "Leader LPC and Follower Satisfaction: A Review," *Organizational Behavior and Human Performance*, 28 (1981), pp. 288–294.
[50]Likert, *New Patterns of Management*.
[51]John K. Kennedy, "Middle LPC Leaders and Contingency Model of Leader Effectiveness," *Organizational Behavior and Human Performance*, 30 (1982), pp. 1–14.
[52]Samuel Shiflett, "Is There a Problem with the LPC Score in Leader Match?" *Personnel Psychology*, 34 (1981), pp. 765–769.

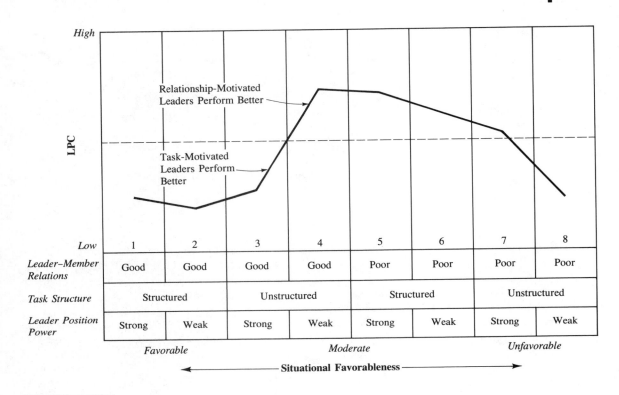

FIGURE 5-6   Summary of Contingency Model Research (SOURCE: Adapted from Fred E. Fiedler and Martin M. Chemers, *Leadership and Effective Management*, © 1974, p. 80. Used by permission of Fred E. Fiedler.)

style.[53] Nevertheless, evidence supports the LPC measure of leadership style,[54] and Fiedler has replied to most of the criticisms of his contingency theory.[55]

Despite these criticisms, Fiedler's contingency model has made a major contribution to the study of leadership for several reasons. First, the contingency model was one of the first approaches to leadership to examine the situation—the people, the task, and the organization. In addition, much research supports the model, and researchers continue to investigate, refine, and extend the theory. Second, the theory implies that leadership should not be thought of as either good or bad. Instead, a more realistic approach is to view an administrator's leadership style as effective in one set of circumstances but ineffective in another. Finally, leadership is a function of the interaction of leadership style and situational dimensions within the organization. There are at least two implications of such a

[53]Ramadhar Singh, "Leadership Style and Reward Allocation: Does the Least Preferred Coworker Scale Measure Task and Relation Orientation?" *Organizational Behavior and Human Performance*, 32 (1983), pp. 178–197.

[54]Michael J. Strube and Joseph E. Garcia, "A Meta-Analytic Investigation of Fiedler's Contingency Model of Leadership Effectiveness," *Psychological Bulletin*, 90 (1981), pp. 307–321.

[55]Fred E. Fiedler, "A Rejoiner to Schriesheim and Kerr's Premature Obituary of the Contingency Model," in J. G. Hunt and L. L. Larson (eds.), *Leadership: The Cutting Edge* (Carbondale: Southern Illinois University Press, 1977).

relationship. Leaders can improve their effectiveness by modifying the situation so that it better fits with their own leadership style, or they can change their leadership style to obtain a better match with the situation. Now let's examine another contingency theory.

Path–Goal Theory

Another widely known contingency theory of leadership is the path–goal theory of leadership effectiveness. **Path–goal theory** is based on the expectancy theory of motivation and emphasizes the leader's effect on subordinate's goals and the paths to achieve the goals. Leaders have influence over subordinate's ability to reach goals, the rewards associated with reaching goals, and the importance of the goals.

The modern development of path–goal theory is usually attributed to Martin Evans and to Robert House and his colleagues.[56] Essentially, the path–goal theory attempts to explain the impact of leadership behavior on subordinate motivation, satisfaction, effort, and performance as moderated by situational factors of the subordinates and the work environment. House's general model and each of its parts are examined in the following sections.

Leader Behavior   Four distinct types of leader behavior comprise House's path–goal model:

- *Directive Leadership.* A **directive leader** lets subordinates know what is expected of them, provides specific guidance concerning what

is to be done and how to do it, sets performance standards, requests that subordinates follow standard rules and regulations, schedules and coordinates work, and explains his role as leader of the group. Directive leadership is similar to the Ohio State researchers' initiating structure.

- *Supportive Leadership.* A **supportive leader** is friendly, approachable, and concerned with the needs, status, and well-being of subordinates. A supportive leader treats subordinates as equals and frequently goes out of her way to make the work environment more pleasant and enjoyable. This leadership style is similar to what the Ohio State researchers call consideration.

- *Participative Leadership.* A **participative leader** consults with subordinates concerning work-related matters, solicits their opinions, and frequently attempts to use subordinates' ideas in making decisions.

- *Achievement-Oriented Leadership.* An **achievement-oriented leader** sets challenging goals for subordinates, emphasizes excellence in performance, and shows confidence in subordinates' ability to achieve high standards of performance.

Numerous research studies in path–goal theory suggest that the same leader can manifest these four styles of leadership in various situations. Unlike Fiedler's contingency model, which considers leadership behavior as unidimensional, path–goal theory views leadership behavior as relatively adaptable.

Situational Factors   Each type of leader behavior works well in some situations but not in others. Two situational factors moderate the relationship between leader behavior and subordinate outcomes. The two situational variables are subordinate characteristics and environmental forces.

With respect to subordinate characteristics, the theory asserts that leadership behavior will be acceptable to subordinates to the extent that subordinates see such behavior as either an immediate source of satisfaction or as instrumental

---

[56]Martin G. Evans, "The Effects of Supervisory Behavior on the Path–Goal Relationship," *Organizational Behavior and Human Performance*, 5 (1970), pp. 277–298; Robert J. House, "A Path–Goal Theory of Leader Effectiveness," *Administrative Science Quarterly*, 16 (1971), pp. 321–339; Robert J. House and Gary Dessler, "The Path–Goal Theory of Leadership: Some Post Hoc and A Priori Tests," in J. G. Hunt and L. L. Larson (eds.), *Contingency Approaches to Leadership* (Carbondale: Southern Illinois University Press, 1974).

to future satisfaction.[57] Subordinate characteristics are seen to partially determine the extent to which subordinates perceive a leader's behavior as acceptable and satisfying. House and Baetz identified three subordinate characteristics:

- *Ability*. An important personal characteristic of subordinates is their perception of their ability to perform a task. For example, subordinates who feel they have low task ability should appreciate directive leadership, whereas subordinates who feel quite capable to perform the task will find directive leadership unnecessary and perhaps irritating.
- *Locus of Control*. Locus of control refers to the degree to which an individual sees the environment as systematically responding to his behavior.[58] Individuals with an internal locus of control believe outcomes are a function of their own behavior. Individuals with an external locus of control believe outcomes are a function of luck or chance. Research suggests that "internals" are more satisfied with participative leadership and "externals" are more satisfied with a directive leadership style.[59]
- *Needs and Motives*. The dominant needs, motives, and personality characteristics of subordinates may influence their acceptance of and satisfaction with alternative leadership styles. For example, subordinates who have a high need for esteem and affiliation should be more satisfied with a supportive leader. Those with a high need for security will be

more satisfied with a directive leader. Furthermore, subordinates with a high need for autonomy, responsibility, and self-actualization will probably be more motivated by a participative leader, and those who are high-need achievers should be more satisfied with achievement-oriented leaders. (See Administrative Advice 5-3.)

With respect to the second situational factor, environmental forces, path–goal theory states: Leadership behavior will be motivational to the extent that (1) it makes satisfaction of subordinate needs contingent on effective performance and (2) it compliments the environment of subordinates by providing the coaching, guidance, support, and rewards that are necessary for effective performance and that may otherwise be lacking in subordinates or in their environment.[60] Environmental forces include three broad aspects of situational factors: subordinate's tasks, the primary work group, and the formal authority system.

- *Tasks*. An important environmental force that moderates the effects of leader behavior on subordinate outcomes is subordinates' tasks. Generally, researchers have classified tasks as highly structured or highly unstructured. Research has provided some evidence that supportive and participative leadership is more likely to increase subordinate satisfaction on highly structured tasks. This is because the tasks are routine and no further direction is necessary. Subordinates should be more satisfied with directive leadership on unstructured tasks because directive behavior can help clarify an ambiguous task for subordinates.[61]
- *Work Group*. The characteristics of work groups may also influence subordinate ac-

[57]Robert House and Mary L. Baetz, "Leadership: Some Empirical Generalizations and New Research Directions," *Research in Organizational Behavior*, 1 (1979), pp. 341–423.

[58]J. B. Rotter, "Generalized Expectancies for Internal Versus External Control of Reinforcement," *Psychological Monographs*, 80 (1966), whole issue.

[59]Avis L. Johnson, Fred Luthans, and Harry W. Hennessey, "The Role of Locus of Control in Leader Influence Behavior," *Personnel Psychology*, 37 (1984), pp. 61–75.

[60]House and Baetz, "Leadership: Some Empirical Generalizations and New Research Directions."

[61]House and Dessler, "The Path-Goal Theory of Leadership."

ADMINISTRATIVE ADVICE 5-3

■

COMPETENT FACULTY NEED SUPERVISION TOO

The concept of "appreciative supervision" maximizes the support and appreciation given to competent subordinates. It commits both the supervisor and the subordinate to an interdependent relationship, in which both parties derive satisfaction and growth. This process is based on eight assumptions and the supervisor's willingness to act on those beliefs when dealing with employees.

- *Employees Know How to Perform Their Jobs.* Begin with the assumption that four of every five employees in any organization are basically competent. These employees don't need direct, continuous supervision. The supervisor's role is to guide, not direct.
- *Employees Want to Know How They Are Doing.* Employees seek feedback that needs to be timely and confidential to be effective. Share what you are thinking; don't wait until you have documentable information. Employees may be in a position to offer alternative courses of action.
- *Employees Want to Meet the Employer's Expectations.* On-the-job success for employees means meeting the needs and expectations of the organization. If you seek changes in policies and procedures, discuss them with employees.
- *Employees Need Opportunities for Growth and Change.* If employees' growth has stagnated, guide them in developing new skills. Consider the professional maturity of each individual.
- *Employees Need Control Over the Work Environment.* Whenever possible, provide latitude within job responsibilities for employees to

make decisions about personal abilities and availability.
- *Employees Possess Valuable Information.* Employees should be provided with the opportunity to evaluate the organization—for example, what needs changing and what should be strengthened. What may not be a problem for supervisors may be for employees and vice versa. Your employees are your most valuable resource.
- *Employees Should Help Set the Direction of Supervision.* What is important to employees should be a priority for the supervisor. Assume employees are in the best position to judge their immediate needs.
- *Employees Want Someone with Whom to Share Their Work Experiences.* Dropping by to visit employees at their workstations is a valuable component of an effective supervisory relationship. Give employees the chance to share experiences.

Source: Adapted from Doreen Cunningham, "Competent Staff Need Your Supervision, Too," *School Administrator*, 46 (1989), pp. 39–40. Used by permission.

---

ceptance of a particular leadership style. For example, the path–goal theory asserts that "when goals and paths to desired goals are apparent because of . . . clear group norms . . . , attempts by the leader to clarify paths and goals would be redundant and

would be seen by subordinates as an imposition of unnecessarily close control."[62]
- *Formal Authority System.* The final environmental force concerns such matters as

[62]Ibid., pp. 29–62.

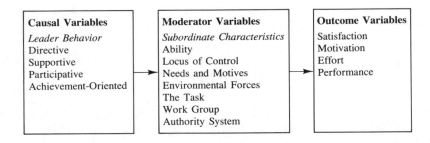

FIGURE 5-7   Relationship of Variables in the Path–Goal Theory

(1) the degree of emphasis on rules, regulations, policies, and procedures governing the performance of tasks; (2) situations of high stress; and (3) situations of great uncertainty. Some examples follow: With tasks (i.e., typing manuscripts) that are self-evident due to mechanization, standards, and procedures, directive leadership may lead to subordinate dissatisfaction. Research suggests directive and supportive leadership will increase subordinate satisfaction in some stressful situations.[63] In environments of uncertainty, leaders may initially use a participatory leadership style to solicit ideas in reaching a decision but later may resort to directive leadership once the final decision is made.

Figure 5-7 summarizes the path–goal theory of leadership effectiveness. As the figure shows, leader behavior moderated by subordinate characteristics and environmental forces results in subordinate motivation, satisfaction, effort, and performance.

Research on Path–Goal Theory   Some research evidence is available concerning path–goal theory. Because many variables in the model exist, simultaneously testing all possible relationships is difficult. Directive, supportive, participative,

and achievement-oriented styles of leadership, as well as the situational factors of the model, seem to make intuitive sense. However, research to date has focused on a limited set of leader behaviors and has tested them in only one or a few situations.[64] In particular, there is substantial evidence that directive leader behavior is most effective in supervising ambiguous, unstructured tasks and that supportive leader behavior is most beneficial in routine, structured tasks.[65] Considerable evidence also indicates that supportive leader behavior will increase motivation and satisfaction for subordinates working on stressful, frustrating, or dissatisfying tasks.[66] Furthermore, path–goal theory appears to work better in predicting subordinate motivation and satisfaction than in predicting performance.[67] Overall, the path–goal theory is important to both school leaders and researchers, for it may provide the road to a better understanding of leadership.

[63]Andrew D. Szilagyi and Henry P. Sims, "An Exploration of the Path–Goal Theory of Leadership in Health Care Environments," *Academy of Management Journal*, 17 (1974), pp. 622–634.

[64]John B. Miner, *Organizational Behavior: Performance and Productivity*, (New York: Random House, 1988).
[65]Chester A. Schriesheim and Angelo S. DeNisi, "Task Dimensions as Moderators of the Effects of Instrumental Leadership: A Two-Sample Replicated Test of Path–Goal Leadership Theory," *Journal of Applied Psychology*, 66 (1981), pp. 589–597.
[66]H. Kirk Downey, John E. Sheridan, and John W. Slocum, "Analysis of Relationships Among Leader Behavior, Subordinate Job Performance, and Satisfaction: A Path–Goal Approach," *Academy of Management Journal*, 18 (1975), pp. 253–262.
[67]Ricky W. Griffin, "Relationships Among Individual, Task Design, and Leader Behavior Variables," *Academy of Management Journal*, 23 (1980), pp. 665–683.

TABLE 5 ▪ 6   Summary of Leadership Styles Extracted from Classic Studies and Contingency Theories

STUDIES/THEORIES	TASK-ORIENTED	EMPLOYEE-ORIENTED
Iowa studies	Authoritarian	Democratic
Ohio State studies	Initiating structure	Consideration
Michigan studies	Job-centered	Employee-centered
Contingencey theory	Task-motivated	Relationship-motivated
Path–goal theory	Directive	Supportive

LEADERSHIP STYLES

The classic leadership studies (trait and behavioral approaches) and the contingency theories of leadership all have direct implications for what style the leader uses in managing human resources. The term *style* is roughly equivalent to the manner in which the leader *influences* subordinates.

In the following sections, we present the most recent approaches that deal directly with style. Before proceeding, however, Table 5-6 presents a summary of the leadership styles extracted from the classic leadership studies and the contingency studies. For ease of presentation, we list the styles under a two-heading continuum labeled task-oriented and employee-oriented. This classification can serve as a background for a more detailed discussion of leadership styles to come.

Leadership-Style Continuum

Robert Tannenbaum and Warren Schmidt[68] elaborated on two styles identified in the earlier trait and behavioral studies of leadership. They conceive of a continuum that runs between *boss-centered leadership* at one extreme and *subordinate-centered leadership* at the other. Between these extremes are five points representing various combinations of managerial authority and subordinate freedom. Figure 5-8 depicts their concept of a **leadership-style continuum**.

Leadership Behaviors   The authors identify five typical patterns of leadership behavior from their model:

1. *Telling*. The leader identifies a problem, considers alternative solutions, chooses one of them, and then tells her followers what they are to do. Members may be considered but do not participate directly in the decision making. Coercion may or may not be used or implied.
2. *Selling*. The leader makes the decision but tries to persuade the group members to accept it. She points out how she has considered organizational goals and the interests of group members, and she states how the members will benefit from carrying out the decision.
3. *Testing*. The leader identifies a problem and proposes a tentative solution. She asks for the reaction of those who will implement it, but she makes the final decision.
4. *Consulting*. The group members have a chance to influence the decision from the beginning. The leader presents a problem and relevant background information. The

[68]Robert Tannenbaum and Warren Schmidt, "How to Choose a Leadership Pattern," *Harvard Business Review*, 51 (1973), pp. 162–180.

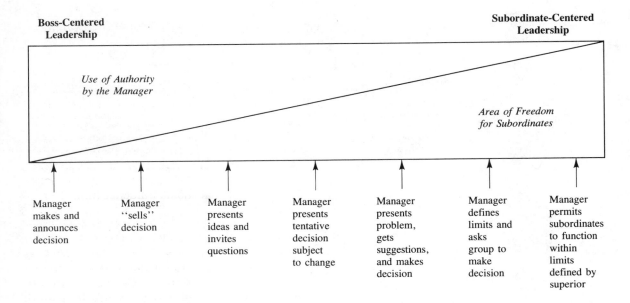

Boss-Centered Leadership

Subordinate-Centered Leadership

Use of Authority by the Manager

Area of Freedom for Subordinates

| Manager makes and announces decision | Manager ''sells'' decision | Manager presents ideas and invites questions | Manager presents tentative decision subject to change | Manager presents problem, gets suggestions, and makes decision | Manager defines limits and asks group to make decision | Manager permits subordinates to function within limits defined by superior |

FIGURE 5-8   Leadership-Style Continuum (SOURCE: Adapted from Robert Tannenbaum and Warren Schmidt, "How to Choose a Leadership Pattern," *Harvard Business Review*, 51 (1973), p. 167. Copyright © 1973 by the President and Fellows of Harvard College. Used by permission.)

group is invited to increase the number of alternative actions to be considered. The leader then selects the solution she regards as most promising.

5. *Joining*. The leader participates in the discussion as a member and agrees in advance to carry out whatever decision the group makes.

Influences on the Leader Tannenbaum and Schmidt assert that a wide range of factors determines whether superordinate-centered leadership, subordinate-centered leadership, or something in between is best. These factors fall into four broad categories: forces in the leader, forces in the group, forces in the situation, and long-run objectives and strategy.

1. *Forces in the Leader*

  (a) His value system: How strongly does he feel that individuals should have a share in making the decisions that affect them? Or, how convinced is he that the

official who is paid or chosen to assume responsibility should personally carry the burden of decision making? Also, what is the relative importance that he attaches to organizational efficiency and personal growth of subordinates?

  (b) His confidence in the group members: Leaders differ in the amount of trust they have in other people generally. After considering the knowledge and competence of a group with respect to a problem, a leader may (justifiably or not) have more confidence in his own capabilities than in those of the group members.

  (c) His own leadership inclinations: Leaders differ in the manner (e.g., telling or team role) in which they seem to function more comfortably and naturally.

  (d) His feelings of security in an uncertain situation: The leader who releases control over the decision-making process reduces the predictability of the outcome. Leaders who have a greater need than others for predictability and stability are more likely to "tell" or "sell" than to "join."

2. *Forces in the Group Members.* Before deciding how to lead a certain group, the leader will also want to remember that each member, like himself, is influenced by many personality variables and expectations. Generally speaking, the leader can permit the group greater freedom if the following essential conditions exist:
   (a) Members have relatively high needs for independence.
   (b) Members have readiness to assume responsibility.
   (c) Members have a relatively high tolerance for ambiguity.
   (d) Members are interested in the problem and feel that it is important.
   (e) Members understand and identify with the goals of the organization.
   (f) Members have the necessary knowledge and experience to deal with the problem.
   (g) Members expect to share in decision making.

3. *Forces in the Situation.* Some of the critical environmental pressures on the leader are as follows:
   (a) The problem itself: Do the members have the kind of knowledge that is needed? Does the complexity of the problem require special experience or a one-person solution?
   (b) The pressure of time: The more the leader feels the need for an immediate decision, the more difficult it is to involve other people.

4. *Long-Run Objectives and Strategy.* As the leader works on daily problems, his choice of a leadership pattern is usually limited. But he may also begin to regard some of the forces mentioned as variables over which he has some control and to consider such long-range objectives as
   (a) Raising the level of member motivation.
   (b) Improving the quality of all decisions.
   (c) Developing teamwork and morale.

(d) Furthering the individual development of members.
(e) Increasing the readiness to accept change.

Generally, a fairly high degree of member-centered behavior is more likely to achieve these long-range purposes. But the successful administrator can be characterized neither as a strong leader nor as a permissive one. Rather, he is one who is sensitive to the forces that influence him in a given situation and one who can accurately assess those that should influence him.

Status of the Model   The Tannenbaum–Schmidt model has not generated any empirical research probably because there are no instruments associated with the formulation. However, from a practical standpoint, the model makes intuitive sense. Tannenbaum and Schmidt's framework can be used to identify various alternative leadership behaviors available to a school administrator and the general classes of factors (influences on the leader) that are relevant in selecting an appropriate leadership style to fit a given situation.

Managerial Grid® Styles

A popular approach to identifying leadership styles of practicing administrators is Robert Blake and Jane Mouton's **Managerial Grid**.[69] They define two dimensions of leader orientation as *concern for production* and *concern for people.* These dimensions are similar to the task-oriented and employee-oriented concepts depicted in Table 5-6.

The Grid portrays five key leadership styles. Concern for production is rated on a 1 to 9 scale on the horizontal axis, while concern for people is rated similarly on the vertical axis (Figure 5-9). The Grid identifies a range of leader orienta-

---

[69]Robert R. Blake and Jane S. Mouton, *The Managerial Grid III: The Key to Leadership Excellence* (Houston: Gulf, 1985).

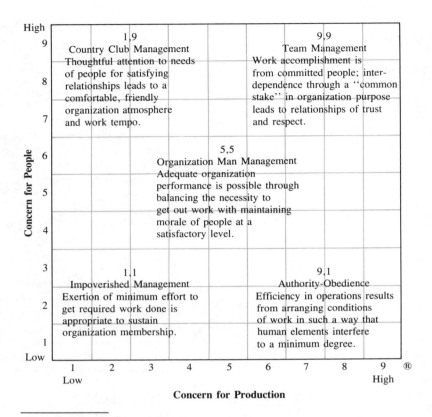

FIGURE 5-9   The Managerial Grid® Figure. (SOURCE: The Managerial Grid Figure from *The Managerial Grid III: The Key to Leadership Excellence*, by Robert R. Blake and Jane Srygley Mouton. Houston: Gulf Publishing Company, Copyright © 1985, page 12. Reproduced by permission.

tions based on the various ways in which task-oriented and people-oriented styles can interact with each other.

Leadership Styles   Although there are eighty-one possible styles in the Grid, the five styles noted in Figure 5-9 and discussed below are treated as benchmarks in the theory. Blake and Mouton view leaders as capable of selecting from among them.

- *9,1—Authority–Obedience*. Leaders concentrate on maximizing production through the use of power, authority, and control.

- *1,9—Country Club Management*. Leaders place primary emphasis on good feelings among colleagues and subordinates even if production suffers as a result.
- *1,1—Impoverished Management*. Leaders do the minimum required to remain employed in the organization.
- *5,5—Organization–Man Management*. Leaders concentrate on conforming to the status quo and maintaining middle-of-the-road or "to-go-along-to-get-along" assumptions.
- *9,9—Team Management*. Leaders use a goal-centered approach to gain high quantity and high-quality results through broad involve-

ment of group members: participation, commitment, and conflict resolution.

Research on the Managerial Grid
The authors of the Grid indicate there is evidence regarding the effectiveness of the 9,9—team management style as judged by groups of administrators from different organizational contexts.[70] Further, the authors recently provided empirical evidence that their Managerial Grid has more predictive validity than additive situational approaches.[71] Finally, Blake and Mouton have developed instruments which are designed to stimulate feedback from colleagues, associates, subordinates, and the like, which enable the targeted person to learn from others how they experience his or her leadership, that is, as 1,9-oriented, 9,1-oriented, 9,9-oriented, and so on. Therefore, the Grid is used to help people analyze the different possibilities and likely results to be achieved by each of the Grid styles and select the one they believe most effective.

Three-Dimensional Leadership Styles

William Reddin developed another useful model for identifying the leadership styles of practicing school administrators.[72] Figure 5-10 shows his relatively elaborate three-dimensional model of leadership effectiveness. By adding an effectiveness dimension to the task behavior and relationship behavior dimensions of the earlier Ohio State leadership models,

Reddin has attempted to integrate the concepts of leadership style with situational demands of a specific environment. As Figure 5-10 shows, when the style of a leader is appropriate to a given situation, it is termed *effective*; when the style is inappropriate to a given situation, it is termed *ineffective*. In the center grid, the four basic leadership styles in the model are related, integrated, separated, and dedicated. Reddin proposes that any of the four basic leadership styles may be effective or ineffective depending on the situation. These effective and ineffective equivalents result in eight operational leadership styles, which we briefly summarize.

The effective styles are as follows:

1. *Developer*. A leader using this style gives maximum concern to relationships and minimum concern to tasks. The leader is seen as having implicit trust in people and concerned mainly with developing them as individuals.
2. *Executive*. A leader using this style gives a great deal of concern to both tasks and relationships. The leader is seen as a good motivator, setting high standards, recognizing individual differences, and using team management.
3. *Bureaucrat*. A leader using this style gives minimum concern to both tasks and relationships. The leader is seen as conscientious and is interested mainly in rules and wants to maintain and control the situation by the use of rules.
4. *Benevolent Autocrat*. A leader using this style gives maximum concern to tasks and minimum concern to relationships. The leader is seen as knowing exactly what she wants and how to get it without causing resentment.

The ineffective styles are as follows:

1. *Missionary*. A leader using this style gives maximum concern to people and relationships and minimum concern to tasks in a situation in which such behavior is inappropriate. The leader is seen as a "do-gooder" who values harmony as an end in itself.

[70]Robert R. Blake and Jane S. Mouton, "Theory and Research for Developing a Science of Leadership," *Journal of Applied Behavioral Science*, 18 (1982), pp. 275–291.
[71]Robert R. Blake and Jane S. Mouton, "Management by Grid Principles or Situationalism: Which?" *Group and Organization Studies*, 6 (1981), pp. 439–455.
[72]William J. Reddin, *Managerial Effectiveness* (New York: McGraw-Hill, 1970).

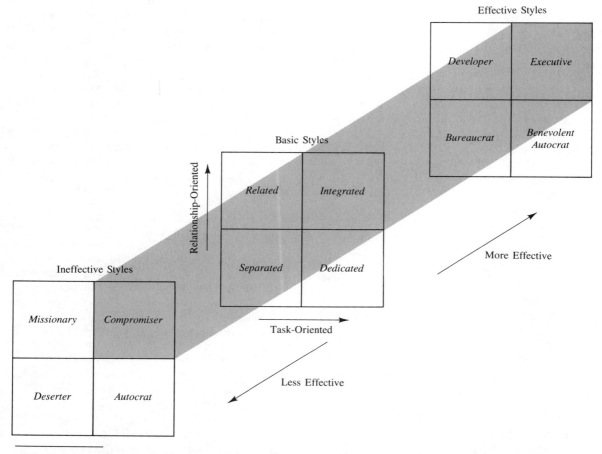

FIGURE 5-10   Reddin's Three-Dimensional Model of Leadership Effectiveness (SOURCE: Adapted from William J. Reddin, *Managerial Effectiveness*, © 1970, p. 230. Used by permission of McGraw-Hill, New York.)

2. *Compromiser*. A leader using this style gives a great deal of concern to both tasks and relationships in a situation that requires emphasis on only one or on neither. The leader is seen as a poor decision maker; he is affected by pressure.

3. *Deserter*. A leader using this style gives minimum concern to tasks and relationships in a situation where such behavior is inappropriate. The leader is seen as uninvolved and passive.

4. *Autocrat*. A leader using this style gives minimum concern to tasks and minimum concern to relationships in a situation in which

such behavior is inappropriate. The leader is seen as having no confidence in others, as unpleasant, and as interested only in the immediate job.

Status of the Three-Dimensional Model   Reddin's model incorporates three theoretical bases discussed previously, namely, leader traits and behaviors, groups, and situational factors. Reddin's model has not been the object of much empirical research. Instead, it has become a very popular technique for use in training administrators in numerous organizational contexts. Using Reddin's sixty-four-item questionnaire, administrators can identify their leadership styles. Primarily, executive-development seminars conducted by Reddin and his colleagues are designed to make participants cognizant of a variety of leadership styles and train leaders to adapt styles to particular situations in order to achieve maximum effectiveness.

Situational Leadership Styles

Another well-known and useful framework for analyzing leadership behavior is Paul Hersey and Kenneth Blanchard's **situational leadership theory**.[73] It is an extension of Tannenbaum and Schmidt's leadership-style continuum, Blake and Mouton's managerial grid, and Reddin's three-dimensional leadership styles. Following the lead of the earlier Ohio State leadership studies, and like the leadership-style continuum, the grid, and the three-dimensional frameworks, situational leadership theory identifies two key leadership behaviors: task behavior and relationship behavior.

- *Task Behavior*. The leader engages in one-way communication by explaining what each subordinate is to do, as well as when, where, and how tasks are to be performed.
- *Relationship Behavior*. The leader engages in two-way communication by providing socio-emotional support, "psychological strokes," and "facilitating behaviors."

Situational Factor: Maturity of Followers   Taking the lead from Fiedler's contingency factors, Hersey and Blanchard incorporated the maturity of followers as a key situational variable in their model. Hersey and Blanchard see two types of maturity as particularly important: job maturity and psychological maturity.

- *Job Maturity*. This refers to a person's maturity to perform the job as influenced by education

[73]Paul Hersey and Kenneth H. Blanchard, *Management of Organizational Behavior*, 5th ed. (Englewood Cliffs, NJ: Prentice-Hall, 1988).

and experience. For example, a teacher or counselor in a public school who has been on the job for many years and is thoroughly competent in all areas of the job would be rated high on job maturity.
- *Psychological Maturity*. This refers to the person's level of motivation as reflected in achievement needs and willingness to accept responsibility. An example would be a university professor who works independently on her research and course preparations for publication and teaching.

Hersey and Blanchard caution that maturity of followers is task-specific. For example, a principal might be a mature follower in a school district situation but be immature as a forward on the school district's basketball team. The two types combine to produce four levels of maturity, which create situations that call for four leadership styles that are combinations of task and relationship behavior.

Leadership Styles   The key for leadership effectiveness in Hersey and Blanchard's model is to match the situation with the appropriate leadership style. Four basic leadership styles are in the model: directing, coaching, supporting, and delegating.

- *Directing Style*. This is a high-task, low-relationship style and is effective when subordinates are low in motivation and ability.
- *Coaching Style*. This is a high-task, high-relationship style and is effective when subordinates have adequate motivation but low ability.
- *Supporting Style*. This is a low-task, high-relationship style and is effective when subordinates have adequate ability but low motivation.
- *Delegating Style*. This is a low-task, low-relationship style and is effective when subordinates are very high in ability and motivation.

Figure 5-11 summarizes the situational leadership theory.

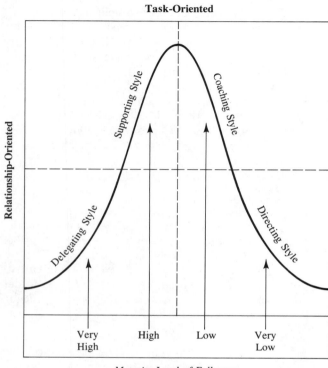

Task-Oriented

Subordinates

M1 = Low Motivation and Ability
M2 = Adequate Motivation but Low Ability
M3 = Adequate Ability but Low Motivation
M4 = Needed Ability and Motivation Are
Present

Leader

Q1 = High Task Behavior
and Low Relationship Behavior
Q2 = High Task Behavior
and High Relationship Behavior
Q3 = Low Task Behavior
and High Relationship Behavior
Q4 = Low Task Behavior
and Low Relationship Behavior

Relationship-Oriented

Supporting Style

Coaching Style

Delegating Style

Directing Style

| Very High | High | Low | Very Low |

Maturity Level of Followers

FIGURE 5-11   Hersey and Blanchard's Situational Leadership Model (source: Adapted from Paul Hersey and Kenneth H. Blanchard, *Management of Organizational Behavior*, 1988, p. 171. Copyrighted materials from Leadership Studies, Inc. Used by permission.)

As Figure 5-11 shows, when subordinates have low motivation (M1), leaders should define roles and direct the behavior of group members (Q1). When subordinates have moderately low motivation (M2), leaders should provide some direction, but they can attempt to persuade subordinates to accept decisions and directions (Q2). When subordinates have moderately high motivation (M3), initial direction is not needed, but group members should share in decision making (Q3). Finally, when subordinates have high motivation (M4), leaders should demonstrate confidence in group members by delegating tasks to them (Q4). The key to the success of situational leadership theory is matching leadership styles to the appropriate people and situations. (See Administrative Advice 5-4.)

Research on Situational Leadership Theory   Until recently, there was almost no empirical research evidence to suggest the validity of the Hersey–Blanchard model. However, two industrial studies have yielded some data that support the theory, and a third educational study provides partial support for Hersey and Blanchard's model. The first industrial study, in a large division of the Xerox Corporation, found that managers who could correctly apply the Hersey–Blanchard theory got better performance from their subordinates, as compared with their

ADMINISTRATIVE ADVICE 5-4

Applying Situational Leadership

School administrators should consider situational leadership styles systematically, and under what circumstances each is appropriate. School administrators can apply the four leadership styles in the following manner:

- *Directing Style*. Give specific instructions and supervise staff members closely. This leadership style is primarily for first-year teachers who need a lot of structure and supervision.
- *Coaching Style*. Explain decisions and solicit suggestions from followers but continue to direct tasks. This leadership style works especially well with nontenured teachers, who are in their second or third year on the job. They're gaining confidence and competence, but they're still getting their feet on the ground.
- *Supporting Style*. Make decisions together with staff members and support their efforts toward

performing tasks. This leadership style works with highly creative teachers. Applying this style can take the form of supporting teachers when they come up with excellent ideas and helping them bring those ideas to fruition.
- *Delegating Style*. Turn over decisions and responsibility for implementing them to staff members. This leadership style works with people who go above and beyond their instructions.

Source: Adapted from Bob Webb, "Situational Leadership: The Key Is Knowing When to Do What," *Executive Educator*, 12 (1990), pp. 29–30. Copyright 1990, the National School Boards Association. Used by permission.

counterparts who could not correctly apply the model.[74] The second industrial study found that managers who received training during seminars in which situational leadership theory was applied scored significantly higher on a final examination than did managers who were taught using traditional methods of instruction.[75]

The third study was a field test of Hersey and Blanchard's situational leadership theory in a school setting. Elementary school principals

training using Hersey and Blanchard's framework. Pretests and posttests were administered to the principals and a sample of their teachers before and after training to determine the effects of training on principals' leadership effectiveness and style range. The study provided only partial support for the Hersey–Blanchard theory. Principals were perceived as more effective three years after training than before training. However, no significant differences were found in principals' effectiveness immediately following training, nor in principals' leadership style range before and after training.[76]

[74]Ronald K. Hambleton and Ray Gumpert, "The Validity of Hersey and Blanchard's Theory of Leadership Effectiveness," *Group and Organization Studies*, 7 (1982), pp. 225–242.

[75]Paul Hersey, Arrigo L. Angelini, and Sofia Carakushansky, "The Impact of Situational Leadership and Classroom Structure on Learning Effectiveness," *Group and Organization Studies*, 7 (1982), pp. 216–224.

[76]Salvatore V. Pascarella and Fred C. Lunenburg, "A Field Test of Hersey and Blanchard's Situational Leadership Theory in a School Setting," *College Student Journal*, 21 (1988), pp. 33–37.

SUMMARY

1. Leadership is the process of influencing followers through the use of power. Using different bases of power results in different reactions from followers.
2. Leadership theories can be classified as trait, behavioral, or contingency.
3. Early trait studies, which compared leaders and nonleaders, led to few consistent findings. Later research on traits of effective leaders has been more fruitful.
4. Recent use of assessment centers to identify potential leaders has led to a revitalization of the trait approach. Now the trait approach has been extended to include job-related skills as well as traits in the identification of potential leaders.
5. The Iowa studies, Ohio State studies, and Michigan leadership studies identified distinct leader behaviors. Although no conclusive results emerged concerning leadership effectiveness, these behaviors have been incorporated into the more recent contingency theories of leadership.
6. The contingency theories of leadership are more complex than the trait and behavioral theories. The complexity arises from the necessity to consider several moderator variables in the process of leadership, such as leader–member relations, task structure, leader position power, subordinate motivation, and path–goal clarity.
7. The contingency theories are based on two different assumptions about leader adaptability. One approach assumes that leaders must change their behavior to fit the situation (House's path–goal theory); the other approach assumes that the leader must change the situation to fit the leader's behavior, which is assumed to be immutable (Fiedler's contingency theory).
8. As outgrowths and concurrent with the contingency theories, the various leadership styles are Tannenbaum and Schmidt's leadership-style continuum, Blake and Mouton's managerial grid, Reddin's three-dimensional leadership styles, and Hersey and Blanchard's situational leadership model.
9. The most important conclusion from leadership theory is that the traits or skills of a leader, leader behaviors, and various situational factors interacting together may ultimately determine a leader's effectiveness.

KEY TERMS

leadership
manager
leader
influence
legitimate power
reward power
coercive power
expert power
referent power
traits
skills
assessment center
authoritarian leadership
democratic leadership
laissez-faire leadership
initiating structure
consideration

production-centered leader
employee-centered leader
contingency theory
path–goal theory
directive leader
supportive leader
participative leader
achievement-oriented leader
leadership-style continuum
managerial grid
three-dimensional leadership style
situational leadership theory

DISCUSSION QUESTIONS

1. What are some common features in most definitions of leadership?
2. Which is more important for a leader to possess: a high degree of position power or a high degree of personal power? Explain.
3. What traits or skills appear to be associated with effective leaders? Support your position.
4. Discuss several different leadership styles and the leadership models associated with each. Be specific.
5. Why is it so important for an administrator to develop the ability to diagnose and evaluate a situation? Explain.

SUGGESTED READINGS

Jay A. Conger, *The Charismatic Leader: Behind the Mystique of Exceptional Leadership* (San Francisco: Jossey-Bass, 1989). A complete discussion of leadership, including some of the great leaders in history.

Larry Cuban, *The Managerial Imperative and the Practice of Leadership in Schools* (Ithaca: State University of New York Press, 1989). A scholarly treatment of leadership that integrates historical, theoretical, and experimental perspectives.

John W. Gardner, *On Leadership* (New York: Free Press, 1989). A masterpiece that appeals to the widest range of audiences and will stimulate further exploration into this crucial human activity.

Daniel E. Griffiths, Robert T. Stout, and Patrick B. Forsyth (eds.), *Leaders for America's Schools: The Report of the National Commission on Excellence in Educational Administration* (Berkeley, CA: McCutchan, 1988). Consists of a report by the National Commission on Excellence in Educational Administration and other papers, commissioned from scholars in the United States, Australia, and Canada, dealing with the practice of leadership.

James M. Kouzes and Barry Z. Posner, *The Leadership Challenge: How to Get Extraordinary Things Done in Organizations* (San Francisco: Jossey-Bass, 1990). A best-selling book on leadership that reveals five basic practices and ten specific behaviors that leadership involves.

John J. Muriel, *Strategic Leadership for Schools: Creating and Sustaining Productive Change* (San Francisco: Jossey-Bass, 1989). A sophisticated use of advanced thinking from business management in understanding critical issues in school administration.

Gary A. Yukl, *Leadership in Organizations*, 2nd ed. (Englewood Cliffs, NJ: Prentice-Hall, 1989). A comprehensive treatment of the topic of leadership, including theories and practical advice on how managers and school administrators can learn to practice effective leadership.

6

DECISION MAKING

FOCUSING QUESTIONS

1 Why is decision making an important activity in school administration?
2 What is rational decision making?
3 How do administrators make decisions?
4 What factors prevent school administrators from making optimal decisions?
5 What are the benefits and problems of using groups to make decisions?
6 How can group decision making be improved?

In this chapter, we attempt to answer these questions concerning decision making in school organizations. We begin our discussion by exploring the importance of decision making in schools. Then we provide some general decision-making models, describe the major steps in the decision-making process, and identify factors that limit rational decision making. We explore the advantages and disadvantages of group decision making and, finally, we examine techniques commonly used to improve group decision making.

THE NATURE OF DECISION MAKING

Decision making, universally defined as the process of choosing from among alternatives, is important to an understanding of educational administration because choice processes play an important role in motivation, leadership, communication, and organizational change. Decision making pervades all other administrative functions as well. Planning, organizing, staffing, directing, coordinating, and controlling all involve decision making.

School administrators at all levels along the hierarchy make decisions. These decisions may ultimately influence the school's clients—the students. All decisions, however, have some influence, whether large or small, on the performance of both faculty and students. Therefore, school administrators must develop decision-making skills because they make many decisions and those decisions will affect the organization. Furthermore, because school administrators are evaluated on the results of their decisions, the quality of the decisions is one criterion in judging administrators' effectiveness. Consider the following scenarios:

1. You are the principal of a small, rural high school, and it is one week away from the beginning of the state basketball tournament. The basketball team has a record of 18–2 for the season and is the favorite to win the Class B State Championship. You have just caught the star player of the basketball team, an all-state candidate, drinking an alcoholic beverage at a local restaurant. This is the player's second offense. According to board of education policy, a second offense carries a penalty of a four-week suspension from the team. The policy has not been consistently enforced by the various athletic coaches.
2. You are the assistant superintendent for business of a large, urban school district. The district operates its budgetary procedures on a variation of program planning budgeting systems (PPBS). There is a $100,000 surplus in this year's research and development account that you must spend before the end of the fiscal year. Three program priorities for the current school year are expansion of the vocational education facilities and curriculum, initiation of a new special education curriculum for the hearing impaired, and a districtwide remediation program for students who fall below the national average on the state-administered standardized achievement tests in the basic skills.
3. You are the superintendent of a wealthy, suburban school district. Student enrollment, increased by 20 percent during the past five years, has occurred primarily in grades 1–5. The current facilities of the school district can no longer accommodate the increased student population. The board of education has discussed several options: Merge with an adjacent urban school district, which has experienced a decline in enrollment; change the grade structure in the district from (K–5, 6–8, 9–12) to (K–4, 5–8, 9–12); build another elementary school; go on double sessions in the elementary schools; or rent one of the buildings from the nearby parochial school.

School administrators at different hierarchical levels and career stages face these problems or variations thereof every day. The elements of each problem differ: for example, athletic disciplinary action, allocation of funds from the research and development unit, and expansion of school facilities. Nevertheless, there is similarity among the scenarios; all require that a decision be made. The quality of the decision reached will not only have an impact on the school's clients but also will determine the school administrator's perceived value to the school district.

MODELS OF DECISION MAKING

Decision making is one type of activity that has been studied extensively through the use of models. Models attempt to describe theoretically and practically how school administrators make decisions. All models characteristically include the concept of decision making as rational behavior. That is, a decision maker will go through a logical sequence of decision-making steps.

Herbert Simon, the Nobel Prize–winning decision theorist, describes the decision-making process in three stages:[1]

1. *Intelligence Activity*. The decision maker searches the environment for conditions calling for decision making. (The term is borrowed from the military meaning of intelligence.)
2. *Design Activity*. The decision maker invents, develops, and analyzes possible courses of action to take.
3. *Choice Activity*. The decision maker selects a particular course of action from among those available.

After analyzing the actual decisions of executives across a spectrum of organizational types and administrative levels, including a school superintendent, Henry Mintzberg and his associates identify three phases in the decision-making process:[2]

1. *Identification Phase*. The decision maker recognizes a problem or opportunity and makes a diagnosis. It was found that severe, immediate problems did not have a very systematic, extensive diagnosis, but mild problems did.
2. *Development Phase*. The decision maker searches for existing standard procedures or solutions already in place or designs a new, tailor-made solution. It was found that the design process was a groping, trial-and-error process in which decision makers had only a vague idea of the ideal solution.
3. *Selection Phase*. The decision maker chooses a solution. There are three ways of making this selection: by the *judgment* of the decision maker; by *analysis* of the alternatives on a logical, systematic basis; and by *bargaining*

when the selection involves a group of decision makers and all the political maneuvering that this entails. Once the decision is formally accepted, an authorization is made.

Peter Drucker, another leading organizational theorist, contends there are six steps in the decision-making process: (1) define the problem; (2) analyze the problem; (3) develop alternative solutions to the problem; (4) decide on the best solution; (5) convert decisions into effective actions; and (6) monitor and assess the results.[3]

Every decision-making model has as its basis some more general model of decision making. Decision-making models can be classified broadly as classical and behavioral. As noted, all models include the concept of decision making as a rational activity. Decision-making models then can be thought of as ranging on a continuum from complete rationality to complete irrationality.

The Classical Decision-Making Model

The **classical model** of decision making assumes that decision making is a rational process whereby decision makers seek to maximize the chances of achieving their desired objectives by considering all possible alternatives, exploring all conceivable consequences from among the alternatives, and then making a decision. The classical model of decision making then is based on the concept of complete **rationality**. According to the classical model, the decision-making process can be broken down into logical steps. Numerous authors have provided their models of the decision-making process, but most include versions of the six steps we have included in our model: identifying problems, generating alternatives, evaluating alternatives, choosing alternatives, implementing decisions, and evaluating decisions (Figure 6-1).

---

[1]Herbert A. Simon, *The New Science of Management Decision* (New York: Harper & Row, 1960).
[2]Henry Mintzberg, Duru Raisinghani, and André Theoret, "The Structure of 'Unstructured' Decision Processes," *Administrative Science Quarterly*, 21 (1976), pp. 246–275.

[3]Peter F. Drucker, *Management: Tasks, Responsibilities, and Practices* (New York: Harper & Row, 1974).

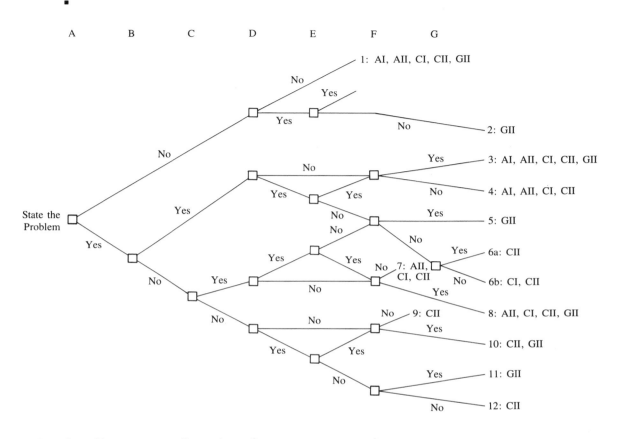

A. Does the problem possess a quality requirement?
B. Do I have sufficient information to make a high-quality decision?
C. Is the problem structured?
D. Is acceptance of the decision by subordinates important for effective implementation?
E. If I were to make the decision by myself, am I reasonably certain that it would be accepted by my subordinates?
F. Do subordinates share the organizational goals to be attained in solving this problem?
G. Is conflict among subordinates likely in preferred solutions?

FIGURE 6-1   The Decision-Making Process

Identifying the Problem   The first step in the decision-making process is identifying the problem. If there is no problem, there is no need to make a decision. A warning of a possible problem is a discrepancy between existing and desired conditions. For example, if a school district establishes an objective that 70 percent of the students will be reading on grade level and if only 30 percent of students are reading on grade level

at the end of the period, there is a gap between actual performance and the desired level of achievement. If the student dropout rate increases 25 percent over the preceding year, if students and parents file numerous complaints about the schools, if faculty grievances significantly increase, if new book and classroom supply deliveries are twelve months past due, and if the local newspaper runs a series of articles about deficiencies in school district operations, there are problems that require decisions.

Identifying problems is more difficult than one might suspect. One writer proposes four steps in problem identification: measure results, compare results to objectives, determine the significance of the difference, and communicate threshold differences to administration.[4] Another acknowledges similar steps in problem formulation: An administrator (1) must be alert to recognize a problem, (2) must determine a level of performance so that actual performance can be measured against it, (3) must divide complex problems into subproblems and set priorities based on the seriousness of the problem, and (4) must specify the problem in terms of what, where, when, and how big the deviations are from the performance standards previously set.[5]

Generating Alternatives   After identifying and defining the problem, the school administrator should generate but not evaluate a list of alternatives. That is, all possible alternatives should be included no matter how ridiculous they may first appear; a choice will be made later. Eliminating alternatives from the list too early decreases the options for the best solution. The administrator must then seek information regarding each alternative and its various consequences that will contribute to solving the problem.

Evaluating Alternatives   In evaluating alternatives, an additional search for information should be done. Joseph Reitz recommends three steps in the process:[6]

1. The decision maker must recognize all possible outcomes from each alternative solution, both positive and negative.
2. The decision maker must assess the value of each outcome, both positive and negative.
3. The decision maker must assess the likelihood of each possible outcome to each alternative.

Estimating the likelihood of each outcome prepares the decision maker to evaluate and compare alternatives, which is done under one of three conditions: certainty, risk, or uncertainty. These conditions force the school administrator into the area of quantitative decision making. An in-depth quantitative analysis of alternatives and their outcomes is beyond the scope of this book. However, we give a brief definition of each term, to clarify the process.

Certainty exists when the decision maker knows exactly what the probabilities of the outcome of each alternative will be. Thus, she must estimate the probabilities of the occurrence of the various outcomes.[7] *Risk* exists when the decision maker estimates the probabilities of the outcome of each alternative. That is, success is not 100 percent assured. Thus, predictions can be made, but risk is associated with the various alternatives.[8] *Uncertainty* exists when the decision maker does not know what the probabilities of the outcome of each alternative will be; that is, the likelihood of success or failure associated with alternatives is not clear.[9] In working through the three conditions of certainty, risk, and uncertainty, the decision maker should rank order all alternatives from best to worst according to their likelihood of providing the greatest payoffs to the school district.

[4]Jonathan Rosenhead (ed.), *Rational Analysis for a Problematic World: Problem Structuring Methods for Complexity, Uncertainty and Conflict* (New York, Wiley, 1990).
[5]Edward F. McClennen, *Rationality and Dynamic Choices: Foundational Explorations* (New York: Cambridge University Press, 1990).
[6]H. Joseph Reitz, *Behavior in Organizations*, 3rd ed. (Homewood, IL: Dow Jones-Irwin, 1989).

[7]Richard M. Oliver and John Q. Smith (eds.), *Influence Diagrams, Belief Nets, and Decision Analysis* (New York: Wiley, 1990).
[8]Keinosuke Fukunaga, *Introduction to Statistical Pattern Recognition*, 2nd ed. (San Diego: Academic Press, 1990).
[9]James M. Antill and Ronald W. Woodhead, *Critical Path Methods in Construction Practice*, 4th ed. (New York: Wiley, 1990).

Choosing an Alternative   The next step in the decision-making process involves choosing the alternative that the school administrator considers most effective; that is, the one that allows the administrator to solve the problem and accomplish the school district's objectives. The choice can be difficult even when outcomes have been evaluated based on some comparable criteria. James March and Herbert Simon, two leading decision theorists, have proposed five types of alternatives:[10]

1. A *good alternative* has a high probability of positively valued outcomes and a low probability of negatively valued outcomes.
2. A *bland alternative* has a low probability of both positively and negatively valued outcomes.
3. A *mixed alternative* has a high probability of both positively and negatively valued outcomes.
4. A *poor alternative* has a low probability of positively valued outcomes and a high probability of negatively valued outcomes.
5. An *uncertain alternative* is one for which the decision maker cannot assess the relative probabilities of outcomes. (This alternative was discussed earlier).

Some combination of these types of alternatives will result in more difficult choices than will other combinations. Consider a school administrator who is faced with two alternatives. If one alternative is good and the other is bland, mixed, poor, or uncertain, then choosing an alternative is easy. Now consider the choice between any other combination of two alternatives, excluding the good alternative. It is difficult to choose between a bland and mixed alternative, a bland and a poor alternative, and so on.

For instance, consider the decision of an athletic director of a major university to hire an interim basketball coach to complete the season because the existing coach suddenly died just prior to the opening of the season. One alternative (uncertain) is to hire a former high school basketball coach with an outstanding record but no experience at the college level. Thus, the coach is virtually untested at the university level. Another alternative (poor) is to hire a mediocre coach from a nearby small college or junior college. A third alternative (mixed) is to hire an outstanding coach who won several NCAA championships but who was fired by his school administration for manifesting erratic and irrational behavior during games and for striking a player. While one would expect a good season, there is also the chance of alienating the school administration and a repeat of the irrational behavior and player abuse. The final alternative (bland) is to select one of the assistant coaches to assume the head coaching position. While skilled in other areas, neither assistant coach possesses the technical court skills nor the personality to motivate players. Such a decision is likely to produce an average season in terms of record and relations with the school's administration and players.

Implementing the Decision   Once a decision is made to choose an alternative solution, it must be implemented. The decision maker will have already considered all conceivable problems that may be associated with the implementation of the solution during the previous step in the decision-making process. However, in school organizations, administrators are dependent on others to implement decisions. That is, a school administrator must have skills not only for problem solving but also for "selling" the decision to those affected by it.[11]

Evaluating the Decision   The decision-making process does not end when the decision is implemented. The school administrator must evaluate the extent to which the solution achieved the school district's objectives. Measuring actual

---

[10]James G. March and Herbert A. Simon, *Organizations* (New York: Wiley, 1958); Reitz, *Behavior in Organizations*.

[11]William R. King et al., *Management Science: A Decision-Support Approach* (Reading, MA: Addison-Wesley, 1990).

performance against performance specified in the objectives is one way of evaluating success. If a discrepancy exists between actual results and expected objectives, then the decision-making process must be recycled. Changes in the alternative that was chosen, how it was implemented, or the determination of objectives are necessary.

For example, it is possible that the objectives established are unrealistic and that no reasonable alternative could result in a successful decision. Such a situation stresses the importance of determining measurable objectives. Unless specific objectives are set, mutually agreed on, and met at all levels of operation, there will be relatively little value or basis for measuring the effectiveness of the school district's decisions.

The Behavioral Decision-Making Model

The classical decision-making model, discussed earlier, characterizes the decision maker as completely rational. More specifically, he is assumed to (1) recognize all possible alternative solutions to the problem, (2) be aware of all possible consequences of each alternative, (3) be able to evaluate the consequences against his value system, (4) be able to rank the alternatives in the order in which they are likely to meet his objectives, and (5) select the alternative that maximizes his objectives.[12] The classical model assumes that the decision maker has perfect information (i.e., is aware of a problem, knows all alternatives and their possible consequences, and possesses a criterion for making the decision) and seeks to maximize some expected objective.

Frequently, school administrators are not aware that problems exist. Even when they are, they do not systematically search for all possible alternative solutions. They are limited by time constraints, cost, and the ability to process information. So they generate a partial list of alter-

native solutions to the problem based on their experience, intuition, advice from others, and perhaps even some creative thought. Rationality is, therefore, limited. Simon coined the term *bounded rationality* to describe the decision maker who would like to make the best decisions but normally settles for less than the optimal.[13]

In contrast to the completely rational model of decision making (classical decision-making model), Daniel Feldman and Hugh Arnold summarize **bounded rationality** as follows:[14]

1. Decisions will always be based on an incomplete and, to some degree, inadequate comprehension of the true nature of the problem being faced.
2. Decision makers will never succeed in generating all possible alternative solutions for consideration.
3. Alternatives are always evaluated incompletely because it is impossible to predict accurately all consequences associated with each alternative.
4. The ultimate decision regarding which alternative to choose must be based on some criterion other than maximization or optimization because it is impossible ever to determine which alternative is optimal.

Satisficing   One version of bounded rationality is the principle of **satisficing**. This approach to decision making involves choosing the first alternative that satisfies minimal standards of acceptability without exploring all possibilities. This is the usual approach taken by decision makers. James March and Simon express it this way: "Most human decision making, whether individual or organizational, is concerned with the discovery and selection of satisfactory alternatives; only in exceptional cases is it concerned

---

[12]Reitz, *Behavior in Organizations*.

[13]Herbert A. Simon, *Administrative Behavior*, 3rd ed. (New York: Free Press, 1976).

[14]Daniel C. Feldman and Hugh J. Arnold, *Managing Individual and Group Behavior in Organizations* (New York: McGraw-Hill, 1983).

with the discovery and selection of optimal alternatives."[15]

Contextual Rationality and Procedural Rationality

March and Simon later proposed two other forms of bounded rationality: contextual rationality and procedural rationality. **Contextual rationality** suggests that a decision maker is embedded in a network of environmental influences that constrain purely rational decision making.[16] Although the school administrator wants to make optimal decisions, these are mediated by such "realities of organizational life as internal and external politics, conflict-resolution requirements, distribution of power and authority, and limits of human rationality."[17] Furthermore, schools have vague and ambiguous goals. This, coupled with the lack of a clearly defined success criteria, leads to policies and procedures designed to maintain stability and control, and the objectives of the school as a social institution are to achieve major changes in the student. These changes are not restricted to cognitive behavior (learning) but include a wide range of social, emotional, physical, and, in some cases, moral behavior. Thus, school administrators must pursue multiple and often conflicting goals, within a network of environmental constraints, that restrict the maximization of goal achievement.[18]

We noted that bounded rationality, satisficing, and contextual rationality limit perfectly rational decision making. This results in the inability of decision makers to "maximize" outcomes. What then can school administrators do to improve their decisions in view of the constraints on complete rationality implied by the classical decision-making model? Simon proposes the principle of **procedural rationality**.[19] Instead of focusing on generating and evaluating all possible alternative solutions to a problem and their consequences, decision makers focus on the procedures used in making decisions. Thus, techniques are perfected and used to make the best possible decisions, including operations research, systems analysis, strategic planning, program planning budgeting systems (PPBS), management information systems (MIS), and so on, each prescribed to improve the reliability of decisions. Rational procedures are not designed to focus on generating and evaluating all available information to solve problems, but they are aimed at adequate acquisition and processing of relevant information.

Retrospective Rationality   **Retrospective rationality** is another major form of decision making.[20] By this we mean that decision makers devote considerable energy in justifying the rationality of decisions they have already made. One author puts it this way: "Now that I have made my choice, I need to find good reasons for it."[21]

Evidence supports the notion that decision makers tend to be defensive about their decisions.[22] Substantial dissonance occurs when a decision turns out to be unsuccessful. For this reason, many organizations do not conduct thorough evaluations of expensive programs that are implemented, for fear of exposing faulty decisions. Another aspect of retrospective rationality is the tendency for decision makers to take personal responsibility for successful decision outcomes while denying responsibility for un-

[15]March and Simon, *Organizations*, pp. 140–141.

[16]James G. March, "Bounded Rationality, Ambiguity, and the Engineering of Choice," *Bell Journal of Economics*, 9 (1978), pp. 587–608.

[17]Thomas J. Sergiovanni et al., *Educational Governance and Administration*, 2nd ed. (Englewood Cliffs, NJ: Prentice-Hall, 1987), p. 159.

[18]Karen S. Cook and Margaret Levi (eds.), *The Limit of Rationality* (Chicago: University of Chicago Press, 1990).

[19]Herbert A. Simon, "Rationality as a Process and as a Product of Thought," *American Economic Review*, 68 (1978), pp. 1–16.

[20]Barry M. Staw, "Rationality and Justification in Organizational Life," in B. M. Staw and L. L. Cummings (eds.), *Research in Organizational Behavior*, Vol 2. (Greenwich, CT: JAI Press, 1980), pp. 45–80.

[21]Bernard M. Bass, *Organizational Decision Making* (Homewood, IL: Irwin, 1983), p. 142.

[22]Gary Johns, *Organizational Behavior: Understanding Life at Work* (Glenview, IL: Scott, Foresman, 1983).

successful ones.[23] For example, students are willing to take full responsibility for good grades, while bad grades are attributed to poor teaching.

Incrementalizing   Another approach to decision making, sometimes referred to as "muddling through," involves making small changes (increments) in the existing situation. Charles Lindblom, its author, distinguishes between completely rational decision making based on the classical model and **incrementalizing**, which is based on successive limited comparisons.[24] The rational approach to decision making involves determining objectives, considering all possible alternative solutions, exploring all conceivable consequences of the alternative solutions, and finally choosing the optimal alternative solution that will maximize the achievement of the agreed-on objectives. Incrementalizing, on the other hand, does not require agreement on objectives, an exhaustive search of all possible alternatives and their consequences, or selection of the optimal alternative. Instead, Lindblom argues that "no more than small or incremental steps—no more than muddling through—is ordinarily possible."[25] In other words, incrementalizing is a process of successive limited comparisons of alternative courses of action with one another until decision makers arrive at an alternative on which they agree.

The Garbage Can Model   Earlier we noted that while the school administrator wants to make optimal decisions, the realities of organizational life—including politics, time constraints, finances, and the inability to process information—limit purely rational decision making. Applying the classical decision-making model

(rational decision making) is particularly troublesome for schools. The technologies of teaching are varied and not well understood. Moreover, schools have multiple and conflicting goals that are vague and ambiguous. And schools lack clearly defined success criteria. Thus, problems and solutions cannot be translated easily into a logical sequence of steps (classical decision-making model).[26] In accordance with this view, David Cohen and his associates conceptualized this decision-making process as a **garbage can model**.[27] As members of a school or school district generate problems and alternative solutions to problems, they deposit them into the garbage can. The mixture is seen as a collection of solutions that must be matched to problems. Participants are also deposited into the garbage can. Mixing problems, solutions, and decision participants results in interaction patterns leading to decisions that often do not follow the classical decision-making model sequence.

A number of studies in educational administration have specified and tested comparative models of decision making, using the classical and behavioral models as one of several. For example, one study found that high schools were more likely to resemble the behavioral model (bounded rationality) than were elementary schools, which more closely resembled the classical model.[28] According to the researchers, because high schools were typically departmentalized and had more diverse goals, they could be characterized as more loosely coupled than elementary schools.

Several other studies address some of the assumptions of bounded rationality. Research on

[23]Anthony G. Greenwald, "The Totalitarian Ego: Fabrication and Revision of Personal History," *American Psychologist*, 35 (1980), pp. 603–618.
[24]Charles E. Lindblom, "The Science of Muddling Through," *Public Administration Review*, 19 (1959), pp. 79–88.
[25]Charles E. Lindblom, "Still Muddling, Not Yet Through," *Public Administration Review*, 20 (1959), p. 517.

[26]Ira Horowitz, *Organization and Decision Theory* (Norwell, MA: Kluwer Academic, 1989).
[27]David M. Cohen, James G. March, and Johan D. Olsen, "A Garbage Can Model of Organizational Choice," *Administrative Science Quarterly*, 17 (1972), pp. 1–25.
[28]William A. Firestone and Robert E. Herriott, "Images of Organization and the Promotion of Change," in R. G. Corwin (ed.), *Research in Sociology of Education and Socialization*, Vol. II (Greenwich, CT: JAI Press, 1981), pp. 221–260.

ADMINISTRATIVE ADVICE 6-1

TIME-MANAGEMENT TIPS

If you are like many harried school administrators, get control of your time by using the following management techniques:

- *Use a Notebook with an Agenda and Calendar and Carry It with You*. If properly implemented, this notebook should evolve into a portable administrative resource center.
- *Start Each Day with a Five-Minute Meeting with Your Secretary*. You can increase your secretarial staff's efficiency greatly by outlining your priorities and goals daily.
- *Go Through Your Mail and In-Box, Handling Any Piece of Paper Only Once*. No communication that comes across your desk should require more than one reading. After you have read it, route it, file it, act on it, or toss it.
- *Delegate*. Deciding what, when, how, and to whom to delegate are formidable administrative decisions.
- *Learn to Say No*. Don't get stuck on tasks and responsibilities that don't correspond to your priorities.
- *Control Visitors, Especially the "Drop-In" Kind*. Instruct your secretary to answer as many questions as possible, refer calls to other appropriate staff, take information from callers, and pass on to you only those calls you need to take.

- *Put a Large Wastebasket to Use*. It usually takes more time to locate vaguely recalled "old treasures" than they are worth. If you can't act on it and it isn't worth filing, throw it out.
- *Streamline Meetings*. Provide each person with an agenda prior to the meeting. Note whether each item is intended as information or requires action.
- *Use Your Subconscious Time to Your Advantage*. Research shows many creative decisions can result from subconscious processing of conscious concerns. Try submitting pending matters to your subconscious at bedtime and let it work on them all night.
- *Clean Off Your Desk Every Night Before You Leave*. A cluttered desk wastes time and is a sure sign of disorganization to anyone who enters your office. Starting the day with a desk piled with yesterday's concerns is demoralizing.

Source: Adapted from Jack J. Bimrose, "Try These Time Management Tips," *School Administrator*, 44 (1987), pp. 22–23. Used by permission.

administrative behavior in schools is consistent in identifying the demands on the administrator as fragmented, rapid fire, and difficult to prioritize. For example, one study noted that the fragmented and unpredictable workday of principals was not conducive to rational decision making.[29] (See Administrative Advice 6-1.)

Vroom–Yetton Normative Model

Victor Vroom and Philip Yetton have devised a sophisticated model of decision making that involves a clear statement of what the leader is supposed to accomplish: (1) decision quality, (2) decision acceptance, and (3) timeliness.[30] The model first identifies five decision-making

[29]Van Cleve Morris et al., *Urban Principal: Discretionary Decision Making in a Large Educational Organization*, Research Report (Chicago: University of Illinois at Chicago Circle, 1981).

[30]Victor H. Vroom and Arthur G. Jago, *The New Leadership: Managing Participation in Organizations* (Englewood Cliffs, NJ: Prentice-Hall, 1988).

styles. Second, it identifies criteria for choosing among the decision-making styles. Third, it describes attributes of decision problems that determine which levels of subordinate participation are feasible. Finally, it offers the school administrator rules for making the final choice from among an array of feasible alternatives.

Decision Effectiveness   As noted, three critical aspects influence overall effectiveness, or **decision feasibility**: quality, acceptance, and timeliness.

Decision Quality. Decision quality refers to the extent to which a decision is effective. Different problems have different quality requirements. For example, decisions such as a technique to evaluate teacher competence, the assignment of teachers to specific tasks, the selection of textbooks and other instructional materials, and the development of policies and procedures for operating a school require high decision quality. Conversely, a decision on what brand of milk to place in the school cafeteria or which teacher to put on a school committee when all are equally qualified requires low decision quality. Generally, when decision quality is important and subordinates have the expertise to make the decision, a participatory decision-making style leads to more effective decisions than does a more autocratic style.

Decision Acceptance. Decision acceptance refers to the extent to which decisions are accepted by those subordinates who must implement them. Even if a leader's decision is high in decision quality, the decision will not be effective if it is not implemented. Thus, school administrators need to consider acceptance just as important as quality in arriving at effective decisions. Research demonstrates that subordinate involvement in decision making is advantageous for arriving at better-quality decisions and for promoting acceptance. House's path–goal model (see Chapter 5) also shows that if subordinates have influence in decision making, they tend to perceive decisions as their own and are motivated to implement them successfully.

Timeliness. Timeliness refers to the amount of time available to the decision maker to arrive at a decision. Participatory decision making is very costly in terms of time. If time is an important factor, the leader may need to choose a more autocratic leadership style. If, however, a long-term development of the skills and competencies of the group is the most important criterion, then choosing a more participative style may be more productive.

Decision-Making Styles   Vroom and Yetton identify and describe five alternative decision-making styles that can be placed on a continuum from highly autocratic to highly participatory (Table 6-1). The styles labeled *A* are basically autocratic, those labeled *C* are consultative, and those labeled *G* are group styles. Roman numerals identify variants of each style. As you study each style in Table 6-1, try to determine which of these styles you used in a given situation. Test this by thinking of leadership situations you have encountered on your job and see if you can classify your styles in terms the Vroom–Yetton taxonomy.

Choosing the Correct Decision-Making Style   According to Vroom and Yetton, one leader can use all five styles as listed in Table 6-1, depending on the situation. As a decision maker, the leader may be autocratic in one situation and participatory in the next. Thus, different types of situations require different types of styles. The key to effective administration is the ability to correctly diagnose the situation and then choose an appropriate decision-making style.

The Vroom–Yetton normative model contains a set of seven diagnostic questions that an administrator can use in determining which decision-making style to choose in any given situation. These diagnostic questions are based on a set of seven rules aimed at simplifying the selection of the appropriate decision-making style. The first three rules focus on the quality of the decision, and the remaining four deal with decision acceptance (Table 6-2).

Vroom and Yetton use a decision tree to relate the seven diagnostic questions, listed at the bot-

TABLE 6 ▪ 1   Five Decision-Making Styles of the Vroom–Yetton Model

STYLE	METHOD
AI	Solve the problem or make the decision yourself using the information available to you at the present time.
AII	Obtain any necessary information from subordinates, then decide on a solution to the problem yourself. You may or may not tell subordinates the purpose of your questions or give information about the problem or decision on which you are working. The input provided by them is clearly in response to your request for specific information. They do not play a role in the definition of the problem or in generating or evaluating alternative solutions.
CI	Share the problem with the relevant subordinates individually, getting their ideas and suggestions without bringing them together as a group. Then *you* make the decision. This decision may or may not reflect your subordinates' influence.
CII	Share the problem with your subordinates in a group meeting where you obtain their ideas and suggestions. Then, *you* make the decision, which may or may not reflect your subordinates' influence.
GII	Share the problem with your subordinates as a group. Together you generate and evaluate alternatives and attempt to reach agreement (consensus) on a solution. Your role is much like that of chairman, coordinating the discussion, keeping it focused on the problem, and ensuring that the critical issues are discussed. You can provide the group with information or ideas that you have but you do not try to "press" them to adopt "your" solution and are willing to accept and implement any solution that has the support of the entire group.

SOURCE: Adapted from Victor H. Vroom and Philip W. Yetton, *Leadership and Decision Making.* © 1973, the University of Pittsburg Press. Used by permission.

tom of the decision tree, to the appropriate decision-making style (Figure 6-2). Starting at the left, the administrator answers each question along the path. At the end of each path is a list of acceptable decision-making styles. Some paths end with one acceptable style; others end with five acceptable styles. To be acceptable, the style must meet the criteria of the seven decision rules that protect quality and acceptance. If more than one style remains after the test of both quality and acceptance, the third most important aspect of a decision—timeliness—determines the single, best style that should be used in a given situation.

Training Administrators in Decision Making   The rationale of the Vroom–Yetton model is that administrators should ask themselves a series of diagnostic questions when they confront a problem situation and select an approach to solving

the problem based on their responses to the diagnostic questions. However, the number of questions and alternative decision-making styles make their problem-solving process complex. Therefore, Vroom has introduced a training program to help administrators learn the prescriptions of his theory.[31] TELOS (marketed by the Kepner Tregoe organization) is a version of this training.[32]

In consultation with Vroom, the TELOS training explains the theory and provides administrators with practice in examining their own decision-making styles. Essentially, the

---

[31]Victor H. Vroom, "Can Leaders Learn How to Lead?" *Organizational Dynamics*, 4 (1976), pp. 17–28.
[32]Blanchard B. Smith, "The TELOS Program and the Vroom–Yetton Model," in J. G. Hunt and L. L. Larson (eds.), *Crosscurrents in Leadership* (Carbondale: Southern Illinois University Press, 1979), pp. 39–60.

program exposes administrators to a standard-ized set of cases and allows them to make a choice among responses. A computer, which generates a detailed analysis of decision-making styles, processes the responses. Administrators receive printouts showing how their decision-making style compares with other trainees in the workshop. They are also able to form profiles of

---

TABLE 6 ■ 2   Rules for Decision-Making Selection

RULES TO PROTECT THE QUALITY OF THE DECISION

1. *Leader information rule*. If decision quality is important and the leader does not possess enough information or expertise to solve the problem by himself, then eliminate AI from the feasible set.
2. *Goal congruence rule*. If decision quality is important and subordinates are not likely to pursue the organization goals in their efforts to solve this problem, then eliminate GII from the feasible set.
3. *Unstructured problem rule*. In decisions in which decision quality is important, if the leader lacks the necessary information or expertise to solve the problem by herself, and if the problem is unstructured, the problem-solving method should provide for interaction among subordinates likely to possess relevant information. Accordingly, eliminate AI, AII, and CI from the feasible set.

RULES TO PROTECT THE ACCEPTANCE OF THE DECISION

4. *Acceptance rule*. If decision acceptance by subordinates is critical to effective implemen-tation and if it is not certain that an autocratic decision will be accepted, eliminate AI and AII from the feasible set.
5. *Conflict rule*. If decision acceptance is critical and if an autocratic decision is not certain to be accepted and disagreement among subordinates in methods of attaining the orga-nizational goal is likely, the problem-solving methods should enable those in disagree-ment to resolve their differences with full knowledge of the problem. Accordingly, under these conditions, eliminate AI, AII, and CI, which permit no interaction among subordi-nates and therefore provide no opportunity for those in conflict to resolve their differ-ences, from the feasible set. Their use runs the risk of leaving some of the subordinates with less than the needed commitment to the final decision.
6. *Fairness rule*. If decision quality is unimportant but acceptance of the decision is critical and not certain to result from an autocratic decision, the decision process must generate the needed acceptance. The decision process should permit subordinates to interact with one another and negotiate over the fair method of resolving any differences with the full responsibility on them for determining what is fair and equitable. Accordingly, under these circumstances, eliminate AI, AII, CI, and CII from the feasible set.
7. *Acceptance priority rule*. If acceptance is critical, but not certain to result from an autocratic decision, and if subordinates are motivated to pursue the organizational goals represented in the problem, then methods that provide equal partnership in the deci-sion-making process can provide greater acceptance without risking decision quality. Accordingly, eliminate AI, AII, CI, and CII from the feasible set.

SOURCE: Adapted from Victor H. Vroom and Philip W. Yetton, *Leadership and Decision Making.* © 1973, the University of Pittsburg Press. Used by permission.

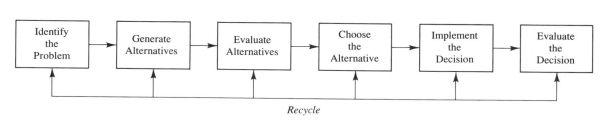

FIGURE 6-2   The Decision Tree (SOURCE: Adapted from Victor H. Vroom and Philip W. Yetton, *Leadership and Decision Making.* © 1973, the University of Pittsburg Press. Used by permission.)

the extent to which they vary their styles. Subsequently, cases are reanalyzed, and small-group discussions take place, where trainees may feel considerable peer pressure to shift their decision-making style. Generally, this pressure causes trainees to adopt new decision-making styles that are more congruent with the Vroom–Yetton theory.

BENEFITS OF GROUP DECISION MAKING

Up to this point, we have been discussing decision making as an individual activity. We pictured a school administrator working at a hectic pace and making decisions under pressure with little time for reflective planning. But more often than not, a number of people participate in important decisions in schools, and they come together to solve school problems. Whether decision making involves individual or group activity, the process requires the individual or group to go through the typical decision-making steps: identifying the problem, generating alternatives, evaluating alternatives, choosing an alternative, implementing the decision, and evaluating the decision. We pointed out, however, that this description of decision making is limited by various forms of bounded rationality and thus misrepresents how decisions are actually made in school organizations.

In the group decision-making process, decisions are the product of interpersonal decision processes and group dynamics.[33] Thus, the school administrator must be concerned with leading the group from a collection of individuals to a collaborative decision-making unit. This implies that school administrators must develop group decision-making skills as well as skills in individual decision making.

School administrators and faculty alike spend large amounts of time participating in committees that are attempting to make decisions. Superintendents are usually chosen by boards of education. Principals are selected by committees consisting of a variety of organizational participants including administrators, teachers, students, and sometimes community members. Faculty committees usually decide on which textbooks to adopt. Formal review committees normally process curriculum modifications. These activities are intended to bring school participants into the organization's decision-making process.

It is believed that group decision making results in a number of benefits over individual decision making, including increased decision quality, creativity, acceptance, understanding, judgment, and accuracy. Experts advise school districts that a proven method to increase school effectiveness is to involve school employees in

---

[33]Bobby R. Patton (ed.), *Decision Making Group Interaction*, 3rd ed. (New York: Harper & Row, 1989).

the decision-making process.[34] With these generalizations in mind, the benefits of participative decision making include the following:[35]

1. *Decision Quality*. A greater sum total of knowledge and information is accessible in a group than in any of its members. Members can often fill in each others' information gaps. Groups are more vigilant, can generate more ideas, and can evaluate ideas better than individuals.

2. *Decision Creativity*. Groups provide a greater number of approaches to a problem because individuals are more likely to be close-minded in their thinking. Because group members do not have identical approaches, each can contribute by getting people to become more open-minded in their thinking. Group participation increases performance. More participation leads to more creative thinking, which often results in more feasible solutions to problems.

3. *Decision Acceptance*. Participation in decision making increases acceptance of the decision or the solution to the problem. This idea is exemplified in the movement toward site-based decision making[36] Site-based decision-making, however, is not viable in school districts that are highly centralized. (See Administrative Advice 6-2).

4. *Decision Understanding*. Group participation increases understanding of the decision. When group members have been involved in the decision-making process, further information about the decision does not have to be provided to them. Moreover, members comprehend the decision better because they were involved in the developmental stages of the decision process.

5. *Decision Judgment*. Groups are more effective at establishing objectives, identifying alternatives, and evaluating alternatives because of the increased knowledge and viewpoints available to them.

6. *Decision Accuracy*. Because group members evaluate each other's thinking, major errors, "bloopers," and "glitches" tend to be avoided. Poor or nonfeasible alternatives are more likely to be spotted.

Do groups actually make better decisions than individuals? The discussion here suggests that they do. Reviews of research on the benefits of group decision making, however, are inconsistent. Research related specifically to the relationship between participative decision making and decision outcomes reveals ambiguity or nonsupport for the relationship.[37] Most research in this area assumes the benefits of teacher participation as a given.[38] The benefits of group decision making are probably not directly related to decision outcomes but instead are more associated with morale and job satisfaction.[39] One review of research concludes that "groups usually produce more and better solutions to problems than do individuals working alone."[40] And two prominent consultants claim the benefits of participatory decision making over individual

[34]John I. Goodlad (ed.), *The Ecology of School Renewal* (Chicago: University of Chicago Press, 1987); Kenneth A. Sirotnik and Jeannie Oaks (eds.), *Critical Perspectives on the Organization and Improvement of Schooling* (Boston: Martinus Nijhoff, 1986).

[35]Andrew J. DuBrin, *Foundations of Organizational Behavior: An Applied Perspective* (Englewood Cliffs, NJ: Prentice-Hall, 1984).

[36]Kenneth A. Sirotnik, "The School as the Center of Change," in T. J. Sergiovanni and J. H. Moore (eds.), *Schooling for Tomorrow: Directing Reforms to Issues That Count* (Needham Heights, MA: Allyn and Bacon, 1988), pp. 89–113.

[37]James A. Conway, "The Myth, Mystery and Mastery of Participative Decision Making in Education," *Educational Administrative Quarterly*, 20 (1984), pp. 11–40.

[38]Stephen J. Andriole, *Handbook of Decision Support Systems* (Blue Ridge Summit, PA: TAB Books, 1990).

[39]Wayne K. Hoy and Cecil G. Miskel, *Educational Administration: Theory, Research and Practice*, 4th ed. (New York: McGraw-Hill, 1991).

[40]Malcolm E. Shaw, *Group Dynamics*, 3rd ed. (New York: McGraw-Hill, 1981), p. 78.

ADMINISTRATIVE ADVICE 6-2

■

QUESTIONS DISTRICTS SHOULD ASK BEFORE IMPLEMENTING SITE-BASED DECISION MAKING

Site-based decision making means creating ownership for those responsible for carrying out decisions by involving them directly in the decision-making process. Before implementing site-based decision making, school districts should ask the following questions:

- What do we mean by site-based decision making?
- What roles need to be redefined, and how will we provide the necessary training and support?
- What are the parameters, expectations, or limitations of local site-based decision making?
- What do we know about the change process, and how does this apply to our situation?
- To what degree will variations and differences among schools within the district be accommodated?

- What underlying conditions must be present for site-based decision making to work? How can we clarify and communicate them?
- What can we learn from other organizations about making the transition?

Source: Adapted from Cynthia R. Harrison, Joellen P. Killion, and James E. Mitchell, "Site-Based Management: The Realities of Implementing," *Educational Leadership*, 46 (1989), pp. 55–58. Used by permission of the Association for Supervision and Curriculum Development. Copyright © 1989 by ASCD.

decision making.[41] The conclusions of the latter three works are qualified by the exact nature of the problem being solved and the composition of the group making the decision. More specifically, groups should perform better than individuals when (1) group members differ in relevant skills and abilities, as long as they don't differ so much that conflict occurs; (2) some division of labor can occur; (3) memory of facts is an important issue; and (4) individual judgments can be averaged to arrive at a group position.[42] (See Administrative Advice 6-3.)

Controversy, however, arises when traditional roles are shifted, as the PRO/CON Debate points out.

PROBLEMS IN GROUP DECISION MAKING

We have pointed out the potential benefits of group decision making over individual decisions; however, the social nature of group processes can negatively affect performance. More specifically, three tendencies in particular can damage group decision processes; groupthink, risky shift, and escalation of commitment.[43]

Groupthink

Irving Janis coined the term **groupthink**, which happens when in-group pressures lead to a de-

[41]Colin Eden and Jim Radford (eds.), *Tackling Strategic Problems: The Role of Group Decision Support* (Newbury Park, CA: Sage, 1990).

[42]Johns, *Organizational Behavior: Understanding Life at Work*.

[43]John B. Miner, *Organizational Behavior: Performance and Productivity* (New York: Random House, 1988).

ADMINISTRATIVE ADVICE 6-3
∎
COLLABORATIVE DECISION MAKING

Does involving teachers in decision making really improve functioning, or is it just another fashionable theory? The current reform movement in education suggests that it does. Here are some characteristics of a collaborative style. Administrators may want to check these against their own decision-making behavior. In the collaborative style, the supervisor

- Works with subordinates to identify and resolve teaching-related problems; guides and assists them in setting the standards and goals.
- Helps subordinates set challenging goals for themselves by channeling and molding their own motivation.
- Educates subordinates to check on their own performance and promotes self-evaluation; encourages their achievements and counsels them on how to learn from their failures.

- Provides opportunities for subordinates to pursue and move into areas of growth and development.
- Mediates conflict by interpreting rules rationally, explaining their usefulness and the logical consequences of violating them.
- Allows subordinates to develop and install new methods and helps them do it; induces *their* innovation.

Source: Adapted from Kenneth J. Tewel, "Collaborative Supervision: Theory into Practice," *NASSP Bulletin*, 73 (1989), p. 76. Used by permission.

---

terioration in mental efficiency, poor testing of reality, and lax moral judgments.[44] It tends to occur in highly cohesive groups in which the group members' desire for consensus becomes more important than evaluating problems and solutions realistically. An example would be the top administrative cabinet (the superintendent and her associate superintendents) of a school district who have worked together for many years. They know each other well and think as a cohesive unit rather than as a collection of individuals. Similarly, when a group of teachers collectively decides to go on strike, the decision may be a product of groupthink. Janis identifies eight symptoms of groupthink:[45]

1. *Invulnerability*. Most or all group members develop an illusion of invulnerability, which causes them to become overly optimistic and take extreme risks.
2. *Rationalization*. Group members collectively rationalize in order to discount warnings that might lead them to reconcile their assumptions before they recommit themselves to their past policy decisions.
3. *Morality*. Group members develop an unquestioned belief in the group's inherent morality, inclining the members to ignore ethical or moral consequences of their decisions.
4. *Stereotyping*. Group members develop stereotyped views of opposition leaders as too evil to warrant genuine attempts to negotiate or as too weak and stupid to counter whatever risky attempts are made to defeat their purposes.
5. *Pressure*. Group members apply direct pressure on any member who expresses strong

---

[44]Irving L. Janis, *Groupthink: Psychological Studies of Policy Decisions and Fiascoes*, 2nd ed. (Boston: Houghton Mifflin, 1982).

[45]Ibid.

PRO/CON DEBATE

■

PRINCIPAL POWER

With the introduction of collective negotiations into most educational workplaces in the late 1960s, principals' roles changed. For the last twenty years, principals have administered the negotiated contract in their buildings. Many principals who have served both before and after collective negotiations indicate that their decision-making discretion was limited by the constraints of union contracts. In the 1990s, the school as a workplace will be altered again in the area of principal decision making. Employee participation in decision making is evident in the most innovative recent contracts.

QUESTION Does teacher participation in decision making enhance principals' power?

ARGUMENTS PRO

1   Power increases when it is shared. When principals share decisions with other stakeholders in the system (teachers, parents, students), all become more responsible for outcomes.

2   By becoming facilitators of the decision-making process, principals enhance their personal power as well as their role power.

3   Principals who are experienced in shared decision making point out that, like the students who participate in establishing rules of behavior in the classroom, teachers are tougher on themselves than are principals.

4   As teachers assume greater responsibility for improving the educational environment of the school, principals become the leaders of leaders. The principal leads rather than manages.

5   Principals' roles will change for the better. For example, most articles in professional journals on shared decision making are written by administrators or administrator–teacher teams.

6   The national reform literature is filled with recommendations that teachers assume more responsibility and accountability for schooling. Principals who accommodate this call will increase their stature in the community.

ARGUMENTS CON

1   If principals are accountable for everything that happens in their buildings, they should have the power to control people, resources, events, and plans.

2   Principals can only effect desired outcomes if they have the role power to do so.

3   Teacher tenure puts serious limits on principals' power to deal with weak teachers. If principals' power to supervise teachers diminishes, the quality of classroom instruction will decrease.

4   If teachers are responsible for school decisions, principals will act less as instructional leaders and more as managers.

5   Few teachers are willing to make school decisions. They expect principals to support their work in the classroom by dealing with the traditional tasks of budgeting, hiring, firing, disciplining, and monitoring.

6   Parents expect someone to be in charge of the school. When they have concerns about their children, they want someone to make immediate decisions. Parents will view principals as weak if principals must share in decision making.

arguments against any of the group's stereo-types, illusions, or commitments, making clear that this type of dissent is contrary to what is expected of all loyal members.

6. *Self-Censorship*. Group members censor themselves from any deviations from the apparent group consensus, reflecting each member's inclination to minimize to himself the importance of his doubts and counterarguments.

7. *Unanimity*. Group members perceive a shared illusion of unanimity concerning judgments conforming to the majority view (partly resulting from self-censorship of deviations, augmented by the false assumption that silence means consent).

8. *Mindguards*. Some group members appoint themselves to protect the group from adverse information that might shatter their shared complacency about the effectiveness and morality of their decisions.

The likelihood that groupthink will emerge is greatest when: (1) the group is cohesive, (2) the group becomes insulated from qualified outsiders, and (3) the leader promotes her own favored solution.[46] In suggesting ways of avoiding groupthink, Janis hopes to reduce cohesiveness and open up decision activity in various ways. One way is to select ad hoc groups to solve problems; in this way, the members do not already belong to a cohesive group. Another approach is to have higher-level administrators set the parameters of the decision. Still another method is to assign different groups to work on the same problem.[47] And, finally, different group decision-making techniques can be used to limit the effects of groupthink and other problems inherent in group decision making. Nine suggestions for avoiding groupthink are as follows:[48]

1. The leader of a policy-forming group should assign the role of critical evaluator to each member, encouraging the group to give high priority to airing objections and doubts.

2. The leaders in an organization's hierarchy, when assigning a policy-planning mission to a group, should be impartial instead of stating their preferences and expectations at the outset.

3. The organization should routinely follow the administrative practice of setting up several independent policy-planning and evaluation groups to work on the same policy question, each carrying out its deliberations under a different leader.

4. Through the period when the feasibility and effectiveness of policy alternatives are being surveyed, the policy-making group should from time to time divide into two or more subgroups to meet separately, under different chairpersons, and then come together to reconcile their differences.

5. Each member of the policy-making group should periodically discuss the group's deliberations with trusted associates in his own unit of the organization and report their reactions back to the group.

6. One or more outside experts or qualified colleagues within the organization who are not core members of the policy-making group should be invited to each meeting on a staggered basis and should be encouraged to challenge the views of the core members.

7. At each meeting devoted to evaluating policy alternatives, at least one member should be assigned the role of devil's advocate, expressing as many objections to each policy alternative as possible.

8. Whenever the policy issue involves relations with a rival organization, a sizable block of time should be spent surveying all warning signals from the rivals and constructing alternative scenarios of the rivals' intentions.

9. After reaching a preliminary consensus about what seems to be the best policy alternative, the policy-making group should hold a second-chance meeting at which the

[46]Herve Moulin, *Axioms of Cooperative Decision Making* (New York: Cambridge University Press, 1989).
[47]R. Dennis Middlemist and Michael A. Hitt, *Organizational Behavior: Managerial Strategies for Performance* (St. Paul: West, 1988).
[48]Janis, *Groupthink: Psychological Studies of Policy Decisions and Fiascoes*.

members are expected to express as vividly as they can all their residual doubts and to rethink the entire issue before making a definitive choice.

Risky Shift

Problem solving in groups always involves some degree of risk. One can never be certain whether a decision made in a group would be the same as a decision made by an individual. This raises an interesting question: Do groups make decisions that are more or less risky than individual decisions? Or is a group decision simply the average of the individuals in the group?

In the 1960s, James Stoner initiated research on the amount of risk taken by groups in making decisions. Stoner tested the hypothesis that group decisions would be more cautious than individual decisions. He compared individual and group decisions using a series of hypothetical cases developed to measure an individual's propensity for risk taking. The alternative choices provided in each case ranged from relatively cautious with moderate payoffs to relatively risky with higher payoffs. For example, situations ranged from a football team playing cautiously for a tie or risky for a win to a graduate student choosing to pursue a Ph.D. degree in chemistry at one of two universities. Contrary to Stoner's prediction, the group decisions were consistently riskier than individual decisions.[49] This finding has been called the **risky-shift** phenomenon in group decision making.

Several explanations have been proposed for this risky-shift phenomenon:

- Making a decision in a group produces a diffusion of responsibility. Because no single person is held accountable for a bad decision, the group takes greater risks. Blame for a bad decision can then be shared with others; in fact, individuals may shift the blame entirely to others.
- Leaders of groups are greater risk takers than other members and so are more likely to persuade others to become more risky.
- Group discussion leads to a more thorough examination of the pros and cons of a particular decision than individual decision making. Consequently, greater familiarization with all aspects of a problem leads to higher risk levels.
- Risk taking is socially desirable in our culture, and socially desirable qualities are likely to be expressed in a group rather than individually.[50]

Subsequent research refutes the conclusion that groups consistently take greater risk than individuals. For some groups and some decisions, cautious shifts were observed; that is, groups arrived at decisions that were less risky than those of individuals. Thus, both risky and cautious decisions are possible in groups. A key factor in determining which kind of shift occurs—more risky or more cautious—is the position assumed by the members before group interaction occurs. If the members lean initially toward risk, group discussion results in a shift toward greater risk; and if members lean initially toward caution, discussion leads to a cautious shift. That is, group discussion tends to polarize the initial position of the group.[51] This phenomenon, called *group polarization*, is a reality in group decision making, but risky shift is more prevalent. Risky shift and group polarization are aspects of group decision making worth the attention of school administrators. In both cases, variance in individual decisions is reduced in groups.

---

[49]James A. Stoner, "Risky and Cautious Shifts in Group Decisions: The Influence of Widely Held Values," *Journal of Experimental Social Psychology*, 4 (1968), pp. 442–459.

[50]Richard M. Hodgetts and Steven Altman, *Organizational Behavior* (Philadelphia: Saunders, 1979).

[51]Robert F. Bordley, "A Bayesian Model of Group Polarization," *Organizational Behavior and Human Performance*, 32 (1983), pp. 262–274.

Escalation of Commitment

Escalation of commitment is closely related to retrospective rationality. Whereas retrospective rationality occurs in individuals exclusively, escalation of commitment can occur among individuals as well as among groups.[52] This phenomenon deals with the tendency of groups to escalate commitment to a course of action in order to justify their original decision. For example, a board of education makes a decision to renovate a high school building rather than build a new one. As the project progresses, the board soon becomes aware that the renovation will cost considerably more money than it would cost to build an entirely new structure. The decision makers continue to commit additional resources into what obviously was a poor decision. It is important for school administrators to recognize that groups making decisions face similar problems as those faced by individuals making decisions.

GROUP DECISION-MAKING TECHNIQUES

Because decision making in schools is frequently based on group participation, several techniques have been developed to improve the process. Five important techniques for group decision making are brainstorming, nominal group technique, the Delphi technique, devil's advocacy, and dialectical inquiry.

Brainstorming

Brainstorming, developed by Alex Osborne over thirty years ago, is a technique for creatively generating alternative solutions to a problem.[53] The unique feature of brainstorming is the separation of ideas from evaluation. Earlier, we noted the importance of generating a wide variety of new ideas during the generating alternatives step of the decision-making process (see Figure 6-1). This increases the number of alternatives from which school administrators can choose when evaluating alternatives and making their decisions. People tend to evaluate solutions to problems when they are proposed, which often eliminates many creative and feasible ideas from further consideration. The following rules are central to the technique:[54]

1. *Do Not Evaluate or Discuss Alternatives*. Evaluation comes later. Avoid criticism of one's own or others' ideas.
2. *Encourage "Freewheeling."* Do not consider any idea outlandish. An unusual idea may point the way to a truly creative decision.
3. *Encourage and Welcome Quantities of Ideas*. The greater the number of ideas generated, the greater the number of useful ideas will remain after evaluation.
4. *Encourage "Piggybacking."* Group members should try to combine, embellish, or improve on an idea. Consequently, most of the ideas produced will belong to the group and not to a single individual.

As an idea-generating technique, group brainstorming may not be any more effective than individual brainstorming. However, the technique is in widespread use today in all types of organizations, including schools.

Nominal Group Technique

Another technique that can be used in group decision making, which incorporates some of the features of brainstorming, is the **nominal**

[52]Max H. Bazerman, Toni Giulano, and Alan Appelman, "Escalation of Commitment in Individual and Group Decision Making," *Organizational Behavior and Human Performance*, 33 (1984), pp. 141–152.

[53]Alex Osborn, *Applied Imagination* (New York: Scribner, 1957).
[54]Ronald N. Taylor, *Behavioral Decision Making* (Glenview, IL: Scott, Foresman, 1984).

group technique.[55] As in brainstorming, individuals are brought together to develop a solution to a problem. Unlike brainstorming, the nominal group technique is concerned with both the generation of ideas and the evolution of these ideas. The process of decision making in nominal groups has six steps:[56]

1. *Silent Generation of Ideas*. Allow five to ten minutes for this phase. The problem should be posted on a flip chart in the front of the room. Group members are asked to solve the problem on the chart. They are cautioned not to talk to or look at the worksheets of other participants.

2. *Round-Robin Recording of Ideas*. The leader circulates around the room eliciting one idea from each group member and recording it on the flip chart. This continues, round-robin fashion, until all ideas are exhausted. The chief objective of this step is to get before the group an accurate list of ideas that can serve as a compilation of group ideas.

3. *Discussion of Ideas*. Each idea on the flip chart is discussed in the order it appears on the chart. The leader reads each item and asks the group if there are any questions, needs for clarification, agreement, or disagreement.

4. *Preliminary Vote on Item Importance*. Each participant makes an independent judgment about the alternatives by rank ordering them secretly on three-by-five-inch cards. The average of these judgments is used as the group's decision. The nominal group process may end here, or the decision may be further refined through discussion and revoting.

5. *Additional Discussion*. The voting patterns are analyzed and reasons examined to determine if a more accurate decision can be made.

6. *Final Vote*. The final voting occurs in the same manner as the preliminary vote, by secret rankings. This action completes the decision process and provides closure.

As noted, the nominal group technique separates ideation from evaluation. Ideas are generated nominally (without verbal communication). This prevents inhibition and conformity, which we noted in the phenomenon of groupthink. Evaluation occurs in a structured manner that allows each idea to get adequate attention.

The research on the effectiveness of the nominal group technique is encouraging. In terms of the number and quality of ideas generated, studies indicate that nominal group technique is superior to both ordinary group decision making and brainstorming.[57] Furthermore, nominal group techniques often facilitate the implementation of decisions.[58] In any event, the nominal group technique provides for both greater expression and evaluation of creative ideas by group members than either brainstorming or ordinary group decisions. Despite the research support for the nominal group technique, many school administrators still do not take advantage of its benefits in group decisions.

Delphi Technique

Researchers at the Rand Corporation developed the **Delphi technique** in the 1960s.[59] Unlike

[55]André L. Delbecq, Andrew H. Van de Ven, and David H. Gustafsen, *Group Techniques for Program Planning: A Guide to Nominal Group and Delphi Processes* (Glenview, IL: Scott, Foresman, 1975); Mark J. Martinko and Jim Gepson, "Nominal Grouping and Needs Analysis," in F. L. Ulschak (ed.), *Human Resource Development: The Theory and Practice of Needs Assessment* (Reston, VA: Reston Publishing, 1983), pp. 101–110.
[56]Delbecq, Van de Ven, and Gustafsen, *Group Techniques for Program Planning*.

[57]J. Keith Murnighan, "Group Decision Making: What Strategies Should You Use," *Management Review*, 70 (1981), pp. 55–64.
[58]Sam E. White, John E. Dittrich, and James R. Lang, "The Effects of Group Decision-Making Process and Problem Solving–Situation Complexity on Implementation Attempts," *Administrative Science Quarterly*, 25 (1980), pp. 428–440.
[59]Norman Dalkey, *The Delphi Method: An Experimental Study of Group Opinion* (Santa Monica, CA: Rand Corporation, 1969).

brainstorming and the nominal group technique, the Delphi approach relies completely on a nominal group; that is, participants do not engage in face-to-face discussions. Instead their input is solicited by mail at their various home bases, thus allowing the polling of large numbers of experts, clients, administrators, or constituencies who are removed from the organization by distance and scheduling problems. For example, suppose the superintendent of schools of a large urban school district wishes to evaluate the curriculum in the basic-skills areas. Selected members of the student body, administration, faculty, community, and nationally renowned experts could participate in the various phases of the Delphi process.

The Delphi technique has many variations, but generally it works as follows:[60]

1. The organization identifies a panel of experts, both inside and outside the organization, and solicits their cooperation.
2. Each member of the panel receives the basic problem.
3. Each individual expert independently and anonymously writes comments, suggestions, and solutions to the problem.
4. A central location compiles, transcribes, and reproduces the experts' comments.
5. Each panelist receives a copy of all the other experts' comments and solutions.
6. Each expert provides feedback on the others' comments, writes new ideas stimulated by their comments, and forwards these to the central location.
7. The organization repeats Steps 5 and 6 as often as necessary until consensus is reached or until some kind of voting procedure is imposed to reach a decision.

Success of the Delphi technique depends on the expertise, communication skills, and motivation of the participants and the amount of time the organization has available to make a decision.

There are several benefits of the Delphi approach. First, it eliminates many of the interpersonal problems associated with other group decision-making approaches. Second, it enlists the assistance of experts and provides for the efficient use of their time. Third, it allows adequate time for reflection and analysis of a problem. Fourth, it provides for a wide diversity and quantity of ideas. And, finally, it facilitates the accurate prediction and forecasting of future events.[61] The major objectives of the Delphi technique include the following:[62]

- To determine or develop a range of possible program alternatives
- To explore or expose underlying assumptions or information leading to different judgments
- To seek out information that may generate a consensus among the group members
- To correlate informed judgments on a subject that spans a wide range of disciplines
- To educate group members concerning the diverse and interrelated aspects of the subject

Today, numerous organizations in business, government, the military, health-care agencies, and schools are using the Delphi technique. Research shows that the technique is superior to ordinary group decision making in terms of the number and quality of ideas generated and group members' overall satisfaction.[63] The major disadvantage of the Delphi technique is the amount of time involved in going through the questionnaire phases of the process. Variations of the Delphi technique have been used to overcome this problem.

---

[60]Linda N. Jewell and H. Joseph Reitz, *Group Effectiveness in Organizations* (Glenview, IL: Scott, Foresman, 1981).

[61]Gustave Rath and Karen Stoyanoff, "The Delphi Technique," in F. L. Ulschak (ed.), *Human Resource Development: The Theory and Practice of Needs Assessment* (Reston, VA: Reston Publishing, 1983), pp. 111–131.

[62]Delbecq, Van de Ven, and Gustafsen, *Group Techniques for Program Planning.*

[63]Murnighan, "Group Decision Making: What Strategies Should You Use?"; Rath and Stoyanoff, "The Delphi Technique."

One special type of Delphi approach is a procedure called *ringi* used by the Japanese. This version of the Delphi technique involves the circulation of a written document from member to member, in nominal group fashion, for sequential editing until no more changes are required and each participant has signed off the final document. Another Japanese variation of the Delphi technique is assigning parts of the problem to each of several subgroups who prepare responses for their assignments. This version differs from the pure Delphi approach in that the written minireports are then circulated among the group members before face-to-face discussion starts. In essence, the latter Japanese version of the Delphi technique combines with simple group decision making.

Devil's Advocacy

Devil's advocacy, another technique for improving the quality of group decisions, introduces conflict into the decision-making process. Janis suggests that this concept is an antidote for groupthink. Earlier, we noted that groupthink results in inhibitions and premature conformity to group norms. Devil's advocacy can nullify these and other group phenomena to which group members are subjected. After a planning group has developed alternative solutions to a problem, the plan is given to one or more staff members, with instructions to find fault with it. "If the plan withstands the scrutiny of the devil's advocates, it can be presumed to be free of the effects of groupthink . . . and thus viable."[64] Although devil's advocacy can be used as a critiquing technique after alternative solutions to a problem have been developed, it can

also be used during the early stages of the decision-making process. For example, during a decision-making session one member could be assigned the role of devil's advocate, expressing as many objections to each alternative solution to a problem as possible.[65]

Dialectical Inquiry

Like devil's advocacy, **dialectical inquiry** is an alternative approach for controlling group phenomena in decision making such as groupthink. The process can be described as follows:[66]

1. The process begins with group formation of two or more divergent groups to represent the full range of views on a specific problem. Each group is made as internally homogeneous as possible; the groups, however, are as different from one another as possible. Collectively they cover all positions that might have an impact on the ultimate solution to a problem.
2. Each group meets separately, identifies the assumptions behind its position, and rates them on their importance and feasibility. Each group then presents a "for" and an "against" position to the other groups.
3. Each group debates the other groups' position and defends its own. The goal is not to convince others but to confirm that what each group expresses as its position is not necessarily accepted by others.
4. Information, provided by all groups, is analyzed. This results in the identification of information gaps and establishes guidelines for further research on the problem.
5. An attempt to achieve consensus among the positions occurs. Strategies are sought that will best meet the requirements of all positions that remain viable. This final step per-

[64]Miner, *Organizational Behavior: Performance and Productivity*, pp. 307–308.

[65]David M. Schweiger and Phyllis A. Finger, "The Comparative Effectiveness of Dialectical Inquiry and Devil's Advocacy: The Impact of Task Biases on Previous Research Findings," *Strategic Management Journal*, 5 (1984), pp. 335–350.

[66]Vincent P. Barabba, "Making Use of Methodologies Developed in Academia: Lessons from One Practitioner's Experience," in R. H. Kilmann et al. (eds.), *Producing Useful Knowledge for Organizations* (New York: Praeger, 1983), pp. 147–166.

mits further refinement of information needed to solve the problem.

Although agreement on an administrative plan is a goal of this approach, a full consensus does not always follow. Nevertheless, the procedure can produce useful indicators of the organization's planning needs.

SUMMARY

1. Decision making is a process of choosing from among alternatives. All decision-making models include the concept of rational activity. Decision-making models can be thought of as ranging on a continuum from perfect rationality (classical model) to nonrationality (behavioral model).
2. Rational decision making consists of several steps: identifying problems, generating alternatives, evaluating alternatives, choosing the optimal alternative, implementing the decision, and evaluating the decision.
3. Although school administrators want to make the best decisions, the realities of school life affect rational decision making. These include internal and external politics, conflict-resolution techniques, distribution of power and authority, time constraints, cost, the inability to process information, and other limits of human rationality.
4. There are advantages of group decision making in schools. Groups have the potential to generate and evaluate more ideas, and once a decision is made, acceptance will be easier.
5. The disadvantages of group decision making include groupthink, risky shift, and escalation of commitment.
6. Techniques to improve group decision making include brainstorming, the nominal group technique, the Delphi technique, devil's advocacy, and dialectical inquiry.

KEY TERMS

decision making
classical model
rationality

identifying problems
generating alternatives
evaluating alternatives

choosing an alternative
implementing the decision
evaluating the decision
behavioral model
bounded rationality
satisficing
contextual rationality
procedural rationality
retrospective rationality
incrementalizing
garbage can model

decision feasibility
groupthink
risky shift
escalation of commitment
brainstorming
nominal group technique
Delphi technique
devil's advocacy
dialectical inquiry

DISCUSSION QUESTIONS

1. Give an example of a decision-making situation with which you are familiar and illustrate how the problem was solved.
2. What are the basic assumptions of the classical model of decision making? Describe the steps that occur in the decision-making process.
3. Should school administrators attempt to make decisions according to the classical model? Why or why not?
4. What are the major benefits of using groups for decision making?
5. What group techniques can be used to improve group decision making?

SUGGESTED READINGS

Karen S. Cook and Margaret Levi (eds.), *The Limit of Rationality* (Chicago: University of Chicago Press, 1990). Provides a systematic examination of the limits of rationality in decision making from the perspective of management.

Colin Eden and Jim Radford (eds.), *Tackling Strategic Problems: The Role of Group Decision Support* (Newbury Park, CA.: Sage, 1990). Consultants from a wide variety of organizational settings explore key issues in the provision of effective decision support.

Mary E. Guy, *Ethical Decision Making in Everyday Work Situations* (Westport, CT.: Greenwood, 1990). Provides an up-to-date guide on ethical considerations in managerial decision making.

William R. Kind et al., *Management Science: A Deci-sion-Support Approach* (Reading, MA.: Addison-Wesley, 1990). A clear and concise approach to group-decision support.

Edward F. McClennen, *Rationality and Dynamic Choice: Foundational Explorations* (New York: Cambridge University Press, 1990). Describes the whole process of decision making from identifying the problem to evaluating the decision.

Richard M. Oliver and John Q. Smith (eds.), *Influence Diagrams, Belief Nets, and Decision Analysis* (New York: Wiley, 1990). Provides an excellent introduction to methods for conducting rigorous analysis of decision probability and choice using statistical models.

Warren J. Pelson et al., *Tough Choices: The Decision-Making Styles of America's Top 50 CEO's* (Homewood, IL.: Dow Jones-Irwin, 1989). Offers a crisp, condensed, and up-to-date digest of the decision-making styles used by the top CEO's in America.

7

COMMUNICATION

In this chapter, we attempt to answer these questions concerning communication in school organizations. We begin our discussion with a brief treatment of the importance of communication in schools. Then we examine the process and patterns of verbal and nonverbal communication. Next, we identify and describe some common barriers to communication. Finally, we discuss some useful techniques for overcoming these communication barriers.

THE IMPORTANCE OF COMMUNICATION

Anyone who walks through a school will observe numerous communication activities taking place. Secretaries type letters, memoranda, and reports; others talk on the telephone; a parent conference is underway in the assistant principal's office; the principal is in an evaluation conference with a teacher; other meetings are in session; teachers and students exchange information in classrooms; other students use the computer terminals in another part of the building; the library buzzes with activity; and a number of other communication activities, using a variety of media, are observable.

Communication, the lifeblood of every school organization, is a process that links the individual, the group, and the organization. To be sure, communication mediates inputs to the organization from the environment and outputs from the organization to the environment. As Chester Barnard asserted, communication occupies a central place in organizations "because the structure, extensiveness, and scope of organization are almost entirely determined by communication techniques."[1] Or as Daniel Katz and Robert Kahn put it, communication is the "essence of organizations."[2]

The administrator of today's school organization has a multifaceted job, which includes setting objectives, organizing tasks, motivating employees, reviewing results, and making decisions. School administrators plan, organize, staff, direct, coordinate, and review. Tasks cannot be accomplished, objectives cannot be met, and decisions cannot be implemented without adequate communication.

The centrality of communication to the overall job of the administrator is evident when we consider how much time administrators spend communicating in organizations. The results of two separate studies of executives across a spectrum of organizational types and administrative levels indicate that administrators spend 80 percent of their time in interpersonal communica-tion.[3] Similar findings ranging from 70 to 80 percent have been reported for elementary school principals, high school principals, and school superintendents.[4] School administrators therefore need a clear understanding of the process of communication.

THE COMMUNICATION PROCESS

The **communication process** involves the exchange of information between a sender and a receiver. Figure 7-1 shows the key components of the communication process, which involves a sequence of steps: ideating, encoding, transmitting, receiving, decoding, and acting. In simple terms, the sender encodes an idea into a message and transmits the message to a receiver who decodes the message and acts.[5] Barriers to communication can occur at any step in the process but most frequently occur between transmission and reception and between receiving and decoding. Barriers to communication and techniques for overcoming them are discussed later in the chapter. Although feedback is not present in all cases, it is necessary to ensure effective communication.

---

[1]Chester I. Barnard, *The Functions of the Executive* (Cambridge, MA: Harvard University Press, 1938), p. 91.

[2]Daniel Katz and Robert L. Kahn, *The Social Psychology of Organizations*, 2nd ed. (New York: Wiley, 1978), p. 223.

[3]Edward E. Lawler, Lyman W. Porter, and A. Tennenbaum, "A Manager's Attitude Toward Interaction Episodes," *Journal of Applied Psychology*, 52 (1968), pp. 423–439; Henry Mintzberg, *The Nature of Managerial Work* (New York: Harper & Row, 1973).

[4]John T. Kmetz and Donald J. Willower, "Elementary School Principals' Work Behavior," *Educational Administration Quarterly*, 18 (1982), pp. 62–78; William J. Martin and Donald J. Willower, "The Managerial Behavior of High School Principals," *Educational Administration Quarterly*, 17 (1981), pp. 69–90; Nancy J. Pitner and Rodney T. Ogawa, "Organizational Leadership: The Case of the Superintendent," *Educational Administration Quarterly*, 17 (1981), pp. 45–65.

[5]James C. McCroskey, Virginia P. Richmond, and Robert A. Stewart, *One on One: The Foundations of Interpersonal Communication* (Englewood Cliffs, NJ: Prentice-Hall, 1986).

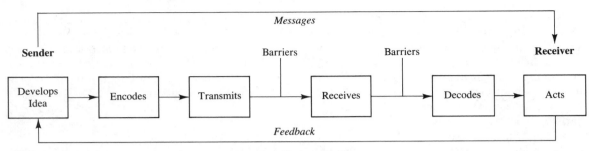

FIGURE 7-1   The Communication Process

Ideating

Senders in a school district can be central office administrators, building administrators, faculty members, departments within a school, a school, or the school district itself. Administrators communicate with other administrators, subordinates, students, the board of education, and members of the community. Faculty members communicate with administrators, staff, students, parents, and the community. Communications within the school district are important ways of coordinating the tasks of superintendents, assistant superintendents, directors, coordinators, supervisors, principals, and teachers. Communications within school buildings help coordinate the work of faculty and staff. School districts communicate with employees at all levels: unions, the community, the school board and local, state, and federal governments. The first step is **ideating**—developing an idea, message, or information to transmit to some individual or group.

Encoding

Encoding symbolizes the ideas that the sender wishes to transmit. Symbols (words, nonverbal cues, or even pictures and diagrams) are designed to communicate only messages. Meaning cannot be transmitted because it lies in the sig-

nificance that the encoder attributes to the syı. bol. The receiver of the message will also assign meaning to that symbol. The greater the agreement between the sender and the receiver regarding the meaning of the symbols, the greater the probability of understanding between the two parties. It is important therefore that school administrators select symbols that have mutual meaning for them and their intended receivers.

Transmitting

Once the message is developed, **transmitting** is the next step by one of several methods including memoranda, telephone, closed-circuit television, computers, board policy statements, and face-to-face communication. Unintended messages such as silence or inaction on particular issues are not as obvious. And such nonverbal cues as hand gestures, body position, facial expression, and voice intonation also communicate messages.

Receiving

Receiving is the next step, which requires that the receiver be a good listener if the message is oral. If the message is written, the receiver must be attentive to its stated and implied meaning.

Decoding

Decoding is the translation of a received message into a perceived or interpreted meaning. Because meaning cannot be transmitted, it cannot be received. Therefore, receivers must take transmitted messages and give meaning to the them. Barriers to communication can occur at any stage of the communication process, but they are most prevalent during the decoding step.

Acting

Acting is the final step in the communication process. The receiver can ignore the communication, store it for possible action later, or do something else with it. The receiver, however, should give feedback to the sender that the message was received and understood.

NONVERBAL COMMUNICATION

We communicate as many messages nonverbally as we do verbally. **Nonverbal communication**—the way we stand, the distance we maintain from another person, the way we walk, the way we fold our arms and wrinkle our brow, our eye contact, being late for a meeting—conveys messages to others. However, we need not perform an act for nonverbal communication to occur. We communicate by our manner of dress and appearance, the automobile we drive, and the office we occupy.[6]

Nonverbal communication comes in many forms: *kinesis* (body movements and position), *paralanguage* (voice qualities), *proxemics* (space and proximity), and *chronemics* (determination and definition of time).

Kinesis applies to ways in which facial expressions, the use of hands, arms, and legs, and posture affect communication.[7] What is your facial expression when you talk to others? What are your body gestures? Even a person's clothing can be important. For instance, John Molloy points out that the "most authoritative pattern is the pinstripe, followed in descending order by the solid, the chalk stripe and the plaid." "If you need to be more authoritative," says Molloy, "stick with dark pinstripes."[8]

Besides the truly silent aspects of kinesis, people say things in ways that are important aspects of nonverbal communication. Sometimes referred to as paralanguage, these include voice quality, volume, speech rate, pitch, nonfluences ("ah," "um," or "uh"), laughing, yawning, and the like. Also, *who* says a word (e.g., whether the boss or a colleague asks for "volunteers") and in what *environmental context* it is said (e.g., in the boss's office or out on the golf course) make a difference.[9]

Proxemics refers to the physical environment of communication and deals with space, including location. For example, how close do you stand to someone in normal conversation?

Edward Hall, an anthropologist, suggests that in the United States there are definable *personal space zones*:[10]

1. *Intimate Zone (Zero to Two Feet)*. To be this close, we must have an intimate association with the other person or be socially domineering.
2. *Personal Zone (Two to Four Feet)*. Within this zone, we should be fairly well acquainted with the other individual.
3. *Social Zone (Four to Twelve Feet)*. In this zone, we are at least minimally acquainted with the other person and have a definite purpose

---

[6]Judy Burgoon et al., *Nonverbal Communication: The Unspoken Dialogue* (New York: Harper & Row, 1988).

[7]Michael Argyle, *Bodily Communication*, 2nd ed. (Madison, CT: International Universities Press, 1988).

[8]John T. Molloy, *Dress for Success* (New York: Warner, 1975), p. 46.

[9]Fred Luthans, *Organizational Behavior*, 5th ed. (New York: McGraw-Hill, 1989).

[10]Edward T. Hall, *The Silent Language* (Westport, CT: Greenwood, 1980).

for seeking to communicate. Most behavior in the business world occurs in this zone.

4. *Public Zone (Beyond Twelve Feet)*. When people are more than twelve feet away, we treat them as if they did not exist. We may look at others from this distance, provided our gaze does not develop into a stare.

Related to the notion of personal space zones is the concept of *physical space*. For example, employees of higher status have better offices (more spacious, finer carpets and furniture, and more windows) than do employees of lower status. Furthermore, the offices of higher-status employees are better protected than lower-status employees. Top-executive areas are typically sealed off from intruders by several doors, assistants, and secretaries. Moreover, the higher the employee's status, the easier they find it to invade the physical space of lower-status employees. A superior typically feels free to walk right in on subordinates, whereas subordinates are more cautious and ask permission or make an appointment before visiting a superior.[11]

Chronemics, or the use of time, is another form of nonverbal communication.[12] For example, being late for a meeting may convey any number of different messages including carelessness, lack of involvement, and lack of ambition. Yet, at the same time, the late arrival of high-status persons reaffirms their superiority relative to subordinates. Their tardiness symbolizes power or having a busy schedule.[13]

You cannot not communicate. Everything that you do is a form of communication, verbal and nonverbal. The way you walk, your facial expression, and your silence are interpreted by others,

so you might as well do it right. (See Administrative Advice 7-1.)

DIRECTION OF COMMUNICATION

Communication is interlinked with most of the processes that take place in school districts, such as planning, organizing, staffing, directing, coordinating, and reporting. The purpose of organizational communication is to provide the means for transmitting information essential to goal achievement. Much of this **communication flow** is carried in four distinct directions (Figure 7-2): downward, upward, horizontally, and diagonally.[14] The other major communication flow is the grapevine.

Downward Communication

Hierarchical systems like large school districts tend to use downward communication, in which people at higher levels transmit information to people at lower levels in the school district. The communication can take place among different groups of senders and receivers, including superintendent to assistant superintendents, assistant superintendents to principals, principals to department heads, department heads to teachers, or any other combination of superior to subordinate.

For example, the school district's superintendent might instruct the assistant superintendent of instruction to prepare for a new personnel evaluation system mandated by the state. In turn, the assistant superintendent would provide specific instructions to the principals, who would inform the teachers accordingly. Downward communication is necessary to help clarify the school district's goals, provide a sense of mission, assist in indoctrinating new

[11]Don Hellriegel, John W. Slocum, and Richard W. Woodman, *Organizational Behavior*, 5th ed. (St. Paul: West, 1989).

[12]Mark L. Knapp, *Essentials of Nonverbal Communication* (New York: Holt, Rinehart & Winston, 1980).

[13]Robert P. Vecchio, *Organizational Behavior* (New York: Dryden, 1988).

[14]John B. Miner, *Organizational Behavior: Performance and Productivity* (New York: Random House, 1988).

ADMINISTRATIVE ADVICE 7-1

■

WAYS TO PROMOTE EFFECTIVE COMMUNICATION

The importance of communication throughout the school environment is axiomatic. The potential payoff of effective communication is enormous in terms of the productivity and attitudes of faculty and students. Ten ways that school administrators can promote effective communication are as follows:

■ *View Everything You Do As a Form of Communication*. The role of the school administrator is one of communicator—both sender and receiver. Viewing your actions in this framework should make you aware of the significance of your messages, how they are presented, and how they will be perceived by others.

■ *Be Aware That Communication Is Often the First Step in Preventing and Solving Problems*. Communication, however, does not work by itself; it exists in a context—something preceded it and something will follow it. This realization should determine what kind of communication is appropriate and if more communication on a topic is needed.

■ *Want to Communicate with Others*. A great number of communication flaws will be overlooked if the school administrator is perceived as wanting to talk and listen to others.

■ *Model Effective Communication*. Whatever the purpose, spoken communication should express ideas clearly, use language effectively, contain carefully reasoned and well-supported ideas, be adapted to the listeners, and be presented in an effective and interesting manner. Administrators must have listening skills as well.

■ *Adapt to the Communications Needs of Others*. First, recognize the varying needs others have for communication. Second, relate your topic to listeners by being certain they understood the relevance of the topic for them.

■ *Want Others to Communicate Among Themselves*. The principal who wants an open-communication environment must support and encourage communication among all those in the school.

■ *Provide Opportunities for Communication*. Ways to facilitate communication include planning meetings with agendas; setting aside time for one-on-one, small-group, and large-group discussions; organizing debates and forums on controversial issues; scheduling faculty retreats; and the like.

■ *Provide In-Service Programs on Communication Topics*. Teachers can learn the principles of communications and develop strategies for more effective communication by attending in-service workshops.

■ *Reward Effective Communication*. Praise, merit pay, comments on assessment forms, and emphasis on communication ability as a criterion for selection for valued positions and duties can reward effective communication.

■ *Make Sure That Students Are Taught Communication Skills*. All students should be taught in reading and writing as well as in speaking and listening.

Source: Adapted from Mary Bozik, "Ten Ways That Principals Can Promote Effective Communication," *Principal*, 69 (1989), pp. 34–36. Copyright 1989, the National Association of Elementary School Principals. Used by permission.

employees into the system, inform employees about educational changes impacting the district, and provide subordinates with data concerning their performance.

Downward communication occurs easily, but it is frequently deficient. One problem is that subordinates select from among the various directives transmitted from above those most in

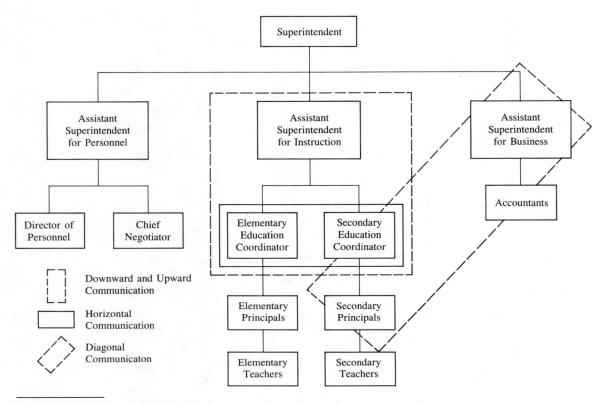

FIGURE 7-2   School District Communication Flows

keeping with their perceptions of their bosses' character, personality, motivation, and style and give them priority. Another problem is that not enough time and effort are devoted to learning whether messages sent from above have been received and understood. A third problem is that those at the top of the hierarchy may shut off this channel at times and on certain subjects, that is, withhold information on a need-to-know basis.[15] And, finally, downward communication tends to dominate in mechanistic organizations as opposed to organic systems, which are char-acterized by more open and unidirectional flows of information.[16]

One author has identified three ways for administrators to improve downward communication:[17]

1. School districts should adopt communication-training programs for all administrative personnel. Most school administrators could benefit greatly from learning better ways of

[15]Lawrence F. Frey et al., *Investigating Communication* (Englewood Cliffs, NJ: Prentice-Hall, 1990).

[16]Samuel B. Bacharach, Peter Bamberger, and Sharon C. Conley, "The See-Saw Metaphor and Managing Professionals," unpublished paper, Cornell University, 1988.

[17]Phillip V. Lewis, *Organizational Communication: The Essence of Effective Management* (New York: Wiley, 1987).

communicating, as well as developing more effective listening skills.

2. School administrators should get out of their offices and talk to employees on "the firing line." Two authors refer to this technique as management by wandering around (MBWA).[18] It allows administrators to become more aware of the needs of their subordinates.

3. School administrators should conduct regular supervisory–subordinate discussions. Such participative interactions will help administrators identify, analyze, and solve problems collaboratively with subordinates.

Upward Communication

This type of communication also follows the hierarchical chart and transmits information from lower to higher levels in the organization. For example, a teacher might conceive of a new course in social studies. The teacher would pass this information upward to the department head who would in turn pass the information to her immediate supervisor who would then inform the superintendent. Upward communication is necessary to provide administrators with feedback on downward communication, monitor decision-making effectiveness, gauge organizational climate, deal with problem areas quickly, and provide needed information to administrators.

For several reasons, upward communication is difficult to achieve. Upward communication is usually subject to filtering and distortion because subordinates do not want their superiors to learn anything that may be potentially damaging to subordinates' careers.[19] This tendency is likely to increase when subordinates do not

trust supervisors. Furthermore, highly cohesive groups tend to withhold information from superiors that might be damaging to the group as a whole.[20] However, all subordinates tend to distort upward communication somewhat less under a participatory management system than under an authoritative system.[21] Other research shows that lower-level subordinates perceive much less openness to upward communication than is perceived at higher levels in the organization. In fact, "higher-level managers involve their subordinates more in the decision-making process and thus expect upward communication more than do lower-level managers."[22] Similar findings have been reported in educational settings.[23]

Other research recommends four practices to improve upward communication: employee meetings, open-door policy, employee letters, and participation in social groups.[24]

Employee Meetings   These meetings attempt to probe job problems, needs, and administrative practices that help and hinder subordinate job performance. These meetings, sometimes referred to as "quality circles," provide feedback to

[18]Larry Frase and Robert Hetzel, *School Management by Wandering Around* (Lancaster, PA: Technomic, 1989).

[19]Ray Blair, *Introduction to Professional Communication* (Englewood Cliffs, NJ: Prentice-Hall, 1989).

[20]Rebecca Blair, Karlene H. Roberts, and Pamela McKechnie, "Vertical and Network Communication in Organizations: The Present and the Future," in R. D. McPhee and P. Thompkins (eds.), *Organizational Communication: Traditional Themes and New Directions* (Beverly Hills, CA: Sage, 1985), pp. 55–77.

[21]Philip R. Cohen et al. (eds.), *Intentions in Communications* (Cambridge, MA: MIT Press, 1990).

[22]R. Dennis Middlemist and Michael A. Hitt, *Organizational Behavior: Managerial Strategies for Performance* (St. Paul: West, 1988), p. 321.

[23]Edwin M. Bridges and Maureen T. Hallinan, "Subunit Size, Work System Interdependence, and Employee Absenteeism," *Educational Administration Quarterly*, 14 (1978), pp. 24–42; Cecil Miskel, David McDonald, and Susan Bloom, "Structural and Expectancy Linkages Within Schools and Organizational Effectiveness, *Educational Administration Quarterly*, 19 (1983), pp. 49–82.

[24]Keith Davis and John W. Newstrom, *Human Behavior at Work: Organizational Behavior*, 7th ed. (New York: McGraw-Hill, 1985).

administrators and encourage subordinates to submit ideas to supervisors. As a consequence, subordinates feel a sense of personal worth and importance because administrators listen to them. By opening channels upward, administrators help the flow and acceptance of communication downward. Also, subordinates' attitudes improve, and turnover declines.

Open-Door Policy An open door policy is a statement that encourages subordinates to walk in and talk to administrators many levels up the hierarchy. Generally, however, subordinates are encouraged to see their immediate supervisors first. Then if their problem is not resolved at that level, they are free to approach higher-level administrators. Bringing a problem to one's immediate supervisor first should alleviate resentment among administrators who are bypassed when subordinates skip several administrative levels in the hierarchy. The goal of an open-door policy—to facilitate upward communication—has merit but is often difficult to implement because psychological barriers often exist between superiors and subordinates. Some subordinates do not want to be identified as having a problem or lacking information. A more effective open-door procedure is for administrators to get out of their offices and observe firsthand what is happening in the organization. This was referred to earlier as management by wandering around.

Employee Letters Programs that use employee letters or suggestions serve as a type of written open-door policy. This direct and personal method provides subordinates with the opportunity to present their ideas to administrators. To increase the effectiveness of this procedure, submissions can be anonymous, all submissions must be answered, and replies must be delivered without delay. Replies can be directed to the appropriate lower-level administrator or, in cases where the communicator is anonymous, responses can be deposited in an "answer box," similar to a suggestion box in which employees communicate with superiors.

Participation in Social Groups This method provides excellent opportunities for unplanned upward communication. Information at these activities is shared informally between subordinates and superiors. Examples include departmental parties, sports events, picnics, golf outings, and other employer-sponsored activities. The major barrier to such activities is lack of attendance; that is, those who need to share information the most may not attend the activities. Although upward communication is not the primary goal of these activities, it is certainly an important by-product. It is also a means of enhancing employee morale. Other approaches are job-satisfaction surveys, grievance or complaint procedures, counseling programs, exit interviews, discussions with union representatives, consultative supervision, and suggestion systems.

Horizontal Communication

Horizontal communication takes place between employees at the same hierarchical level. This type of communication is frequently overlooked in the design of most organizations. Integration and coordination between units in an organization is facilitated by horizontal communication. At the upper levels of a school district, for example, the assistant superintendents for instruction, business, and personnel will coordinate their efforts in arriving at an integrated strategic plan for the district. In a high school, meanwhile, the department chairpersons will work together in developing a curriculum for the entire school. Likewise, in a school of education of a large university, it is common to observe departments coordinating their efforts for the purpose of ensuring that all units of the school are working toward the same general goals. This horizontal communication is frequently achieved through cross-functional committees or council meetings, groups or liaison positions that tie together units horizontally, and informal interpersonal communication.

Besides providing task coordination, horizontal communication furnishes emotional and social support among peers. In effect, it serves as a socialization process for the organization. The more interdependent the various functions in the organization, the greater the need to formalize horizontal communication.

Diagonal Communication

Diagonal communication is important in situations in which participants cannot communicate effectively through other channels. For example, the assistant superintendent for business of a large, urban school district may wish to conduct an instructional program cost analysis for each high school. One part of the analysis involves having each high school principal send a special report directly to the assistant superintendent for business, rather than go through the traditional, circuitous channels of assistant superintendent for instruction to the coordinator of secondary education to the high school principals and back again. Thus, the flow of communication would be diagonal rather than vertical (downward and upward). In this instance, diagonal communication minimizes the time lag in securing the needed data. The four directions of organizational communication flows are shown in Figure 7-2.

The Grapevine

When the shortcomings of the four types of organizational communication become apparent, employees build their own channels of communication, **grapevines**. Also grapevines exist in all large organizations regardless of communication flow. This particular communication flow does not appear on any organizational chart, but it carries much of the communication in the organization. The term *grapevine* applies to all informal communication including institutional information that is communicated verbally between employees and people in the community. It coexists with the administration's formal communication system. Therefore, school adminis-

trators should learn to integrate grapevine communication with formal communication.

Because the grapevine is flexible and usually involves face-to-face communication, it transmits information rapidly. Moreover, nearly five out of every six messages are carried by the grapevine rather than through official channels.[25] And in normal work situations, well over 75 percent of grapevine information is accurate.[26]

The grapevine has both positive and negative features. According to Deal and Kennedy and others, its positive features include the following:[27]

- Keeps subordinates informed about important organizational matters.
- Gives school administrators insights into subordinates' attitudes.
- Provides subordinates with a safety valve for their emotions.
- Provides a test of subordinates' reactions to a new policy or procedural change without making formal commitments. (School administrators have been known to "feed" ideas into the grapevine in order to probe their potential acceptance by subordinates.)
- Helps build morale by carrying the positive comments people make about the school district.

One of the negative features of the grapevine, the one that gives the grapevine its poor reputation, is rumor. A rumor is an unverified belief that is in general circulation. Because the information cannot be verified, rumors are susceptible to severe distortion as they are passed from person to person within the organization. One

---

[25]John M. Ivancevich, James H. Donnelly, Jr., and James L. Gibson, *Managing for Performance* (Dallas: Business Publications, 1980); Lewis, *Organizational Communication: The Essence of Effective Management.*
[26]Davis and Newstrom, *Human Behavior at Work: Organizational Behavior.*
[27]Terrence Deal and Allen Kennedy, *Corporate Cultures* (Reading, MA: Addison-Wesley, 1984); Karl Albrecht and Ron Zemke, *Service America* (Homewood, IL: Dow Jones–Irwin, 1985).

way to minimize the spread of rumors is to improve other forms of communication. If school administrators provide information on issues relevant to subordinates, then damaging rumors are less likely to develop.

Joseph Licata and Walter Hack examined grapevine structures among principals and report that grapevine linkages differed between elementary and secondary school principals. In elementary schools, where relationships are closer, principals tended to communicate informally; in high schools, where the structure is more formal, principals built the grapevine around professional survival and development.[28]

As important as communication is, few school administrators and schools make an effort to systematically organize, coordinate, and evaluate their communication system. (See Administrative Advice 7-2.)

COMMUNICATION NETWORKS

As noted, organizational communication can be transmitted in a number of directions: downward, upward, horizontally, diagonally, and through the grapevine. These communications can be formal or informal; whether formal or informal, the actual pattern and flow of communication connecting senders and receivers are called communication networks. Because this system contains all the communication of the organization, these networks have a pervasive influence on the behavior of individuals functioning within them.

Network Patterns

Network patterns are derived from laboratory experiments in which the structure of the groupings can be manipulated by the experimenter. Figure 7-3 depicts five of the more frequently used networks (wheel, chain, Y, circle, and star). The major difference among the networks is the degree to which they are centralized or decentralized.[29] Each network pattern is discussed in turn.[30]

The *wheel network*, a two-level hierarchy, is the most structured and centralized of the patterns because each member can communicate with only one other person. For example, a superintendent of schools and those who are his immediate subordinates (assistant superintendent for business, instruction, personnel, and assistant to the superintendent), probably form a wheel network. The superintendent is A and his assistant superintendents are B, C, D, and E, respectively. The four subordinates send information to the superintendent, and the superintendent sends that information back to them, usually in the form of decisions.

The *chain network* ranks next highest in centralization. Only two people communicate with one another, and they in turn have only one person to whom they communicate. Information is generally sent through such a network in relay fashion. A typical chain network would be one in which a teacher (B) reports to her department head (C), who in turn reports to the principal (A), who reports to the assistant superintendent for instruction (D), who reports to the superintendent (E). Another example is the grapevine through which information passes throughout a school building or district between different departments and organizational levels.

The *Y network* is similar to the chain except that two members fall outside the chain. In the Y network, for example, members A and B can send information to C, but they can receive information from no one. C and D can exchange information; E can receive information from D but cannot send any information. For example, two assistant principals (A and B) report to the

---

[28]Joseph W. Licata and Walter G. Hack, "School Administrator Grapevine Structure," *Educational Administration Quarterly*, 16 (1980), pp. 82–99.

[29]H. Joseph Reitz, *Behavior in Organizations*, 3rd ed., (Homewood, IL: Dow Jones-Irwin, 1989).

[30]Lewis, *Organizational Communication: The Essence of Effective Management*.

ADMINISTRATIVE ADVICE 7-2

■

EVALUATING THE EFFECTIVENESS OF YOUR SCHOOL'S COMMUNICATIONS

To thoroughly and comprehensively evaluate the communications effectiveness of your school, follow the essential components of the communication process:

- *Promote the Communication Climate.* A feeling of mutual trust must exist among fellow workers and between management and employees.
- *Open Communication Channels.* Upward, downward, horizontal, and informal communications provide effective results.
- *Use a Wide Variety of Communication Methods.* Different communication methods can convey information that is appropriate to the situation.
- *Plan Communication Timing.* The carefully planned and coordinated timing of important messages increases their effectiveness.
- *Adapt Message Content.* Particular receivers and situations require different wording.

- *Encourage Feedback to Communications.* The senders of messages view the securing of feedback as essential and encourage it.
- *Know Your Sources of Information.* The sources of important information must be knowledgeable (well-informed) and credible (believable).
- *Nurture Superior–Subordinate Communications.* Both superiors and subordinates must understand goals, standards, and priorities.

Source: Adapted from Walter St. John, "Evaluating the Effectiveness of Your Organizations's Communications," *NASSP Bulletin*, 73 (1989), pp. 99–109. Used by permission.

principal (C). The principal, in turn, reports to the assistant superintendent (D), who reports to the superintendent (E).

The *circle network*, a three-level hierarchy, is very different from the wheel, chain, and Y networks. It is symbolic of horizontal and decentralized communication. The circle gives every member equal communication opportunities. Each member can communicate with persons to their right and left. Members have identical restrictions, but the circle is a less restricted condition than the wheel, chain, or Y networks. For example, the circle network has more two-way channels open for problem solving (i.e., five) than the four channels of the aforementioned networks. In the circle network, everyone becomes a decision maker.

The *star network* is an extension of the circle network. By connecting everyone in the circle

network, the result is a star, or all-channel, network. The star network permits each member to communicate freely with all other persons (decentralized communication). The star network has no central position, and no communication restrictions are placed on any member. A committee in which no member either formally or informally assumes a leadership position is a good example of a star network.

Effectiveness of Different Networks   The importance of a communication network lies in its potential effects on such variables as speed, accuracy, morale, leadership, stability, organization, and flexibility. Table 7-1 summarizes the findings of most research that has been done on communication networks.

Studies in communication networks show that the network effectiveness depends on situ-

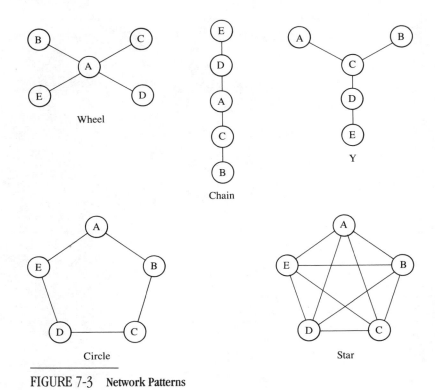

FIGURE 7-3   Network Patterns

ational factors.[31] For example, centralized networks are more effective in accomplishing simple tasks, whereas decentralized patterns are more effective on complex tasks. In addition, the overall morale of members of decentralized networks is higher than those of centralized networks. This finding makes sense in view of the research indicating that employees are most satisfied with their jobs when they have participated in decision making about them. Moreover, research shows that a member's position in the network can affect personal satisfaction. Members in more central positions in the network tend to be more satisfied.[32]

Network Analysis

Besides network patterns, another method to help school administrators analyze communication flows and patterns is network analysis. In **network analysis**, communication flows and patterns are analyzed between units and across hierarchical positions. Network analysis uses survey sociometry rather than controlled laboratory experiments to identify cliques and certain specialized roles of members in the communication structure of real-life organizations.

To illustrate, consider the communication network for a hypothetical school district.[33] Fig-

[31]John R. Bittner, *Fundamentals of Communication*, 2nd ed. (Englewood Cliffs, NJ: Prentice-Hall, 1988).

[32]Daniel J. Brass, "Being in the Right Place: A Structural Analysis of Individual Influence in an Organization," *Administrative Science Quarterly*, 29 (1984), pp. 518–539.

[33]Our hypothetical illustration is similar to the data provided in the description of the network analysis by Everett M. Rogers and Rekha Agarwala Rogers, *Communication in Organizations* (New York: Fress Press, 1976).

TABLE 7 ▪ 1   Summary of Research on Communication Networks

CHARACTERISTIC	CIRCLE	CHAIN	WHEEL	STAR
Speed	Slow	Fast	Very fast	Slow/fast
Accuracy	Poor	Good	Good	Poor/excellent
Morale	High	Low	Very low	Very high
Leadership stability	None	Marked	Very pronounced	None
Organization	Unstable	Emerging stability	Very stable	Unstable
Flexibility	High	Low	Low	High

SOURCE: Adapted from Phillip V. Lewis, *Organizational Communication: The Essence of Effective Management,* © 1987, p. 53. Used by permission of John Wiley & Sons, New York.

ure 7-4 presents a formal organizational chart showing the hierarchical positions occupied by twenty-two people in three divisions of the school district. The numbers within the boxes represent individuals in the school district. Person 1 at the top of the hierarchy is the superintendent of schools. The three people immediately below him are the assistant superintendents of the three divisions: personnel, instruction, and business. The remaining individuals are employees in each division. This chart represents the formal structure of communications within the school district. Through network analysis, Figure 7-5 shows a communication network and contrasts it with the school district's formal structure (Figure 7-4).

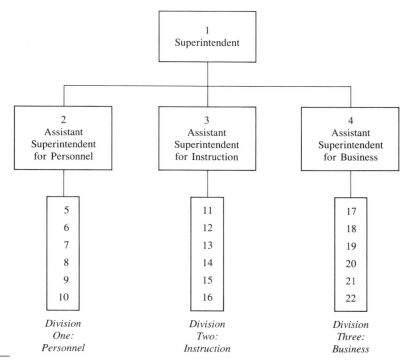

FIGURE 7-4   Formal Organizational Chart of a Hypothetical School District

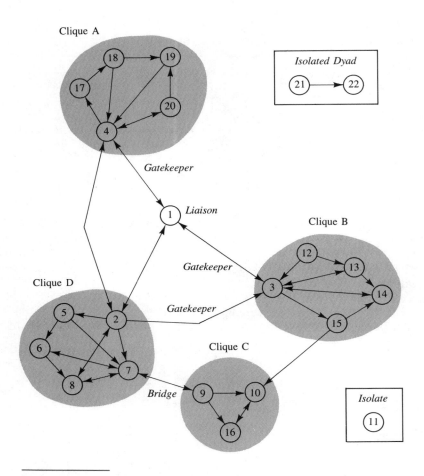

FIGURE 7-5   Communication Network of a Hypothetical School District

As Figure 7-5 shows, Person 1 (the superintendent) frequently communicates with Persons 2, 3, and 4, the assistant superintendents for personnel, instruction, and business, respectively. His communications with other lower-level members are less frequent or nonexistent. Figure 7-5 also identifies cliques in the communication network of the twenty-two members on the basis of intercommunication patterns among them. The lines indicate patterned communication contacts. Some communication contacts are two-way (↔), and some are one-way (→). Two-way arrows connect Persons 1 and 4, 1 and 2, 1 and 3, and 2 and 4, while one-way communications exist between Persons 2 and 3, 4 and 17, and so on.

There are four cliques in the school district: A, B, C, and D. "A *clique* is a subsystem whose elements interact with each other relatively more frequently than with other members of the communication system."[34] Clique A is composed of Persons 4, 17, 18, 19, 20; Clique B is composed of Persons 3, 12, 13, 14, and 15; and so on. Most clique members in a network are usually rela-

---

[34]Ibid., p. 130.

tively close to each other in the formal hierarchy of the organization. However, a school district's actual communication network can be very different from the pattern of communication established by its formal organizational structure. Four main communication roles have emerged in network analysis: gatekeepers, liaisons, bridges, and isolates.

Person 1, the superintendent, is dependent on Persons 2, 3, and 4, the three assistant superintendents, for access to communication flows. The three superintendents are also *gatekeepers*, having the capacity to control information moving in either direction between the superintendent and the rest of the school district. Person 1 also serves as a *liaison* (an individual who interpersonally connects two or more cliques within the system without himself belonging to any clique) who connects Clique A, Clique B, and Clique D. If this liaison were removed from the network, it would be a much less interconnected system. Person 7 is a *bridge*, a person who is a member of one communication clique and links it, via a communication dyad, with another clique. Thus, Person 7 is a member of Clique D and communicates with Person 9, who is a member of Clique C. Person 11 is an *isolate* (an individual who has few communication contacts with the rest of the system) and is virtually cut off from communication. Person 21 has an ingroup relationship in an isolated dyad with Person 22.

Patrick Forsyth and Wayne Hoy studied communication isolates in five secondary schools. Results indicated that communication isolates tend to be separated from perceived control, the school's control structure, respected colleagues, and sometimes friends.[35] A subsequent study of communication isolates in elementary schools reports similar findings, except that isolation from friends was not related to isolation from formal authority.[36] In another study of commu-

nication networks in one high school and five elementary schools, using sociometry and frequency surveys of communication, results indicate more frequent communication contacts in elementary schools as compared with high schools. According to this study, three factors affect horizontal communication patterns in schools: level and size of school, specialization, and proximity.[37]

In sum, we have identified and described individuals who have potential influence in the informal communication network and their roles in interpersonal communication in school districts. School administrators entering a school district would be well advised to establish good interpersonal relationships with gatekeepers, liaisons, and bridges. Furthermore, being cognizant of the potentially destructive aspect of isolates who often become alienated and exhibit detrimental behaviors dysfunctional to the school district is vital. Knowledge of communication networks can serve as useful interpersonal communication sources. More important, such knowledge can determine the success or failure of a school administrator on the job. School administrators, who must communicate with several groups (parents, nonparents, students, staff members, other administrators, school board members, community groups, and the media), can develop effective communication strategies. (See Administrative Advice 7-3.)

However, problems could arise when effective communication evolves to overinvolvement, particularly from parents (see the PRO/CON Debate).

BARRIERS TO COMMUNICATION

Effective communication plays a vital role in accomplishing the goals of the school district. However, barriers may interfere with effective communication and include frames of reference, filtering, structure, information overload, semantics, and status differences.

[35]Patrick B. Forsyth and Wayne K. Hoy, "Isolation and Alienation in Educational Organizations," *Educational Administration Quarterly*, 14 (1978), pp. 80–96.

[36]Arlene E. Zielinski and Wayne K. Hoy, "Isolation and Alienation in Elementary Schools," *Educational Administration Quarterly*, 19 (1983), pp. 27–45.

[37]W. W. Charters, "Stability and Change in the Communication Structure of School Facilities," *Educational Administration Quarterly*, 3 (1967), pp. 15–38.

■

COMMUNICATION STRATEGIES

The following communication strategies are designed to enhance a school district's communications network.

CALLING ALL PARENTS

- *Weekly Newsletter*. Prepare a weekly newsletter to parents.
- *Special Announcements*. Announce plays, honors, assemblies, class trips, and other special events.
- *Videotapes*. Videotape presentations students make in class so parents can see them later.
- *Annual Packet*. In August send parents a packet containing general information about the coming school year and information specific to each student's program.

LINKING SCHOOL AND COMMUNITY

- *Grandparents' and Senior Citizens' Day*. Plan events especially for them and coordinate these events with some major school activity such as an art show or science exhibition.
- *Newspaper Coverage*. Provide local newspapers with a constant flow of information about the school.
- *Radio*. Spread school news through the radio. Encourage staff members to appear on talk shows to describe special programs.
- *Television*. Hook up with the local cable network to provide a series of programs about the school system.
- *School System Profile*. Every third year, produce a brochure, which is distributed across the county and state, about the school system.
- *District Newspaper*. Once or twice a year, distribute a four-page newspaper to all residents of the community.
- *Speakers' Bureau*. Develop a speakers' bureau of faculty and administrators who offer to speak on a variety of school topics.
- *Memberships*. Hold membership in several organizations and serve on the boards of several service groups.

- *Telephone-Answering System*. Install answering devices on all office telephones in the school district.

KEEPING THE SCHOOL BOARD INFORMED

- *Weekly Board Newsletters*. Send board members weekly newsletters identifying important topics and giving a bit of background on each (prepared by the superintendent).
- *Monthly Board Report*. Prior to a school meeting, prepare a package of information pertinent to the agenda items, for each board member (prepared by the superintendent).

BUILDING RAPPORT WITH THE STAFF

- *Principals' Newsletters*. Assure a continuous flow of information at the building level.
- *Superintendent's Newsletters*. Distribute a weekly newsletter to staff once a week.
- *Meetings*. Hold regularly scheduled staff meetings.

COMMUNICATING WITH STUDENTS

- *Student Broadcasts*. Address students through an intercom system or a closed-circuit television network in the school.
- *Meetings and Rallies*. Hold student meetings and rallies, which create a sense of community and enthusiasm for school life.
- *Magazines*. Encourage students at all levels to put together magazines about their school experiences for each other, their parents, and the community.

Source: Adapted from Joan D. Abrams, "Pass it on: School P.R. Doesn't Have to Be Costly," *Executive Educator*, 11 (1988), pp. 18–20. Used by permission.

Frames of Reference

People can interpret the same communication differently, depending on their learning, culture, and experience. This type of communication barrier is related to the encoding and decoding components of the communication process discussed earlier. If the sender and receiver have a common **frame of reference**—that is, when the encoding and decoding of a message is similar—communication is likely to be effective. If, on the other hand, the communicators have different frames of reference, communication is likely to become distorted.[38] For example, people raised in different cultures may react quite differently to the same message. Other examples of different frames of reference in a school district may include those of superintendent and principal, principal and teacher, teacher and student, and management and union. While neither of these groups is right or wrong, each group has unique experiences, and each plays a different role, which often results in unintentional distortions of the communication between them, in the school district.

Filtering

Another barrier to effective communication is **filtering**, a process that occurs as information is transmitted from one level to another. It involves the transmittal of partial information by the sender. Filtering can occur in either direction, that is, during downward or upward flows of communication.

During downward communication flows, unintentional filtering can occur because of errors in encoding or decoding messages. Differences in learning, culture, and experiences may ac-

count for unintentional filtering. Intentional filtering occurs when a sender assumes that parts of a message are not needed by the receiver. This can result in distortions of the original meaning of the message. Research shows that administrators may be reluctant to transmit negative information downward. For example, subordinates who had good performance ratings were more likely to be informed of those ratings than subordinates who had poor ratings.[39] Also administrators may be reluctant to communicate positive information if they feel the subordinate will use it one day to support a claim against the organization or to oppose the administration sometime in the future.

Given this finding, it is not surprising that administrators and their subordinates sometimes have differing perceptions concerning subordinate performance ratings. Filtering by school administrators can also be a constructive means of uncertainty absorption, according to James March and Herbert Simon.[40] Administrators may intentionally withhold information that they feel might create anxiety in subordinates and thus result in a decrease in subordinates' productivity.

In school districts, filtering problems occur more often in upward communication than in downward communication. Because administrators are in a position to withhold rewards, subordinates manipulate unfavorable information flowing upward in the school district. The reason for such filtering should be obvious. Administrators make merit evaluations, give salary increases, and promote employees based on the information they receive from subordinates. Research indicates that subordinates with strong aspirations for upward mobility are especially likely to filter information in upward communi-

---

[38]John D. Hatfield and Richard C. Huseman, "Perceptual Congruence About Communication as Related to Satisfaction: Moderating Effects of Individual Characteristics," *Academy of Management Journal*, 25 (1982) pp. 349–358.

[39]Gary Johns, *Organizational Behavior: Understanding Life at Work* (Glenview, IL: Scott, Foresman, 1983).
[40]James G. March and Herbert A. Simon, *Organizations* (New York: Wiley, 1958).

PRO/CON DEBATE

■

PARENT INVOLVEMENT

Parent–teacher organizations and booster clubs provide many schools with volunteer assistance in classrooms, school libraries, and school offices. In some communities, their fund-raising abilities supply instructional, athletic, and musical equipment beyond the scope of the school budget. These resources provide visible support for schools, but they are not intended to impact directly on school policy or curriculum. Recently, the literature recommends parent involvement on school and district committees so that parents can influence decisions about schooling.

QUESTION When parents sit on district and school committees, does this communication channel enhance the relationship between school and community?

ARGUMENTS PRO

1 Parents and educators are partners in the child's development. A partnership suggests separate but equal contributions and shared responsibility. Parents deserve greater access to the inner workings of schools. The relationship between school and community will only improve when schools provide vehicles for access.

2 Parents, especially the urban poor who were themselves not successful in school, are disenfranchised stakeholders in the educational system. They have a vested interest in the welfare of their own children but are intimidated by school policies and procedures. These parents need nonthreatening interactions with educators. Service on committees provides an arena for work on mutual goals and the development of positive attitudes.

ARGUMENTS CON

1 The school acts *in loco parentis*, in place of the parent. School personnel have the responsibility for providing educational service and are certified to do so by the state. Frequently, parents are the problem, not the solution. Their access to school matters should be limited.

2 Most parents are concerned about their child's education, but, with changes in families (mothers working outside the home, single parents, etc.), many are too busy. In some settings, parents ignore or are hostile toward educators. They do not participate voluntarily in school-sponsored events such as open house. Those who need to volunteer won't.

cation. Moreover, subordinates who distrust their superiors and lack security will filter their messages. And those who desire to impress their superiors to achieve a promotion will manipulate unfavorable information about themselves.[41]

---

[41]Fredric M. Jablin et al. (eds.), *Handbook of Organizational Communication* (Newbury Park, CA: Sage, 1987).

Structure

The **structure** of the school district can affect the quality of communications within it. A tall structure is one in which there are many hierarchical levels of authority. Generally, communication efficiency decreases with the number of levels through which information must pass before reaching its intended receiver. The reason is fairly simple: The more levels of adminis-

Pro/Con Debate (continued)

3 Through involvement on district and school committees, parents provide the client's view of the educational system. Traditionally, this viewpoint has been sought only rarely. The relationship between school and community is enhanced because the client's perspective is valued.

3 Most of what parents know about the school they learn from their own children. They overgeneralize on the basis of that limited data. Their motivation is to improve conditions for only their child. They have little interest in supporting procedures that benefit the general welfare. Because committees act for the general good, parents are thwarted in their efforts. In the long run, the school–community relationship worsens.

4 When parents are oriented to their role in governance, they develop the knowledge and skills they need to operate well in committee structures. A period of orientation and training increases mutual understanding between parents and teachers.

4 Parents lack the educational expertise to understand the complex issues raised on committees. School–community relations will worsen because parents cannot participate on an equal footing with professional educators.

5 Parents have too few opportunities to interact with schools in a positive, professional manner. Through involvement such as service on committees, parents will observe that teachers are skilled problem solvers.

5 Parents have ample opportunity to observe and interact with teachers on matters related to their children's instruction. However, parents are often intimidated by teachers' knowledge. When working together on committees, they will see teachers as formal and distant.

---

tration through which a message must be transmitted, the greater the danger that it will be changed, modified, shortened, amended, or misinterpreted or will totally fail to reach its receiver.[42] The tall structure is very useful for horizontal communication flow. Individuals tend to communicate more at their own level than to attempt to circumvent levels and converse with others at the top and bottom of the hierarchy. Thus, communication among colleagues is good, but upward and downward communication is frequently poor and distorted.[43]

A flat structure, which has few levels between the top and bottom of the hierarchy, has many people at the bottom. It is relatively easy to get a message from the bottom to the top of the hierarchy in a flat structure. This provides a partial explanation of why face-to-face communication works more effectively in small rather than in large school districts. Direct channels can be used more readily because fewer levels of administration have to be penetrated.[44] For example, in very small school districts, board members often speak directly to building principals or teachers, bypassing the superintendent. Similarly, in small school districts, teachers often communicate directly with board members, violating the

[42]Bernard Rosenblatt, T. Richard Cheatham, and James T. Watt, *Communication in Business*, 2nd ed. (Englewood Cliffs, NJ: Prentice-Hall, 1982).

[43]McCroskey, Richmond, and Stewart, *One on One: The Foundations of Interpersonal Communication*.

[44]DuBrin, *Foundations of Organizational Behavior: An Applied Perspective*.

formal hierarchy. Furthermore, in a flat structure, there is less gatekeeping, and vertical (upward and downward) communication between superior and subordinate is better.

An example of a tall structure might be the New York City public schools, and an example of a flat structure might be a small, rural elementary school. The New York City public schools has many levels of authority, with smaller units under each; the typical small, rural elementary school has a principal and several teachers. One disadvantage of the flat structure is that the head administrator might suffer from information overload because the span of control in a flat structure is generally greater than in a tall structure.[45]

Information Overload

In today's complex school organizations, school administrators are frequently overloaded with more information than they can handle effectively. This **information overload** occurs for several reasons. First, school districts face higher levels of uncertainty today because of increasing turbulence in the external environment.[46] School districts respond by obtaining more information to reduce the uncertainty. Second, increased role specialization and task complexity create a need for more information. For example, school districts employ counselors, social workers, school psychologists, business managers, personnel directors, professional negotiators, and curriculum directors, to name only a few. In the curriculum area of special education alone, there are teacher specialists in emotionally disturbed (ED), learning disabilities (LD), educable mentally handicapped

(EMH), physically handicapped and other health impairments (PHOHI), multiply handicapped (MH), orthopedically handicapped (OH), and severely and profoundly handicapped (SPH).[47] The wide variety of specialists provide needed information to accomplish a complexity of tasks. This specialization results in additional demands to process the increased amount of information. Third, advances in communication technology, such as the use of computers, increases the quantity of information and data available. As a result, administrators are deluged with information; they cannot absorb or adequately respond to all of it. Thus, they select parts of it, which often results in incomplete or inaccurate information on which to make decisions. The problem today is not a scarcity but an overabundance of information that can be processed effectively.

One research team identifies seven categories of response to communication overload: *omitting*—failing to process some of the information; *erroring*—processing information incorrectly; *queuing*—leveling the peak loads by delaying until a lull occurs; *filtering*—separating out less relevant information; *approximating*—categorizing input and using a general response for each category; *employing multiple channels*—introducing alternative channels for information flow; and *escaping*—avoiding the information.[48]

Semantics

The same words may have different meanings to different people. Thus, it is possible for a school administrator and her subordinates to speak the same language but still not transmit understanding. As defined previously, communication is the transmission of information from a sender

---

[45]David D. Van Fleet, "Span of Management Research and Issues," *Academy of Management Journal*, 26 (1983), pp. 546–552.

[46]R. Bruce McPherson, Robert L. Crowson, and Nancy J. Pitner, *Managing Uncertainty: Administrative Theory and Practice in Education* (Columbus, OH: Merrill, 1986).

[47]Special education nomenclature varies from state to state.

[48]Robert E. Callahan, C. Patrick Fleenor, and Harry R. Knudson, *Understanding Organizational Behavior: A Managerial Viewpoint* (Columbus, OH: Merrill, 1986).

to a receiver through the use of common symbols. However, one cannot transmit understanding; one can only transmit information in the form of words, which are the common symbols conveying ideas, facts, and feelings. **Semantics** can be a communication barrier because of the misinterpretation of words. Meanings are not in the words but in the minds of the people who receive them.

Meanings of concrete words do not differ much from sender to receiver. Little misunderstanding arises when we speak of typewriter, computer, paper, or book. Because words such as love, happiness, and virtue are more abstract, more misunderstandings are likely to occur. Similarly, words that evoke emotional responses, like liberal and conservative, are prime candidates for greater misunderstandings.

One reason for semantic differences relates to the use of numerous specialists who tend to develop their own professional jargon. This special language can provide in-group members with feelings of belongingness, cohesiveness, and even self-esteem. And it can enhance effective communication within the group. However, the use of in-group language can often result in barriers to communication for outsiders. For example, special education teachers use abbreviations like LD (learning disabilities), ED (emotionally disturbed), EMH (educable mentally handicapped), and IEP (individualized education plan), which is common terminology among these professionals. Such abbreviations or terms will probably have little meaning to people outside this specialized group.

Status Differences

Another barrier to communication is **status difference**, which exists within every school district. School districts create status differences through titles, size of office, carpeting, office furnishings, stationery, private secretary, a reserved parking space, salary, and the formal or-

ganizational chart. Regardless of the symbols, status interferes with effective communication between personnel at different levels of the hierarchy. The status of superordinate–subordinate relationships, for example, inhibits the free flow of information vertically (upward and downward).

The higher one's status in the school district, the less likely he will have effective communications with personnel a few levels removed. In general, individuals who have higher status also receive more communication demands on them. Out of necessity, they must limit their communications to those who have direct influence on them—that is, their direct supervisors and subordinates. For example, the superintendent needs to be more concerned with establishing communications with the assistant superintendents directly under her as well as with the board of education, who is directly above the superintendent. Such a communication pattern was outlined previously. Recall that the superintendent communicated frequently with his assistant superintendents. However, the superintendent's communication with other lower-level personnel was less frequent or nonexistent (see Figure 7-5).

Thus, as shown in network analysis, communication between higher-status personnel and lower-status personnel tends to be limited, and the messages that subordinates send upward in the hierarchy tend to be positive (filtering). Moreover, subordinates may be reluctant to express an opinion that is contrary to their supervisor's. One reason for this behavior is that the administration has the power to grant and withhold rewards such as merit evaluations, salary increases, promotions, and better work assignments. School administrators, because of time constraints, indifference, or arrogance, may actually strengthen status differentials by not being open to feedback or other forms of upward communication. However, when the status differences become too great, communications decrease, and subordinates initiate less communication with superiors.

OVERCOMING BARRIERS TO COMMUNICATION

Effective communication requires a sustained effort on the part of both school administrators and employees to overcome communication barriers and to arrive at mutual understandings. Although there should be some responsibilities on both sides, successful communication seems to lie primarily with school administrators because they are the ones to develop a two-way communicative climate. In an attempt to overcome some of the communication barriers, we examine five communication skills—repetition, empathy, understanding, feedback, and listening—that are a means of improving school district communications.

Repetition

One of the most frequently used techniques of effective communication is repetition. **Repetition** involves sending the same message over and over again, using multiple channels (e.g., telephone call, face-to-face discussion, memorandum, or letter). Most communication is subject to some distortion. By using two or more channels to transmit a message, communication failure is less likely to occur. For example, a personal discussion can be followed up with a memorandum or letter. Here both written and oral channels are used. The sender has gained the attention of the receiver as a result of face-to-face communication. The sender and receiver also have written records of the conversation for future reference and to stipulate all details of the conversation. Similarly, sending minutes of a meeting to participants is using repetition and multiple channels of communication to ensure understanding. Similarly, it is customary in large school districts for school administrators to use multiple channels to communicate the results of a subordinate's performance evaluation. The subordinate first receives a verbal explanation of the results that is accompanied or followed by a written statement, which the superior and subordinate sign as an indication that each has read and understands its content.

Empathy

Effective communication means that the sender can make predictions about how the receiver will respond to a message. The sender can accomplish this by visualizing the receiver's frame of reference into the transmission of the message. In other words, a school administrator should place herself figuratively in the shoes of the subordinate and attempt to anticipate personal and situational factors that might influence the subordinate's interpretation of the message. For superintendents to communicate effectively with assistant superintendents, for assistant superintendents to communicate effectively with principals, for principals to communicate effectively with faculty, and for faculty to communicate effectively with students, empathy is an important ingredient and can reduce many of the aforementioned barriers to communication. **Empathy** is a technique for understanding the other person's frame of reference. The greater the gap between the learning, the culture, and the experiences of the sender and the receiver, the greater the effort that must be made to find a common ground of understanding.

Understanding

Earlier we said that communication is effective to the extent that both the sender and the receiver have high agreement in their understanding of a transmitted message. School administrators must remember that effective communication involves transmitting **understanding** as well as messages. Regardless of the communication channel used, messages should contain simple, understandable language. School administrators must encode messages in words and symbols that are understandable to the receiver.

As noted, understanding cannot be communicated; only messages can. This is the idea behind the concept of readability popularized by Rudolf Flesch.[49] Readability seeks to make writing and speech more understandable. Flesch and others developed readability formulas that can be applied to written and oral communication alike. Some research has found that much written communication that is transmitted to employees is rated as beyond the level of satisfactory reading for typical adults.[50]

Feedback

Feedback ensures effective communication and determines the degree to which a message has been received and understood. This two-way communication, in which the sender and the receiver arrive at mutual understanding, contrasts with one-way communication of the kind that occurs in most downward communication. In downward communication, for example, distortions often occur because of insufficient opportunity for feedback from receivers. For example, when the superintendent distributes a memorandum on an important board policy to all professional personnel in the school district, this act alone does not guarantee that communication has taken place. One might expect feedback in the form of upward communication to be encouraged more in school districts that use participatory management, site-based management, and site-based decision-making practices. School districts need effective upward communications if their downward communications are to be effective. Some studies report numerous benefits of two-way communication (feedback) over one-way communication. For example, although two-way communication is more time-consuming than is one-way communication, it provides increased satisfaction and

is recommended in all but the simplest and routine transmission of information.[51]

Written messages provide much less opportunity for feedback than does face-to-face communication. When possible, school administrators should use face-to-face communication because this approach allows the individuals communicating with each other to receive both verbal and nonverbal feedback. Brief, straightforward questions such as the following can be helpful in eliciting feedback from subordinates about the reception of a message: How do you feel about my statement? What do you think? What did you hear me say? Do you see any problems with what we have talked about?[52] Such attempts to elicit feedback from a receiver of a message can avoid misunderstandings between a sender and a receiver.

Some guidelines that school administrators can use to elicit feedback from subordinates include the following:[53]

- Promote and cultivate feedback, but don't try to force it.
- Reward those who provide feedback and use feedback received.
- Whenever possible, go straight to the source and observe the results—don't wait for feedback.
- Give feedback to subordinates on the outcome of the feedback received. Thus, the school administrator elicits feedback, uses it, and feeds back its results to subordinates.

Listening

Earlier, we noted that school administrators spend over 70 percent of their time communicating. Moreover, estimates indicate that over 30

[49]Rudolf Flesch, *The Art of Readable Writing*, rev. ed. (New York: Harper & Row, 1974).
[50]Richard L. Enos (ed.), *Oral and Written Communication* (Newbury Park: CA: Sage, 1990).

[51]Donald Walton, *Are You Communicating? You Can't Manage Without It* (New York: McGraw-Hill, 1989).
[52]DuBrin, *Foundations of Organizational Behavior: An Applied Perspective.*
[53]Middlemist and Hitt, *Organizational Behavior: Managerial Strategies for Performance.*

ADMINISTRATIVE ADVICE 7-4

■

LISTENING STYLES

One way of viewing listening is to look at listening styles. Six listening styles, which have been developed by Performax Systems International, can help school administrators improve their listening skills.

- **Leisure Listener.** This listener is very relaxed and tunes in primarily to what is pleasant. To be more effective, a leisure listener needs to avoid wandering off on tangents and to focus on the task at hand. This listener should also be willing to listen to important information, even if it is unpleasant and makes her uncomfortable.
- **Inclusive Listener.** This listener takes in everything, wanting to understand the main ideas of the speaker in order to be comfortable. To be more effective, an inclusive listener needs to avoid getting impatient with ramblers, to stop trying to take in everything, and to concentrate more on analyzing and evaluating the message.
- **Stylistic Listener.** This listener tunes in to the mannerisms and dress of the speaker and wants to know the speaker's background and credentials. This listener also tends to place the speaker in a favorable or unfavorable category. To be more effective, a stylistic listener needs to avoid stereotyping and to pay more attention to the content that is being presented.
- **Technical Listener.** This listener is very tuned in to processing information and is listening or gathering specific data within a narrow but in-depth listening range. To be more effective, a technical listener needs to avoid tunnel listening and to become more inclusive. This listener

would also profit by paying more attention to nonverbal cues and being more open to the emotions of the speaker.
- **Emphatic Listener.** This listener is looking for the unstated message and needs to understand the emotions of the speaker before becoming comfortable with the interpersonal communications. To be more effective, an emphatic listener needs to focus on the task at hand, realizing that the content of the message is important as well as the emotions.
- **Nonconforming Listener.** This listener analyzes, evaluates, and has a tendency to agree or disagree quickly. This listener also tends to challenge the speaker and listens for supporting data to use in agreement or disagreement. (This is different from the technical listener who gathers supporting data to apply to a specific task situation.) To be more effective, a nonconforming listener needs to avoid hasty judgments and to look for points of agreement early in the speaker's message. This person also has a tendency to overprotect stimuli and assign a deeper meaning than was intended.

Source: Adapted from Frank W. Freshour, "Listening Power: Key to Effective Leadership," *Illinois School Research and Development*, 26 (1989), pp. 17–23.

percent of an administrator's day is spent devoted to listening. More important, tests of listening comprehension suggest that these individuals listen at only 25 percent efficiency.[54]

[54]Robert N. Bostrom, *Listening Behavior: Measurement and Applications* (New York: Guilford Press, 1989).

Listening skills affect the quality of colleague and superordinate–subordinate relationships in schools. (See Administrative Advice 7-4.)

Successful communication therefore requires effective **listening** on the part of both the sender and the receiver. The receiver must listen to receive and understand the sender's messages; and the sender must listen to receive and understand the receiver's feedback. Often listening is the weak link in the chain of two-way communication. Many people do not work actively at listening well. One author emphasizes that listening is an active process that demands a great deal of concentration and effort.[55] Recently, some organizations have designed training programs, which explore techniques for improving listening skills.[56] For example, the following guidelines can be helpful to school administrators:[57]

- *Stop talking.*
- Put the talker at ease.
- Show the talker you want to listen.
- Remove distractions.
- Empathize with the talker.
- Be patient.
- Hold your temper.
- Go easy on argument and criticism.
- Ask questions.
- *Stop talking.*

Note that the first and last rule for good listening is to "stop talking." Some researchers estimate that administrators spend as much as 85 percent of time devoted to communicating—in talking.[58] This does not leave much time for listening and feedback. School administrators must realize that effective communication involves understanding as well as being understood.

Lee Iacocca stresses the importance of listening, Tom Peters and Nancy Austin suggest that service to clients is the foundation of listening, and Paul Hersey and Kenneth Blanchard make numerous references to listening in their situa-

tional leadership theory.[59] And numerous reform reports—including *A Nation at Risk*, the Holmes Group, the Carnegie Task Force on Teaching as a Profession, and the Governor's Report—all recommend formal instruction in listening skills in schools.

SUMMARY

1. Communication is an important skill because school administrators spend over 70 percent of their time communicating.
2. The communication process is continuous and involves six steps: ideating, encoding, transmitting, receiving, decoding, and acting. Nonverbal communication involves encoding and decoding body language, vocal cues, use of time, and spatial relationships to more effectively understand verbal messages.
3. Communications within school organizations flow in four primary directions: downward, upward, horizontally, and diagonally. These communication flows are more likely to occur in open than in closed organizational climates.
4. The major informal communication flow in school organizations is called the grapevine. The grapevine carries both accurate information and rumors.
5. Whether formal or informal, the actual pattern of communication connecting role incumbents within school organizations is called a network. A school organization's network is often quite different from the pattern of relationships established by its formal structure.
6. The barriers to effective communication include differing frames of reference, filtering, structure, information overload, semantics, and status differences. Techniques for overcoming barriers to effective communication include repetition, empathy, understanding, feedback, and listening.

[55]Bruce Benward, *Ear Training: A Technique for Listening*, 3rd ed. (Dubuque, IA: Brown, 1987).

[56]Larry Barker, *Listening Behavior* (Dillon, CO: Spectra, 1990).

[57]Kay Dans, *Human Behavior at Work* (New York: McGraw-Hill, 1972).

[58]Middlemist and Hitt, *Organizational Behavior: Managerial Strategies for Performance*.

[59]Paul Hersey and Kenneth H. Blanchard, *Management of Organizational Behavior*, 5th ed., (Englewood Cliffs, N.J.: Prentice-Hall, 1988); Lee Iacocca and William Novak, *Iacocca: An Autobiography* (Toronto: Bantam Books, 1984); Thomas J. Peters and Nancy Austin, *A Passion for Excellence: The Leadership Difference* (New York: Random House, 1985).

Key Terms

communication process
ideating
encoding
transmitting
receiving
decoding
acting
nonverbal communication
communication flow
grapevine
network pattern

network analysis
frame of reference
filtering
structure
information overload
semantics
status differences
repetition
empathy
understanding
feedback
listening

Discussion Questions

1. Select a communication you have had recently and analyze it using the model shown in Figure 7-1.
2. Using network analysis, develop a communication network for your school. Compare your communication network with the formal structure of the school.
3. Why is it difficult to obtain accurate information from upward and downward communication flows?
4. What are six barriers to effective communication in school organizations? And what are some techniques for overcoming these barriers?
5. Observe the nonverbal communication behavior of organizational participants for fifteen minutes. Explain the nonverbal behavior you observe. Is there any inconsistency between nonverbal and verbal behaviors?

Suggested Readings

Patricia Calvert (ed.), *The Communicator's Handbook: Techniques and Technology* (Gainesville, FL.: Maupin House, 1990). Presents a thorough overview to the basics of communication.

Philip R. Cohen et al. (eds.), *Intentions in Communications* (Cambridge, MA.: MIT Press, 1990). Provides managers with an excellent guide to the hidden meanings behind what people say during organizational communication.

Eugene V. Donaldson, *Predictable Communication Strategies* (Los Angeles: Outcomes Unlimited, 1990). Describes the whole process of communication from ideation to activity, including barriers and methods of overcoming these.

Richard L. Enos (ed.), *Oral and Written Communication: Historical Approaches* (Newbury Park, CA.: Sage, 1990). An array of essays by an international team of contributors that explore the diversity and depth of oral and written communication.

Lawrence F. Frey et al., *Investigating Communication Strategies* (Englewood Cliffs, NJ: Prentice-Hall, 1990). Provides scholars, practitioners, and students with an invaluable, state-of-the-art research tool.

Sonya Hamlin, *How to Talk So People Listen: The Real Key to Job Success* (New York: Harper & Row, 1989). Provides practical and relevant information concerning professional communication in the workplace from the standpoint of management.

Donald Walton, *Are You Communicating? You Can't Manage Without It* (New York: McGraw-Hill, 1989). A valuable addition to the existing professional communication literature.

8

ORGANIZATIONAL CHANGE

In this chapter, we attempt to answer these questions concerning change in school organizations. We begin our discussion by examining the open-systems model, which provides a useful framework for understanding the change process in schools. We discuss internal and external pressures for change in schools. We examine the major sources of resistance to change and how to overcome them. Force-field analysis serves as a useful model in exploring the complex nature of change. Finally, we present and analyze various approaches to change, including individual and group strategies.

During the last decade, the prominent approach in organizational theory has moved from an emphasis on innovation in organizations to frameworks for change based on an organization's strategy in human resource management and on the determinism experienced by external and internal environments. This new approach to organizational change stems in part from contemporary thinking about organizational management. Both business and education are beginning to incorporate the principles of Theory Z management.[1] Such management is likely to concern itself with such issues as the empowerment of teachers, the improvement of the quality of work life, and the forging of strong linkages between school and community. When such principles are introduced in schools, they probably represent a change from existing practice. But what causes such changes to take place?

Previously, we used the term *social system* to refer to aggregates of human relationships such as schools, school districts, and communities. We pointed out the impact of the external environment on each of these social systems. Put another way, nearly all social systems are open systems. We will elaborate on the concept of **open systems** because it has considerable utility in understanding organizational change in school organizations.

SCHOOLS AS OPEN SYSTEMS

We can view social systems, such as school organizations, as a linkage of inputs (materials, information, or people) from sources in the external environment, a transformation process (a technical–human organization), and outputs (products and services). The system may include one or more feedback loops for control. For example, feedback from the internal and external environments that the output is substandard could lead to change in either the transformation process or the inputs, or both. Effectiveness of the organization is thus based on adaptation to both internal and external forces (Figure 8-1).

Daniel Katz and Robert Kahn provide one of the most comprehensive descriptions of the open-systems perspective. They suggest nine

common characteristics shared by all open systems:[2]

1. *Importation of Energy.* Open systems take in energy from the outside environment in the form of people, materials, and information.
2. *The Throughput.* Open systems transform the imported energy. The organization builds a product, trains people, provides a service, or processes materials.
3. *The Output.* Open systems export a product into the outside environment. In a school, the output may be students' knowledge, skills, abilities, and attitudes.
4. *Cycles of Events.* In open systems, the pattern of activities is recycled. The export of a product furnishes energy for the cycle to repeat. In a school system, the importation of resources (people, materials, and information) is used to teach students who are then exported into the outside environment. These graduates continue to contribute energy to the school system in the form of resources (financial, human, or material). The importation of new energy into the system triggers a new cycle.
5. *Negative Entropy.* Entropy, a law of nature, stipulates that all forms of organization move toward death or disorganization. Because the open system can import more energy than it uses, it can survive and expand. However, not all organizations continue to import more energy than they expend. Consequently, many organizations go out of business each year.

Public schools are a special type of organization, which have been classified as "domesticated" organizations.[3] Put another way, public schools are protected and secure in

[1]William G. Ouchi, *Theory Z: How American Business Can Meet the Japanese Challenge* (Reading, MA: Addison-Wesley, 1981).

[2]Daniel Katz and Robert L. Kahn, *The Social Psychology of Organizations* (New York: Wiley, 1978).
[3]Richard O. Carlson, "Environmental Constraints and Organizational Consequences: The Public School and Its Clients," in D. E. Griffiths (ed.), *Behavioral Science and Educational Administration* (Chicago: University of Chicago Press, 1964), pp. 262–276.

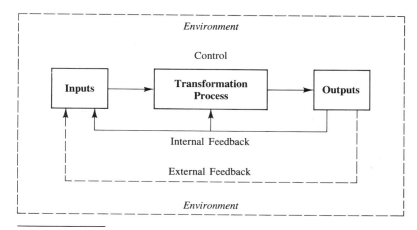

FIGURE 8-1   Open-Systems Model

many ways. For example, their clients (students) must participate in the organization, and the organization will be protected regardless of its performance.[4] Furthermore, although public schools must compete for public funds, they are virtually assured by law that they will not go out of business.

6. *Feedback.* The information coming into an organization is coded and selected so that the organization does not receive more information than it can process. Information provides signals from the environment, and negative feedback indicates deviations from what the environment desires. This is a control mechanism.

7. *Dynamic Homeostasis.* There is a continuous inflow from the environment, but the ratio tends to remain relatively equal. This process serves to preserve the character of the system and to maintain it in equilibrium.

However, the equilibrium is not stationary. For example, as the goals of the organization change, a new character may develop that will serve as a new homeostatic basis.

8. *Differentiation.* Open systems tend toward elaboration of roles and specialization of function. Roles in schools—including those of superintendents, principals, teachers, and other specialists—are illustrative of this tendency.

9. *Equifinality.* Multiple means to the same ends exist within open systems.

Figure 8-1 depicts an open system interacting with the external environment and highlights open-system characteristics. The figure shows that, as open systems, organizations possess aspects of interdependency and interaction of components within an identifiable wholeness.

Each component (inputs, transformation process, outputs, and the external and internal environments) must be successfully managed and linked if the organization is to be effective. For example, to focus more attention on the technical–human organization (transformation process) and to ignore how the external environment is reacting to the product and services provided by the organization can result in serious

[4]There is a trend underway for state departments of education to seize control of academically deficient school systems. See Connie Leslie, Tony Emerson, and Pat Wingert, "Very Hostile Takeovers: States May Step in When Local Schools Fail," *Newsweek,* March 13 (1989), pp. 61–64.

consequences. Similarly, to focus on inputs or to concentrate on outputs while ignoring the effectiveness of the technical–human organization can also lead to serious consequences.

We have all seen school administrators jeopardize a school district by spending all their energies on inputs or on outputs while paying little attention to employee motivation, the quality of leadership, methods of decision-making, and internal communications. As a result, school faculty exhibits low morale and job satisfaction, interpersonal conflict, and disillusionment with the leadership of the school or school district. These are examples of not providing adequate attention to feedback and managing the interrelationships of the component parts of the social system.[5]

PRESSURES FOR ORGANIZATIONAL CHANGE

What causes changes to take place in school organizations? Generally, pressures on schools to change emanate from the external and internal environment. These include government intervention in education, society's values, changing technology and knowledge explosion, and administrative processes and the fulfillment of employee's needs.

Government Intervention in Schools

For a number of years prior to the Reagan administration, the federal government continued to increase its intervention in educational policy-making. Much of this intervention in educational matters was evidenced in legislation deal-

ing with civil rights and equal educational opportunity, school district desegregation, and programs for the handicapped and economically disadvantaged. While much of the federal intervention in educational matters described herein still exists, President Bush has de-emphasized the role of the federal government in educational matters; he has provided state and local education leaders with more latitude in educational policy-making.

Nevertheless, between the release of *A Nation at Risk* in 1983 and two other prestigious, national reports issued by the Holmes Group and the Carnegie Task Force on Teaching as a Profession in 1986, state legislatures enacted more than 700 statutes regulating education.[6] This mass of legislation imposed by the states usurped the authority of teachers, administrators, and local communities. The second wave of school reform, precipitated by the latter two national reports, viewed the local school as the center of change.[7] Instead of top-down hierarchical reform initiated at the state level, change efforts would be tailored to the needs of local schools and communities.

Society's Values

Changes in society's values also illustrate the impact of the external environment on organizational change. Society's values are evidenced in employee attitudes and expectations. For example, we noted that Herzberg's hygiene factors (salary, job security, working conditions, supervision, organizational policies, and status) are expected as givens by employees in today's schools; that is, the absence of these factors results in employee job dissatisfaction.

---

[5]For further information on the nature of open systems, see Wendell L. French and Cecil H. Bell, *Organization Development: Behavioral Science Interventions for Organization Improvement,* 4th ed. (Englewood Cliffs, NJ: Prentice-Hall, 1989).

[6]Mary Hatwood Futrell, "Mission Not Accomplished: Education Reform in Retrospect," *Phi Delta Kappan,* 71 (1989), pp. 9–14.

[7]Kenneth A. Sirotnik, "The School as the Center of Change," in T. J. Sergiovanni and J. H. Moore (eds.), *Schooling for Tomorrow: Directing Reforms to Issues That Count,* (Needham Heights, MA: Allyn and Bacon, 1989), pp. 89–113.

A recent extension of Herzberg's work is the concept of *quality of work life*. By this we mean the extent to which employees are able to satisfy their needs through their participation in the organization. Management and unions alike have taken an active role recently in effecting organizational change designed to improve the quality of work life.[8]

Society's values also influence government legislation, which in turn places external pressures on school districts to change. For example, during the 1960s and early 1970s, the values of equity and efficiency dominated the national agenda as bases for educational policy-making. Beginning in the late 1970s, the federal preoccupation with equity began to give way to the "excellence movement" in U.S. schools. And by the 1980s, the Reagan administration continued to emphasize excellence in schools and to deemphasize equity and the federal government's role in educational policy-making.[9] This emphasis on excellence and state and local involvement in educational policy-making has continued under the Bush administration. However, the new agenda for educational reform in the 1990s is likely to have a combined focus on excellence and *equity*. In the latter case, attention will be given to the educational needs of rapidly growing minority groups, the recruitment of minority teachers and administrators, and the psychological health of youngsters in a nation plagued by drug abuse, teenage suicide, and AIDS.[10]

Technological Change and Knowledge Explosion

Another source of external pressure for change is the technological explosion all organizations are experiencing. This pressure is due in part to research and development efforts within organizations. For example, many large, urban school districts now have research and development departments as part of their organizational structures. However, a great deal of technological development occurs outside the organization. This development is the result of governmental-sponsored research efforts and the efforts of numerous educational organizations including the American Association of School Administrators (AASA), National Association of Secondary School Principals (NASSP), National Association of Elementary School Principals (NAESP), Cooperative Program in Educational Administration (CPEA), University Council for Educational Administration (UCEA), National Council of Professors of Educational Administration (NCPEA), National Academy for School Executives (NASE), Association for Supervision and Curriculum Development (ASCD), National Society for the Study of Education (NSSE), and the American Educational Research Association (AERA).

Concurrently with the development of new technologies is an explosion of knowledge. More people than ever before are attending college, and a large percentage of the population is receiving graduate degrees. Higher education is no longer reserved for the elite few. There is also a growing emphasis on continuing education courses offered on university campuses across the country, and nontraditional students (older students) are returning to junior colleges and four-year institutions. New technologies require the development of knowledge to implement the technology. Thus, the interaction of new technology and the knowledge required to generate the technology into the organization compounds the rate of technological change exponentially.

Processes and People

Pressures in the internal environment of the organization can also stimulate change. The two most significant internal pressures for change

---

[8]Fred Massarik (ed.), *Advances in Organization Development Vol. 1* (Norwood, NJ: Ablex, 1990).

[9]Larry Cuban, "Reforming Again, Again, and Again," *Educational Researcher,* 19 (1990), pp. 3–13.

[10]Thomas R. McDaniel, "Demilitarized Public Education: School Reform in an Era of George Bush," *Phi Delta Kappan,* 71 (1989), pp. 15–18.

come from processes and people. Processes that act as pressures for change include communications, decision making, leadership, and motivational strategies, to name only a few. Breakdowns or problems in any of these processes can create pressures for change. Communications may be inadequate; decisions may be of poor quality; leadership may be inappropriate for the situation; and employee motivation may be nonexistent. Such processes reflect breakdowns or problems in the transformation process of the open-systems model (see Figure 8-1) and may reflect the need for change.

Some symptoms of people problems are poor performance levels of teachers and students, high absenteeism of teachers or students, high dropout rates of students, high teacher turnover, poor school–community relations, poor management–union relations, and low levels of teacher morale and job satisfaction. A teacher's strike, numerous employee complaints, and the filing of grievances are some tangible signs of problems in the internal environment. These factors provide a signal to school administrators that change is necessary. In addition, internal pressures for change occur in response to organizational changes that are designed to deal with pressures for change exerted by the external environment.

In short, many organizational changes are influenced by external and internal environmental pressures. The way in which these pressures are foreseen and administered is critical to the organization's effectiveness. The external and internal pressures for change require effective strategic planning to ensure that the organization is able to adapt to changes as they occur. (See Administrative Advice 8-1.)

RESISTANCE TO CHANGE

Pressures on school organizations to change are presently occurring and demand some response from their members. But, many of the problems associated with change concern the forces resisting it—that is, the forces for maintaining the status quo or equilibrium. Two major issues concern the resistance to change: the causes of resistance and ways of reducing resistance.

Causes of Resistance to Change

Organizational change is an attempt by school executives to improve the effectiveness of schools. These attempts to change schools result in different responses from organizational members. One typical response to any change is resistance. School administrators need to understand the common causes of resistance to change.[11] These include interference with need fulfillment, fear of the unknown, threats to power and influence, knowledge and skill obsolescence, organizational structure, limited resources, and collective bargaining agreements.

Interference with Need Fulfillment   Changes that interfere with a person's economic, social, esteem, or other needs are likely to meet with resistance. People usually resist changes that could lower their income or job status, such as termination or a demotion. Besides the fulfillment of economic and esteem needs, people work for social reasons. The social relationships that develop in the organization are often more important to its members than is commonly realized. For example, even such seemingly minor changes as relocating employees within the same building or school district may affect social-status relationships and result in resistance.

Fear of the Unknown   People like stability. They may have invested a great deal of time and effort in the current system. They have established a normal routine in performing their jobs. They have learned what their range of duties are and

[11]Urs E. Gattiker, *Technology Management in Organizations* (Newbury Park, CA: Sage, 1990).

ADMINISTRATIVE ADVICE 8-1

PLANNING FOR CHANGE

In planning for change, high morale and positive feelings of the staff are essential. Teachers who like their work environment and respect and appreciate the school leadership are more likely to participate and devote more time for constructive change. Below are the ten most frequent suggestions made by 150 teachers (East Baton Rouge, Louisiana, school district) for school administrators to exhibit to help teachers acquire a positive mental attitude toward change.

- Ensure that the first faculty meeting is carefully organized. Avoid long drawn-out meetings and use visual aids to emphasize points rather than long readings and unimaginative lectures.
- Encourage teacher input and involvement; give teachers opportunities to become instrumental in the school's organizational structure. Allow them to have input in establishing guidelines.
- Be fair and impartial to the entire staff, enforcing rules and regulations for all teachers. Be firm but fair.
- Be visible around the school campus so teachers are not intimidated by the administrative hierarchy. Some rapport with the students, teachers, and staff members on an informal level will encourage cooperation from everyone.
- Give positive reinforcement as often as possible. Expound on teachers' strengths as well as their weaknesses.

- Project a positive mental attitude.
- Minimize paperwork; maximize actual teaching time.
- Ensure that all equipment and facilities are in proper working order and that teachers know how and where to locate all materials, supplies, and equipment.
- Ensure that teachers know exactly what you expect of them. Present expectations clearly and positively. Be sure new teachers are thoroughly acquainted with all rules, regulations, policies, and procedures.
- Assign teachers to classes in which they are certified to teach. Try to accommodate teachers in classes they prefer to teach, when possible.

Source: Adapted from Frank B. Cortez, "Planning Ahead for a Good School Year," *NASSP Bulletin*, 73 (1989), p. 118. Used by permission.

---

what their supervisor's expectations are for performing these duties. They have some idea of the routine problems that may surface in the performance of their jobs. That is, they have learned how to perform their jobs successfully, how to get good performance ratings from their supervisors, how to interact with their work group, and so on. Put another way, the present system has a high degree of certainty.

Changes in established work routines or job duties create some potential unknowns. For example, employees may fear that they will not be able to perform up to their previous standards.

They may have to learn a new job. They may have to learn to adjust to a new supervisor's expectations. They may have to adjust to a new work group. They may have to make new friends. When a change occurs, the normal routine is disrupted, and the employee must begin to find new and different ways to function within the environment.

Threats to Power and Influence Resistance can also occur because the proposed changes may reduce one's power and influence in the organization. One source of power in organizations is the control of something that other people need, such as information or resources. Individuals or groups who have established a power position in an organization will resist changes that are felt to reduce their power and influence. For example, a superintendent of schools whose school district is threatened with consolidation with another school district will resist the merger in order to maintain his current position. Similarly, the trend toward management information systems (MIS) in today's school districts, which makes more information available to more school district members, is likely to be resisted by top-level administrators. These administrators would lose this source of influence and power if MIS were implemented.

Knowledge and Skill Obsolescence

Somewhat related to threats to power and influence is knowledge and skill obsolescence. While the former usually applies to management, the latter can apply to any member of the organization's hierarchy. Employees will resist organizational changes that make their knowledge and skills obsolete. For example, consider the school bookkeeper who has mastered a complex accounting system over a long period of time. The superintendent of schools announces the implementation of a new computerized accounting system that is reputed to be easier and more efficient. The bookkeeper is threatened by a change to a new computerized system and will likely resist the change because her identity is the mastery of the old and more complex accounting system.

Organizational Structure

In Chapter 2, we characterized the school district as a bureaucratic organizational structure. Like all modern organizations, schools have many of the characteristics of an ideal bureaucracy—a hierarchy of authority, a division of labor and specialization, rules and regulations, impersonality in interpersonal relationships, and a career orientation. In fact, the very meaning of organization implies that some degree of structure must be given to groups so that they can fulfill the organization's goals. However, this legitimate need for struc-

ture can be dysfunctional to the organization and serve as a major resistance to change.[12] For example, schools typically have narrowly defined roles; clearly spelled out lines of authority, responsibility, and accountability; and limited flows of information from the top to the bottom of the hierarchy.

Recall from Chapter 7 that an emphasis on the hierarchy of authority causes employees to feed back only positive information to superiors concerning their jobs. The avoidance of negative feedback by subordinates hampers school administrators from identifying subordinates' concerns and needed changes in the organization. Also recall that the taller the organizational structure is, the more numerous the levels through which a message must travel. This increases the probability that any new idea will be filtered as it travels upward through the hierarchy because it violates the status quo in the school or school district.

Limited Resources

Some school districts prefer to maintain the status quo, whereas others would change if they had the available resources. Generally, change requires resources: capital and people with the appropriate skills and time. A school district may have identified a number of innovations that could improve the effectiveness of the district operation. However, the district may have to abandon the desired changes because of inadequate resources. We are certain that you can identify a number of local school district innovations, as well as those initiated by the federal and state governments, that have been deferred or completely abandoned due to resource limitations.

Collective Bargaining Agreements

The most pervasive changes in educational policy matters have been brought about by the practice of negotiating formally with the teachers' union and other employee unions in a school district. Agreements between management and union

---

[12]Fred C. Lunenburg, "Factors Affecting Educational Innovation," *EDUCARE Journal,* 3 (1975), pp. 19–23.

usually impose obligations on participants that can restrain their behaviors. Collective bargaining agreements are a good example. That is, ways of doing things that were once considered management prerogatives may become subject to negotiation and be fixed in the collective bargaining agreement. Some examples include salaries, cost-of-living adjustments (COLA), class size, teacher transfer, school calendar, class hours, evaluations, and promotions. Such agreements restrain the behavior of school administrators from implementing desired changes in the system.

After years of ignoring, denying, and placing blame on their clients for troubled schools, U.S. school systems are realizing that it is time to trace the problem of declining school systems. Schools are beginning to examine their own situations and seek new answers. They are acknowledging their internal difficulties with slipping technological leadership, inadequate teaching processes, obsolete and excessive management approaches, and an overall low rating in the quality of student outcomes. (See Administrative Advice 8-2.)

Reducing Resistance to Change

Earlier, we focused on change as it relates to social systems, more specifically to open systems. Change must involve attention to several interacting linkages that constitute an entire social system, a whole or gestalt (see Figure 8-1). Moreover, an open system is in a state of quasi-stationary equilibrium; that is, as the goals of a social system change, the equilibrium will change.

To better understand resistance to change, Kurt Lewin developed the concept of **force-field analysis.**[13] He looks upon a level of behavior within an organization not as a static custom but as a dynamic balance of forces working in opposite directions within the organization. He

believes that we should think about any change situation in terms of driving forces or factors acting to change the current condition (pressures for change) and resisting forces or factors acting to inhibit change (resistance to change). These forces may originate in the internal or external environment of the organization or in the behavior of the change agent.

School administrators must play an active role in initiating change and in attempting to reduce resistance to change. School administrators can think of the current condition in an organization as an equilibrium that is the result of driving forces and resisting forces working against each other. Change agents must assess the change potential and resistance and attempt to change the balance of forces so that there will be movement toward a desired condition. There are three ways of doing this: increasing the driving forces, reducing the resisting forces, or considering new driving forces.

Lewin points out that increasing one set of forces without decreasing the other set of forces will increase tension and conflict in the organization. Reducing the other set of forces may reduce the amount of tension. While increasing driving forces is sometimes effective, it is usually better to reduce the resisting forces because increasing driving forces often tends to be offset by increased resistance. Put another way, when we push people, they are likely to push back. Figure 8-2 illustrates the two sets of forces—pressures for change and resistance to change. This is the type of situation that school administrators face and must work with on a daily basis when attempting to effect change.

As Figure 8-2 shows, change results when an imbalance occurs between the ratio of driving forces and resisting forces. Such an imbalance alters the existing condition—hopefully in the direction planned by the school administrator—into a new and desired condition. Once the new, desired condition is reached, the opposing forces are again brought into equilibrium. An imbalance may occur through a change in the velocity of any force, a change in the direction of a force, or the introduction of a new force.

[13]Kurt Lewin, *Field Theory in Social Sciences* (New York: Harper & Row, 1951).

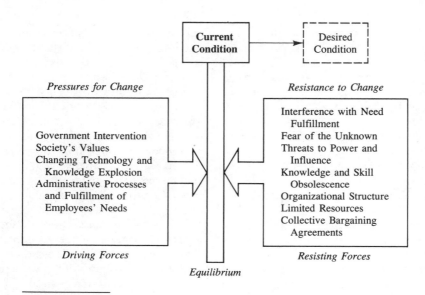

FIGURE 8-2   Pressures for Change and Resistance to Change

Moreover, change involves a sequence of organizational processes that occurs over time. Lewin suggests this process typically requires three steps: unfreezing, moving, and refreezing.[14]

1. *Unfreezing.* This step usually means reducing the forces acting to keep the organization in its current condition. Unfreezing might be accomplished by introducing new information that points out inadequacies in the current state or by decreasing the strength of current values, attitudes, and behaviors. Crises often stimulate unfreezing. Examples of crises are significant increases in the student dropout rate, dramatic enrollment declines, shifts in population within a school district, a sudden increase in teacher or middle-management turnover, a costly lawsuit, and an unexpected teacher strike. Unfreezing may occur without crises as well. Cli-

mate surveys, financial data, and enrollment projections can be used to determine problem areas in a school district and initiate change to alleviate problems before crises erupt.

2. *Moving.* Once the organization is unfrozen, it can be changed. This step usually involves the development of new values, attitudes, and behaviors through internalization, identification, or change in structure. Some changes may be minor and involve a few members—such as changes in recruitment and selection procedures—and others may be major, involving many participants. Examples of the latter include a new evaluation system, restructuring of jobs and duties performed by employees, or restructuring the school district, which necessitates relocating faculty to different school sites with the system.

3. *Refreezing.* The final step in the change process involves stabilizing the change at a new quasi-stationary equilibrium. Changes in organizational culture, changes in group norms, changes in organizational policy, or

---

[14]Jitendra V. Singh (ed.), *Organizational Evolution: New Directions* (Newbury Park, CA: Sage, 1990).

ADMINISTRATIVE ADVICE 8-2

■

KEYS TO SUCCESS OF AN ORGANIZATIONAL CHANGE EFFORT

A broad look at large-scale organizational change efforts reveals some interesting patterns. Successful change efforts seem to have three basic characteristics that program designers should keep in mind.

■ *They Establish Need.* Before initiating any substantial actions, those who will be affected by the change (starting with the top organizational levels) must clearly recognize the need for change. Without that incentive, change efforts may encounter organizational inertia or even active resistance.

■ *They Involve People.* Relevant administrator and teacher groups need to be involved in shaping, even inventing, the change effort. It is equally important to tailor the effort to the unique situation and style of each organization. "Off-the-shelf" programs imported from other organizations or consulting firms tend to inspire less involvement and may produce more "sloganeering" and simulated compliance than actual change.

■ *They Sustain Commitment.* Top leadership must lead the process actively and demonstrate a strong and sustained commitment to it. Without patience, persistence, and consistency, subordinates probably will view the change process as just another "program-of-the-month."

The Down Side. Change programs that do not do well tend to have equally consistent characteristics:

■ Top-level administrators look to the effort for a semiquick fix or do it because "everyone else is doing it."

■ Administration is most interested in "OP" (other people's) change. The attitude is, "Try it–it's good for you," but administration is unwilling to take the tough first step: examining and changing its own processes.

■ When early half-hearted efforts produce disappointments (or even successes), administration turns its attention elsewhere, leaving the effort to be run by specialists or staff personnel.

Source: Adapted from Jon E. Cornell and Stanley M. Herman, "The Quality Difference," *Training and Development Journal,* 43 (1989), pp. 55–57. Copyright 1989 *Training and Development Journal,* American Society for Training and Development. Used by permission.

modifications in organizational structure often accomplish this.

Figure 8-2 illustrates force-field analysis that shows both the pressures for change and resistance to change within a school setting. School administrators can use six specific methods to reduce resistance to change: participation, communication, support, rewards, planning, and coercion.

Participation   One of the best methods for reducing resistance to change is to involve those who will be affected by the change to participate in planning, design, and implementation. There are at least three explanations for the effect of participation in reducing resistance to change: (1) As those affected by the change plan, design, and implement it, new ideas and information can be generated. The increased information is likely to result in a more effective change; (2) participation builds ownership for the change, thus leading to a commitment to see the change successfully implemented; and (3) by providing information about the nature and consequences of the change, anxiety about the unknown is reduced, and rumors are stifled.[15]

Communication   Another method for reducing resistance to change involves communicating and explaining to employees the nature of and need for the change. In explaining the need, administrators are advised to explain the effects the change will have on employees. This too will lessen employees' fear of the unknown. Employees who are informed about the logic behind administrative decisions are more likely to support new ideas.[16]

Support   Effective implementation of a change requires support from top-level administrators such as the superintendent of schools and his cabinet. Support from the superintendent usually means that administrators lower in the organization's hierarchy, such as building principals, will be committed to the change. It is particularly important for building principals to manifest *supportive* and *considerate* leadership behaviors when change is being implemented. This type of leader behavior includes listening to subordinates' ideas, being approachable, and using employee ideas that have merit. Supportive leaders go out of their way to make the work environment more pleasant and enjoyable. For example, difficult changes may require training to acquire new skills necessary to implement the change. Administrators need to provide such training.[17] In short, when procedures are established to implement changes smoothly, less resistance is likely to be encountered.

Rewards   When change is imminent, most people say, "What's in it for me?" Subordinates are less likely to resist changes that will benefit them directly.[18] For example, during collective bargaining between the board of education and the teachers' union, certain concessions can be given to teachers in exchange for support of a new program desired by management. Such concessions may include salary increases, bonuses, or more union representation in decision making. Administrators can also use standard rewards such as recognition, increased responsibility, praise, and status symbols. Thus, building in rewards may help reduce subordinates' resistance to a change.

Planning   Prospective changes should be well planned in advance. Change inevitably leads to subordinate anxiety about new expectations and fear of the unknown. The proposed change may require new performance levels. Therefore, performance levels need to be given careful consideration by administrators when planning a change. Performance levels that are set too low can negatively affect performance. On the contrary, performance levels that are set too high can result in frustration and low performance.[19] Moreover, introducing change incrementally can lessen the impact of change on subordinates and allow them time to adjust to new expectations and conditions.[20]

Coercion   When other methods have failed, coercion can be used as a last resort. Some changes require immediate implementation. And top-level administrators may have considerable power. Such instances lend themselves

---

[15]Chris Argyris, *Overcoming Organizational Defenses* (Needham Heights, MA: Allyn and Bacon, 1989).

[16]Robert E. Callahan, C. Patrick Fleenor, and Harry R. Knudson, *Understanding Organizational Behavior: A Managerial Viewpoint* (Columbus, OH: Merrill, 1986).

[17]Richard A. Schmuck and Philip J. Runkel, *Handbook of Organization Development in Schools,* 3rd ed. (Prospect Heights, IL: Waveland Press, 1988).

[18]Edward E. Lawler, *Pay and Organization Development* (Reading, MA: Addison-Wesley, 1981).

[19]George L. Morrissey, Patrick J. Below, and Betty L. Acomb, *The Executive Guide to Operational Planning* (San Francisco: Jossey-Bass, 1988).

[20]Robert E. Hoskisson and Craig S. Galbraith, "The Effect of Quantum Versus Incremental M-Form Reorganization on Performance: A Time-Series Exploration of Intervention Dynamics," *Journal of Management,* 11 (1985), pp. 55–70.

more readily to administrators using coercion to gain compliance to changes. Subordinates can be threatened with job loss, decreased promotional opportunities, no salary increases (this technique is used infrequently in public schools), or a job transfer to achieve compliance with a change. There are, however, negative effects of using coercion, including frustration, fear, revenge, and alienation. This in turn may lead to poor performance, dissatisfaction, and turnover.[21]

Changing the Roles of Stakeholder Groups

Producing substantial, positive change in our schools requires changes in the roles of school personnel. School administrators can successfully manage change if they follow a process designed to guide their efforts, which involves restructuring the roles of the school district's major stakeholder groups. (See Administrative Advice 8-3.)

Staff development programs can also provide positive change. However, some claim that, because they are professionals, teachers will voluntarily increase their knowledge and should not be coerced to participate (see the PRO/CON Debate).

INDIVIDUAL APPROACHES TO CHANGE

One way to improve an organization's effectiveness is to enhance an individual's functioning within the organization. This involves two basic types of approaches. The first type is aimed at changing the job or the person's perception of the job. The objective is to make the job more intrinsically satisfying to the employee. The second type is aimed at changing the person. The approaches we discuss are job enrichment, laboratory training, behavior modification, and transactional analysis. These change strategies are important, but not all of them might be used in a specific change program. Understanding the strategies and when to use them is necessary for change agents.

Job Enrichment

Frederick Herzberg's motivation–hygiene theory has stimulated programs in job enrichment in many organizations. Herzberg feels that the challenge to organizations is to emphasize motivation factors while ensuring that the hygiene factors are present. He refers to job enrichment as the method for achieving such a condition.[22] **Job enrichment** focuses on achieving organizational change by making jobs more meaningful, interesting, and challenging.

Expanding on the earlier work of Herzberg, Richard Hackman and Greg Oldham provide an explicit framework for enriching jobs.[23] Based on their own research and the work of others, they developed a job-characteristics model (Figure 8-3). As the figure shows, five core job characteristics create three critical psychological states that in turn lead to a number of employee outcomes. The employee's knowledge and skills, growth-need strength, and satisfaction with context factors moderate the linkage among the job characteristics, the psychological states, and the outcomes.

---

[21] Richard W. Woodman and William A. Pasmore (eds.), *Research in Organizational Change and Development,* Vol. 1 (Greenwich, CT: JAI Press, 1987).

[22] Frederick Herzberg, "One More Time: How Do You Motivate Employees?" *Harvard Business Review,* 65 (1987), pp. 109–120.

[23] J. Richard Hackman and Greg R. Oldham, *Work Redesign* (Reading, MA: Addison-Wesley, 1980).

■

A NEW WAY OF THINKING

The movement toward school improvement necessitates changes in the duties of school board members, central office administrators, principals, and teachers. There are changes in the way these key groups make decisions about change and improvement in the schools. The new duties of these key decision-making groups are as follows:

DUTIES FOR PRINCIPALS

- Ensure the positive climate necessary for gaining commitment to school improvement decisions.
- Involve staff and students in developing goals and program plans for improvement.
- Ensure that staff development programs are related to school-improvement goals.
- Participate in staff development with their faculties.
- Ensure that the design of the school-improvement plan addresses the major educational problems in their schools.
- Implement and evaluate school instructional improvement with their planning teams.

DUTIES FOR TEACHERS

- Work collaboratively with the principal, central office staff, and representative parents (and in high schools, students) to consider district and school priorities and to select goals to achieve over the next four or five years.
- Help identify the programs and practices necessary to achieve their school goals.
- Assist in the implementation of these programs and practices by participating in staff development designed to help them achieve their goals.
- Conduct in-service programs for their peers.
- Help collect and interpret evaluation data related to their improvement goals.
- Assist the principal in managing the resources to ensure their improvement plans are successful.

DUTIES FOR SCHOOL BOARD MEMBERS

- Establish and revise current policies to promote and support effective decision making and im-

provement of programs and practices in district schools.
- Identify improvement goals to address major educational problems affecting the district.
- Identify any improvement goals that all schools must address.
- Establish a climate supportive of school-based improvement.
- Establish performance expectations for central administration that support school-based improvement.
- Monitor progress toward achieving the district's goals.
- Allocate funds to support the achievement of the district's improvement goals.
- Serve as public advocates for both the school-improvement process and the effort to achieve the district's improvement goals.

DUTIES FOR CENTRAL OFFICE PERSONNEL

- Translate board policy and priority goals for improvement into short- and long-range district plans for implementation.
- Provide data related to the district's major problems and goal areas identified by the board.
- Provide and manage district resources to support school instructional improvement plans.
- Approve and monitor school instructional improvement plans.
- Evaluate all aspects of the district-improvement operation.
- Provide staff development to accomplish desired goals and objectives of approved school-improvement plans.
- Model, in all aspects of their operations, the behaviors expected of principals and their school-based improvement teams.

Source: Adapted from Sarah D. Caldwell and Fred H. Wood, "School-Based Improvement—Are We Ready?" *Educational Leadership*, 46 (1988), pp. 50–53. Copyright © 1985 by the Association for Supervision and Curriculum Development. Used by permission.

PRO/CON DEBATE

■

STAFF DEVELOPMENT

In recent years, staff development proponents have argued that all planned change efforts require a staff development component. A staff development infrastructure has emerged: staff developers, which are new roles in school districts; teacher centers and principal centers; and LEAD centers which are funded by the Department of Education. In every school district, someone's job description includes responsibility for staff development. College courses on staff development are filled. Is this allocation of resources justified?

QUESTION Is staff development essential to planned organizational change?

ARGUMENTS PRO

1 Leaders of high-performing educational systems recognize that schooling is a labor-intensive industry. Any planned change must reorient the people who perform the work and pursue the mission. Massive changes require massive staff development components that support staff through the stages of change and learning.

2 Teachers may not choose to learn what they need to learn. A teacher's knowledge base, like that of all professionals, becomes obsolete. The organization bears a major responsibility for ensuring the currency of teachers' professional knowledge in the areas it identifies as essential.

3 School district's staff development programs are often fragmented with many teachers taking different courses. Staff-development programs should focus on a limited numbered of programs. Teachers are more apt to apply staff development information if districts support teachers as they use ideas and discuss results with colleagues.

4 Staff development is long overdue. Without constant infusions of staff development knowledge and expertise, the educational enterprise will not stay current.

5 Organizations in all sectors have devised structures so they can to do their work and train their people. Innovative school districts have developed new structures to support staff development. More structures will emerge as staff development is institutionalized.

ARGUMENTS CON

1 Successful planned change in organizations is a function of good planning, well-chosen models, the involvement of participants, and well-conducted formative evaluations. The change itself is a learning process. People learn best by doing, not by listening to speakers or attending workshops.

2 Educators are highly trained. Most have many degrees and licenses. If teachers need more professional background, school districts should work with colleges to improve preservice programs. Graduates should be taught to continue learning on their own throughout their careers.

3 Educators do not need to be told what to learn. They are highly socialized professionals who know what they need to know and when they need to know it. By reading, attending professional conferences, working with their peers, and reflecting on their work with students, teachers learn theoretical models and techniques.

4 Staff development is another fad. It will go the way of open-space schools and individualized instruction.

5 Massive staff development is too expensive and time-consuming. While the full-time staff is away learning, classrooms operate with substitute teachers and schools make do with part-time administrators. Planned change that requires staff development is not cost effective.

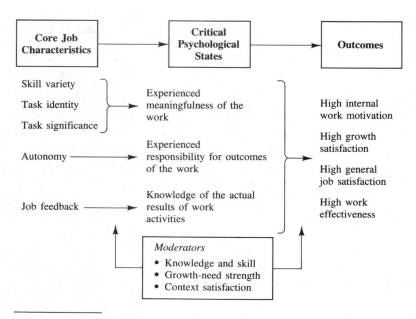

FIGURE 8-3   Job-Enrichment Model (Source: Adapted from J. Richard Hackman and Greg R. Oldham, *Work Redesign,* © 1980, p. 90. Used by permission of Addison-Wesley Publishing Co., Inc., Reading, MA)

The five job characteristics that are essential to job enrichment are

1. *Skill variety* is the degree to which a job requires a variety of different activities in carrying out the work, which involves the use of a number of different skills and talents of the employee.
2. *Task identity* is the degree to which a job requires completion of a "whole" and identifiable piece of work, that is, doing a job from beginning to end with a visible outcome.
3. *Task significance* is the degree to which the job has a substantial impact on the lives of other people, whether those people are in the immediate organization or in the external environment.
4. *Autonomy* is the degree to which the job provides substantial freedom, independence, and discretion to the individual in scheduling the work and in determining the procedures to be used in doing the work.

5. *Job feedback* is the degree to which carrying out the work activities required by the job provides the individual with direction and clear information about the effectiveness of her performance.[24]

Skill variety, task identity, and task significance together affect "experienced meaningfulness of the work." Autonomy and feedback independently affect the other two psychological states, respectively, "experienced responsibility for outcomes of the work" and "knowledge of the actual results of the work activities." And according to Hackman and Oldham, only employees who have job-related knowledge and skills, high growth-need strength, and high satisfaction with context factors (Herzberg's hygienes) are likely to be affected in the manner specified in the model.

[24]Ibid.

Hackman and Oldham have developed the job diagnostic survey (JDS) to diagnose the job dimensions in their model (see Figure 8-3) and to determine the effect of job changes on employees.[25] Thus, the job dimensions in the job-enrichment model can be combined into the following mathematic expression, which explains the relative impact of change in each dimension of the Hackman–Oldham model:

$$MPS = \frac{\text{Skill variety} + \text{Task identity} + \text{Task significance}}{3} \times \text{Autonomy} \times \text{Feedback}$$

The motivation potential score (MPS) formula sums the scores for skill variety, task identity, and task significance and divides the total by three. The combination of these three job characteristics is equally weighted, with autonomy and feedback considered separately. The result is an overall measure of job enrichment.

Laboratory Training

Lewin was instrumental in the development of **laboratory training,** also known as sensitivity training or T-groups.[26] The National Training Laboratories (NTL) developed and refined laboratory training in 1946. From this beginning, training has emerged as a widely used organizational strategy aimed at individual change, which generally takes place in small groups.

Goals of Laboratory Training   Based on an extensive review of the literature, two researchers have outlined six basic objectives common to most laboratory training sessions:

1. To increase understanding, insight, and self-awareness about one's own behavior and its impact on others, including the ways in which others interpret one's behavior

2. To increase understanding and sensitivity about the behavior of others, including better interpretation of both verbal and nonverbal cues, which increases awareness and understanding of what the other person is thinking and feeling

3. To improve understanding and awareness of group and intergroup processes, both those that facilitate and those that inhibit group functioning.

4. To improve diagnostic skills in interpersonal and intergroup situations, which is attained by accomplishing the first three objectives

5. To increase the ability to transform learning into action, so that real-life interventions will be more successful in increasing member effectiveness, satisfaction, or output

6. To improve an individual's ability to analyze her own interpersonal behavior, as well as to learn how to help herself and others with whom she comes in contact to achieve more satisfying, rewarding, and effective interpersonal relationships[27]

These objectives point out that laboratory training can be a useful strategy for bringing about organizational change. School districts that are experiencing problems with communications, coordination, or excessive and continuing conflict in interpersonal relationships may benefit from laboratory training as a means of improving individual and organizational effectiveness.

Design of Laboratory Training   Laboratory training groups (T-groups) typically consist of ten to fifteen members and a professional trainer. The duration of T-group sessions range from a few days to several weeks. The sessions are usually conducted away from the organization, but some

[25]J. Richard Hackman and Greg R. Oldham, "Development of the Job Diagnostic Survey," *Journal of Applied Psychology,* 60 (1975), pp. 159–170.

[26]For a discussion of laboratory training, see Robert T. Golembiewski and Alan Kiepper, *High Performance and Human Costs: A Public Sector Model of Organizational Development* (New York: Praeger, 1988).

[27]John P. Campbell and Marvin D. Dunnette, "Effectiveness of T-Group Experience in Managerial Training and Development," *Psychological Bulletin,* 70 (1968), pp. 73–104.

occur on university campuses or on the premises of large business organizations. Laboratory training stresses the process rather than the context of training and focuses on attitudinal rather than conceptual training.

The four basic types of training groups are stranger, cousin, brother, and family laboratories. In stranger T-groups, members are from different organizations and therefore are unknown to each other before training. An example would be several superintendents from different districts. Cousin laboratories consist of members taken from a diagonal slice of an organization, which cuts across two or three vertical hierarchical levels without a superior and subordinate being in the same group. An example would be the coordinator of secondary education and elementary school principals from the same district. Brother laboratories include members who occupy similar horizontal roles in an organization but without superiors and subordinates in the same group. For example, a group of principals from the same district would be brothers. In the family laboratory, all members belong to the same subunit of an organization. The superintendent of a school district and his administrative cabinet or the principal of a school and her department heads are examples of a family training group.

The trainer may structure the content of the laboratory training by using a number of exercises or management games or follow an unstructured format in which the group develops its own agenda. Robert Blake and Jane Mouton were among the first trainers to modify the unstructured format into an instrumental one.[28]

Stranger laboratory groups with an unstructured format were the classic form of T-groups used during the early beginnings of laboratory training. However, the difficulty encountered in applying interpersonal skills acquired away from the organization to the home-base organization when participants returned has led to the use of cousin and family groups in recent years. In fact, there has been a movement recently away from laboratory training groups and toward team building. This more recent application of T-groups as been exemplified in the work of Chris Argyris, an early proponent of laboratory training.[29] Thus, laboratory training is often used today as part of more complex organizational change strategies.

Behavior Modification

Behavior modification has its roots in B. F. Skinner's theory of operant conditioning, which emphasizes the effect of environmental influences on behavior.[30] More recently, a social-learning approach has been suggested as a more comprehensive theoretical foundation for applying behavior modification in organizations.[31] Thus, organizational behavior modification is the process of changing the behavior of an employee by managing the consequences that follow his work behavior.

Fred Luthans's S-O-B-C model provides a useful way of viewing the behavior modification process.[32] Based on a social learning approach, the behavior modification process recognizes the interaction of four parts: S (stimulus), O (organism or employee), B (behavior), and C (consequences) (Figure 8-4).

Stimulus   The S in the model refers to stimulus, which includes internal and external factors, mediated by learning, that determines employee behavior. External factors include organizational

[28]Susan A. Mohrman and Thomas G. Cummings, *Self-Designing Organizations: Learning How to Create High Performance* (Reading, MA: Addison-Wesley, 1989).

[29]Chris Argyris, *Reasoning, Learning, and Action: Individual and Organizational* (San Francisco: Jossey-Bass, 1982).

[30]B. F. Skinner, *About Behaviorism* (New York: Knopf, 1974).

[31]Fred Luthans and Robert Kreitner, *Organizational Behavior Modification and Beyond: An Operant and Social Learning Approach* (Glenview, IL: Scott, Foresman, 1985).

[32]Fred Luthans, *Organizational Behavior,* 5th ed. (New York: McGraw-Hill, 1989).

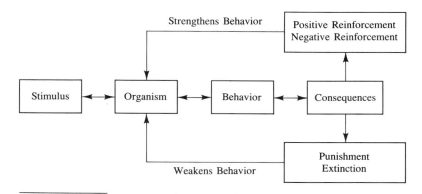

FIGURE 8-4   S-O-B-C Model (Source: Adapted from Fred Luthans, *Organizational Behavior,* 5th ed., © 1989, p. 15. Used by permission of McGraw-Hill, Inc., New York)

structure and organizational and administrative processes interacting with the structure: decision making, control, communication, power, and goal setting. Internal factors include planning, personal goals, self-observation data, stimulus removal, selective stimulus exposure, and self-contracts.[33]

Organism   The O in the model refers to the organism, or school employee. The internal and external factors in the situation constitute the organizational environment in which the school employee operates. School employees can be thought of as consisting of cognitive and psychological processes. For example, much of what we discussed about motivating behavior with need theories, expectancy theory, equity theory, goal setting, and management by objectives applies to this part of the model.

Behavior   The B in the model represents employee behavior. The study of the organizational environment (S) and the school employee (O) leads to a better understanding of the school employee's behavior—the overt and covert responses to the organizational environment. Behavior includes verbal and nonverbal com-

munication, actions, and the like. In schools we are specifically interested in work behaviors such as performance, attendance, promptness, participation in committees, superordinate–subordinate relations, interaction among colleagues, or leaving the organization.

Consequences   The C part of the model represents the consequences that result from employee behavior. The study of behavioral consequences can help improve the prediction and control of employee behavior, but this is a very simplified generalization. Social-learning theorists place more emphasis on internal states and processes when explaining job behavior than the so-called radical behaviorists.[34] However, approaches such as self-management are insufficient in producing a coordinated organizational behavior modification effort. As shown in the model, behavior is a function of internal and external cues and consequences that follow a given behavior. Some types of consequences strengthen behavior while others weaken it.

Contingencies of Reinforcement   Changing the interrelationships among organizational environ-

[33]Luthans and Kreitner, *Organizational Behavior Modification and Beyond.*

[34]Robert Kreitner and Fred Luthans, "A Social Learning Approach to Behavioral Management: Radical Behaviorists' Mellowing Out," *Organizational Dynamics,* 13 (1984), pp. 47–65.

ment (*S*), employee (*O*), behavior (*B*), and consequences (*C*) is referred to as managing the *contingencies of reinforcement*.[35] As Figure 8-4 shows, the consequences that strengthen behavior are positive reinforcement and negative reinforcement. The consequences that weaken behavior are extinction and punishment.

Positive reinforcement involves following a desired behavior with the application of a pleasant stimulus, which should increase the probability of the desired behavior. Examples of positive reinforcement in a school setting include promotions, salary increases, merit raises, praise, more desirable work assignments, awards, or simply smiles. All reinforcement strategies, however, are specific to a given individual or situation.

Negative reinforcement involves the removal of an unpleasant stimulus on the appearance of a desired behavior, which should increase the probability of that behavior. For example, a football coach of a major university requires all football players to attend an early Sunday morning practice whenever their performance in a game falls below a minimum level. The players will strive for a high performance level in the next game to avoid the unpleasant, early Sunday morning practice.

Extinction involves removing a reinforcer that is maintaining some undesired behavior. If the behavior is not reinforced, it should gradually be extinguished. For instance, suppose you have an assistant who enjoys talking about her personal life for fifteen or twenty minutes *every* time you come into the office. In the past, you have been polite and have listened attentively as she related her personal experiences. In essence, you have been positively reinforcing her behavior. To extinguish her undesired behavior, you must ignore all conversations after exchanging some brief courtesies, turn around, and walk out of the office. This should dissipate the undesired

behavior that is interfering with the performance of her work.

Punishment involves following an unwanted behavior with the application of some unpleasant stimulus. In theory, this should reduce the probability of the undesired behavior. Examples of punishment include oral reprimands, written warnings, suspensions, demotions, and discharge. While punishment may eliminate undesirable employee behavior in the short run, long-term, sustained use of punishment is dysfunctional to the organization.[36]

Steps in Organizational Behavior Modification   Luthans and Kreitner suggest five steps for using organizational behavior modification to change employee-behavior patterns.[37]

Step 1. *Identify Significant Performance-Related Behaviors*. The principal and the teachers begin by identifying and describing the changes they desire to make. The analysis includes identification of significant performance-related behaviors that can be observed, counted, and specified precisely. The teacher or the principal can do the identification process. In either case, it requires training to identify behaviors for which reinforcement strategies can be used.

Step 2. *Measure Performance-Related Behaviors*. Obtain prior to learning, baseline measurements of the frequency of the desired target behaviors. Use tally sheets and time sampling to gather the data. In a school setting, select for assessment observed classroom performance, work-assignment completions, participation in committees, student achievement, advisement, publications, absences, service to the community, curriculum writing, and complaints. Establish some preliminary period of assessment as a baseline.

---

[35]B. F. Skinner, "Whatever Happened to Psychology as the Science of Behavior?" *American Psychologist*, 42 (1987), pp. 780–786.

[36]Janice M. Beyer and Harrison M. Trice, "A Field Study of the Use and Perceived Effects of Discipline in Controlling Work Performance," *Academy of Management Journal*, 27 (1984), pp. 743–764.
[37]Luthans and Kreitner, *Organizational Behavior Modification and Beyond*.

Step 3. *Analyze the Antecedents and Consequences of Behaviors.* The behavior to be changed is often influenced by prior occurrences (antecedents) and has some identifiable consequences. For example, a particularly ineffective teacher may be a case for study. The teacher lacks effective instructional techniques, has poor rapport with students, complains incessantly about administrative policies and procedures, and adversely affects the performance and attitudes of colleagues. During this step, the principal identifies existing contingencies of reinforcement to determine when the behaviors occur, what causes them, and what their consequences are. Effective behavior change in the teacher requires replacement or removal of these reinforcing consequences.

Step 4. *Implement the Change Approach.* Use positive reinforcement, negative reinforcement, extinction, and punishment to change significant performance-related behaviors of teachers or other employees. In other words, develop an intervention strategy, then apply the strategy using suitable contingencies of reinforcement. Finally, maintain the behaviors with appropriate schedules of reinforcement, including variable ratio, fixed ratio, variable interval, and fixed interval. [38]

Step 5. *Evaluate Behavior Change.* Evaluate the effectiveness of behavior modification in four areas: reaction of the teachers to the approach, learning of the concepts programmed, degree of behavior change that occurs, and impact of behavior change on actual performance. In evaluating the success or failure of the behavior modification program, compare the original baseline measurements with outcome measurements of behavior. If it becomes apparent at Step 5 that the intervention strategy implemented in Step 4 has not resulted in the desired impact, start the process over again at Step 1.

---

[38]For more information on schedules of reinforcement, see Luthans, *Organizational Behavior.*

Transactional Analysis

Eric Berne developed **transactional analysis** for use in psychotherapy.[39] It was further popularized in the best-selling books *Games People Play* and *I'm OK — You're OK.*[40] More recently, managers have used transactional analysis as an organizational change technique.[41]

Transactional analysis is concerned with three areas of analysis: structural analysis—the analysis of individual personality; time structuring—the analysis of the way people structure their time; and life scripts—the analysis of the roles that people learn to play in life. The focus in organizational change has been on structural analysis and time structuring.

Structural Analysis   The personality of each person is made up of ego states. Berne defines an ego state as "a consistent pattern of feeling and experience directly related to a corresponding consistent pattern of behavior."[42] Although school administrators cannot direct ego states, they can observe behavior and from this infer which of the three ego states is operating at any given time. This should help them better understand others in the workplace and the reasons for their behavior.

The three ego states—the Parent, the Adult, and the Child—are common to all people, but the content of each is unique to each individual, based on her background and experiences.

- The *Parent ego state* derives from one's parents or other powerful figures in one's childhood. It is expressed toward others as nurturing, critical, or standard-setting be-

---

[39]Eric Berne, *Transactional Analysis in Psychotherapy* (New York: Grove Press, 1961).

[40]Eric Berne, *Games People Play* (New York: Grove Press, 1964); Thomas A. Harris, *I'm OK — You're OK* (New York: Harper & Row, 1969).

[41]Dorothy Jongeward and Contributors, *Everybody Wins: Transactional Analysis Applied to Organizations* (Reading, MA: Addison-Wesley, 1973).

[42]Eric Berne, *What Do You Say After You Say Hello?* (New York: Grove Press, 1972), p. 11.

havior. A school administrator exhibiting a Parent ego state tends to talk down to subordinates and to treat them like children.

- The *Adult ego state* reflects maturity, objectivity, problem analysis, logic, and rationality. It is oriented toward objective information gathering, careful analysis, generating alternatives, and making logical choices. A school administrator who behaves fairly and objectively in dealing with subordinates is exhibiting an Adult ego state.

- The *Child ego state* derives from one's experiences as a child. This ego state can range from being submissive and conforming to being insubordinate, rebellious, emotional, or perhaps inadequate.

Time Structuring   Another focus of transactional analysis is the way in which people structure their time. There are six basic ways to structure time: withdrawal, rituals, pastimes, activities, games, and authenticity.[43]

1. *Withdrawal* can be either physical or psychological. Examples include walking away from an argument (physical), withdrawing to avoid pain and punishment (physical), withdrawing to think through a problem and examine alternatives (psychological), or daydreaming (psychological).

2. *Rituals* are stylized transactions, such as "Good morning, how are you?" Such a rhetorical question suggests the response, "Fine, how are you?" Such interchanges have little meaning except to recognize the other person. Should the receiver of the message actually respond to the question, the sender would be distressed because no answer is expected.

3. *Pastimes* are nonstylized transactions that have a repetitive quality. Discussing the weather or politics during social occasions are examples.

4. *Activities* consist of transactions centered on getting work done. Work fulfills various needs in people, such as recognition and accomplishment. We all know of cases where people die shortly after retirement. Explanations for this phenomenon include people's loss of a constructive way of structuring time and feeling worthwhile and important to society.

5. *Games* are "sets of ulterior transactions, repetitive in nature, with well-defined psychological payoff."[44] People use games to avoid authenticity or intimacy. Other books provide several descriptions of games.[45] Therefore, we describe only a few of the more well-known games used in organizations. Superior and subordinate frequently play "blemish." For example, a principal brings in a report to the superintendent, and he quickly skims it. Regardless of how good the report is, the superintendent finds one or more "blemishes" in it and points these out to the principal. In this way, the superintendent maintains his power position. This game can be played at any level along the hierarchy (principal–department head, department head–teacher, teacher–student). Another game in which the superior maintains a power position is called "Yes, but. . . ." For example, the superintendent asks her principals for input in solving a problem. Each suggestion from the principals is followed with a "Yes, but . . . " response from the superintendent. Finally, there is the game of NIGYYSOB (Now I've Got You, You SOB). In this game, one employee lures another into a work situation (for example, a superintendent and principal) in which the victim, the subordinate, is programmed for failure. When the mistake occurs, the superintendent pounces on the principal, which results

[43]Muriel James and Dorothy Jongeward, *Born to Win* (Reading, MA.: Addison-Wesley, 1971).

[44]Berne, *What Do You Say After You Say Hello?*, p. 23.
[45]Berne, *Games People Play;* Fred Luthans and Mark J. Martinko, *The Practice of Supervision and Management* (New York: McGraw-Hill, 1979).

in embarrassment, a reprimand, or even dismissal.

6. *Authenticity* refers to transactions that are devoid of game playing and exploitation of people.

Andrew Halpin and Don Croft are two early researchers who recognized the significance of authenticity in organizational behavior.[46] The chief consequence of their research on organizational climate was identifying the pivotal importance of authenticity in schools.[47] Later, James Henderson and Wayne Hoy, after an extensive review of the literature, identified three basic aspects of leader authenticity in schools: accountability, nonmanipulation, and salience of self over role.[48]

Accountability is the aspect of authenticity that describes the leader as accepting responsibility and admitting errors. The authentic leader accepts responsibility for his own actions as well as those of subordinates and admits mistakes when they are made. On the other hand, inauthentic leaders are unwilling to accept responsibility and admit mistakes; they blame others and circumstances for their shortcomings and failures.

Nonmanipulation of subordinates reflects the perception of subordinates that their leader avoids exploiting them. Authentic leaders are seen as those who avoid manipulating others as if they were objects. Whereas inauthentic leaders are perceived as dealing with subordinates as if they were things.

Salience of self over roles, refers to the ability to break through the barriers of role stereotyping and behave in congruence with personal and situational needs. Authentic leader behavior is relatively unconstrained by traditional role requirements. Inauthentic leaders, in contrast, adhere to the narrow behavior of their job description, never allowing self to override the routinized behavior of the office.

In a follow-up study, Hoy and William Kupersmith report that perceived leader authenticity was related to commanding trust and loyalty from teachers.[49] They conclude that an atmosphere of trust facilitates organizational change in schools. They reason that one of the major impediments to change in schools is the fear that administration-proposed changes have a hidden agenda and will result in negative consequences for subordinates. "An atmosphere of trust in schools can . . . produce a climate conducive to change." Open and authentic behaviors foster trust, which in turn is likely to reduce resistance to change.[50]

How does transactional analysis relate to organizational change? People are trained in seminars to identify dysfunctional aspects of transactional analysis: time structuring, analysis of transactions, and structural analysis. The assumption is that this knowledge will make school administrators more effective in their relationships with faculty and in collegial relationships among the faculty. Increased effectiveness in interpersonal relations in schools should help to reduce resistance to change efforts proposed by school administrators.

School-improvement efforts are taking place throughout the United States. Many individuals are contributing their time and expertise: teachers, principals, curriculum specialists, school board members, and parents. But a person who is often overlooked as a key figure in school reform is the superintendent. Recent indicators suggest that the superintendent of schools is being seen as the "key" player in the

---

[46]Andrew W. Halpin and Don B. Croft, *The Organizational Climate of Schools* (Chicago: University of Chicago Press, 1963).

[47]Andrew W. Halpin, *Theory and Research in Administration* (New York: Macmillan, 1966).

[48]James E. Henderson and Wayne K. Hoy, "Leader Authenticity: The Development and Test of an Operational Measure," *Educational and Psychological Measurement*, 3 (1983), pp. 63–75.

[49]Wayne K. Hoy and William Kupersmith, "Principal Authenticity and Faculty Trust: Key Elements in Organizational Behavior, *Planning and Changing*, 15 (1984), pp. 80–88.

[50]Ibid., p. 87.

ADMINISTRATIVE ADVICE 8-4

■

THE SUPERINTENDENT: A KEY PLAYER IN SCHOOL REFORM

The type of instructional leadership that enhances school-based improvement includes not only the use of symbolic leadership but also district leadership that comes from a total commitment to improving the results of student learning. Specifically, the superintendent must

- Demonstrate a thorough and up-to-date understanding of the teacher effectiveness and instructional improvement research.
- Demonstrate a commitment to community education that fosters active support and involvement.
- Establish an ongoing self-renewal program for all professional staff, both on a group and individual basis.
- Develop an organizational culture that fosters, values, and rewards experimentation.
- Implement a decision-making process that focuses on instruction and student learning first and foremost at the expense of expediency or tradition, when necessary.
- Demonstrate the application of research and collaboration in everyday practice.

- Insist on the development of clearly stated and concise district and building goals.
- Establish mechanisms to monitor curriculum and instruction systematically.
- Become directly involved in the supervision and assessment of instruction.
- Provide impetus for establishing a clear instruction and curriculum focus.
- Demonstrate positive modeling behavior at every opportunity.
- Develop a budget that reflects the district's commitment to instructional improvement.

Source: Source: Adapted from David F. Hendrix, "Spotlight on Superintendents in School Reform," *School Administrator*, 4 (1988), pp. 17–18. Used by permission.

---

effort to improve education. (See Administrative Advice 8-4.)

GROUP APPROACHES TO CHANGE

In the discussion of individual approaches to change, we focused on improving a department, school, or school district by making its members more effective individually. However, educational institutions are more than an aggregate of individuals. Effective school performance depends on the ability of individual members to operate as effective groups.

Now, we focus on approaches to change that aim at improving the performance of groups: role analysis technique, intergroup problem solving, process consultation, survey feedback, and strategic planning.

Role Analysis Technique

Ishwar Dayal and John Thomas are usually credited with the development of the **role analysis technique** over twenty years ago.[51] The tech-

---

[51]Ishwar Dayal and John M. Thomas, "Operation KPE: Developing a New Organization," *Journal of Applied Behavioral Science*, 4 (1968), pp. 473–506.

nique clarifies role expectations and obligations of team members. In schools people fill different specialized roles: for example, board of education, superintendent, principals, teachers, and other specialists. This division of labor brings about the school district's goals. In many school districts, people lack a clear understanding of what is expected of them and the types of support they can expect from other personnel, which can hinder performance. The role analysis technique can be used in new teams in which initial roles need to be analyzed, as well as in established teams in which role ambiguity exists. In a series of steps, role incumbents and team members define and delineate their roles.

Step 1: Defining Roles Each person in succession defines her role, its place in the school district, the rationale for its existence, and its place in achieving the overall goals of the district. The entire team openly discusses these specifications, which are listed on a chalkboard. Behaviors are added and deleted until the group and the role incumbent are satisfied with the defined role.

Step 2: Examining Expectations Each role incumbent lists his expectations of the other roles in the group that most affect the incumbent's own role performance. The entire group then discusses, modifies, and agrees on these expectations.

Then the group discusses what it expects from each role incumbent. Finally, the group and each role incumbent discuss, modify, and agree on these expectations of others.

Step 3: Summarizing Roles Each role incumbent makes a summary of the job as it has been defined. This role profile represents a compilation of the discussions in Steps 1 and 2. According to Dayal and Thomas, the role profile "consists of (a) a set of activities classified as to the prescribed and discretionary elements of the role, (b) the obligation of the role to each role in its set, and (c) the expectations of this role from others in its set . . . [and] provides a comprehen-

sive understanding of each individual's 'role space.' "[52]

Many consultants have had success with the role analysis technique because it constitutes a nonthreatening activity with high payoff for team members. Team members like the technique because it allows them to know what other people in the school district are doing and how that relates to their own roles. Furthermore, because of the public exposure and scrutiny of each role in the school district, role analysis ensures commitment to these roles.

Intergroup Problem Solving

A school is a composite of various units or groups. In a high school, there are several academic departments: English, social studies, mathematics, science, and so on. In an elementary school, there may be grade-level divisions, teams, or departments. It is important that these groups perceive their goals as being relatively congruent with the goals of the school. Occasionally, groups or units of the school come into conflict. Similar conflicts often develop in school districts between line and staff, central office and school buildings, and union and management.

Research has identified the dynamics of intergroup conflict.[53] The competitive nature of groups can affect the total productivity of a school or school district. During competition each group becomes more cohesive. Internal differences are set aside, and members strengthen their loyalty and identification with their group. Group members view each other as more and more similar and other groups as more and more different. Each group becomes more structured and places demand for conformity on its mem-

[52]Ibid., p. 488.
[53]Michael K. Mach and Jean M. Bartunek, *Creating Alternative Realities at Work: A Cognitive Perspective for Understanding and Managing Organizational Change* (New York: Ballinger, 1989).

bers in order to present a united front against the other group(s). Distortions in perception of the other group(s) come into play to justify attitudes concerning other group(s). In other words, each group views the other as the enemy, and hostility increases while communication decreases.

The negative consequences of intergroup conflict causes school administrators to seek resolution. One method for resolving such intergroup conflict is **intergroup problem solving**.[54] The following represent the general pattern of activities.

Step 1: Meeting Jointly   The administrators of the two groups (or the total membership) meet with a consultant, who asks if the relations between them are hostile and can be improved. If the groups confirm this, the intergroup problem-solving process begins. (The use of an outside change agent is highly recommended because in these situations a mediating influence may be necessary to create a common ground between the groups.)

Step 2: Identifying the Problem(s)   The two groups meet in separate rooms and develop two lists. In one list, they provide their perceptions, attitudes, feelings, and opinions of the other group. The list includes answers to questions such as: What is the other group like? What do they do that upsets us? In the second list, the group attempts to predict what the other group is saying about them. The list includes answers to questions such as: What does the other group dislike about us? How does the other group see us?

Step 3: Sharing Information   The two groups come together to share the information on their respective lists. Group A reads its list of how it sees Group B and what it dislikes about Group

B. Then Group B does the same. The change agent does not permit discussion to take place during this step; the two groups can pose and respond to only questions of clarification. Next, Group A reads its list of what it expected Group B would say about it, and Group B reads its list of what it expected Group A would say.

Step 4: Analyzing Information   The two groups return to their separate rooms to discuss what they have learned about themselves and the other group. Frequently, the groups discover that the hostility and friction between them rests on misperceptions and miscommunication, as revealed by the lists. The problems between the two groups are seen to be fewer than perceived initially. After this discussion, each group is given the task of preparing a list of priority issues that remain unresolved between the two groups.

Step 5: Resolving the Problem(s)   The two groups meet together again to share and discuss their lists with each other. After this discussion, both groups work together to prepare one list of the unresolved issues and problems. Also, together they generate action steps for resolving the issues and assign responsibilities for the actions. These steps indicate who will do what and when.

Step 6: Following Through   As a follow-up to the intergroup problem-solving strategy, it is usually desirable to have a meeting of the two groups or their leaders to determine whether the action steps have occurred.

Process Consultation

Process consultation is a set of activities, provided by a consultant, that helps members of an organization to perceive, understand, and act on process events that occur in their work environment.[55] The process consultant helps the orga-

---

[54]Robert R. Blake and Jane S. Mouton, *Solving Costly Organizational Conflicts: Achieving Intergroup Trust, Cooperation, and Teamwork* (San Francisco: Jossey-Bass, 1984).

[55]Edgar H. Schein, *Process Consultation, Volume I: Its Role in Organization Development*, 2nd ed. (Reading, MA: Addison-Wesley, 1988).

nization's participants obtain insight into the organizational processes, of the consequences of these processes, and of the mechanisms by which they can be changed. The ultimate goal is to help the organization diagnose its problems and generate a solution. The consultant may be a competent member of the organization skilled in process activities or a professionally trained outside consultant.

Process consultation is aimed primarily at five important organizational processes: communication, functional roles of group members, decision making, group norms and growth, and leadership. The process consultant observes organizational processes firsthand, by sitting in on meetings, observing negotiations between employees or groups, and observing daily activities.

Communication   School administrators must understand the nature and style of the communication process in the organization. The process consultant can help the administrator understand the organization's communication system. In observing a communication pattern, the process consultant examines who communicates to whom, for how long and how often, what is communicated, and how messages are transmitted. The examination of the nature and style of communication, at both the overt and covert levels and nonverbal communication patterns can be informative. The process consultant records this information in a log. In this way, the consultant provides nonevaluative-descriptive feedback to the school district concerning possible communication problems, thereby helping the district find solutions.

Functional Roles of Group Members   School administrators need to understand role functioning among group members. Three functional roles that need to be performed if a group is to be effective are self-related activities such as self-identity, influence, and power; task-related activities such as obtaining and providing information, coordinating, setting standards, and evaluating; and group-maintenance activities,

which include encouraging, supporting, harmonizing, and compromising.

The process consultant observes the different roles that organizational members assume when they are interacting in a group. For example, preoccupation with self-interests or power struggles can be dysfunctional to school district effectiveness. And an overemphasis on task-related activities to the exclusion of sufficient group-maintenance activities can result in organizational goal suffering as well. The process consultant can help the school district identify and diagnose these group dysfunctions.

Decision Making   An important component of effective groups is decision making. Effective groups identify problems, examine alternatives, make decisions, and implement decisions. There are several methods of making decisions. One method is to ignore a suggestion made by a group member, that is, refuse to discuss it. This approach has dysfunctional consequences for the organization. Another is to place decision-making power in the hands of the person in authority. Such decisions are made by minority rule; for example, the leader makes a decision and turns to subordinates who willingly comply. A third method is by majority rule or consensus. The process consultant can help school districts understand how decisions are made, the consequences of different decision-making methods, and how to diagnose which method may be most effective in a given situation.

Group Norms and Growth   School administrators need to understand the process of group norms and how these norms affect group functioning. Groups of people who work together develop group norms or standards of behavior. For instance, there may be an explicit norm that group members can express their ideas freely, but the implicit norm also suggests that a member does not contradict the ideas of certain other (powerful) group members. The process consultant can help the school district understand the group's norms and the effect of these norms on group functioning.

Leadership The process consultant can help the group understand different leadership styles and help school administrators adjust their style to better fit the situation. The idea is to enable the administrator to get a better understanding of her own behavior and the group's reaction to that behavior. Such knowledge can help the administrator change her behavior to fit the situation.[56]

Process consultation, then, is aimed at facilitating organizational change by helping educational administrators to become aware of the processes of change, the consequences of these processes, and the mechanisms by which they can be changed.

Survey Feedback

Survey feedback is an organizational approach to change that involves collecting data (usually by means of a survey questionnaire) from members of a work group or whole organization, analyzing and summarizing the data into an understandable form, feeding back the data to those who generated it, and using the data to diagnose problems and develop action plans for problem solving.[57]

Similar to process consultation in some respects, survey feedback places greater emphasis on the collection of valid data and less emphasis on the interpersonal processes of individual work groups. Instead, survey feedback focuses on the relationships between administrative personnel and their subordinates at all levels of the hierarchy.

If used properly, attitude surveys can be a powerful tool in school-improvement efforts. Change agents who use survey feedback point out that most attitude surveys are not used prop-

erly. At best, most give higher-level administrators some data for changing practices or provide a benchmark against which to compare trends. At worst, they are filed away with little consequence for school improvement.

Survey feedback has two major phases. Collecting data is only part of the process; providing appropriate feedback to the organization's members is equally significant. Figure 8-5 outlines the six steps involved in survey feedback, which are described next.[58]

Step 1: Preliminary Planning Organizational members at the top of the hierarchy are involved in the preliminary planning. Surveys used in organizational change efforts are usually constructed around a theoretical model. This allows the user to rate himself or the organization in terms of the theory. When the approach involves a theoretical model, commitment to the model must be obtained. If top management does not accept the theoretical model undergirding the survey, the approach will likely fail no matter how effective the effort is toward gathering data.

Step 2: Data Gathering A questionnaire is administered to all organizational members. The best-known survey-feedback instrument is the one developed by the Institute for Social Research (ISR) at the University of Michigan.[59] The questionnaire generally asks the respondents' perceptions on such organizational areas as communications, goal emphasis, leadership styles, decision making, coordination between departments, and employee attitudes. The ISR instrument, a standardized questionnaire, permits the additions of questions that may be of interest to the organization under study. However, many organizations, including schools, de-

[56]Edgar F. Huse and Thomas G. Cummings, *Organization Development and Change*, 3rd ed. (St. Paul: West, 1985).

[57]Edward J. Conlon and Lawrence O. Short, "Survey Feedback as a Large-Scale Change Device: An Empirical Examination," *Group and Organization Studies*, 9 (1984), pp. 399–416.

[58]David G. Bowers and Jerome L. Franklin, *Survey-Guided Development: Data-Based Organizational Change* (La Jolla, CA: University Associates, 1977).

[59]James C. Taylor and David G. Bowers, *Survey of Organizations: A Machine Scored Standardized Questionnaire Instrument* (Ann Arbor: Institute for Social Research, University of Michigan, 1972).

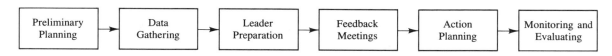

FIGURE 8-5   Steps Involved in Survey Feedback

velop their own questionnaires that are specific to their individual needs rather than relying on a standardized instrument.

Step 3: Leader Preparation   Once the data have been obtained from the questionnaire, an external or internal change agent helps school administrators understand the data and instructs them on how to present the data to the work group. Data are then fed back to the top-administrative team and then down through the hierarchy in functional teams.

Step 4: Feedback Meetings   Each superior conducts group feedback meetings with his subordinates in which the data are discussed and in which subordinates are asked to help interpret the data, plans are made for making constructive changes, and plans are made for introducing the information at the next lower level of subordinates.

For example, the superintendent of schools and the major divisional assistant superintendents meet and compare the survey findings for each of the district's functional areas—such as personnel, business, instruction, and research and development. Each assistant superintendent can see the summary data for her division and for the total school district. Problems unique to each division, the implications of the findings, and themes common to the total organization are discussed.

The next series of feedback meetings occur as each assistant superintendent meets with building principals or other subordinates to discuss survey data specific to each. The process continues until department heads discuss with teachers or other school personnel the issues raised in each work group by the survey data.

Step 5: Action Planning   The fact that a discrepancy exists between the actual state of the organization and the ideal theoretical model does not in and of itself provide sufficient motivation to change. Organizational members must be made aware of how the change can be effected. Thus, resources are allocated to implement the changes in accordance with the needs indicated by the group feedback meetings and the systematic diagnosis of the data by the change agent and top-level administrators.

Step 6: Monitoring and Evaluating   The change agent helps organizational members develop skills that are necessary to move the organization toward their goals. Some of these skills include listening, giving and receiving personal feedback, general leadership techniques, problem solving, goal setting, and diagnosing group processes. Additional questionnaires are administered and analyzed to monitor the change process. And, finally, the school district is formally reassessed to evaluate change, again using questionnaire data.

Strategic Planning

Constantly changing social and economic conditions affect organizations, necessitating the imperative to plan ahead. Organizations must anticipate the turbulence of future years and preplan processes for achieving their objectives; implicit in these processes is environmental scanning.[60]

---

[60]Tom Peters, *Thriving on Chaos: Handbook for a Management Revolution* (New York: Harper & Row, 1988).

Strategic planning involves identifying the mission of an organization; recognizing internal and external forces that impact the organization; analyzing those forces to determine the effects they have on the organization's ability to accomplish its mission; developing strategies for dealing with them, including a framework for improvement and restructuring of programs, management, participation, and evaluation; and instituting action plans to carry out those strategies and achieve the organization's mission.[61]

Many authors do not discriminate between long-range planning and strategic planning. Strategic planning goes beyond a mechanistic series of planning procedures. Its power lies in its capacity to create dissonance in people, upset traditional views, identify new possibilities, and pose new questions. In this sense, "strategic planning is a management process for changing and transforming organizations."[62]

Shirley McCune outlines the structural differences between strategic planning and long-range planning. Although both types of planning are concerned with the future, long-range planning typically begins with an assumption that an organization will remain comparatively stable; it seeks to develop internal goals and projections based on that assumption. Strategic planning, on the other hand, begins with a recognition of the external environment as an important consideration of the planning process, and the actions initiated to effect plans are based on an analysis, synthesis, and evaluation of this environment. Table 8-1 shows other differences between strategic planning and long-range planning.

Business has devoted a great deal of attention to strategic planning.[63] Only recently has any emphasis been placed on the study of strategic planning in school settings. In a study of 127 school districts in Kentucky, researchers found relationships between strategic planning and student achievement in reading, language arts, and mathematics at several grade levels. None of the relationships was strong, however. In addition, the researchers found a direct relationship between strategic planning and both school district wealth and per-pupil expenditures. That is, the higher the assessed property value per child and the greater the percentage of revenue from local sources supporting education, the more likely the school district is engaged in strategic planning efforts.[64]

SUMMARY

1. We have described the change process in schools using an open-systems framework. An open system has three basic, recurring cycles: inputs, a transformation process, and outputs. The internal and external environment impact on the three basic cycles of the open-systems model.

2. Schools face pressures for change, including government intervention, changes in society's values, changing technology and knowledge explosion, and administrative processes and employees' needs.

3. Schools also resist change. Resistance can stem from several sources, including interference with need fulfillment, fear of the unknown, threats to power and influence, knowledge and skill obsolescence, organizational structure, limited resources, and collective bargaining agreements.

4. Methods schools can use to reduce resistance to change include participation, communication, support, rewards, planning, and coercion.

5. The major approaches to change can be classified as individual and group. Individual approaches to change include job enrichment, laboratory training, behavior modification, and transactional analysis. Group approaches to change include role analysis technique, intergroup problem solving,

[61]William J. Cook, *Bill Cook's Strategic Planning for America's Schools* (Arlington, VA: American Association of School Administrators, 1988).

[62]Shirley D. McCune, *Guide to Strategic Planning for Educators* (Alexandria, VA: Association for Supervision and Curriculum Development, 1986), p. 32.

[63]Robert G. Dyson, *Strategic Planning: Models and Analytical Techniques* (New York: Wiley, 1990).

[64]Vickie Basham and Fred C. Lunenburg, "Strategic Planning, Student Achievement, and School District Financial and Demographic Factors," *Planning and Changing*, 20 (1989), pp. 158–171.

TABLE 8 ■ 1   Comparison of Strategic Planning and Long-Range Planning

STRATEGIC PLANNING	LONG-RANGE PLANNING
1. Assumes an open system whereby organizations must constantly change as the needs of the larger society change.	1. Assumes a closed system within which short-range plans or blueprints are developed.
2. Focuses on the process of planning, building a vision, external environment, organizational capacity, staff and community education.	2. Focuses on the final blueprint of a plan, internal analysis.
3. Is done by a small group of planners with widespread involvement of stakeholders.	3. Is done by a planning department or professionals.
4. Uses current and projected trends to make current decisions.	4. Uses existing data on which to project future plans.
5. Emphasizes changes outside the organization, organizational values, and proactive action.	5. Emphasizes internal changes, planning methods, and inside-out planning.
6. Focuses on what decision is appropriate today, based on an understanding of the situation five years from now.	6. Focuses on organizational goals and objectives five years from now.
7. Depends upon intuitive and creative decision making as to how to guide the organization over time in an everchanging environment and an organization-wide process that anticipates the future, makes decisions, and behaves in light of an agreed-on vision.	7. Depends on detailed and interrelated data sets, agency plans, and extrapolations of current budgets.

SOURCE: Adapted from Shirley D. McCune, *Guide to Strategic Planning for Educators,* © 1986, p. 35. Used by permission of Association for Supervision and Curriculum Development, Alexandria, VA.

process consultation, survey feedback, and strategic planning.

6. In practice, the approaches are generally used in combination to affect organizational change in schools.

KEY TERMS

open systems

force-field analysis

job enrichment

laboratory training

behavior modification

transactional analysis

role analysis technique

intergroup problem solving

process consultation

survey feedback

strategic planning

DISCUSSION QUESTIONS

1. Explain why the change agent must consider the open-systems framework when considering organizational change efforts.

2. Using force-field analysis, diagnose your school district, university, or other educational institution. Describe the pressures for change and the forces resisting change. Which forces would lend themselves to change? Which would make your organization more effective?

3. Discuss several methods organizations can use to overcome resistance to change.

4. Based on your own experience, describe an educational institution that needs change. Which of the approaches to change presented in this chapter

would you use to make the organization more effective?

5. Explain why schools normally need to use a combination of approaches (i.e., individual and group) in order to effect change. Cite examples where appropriate.

SUGGESTED READINGS

James A. Belasco, *Teaching the Elephant to Dance: Empowering Change in Your Organization* (New York: Crown, 1990). Provides an excellent introduction to strategies for effecting change in organizations.

Urs E. Gattiker, *Technology Management in Organizations* (Newbury Park, CA: Sage, 1990). Interdisciplinary and cross-national, this richly diverse volume integrates theories, research, and models of organizational change from such fields as economics, engineering, organizational behavior, psychology, sociology, and industrial relations.

David Jaffee, *Levels of Socio-Economic Development Theory* (Westport, CT: Greenwood, 1990). Provides a systematic examination of the impact of socioeconomic status levels on the change process.

Ronnie Lessem, *Developmental Management: Learning to Manage with Vision* (Cambridge, MA: Basil Blackwell, 1990). Presents a thorough overview to the basics of organizational change and a guide to designing effective productivity measures.

Karen Seashore Louis and Matthew B. Miles, *Improving the Urban High School: What Works and Why* (New York: Teachers College Press, 1990). Evolutionary planning, vision building, getting and managing resources, and problem coping are articulated with great power.

Fred Massarik (ed.), *Advances in Organization Development, Vol. 1* (Norwood, NJ: Ablex, 1990). Provides an excellent introduction to strategies for changing an organization, including the latest theory and research.

Jitendra V. Singh (ed.), *Organizational Evolution: New Directions* (Newbury Park, CA: Sage, 1990). Addresses organizational change by examining the process of continual change within organizations, including founding, disbanding, growth, and change.

III

THE STRUCTURAL FRAMEWORK FOR EDUCATION

9

THE FEDERAL GOVERNMENT AND EDUCATION

We attempt to answer these questions by first exploring the relationship between the federal government and education. Then we examine congressional influence on education and the various federal programs designed to enhance learning. We next consider the role of the federal courts and, finally, discuss the national reform movement in education.

THE FEDERAL ROLE IN EDUCATION

A national system of education does not exist in the United States in the same sense that it does in England, France, Germany, Japan, or the Soviet Union. Education in the United States is considered a state and/or local function; there are fifty different state systems, and many differences exist among local school systems within the same state. In total, there are some

15,000 different local school districts—each with their own philosophy and goals.

The U.S. Constitution makes no mention of public education, but the Tenth Amendment to the Constitution reserves to the states all powers not specifically delegated to the federal government or prohibited to the states by the Constitution. This amendment is the basis for allocating primary legal responsibility for public education to the states. However, the states have delegated to the local districts the responsibility of the practical day-to-day operation of school districts.

The schools have always been a provincial domain of the towns and cities of the United States, rooted in the colonial tradition of the nation, but the federal government has always had some say in public education. Beginning with the land grants that antedated the U.S. Constitution and highlighted by the welfare clause of the Constitution (Article I, Section 8), which gives Congress the power to tax for the general good and for broad social purposes, education has always been the federal government's concern. Although education is not specifically spelled out by Article I, the language is general enough for the government to use public tax monies to support the nation's schools and school programs and to enact educational laws for the welfare of the people.

CHANGING ROLES IN THE FEDERAL GOVERNMENT AND EDUCATION

To fully understand the federal government and its relations with the schools, one must understand that there has been a gradual shift from the historical **separation of powers** between the federal government and states—toward the federal government playing a greater role in education and social areas. Recently, there has been a trend toward greater decentralization at the federal level and sharing of educational re-

sponsibilities and functions between the federal government and states. At the same time, there is a countertrend to develop national goals and standards in education, a shift toward greater nationalization of the curriculum, as part of the reform movement to upgrade education.[1]

The first 150 years of U.S. education can be considered the period of **dual federalism,** whereby the founding fathers' majority view to limit the federal government at all levels and most functions prevailed. During this period, federal programs and activities in education were passive and uncoordinated. Sometime around the Great Depression and the Roosevelt administration the next period evolved, called **national federalism.**[2] Economic and social circumstances of the day called for greater federal intervention, first in the area of labor legislation and relief acts in education and public works; followed by educational legislation for the Cold War and Sputnik period of the late 1940s and 1950s; and then the War on Poverty and civil rights movement that impacted on schools and society in the 1960s and 1970s. What became apparent during this national federalism period was that national action and national coordination of programs and activities were needed to resolve many problems that extended beyond the boundaries of state and local governments. National identity and national welfare were at stake, and there were dramatic increases in federal commitment to education.

---

[1]Howard Gardner, "National Education Goals and the Academic Community," *Education Digest,* 60 (1990), pp. 41–43; "Themes of Educational Leadership for 1990–91," *Educational Leadership,* 47 (1990), p. 78. Also see Albert Shanker, "The End of the Traditional Model of Schooling," *Phi Delta Kappan,* 71 (1990), pp. 344–357.

[2]Roald F. Campbell et al., *The Organization of the American Schools,* 6th ed. (Columbus, OH: Merrill, 1990). It should be noted, however, that Campbell and his associates put the beginning of this second period at the time of the Civil War and the "due process" clause of the Fourteenth Amendment.

Current Period: 1980s and 1990s

Starting in the 1980s under President Reagan and continued by President Bush, a **new federalism** evolved, which called for a dramatic shift in federal policy and programs. Driven by a belief that the federal government was too meddlesome and involved in too many activities and regulations, Reagan and Bush reduced federal funds (vis-à-vis inflation), activities, and regulations in education as well as other social sectors of the economy.[3] In addition, monetary and program responsibilities were shifted to state (and local) agencies. Federal rules and regulations governing education were revoked or more loosely enforced.

The new federalism, according to two educators, can be viewed in terms of three policy moves by the executive branch of government: (1) deregulation, the reduction of federal bureaucratic rules and regulations; (2) consolidation, the reduction of government proliferation of agencies and programs; and (3) cutbacks, the move to reduce social and educational spending.[4] Similarly, David Clark analyzed the new federalism in terms of five policy shifts—or what he termed the "five *D*s" in education: (1) diminution, reduction of federal expenditures in education; (2) deregulation, revocation of federal enforcement of rules and regulations; (3) decentralization, the belief that the ills of education are related to federal intrusion into what should be a state or local responsibility; (4) disestablishment, limiting the powers of the Department of Education and other federal agencies; and (5) de-emphasis, the sum of the preceding aspects or the narrowing of the focus and scope of the federal role in education.[5]

The new federalism shows up in the Reagan–Bush administrations—despite the rhetoric about the need to bolster education and human capital. First, there has been a shift in priorities from human, social, and educational concerns to big business and military interests. It shows up in their lack of formal policy regarding education and in the belief that the federal government should be involved less, not more, in the education of the nation's children and youth. It shows up in Reagan's unsuccessful attempt to eliminate the Department of Education and in Bush's replacement of the high-profile, assertive Secretary of Education, William Bennett, by the relatively unknown Secretary Lauro Cavazos.

The new federalism also surfaces in terms of the growing demise of egalitarianism as a national policy. It is evidenced in a reduction in programs for big-city schools, especially those for minority and low-income groups, and an increase in federal programs that coincide with national need—say, in areas of math and science education and high technology. By the mid-1980s, for example, only 20 percent of Chapter 2 block-grant monies (funds earmarked by the federal government for the states) were being dedicated to compensatory and basic-skills programs.[6] Many people now feel that the nation's urban schools will be shortchanged under the guise of educational reform and educational efficiency.

While the new federalism has been reshaping education, another conservative trend, the **na-**

---

[3]Norman Amaker, "Reagan Record on Civil Rights," *Urban Institute Policy and Research Report,* 18 (1988), pp. 15–16; Allan C. Ornstein, "The Changing Federal Role in Education," *Kappa Delta Pi Record,* 21 (1985), pp. 85–88.

[4]Paul T. Hill, "The Federal Role in Education: A Strategy for the 1990s," *Phi Delta Kappan,* 71 (1990), pp. 398–402; Ornstein, "The Changing Federal Role in Education."

[5]David L. Clark and Mary A. Amiot, "The Reagan Administration and Federal Education Policy," *Phi Delta Kappan,* 63 (1981), pp. 258–262; David L. Clark, Terry A. Astuto, and Paula M. Rooney, "The Changing Structure of Federal Education Policy in the 1980s," *Phi Delta Kappan,* 65 (1983), pp. 188–193.

[6]"Congressmen Call for Tighter Controls on Chapter 2 Funds," *Phi Delta Kappan,* 68 (1986), p. 89; Michael S. Knapp et al. "Prospects for Improving K–12 Science Education from the Federal Level," *Phi Delta Kappan,* 70 (1988), pp. 677–683.

tional standards movement, has been gaining momentum. This movement shows a deepening concern for declining student scores on national and international achievement tests and for the declining quality of the teaching work force as evidenced by a large percentage of entry teachers having difficulty passing basic-skill tests.[7] There is also concern for investment in human capital and the nation's economic decline and lack of international competitiveness. A new consensus is developing—one that promotes national needs and goals as more important than local or pluralistic needs and goals, supports more rigorous teacher training and national testing and professional standards for teachers, and seeks a common core of subjects, content, and values in the Adler–Bloom–Hirsch mode.

Thus, President Bush, while he has been criticized for a federal school budget as being well below what is needed to keep up with inflation, calls himself the "Education President" and has outlined seven program areas that center mostly around national standards for achievement and excellence in education: (1) merit schools, (2) magnet schools of excellence, (3) alternative certification of teachers and principals, (4) teacher excellence, (5) student excellence in science and math, (6) drug-free schools, and (7) endowments for black colleges.[8]

Within the context of nationalization of standards, some critics are asking why raise standards if students cannot meet them? Why talk about a nationalized set of goals or curriculum when the focus has always been on local control of the schools and when there is little agreement on goals, standards, or requirements among the fifty states and more than 15,000 school dis-

tricts? Why talk about a national commitment to educational reform when the federal government is reducing educational spending in real dollars?

Clarifying the Federal Role in Education

The federal government's role in education is compelling because how we educate our children and youth will determine the kind of nation we become. The issue is not whether we do or do not reduce the federal role or nationalize standards in education; the issue is to clarify and determine how the federal government can and should use its resources and dollars to effectively promote schools and other social institutions. Federal leadership should support and work with state and local agencies, not for the purpose of promoting the needs of one group versus another group but for the priorities of all of us—as a people or nation.

Table 9-1 outlines a set of priorities set forth by the National School Boards Association (NSBA). The priorities suggest that we are at a critical period in our history, where policies and actions in education by the federal government can enhance or hinder our future. The priorities suggest that federal leadership can work hand-in-hand with local school districts and that the focus should be on enhancing academic achievement for all students and ensuring that students with special needs have equal opportunity to succeed. In no way should the priorities suggest that schools be nationalized or that the federal government establish national standards of educational performance; this is certainly not the goal of the NSBA, which represents some 97,000 local school board members, prefers a local school focus for reform, and values local educational efforts.

According to one observer, the federal role in education should be based on helping local schools and school districts build consensus and

[7]Gary A. Griffin, "The Future of Teachers and Teaching," *Peabody Journal of Education,* 68 (1990), in print, pp. 74–87. Allan C. Ornstein, "National Reform and Instructional Accountability," *High School Journal,* 74 (1990), in print.
[8]"Bush Calls for New Programs," *AASA Leadership News,* 15 April 1989, pp. 1–2.

TABLE 9 ▪ 1   Priorities for Future Federal Role in Education

Define Federal Responsibilities

1. Establish a revolving fund for low-cost construction and renovation of schools.
2. Establish research and development programs in mathematics, science, and foreign languages.
3. Expand the dissemination of research to state and local policymakers.
4. Establish a national panel for continually reviewing educational research and making recommendations to the president and Congress.
5. Create a matching public- and private-funding program to expand research and library facilities.
6. Strengthen teacher training in areas of critical national interest (such as math, science, and English).
7. Provide technical assistance and information to local schools on how children learn.

Increase our Competitive Edge

1. Offer technical assistance to enable local school districts to use the latest advancements in educational technology.
2. Provide additional funding to improve math, science, foreign language, international studies, and technology.
3. Supplement state aid to school districts for vocational education that focuses on labor shortages in the national interest.
4. Provide additional funding for dropout prevention.
5. Provide new funding for adult literacy programs.

Promote Effective Use of Technology

1. Underwrite technical assistance for computer and electronic software materials.
2. Encourage transfer of technology into the classroom.
3. Fund a satellite-based educational program to serve the nation in important areas such as drug–alcohol abuse, bilingual education, and AIDS education.
4. Increase assistance for training teachers to work with technologies in classrooms and schools.
5. Monitor and coordinate federal efforts in educational technology.
6. Remove regulatory provisions that prevent investment in technological development.

Strengthen the Quality of Teachers

1. Establish incentive programs to attract promising future teachers in both inner-city and rural areas.

---

confidence in educating their clients. Many educational problems are both national and local.[9] The problem is national because it occurs in many parts of the country and because world and national events help construct it. It is also local in the sense that the composition and needs of the student population differ from place to place and that local efforts and resources are

needed to resolve the problem. If local efforts and resources are not funneled, then the services or personnel will not be provided.

A new federal strategy is needed—one that stimulates local school planning and reform and supplements local efforts and resources. Table 9-2 shows eleven services that the federal government has performed in recent years—sometimes vigorously, sometimes reluctantly. As part of the 19th Annual Gallup Poll, a nationwide

---

[9]Hill, "The Federal Role in Education."

TABLE 9 ■ 1   Continued

Strengthen the Quality of Teachers (continued)

2. Develop new recruiting programs where there is special national interest such as math, science, and foreign languages.
3. Strengthen support of international education and exchange programs for teachers.
4. Underwrite educational programs for outstanding teachers.
5. Provide grants for teachers to work in research projects, especially with at-risk students.

Reduce the Risk for Special-Needs Students

1. Provide adequate funding for state and local educational agencies to implement federal mandates.
2. Reject proposals inconsistent with equal educational opportunity.
3. Increase funding for Head Start, Chapter I, bilingual education, education of the handicapped, immigration education, and school nutrition.
4. Initiate nationwide literacy campaigns for at-risk youth and their parents.
5. Expand dropout-prevention programs, as well as extended day, year, and preschool programs.
6. Provide English (and reading) instruction summer programs with jobs for limited-English-speaking youth.

Improve Rural Education

1. Support distance learning and related applications of technology in rural areas.
2. Provide assistance for vocationally oriented and farm-related programs suited for the future.
3. Coordinate interagency efforts to support rural education.
4. Provide funding for research on rural education.
5. Disseminate information to rural policymakers and the public in general.

Provide Opportunity in Urban Schools

1. Focus on early childhood education by providing sufficient funds.
2. Provide funds for language-oriented programs.
3. Provide discretionary funds to local schools to expand preschool, after school, day-care, and summer programs in low-income areas.
4. Develop a national policy for urban education to be coordinated with housing, health, welfare, crime, and drug abuse.

SOURCE: Adapted from National School Boards Association, *A National Imperative: Educating for the 21st Century,* © 1989, pp. 3–16. Used by permission of National School Boards Association, Alexandria, Va.

sample of professional educators and parents were asked whether these were services they thought the federal government should do. The results are shown. Note the strong agreement on most matters, except Item 8, dealing with equal opportunities for minority groups and women; Item 9, national minimum educational standards; and Item 11, national testing program. Obviously, it is the areas of disagreement between the professionals and public that should

concern both groups as well as administrative leaders.

The Department of Education

Although many different federal agencies (thirteen departments and about fifteen other agencies or units) are involved in some type of educational program or activity, the U.S. De-

TABLE 9 ▪ 2   Services That the Federal Government Should Perform

	YES		NO		DON'T KNOW	
	Professionals (%)	Public (%)	Professionals (%)	Public (%)	Professionals (%)	Public (%)
1. Advise and encourage state and local educational systems to deal with important national problems in education, such as illiteracy and poor math achievement.	83	83	14	10	3	7
2. Identify important national problems in education, such as illiteracy and poor math achievement.	81	81	15	12	4	7
3. Collect and report information and statistics that measure educational performance in the nation.	80	73	16	18	4	9
4. Fund research and development in areas of need, such as the curriculum and teaching methods.	77	72	18	19	4	9
5. Fund programs to deal with important national problems in education, such as illiteracy and poor math achievement.	73	78	22	15	5	7
6. Provide financing for scholarships and fellowships for college students.	70	72	24	20	6	8
7. Provide recognition and awards for high achievement by students, teachers, and schools.	68	76	27	17	5	7
8. Promote educational programs intended to help solve such social problems as poverty and equal opportunities for minorities, women, and the handicapped.	67	80	22	12	6	8
9. Require states and local school districts to meet minimum educational standards.	53	84	43	10	4	6
10. Provide financial aid to the states through block grants that can be used for education or for any other purpose.	50	57	43	30	6	13
11. Support a national testing program for public school students.	31	74	63	17	6	9

SOURCE: Adapted from Stanley M. Elam, "Differences Between Educators and the Public on Questions of Education Policy," *Phi Delta Kappan,* 69 (1987), p. 296. Used by permission.

TABLE 9 ■ 3   Federal Funds for Department of Education Programs (in Thousands)

	1970	1980	1989
K–12 programs	$2,719,204	$ 6,629,095	$ 8,853,527
Higher-education programs	3,447,697	10,939,494	11,904,175
Research programs	87,823	78,742	80,479
TOTAL:	6,254,724	17,647,331	20,838,181

SOURCE: *Digest of Education Statistics, 1989* (Washington, D.C.: Government Printing Office, 1989), Table 304, pp. 336–340.

NOTE: Until 1980 the department was called the Office of Education.

partment of Education is the major agency through which the federal government demonstrates its commitment to education. Of the thirteen departments, it receives 45 percent of all federal funds for education. However, Table 9-3 shows a dramatic decline in funding in real dollars for the department since 1980, when the "new federalism" first surfaced. After increasing more than 60 percent in real dollars (after inflation) between 1970 and 1980 for elementary and secondary education, as well as higher education, funds between 1980 and 1989 for elementary/secondary education declined in real dollars 17 percent; for higher education, it fell by 27 percent.[10]

When the Department of Education was formed in 1867, its commissioner had a staff of three clerks and a total of $18,600 to spend. From these humble beginnings, the department has grown to more than 4525 employees and annual expenditures of $24.1 billion in 1989. The department presently administers over 200 separate programs, spending about $21 billion on these programs.[11]

The original purpose of the department was to collect and disseminate statistics and facts and to promote the goals of education throughout the country. Even though it was known as the Department of Education, the commissioner was not a member of the president's cabinet. In fact, the department was attached to the Department of Interior in 1868 and given the status and name of a bureau.

In 1929 the title Office of Education was adopted; ten years later, the office was transferred to the Federal Security Agency. In 1953, the Office of Education was transferred again, this time to the newly formed Department of Health, Education, and Welfare (HEW). The Office of Education continued to perform its original functions, and additional responsibilities and program activities were added by various acts of Congress or by order of the president. In particular, it assumed new responsibilities of (1) administering grant funds and contracting with state departments of education, school districts, colleges, and universities; (2) engaging in educational innovation, research, and development; and (3) providing leadership, consultative, and clearing-house services related to education.

In 1979, after much congressional debate, a Department of Education (DOE) was signed into law by President Carter, which declared that education was the "biggest single national investment" and that the creation of the depart-

[10]*Digest of Education Statistics, 1989* (Washington, D.C.: Government Printing Office, 1989), Figure 20, p. 333.
[11]*Digest of Education Statistics, 1989*, Table 305, p. 342; telephone conversation with Thomas Skelly, director of Budget Systems Division, Department of Education, January 18, 1990.

ment was the "best move for the quality of life in America for the future." The president, at that time, was reflecting the growing concern among educational reformers that linked the development of human capital (an educated populace) with the prosperity and growth of the nation. A secretary of education was named, Shirley Hufstedler, with full cabinet-level status, and the department officially opened in 1980.

The establishment of a Department of Education with full cabinet status has long been a goal of many professional organizations, especially the American Association of School Administrators (AASA), National Association of Secondary School Principals (NASSP), National Association of Elementary Principals (NAEP), American Federation of Teachers (AFT), and National Education Association (NEA). In theory there now exists a person (the Secretary of Education) with potentially widespread visibility and influence, and with cabinet status, who can exert persuasion and pressure in political and educational circles and who is in charge of educational policy at the federal level and the promotion of programs to carry out these policies.

Although President Reagan almost eliminated the Department of Education and reduced staff by one-third between 1980 and 1985,[12] it was during his administration that the department gained in stature and visibility due to the outspoken and controversial William Bennet, the secretary of education between 1985 and 1988. Bennett stated forceful positions on several educational issues, including but not limited to academic standards, moral education, school discipline, computer literacy, school prayer, drug education and getting drugs out of schools, teacher accountability and teacher testing, and teaching essential knowledge for a democratic society and national pride. His critics, in fact, labeled him as a "bully" and charged that he used his office as a "bully pulpit."

The current secretary, Lauro Cavazos, who replaced Bennett, is a much less visible and controversial person—better fitting into the low-profile Bush administration and being more popular with the minority community who Bennett sometimes alienated because of his concern for excellence rather than equity. Cavazos's main focus seems to be on increasing compensatory funding for disadvantaged populations, funding for bilingual groups, dealing with illiteracy and expanding remedial education, and taking steps to reduce the dropout rate.[13] At the same time, he has made a commitment to national standards of performance by advocating such "targets" as (1) increasing the high school graduation rate to 90 percent; (2) promoting early intervention programs; (3) defining student standards for advancing from elementary, junior, and high school levels; (4) improving class attendance; (5) increasing completion of homework assignments; and (6) improving the use of classroom time. In line with the Bush philosophy to reduce school spending, the Secretary of Education pledged no money and put the onus "at the local level . . . town halls, and state capitals across the country" to speed reform and upgrade standards.[14]

Office of Educational Research and Improvement

Established in 1985, the Office of Educational Research and Improvement (OERI) is part of the Department of Education. It replaced the National Institute of Education (NIE), which had been established in 1972, and also merged

---

[12]Telephone conversation with Thomas Skelly, director of Budget Systems Division, Department of Education, February 23, 1989.

[13]Lauro F. Cavazos, "Education: The Future Begins Today." Paper prepared for delivery before the U.S. Department of Education Forum, January 18, 1989; Edward B. Fiske, "Reagan's Education Secretary Will Continue Under Bush, But Will Reagan's Policies?" *New York Times,* 7 December 1988, p. 14.

[14]Letter to school board presidents by Lauro F. Cavazos. Released by U.S. Department of Education, August 19, 1989.

the functions of the Center for Educational Statistics (which publishes many of the government surveys and projections in education) and the **National Assessment of Educational Progress** (which analyzes and reports student educational progress). Like the old NIE, OERI's primary focus is on research and development and on programs to improve educational practices; but OERI is bureaucratically more streamlined than its predecessor.

The early years of OERI have been difficult. Many members of Congress have been disappointed by the agency's lack of direction and action; many also feel that educational research has produced little of value. Similar problems plagued the NIE and led to its eventual demise. The lack of confidence in educational research, combined with the federal government's desire to transfer many educational responsibilities to the states, has made it hard for OERI to build support in the political community. In line with other federal cutbacks in the human and educational sectors, OERI has had its budget requests pared down during the 1980s. The budget for fiscal year 1990 was $231.8 million, slightly up from $185 million in 1985 when the office was first established.[15]

Even among educators, OERI has not received much support. The agency has not overcome the communication gap between researchers and practitioners, and few people in schools and colleges even realize that OERI exists. There has been little discussion of the agency in the professional literature.

It is hoped that the recent national concern over éducation will spill over to research in education and thus give an assist to OERI. Writing in 1987, Chester Finn, the first OERI director, suggested that the agency (1) provide leadership in educational research and development, (2) promote excellence and equality in education, (3) make the schools more productive and effi-

cient, and (4) translate research into practical benefits.[16]

Assistant Secretary of Education Christopher Cross, the current OERI director, is unknown to the educational research and school community (compared to Finn, who was highly visible, outspoken, and well known among educators). Cross has not clarified his position about the mission of the agency.[17]

CONGRESSIONAL INFLUENCE ON EDUCATION

Although the framers of the Constitution gave the states primary responsibility to maintain and operate the schools through its Tenth Amendment, they also provided another important provision that Congress could "provide for the . . . general welfare of the United States."

Congress remained in the background for the first 150 years, at least in terms of supporting and enacting educational legislation. But a sense of national need, starting in the mid-1930s with the depression, required Congress to strengthen school support and enact laws. For example, between 1787 and 1937, Congress enacted only 14 major educational laws. During the last 50 years, however, more than 110 major laws were passed.[18]

The federal government, particularly Congress, never completely ignored schools and colleges; but the fact they remained in the background was welcomed by most state legislatures who wished to maintain control over education. Most administrative organizations such as the National School Boards Association

[15]Telephone conversation with Thomas Brown, director of Operations, Office of Educational Research and Improvement, January 6, 1990.

[16]Chester Finn, "Education That Works: Make the Schools Complete," *Harvard Business Review*, 14 (1987), pp. 63–68; Finn, "Governing Education," *Educational Policy*, 16 (1987), pp. 303–320.
[17]David Hill, "What Has the 1980s Reform Movement Accomplished?" *Education Digest*, 60 (1990), pp. 3–6.
[18]*Digest of Education Statistics, 1990* (Washington, D.C.: Government Printing Office, 1990).

(NSBA) also welcomed federal indifference. NSBA stated that "public education is a local function [and that] school boards are accountable directly to the communities which select them." Yet, the federal government has a major role to play: to provide a clear mission and sufficient resources so that "local administrators and teachers [can link] the schoolhouse to broader national and global priorities."[19]

While the NSBA "recognizes that special assistance and general aid are appropriate federal activities," it urges that local schools "not be subject to federal regulation."[20] Similarly, the Council of Chief State School Officers (CCSSO) maintains that the federal government should ensure that education serves the goals of the nation, but "the governance of education has been and should remain a matter of states to decide. The interests of children [and] youth . . . are best served when state and local agencies work together . . . [and when] federal funds are used in conjunction with state and local funds."[21]

With regard to the NSBA, emphasis is put on the local level in terms of responsibility. The CCSSO, as representatives of state educational agencies, puts the emphasis at the state level. However, both groups are concerned with national priorities and would like to see the federal government play a more active role in improving and funding educational programs, while not subjecting the states or local school districts to federal requirements or regulations. The new challenge is for the federal government to support its investment in human capital—that is, education of its people—in order for the nation to remain viable and compete internationally. State and local resources are insufficient to support high-quality investment in education; they need federal support and involvement but not control.

FEDERAL PROGRAMS AND ACTIVITIES IN EDUCATION

Until the mid-twentieth century, the federal government gave very little financial assistance to the states (or local schools) for the education of students. This attitude was in line with the majority belief that the federal government should have little to do with education and that education is a state responsibility. One might characterize federal programs and activities as passive and uncoordinated during this period. This is not to say that the federal government had no influence on education. National laws and federal programs had a significant impact on the way education developed in the United States. But what must be kept in mind is that these programs and acts were uncoordinated; they were not part of a broadly conceived national plan for education. After Sputnik in 1957, however, as national policy became more closely linked to education, federal funding dramatically increased and steadily involved specific educational targets. This growth in federal funding lasted until the 1980s.

Grants for Schools

The **Northwest Ordinances** of 1785 and 1787 are the first instances of federal assistance to education. The Northwest Ordinance of 1785 divided the Northwest Territory into townships and each township into thirty-six sections; it reserved the sixteenth section "of every township for the maintenance of public schools within the said township." The Ordinance of 1787 stated that "schools and the means of education shall forever be encouraged" by the states. The federal government thus demon-

---

[19]National School Boards Association, *A National Imperative: Educating for the 21st Century.* (Washington, D.C.: NSBA, 1989), p. 3.

[20]*Resolutions of the National School Boards Association: 1988–89.* (Washington, D.C.: NSBA, 1989), p. 1.

[21]Council of Chief State School Officers, *Council Policy Statements 1988* (Washington, D.C.: CCSSO, 1988), pp. 3, 5.

strated its commitment to education while ensuring the autonomy of state and local schools. As a result of these ordinances, thirty-nine states received over 154 million acres of land for schools from the federal government.[22]

Grants for Colleges

Seventy-five years were to pass before another major federal educational program was enacted. This program involved institutions of higher learning, not elementary and secondary schools. In the **Morrill Act** of 1862, federally owned lands totaling 30,000 acres were set aside for each state, with the provision that the income from the sale or rental of these lands was to be used to establish colleges for the study of agriculture and mechanical arts. A total of 6 million acres of federal lands was given to the states. These "people's colleges," or land-grant institutions, were to become the great multipurpose state universities that now enroll students from all segments of society. The Morrill Act demonstrated that the federal government would take action in education for the good and welfare of the nation; it also marked the beginning of meaningful federal influence on higher education.

Vocational Education Acts

The third phase of federal activity in public education came with the conditional grants for highly specific purposes in public secondary schools. The **Smith–Hughes Act** of 1917 provided money grants for vocational education, home economics, and agricultural subjects. The original act called for federal appropriations to be matched by state or local educational agencies. It was extended by various acts between 1929 and 1984; the 1984 legislation, called the Perkins Vocational Education Act, extended funding until fiscal year 1989 and included people with handicaps, single parents, homemakers, and the incarcerated among its beneficiaries.

The 1917 federal vocational act marked the federal government's first annual appropriation for public secondary education. The 1963 federal vocational act appropriated $235 million for vocational training, quadruple the annual appropriations of the original Smith–Hughes Act;[23] by 1989 the annual federal funding for vocational programs had reached $974 million.[24]

Relief Acts

The fourth phase of federal activity emerged during the Great Depression. Federal interest in schools at that time was only incidental to greater concerns for the welfare of unemployed youth from ages sixteen to twenty-five. The Civilian Conservation Corps (CCC) was organized in 1933 for unemployed males ages seventeen to twenty-three. More than half of the youth who joined had never finished grade school, and a substantial number were practically illiterate. The act provided federal appropriations for the education and vocational training of more than 3 million youth until it was abolished in 1943. Almost a generation passed before the CCC idea was brought back as a part of the Job Corps in the mid-1960s.

Other federal programs of the depression era included the National Youth Administration (1933), which provided welfare and training programs for unemployed youth ages sixteen to twenty-five, as well as financial aid for needy students attending secondary schools and colleges; Federal Emergency Relief Administration (1933), which allocated funds for the employ-

---

[22]Ellwood P. Cubberley, *Public Education in the United States,* rev. ed. (Boston: Houghton Mifflin, 1934).

[23]*The Condition of Education, 1983* (Washington, D.C.: U.S. Government Printing Office, 1983), Table 3.8, p. 152.

[24]*Digest of Education Statistics, 1989,* Table 307, p. 344.

ment of unemployed rural teachers; Public Works Administration (1933) and Works Progress Administration (1935), both of which provided federal money for school construction and repairs, amounting to 30 to 45 percent of the national allocation of funding of new schools from 1933 to 1938. All federal relief agencies were terminated by the mid-1940s. Although some educators were concerned about possible federal domination of public schooling during the 1930s, these fears subsided; the communities that had participated in these programs were in a better position to meet the classroom shortage that occurred after World War II.[25]

War Acts

The fifth phase of federal activity took place during World War II and the immediate postwar period. Three major bills were passed at this time.

1. The Lanham Act (1941) provided aid for construction and maintenance of local schools in areas where military personnel resided or where there were extensive federal projects.
2. The Occupational Rehabilitation Act (1943) provided educational and occupational assistance to disabled veterans.
3. The Servicemen's Readjustment Act (1944), commonly called the **G.I. Bill,** provided funds for the education of veterans and enabled hundreds of thousands of Americans to attend institutions of higher learning or special-training schools.

The benefits of the G.I. Bill were extended to the Korean and Vietnam conflicts. Direct aid, totaling more than $10 billion, has helped more than 7.5 million veterans to attend institutions of higher learning or special-training schools. The G.I. Bill, along with the baby boom, was a major factor in the growth and expansion of American colleges, including community colleges. In 1989 more than $600 million in tuition assistance was granted to veterans.[26]

National Defense Education Act

The Cold War and the Soviet launching of Sputnik in 1957 increased pressure for better schools and federal funding. This led to the sixth phase of federal education legislation, particularly the **National Defense Education Act** (NDEA) of 1958. The act stressed the importance of education to the national defense, and funding was earmarked for educational programs that enhanced "the security of the nation . . . and [developed] the mental resources and technical skills of its young men and women."

This broad act emphasized improvement of instruction in science, mathematics, foreign languages, and other critical subjects; provided college and university students loans and scholarships; funded numerous teacher-training programs, including those for teaching the disadvantaged; stimulated guidance and counseling programs; and promoted curriculum reform and programs in vocational and technical education. By 1960 the federal government was spending nearly $240 million annually on NDEA programs; in the mid-1960s, the act was extended to include history, geography, English, and reading as critical subjects.[27]

Compensatory Education Acts

The 1960s and 1970s brought a new emphasis on equality in education and represents the seventh stage of federal programs. With the War on

---

[25]Marvin Lazerson, *American Education in the Twentieth Century* (New York: Teachers College Press, 1987); Joel Spring, *The Politics of American Education* (New York: Longman, 1988).

[26]*Digest of Education Statistics, 1989,* Table 304, p. 337.
[27]Allan C. Ornstein, *Education and Social Inquiry* (Itasca, IL: Peacock, 1978); S. Alexander Rippa, *Education in a Free Society,* 6th ed. (New York: Longman, 1988).

Poverty and the spread of the civil rights movement, national policy became linked to education, as the government targeted specific groups—namely, minorities and the poor—and created specific policies to improve their educational opportunities. The federal government took on an active and coordinated posture with reference to education as it substantially increased its contributions to a variety of targeted programs and increased its regulations over specific policies.

The most important act of this period was the **Elementary and Secondary Education Act** (ESEA) of 1965, part of President Johnson's Great Society. It focused on compensatory programs for the disadvantaged student, immediately providing $1 billion for the first year. In 1980, at the height of its funding, monies totaled $3.5 billion, or about $300 per disadvantaged child; from 1965 to 1980, $30 billion had been appropriated. (Appropriations for the disadvantaged fluctuated between $3.1 and $4.4 billion from 1981 to 1989. Considering inflation, this was a drop in real dollars that reflected the general cutbacks in education by the federal government during this period.)[28]

Most grants for compensatory education are earmarked for urban disadvantaged students, now called at-risk students, and tend to fall in one of the six following programs:

1. *Early Childhood Education.* Head Start and Follow-Through are the most common programs under this category. Whereas Head Start attempts to help disadvantaged children receive "readiness" for the first grade, Follow-Through concentrates on sustaining readiness and supplementing in the primary grades whatever gains were made by the children who had a year's experience in Head Start.

2. *Reading, Language, and Basic-Skills Development.* Most compensatory funding (nearly 50 per-

cent) deals directly with improvement of basic skills in reading, language, and communication skills. This includes reduced class sizes, special tutoring programs, and special materials and personnel.

3. *Guidance and Counseling Programs.* These programs provide various social, psychological, health, and vocational services for the disadvantaged. Social workers, school psychologists, and community aids have been involved to help bridge the gap between school and home.

4. *Dropout-Prevention Programs.* Along with vocational and career education, a number of programs have aimed at preventing students from dropping out of school: work–study programs, on-the-job training programs, and financial incentives. Some of these programs are incorporated into the regular secondary school programs; others are offered in special centers in the community.

5. *Personnel Training.* Funds provide for a great many preservice and in-service training programs to help teachers and administrators gain insight into teaching the disadvantaged. Many of the in-service programs today are funded as part of staff-development programs in collaboration with schools and colleges.

6. *Higher Education.* Special programs in this area include identifying students of college potential early in the secondary schools and enriching their learning experience in the summer; accepting special provisions and lower academic requirements for college admission; using admission criteria that allow open enrollment in two-year and four-year colleges; and offering special scholarships, loans, and jobs.[29]

---

[28]*Digest of Education Statistics, 1983–84* (Washington, D.C.: Government Printing Office, 1983), Table 144, p. 174; *Digest of Education Statistics, 1989*, Table 307, p. 344.

[29]Allan C. Ornstein and Daniel U. Levine, "Compensatory Education: Can It Be Successful? What are the Issues?" *NASSP Bulletin*, 65 (1981), pp. 1–15; Ornstein and Levine, "Social Class, Race, and School Achievement," *Journal of Teacher Education*, 40 (1989), pp. 17–23.

Title IX

Title IX (Public Law 92–318) of the 1972 Education Amendments to the Civil Rights Act prohibits discrimination against women in educational programs receiving federal assistance. Part of the movement toward equality of opportunity, this legislation (and later acts such as the Women's Educational Equity Act of 1974) and a host of affirmative action rulings enforced by the Office of Civil Rights (which is also under the jurisdiction of the Department of Labor) evolved out of the **Civil Rights Act** of 1964 to include women's rights and concerns.

Federal control over these school matters is implicitly stated by the regulations governing Title IX and outline in detail what schools and colleges must do in terms of making available sports programs and facilities and in the hiring of women to prevent sex discrimination and possible loss of federal funds. Individuals and organizations can challenge any discriminatory practice by contacting the local agency of the Office of Civil Rights or Department of Labor. Moreover, Title VII of the Civil Rights Act of 1964, covers *all* educational institutions regardless of whether they receive federal funds or not. The latter condition reflects the fact that the U.S. Supreme Court has ruled that education is a right, guaranteed by the Constitution, and therefore it extends federal influence over schools and colleges.[30]

Bilingual Education

Bilingual education, which provides instruction in the native language of non-English-proficient students, has been expanding in U.S. public schools—in part due to federal policy. In 1968 Congress passed the **Bilingual Education Act** and amended it in 1974 to ensure that instruc-

tion be given in English or the native language of the child, whichever is more suitable, "to allow the child to progress effectively through the educational system."

Much of bilingual educational expansion is based on the 1974 U.S. Supreme Court ruling in *Lau v. Nichols* that requires schools to help students who "are certain to find their classroom experiences wholly incomprehensible" because they do not understand English; Congressional appropriations for bilingual education increased from $7.5 million in 1969 to $197 million in 1989.[31] Although the federal and state governments fund bilingual projects for more than sixty language groups speaking various Asian, Indo-European, and Native American languages, the large majority (about 70 percent) of children in these projects are Hispanic.

Although this country continues to attract hundreds of thousands of immigrants from around the world each year, Hispanics represent the fastest growing ethnic population in the country. In 1980, 15 million was the legal Hispanic population. Based on current immigration and fertility trends, shown in Table 9-4, the Hispanic population should reach 30 million in the year 2000 (10.8 percent of the total population) and 47 million in 2020 (14.7 percent), surpassing the U.S. black population (14 percent) as the largest minority group. On the heels of the Hispanic population is the Asian group—the next fastest growing minority group. It is expected to total 12 million in 2000 (4.3 percent) and 20 million in 2020 (6.3 percent) compared to 4 million (2 percent) in 1980.[32] The composition of the United States is undergoing considerable ethnic change—due largely to immigration trends—and the federal government is responding in the schools by requiring that the states

---

[30]Michael W. La Morte, *School Law: Cases and Concepts* (Englewood Cliffs, NJ: Prentice-Hall, 1990); Richard D. Strahan and L. Charles Turner, *The Courts and the Schools* (New York: Longman, 1988).

[31]*Digest of Education Statistics, 1989,* Table 305, p. 342.

[32]L. F. Bouvier and C. B. Davis, *The Future Racial Composition of the United States* (Washington, D.C.: Population Reference Bureau, 1982); Allan C. Ornstein, "Enrollment Trends in Big-City Schools," *Peabody Journal of Education,* 69 (1991), in print.

TABLE 9 ▪ 4   Total U.S. and Minority Population, Based on Current Immigration Rates and Fertility, 1980–2020 (in Millions)

	1980		2000		2020	
	Number	%	Number	%	Number	%
White (non-Hispanic)	181.0	79.9	200.3	71.7	205.6	64.9
Black	26.5	11.7	36.4	13.0	44.4	14.0
Hispanic	14.6	6.5	30.3	10.8	46.6	14.7
Asian	4.4	2.0	12.1	4.3	20.3	6.3
TOTAL:	226.5	100.0	279.1	100.0	316.9	100.0

SOURCE: Adapted from Allan C. Ornstein, "Urban Demographics for the 1980s: Educational Implications," *Education and Urban Society*, 16 (1984), Table 2, p. 486. Used by permission.

and local educational agencies meet the needs of these children.

Bilingual education has been expanding partly because the federal Office of Civil Rights (OCR) has been insisting that special educational opportunities be improved for limited-English-proficient (LEP) and non-English-proficient (NEP) students. Controversies over bilingual education have become somewhat embittered as federal and state actions have led to the establishment of various bilingual programs. There are arguments between those who would "immerse" children in an English-language environment and those who believe initial instruction will be more effective in the native language. On the one side are those who favor maintenance because they believe this would help build a constructive sense of identity, and there are those who believe that cultural maintenance is harmful because it separates groups from one another or discourages students from mastering English well enough to function successfully in the larger society.[33]

Adherents and opponents of bilingual education also differ on the related issues of whether

bilingual programs sometimes or frequently are designed to provide teaching jobs for native-language speakers and whether individuals who fill these jobs are competent in English. Observers who favor bilingual/bicultural maintenance tend to believe that the schools need many adults who can teach LEP or NEP students in their own language, whereas observers who favor transitional programs feel that very few native-language or bilingual speakers are required to staff a legitimate program.

Education for the Handicapped

Federal legislation focusing on the rights of handicapped persons and governing much of the subsequent activity in educating handicapped students was spelled out in three major laws: the Rehabilitation Act of 1973, Public Law 93–380 in 1974, and **Public Law 94–142** (the Education for All Handicapped Children Act) in 1975.

The Rehabilitation Act provided that no "program" or "activity" receiving federal assistance can exclude or discriminate against persons solely because of their handicaps. PL 93–380 authorized increased levels of aid to states for the implementation of special education services and set forth due process requirements to protect the rights of affected children and their

[33]James Crawford, "Bilingual Education," *Education Week*, 1 April 1987, pp. 1–14; August E. Hawkins and Robert T. Stafford, "Elementary and Secondary School Improvement Amendments of 1988," *Congressional Record—House*, 13 April 1988, pp. H1488–1608.

TABLE 9 ▪ 5   Number of Students Receiving Public Educational Services by Type of Handicap, 1978 and 1988

HANDICAP	1978	1988
Learning disabled	964,000	1,928,000
Speech impaired	1,223,000	953,000
Mentally retarded	935,000	582,000
Emotionally disturbed	288,000	373,000
Hard of hearing/deaf	85,000	56,000
Orthopedically handicapped	87,000	47,000
Other health impaired	135,000	45,000
Visually handicapped	35,000	22,000
Multihandicapped	—	77,000
Deaf–blind	—	1,000
Preschool handicapped (three to five years old)	—	363,000
TOTAL: (all conditions)	3,751,000	4,446,000
PERCENTAGE OF PUBLIC SCHOOL ENROLLMENT	8.6	11.1

SOURCE: *Digest of Education Statistics, 1989* (Washington, D.C.: Government Printing Office, 1989), Table 45, p. 59.

families. PL 94–142 set forth as national policy the goal that "free appropriate public education . . . must be extended to handicapped children as their fundamental right."

As indicated in Table 9-5, the total number of handicapped students served by public funds has increased over ten years, from 3.8 million to 4.4 million (or 11 percent of the public school enrollment), with more than two-thirds (68 percent) being served in regular classes (part-time or full time); 24 percent are in self-contained classes, and the remaining are in special schools or facilities.[34] The growth of handicapped students has been associated with the civil rights movement and its concern with making equal educational opportunity available to all students, not that more of our students have become handicapped. Although *Brown v. Board of Education* in 1954 addressed the segregation of black students in separate schools, it also served as a precedent in establishing the rights of students with handicaps to be provided with equal edu-

cational opportunity under the umbrella notion of **mainstreaming.**

In terms of costs, special education expenditures rose steadily in the 1970s and 1980s. The average cost of educating a child with handicaps is much higher than the national average for a nonhandicapped child, about double the national average of $4500 in 1989.[35] Although federal law requires local school districts to provide free appropriate education, the federal government has contributed relatively few dollars to this effort. Federal expenditures for special education increased from $75 million in 1969 to little more than $4.2 billion in 1989, but the latter amount represents only a few hundred extra dollars per child.[36] Thus, special education

[34]*Digest of Education Statistics 1989*, Table 46, p. 60.

[35]*Estimates of School Statistics 1988–89* (Washington, D.C.: National Education Association, 1989), Table 2, p. 7; *Eleventh Annual Report to Congress on the Implementation of the Education of the Handicapped Act* (Washington, D.C.: Government Printing Office, 1989).

[36]*Digest of Education Statistics, 1989*, Table 305, p. 342.

mandates place a heavy financial burden on the states and local educational agencies (which many school districts find burdensome).

Educational Consolidation and Improvement Act (ECIA)

At the insistence of the Reagan administration, Congress changed the long-term direction and method of federal funding of education from categorical grants (funds for specific groups and designated purposes) to **block grants** (funds for general purposes without precise categories).

Categorical grants were an important feature of federal involvement in education during the mid-1960s and 1970s. But Chapter 2 of the federal ECIA of 1981 replaced categorical grants for twenty-eight separate educational programs (at which Title I funding was specifically aimed and was the most popular) with one block grant that state and local educational agencies could use for broadly defined educational purposes. (Categorical grants for vocational, bilingual, and handicapped students were saved due to extensive pressuring from interest groups.) This move should be seen as part of the trend toward a new federalism, reflecting increased conservatism that reduced federal spending in real dollars (taking inflation into account), reduced federal bureaucracy and centralization, and shifted many social and educational programs from the national to the state governments.[37]

As a result of the act, funds have shifted from grants based on need, which mainly served disadvantaged students and urban school districts, to state-devised formulas based on student enrollments. The programs fall into one of three broad categories: (1) basic skills development in reading, writing, and math; (2) services for staff and school support such as staff training, in-structional equipment, testing and evaluation, as well as desegregation; and (3) special projects, including those related to career education, parental involvement, and gifted and talented students. There is also a special provision for support of "secular" or "neutral services" of nonpublic schools such as transportation, school lunches, and instructional materials, media, and equipment.

Observers cite a number of advantages of the block-grant approach for educational programs. It has reduced the amount of paperwork required to get a grant (from twenty to thirty pages for a $50,000 program to four to six pages), simplified the administration of grant monies, and enabled school districts to cut down the bureaucracy devoted to grants. Instead of submitting applications to several different federal agencies, a school district now has to interact only with its own state's educational agency. The block-grant approach has also enhanced the role of local administrators in determining how resources will be used. (See Administrative Advice 9-1.) Finally, under the old system, some school districts were continually unsuccessful at competing for federal grants, whereas others became very skillful at the process. Block grants, according to their supporters, have reduced this kind of competition among districts.[38]

On the other hand, critics point out that the states have failed to pick up some of the programs formerly funded by the federal government. Many states have chosen to distribute funds to local schools on a per-child basis rather than on the basis of need. The "winners" under the block-grant approach have included small-town and rural school districts; the "losers" have

[37]Denis P. Doyle and Bruce C. Cooper, *Federal Aid to the Disadvantaged* (New York: Falmer Press, 1988); Alan J. De Young, *Economics and American Education* (New York: Longman, 1989).

[38]Richard F. Elmore, "Differential Treatment of States in Federal Education Policy," *Peabody Journal of Education*, 60 (1982), pp. 34–52; Anne H. Hastings, "Snipping the Strings: Local and State Administrators Discuss Chapter 2," *Phi Delta Kappan*, 65 (1983), pp. 194–198; and Michael S. Knapp and Rhonda A. Cooperstein, "Early Research on the Federal Education Block Grant," *Educational Evaluation and Policy Analysis*, 4 (1986), pp. 121–137.

ADMINISTRATIVE ADVICE 9-1

■

DEALING WITH THE POLITICS OF BLOCK GRANTS

A critical issue for school administrators is to deal with the reduction in federal funding and in other policy areas. Cuts in federal programs and efforts to deregulate these programs pose new challenges to school districts in the way they deal with state agencies. The states tend to view the block grants as an opportunity to increase their policy-making role in education, and local school administrators must learn the new policies and procedures in order to obtain their share of funds. Below are some practical suggestions:

- Determine which federal programs the federal government will continue to fund and which the states will fund.
- Determine how local school programs have to be modified to reflect changes in federal guidelines.
- Determine which local school programs have to be modified to reflect changes in state guidelines.
- Decide on how to modify those programs to meet state guidelines.
- Decide what, if any, state guidelines conflict with federal mandates. For those that conflict, ask the state to clarify the specific guidelines.
- Determine how block grants to local school districts will be distributed and monitored.
- Determine what part of the local school program will receive greater scrutiny by the state. Make appropriate adjustments.

- Reduce central personnel who had to be hired to cope with prior red tape of categorical grants.
- Organize a staff-development program to enhance block-grant funding for local school districts; collaborate with teachers, administrators, and community members.
- Design your block-grant program around the characteristics and needs of your school district; look at practical matters—budget, staff size, number of students, grade levels, and the like.
- Maintain broad-based political pressure for continually increasing the funding of block grants in your school district.
- Keep in contact with the state legislature and state department of education to determine policy or program shifts in block grants; hire a local ombudsman or consultant to build communication links with state agencies.

often been urban districts with high percentages of minority and disadvantaged students. Districts under court-ordered desegregation that previously received federal funds also have taken large cuts. Many critics contend that the federal government began providing its services and programs in the first place because states did not accept those responsibilities. For example, before block grants went into effect, the **Council of Great City Schools** (a coalition that includes the forty-four largest urban school districts) depended on Washington for 16 percent

of school revenues, compared to a national average of 8 percent. This need for federal funds, some critics argue, derived from the states' lack of attention to the problems of big-city schools.[39]

[39]Knapp and Cooperstein, "Early Research on the Federal Education Block Grant"; telephone conversation with Michael Casserly, legislative and research associate, Council of Great City Schools, January 6, 1988; and Thomas Timar, "The Politics of School Restructuring," *Phi Delta Kappan*, 71 (1989), pp. 264–275.

However, the intense interest in winners and losers seems to be waning, and educators now seem more concerned with the variety of the block grant's contributions to local schools and the way funds are distributed from the state to the local level. At present, urban schools (with large percentages of disadvantaged children) overwhelmingly use block-grant money for reading and language programs, whereas rural and suburban schools use the money for books, materials, and computer hardware and software.[40] Another major concern is whether block grants will survive if the federal government continues to de-emphasize spending for social and educational programs.

National Assessment of Education Progress (NAEP)

The NAEP is a representative nationwide study conducted since 1969 to gather information about selected levels of achievement of nine-, thirteen-, and seventeen-year-olds and young adults (twenty to twenty-five years) in ten learning areas. Different learning areas are assessed each year, and all areas have been assessed periodically in order to measure possible changes in educational achievement.

Originally operated by the Education Commission of the States (ESC), an interstate information center with headquarters in Denver, in 1983 NAEP's operation was transferred under the jurisdiction of the Educational Testing Service (ETS), supported by federal funds. It is generally oriented toward two broad goals: equalization of educational opportunity and increased educational productivity.[41] With a budget of more than $9.5 million a year, it fills a national need for providing information on the performance levels of the nation's students in thirty states, and by 1992 it will be expanded to forty-one states.[42]

The reading, writing, math, and science scores are considered the most important tests. The scores are sometimes used by school districts as a report card about their students' performance and as a yardstick for comparisons with other school districts in the state or nation. Moreover, in more than three-fourths of the states that have their own testing programs, such examinations are often patterned after the NAEP tests. (See Administrative Advice 9-2.)

Important Variables The scores on the tests strongly correlate with social class, family conditions, and ethnicity. For example, the average reading-proficiency score of seventeen-year-olds whose parents have not graduated from high school (an indicator of social class) was almost identical to the average score of thirteen-year-olds whose parents have attended college. Only 20 percent of seventeen-year-olds whose parents did not complete high school scored in 1984–1985 above the "adept" level, compared with 52 percent of those with parents who had postsecondary education.[43] Similar patterns are found for science and math.

The average reading-proficiency score of students from homes with "many" reading materials (at least four books or magazines) is consistently 5 to 7 percent above the mean at all three age levels; those with "few" (one or two books or magazines) or "none" are 5 to 7 percent below the mean (Table 9-6). At all grade levels, except age nine, reading scores are affected by the hours of television watching per day. Television viewing tends to correlate with lower reading scores, and the scores become progressively

---

[40]*Congressional Record—House,* 13 April 1988, pp. H1488–1608.

[41]James W. Guthrie and Rodney J. Reed, *Educational Administration and Policy* (Englewood Cliffs, NJ: Prentice-Hall, 1986); Thomas Timar and David Kirp, *Managing Educational Excellence* (New York: Falmer Press, 1988).

[42]Telephone conversation with Eugene Owen, project director of NAEP, February 24, 1989.

[43]NAEP, *The Reading Report Card* (Princeton, NJ: Educational Testing Service, 1985). p. 71.

TABLE 9-6 NAEP Reading Scores of Students By Selected Characteristics

SELECTED CHARACTERISTICS	AGE 9			AGE 13			AGE 17		
	Reading Scores For			Reading Scores For			Reading Scores For		
	1974–1975	1978–1980	1983–1984	1974–1975	1978–1980	1983–1984	1974–1975	1978–1980	1983–1984
All participants	209.6	213.5	213.2	254.8	257.4	257.8	284.5	284.5	288.2
Reading material in the home									
0–2 items	195.8	199.3	201.0	232.9	239.2	241.2	257.2	264.5	266.7
3 items	211.5	214.7	217.3	248.7	253.0	255.8	276.2	279.4	283.4
4 items	222.2	224.6	225.9	265.3	265.4	265.8	292.6	291.3	294.7
Television watched per day									
0–2 hours	—	217.4	219.6	—	261.3	266.8	—	288.2	295.3
3–5 hours	—	220.0	219.8	—	256.4	261.9	—	278.2	284.4
6+ hours	—	208.8	202.2	—	243.8	246.2	—	263.7	270.1

SOURCE: *Digest of Education Statistics, 1989* (Washington, D.C.: Government Printing Office, 1989), Table 95, p. 108.

lower for thirteen- and seventeen-year-olds after two hours a day of television watching. For nine-year-olds, television watching has a neutral effect until viewing reaches six hours a day[44]— suggesting, at that age (or younger), children may learn as much vocabulary and linguistic concepts by watching television as by engaging in other activities. Some observers point out, however, that older students (thirteen- and seventeen-year-olds) who are poor readers may simply choose to watch more television.

Reading and Math Scores
As many as 63 percent of white students score above 300, or the "adept" category, in reading—compared to 41 percent of Hispanics and 24 percent of blacks.[45] (Actually, this percentage is a considerable improvement for blacks compared with past years, perhaps reflecting the effects of the nation's continuous efforts in compensatory reading programs.) In math 350 is considered "adept"; only 27 percent of white students fall into this category, compared to 11 percent of Hispanics and 2 percent of blacks.[46] Most observers maintain that social-class factors interact with ethnicity and that environmental conditions are more powerful factors than ethnic/racial indicators.

In general, more than 40 percent of thirteen-year-olds and 16 percent of seventeen-year-olds attending school (many lower achievers have already dropped out) have not acquired "intermediate" reading proficiency, that is, 250+; this means they cannot search for specific information, interrelate ideas, or make generalizations about the materials or text they are reading in their subjects. Only 5 percent of students age seventeen are advanced readers (350+),[47] and less than 1 percent of thirteen-year-olds are ca-

[44]*The Condition of Education, 1987* (Washington, D.C.: Government Printing Office, 1987), Table 1.29, Chart 1.29, pp. 68–69; *Digest of Education Statistics, 1987* (Washington, D.C.: Government Printing Office, 1987), Table 73, p. 87.

[45]*Digest of Education Statistics, 1988*, Table A8, p. 333; *Digest of Education Statistics, 1989*, Tables 97 and 103, pp. 110, 115.

[46]Ibid.

[47]NAEP, *The Reading Report Card.* Also see *What Works: Research About Teaching and Learning* (Washington, D.C.: Government Printing Office, 1986).

ADMINISTRATIVE ADVICE 9-2

■

CONSIDERATIONS FOR IMPROVING YOUR SCHOOL'S (SCHOOL DISTRICT'S) NAEP SCORES

The NAEP currently provides indicators of how well schools are doing in producing academic outcomes. School administrators can compare their school or district scores with other U.S. schools. But the data do not tell administrators (or legislators) which aspects of schooling have contributed to educational success. Current reporting procedures may tell administrators their schools should try harder, but not what efforts are likely to be effective.

School administrators might appropriately study the following input variables (over which they have partial control) in order to associate variations in student achievement among their schools and/or school districts.

- *Teachers' Educational Background.* This variable might include such items as highest degree earned, institutional type, major field of study, number of education courses, and membership in professional organizations.
- *Teachers' Salary and Experience.* It seems plausible that higher salaries and more years of experience would directly correlate with student achievement. However, the need is to prove the so-called obvious, which may or may not be so obvious to everyone.
- *Administrators' Background.* Is the ratio of students to school or district administrators related to achievement (should numbers be reduced)? Is the administrators' educational background a factor, years of experience, or salary related to student achievement?
- *Instructional Time.* Variables related to instructional time include the number and length of school days, the number of hours of instruction per term (year) in a given subject and in a given unit or content area, academic time versus nonacademic time in school, the amount of time wasted in school, and the amount of time students are actually engaged in academic tasks.
- *Textbooks.* The textbook seems to be the number-one content indicator of the curriculum. Clearly, the text influences what is covered and not covered by the curriculum. The amount of time the text is used in the classroom and for

homework, the content of the text, and the reading level of the text need to be analyzed.
- *Class size.* This variable is believed to affect achievement, especially at lower grade levels and in classrooms of fifteen or fewer students. Others contend that not until class size is reduce to five students are noticeable effects realized.
- *Classroom Group.* The homogeneity/heterogeneity of the classroom (in terms of gender, ethnicity, social class, and prior achievement scores) is believed to affect student achievement. Most educators contend that heterogeneity is positively correlated with student achievement among low-achieving students while not adversely affecting high achievers.
- *Homework.* The need is to establish what type of homework and how much homework for what type of subjects and students are likely to be most effective. How much homework by prior achievement and grade level is appropriate? What are the best methods for grading homework? How much time should elapse between homework tasks and homework review? Should homework be assigned to introduce or review new concepts, for whom, and in what subjects or grades?
- *Tracking.* How does tracking affect high-achieving, moderate-achieving, and low-achieving students? How does tracking affect students in reading, math, or other subjects? How does

(continued)

Administrative Advice 9-2 (continued)

tracking impact on students by ethnicity and social class?

■ *Courses Taken.* Tracking also influences to some extent courses taken by students that in turn influences information learned and achievement scores. The effects of tracking on achievement should include students' gender, ability, and social class, as well as school size and geographical location.

■ *School Size and Condition.* Is small better or worse? Is the condition or the age of the school

related to student achievement? Do large libraries, pools, auditoriums, gymnasiums, ball fields, parking lots—all those nice expensive items—mean anything in terms of student outcomes?

Source: Adapted from Allan C. Ornstein, "In Pursuit of Cost-Effective Schools," *Principal,* 71 (1990), pp. 28–30; Ornstein, "School Finance in the 90s," *American School Board Journal,* 177 (1990), pp. 36–40; and Daniel P. Resnick and Lauren P. Resnick, "Understanding Achievement and Acting to Produce It," *Phi Delta Kappan,* 69 (1988), pp. 576–579.

pable of reading and understanding the *New York Times* or *Wall Street Journal.*

As for math, only 18 percent of thirteen-year-olds and 51 percent of seventeen-year-olds can perform moderately complex math procedures, and only 1 percent of thirteen-year-olds and 7.4 percent of seventeen-year-olds can perform multistep problems.[48] On the Scholastic Aptitude Test scores and international aptitude tests, the U.S. student scores are even worse (see p. 268).

The dismal performance record of the nation's students on these tests, especially minority students whose enrollments are increasing each year, may be an eye opener for some administrators. Their test outcomes raise questions about the responsibility and role of school leaders as well as parents. Do we pass the buck—and say that's the job of teachers—or merely try to transfer the finger of responsibility to parents or students? Do school administrators have adequate time to deal with teaching and instructional matters or even want to, despite what they might say publicly, given the need and sometimes urgency to deal with managerial, fiscal, personnel, and community issues?

---

[48]*Digest of Education Statistics, 1989,* Table 103, p. 115.

NATIONAL REFORM OF EDUCATION

The rapid expansion of federal influence in education coincides with national reform, based on perceived problems of society and what is in the best interests of the nation. What educational policies the president puts on his agenda, what educational programs Congress establishes and funds, and how the Supreme Court interprets the Constitution on educational matters create a national policy in education.

National priorities in the 1960s and 1970s for the most part focused on educational equality, whereby the definition of minority status was expanded beyond traditional minority and disadvantaged groups to also include bilingual and handicapped groups, as well as women. The notion of equality was enlarged from its original meaning that for the first 175 years of the nation's history was conceived as **equality of opportunity,** that is, free and universal education for all groups. If you took advantage of schools, great; if not, you had the opportunity—and society was not to blame.

The modern view of equality now includes (1) equality based on spending additional monies for special programs and personnel, illustrated by compensatory funding; (2) equality based on racial composition, as suggested by school desegregation and integration; (3) equality based on outcomes for students with similar backgrounds, spearheaded by the accountability movement and school finance reform; and (4) equality based on equal outcomes for students (and adults) with unequal backgrounds and abilities, expressed by affirmative action and quotas.

Once we start to define inequality in terms of equal outcomes (both cognitive and economic), we start comparing racial, ethnic, religious, and gender groups. In a heterogeneous society like ours, this results in some hotly contested issues—including how much to invest in human capital (and for how much gain), how to determine the cost effectiveness of social and educational programs, who should be taxed and how much, how should money be redistributed, to what extent are we to handicap our brightest and most talented minds (the swift runners) to enable those who are slow to finish at the same time, and whether our policies result in reverse discrimination or hinder excellence. Indeed, we cannot treat these issues lightly because they affect most of us in one way or another and lead to questions over which wars have been fought.

All these issues involve balancing acts and the effect these balancing acts have on individuals, groups, and society. Many of us have our own ideas about equality and excellence in education—and the nine wise judges on the U.S. Supreme Court are supposed to be able to render decisions involving these matters. Many of us are unable to agree on what is equitable and just and how much we can stretch the embodiment of reform ideas or the fiber of society. Too much egalitarianism can lead to mediocrity, indifference, and economic decline within society. On the other hand, excellence carried too far can create wide social and economic gaps, hostilities among groups, and a stratified society with a permanent underclass. The idea is to search for the "golden mean."

The issues raised here directly affect the type of society we are and the society we are to become. As school administrators, we are com-

pelled to carry out the law of the land and, more precisely, to carry out the policies of the school board. The best for which we can hope is for an enlightened school board, whose members understand and abide by the law. Administrators are compelled, by virtue of their job, to deal with pressure groups and community groups that often have their own agenda and interpretation of what is right. Indeed, questions that deal with equality and excellence have no easy answers, and they will continue to plague us all, including principals and superintendents who must make school decisions that affect students, teachers, and other administrators.

The Call for Excellence

In the mid-1980s, the pendulum swung from the left to the right, from equality to excellence; national attention turned to the need for higher academic standards: tougher subjects, rigorous testing, and stiffer high school graduation and college admission requirements. The educational dimensions of and reasons for this new movement were amply documented in a number of policy reports released between 1983 and 1990. Many of them (including the most famous of these reports, *A Nation at Risk*) were written and distributed by the federal government, and all called for reforms to improve the quality of education in the United States. The background data to these reports are depressing.

1. Schools and colleges have shifted away from requiring students to take what had been the standard academic core curriculum for graduation twenty years ago: foreign language, mathematics, science, English, and history. Elective courses and remedial courses have replaced many standard academic courses.

2. Requirements for graduation have been lowered; fewer students are enrolled in rigorous or even academic courses. (According to a National Science Foundation report, only 9 percent of U.S. high school graduates took one year of physics; 16 percent took one year of chemistry; less than 5 percent studied a

foreign language beyond the first year; and only 15 percent studied a language at all.)

3. Grade inflation is on the rise, and students are required to complete less homework (75 percent of high school students completed less than one hour of homework a night).

4. Average achievement scores on the **Scholastic Aptitude Test** (SAT) demonstrate a virtually unbroken decline from 1963 to 1988. Average verbal scores fell over 40 points (466 to 428), and mathematics scores dropped nearly 20 points (492 to 471).[49]

5. International comparisons of student achievement, completed in the 1970s, reveal that on nineteen academic tests U.S. students were never first or second and, in comparison with other industrialized nations, were last seven times. In 1988 they scored last in math (averaging 94 points below first-ranked Korea) and next to last in science (averaging 71 points below first-ranked Korea). U.S. students also scored last in geographical knowledge; more than one-third lower than their first-ranked counterparts in Sweden.[50]

6. Some 23 to 25 million U.S. adults are functionally illiterate by the simplest tests of everyday reading and writing.

7. About 13 percent of all seventeen-year-olds in the United States are considered functionally illiterate, and this illiteracy rate jumps to 40 percent among minority youth.

8. Business and military leaders complain that they are required to spend millions of dollars annually on costly remedial education and training programs in the basic skills, or three Rs. Between 1975 and 1985, remedial mathematics courses in four-year colleges increased by 72 percent and by 1985 constituted one-fourth of all mathematics courses taught in these institutions. As many as 25

percent of the recruits in the armed forces cannot read at the ninth-grade level.[51]

9. All these sordid figures pile up and stare at us, despite the fact that our student–teacher ratios were 17:1 in 1988, which put us seventh lowest in the world (whereas such countries as Japan and Korea have over 30:1 student–teacher ratios) and that our pupil expenditures for education were the second highest in the world (about $300 less than first-ranked Switzerland).[52]

These deficiencies have come to light at a time when the demand for highly skilled military personnel and workers in labor and industry is accelerating rapidly and amidst growing concern that the United States is being overtaken by other nations in commerce, industry, science, and technology.

Table 9-7 summarizes the major policy reports. Seven of these twelve emphasize the need to strengthen the curriculum in the core subjects of English, math, science, social studies and foreign language. The focus is thus on a common curriculum. Technology and computer courses are mentioned often, either as components of science or math or as a separate subject area (sometimes referred to as the fourth R). High-level cognitive and thinking skills are also stressed. Most of the reports are also concerned with programs and personnel for disadvantaged students and students with learning disabilities, although this message is not always loud and clear.

Eleven reports emphasize tougher standards and tougher courses, and eight out of the twelve propose that colleges raise their admission requirements. Most of the reports also mention increasing homework, time for learning, and time in school, as well as instituting more rigor-

[49]Ibid., Table 108, p. 120.

[50]*The Condition of Education, 1989*, Vol. 1 (Washington, D.C.: Government Printing Office, 1989), Charts 1.3 and 1.5, pp. 13, 17; *Digest of Education Statistics, 1989*, Tables 347 and 349, pp. 390–391.

[51]Allan C. Ornstein, "The National Reports on Education: Implications for Directions and Aims," *Kappa Delta Pi Record*, 21 (1985), pp. 58–64.

[52]*The Condition of Education, 1989*, Chart 1.18, p. 107; *Digest of Education Statistics 1989*, Table 340, p. 385. Also see John Hood, "Education: Money Isn't Everything," *Wall Street Journal*, 9 February 1990, p. 14.

ous grading, testing, homework, and discipline. They mention upgrading teacher certification, increasing teacher salaries, increasing the number of and paying higher salaries for science and math teachers, and providing merit pay for outstanding teachers. Overall, most stress academic achievement (not the whole child) and increased productivity (not relevancy or humanism).

Most of the reports express concern that the schools are pressed to play too many social roles; that the schools cannot meet all these expectations; and that the schools are in danger of losing sight of their key role—teaching basic skills and core academic subjects, new skills for computer use, and higher-level cognitive skills for the world of work, technology, and military defense. Many of the reports, concerned not only with academic productivity but also with national productivity, link human capital with economic capital. Investment in schools would be an investment in the economy and in the nation's future stability. If education fails, so does our work force and nation. Hence, it behooves the business, labor, and government to work with educators to help educate and train the U.S. populace.

Despite criticisms by some members of the educational community that the reports are too idealistic and unrealistic, that they put too much emphasis on excellence at the expense of equality and equity, and that they are enormously expensive to implement,[53] the reports have captured national attention, spotlighted nationwide concern for the quality of education, and have upgraded nationwide school standards. Publication and discussion of these and other national reports and studies have reinforced and accelerated many federal, state, and local activities designed to improve education. (See Administrative Advice 9-3.)

Need for Caution

Administrators must understand the broad sweep of change and improvement, which come and go like a pendulum, and that schools have been burdened by the rest of society with roles and responsibilities that other agencies and institutions no longer do well, or, for that matter, want to do.[54] The schools are seen as ideal agencies to solve the nation's problems and to reform or change what ails us. With this perspective, many people refuse to admit their own responsibilities in helping children and youth develop their individual capacities and adjust to society. Similarly, parents and policymakers alike often expect administrators and teachers to be solely responsible for carrying out reform.

Seasoned administrators have learned, sometimes the hard way, there are no "magic bullets" for reforming schools; there is no one policy or single combination of policies that will automatically lead to answers or transform ineffective schools into effective ones. School life, as in the case of human life, is much more complicated. Over and over, reform measures that have been imposed on school officials by the federal government and other reform groups have failed. As one author notes, "The freeway of American education is cluttered with the wrecks of famous bandwagons."[55]

In the 1950s, for example, the Ford Foundation invested $250 million in innovative programs before it asked for results—and then found out the projects did not work.[56] In the early 1970s, when the U.S. Office of Education evaluated more than 1200 of its own compensatory programs and after spending more than $1 billion in less than two years, only 10 had solid

[53]*The Cost of Reform* (Arlington, VA: American Association of School Administrators, 1984); Joe Nathan, "Implications for Educators of *Time for Results*." *Phi Delta Kappan*, 68 (1986), pp. 197–201.

[54]Ornstein, "National Reform and Instructional Accountability."

[55]Ron Brandt, keynote address to Washington State Association for Curriculum Development and Supervision, Seattle, February 11, 1983.

[56]*A Foundation Goes to School* (New York: Ford Foundation, 1972).

TABLE 9▪7   Overview of Reports on Excellence in Education

REPORT AND SPONSOR	CURRICULUM OBJECTIVES	CONTENT EMPHASIS	SCHOOL ORGANIZATION	GOVERNMENT–BUSINESS ROLE
Academic Preparation for College, The College Board	Improve student competencies in reading, writing, speaking, listening, reasoning, math, and study skills Raise college entrance standards	English, math, science, computers, foreign language	Stress study and independent learning Incentives to students	Develop a national standard for academic achievement in secondary education
Action for Excellence, Education Commission of the States	Establish minimum competencies in reading, writing, speaking, listening, reasoning, and economics Strengthen programs for gifted students Raise college entrance standards	English, math, science, foreign language, history, computer literacy	Consider longer school day Emphasize order and discipline More homework More rigorous grading with periodic testing Independent learning	Foster partnerships between private sector and education Increase federal funds for education
Educating Americans for the 21st Century, National Science Foundation	Devote more time to math and science in elementary and secondary schools Provide more advanced courses in science and math Raise college entrance standards	Math, science, technology, computers	Consider longer school day, week, and/or year Twelve-year plan for math and science	Federal input in establishing national goals for education Increase NSF role in curriculum development and teacher training
High School, Carnegie Foundation for Achievement in Teaching	Mastery of language, including reading, writing, speaking, and listening Expand basic academic curriculum Student transition to work and further education Strengthen graduation requirements	Core of common learning, including English, history, civics, math, science, technology Computer literacy	Improve working conditions for teachers Utilize technology to enrich curriculum Flexible schedules and time allotments One track for students School–community learning activities Greater leadership role for principal	More "connections" between school and community, business, and universities Increase parent and community coalitions with and service to schools Utilize retired personnel from business and colleges Federal scholarships for science and math teachers

TABLE 9 ▪ 7 Continued

REPORT AND SPONSOR	CURRICULUM OBJECTIVES	CONTENT EMPHASIS	SCHOOL ORGANIZATION	GOVERNMENT– BUSINESS ROLE
Making the Grade, Twentieth Century Fund	Improve basic-skill programs Improve learning in English, math, and science Initiate general programs for students with learning problems and a voucher program for the disadvantaged	Basic skills English, math, and science Computer literacy	Reward teacher performance Special programs for poor, minority, handicapped, bilingual, and immigrant students	Increase federal aid for special programs for disadvantaged student populations Increase federal aid for programs to develop scientific literacy among all students and advanced math and science for academically able secondary students
A Study of High Schools, National Association of Secondary School Principals	Reduce traditional subject matter Emphasize higher-order thinking skills	Interdisciplinary curriculum Problem-solving activities and learning experiences	Eliminate age grouping Eliminate teacher specializations Incentives to students Out-of-school learning activities	Federal support for special students, including learning disabled and gifted
A Nation At Risk, National Commission on Excellence in Education	Improve textbooks and other instructional materials Provide more rigorous courses in vocational education, arts, and science Strengthen graduation requirements Raise college entrance requirements	Five new basics: English, math, science, social studies, and computer science	Consider seven-hour school day Tighten attendance and discipline More homework More rigorous grading and periodic testing Group students by performance rather than age	Federal cooperation with states and localities Meet needs of disadvantaged student populations as well as gifted and talented National standardized tests in context with national interest in education
The First Lesson: A Report on Elementary Education in America, The Secretary of Education	Improve basic skills for young children Improve complex learning tasks and abilities for higher-grade children Increase knowledge base essential for democratic society and national identity Improve textbook and workbook writing and selection Raise academic standards	Basic skills, especially reading through phonics Problem-solving skills in mathematics and hands-on learning and discovery in science Unified sequence stressing history, geography, and civics Computer literacy and cultural literacy	Lengthen school day More homework More rigorous testing Parental choice in children's schools Reward teacher performance	Communitywide and parental responsibility in education Teacher and school accountability Improve training programs for elementary teachers; emphasis on arts and science rather than methods courses

(continued)

TABLE 9 ▪ 7   Continued

REPORT AND SPONSOR	CURRICULUM OBJECTIVES	CONTENT EMPHASIS	SCHOOL ORGANIZATION	GOVERNMENT– BUSINESS ROLE
The Early Years, Carnegie Foundation for the Advancement of Teaching	Focus on plight of at-risk children, the nation's underclass Emphasis on basic skills Priority on childhood education	Language development, including reading, writing, and listening skills	Flexible school schedules reflecting changing family and work patterns Longer school day and school year Reward teacher performance; attract better teachers Parental choice for after school and summer programs; end of traditional summer vacation	Increased federal aid for education of at-risk children Increased role of business and industry Greater involvement of teachers in decision making, increased pay
Time for Results: The Governors' 1991 Report on Education, National Governors' Association	Focus on teenage pregnancy, school dropouts, adult illiteracy, and drug abuse Improve school leadership and management Better use of technology in the classroom Increase state role and responsibility in education Higher academic standards at all grade levels	Basic skills, math, science, and technology Research and development in education	Kindergarten for all children; early childhood programs for all at-risk children Parental education programs Parental choice in selecting children's school Reliable and valid assessment of student performance Year-round schooling Reorganize and regulate schools and school districts that are "academically bankrupt"	National school board to certify teachers Increased pay and accountability for teachers and principals Improved teacher training and educational leadership programs Greater involvement in education of local leaders, teachers, parents, citizens, and business people Greater state role, regulation, and spending in education Annual progress reports until 1991 on what each state is doing to carry out educational reform

empirical data that demonstrated their success.[57] Over and over, some critics conclude that, with regard to school reform and compensatory programs, we have been spending too much and not getting enough in return. What often occurs

is some marginal improvement in the beginning—then gradually diminishment until input (time and money) is wasted because there is virtually no increase in output.[58] A "flat area"—less output in relation to input—is reached eventually, or even worse, there is no return. The same kind of criticism has been leveled at school

[57]*Compensatory Education and Other Alternatives in Urban Schools* (Washington, D.C.: Government Printing Office, 1972); Richard L. Fairley, "Accountability's New Test," *American Education,* 5 (1972), pp. 33–35.

[58]Allan C. Ornstein, "In Pursuit of Cost-Effective Schools," *Principal,* 70 (1990), pp. 28–30.

TABLE 9 ▪ 7   Continued

REPORT AND SPONSOR	CURRICULUM OBJECTIVES	CONTENT EMPHASIS	SCHOOL ORGANIZATION	GOVERNMENT–BUSINESS ROLE
The Disappearing Quality of the Workforce: What Can We Do to Save it? National Alliance of Business	Educate all youth in basic skills Provide students with high-level skills required for our information and service economy Face our educational problems Restructure education; provide financial support Increase the quality of the nation's work force	Basic skills Critical thinking skills Tutoring programs Raise academic standards and high school graduation requirements	Reduce school dropout rates Increase attendance rates Improve national test scores and achievement levels Increase adopt-a-school programs Teacher–administrative accountability Staff development/mentor programs	Business leaders must take an active role in implementing educational reform Collaborative efforts between business and educational groups Reshape education at state and local levels Involve citizen, parent, political, and business groups
Investing in People: A Strategy to Address America's Workforce Crisis, U.S. Department of Labor	Commitment to basic skills and literacy Invest in human capital Increase federal and business support in educational and human resource programs Upgrade work force quality Upgrade high school graduation, college entry, and labor-market standards Develop national goals and timetables to improve education training.	Basic-skill programs for dropouts Literacy programs for illiterate adults Lifetime education and training Combine vocational and technical education	Reduce dropout rates Increase attendance rates Increase parent participation Increase business community presence in schools Reduce competitive learning; increase cooperative learning More rigorous teacher training and testing of new teachers	Partnerships between business, labor, and government at all levels Business to fund incentive-programs to improve teacher–school performance Increase government and training programs to address needs of private sector and labor Tax credits for educational and training programs for private sector

reform in general, although the reasons and responsibilities vary according to the critics' politics and view of the social world.

We, as administrators, need to remember to go slow in the beginning of reform, to weigh the risks and rewards before making decisions, and to search for a balance—where there is no extreme emphasis on subject matter or student's sociopsychological needs, no extreme emphasis on one or two subjects at the expense of others, or no extreme emphasis on excellence or equality. What we need is a prudent social policy, one that is politically and economically feasible and that serves the needs of students and society. Implicit in this view of education is that too much emphasis on any one policy, sometimes at the expense of another, may do harm and cause conflict. How much we emphasize one policy, under the guise of reform or whatever reason, is critical because no one society can give itself over to extreme "isms" or political views and still remain a democracy. The kind of society into which we evolve is in part reflected in our educational system, which is influenced by the policies that we eventually define and develop. (See PRO/CON debate.)

ADMINISTRATIVE ADVICE 9-3

■

BLUEPRINT FOR LOCAL ACTION

Schools belong to many constituents—students, parents, community members, and policy-making groups. Regardless of the federal government's role in education, school principals and central administrators must learn to take action: by seeing the "big picture," involving others, and putting their own ideas into context with needs and interests of others and the norms of the community. Instant reform or change rarely succeeds; it must be tested and refined over time. Action must be built on a secure foundation, well planned and coordinated, and be realistic. Below is a general blueprint for local action.

COMMUNICATION

Open channels of communication with all concerned parties for the purpose of exchanging ideas and concerns by

- Meeting with teachers, parents, students, and administrators.
- Meeting with the PTA, service clubs, religious groups, elected officials, and representatives of the teachers' association.
- Meeting with other administrators from within the district and/or neighboring districts to determine areas of common need.
- Visiting classrooms to observe programs in action.

ASSESS THE CURRENT SITUATION

Analyze the present educational program and the factors that affect the operation of the program by examining

- The fundamental characteristics of the community.
- The factors limiting operation.
- The strengths that should be maximized.
- The weaknesses that must be addressed.
- The implied and stated needs and desires of the staff and community.
- The extent of staff and community involvement in decision making.
- The coordination of the instructional program, student achievement, personnel policies, pupil personnel practices, supporting services, methodology, instructional materials, and staff development.
- Physical facilities, professional negotiations, administrative management, budgetary procedures, board operations, and school–community relations.
- The pressures generated from within and from without the system.

DESIGNING A PLAN OF ACTION

Translate the particular needs of the school community into an action plan that takes into consideration

- Resources that can reasonably be provided.
- The manner in which the timing and details are to be communicated to those involved.
- Educational priorities.
- Alternative programs or routes for attaining the goals.
- Specific activities and procedures that will enable people to attain their goals.
- The relationship between the financial expenditures and the expected learning outcomes.
- Necessary staff-orientation and -training procedures.
- Techniques used to measure the effectiveness of the educational program.
- Methods to be used for informing parents of the progress of the program.
- Specific performance standards and a completion timetable.

Administrative Advice 9-3 (continued)

IMPLEMENTATION

Apply the principles, procedures, and activities that are directed at more adequately meeting the needs of the students by

- Using the available work force most effectively.
- Developing an administrative structure that emphasizes delegation of responsibility, follow-through, accountability, and an overlapping communications link.
- Building a system for regularly reviewing and revising the program.

- Developing the machinery for the systematic self-assessment of staff.
- Projecting plans over a period of several years.
- Communicating with parents on a regular basis through periodic newsletters.
- Organizing a cabinet who will serve in both an advisory and policy capacity.

Source: Adapted from Lawrence Rodes and David Pearlman, "Starting on the Right Foot," *NASSP Bulletin*, 73 (1989), pp. 76–77. Used by permission.

In the final analysis, administrators must understand that they are continuously faced with managerial decisions and that policy is important in determining these decisions. Unfortunately, some administrators forget to test their notions of management and leadership against the school district's mission statement or philosophy. It is common to find administrators developing elaborate lists of goals with little or no consideration to the overall mission or philosophy of the school district.

Schools reflect community norms, and administrators must learn the "rules of the game" or how the game is played in the local community. When local policy and ensuing programs are out of sync with state or national policies and programs, the administrator's decisions are more difficult, and the needs for balance and change are greater.

SUMMARY

1. The federal role in education has dramatically increased for most of this century, especially between the Roosevelt and Carter years. Since the 1980s, however, federal involvement in education has been reduced—highlighted by the "new federalism."

2. The Department of Education (DOE) was established in 1980, with full-cabinet status. Secretary Bennett added visibility and prestige to the department, even though many of his views on education were considered controversial.

3. Federal programs and activities in education were uncoordinated until the enactment of the relief acts during the depression and War Act during World War II. After Sputnik and with the War on Poverty and civil rights movement, national policy became linked to education, and federal funding dramatically increased.

4. The growth in federal funding leveled off in the 1980s, and the Educational Consolidation and Improvement Act (ECIA) of 1981 shifted much of the federal responsibility for education programs to the states. Instead of basic need, monies were mainly earmarked on the basis of student enrollment.

5. The "winners" of the current shift in funding were small towns and rural school districts, as well as the Sunbelt states of the South and West. The "losers" were the urban school districts of the Frostbelt, namely, the Northeast and Midwest.

6. The National Assessment of Education Progress (NAEP) portrays a dim picture of student achievement in the United States. The study focuses on achievement levels of nine-, thirteen-, and seven-

PRO/CON DEBATE

■

YEAR-ROUND SCHOOLING

The United States is one of the few industrialized nations where summer breaks last from ten to fifteen weeks. In Japan summer breaks average from five to eight weeks. In a year-round school model, more short vacations replace one long vacation; children receive more days of instruction per year.

QUESTION Should year-round schooling be implemented?

ARGUMENTS PRO

1 The federal government has an important role to play in ensuring that America regains its competitive edge in international markets. We compare our students' achievement with that of other nations. Students are at a disadvantage if they receive fewer days of instruction.

2 Prolonged summer vacations are an artifact of an agricultural era when children helped the family care for summer crops. Today most parents work year round; they have to make special arrangements for summer activities for their children.

3 At-risk students benefit from attending school year round. Studies indicate that at-risk students lose ground over a long summer break. A year-round school schedule would be one more way for the federal government to support children in educational need.

4 A year-round school is cost-efficient because the physical plant is available during the summer. Having schools stand empty costs the taxpayers money.

5 A year-round program would provide more flexibility in scheduling. Recent curricular reforms have imposed educationally sound but difficult-to-schedule mandates. A year-round program would allow more opportunities for elective and exploratory courses.

ARGUMENTS CON

1 The federal reform effort should be restricted to activities that support local and state initiatives. Educational decisions are best made by local citizens who understand the needs of the local community.

2 Summer breaks are a way of life in the United States. Many children cherish such activities as day and residential camps. Many families plan summer vacation trips and activities; these are a mainstay of family bonding. Much is lost when a treasured tradition is eliminated.

3 The federal government has a long tradition of supporting at-risk youngsters. These programs are in place all across the country. It is redundant to develop additional programs, even worse to put too much stress on children.

4 A year-round school schedule is economically unfeasible. Personnel costs are the largest part of any school budget. If teachers were employed during the summer, their salaries would increase by 20 or 25 percent. The extra expense would strain educational budgets.

5 The summer break without students is the time when school buildings are maintained and renovated. In a year-round model, schools would always be open; instruction would be periodically interrupted for maintenance purposes.

teen-year-olds, as well as young adults (twenty to twenty-five years); ten areas of achievement are reported.

7. The national reform movement in education has shifted educational policy from equality to excellence. The current demand for excellence is highlighted by a series of policy reports for national consumption. Of all the reports, *A Nation at Risk,* the best-known one, started the movement.

KEY TERMS

separation of powers

dual federalism

national federalism

new federalism

national standards movement

National Assessment of Educational Progress

Northwest Ordinances

Morrill Act

Smith–Hughes Act

G.I. Bill

National Defense Education Act

Elementary and Secondary Education Act

Title IX

Civil Rights Act

Bilingual Education Act

Public Law 94–142

mainstreaming

block grant

Council of Great City Schools

equality of opportunity

Scholastic Aptitude Test

DISCUSSION QUESTIONS

1. How can administrators effect changes at the federal level?
2. What are the advantages and disadvantages of the "new federalism"?
3. What are the arguments for and against shifting educational responsibility from the federal government to the states?
4. What are the arguments for and against Title IX, handicapped education legislation, and bilingual education legislation?

5. How can administrators balance the policies of equality and excellence when local community interests take a strong position on one of the two sides of the continuum? Should administrators try to maintain a balance in the face of strong community support for one position?

SUGGESTED READINGS

William L. Boyd and James G. Cibulka, *Private Schools and Public Policy* (New York: Falmer Press, 1989). Policy relationships between public and private schools in the United States and other industrialized countries.

Daniel E. Griffiths, Robert T. Stout, and Patrick B. Forsyth (eds.), *Leaders for America's Schools* (Berkeley, CA: McCutchan, 1988). How policymakers influence schools and educational administrators.

James W. Guthrie and Rodney J. Reed, *Educational Administration and Policy* (Englewood Cliffs, NJ: Prentice-Hall, 1986). How school administrators function in context with the political structure.

Bruce R. Joyce, *Improving America's Schools* (New York: Longman, 1986). The role of federal and state initiatives, as well as active administrative leadership, in improving and redesigning the nation's schools.

Joel Spring, *The Sorting Machine Revisited: National Educational Policy Since 1945,* 2nd ed. (New York: Longman, 1989). A critical analysis of national educational policy from the Cold War to the present.

Tommy M. Tomlinson and Herbert J. Walberg (eds.), Academic Work and Educational Excellence (Berkeley, CA: McCutchan, 1986). A series of essays on how to improve schools and educational productivity.

Frederick Wirt and Michael W. Kirst, *Schools in Conflict: The Politics of Education,* 2nd ed. (Berkeley, CA: McCutchan, 1989). The role of the federal and state governments in influencing educational policy at the local level.

10

THE STATE ROLE IN EDUCATION

In this chapter, we attempt to answer these questions by first discussing the roles that state officials—the governor, legislature, and courts—have in setting and enforcing policy. Then we examine the structure of state boards and departments of education and its chief executive, the chief state school officer. Finally, we explore reform movements for education and present guidelines for reform.

THE GOVERNMENT AND EDUCATION

Every state, today, by constitution, statute, and practice assumes that education is the function of the state; moreover, federal and state courts have supported this interpretation. The federal government's powers related to education have been delegated to the states, through the Tenth Amendment of the Constitution. Indeed, this is a dramatic difference from what exists in most parts of the world, including almost every industrialized nation, where the schools are centralized and controlled by the federal government and usually through a ministry of education.

Each state in the United States has legal responsibility for the support and maintenance of the public schools within its borders. Local school boards, as we will see in the next chapter, are considered creatures of the state and have been devised for the purpose of running a system of schools. Being responsible for the schools, the state enacts legislation; determines school taxes and financial aid to local school districts; sets minimum standards for training, certification, and salaries of personnel; decides on curriculum (some states establish minimum requirements, others establish recommendations); provides special services (such as transportation and free textbooks); and provides funding through block grants and various aid formulas.

The state school code is a collection of laws that establish ways and means of operating schools and conducting education in the state. The state, of course, cannot enact legislation that is contrary to or conflicts with the federal Constitution. State statutes can be divided into two groups: mandatory laws that establish a minimum criteria or program of education and permissive laws that define the functions that are delegated to the school district under appropriate conditions.

STATE HIERARCHY OF EDUCATION

Although state constitutions and statutes provide for the establishment of a uniform system of schools, provisions in most states are detailed concerning state–local powers and authority and methods of school operation. The typical state hierarchy consists of three branches, as with the federal government: (1) executive or governor, (2) legislative or state legislature, and (3) judicial or state courts.

The governor usually depends on a group of advisors and consultants to report on educa-

tional matters. The state legislatures have created a **state education agency** consisting of a state board of education, chief state officer, and state department of education. The relationship between the state education agency and local school districts has changed over time to reflect new problems and concerns. During the 1980s, for example, with the new federalism, the state legislature and its education agency have taken on a more active role in educational reform. The state courts have also become increasingly active with regard to educational matters.

The Governor

Although the powers of governors vary widely, their authority on educational matters is spelled out in law. Usually, the governor is charged with the responsibility of formulating educational budget recommendations to the legislature. In many states, the governor has legal access to any accumulated balances in the state treasury, and these monies can be used for school or college purposes.

The governor (and state legislature) has available staff members and agencies to help analyze and interpret data and can obtain additional information on matters of educational concern as needed. The governor can appoint or remove administrative school personnel at the state level. These powers often carry restrictions, such as approval by the legislature. In a majority of states, the governor can appoint members to the state board of education and, in a few states, the chief state officer. Except in North Carolina, a governor can "kill" educational measures through his veto powers or threaten to use the veto to discourage the legislature from enacting laws he opposes—or at least encourage the legislature to modify a pending bill.

The governor, in today's political arena, will invariably have an educational platform during the election campaign. Thus, all candidates will make specific commitments and promises for education. These platforms vary widely—from a promise to reduce educational spending or to increase it, a pledge for increasing educational equality such as increased prekindergarten programs or college scholarships for minority and needy students on one hand to increased quality and productivity in math, science, and technical education.

The successful gubernatorial candidate must listen to different lobby groups, and the various educational administrative associations recognize the importance of gaining the ear of each candidate. In recent years, the National School Boards Association, National Chief States School Organization, and American Association of School Administrators have increased their lobby efforts and funding to help elect candidates who support their political views on education.[1] In most states, however, the lobby efforts are focused on state legislative officials—at least once the governor is elected.

If the governor chooses to take a visible or outspoken position on educational matters, this influence will be felt. Some people in the legislature may consider it interference, and others may welcome it. Indeed, there have been a growing number of cases—especially dealing with money matters—in which education was used as part of a political struggle between the governor and legislature.[2]

Time for Results   In a recent and sharp departure from tradition, the fifty governors issued a joint report that stated their willingness to act as "strong and eager partners in education reform."[3] Their influence is obvious, and never before have they so dramatically shown their willingness to work with educators.

The report focuses on the concerns of governors and examines the relationship of education, jobs, and their states' economies.[4] They consider a highly educated populace vital to economic development within their respective states (and for the nation); those states that have invested in education have also developed new industry and an enlarged tax base. All this background is essential for understanding the governors' readiness to take a firm stand on educational reform and to earmark increased spending for educational spending.

At the same time, state governments that have invested large sums of money in education do not want well-educated students to leave their states for jobs elsewhere. This is especially the case in the Frostbelt, the regions of the Northeast and Midwest, that have witnessed a large outmigration of young adults (who were educated by state monies) to the Sunbelt: the Southeast, Southwest, and West, in the last twenty years.[5] The basic elements of the report are listed below.

1. *Changes in the U.S. Student Population.* The growing number of low-income minority and limited-English-proficient children–that is, **children at risk**—strains teachers and schools and makes it harder to achieve educational results. For this reason, the report urges schools to improve education for all students, especially for children at risk and at the lower grade levels. A related recommendation is that there be one teacher for every fifteen students in kindergarten through grade 3.

2. *Changes in the Family.* Single-parent households, mothers who work outside the home,

[1]Telephone conversation with Jay Goldman, director of public information, National Chief States School Organization, March 8, 1989; telephone conversation with Bill Tanner, director of public relations, National School Boards Association, February 12, 1990.

[2]Jeffrey L. Miller, W. Henry Cone, and Brenda G. Adkins, "The Tax Breaks Double Bind," *American School Board Journal,* 177 (1990), pp. 42–43; Allan C. Ornstein, "School Finance in the 1990s," *American School Board Journal,* 177 (1990), pp. 36–40.

[3]*Time for Results: The Governors' 1991 Report on Education* (Washington, D.C.: National Governors' Association, 1986), p. 60.

[4]Joe Nathan, "Implications for Educators of *Time for Results,*" *Phi Delta Kappan,* 68 (1986), pp. 199–201.

[5]Allan C. Ornstein, "Decline of the Frostbelt," *Dissent,* 30 (1983), pp. 366–374; Ornstein, "Regional and Urban Population and Student Enrollment Trends," *Journal of Research and Development in Education,* 18 (1985), pp. 19–28.

and low-income families have grown. This has shown a related decline in family structure and/or responsibility for raising and educating children. The report is also concerned with the decreasing proportions of families with school-age children and middle-class families with more than one child; these trends may lead to a decline in the level of support for education. The governors would like to increase parent–community involvement in the schools by making more extensive use of school facilities.

3. *Teachers and Teaching.* The governors recognize that the crux of school reform is an improved teaching force. With this in mind, the report recommends improved teaching training and teacher selection, increased teacher salaries, and higher performance standards for teachers.

4. *Curriculum and Instruction.* The governors see a need to improve the curriculum and to make better use of our instructional technology. They urge educators to upgrade curriculum content, textbooks, and graduation requirements. They also wish to make better use of computers, videotapes, television, and robots to enhance student learning.

5. *Reform Methods.* The report acknowledges that there is no one best reform method and that different states will opt for different reform strategies. The governors are in agreement, however, that students need more than a basic-skills education. They must be good problem solvers and creative thinkers. Nothing less will permit our country to maintain its standard of living and solve its national problems.

6. *Financial Support.* The governors' report notes a willingness on the part of the public to spend more money on education, but only if improvement is likely to follow. The governors are willing to work for increased spending for education, but they want educators to show results in student achievement, attendance, and retention of learning.

The criticisms leveled at the report are similar to the other national reports on reform, that is, the governors' report is too idealistic, unrealistic, and calls for too many expensive reforms; moreover, the report glosses over the resistance to and realities of change. For example, how do we get more students to be problem solvers and creative thinkers when an increasing number arrive at our school doors with basic cognitive deficits—they are unable to perform simple reading, writing, and computing exercises.

The governors now meet on a continual basis to discuss vital education issues. In general, their concerns are economic and the belief that education has put this country in a terrible competitive disadvantage. They reaffirm that the federal government's role in education is limited and should stay that way. However, within these limits, it should do more than it does to support research and programs to restructure schools (in particular, keep them open all year round, provide increased teacher and administrative empowerment, and upgrade standards in general as well as math and science programs).

In their recent round-table discussion, the governors established a 6-point plan for education by the year 2000: (1) high school graduation rates will rise to 90 percent [presently at 75 percent]; (2) U.S. students will be first worldwide in math and science [presently at the bottom of the industrialized rankings]; (3) every adult will be literate [about 25 million are currently classified illiterate]; (4) every school will be drug-free [probably the exact opposite is currently true for every middle, junior, and senior high school]; (5) students will be tested nationwide in major subjects and in grades, 4, 8, and 12, to be accompanied by graduation requirements [the majority of states currently assess most programs and have mandated minimal exit competency tests]; and (6) preschool programs will include increased parental training and nutrition education [only 25 percent of disadvantaged students are enrolled in preschool programs due to cuts in federal and state funds in this category].[6]

---

[6]Debbie Howlett and Mimi Hall, "Govs: Give Schools' Dividend," *USA Today,* 26 February 1990, p. 39. Bracketed statements denote editorial remarks by the author.

There is no mention of funding or who will pay for it, but the fact is that money is needed to implement these recommendations. Many governors seem willing to step up investment in human capital if convinced that investments are being made effectively and fairly. However, it is hard to demonstrate the worth of our educational policies and programs—that is, what works—because of the complexity of the human condition and the numerous variables that influence our educational environment. Hence, the governors are left with a good deal of softness, faith, and testimonial views as to "what works" as they prepare their educational investment strategy for the year 2000.

State Legislatures

With the exception of Nebraska (which has a unicameral arrangement), every state has a two-house legislative body. There is much variation in size and resources, however. Membership in the state Senate ranges from a low of 21 in Nevada to a high of 67 in Minnesota, with most states electing 30 to 40 state senators. Membership in the state House ranges from 40 in Alaska to 400 in New Hampshire, with most states electing 100 to 125 state House members.[7] Nationwide, the state legislative staff size has grown from 27,000 state workers (average size of 519) in 1979 to 34,000 (average size of 680) in 1988, despite the fact the financial conditions of most states worsened during this period. Vermont and South Dakota are the only states with fewer than 100 staff members, whereas California and New York have 3000 or more staff members.[8] The typical state legislator is a white male (about 15 percent are female and another 15 percent are minority) who is an attorney by profession or businessperson and whose pay ranges from $100 a year in New Hampshire to $57,500 in New York.[9]

In most states, the legislature is responsible for establishing and maintaining the public schools and has broad powers to enact laws pertaining to education. These powers are not unlimited; there are restrictions in the form of federal and state constitutions and court decisions. But within these parameters, the legislature has the full power to decide basic school policy in the state. (See Administrative Advice 10-1.)

The state legislature usually determines how the state boards of education will be selected, what their responsibilities will be, how the chief state officer will be selected, what the duties of this office will be, what the functions of the state department of education will be, what types of local and regional school districts there will be, and what the methods of selection and powers of local school boards will be. The legislature usually decides on the nature of state taxes for schools, the level of financial support for education, and the taxing power for schools to be allocated on a local or municipal level. The legislature may determine what may or may not be taught, how many years of compulsory education will be required, the length of the school day and school year, and whether there will be state community colleges and adult and vocational schools. The legislature may also determine staff and student policies and testing and evaluation procedures, authorize school programs, set standards for building construction, and provide various auxiliary services (e.g., student transportation and school lunches). Where the legislature does not enact these policies, they are usually the responsibility of the state board of education.

The system tends to operate much more effectively when the legislature focuses on broad policies such as financing and organization of

[7]"1989 Elections," *State Legislatures*, 15 (1989), p. 25.
[8]Brian Weberg and Beth Bazar, *Legislative Staff Services: 50 State Profiles* (Denver: National Conference of State Legislatures, 1988), Table 5, p. 9.

[9]Beth Bazar, *State Legislators' Occupations: A Decade of Change* (Denver: National Conference of State Legislatures, 1987); "Pay Our Public Officials," *USA Today,* 9 February 1989, p. 69.

ADMINISTRATIVE ADVICE 10-1

■

STATE ASSISTANCE FOR IMPROVING SCHOOLS AND SCHOOL ADMINISTRATORS

Bill Clinton is governor of Arkansas and chairman of the Governor's Task Force on Leadership and Management. He contends that strong leaders create strong schools and that it is up to local school administrators to advance school reform in their own districts. To promote reform or change the structure of schools, he advises a number of long-term recommendations that the states (governor or legislator) and administrative organizations can implement together. These recommendations deal with how principals are trained, certified, and rewarded, as well as with incentives and assistance to promote school effectiveness.

- Begin a dialogue to determine the state's broad goals for education and identify ways in which schools can achieve those goals.
- Revise state selection and certification requirements to skills and knowledge needed by effective principals.
- Match the content of state-approved educational administration programs to the training needed by effective principals.
- Develop a system to evaluate principals effectively and accurately.
- Provide in-service training to school administrators through state-sponsored training centers or higher-education institutions.
- Provide incentives and technical assistance to school districts to promote school-site management and improvement.

- Collect statewide information on the process and the outcomes of schooling.
- Reward principals and schools for performance and effectiveness.
- Highlight success by documenting and disseminating effective administrative strategies and models.
- Be patient and remain committed; school improvement takes time, and it can take several years for new ideas to become routine.

Source: Adapted from Bill Clinton, "Who Will Manage the Schools?" *Phi Delta Kappan*, 68 (1986), pp. 208–210. Used by permission.

---

schools, thus delegating enforcement of defensive criteria and operation of schools to the various state education agencies. The legislature only establishes the minimums in public education, with the proviso that local school districts may exceed these minimum yardsticks. There should be a partnership concept between those who establish legal requirements and basic policies for a state educational system—that is, the legislature—and those who are responsible for implementing the will of the legislature:

the state agencies (state board of education, state department of education, and state chief officer).[10]

State Interest and Lobby Groups   State legislative officials respect the prevailing political climate

---

[10]Stephen J. Knezevich, *Administration of Public Education*, 4th ed. (New York: Harper & Row, 1984); Catherine Marshal, Douglas Mitchell, and Frederick Wirt, *Culture and Education Policy in the United States* (New York: Falmer Press, 1989).

and wishes of the people with respect to education and other policy issues. In effect, the people elect state legislatures and speak through the laws enacted by the officials they have elected. All representatives in the state legislatures understand the necessity of listening and responding to the wishes of the people in their district—if they wish to be reelected.

The role of educational groups in the state political process usually takes one of two different forms: **political action committees** (PACs) to financially support, volunteer time, or endorse candidates for election and educational groups—including administrative associations, teacher associations, parent associations, and special-interest groups (such as those concerned with bilingual education, handicapped education, and vocational education). All recognize the need for coalition building and to work toward, as well as sometimes challenge or spearhead, policies that affect education.

Another important function of interest groups is their lobbying efforts—both *direct,* face-to-face presentations and *indirect* contacts by mail and telephone.[11] Because education is a state responsibility, rather than a federal one, education lobbyists—whether groups of people or associations—focus on state legislatures. And, because education is usually the largest expenditure item in the state budget (about 60 percent on a total state-by-state basis when transportation is omitted),[12] it makes the existence of educational interest groups and their lobby efforts an important element of the political arena and policy-making process at the state level.

The state legislature's time is often consumed by formal and informal meetings and conferences, pertaining to educational matters, with staff, consultants, other government officials, and constituents. Many people do not recognize or realize just how much lobbying is done over educational issues; failure for school administrators to understand this political process puts them in a vulnerable position on matters that directly affect their school districts and the students they are responsible for educating.

To lobby effectively, an education interest group should (1) know what goals it wishes to emphasize, (2) have feasible goals, (3) designate a primary spokesperson to avoid conflicting signals or information, (4) be willing to consider compromise, (5) look to broaden its "friends" and "allies" to get certain bills passed, (6) know when to use the press or television and when to listen or quietly negotiate, and (7) not become too closely tied with one political party.[13]

Ideally, lobby groups should have an ongoing relationship with important government officials. If information, news releases, and reports on issues are provided on a regular basis by a pressure group (or an administrative association), government officials often request the input of the group when that particular issue becomes active or part of a pending bill. Also, a cordial and working relationship with the legislative staff helps provide insight into how receptive the members of the group (or association) will be to particular policies or recommendations that might be advanced by the particular legislator or interest group. This is how political networks and relationships develop. The fact that administrative groups such as the National School Boards Association or American Association of School Adminstrators (as well as teacher groups such as the American Federation of Teachers and National Education Association) have had access to federal policymakers makes them sometimes remiss with state officials; that

[11]Denis P. Doyle and Terry W. Hartle, *Excellence in Education: The States Take Charge* (Washington, D.C.: American Enterprise Institute, 1985); Harry Hatry et al., *Program Analysis for State and Local Governments,* 2nd ed. (Washington, D.C.: Urban Institute, 1987).

[12]John R. Curley, "Education Interest Groups and the Lobbying Function in the Political Process," *Urban Education,* 23 (1988), pp. 162–172; telephone conversation with John Meyer, director of education affairs, National Conference of State Legislatures, March 6, 1989.

[13]Curley, "Education Interest Groups and the Lobbying Function in the Political Process"; Allan C. Ornstein, "The Changing Status of the Teaching Profession," *Urban Education,* 23 (1988), pp. 261–279.

is, there is need for national administrative groups to develop access to policymakers at the state level—where the action is on school affairs.

State Courts

All states have constitutional provisions pertaining to education but leave the details, policies, and provisions to legislative bodies. There is no national uniformity in the state court organization. At the lowest level, most states have a court of original jurisdiction, often referred to as a *municipal* or *superior court* where cases are tried. Adverse decisions can be appealed to the next level, usually called the *appellate court,* by the losing side. This court reviews the trial record from the lower court and additional materials submitted by both sides; it assumes that appropriate laws were properly applied at the lower court level. Should any one side still not be satisfied, another appeal can be made to the state's highest court, often called the *state supreme court.* The decision of this court is final unless an issue involving the U.S. Constitution has been raised. The U.S. Supreme Court can be petitioned to consider such an issue; this is a growing trend in issues involving education.

State court decisions have force only in the area served by that particular court. For this reason, it is possible to find conflicting rules in different circuits. Judges often look to previous law, and in surrounding court circuits, in rendering decisions. Similarly, a state supreme court decision in one state may conflict with a decision of the court in another state; decisions rendered in one state are not binding in another state. Nevertheless, there is a good deal of consistency among the states in matters dealing with education.

State courts have generally rendered decisions upholding the following:

1. Public education is a state function, and that control and operation of the schools (and state colleges) is vested in the power and law-making agencies of the state.

2. The state controls education and operates schools for the general good of the people and society.

3. The legislative power extends to nonpublic schools, but it has limitations as expressed by the separation of state and religion and in the First Amendment, which protects religious expression.

4. The state legislature is the main body for exercising control over public schools and colleges and enacting educational laws.

5. This law-making body decides how it wishes to determine or distribute authority among the state education agencies (state board of education or state department of education) or local school districts (including local school boards).

6. Local school boards are creatures of the state and have no inherent powers of government, other than those given to them by the legislature.

7. State agencies and state officers are also creatures of the state with no inherent powers of government, other than those given to them by the legislature (or sometimes by the governor).

8. Legislative power extends to financial concerns, rooted in the **Kalamazoo decision** of 1874, and it has the power to define the method of allocation of state funds for schools.

9. States have the right (through one of their education agencies) to prescribe job qualifications and require certification and testing of personnel so long as they are not discriminatory.

10. Tenure and employment constitute a contract between the local school district (not the state) and the administrators (teachers).[14]

[14]Ralph W. Kimbrough and Michael Y. Nunnery, *Educational Administration,* 3rd ed. (New York: Macmillan, 1988); Michael W. La Morte, *School Law: Cases and Concepts* (Englewood Cliffs, NJ: Prentice-Hall, 1990); and Frederick M. Wirt and Michael W. Kirst, *Schools in Conflict: The Politics of Education* (Berkeley, CA: McCutchan, 1989).

In all cases, the authority of state to pre-scribe policies is upheld so long as they do not conflict with federal or state constitutional provisions.

In many relationships between officials of the state and those at the school district level, differences evolve that are carried into court—such as matters dealing with school desegregation, school finance, school prayer and Bible reading, teacher and student rights, and affirmative action. Often these cases have gone beyond the state supreme courts to the federal courts. Many other issues end up in state courts because they have little to do with the U.S. Constitution. These issues mainly deal with compulsory attendance, administrator or teacher fitness, teacher strikes, teacher gay rights, school negligence, child abuse, educational malpractice, copyright laws, computer ethics, and an AIDS school policy.

STATE EDUCATION AGENCIES

All states recognize the importance of establishing a state education agency, or what is sometimes called a state system of education. The idea of a state education agency is based on the Northwest Ordinances of 1785 and 1787, which enabled territories to transform into states, subject to many conditions including a system of public education to be implemented through the state.

Until the mid-twentieth century, the role of the state education agency was limited, and leadership in public education was mainly expressed at the local level. We illustrate this with two historical examples: (1) Horace Mann's idea of a system of public education supported by public money and controlled by the state was slow to be accepted beyond Massachusetts and Connecticut in the 1820s; (2) as late as 1930, only 17 percent of total school revenues came

from state sources compared with 83 percent from the local level.

The state education agency is a system comprising the state board of education, chief state school officer, and state department of education. In most cases, the governor appoints the state board of education, and the latter usually appoints the chief state school officer. In a few states, voters elect members of the state board of education and chief state school officer. The state department of education usually consists of career educators, and a few leadership and directorship posts are filled by the chief state school officer.

The State Board of Education

The state board of education is usually the most influential and important state education agency. Almost all states have some sort of state board of education, which is dependent on the state legislature for appropriations and authority and serves an advisory function for the legislature. (New York's Board of Regents is perhaps the strongest and most respected state board of education.) In addition, most states have a separate governing board for the public schools, grades K to 12, and for state colleges and universities; thus, there are often two separate state boards, one for elementary and secondary education and another for higher education.

With the exception of Wisconsin, all states have boards of education. As of 1988, thirty-three were appointed by the governor of the state, thirteen were elected by popular vote (this method has increased during the last twenty years), two (New York and South Carolina) were appointed by state legislatures, and in one state (Washington) the local school board members elected the state board. The number of members of state boards ranges from three in Louisiana and Mississippi to twenty-four in Texas, with a nine-member board occurring most frequently. (An odd number of members eliminates tie votes.) The term of appointment or election ranges from three to nine years, with most states at the four- to five-year range.[15]

There is some controversy involving the method of how the state board of education members acquire their position. The controversy centers on the merits of election versus gubernatorial appointment. The rationales for election are the following: It provides the people with a direct voice in educational policy; the governor tends to appoint people who agree with her views; it enhances political representation of the people; and gubernatorial appointments concentrate too much power in the hands of one official, whereas elections provide for a system of checks and balances.[16]

The major reasons for appointment are: Well-qualified people are more inclined to accept appointment than be a candidate in an election, appointment tends to lessen controversy between the governor and board, appointment tends to ensure that the governor will have a continued interest in education, and an election provides the opportunity for interest groups to finance and influence candidates.[17]

Whereas state boards were originally dominated by white males, their composition has changed dramatically in the past two decades. A survey of board members conducted in 1967 showed that only 18 percent were women and 3 percent were minorities.[18] By 1982, 34 percent of board members were women, and 16 percent

were minorities.[19] This trend toward greater heterogeneity is important; it broadens the perspectives of board members and ensures that boards reflect a wide range of political, social, and educational concerns.

One survey of state boards shows that most members tend to be older (88 percent were age forty or older) and well educated (99 percent have at least some postsecondary education, and 57 percent have a degree beyond the bachelor's). The voluntary nature of service on a state board means that the members must have the time and resources to participate. As a result, the survey found that most board members who were in the work force described their occupation as managerial (25 percent) or professional (50 percent); and those not in the paid work force were either retired (11 percent) or homemakers (12 percent) with a history of voluntary service.[20]

The precise duties and functions of state boards of education vary, but generally the boards are charged with the following functions:

1. Adopting and enforcing policies, rules, and regulations necessary to implement legislative acts related to education
2. Establishing qualifications and appointing personnel to the state department of education
3. Setting standards for teacher and administrative certificates
4. Establishing standards for accrediting schools
5. Managing state funds earmarked for education
6. Keeping records and collecting data needed for reporting and evaluating
7. Adopting long-range plans for the development and improvement of schools
8. Creating advisory bodies as required by law

[15]*Overview of State Education Governance Structure* (Alexandria, VA: National Association of State Boards of Education, 1989); telephone conversation with Tim Callahan, director of public affairs, National Association of State Boards of Education, January 9, 1989; August 23, 1990.

[16]Kimbrough and Nunnery, *Educational Administration.*

[17]Ibid.

[18]Gerald Stroufe, "An Examination of the Relationship Between Methods of Selection and the Characteristics and Self-Role Expectations of State School Board Members" (Doctoral dissertation, University of Chicago Press, 1970).

[19]Dinah Wiley, *State Boards of Education* (Arlington, VA: National Association of State Boards of Education, 1983), Tables 1, 2, pp. 15–16.

[20]Ibid.

9. Advising the governor or legislature on educational matters

10. Appointing the chief state school officer, setting minimum salary schedules for teachers and administrators, and adopting policies for the operation of institutions of higher learning.[21]

Chief State School Officer   The chief state school officer (sometimes known as the state superintendent or commissioner of education) serves as the head of the state department of education and, in most cases, is also the chief executive of the state school board. He is usually a professional educator.

The first chief state officer's position was established in New York in 1812, with the title "superintendent of common schools," and his duties revolved around coordination and management. Perhaps the two most famous chief state officers were Horace Mann, the first Massachusetts "commissioner of education," who spearheaded the common school movement in the mid-1820s and Henry Barnard, the first Connecticut commissioner in 1838, who adopted many of the progressive ideas of Mann and later became the first U.S. commissioner of education from 1867 to 1870.[22]

After Mann popularized the role of commissioner, the position increased rapidly so that by 1859 this post was found in twenty-four states.[23] To be sure, the role of state school officer came into being many decades after local school districts within the states were in operation.

The office is filled in one of three ways: in 1989, seven states filled the position through appointment by the governor, twenty-nine states through appointment by the state board of education, and fourteen states by popular election.[24] The duties of the chief state school officer and the relationship between that position and the state board and state department vary from state to state. They usually depend on whether the official was appointed or voted into office. When the chief officer is elected, she tends to have more independence.

As of 1990, only one chief state school officer, Andrew Jenkins of the District of Columbia, was black; however, there were six female chief officers (Arizona, Arkansas, Florida, Maine, Montana, and Washington).[25] The increasing number of women as chief state school officers represents a noticeable change, just in the last ten years,[26] and a departure from the "old-boy network," which is common in school administration.

Because of differences in method of selection and in the legal relationship between the state board of education and the chief state officer, the responsibilities of the chief state officer vary widely. However, the major responsibilities associated with the office are likely to include the following duties:

1. Serving as the chief administrator of the state department of education

2. Selecting personnel for the state department of education

3. Recommending and administering an educational budget for the state department of education

4. Ensuring compliance with state educational laws and regulations

[21]*State Boards of Education in an Era of Reform,* Final Report of the National Association of State Boards of Education (Alexandria, VA: National Association of State Boards of Education, 1987); *State Policy Data Book* (Arlington, VA: State Policy Research, 1986). Also see Allan C. Ornstein and Daniel U. Levine, *Foundations of Education,* 4th ed. (Boston: Houghton Mifflin, 1989).

[22]Lawrence A. Cremin, *The Republic and the School* (New York: Teachers College Press, 1957); E. P. Cubberley, *The History of Education* (Boston: Houghton Mifflin, 1920).

[23]Knezevich, *Administration of Public Education.*

[24]*Directory of Chief State School Officers 1990* (Washington, D.C.: Council of Chief State Officers, 1990); "State Board of Education, 1989." Paper prepared by the Association of State Boards of Education, February 1990.

[25]*Directory of Chief State School Officers 1990.*

[26]Telephone conversation with Jay Goldman, director of public information, National Chief States School Organization, March 7, 1989.

5. Explaining and interpreting the state's school laws
6. Deciding impartially controversies involving the administration of the schools within the state
7. Arranging the studies, committees, and task forces as deemed necessary to identify problems and recommend solutions
8. Reporting on the status of education within the state to the governor, legislature, state board of education, and the public
9. Recommending improvements in educational legislation and policies to the governor and state legislature
10. Working with local school boards and administrators to improve education within the state.[27]

State Departments of Education

Another major state education agency is the state department of education, which usually operates under the direction of the state board of education and is administered by the chief state school officer. Traditionally, the primary function of state departments of education was to collect and disseminate statistics about the status of education within the state. Since the 1950s, they have enlarged their services and functions to include (1) accrediting schools; (2) certifying teachers; (3) apportioning funds; (4) overseeing student transportation and safety; (5) monitoring state regulations; (6) conducting research, evaluating programs, and issuing reports; and (7) monitoring federally funded programs to ensure compliance with regulations.[28]

During recent decades, state departments have had to grapple with controversial issues such as desegregation, compensatory education, bilingual and handicapped education, student rights and unrest, school finance reform and fiscal crises, aid to minority groups, declining enrollments, collective bargaining, accountability, competency testing, and certification for teachers and principals. The federal government, the courts, and active interest groups have joined in the fray and wrestled with many educational or school issues—forcing governors and legislators to increase the staff budget and functions of state departments of education.

State departments of education, once innocuous and invisible, have doubled and tripled in size and have assumed new responsibilities in administering complex programs. In 1900 there were a total of 177 staff department employees nationwide, and 47 were chief state school officers.[29] In 1962 ten states had departments of more than 100 professionals, and twenty-one had fewer than 50 staff members; in two states, the staff exceeded 1000.[30] By 1982 only six states (Delaware, Idaho, Nevada, South Dakota, North Dakota, and Wyoming) had professional staffs of fewer than 100, and six states (California, Connecticut, Michigan, New Jersey, New York, and Texas) had staffs of more than 1000.[31]

As a general rule, the more populated the state and/or the larger the number of local school districts in the state, the higher the degree of centralization and the larger the state department staff. Less populated states and states with fewer school districts have smaller and decentralized staffs. Although some divisional administrators of these departments change with changes of political party control or with a change in the chief officer, the professional staff—such as researchers and statisticians, curriculum and supervisory specialists, and

[27]Roland Campbell et al., *The Organization and Control of American Schools,* 6th ed. (Columbus, OH: Merrill, 1990); Stephen L. Jacobson and James A. Conway (eds.), *Educational Leadership in the Age of Reform* (New York: Longman, 1990); Jerome T. Murphy, *State Leadership in Education: On Being a Chief State Officer* (Washington, D.C.: Washington University Press, 1980); and Allan C. Ornstein, *Education and Social Inquiry* (Itasca, IL: Peacock, 1978).
[28]James W. Guthrie and Rodney J. Reed, *Educational Administration and Policy* (Englewood Cliffs, NJ: Prentice-Hall, 1986); Ornstein, *Education and Social Inquiry.*

[29]Fred F. Beach and Andrew H. Gibbs, *Personnel of State Department of Education* (Washington, D.C.: Government Printing Office, 1952); Knezevich, *Administration of Public Education.*
[30]Ornstein, *Education and Social Inquiry.*
[31]Wiley, *State Boards of Education.*

clerks and secretaries—are usually career or civil-service employees. By and large, staff members of the state departments of education are recruited from public school personnel and from local school districts and colleges of education.

The leadership role of the state departments of education expanded in the 1980s. The 1981 Education Consolidation and Improvement Act (ECIA) presented states with a broad number of options for spending federal monies allocated to the states. Not only did ECIA give the states more responsibility for determining how and where to spend federal money for education, but it also reduced federal funding and thus put more importance on state funding. This trend is expected to continue in the 1990s.

Reduced federal funding has put added pressure on state departments to spend educational money wisely, to administer the state programs effectively, and to think about where they are going to get extra money to make up for the deficits created by the federal shortfall. In addition, controversial issues in education will not go away, and public groups are becoming more and more aggressive and astute in making their demands felt at the state level. In short, state departments of education must now provide increased leadership and technical assistance to local school districts as well as to state boards of education, state legislators, and governors.

STATE REFORM MOVEMENTS

Not since the wave of school reform that followed Sputnik has education been so prominently on stage at the national and state level, on television, and in local newspapers. Presidential candidates, governors, state legislators, and chief state school officers have all gotten into the act, indicating the high priority of education, the desire to reform it, and the need to allocate more resources for it. Business groups such as Xerox, IBM, and Motorola have recently taken active roles in helping to shape education policy, in part

because jobs are becoming more demanding and complex and the school products (students) are becoming "dumber." Teachers' unions have shifted their focus from the welfare of teacher members to the need to cooperate with school administrators and school board members for purposes of reform; in making this transition, they have shifted the image of union-based organizations to professional organizations and are now willing to work with (not against) administrative associations for institutional welfare.[32]

Between 1983 and 1989, the states have generated more education policies and regulations than the previous twenty years. Nationwide, more than 1000 state statutes affecting some aspect of school reform were enacted between 1985 and 1987.[33] They have come as "waves" with tremendous fanfare, publicity, and controversy attached to the reform measures. These waves have focused on or can be classified into three reform-type packages: (1) academic standards, (2) professional policy, and (3) curriculum development. In general, all three waves have stressed productivity and efficiency, as well as education excellence.

The first wave, dealing with student achievement, has focused on *academic standards;* graduation and college admission requirements; more frequent exit tests; time on task, attendance, and homework; reduced class size; and early childhood education. The second wave, dealing with *professionalism,* has focused on competency-based training, certification and testing requirements, accountability, salary increases, merit pay and career ladders, differen-

---

[32]David T. Kearns, "An Educational Recovery Plan for America," *Phi Delta Kappan,* 69 (1988), pp. 565–570; Albert Shanker, "School Boards Are Being Massacred," *American School Board Journal,* 176 (1989), pp. 29–30. Also see "The Knowledge Gap," *Wall Street Journal* (Education Supplement), 9 February 1990.

[33]Linda Darling-Hammond and Barnett Berry, *The Evolution of Teacher Policy* (Santa Monica, CA: Rand Corporation, 1988); Thomas B. Timar and David Kirp, *Managing Educational Excellence* (New York: Falmer Press, 1988).

tial roles and salaries, evaluation, and staff development. The third category has focused on the *curriculum*—the need to emphasize the basics, computers, and technology; a common core (academic) high school curriculum, especially increased science, math, and foreign language; and business–university–school partnerships.

By 1987 a series of actions had been taken at the state level, largely to improve the quality of education. All states had undertaken academic and curriculum reform (categories 1 and 3), and forty-seven states had undertaken items dealing with professional reform, category 2. Leading the list of reform, forty-five states had increased high school graduation requirements. Especially dramatic increases had occurred in math and science needed for graduation, and six states had added computer literacy as a requirement (Table 10-1). Thirty-seven states had introduced or increased the number of statewide assessment programs, nineteen states required competency tests for high school graduation, and twenty-nine states had raised college entrance requirements. Six states increased the length of the school year, and thirteen states introduced additional instructional time. Thirteen states reduced class sizes, and twelve states started students at a younger age.[34]

By 1988 some forty-eight states had introduced changes in teacher preparation, thirty-four required testing for admission to teacher-education programs, twenty-one required exit tests from teacher-education programs, thirty-seven required testing for initial certification of teachers, and twelve introduced career ladders for teachers.[35] In thirty states, higher teacher

salaries were attributed in part to the national reform movement. As many as twenty states have upgraded the educational and testing requirements of principals since 1983, and others have demanded stricter evaluation and accountability of principals. More than twenty-five states have already introduced centers or academies for principals, to help them improve their leadership and managerial skills.[36]

Models and Strategies for Implementation

The different strategies that states have used to implement reform tend to fall into three distinct approaches—ranging from a traditional, centralized administrative model to a nontraditional, decentralized model:

1. *Rational Planning.* This approach defines discrete problems to be solved, focuses on "right" answers to the specific problems, and relies on "top-down" mandates and decision-making processes.
2. *Market Incentive.* This plan permits bargaining of specific provisions by local school officials, administrators, and teacher groups, as well as local choice.
3. *Political Interaction.* This approach emphasizes the decentralization of authority; relies on delegation, discretion, and dispersion of state authority to local school districts; and combines flexibility in local implementation within certain broad state-articulated requirements and recommendations.[37]

[34]Chris Pipho, "States Move Reform Closer to Reality," *Phi Delta Kappan,* 68 (1986), pp. 1–8; Pipho, "From the State House to the School House," *NASSP Bulletin,* 71 (1987), pp. 71–76. Also see William Chance, *The Education Programs of the United States* (Chicago: MacArthur Foundation, 1986); *The Condition of Education, 1989,* Vol. 1 (Washington, D.C.: Government Printing Office, 1989), Charts 1.29 and 1.30, pp. 69–71, Table 1.29, p. 125.
[35]Allan C. Ornstein, "National Reform and Instructional Accountability," *High School Journal,* 73 (1990),

in print. Also see *The Condition of Education, 1990,* Vol. 1 (Washington D.C.: Government Printing Office, 1990), Table 1.30, p. 127.
[36]Wynn M. Egginton, Thomas S. Jeffries, and Dorothy Kidd-Knights, "State Mandated Tests for Principals: A Growing Trend," *NASSP Bulletin,* 72 (1988), pp. 62–71. Also see the entire issue of *NASSP Bulletin,* 72 (1987) for a description of these centers.
[37]Thomas B. Timar and David L. Kirp, "Education Reform in the 1980s: Lessons from the States," *Phi Delta Kappan,* 70 (1989), pp. 504–511.

TABLE 10 ■ 1   Average Years of Coursework Required for Public High School Graduation, 1981–1982 to 1987–1988

SCHOOL YEAR	MATHEMATICS	SCIENCE	ENGLISH	FOREIGN LANGUAGE	SOCIAL STUDIES
1981–1982	1.6	1.5	3.6	*	2.6
1984–1985	1.9	1.8	3.8	.1	2.8
1987–1988†	2.3	2.0	3.9	.2	2.9
Recommendations of National Commission on Excellence in Education	3.0	3.0	4.0	2.0‡	3.0

SOURCE: Adapted from *The Condition of Education, 1989*, Vol. 1 (Washington, D.C.: Government Printing Office, 1989), Table 1.29, p. 125; Allan C. Ornstein, "National Reform and Instructional Accountability," *High School Journal*, 73 (1990), in print.

*Less than .05 years
†Requirements for seniors graduating in 1988.
‡The commission's recommendations about foreign language applied only to college-bound (not all) students. The other figures represent average requirements for all students.

The first model, exemplified by the states of Florida and Texas, represents a bureaucratic approach, a strong state government, and one that tends to mistrust local authority and discretion. It assumes there is *one best solution* to a problem. The second model, illustrated by California and Washington, is a laissez-faire approach to management, welcomes school-based management, and encourages professional participation. It assumes there is *no one best solution or process* to implement reform. The third one, developed by Michigan and South Carolina, is a middle-of-the-road approach. It integrates the goals and policies of the state with local conditions and practices. The approach establishes a *process* for solving problems *without proposing solutions;* the solutions that evolve are locally based.[38]

Lessons to be Learned   Recent efforts show that education reform, if it is to be successful, cannot come from only one group—politicians, state of-ficials, taxpayers, administrators, or teachers—but cooperation is needed among all groups. Moreover, responsibility is needed at all levels. For example, regardless of how much money is earmarked for increased salaries or merit pay, we need responsible teachers and administrators at the school level. Hence, no one can reform dedication and hard work. Regardless of number or type of student tests, or how much homework is assigned, students (and parents) must make a concerted effort with regard to academic input and performance. Regardless of the motivation or incentives we provide, no student can be compelled to learn; enthusiasm for learning cannot be coerced; learning involves delayed gratification and sweat; it does not come easy and cannot be regulated by a clause, resolution, or mandated statement.

The second lesson to be learned is that education reform, more precisely the success of reform, depends in large measure on the features of the local school: the school organization, school culture, and school ethos. In effect, school as a whole and schooling as a process are interlinked, with a changing and dynamic envi-

[38]Thomas B. Timar and David L. Kirp, *Managing Educational Excellence* (New York: Falmer Press, 1988).

ronment. A broader construct in education that represents this concept of school organization, culture, and ethos is referred to as *school climate*. The concept of a corporation's culture as used by Thomas Peters and Robert Waterman's analysis of the best-run American companies comes near to capturing this whole, too.[39] A more precise term is **subjective culture**, that is, the way the organizational environment or social system operates—its belief systems, structures, stereotype formations, norms, roles, values, rules, and task definitions.[40] The values, beliefs, and behaviors of the school's players—administrators, teachers, students (even parents)—all play a role in determining reform and what will be accomplished at the school level.

The next lesson is, although somewhat oversimplified, the reform measures that states adopt are not likely to make a difference or lead to serious improvement unless the policies are responsive to local needs and pressures and unless the local school environment, including the people, are willing to buy into and adopt those measures. (See Administrative Advice 10-2.)

Although states generally control funding, curriculum requirements, teacher and administrative certification, high school graduation requirements, and even textbook selection in twenty-two states, they still have limited control over the daily operation of schools. (As an example, see the PRO/CON Debate.) State efforts to reform education may be quite visible and vocal and take on many political and economic dimensions, but the dynamics of local schools and school administrators are such that they can torpedo authorized reform policies. State reform, then, must be sensitive to and include the local interpretation and responses to the official version of reform. Educational change must be played out in the classrooms and schools of America, and state-initiated reforms must conform—at least be modified—to local politics, processes, and perceptions.

In California, for example, the manifestation of various local movements in education has been obvious for the last twenty years, starting with the *Serrano* **decision** in school finance. However, the state superintendent of public instruction is able to work closely with local school administrators on an informal and unofficial basis. The success of reform in California is tied more to the superintendent's ability to mobilize local efforts than it is to the specific provisions of state legislative reform.[41] The "old-boy" political network works in the state–local administrative arena in this state.

In Illinois, however, the state department of education failed to consider the influence of local school administrators. When the state's board of higher education voted unanimously (13 to 0) in 1989 to impose tougher admission requirements in the state's public colleges and universities, they were cheered in the chambers as part of the educational reform wave. However, they ran into much opposition from school superintendents in the wealthy suburbs as well as poor cities and small towns. Local school administrators thought students would not have time for nonacademic courses and it would discriminate against students who lack proper education.[42]

The board failed to do its homework and to enlist the advice of the chief state school officer who had a better rapport with the school super-

[39]Thomas Peters and Robert Waterman, *In Search of Excellence: Lessons from America's Best-Run Companies* (New York: Harper & Row, 1982).

[40]Laurence Iannaccone and Richard Jamgochian, "High Performing Curriculum and Instructional Leadership in the Climate of Excellence," *NASSP Bulletin*, 69 (1985), pp. 28–35; R. S. Bhagat and S. J. McQuid, "Role of Subjective Culture in Organizations," *Journal of Applied Psychology Monograph*, No. 67 (1982), pp. 653–658.

[41]Timar and Kirp, "Education Reform in the 1980s: Lessons from the States."

[42]John Camper, "Stricter College Standards OKd," *Chicago Tribune*, 8 March 1989, pp. 1–2. Requirements were upgraded as follows: from two years of math, science, and social studies to three years each; from three years of English to four years, and from zero years to two years of foreign language. Note that in 1983 only three out of eleven state universities had any course requirements at all. Today, as a result of reform, they all have some course requirements for entering freshmen.

ADMINISTRATIVE ADVICE 10-2

■

PRINCIPLES FOR IMPROVING SCHOOLS

A number of "critical factors" or "important principles" result in school effectiveness and excellence. Based on the recent state-initiative programs to improve local schools, as well as the school-reform managerial literature in general, many of these factors or variables are listed below. Hence, we are dealing with principles that school leaders can adapt for improving their own schools.

- The school has a clearly stated mission or set of goals.
- Students are achieving at a level commensurate with their abilities.
- School achievement is closely monitored.
- Provisions are made for *all* students, including tutoring for low achievers and enrichment programs for the talented and gifted.
- Teachers and administrators agree on what is "good" teaching and learning; a general philosophy and psychology of learning prevails, although it may not be clearly stated or labeled by the staff.
- Emphasis on cognition is balanced with concerns for students' personal, social, and moral growth; students are taught to be responsible for their actions and behaviors; every student has a "home base" where teachers advise and provide guidance.
- Teachers and administrators are up-to-date on the knowledge of teaching and learning, as well as knowledge in their specific area or specialty.
- Teachers and administrators expect students to learn and convey these feelings to students and parents.
- Teachers are expected to make significant contributions to school improvement.
- Administrators provide ample support, information, and time for teacher enrichment.
- A sense of teamwork prevails; the staff works together in teams, and there is interdisciplinary and interdepartmental communication.

- Incentives, recognition, and rewards are conveyed to teachers and administrators for their efforts in behalf of the team and school mission.
- The interests and needs of the individual staff members are matched with the expectations of the institution (or school).
- New professional roles are created and others are redefined; the staff has the opportunity to be challenged and creative; there is a sense of professional enrichment and renewal.
- Staff development is planned by staff members to provide opportunities for continuous professional growth—at least on a monthly basis.
- Staff development programs provide a mix for teaching teachers the latest teaching techniques, including how to teach students how to learn so they can eventually learn without the teacher.
- The school environment is safe and healthy; there is a sense of order (not control) in classrooms and hallways.
- Parents and community members are supportive of the school and are involved in school activities.
- The school has a structure and identity of its own in which students, teachers, parents, and community members understand and share.
- The school is a learning center for the larger community, for the young and old, for students and parents alike; it reflects the norms and values of the community, and the community sees the school as an extension of the community.

PRO/CON DEBATE

■

ACADEMICALLY BANKRUPT SCHOOLS

In at least seven states, policies exist for "academic bankruptcy," a condition where a school is declared unable to perform its mission. A bankrupt school is one that is academically deficient and fails to improve, even when a plethora of resources have been poured into it.

QUESTION If states adopt a policy to close academically bankrupt schools, will students be better served?

ARGUMENTS PRO

1   Education is a state responsibility. The state abrogates its responsibility if it allows ineffective schools to continue to serve students.

2   State takeovers are reforms born out of desperation. Somebody has to do something, and states have the right (legally and morally) when local schools fail.

3   It is right and proper for states to establish minimum standards or outcome criteria and to enforce them.

4   The lowest-performing schools tend to be those serving low socioeconomic status students. More low-performing schools stay that way than reverse the trend and improve. We cannot continue to support institutions that produce an underclass of students.

5   In most states, equity of educational opportunity is a serious problem. Students in wealthy districts receive a better education than do those in poor districts. Any measure that supports equity is laudable.

ARGUMENTS CON

1   Local school boards, bearing the burden of responsibility for the operation of schools, are hampered by excessive regulation.

2   There is no evidence that administrators coming in from the state capital (hundreds of miles away in some cases) can do a better job than local officials. The takeover is contrary to many reforms that preach greater local control.

3   If a school is in distress, the state should provide additional resources so that students can learn, not close it so that students are disrupted.

4   If low-performing schools close, the students they serve will be forced to enroll in schools away from their neighborhoods. Research shows that schools are more likely to be effective if there are strong links with parents. Solutions that make parental involvement more difficult are poor solutions.

5   Where will displaced students be served? If there is insufficient space for them in other district schools, will they have the option of attending private schools? This policy is dangerous if it leads toward the privatization of public schooling.

intendents than did the thirteen laypeople of the board. The governor became embroiled in the dispute, and encouraged the board to hold the line.

State–School District Relationship   Policymakers and educators must understand that in some states school reform has involved *billions* of dollars and millions of students, hundreds of thousands of teachers and administrators, and hundreds of provisions. In California, for example, $1 billion was appropriated for each year since 1983.[43] Considering the proportion of stu-

[43]Allan Odden and David Marsh, "How Comprehensive Reform Legislation Can Improve Secondary Schools," *Phi Delta Kappan,* 69 (1988), pp. 593–598.

TABLE 10 ■ 2	Reform Strategies at the School District Level

1. District leaders take an active role and have a shared vision of local reform; they believe that their policies and programs are important, substantive, and sound.
2. District administrators are clear and consistent in the direction they want to go and communicate this commitment to the local schools; the schools are *not* loosely coupled or aimless.
3. All the districts (and schools) increase the school day and year.
4. There is emphasis on curriculum content and effective teaching and instructional strategies.
5. District planning and coordinating teams consist of central office representatives, site administrators, and teachers.
6. District goal setting, development, implementation, and evaluation activities are interrelated and planned for more than one year.
7. School teams composed of site administrators, supervisors, and teachers plan and coordinate similar (as in item 6) activities.
8. Staff development is ongoing, relies heavily on mentor teachers and supervisors, and focuses on curriculum and pedagogical skills.
9. District monitoring focuses on the performance of students, teachers, and school administrators; the results of state assessment programs are used to target problems and modify the curriculum.
10. Assistance is provided to teachers at the classroom level.

SOURCE: Adapted from Michael W. Kirst (ed.), *The Conditions of Children in California* (Berkeley: Policy Analysis for California Education, University of California, 1989); David Marsh and Gregory Bowman, *Comparing School Improvement of Secondary Schools* (Madison: National Center for Effective Schools, University of Wisconsin, 1990).

dents, similar financial and political investment in school reform has characterized states such as Michigan, New Jersey, North Carolina, and Tennessee. Regardless of results, some advocates would like to declare state reform as a great success in order to justify more expenditures for public schools. Others would like to declare schools a failure—and use national and international achievement scores as the acid test. Still others argue for alternative reform packages— often coinciding with the special interests of their own pressure group with whom they identify. To be sure, there are many unanswered questions, and it will take many years to determine if our state initiatives have made substantial change.

In one recent California study of seventeen secondary schools (twelve high schools and five middle–junior high schools) in ten different school districts, a number of successful reform–change strategies seem to be characteristic at the school district level. These and other strategies, listed in Table 10-2, show that district lead-

ership is important but school sites (and teachers and school administrators) are crucial for implementation of school reform. Although commitment to reform and efforts to bring it about were under way in many districts before the state stepped in with its provisions and resources, the state reform legislation strengthened the local desire to focus on school improvement and effectiveness; moreover, the district reform policies became more comprehensive and expanded to include other areas of education and all students. Reforms were typically initiated from the top down (district to school), not a popular idea today among many critics, and tended to result in greater centralization, but principals, supervisors, and teachers played an active role in implementation.[44]

In New York, as part of the Comprehensive School Improvement Planning process, about 1500 schools in more than 100 school districts

---

[44]Ibid.

have seen five principles emerge among reform- and change-minded schools:

1. *Excellence and Equity.* With these two essential philosophical ingredients, emphasis is on both basic skills and advanced level courses.
2. *Research and Evaluation.* Highly prized, research and evaluation use instruments to assess needs, plan improvements, and evaluate results.
3. *Data.* Data are seriously considered, but the information is made clear, simple, and brief before presented.
4. *Site-Based Collaboration and Planning.* Emphasis is on site-based collaboration and planning; that is, the staff is involved in planning and making decisions to ensure their commitment to change.
5. *Instruction.* Emphasis is on instruction while avoiding the tendency to be driven by test data or statewide assessments.[45]

In short, these five generic principles can guide school districts in all parts of the country in their mission pursuits or reform processes.

GUIDELINES FOR REFORM

The theory of school reform, today, recognizes that state-level policymakers, professional associations and people, and local administrative personnel play important roles in producing and maintaining reform measures. These players exist in a vague and uneasy harmony; the fragility of the relationship is increased from efforts to balance state–local policies. Reform measures at the state level require fundamental redefinition of organizational roles and relationships among state education agencies and between state agencies and local school districts. The need for cooperation, vision, and goal setting has become increasingly clear. Next are ten rec-

ommendations for enhancing today's reform efforts:

1. *Develop Comprehensive Reforms.* Reforms should focus on major areas of restructuring school organization, school finance, personnel, curriculum, and student policy. A comprehensive reform package involves the coordinated efforts of several state education agencies and departments within each agency. Reform, to be comprehensive, cannot be based on demands of one internal advocacy group; it must include many diversified groups and agencies within the organization and as many of their services as possible.
2. *Plan Long-Range Reforms.* To have the greatest impact, long-range planning should be built into reform; short-range planning should be developed as part of the feedback process to make adjustments in long-range goals.
3. *Involve Many Agencies Other Than Schools.* Schools cannot be expected to solve all the ills of society; business, universities, local government, community, social and recreational agencies, the home, and mass media have a role to play in reform. Similarly, school administrators can learn from the examples of successful administrators in other organizations. (See Administrative Advice 10-3.)
4. *Consider the Unique Needs of City, Suburban, and Rural School Districts.* The "problems" of schools are different in various geographic settings. Reform in big-city school districts needs to focus on basic problems that deal with student attendance, reading, and discipline. The suburbs often have problems of latchkey children, overstressed and overprogrammed students, and a narrow emphasis on grades and cognitive activities at the expense of socialization and personal development. Reform of rural schools needs to center on inadequate personnel and programs, transportation, and school district sharing plans.
5. *State–City Problems as Mutual Problems.* Often big cities find themselves treated as stepchildren and at the short end of the funds when

---

[45]Thomas F. Kelly, "Five Ways to Make Your Schools Effective," *School Administrator*, 46 (1989), pp. 26, 29.

they have to depend on state agencies because the rural–suburban legislatures often gang up against city interests. Reform measures need to involve cooperation among various state and city institutions and officials. Suburbs, adjacent to the cities, that fail to recognize that the problems and prospects of the city eventually affect their own municipalities are naive about metropolitan trends. By ignoring the inevitable, the suburbs make themselves more vulnerable to the future.

6. *Consider Research and Development as an Integral Part of Reform.* Relations between universities, state education agencies, and local school districts need to be improved in the areas of research and development. Professors have often engaged in research considered to be esoteric and of little value for practitioners; the notion of development— that is, improving products or services— doesn't really exist at the university, state, or local levels because little, if any, competition exists among public schools. Research and development need to be applied to the realities of classrooms and schools—and what concerns practitioners should become the agenda for research and development. Research and development budgets, which often comprise less than 2 percent of a state educational agency or school district's budget, need to be tripled in order to show good faith and produce change.

7. *Structure State Education Agencies to Provide Leadership.* Most state education agencies are increasingly becoming more active in reform; however, with the possible exception of Hawaii, they are not organized to carry out missions and policies at the local level; many policies and programs are regarded as ad hoc—temporary or transitory. Greater stability and institutionalization of departments and units in these agencies are required.

8. *Staff State Education Agencies with Highly Qualified Personnel.* Careers in state education agencies should be seen as important and challenging careers; yet, little attention is given to these jobs by the educational establishment. Failure to recognize that these state educational jobs should be staffed by competent people, who can deal with administrative, supervisory, and technical problems, has created a void in some states; public policy goals that could be achieved often fail to materialize. Plans should be to provide for recruitment of personnel who are qualified to carry out the missions of the respective state organizations. Departments of educational administration and administrative associations (both at the state and national levels) should assume a more active role in preparing public education personnel. Outstanding school superintendents should be recruited for the position of chief state school officer, and his staff should include adequate personnel to accomplish the goals of the office.

9. *Develop State Partnerships at the Regional Level in Six to Ten Different Areas of the Country.* By sharing personnel, programs, and research and development data, state education agencies can save money (instead of duplicating many efforts), resolve some problems that they have trouble dealing with on a separate basis, and engage in comprehensive, intrastate reform. The establishment of a loose regional structure in education, where the states still retain primary identity, provides nearby state education agencies the opportunity to communicate and share ideas that work, draw on the abilities of key personnel, engage in comprehensive staff development and training, and conduct research and development deemed important.

10. *Improve Reform by Forming a Federal Partnership with State Education Agencies.* The federal government has recently shifted too many education responsibilities to the states. Many states have budget problems and cannot afford a comprehensive reform package that costs money; nor do some have the inclination to help out big-city school districts. Increased federal aid to strengthen

ADMINISTRATIVE ADVICE 10-3

■

SCHOOL RENEWAL

From the literature, it is apparent that business ideas related to change and innovation have meaning for schools. Our purpose here is to bring the idea of **self-renewal** in corporations to the attention of education, in particular districtwide administrators and school principals who have great potential for effecting change.

■ *Informed Opportunism.* The leaders of successful companies recognize that an uncertain future carries with it many opportunities for purposeful and productive change. *Implication:* School administrators must learn to recognize and weigh risks and rewards, then take appropriate action.

■ *Empowerment.* Renewing companies value employees as a source of input in decision making and involvement in implementation. *Implication:* School administrators must learn to mobilize and blend the creative energies and ideas of their staff to accomplish the school mission or goals.

■ *Facing the Facts.* Renewing companies seek information; they are interested in good news and bad news. All information (good and bad) is treated as friendly by management because it understands the value of information in terms of decision making. *Implication:* School administrators must learn to value information and build an informal and formal information network. Negative news must be confronted, not ignored, because the problem will not go away by itself.

■ *Learning to Listen.* Renewing companies have administrators that listen; they realize that listening is an active, not passive, activity. *Implication:* School administrators must learn to seek the views of others (not just those closest to them) and listen to all members of their professional staff, as well as parents and community members.

■ *Teamwork and Trust.* Renewing companies place a premium on teamwork and trust because the

problems encountered by the company are often too complex to be solved by one person. *Implication:* School administrators must work hard to build teamwork and trust; it is essential for keeping the organization running smoothly.

■ *Confusion and Change.* Change is a norm in successful companies, and a certain amount of confusion is considered acceptable in highly innovative companies. *Implication:* School administrators need to make change an acceptable, even expected, practice; there should be a continuous flow of ideas and programs—some of which may result in some confusion or surprises at the beginning or evolvement stages.

■ *Attitude and Attention.* Leaders in renewing companies recognize that people need support and attention. *Implication:* School administrators need to provide constructive feedback to staff members and involve them in school activities that they can accomplish and feel good about performing.

■ *Cause and Commitment.* Renewing companies involve their people in worthwhile causes; their leaders inspire a sense of commitment and channel the priorities of the work force in the same direction of the organization. *Implication:* School administrators must build pride and commitment to the school; so-called great education causes or reform ideas should be accepted by the teachers who will be responsible for implementing the causes and ideas of others.

Source: Adapted from Robert H. Waterman, *The Renewal Factor: How the Best Get and Keep the Competitive Edge* (New York: Bantam Books, 1987).

state education agencies is required—paralleling action to improve educational opportunities of inner-city students. In the past, cities carried their needs to the federal government because they could not depend on the states. Only the federal government was willing to mount a comprehensive reform package to save big-city school districts. Although reform should be carried out by the state, and they have that legal responsibility, the federal government must remain highly involved and supportive of the state efforts and provide supplementary funding to whichever city school districts come up short in their dealings with state education agencies.

Finally, policies designed to reform education are no better than the school districts and schools that implement them. The target of reform must always be at the local level, and it must always consider people, for they are the ones who must implement reform. Indeed, every individual who comes into a system or organization plays a multitude of roles; each professional brings to her role her personality as well. Each person has certain needs he expects to fulfill within the system—regardless of whether it is a business, school, hospital, or the like. Rarely is there absolute congruence between institutional roles and expectations and individual personality and needs.

Administrators must recognize they cannot always avoid this conflict; they must manage it. The way they manage it is reflected in the social behavior of their staff and how these people react to change. Table 10-3 may help individual administrators increase their own receptivity to reform, as well as members of their staff. The reform strategies were originally geared for school principals who wanted to make changes and innovations in curriculum. The guidelines, however, are sufficiently generic to apply for all school administrators, including those at the central office, in most phases of reform and innovation.

SUMMARY

1. The state hierarchy of education includes the governor, state legislature, and courts. In recent years, all three groups have taken a more active role in education.
2. Interest groups and lobby groups concentrate their efforts with state legislators who may be undecided on how to vote on issues.
3. With the exception of Wisconsin, all states have state boards of education. State departments of education operate under the direction of the state boards and are headed by the chief state school officer.
4. The chief state school officer, likely called a state superintendent of instruction or state commissioner of education, usually reports to the state department of education and advises the state legislature and governor.
5. The state reform movement in education gained increased momentum during the 1980s and can be categorized into three types of reform: student achievement, professionalism, and curriculum.
6. To facilitate reform at the state level, it is important to consider local school districts and school administrators—their needs and perceptions of reform.

KEY TERMS

state education agency	subjective culture
children at risk	*Serrano* decision
political action committees	self-renewal
Kalamazoo decision	

DISCUSSION QUESTIONS

1. Identify and explain three ways in which the state government is involved in public education.
2. What are the major responsibilities and functions of the state boards of education and state departments of education?
3. What are the major responsibilities of the chief state school officer? How does this compare with

TABLE 10 ▪ 3   Increasing Receptivity to Reform

1. *School Reform Should Be Perceived as a Cooperative Effort.* Cooperation should evolve among teachers, supervisors, and administrators and to a lesser extent students, parents, and community residents. The sense of cooperation is achieved by involving people in the major aspects of planning and implementation.

2. *People Resist Change; People Accept Change.* Most people resist change before they accept it, especially if they are content with the existing program or organization. Administrators need to anticipate initial resistance to change and deal with concerns and questions about change: how people feel about change, conflicts that may surface, what can be done to lessen anxiety, and how to facilitate the change process.

3. *People, Programs, and Organizations Change.* Nothing lasts forever. Schools and society change, and reforms are modified to reflect changes. Change is constant, and educators need to realize that people and programs change, as well as the school as a whole. The need is to play a role in change, rather than be victimized by it or be made powerless by its forces.

4. *Innovations Change.* What is viewed as innovative today, if accepted as part of the school program or organization, will eventually become dated tomorrow. As time passes, contexts change, and modifications are required. Educators should accept the continuous need for change and innovation.

5. *Timing Is Crucial.* If people are satisfied with the status quo and there is little demand for change, then a major reform in the curriculum can rarely be implemented. If the local, state, or federal government perceives a need for change, then a new program addressing this need is likely to be implemented.

6. *Educators Need to Be Rewarded.* Right now, there is little pressure for reform among rank-and-file educators, much less reward for change. Because schools are not competitive, they see little need for improving their products or improving consumer satisfaction. Rewards—either in the form of salary, promotion, or recognition—need to be part of the reform and innovative process of schools.

7. *An Internal Advocacy Group Improves the Chances for Change.* An internal advocacy group at the district office or community level increases the pressure and likelihood for change. When a particular group of educators or community members sees the benefit of a particular program, they will put pressure on the people and the organization for change. Sometimes, however, another group of educators or community residents who are threatened by the advocacy group surfaces. Conflict then arises, and negotiations or modifications are essential before change can be implemented.

8. *Training and Technical Assistance Is Essential.* Continual staff development within the organization and technical assistance from outside the organization (say, the state) are important. However, many teachers don't want to stay after school to receive training or technical assistance and may rely on their contracts for reasons why they don't have to stay late. If necessary, attitudes among the staff may also need to be changed first, before considering staff training or technical assistance.

9. *Administrators Must Understand Their Mission and Priorities.* Many supervisors and administrators lack a clear idea of their school mission and priorities. They see little need for reform or for making it a priority. Reform and innovation should be part of the leadership behaviors that are highlighted among all theoreticians and practitioners, who administer our schools.

10. *Rewards and Risks Must Be Considered.* The political, social, and legal factors related to reform and innovation are important factors that cannot escape the thinking of a wise administrator. Educators must realize that when the rewards are substantial and the risk is minimal, it is worthwhile to pursue change. Most important, school leaders can reduce their risk by understanding the nature of their staff, school district, and community.

SOURCE: Adapted from Allan C. Ornstein and Francis P. Hunkins, "Implementing Curriculum Changes—Guidelines for Principals," *NASSP Bulletin,* 72 (1988), pp. 71–72.

the responsibilities of the local school district superintendent?

4. Explain the concept of state reform in education as it is presently evolving. How can state reform be improved?

5. In terms of Table 10-3, what additional suggestions can you make, based on personal experience, for improving the prospects of change and/or reform?

SUGGESTED READINGS

Michael Cohen, *Meeting the Information Needs of State Education Policymakers* (Alexandria, VA: State Education Policy Consortium, 1985). A survey report of state policymakers and how the states can help improve schools.

Margaret Goertz and Douglass E. Mitchell, *Education Politics for the New Century* (New York: Falmer Press, 1990). Federal and state politics and policies related to educational reform, including business involvement in education for the 1990s.

Robert Kaufman, *Planning Educational Systems: A Results Based Approach* (Lancaster, PA: Technomic, 1988). A systematic, outcome-based method for school planning and school improvement.

David Marsh and Gregory Bowman. *Comparing School Improvement and Recent School Reform* (Madison: National Center for Effective Secondary Schools, University of Wisconsin, 1990). Various phases and strategies for reforming schools in context with state-initiated programs.

Thomas Timar and David Kirp. *Managing Educational Excellence* (New York: Falmer Press, 1988). An assessment of school reform in three states—California, South Carolina, and Texas.

Kenneth A. Sirotnik and John I. Goodlad (eds.), *School–University Partnerships: Concepts, Cases and Concerns.* (New York: Teachers College Press, 1988). These essays examine various school–university collaborative models for improving schools and staff development programs.

Robert H. Waterman, *The Renewal Factor: How the Best Get and Keep the Competitive Edge* (New York: Bantam Books, 1987). Many business examples for success that parallel or are at least relevant to schools.

11

LOCAL SCHOOL DISTRICTS

In this chapter, we attempt to answer these questions by first examining school districts—in particular their size and structure. Then we discuss the structure and duties of the local school board, the responsibilities of the superintendent, and the relationship between the board and the superintendent. Next we explore the role of the central office staff and its obligations to the district and the superintendent. Finally, we discuss the school principal and what makes an effective principal.

STATE AND LOCAL POLICY

The local school district is the basic administrative unit in the education hierarchy, which starts at the federal level and works its way to the state and then local level. For the greater part, the local school district consists of many schools.

Most school districts comprise grades K to 12, with separate elementary and secondary schools; however, a small school district (in a rural or suburban area) may include only grades K to 8 (and consist of one or more elementary and/or middle-grade schools) and a neighboring school district will include grades 9 to 12 (with one or more high schools).

Regardless of the exact school structure within the district, every public school in the United States is part of a local school district. The district is created by the state. The state legislature, subject to the restrictions of the state constitution, can modify a local district's jurisdiction, change its boundaries and powers, or even eliminate it altogether. The local district encompasses a relatively small geographic area and operates the schools for children within a specific community. It is the avenue through which local citizens act in establishing district-wide policies in education. However, because a school district operates to carry out a state function, not a local function, local policies must be consistent with policies set forth in the state school code. The local district can be compared to a limited corporation whose powers are granted by state laws; it has only those powers expressly granted to it and those discretionary powers essential to its operation.

ORGANIZATION OF SCHOOL DISTRICTS

The organization of school districts permits several grade plans and combinations of elementary and secondary schools. Figure 11-1 shows ten common organizational plans; a description for each follows:

1. Plan A shows the traditional 8–4 organizational plan consisting of an eight-year elementary school and a four-year high school.
2. Plan B exemplifies a 4–4–4 district plan, where the first four grades are elementary

school, the next four are middle school, and the final four are high school.
3. Plan C illustrates the 5–3–4 plan, providing a five-year elementary school, and a three-year middle school, and four-year high school. Both Plans B and C are growing in popularity because of the middle-school movement.
4. Plan D shows a 6–2–4 district plan, where grades 1 to 6 comprise the elementary school, grades 7 to 8 comprise the junior high school, and grades 9 to 12 comprise the high school.
5. Plan E is the 3–3–3–3 plan, used in parts of the country that wish to promote school integration at the elementary school level or in rural areas that need to consolidate school facilities. There are also a three-year junior high school and three-year senior high school.
6. Plan F represents a typical 6–3–3 elementary, junior high, and senior high school plan. Plans D, E, and F illustrate the junior high school in relation to elementary school and either high school or senior high school.
7. Plan G is the 6–6 organizational plan consisting of an elementary school for grades 1 to 6 and a combined three-year junior high school and three-year senior high school.
8. Plan H illustrates the 7–5 grade pattern, where the elementary school goes to grade 7, and there is a combined two-year junior high school and three-year senior high school. Plans G and H show the elementary school with a combined junior and senior high school, representative of a small number of U.S. schools.
9. Plan I shows two separate, usually adjacent, districts, where the elementary school grades K to 8 represent one district and the high school grades 9 to 12 represent the other district.
10. Plan J is the 1–12 plan, representative of even a smaller number of schools, usually special schools, alternative schools, one-room schoolhouses, or schools not classified by grade level.

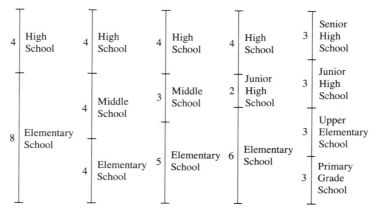

Plan A: 8–4   Plan B: 4–4–4   Plan C: 5–3–4   Plan D: 6–2–4   Plan E: 3–3–3–3

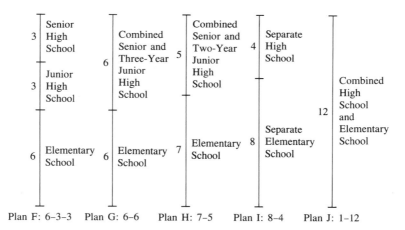

Plan F: 6–3–3   Plan G: 6–6   Plan H: 7–5   Plan I: 8–4   Plan J: 1–12

FIGURE 11-1   **School District Organization by Grades**
SOURCE: Adapted from *Digest of Education Statistics, 1988* (Washington, D.C.: Government Printing Office, 1988), Figure 1, p. 5; James J. Jones, C. Jackson Salisbury, and Ralph L. Spencer, *Secondary School Administration,* © 1969, pp. 96–97, McGraw-Hill, Inc., New York; and Allan C. Ornstein, *An Introduction to the Foundations of Education,* © 1977, Figure 15.1, p. 529, Rand McNally & Co., Chicago.

It is difficult to say which plan is better or worse; it varies with educational philosophy and the conditions in the school district. Most progressive educators or communities prefer a middle grade or junior high school, as a means of putting preadolescent students (who are usually undergoing rapid physical and social changes) under one roof for a number of years to facilitate their growth and development.

Size of School Districts

What is the ideal size for a school district? In terms of minimum size, how many students must be enrolled to justify offering diversified programs, services, and personnel needed to meet modern educational requirements? The studies that suggest optimal size, over the last fifty years, have focused on cost analysis, curriculum offerings, staffing, and student achievement as the most important variables. During this period, the minimum ideal size tends to be at 10,000 to 12,000 students, and the maximum size tends to be 40,000 to 50,000 students.[1] One classic study considered the maximally effective school district to comprise 100,000 students.[2]

Today, small is considered better; the idea is to scale down the school enterprise, whereas in the past big was considered better. Advocates of small school districts and rural schools point out that 5000-student maximums are more cost-effective, have fewer student dropouts (in percentages), higher student SAT and ACT scores, and higher graduation and college entry rates than do school districts with more than 5000 students.[3] Although social class was not controlled in these studies, educational expenditures were. Small school districts, 5000 or fewer students, cluster in the 14th to 30th percentile in per-pupil expenditures but rank in the top 10 percent on nationwide achievement scores and other indicators of student performance (fewer dropouts, more high school graduates).[4]

Other advocates maintain that school districts with 20,000 or fewer students have a significant positive relationship with SAT scores, high school graduation rates, and slightly more favorable pupil–teacher ratios than do districts with more than 20,000 students. Smaller school districts have significantly lower levels of parental income and spend about $250 less per student.[5] In short, "smaller districts . . . appear to achieve better results for students at equal [or less] cost."[6]

Studies of hundreds of school districts nationwide also confirm the relationship of inverse district size and student achievement, after controlling for per-pupil expenditures and social class.[7] Although larger school districts may be more efficient when it comes to spending—that is, per-unit costs decline with a greater number of students served because districts usually purchase more units cheaper and employ fewer teachers and administrators per student—the economies of scale enjoyed by large school districts come at the expense of educational outcomes. Moreover, there are some data to suggest that large school districts are actually inefficient and wasteful.[8] Actually, the dependence of costs

[1]Howard A. Dawson, *Satisfactory Local School Units,* Field Study no. 7 (Nashville, TN: George Peabody College for Teachers, 1934); Mario D. Fantini, Marilyn Gittell, and Richard Magat, *Community Control and the Urban School* (New York: Praeger, 1970); A. Harry Passow, *Toward Creating a Model Urban School System* (New York: Teachers College Press, 1967); and *Summary of Research on Size of Schools and School Districts* (Arlington, VA: Educational Research Service, 1974).
[2]Paul R. Mort and Francis G. Cornell, *American Schools in Transition* (New York: Teachers College Press, 1941); Paul R. Mort, William S. Vincent, and Clarence Newell, *The Growing Edge: An Instrument for Measuring the Adaptability of School Systems,* 2 vols. (New York: Teachers College Press, 1955).
[3]*A Critique of North Carolina Department of Public Instruction's Plan to Mandate School District Mergers Throughout the State* (Raleigh: North Carolina Boards Association, 1986); William Fox, "Reviewing Economies of Size in Education," *Journal of Education and Finance,* 6 (1980), pp. 275–296; John P. Sher, *Education in Rural America: A Reassessment of Conventional Wisdom* (Boulder, CO: Westview, 1977); and Sher, *Class Dismissed: Examining Nebraska's Rural Education Debate* (Lincoln: Lincoln Nebraska Rural Community Schools Association, 1986).

[4]Allan C. Ornstein, "School District and School Size: an Evolving Controversy," *Clearing House,* 63 (1989), pp. 156–158; Ornstein, "Size: Is Bigger Better?" *PTA Today,* 15 (1989), pp. 16–17.
[5]Robert W. Jewell, "School and School District Size Relationships," *Education and Urban Society,* 21 (1989), pp. 140–153.
[6]Ibid., p. 151.
[7]David H. Monk, "Secondary School Size and Curriculum Comprehensiveness," *Economics of Education Review,* 6 (1987), pp. 137–150; Richard Turner et al., "Policy Strategies, Teacher Salary Incentive, and Student Achievement," *Educational Researcher,* 15 (1986), pp. 5–11; and Herbert J. Walberg and William J. Fowler, "Expenditure and Size Efficiencies of Public School Districts," *Educational Researcher,* 16 (1987), pp. 5–15.
[8]Fox, "Reviewing Economies of Size in Education"; Allan C. Ornstein, "Controversy Over Size Continues," *School Administrator,* 46 (1989), pp. 42–43; and Walberg and Fowler, "Expenditure and Size Efficiencies of Public School Districts."

seems U-shaped, with very small and very large school districts spending more per student than moderate-sized districts.

Number of School Districts

Historically, 10,000 students is a large number for a school district. Our schools, we must remember, are an outgrowth of one-room school houses and school districts in the rural United States. With the exception of a few urban areas, even as late as the turn of the twentieth century, most school districts consisted of three, four, or five schools and a few hundred students. As late as 1930, nearly 50 percent of U.S. school districts had fewer than 300 students. By 1988, as many as 26 percent of the school districts (enrolling only 1.3 percent of the nation's students) had fewer than 300 students. Inversely, 4 percent of public school districts were in school districts containing 10,000 or more students. There were only 171, or 1.1 percent, school districts with 25,000 or more students, but they accounted for 11.2 million students, or 28 percent, of the nation's public school enrollment. Table 11-1 shows how school districts today are distributed.

Most of the larger school districts (25,000 or more students) are in California, Florida, Texas, and Maryland, but the states with the largest district averages are, in descending order, Hawaii (163,800 students), Maryland (27,900), Florida (23,200), and Louisiana (12,000). The states with the smallest district averages—that is, less than 1000 students per district—are Oklahoma, Maine, South Dakota, Vermont, Nebraska, and Montana (the lowest with 281 students).[9]

In most cases, the larger school districts are located in or near cities, the largest being the New York City system with approximately 940,000 students, followed by Los Angeles with 590,000 students, Chicago with 420,000 students, and Dade County, Florida, with 255,000 students.[10] (Two other large school districts, Puerto Rico and Hawaii, span an entire territory and state, respectively.) The medium-sized and smaller school districts have followed metropolitan sprawl and tend to be located in the outer ring of the suburbs or in rural areas.

Consolidation of School Districts

The number of school districts in the United States continues to decline. In 1930 there were more than 130,000 school districts. By 1950 the number had shrunk to 83,718; by 1980 to 15,625; by 1990 to 15,500, suggesting a leveling trend (Figure 11-2).

The reduced number of school districts is a result of **consolidation**, the combination of a number of smaller school districts into one or two larger ones. Consolidation is thought to bring about more effective schools by increasing the tax base, quality of professional personnel, breadth of educational programs, special services, and transportation facilities and by reducing overall educational costs per student.[11]

The data on consolidation, however, remain inconclusive. Moreover, consolidating districts usually means closing some schools, and this has proved to be a serious and emotional matter, especially in small and rural school districts where the local school may be a focal point of the community's identity. In many cases, state school officials operating under the assumption that consolidation is cost-effective and enhances student opportunity, have clashed with local

[9]*Digest of Education Statistics, 1988* (Washington, D.C.: Government Printing Office, 1988), Table 70, pp. 85–88; Jewell, "School and District Size Relationships," Table 2, p. 143.

[10]Allan C. Ornstein, "Opening New Schools Depends on More Than Enrollment," *American School Board Journal*, 176 (1989), pp. 40–41.

[11]Richard J. Butler and David H. Monk, "The Cost of Public Schooling in New York State," *Journal of Human Resources*, 20 (1985), pp. 361–380; James Guthrie, "Organizational Scale and School Success," *Educational Evaluation and Policy Analysis*, (1)(1979), pp. 17–27.

TABLE 11 ▪ 1   Distribution of School Districts by Size, 1987–1988

SIZE OF DISTRICT (NUMBER OF PUPILS)	PUBLIC SCHOOL DISTRICTS		PUBLIC SCHOOL STUDENTS	
	Number	Percent	Number	Percent
Total operating districts	15,577	100.0	40,024,000	100.0
25,000 or more	171	1.1	11,166,696	27.9
10,000–24,999	464	3.0	6,844,104	17.1
5000–9999	937	6.0	6,603,960	16.5
2500–4999	1,912	12.3	6,563,936	16.4
1000–2499	3,561	22.9	5,883,528	14.7
600–999	1,796	11.5	1,400,840	3.5
300–599	2,290	14.7	1,006,000	2.5
1–299	4,041	25.9	520,312	1.3
Size not reported	405	2.6	—	—

SOURCE: *Digest of Education Statistics, 1989* (Washington, D.C.: Department of Education, 1989), Tables 36, 80, pp. 47, 90.

townspeople who resent the interference of distant bureaucrats. The process can be demoralizing to students, parents, and the community at large. Local taxpayers, who might normally support plans for saving money, have often refused to endorse consolidation.[12]

Because of this opposition, officials in many states have begun looking for ways to obtain the benefits of consolidation without eliminating schools or districts. One method is for neighboring districts to share programs and personnel. Minnesota, for example, encourages this trend by providing up to 75 percent of the cost of shared secondary school facilities and programs.[13] Iowa provides between 5 and 50 percent extra funding to local school districts that share course offerings, teachers, administrators, and school buildings. In 1987 sixty-seven Iowa school districts shared superintendents, and forty were involved in *whole-share grading* (programs in which all students in a certain grade

are assigned to a single district).[14] In Illinois, Montana, and Nebraska, there is a hold on new consolidation plans, and there are school committees organized to restructure school district sizes.[15]

Some educators contend that consolidation has served its major purpose—eliminating many one-room schools and inefficient small districts—and that this trend will soon pass. But it remains a controversial issue that affects many school districts across the country.

Decentralization

Changes in the urban population after 1950 gave rise to changes in the composition of urban schools. As middle-class and white populations fled to the suburbs—in what became known as the "white flight movement"—the percentages

---

[12]Ornstein, "School District and School Size."
[13]Chris Pipho, "Rural Education," *Phi Delta Kappan*, 69 (1987), pp. 6–7.

[14]*Annual School District Reorganization Report* (Des Moines: Iowa Department of Education, 1987); *Reorganization Feasibility Study* (Des Moines: Iowa Department of Education, 1987).
[15]Ornstein, "Controversy Over Size Continues"; Pipho, "Rural Education."

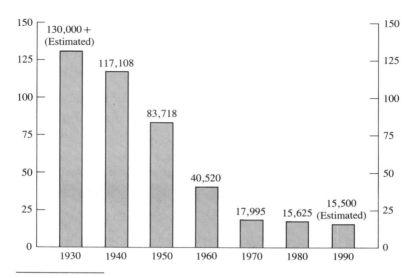

FIGURE 11-2   Declining Number of School Districts, 1930–1990
SOURCE: *Digest of Education Statistics, 1972* (Washington, D.C.: Government Printing Office, 1973), Figure 7, p. 53; *Digest of Education Statistics, 1988* (Washington, D.C.: Government Printing Office, 1988), Table 68, p. 83; and *Educational Directory: Public School Systems, 1980–81* (Washington, D.C.: Government Printing Office, 1980); 1990 estimate is based on authors' projections after speaking with Dr. Vance Grant, specialist in education statistics, Office of Educational Research and Improvement, February 19, 1990.

of low-income and minority residents increased in the cities. As a result, city schools became multiethnic, and many schools in the suburbs became more homogeneous in terms of income and race. By the 1960s, many inner-city ethnic groups, especially blacks, began to feel that the schools did not serve their needs. They began to call for decentralization as a means to greater community involvement in the schools.

By definition, **decentralization** divides the school system into smaller units, but the focus of power and authority remains in a single central administration and board of education. There is usually little controversy over decentralization as long as jobs are not consolidated or expanded on the basis of racial or ethnic patterns. Even professional educators today see a need to reduce school bureaucracy and to accept decentralization because it allows the professional educators to retain power. At the same

time, school critics and minority spokespersons believe that decentralization will give the people greater access to the schools.

Consequently, while many small and rural school districts have been consolidated in recent decades, many large urban districts have decentralized their schools. A nationwide survey on decentralization of school systems with 50,000 or more students was conducted in 1980.[16] Data on some sixty-six out of sixty-nine school districts in that group (96 percent return rate) were reported. Of the sixty-six districts, forty-two (67 percent) reported they were decentralized. Larger school districts (100,000 or more students) had decentralized more than smaller ones (50,000 to 99,999 students). For example, twenty

---

[16]Allan C. Ornstein, "Decentralization and Community Participation Policy of Big School Systems," *Phi Delta Kappan,* 62 (1980), pp. 225–257.

out of twenty-two (91 percent) of the larger ones had decentralized, whereas only twenty-two out of forty-four (50 percent) enrolling fewer than 100,000 students were decentralized.

The decentralized unit names were largely confined to three terms. Twenty-eight referred to *areas* (67 percent adjusted percentage); seven to *districts* (17 percent), including community districts and subdistricts; and six referred to *regions* (14 percent). One district (2 percent) used the term *zone*. The number of decentralized units varied from as few as two areas in Oakland, California, and Portland, Oregon, to as many as thirty-two community districts in New York City, with four decentralized units the most frequent plan in fourteen school districts (33 percent adjusted percentage) and three units second most frequent in ten districts (24 percent). The number of decentralized units averaged 5.6, with larger districts (100,000 plus students) averaging 7.7 and smaller ones (fewer than 100,000 students) averaging 3.9.[17]

In a companion study, seventeen reasons were given for decentralization. The top eight reasons, in order of priority and representing 79 percent of the responses, are the following:

1. To enhance school–community relations
2. To provide greater community input at the local level
3. To provide local schools with more field and resource personnel
4. To provide efficient maintenance and support for local schools
5. To reduce administrative span of control
6. To provide greater linkages between local schools and the central school board
7. To redirect spending for local school needs
8. To provide greater curriculum continuity from kindergarten through grade 12.[18]

Oddly enough, little evidence supported these reasons for decentralization. Very few of the school systems have conducted evaluations of their new organizational models or tested the assumptions, goals, and recommendations related to decentralization. Little hard evidence supports the assertion that school decentralization improves education.[19]

In 1988 the number of school districts with 50,000 or more students had decreased to sixty-two; in a follow-up study to the 1980 study, data were obtained from fifty-one districts (82 percent response rate). Only sixteen school districts (31 percent) purported to be decentralized, although three others had recently moved from decentralization to centralization. Even with school districts that purported to be decentralized, they were actually more centralized than decentralized in organizational hierarchy and administrative positions. Table 11-2 reports data concerning the sixteen large school districts that were decentralized in 1988. The table shows that four out of sixteen school districts claiming to be decentralized (Palm Beach, Florida; New Orleans; Jefferson County, Colorado; and Cleveland) are strongly committed to centralization. This is based on the fact that their central administrative staffs are each 10.8 to 21.5 times greater than their respective decentralized staffs. The majority of the school districts, ten out of sixteen, are moderately more centralized than decentralized. Their centralized administration is 1.5 to 4.0 times greater than their decentralized administration.

Only two school districts, New York City and St. Louis, were seemingly more committed to decentralization than centralization by virtue that their administrative positions were greater at the decentralized level than the centralized level. This fact is represented by the ratios of less than 1 of the two districts in the table. Hence, a school district planning to study decentraliza-

---

[17]Ibid.

[18]Allan C. Ornstein, "Decentralization and Community Outlook," *Educational Forum*, 46 (1981), pp. 45–54; Ornstein, "Decentralization—Is It Working?" *Elementary School Principal*, 61 (1981), pp. 24–27. Also see Daniel U. Levine and Robert J. Havighurst, *Society and Education*, 7th ed. (Needham Heights, MA: Allyn and Bacon, 1989).

[19]Jim S. Fuerst, "School Decentralization Has Poor Track Record," *Chicago Sun Times*, 22 April 1989, p. 20; Ornstein, "Decentralization and Community Outlook."

TABLE 11 ▪ 2   Centralization–Decentralization Ratios of School Districts Comprising 50,000 or More Students

	SCHOOL ENROLLMENT	NUMBER OF CENTRAL ADMINISTRATORS	NUMBER OF DECENTRALIZED ADMINISTRATORS	RATIO OF CENTRALIZED AND DECENTRALIZED ADMINISTRATORS
New York	939,933	2100	3730	+ 0.56
Los Angeles	592,273	340	101	+ 3.37
Chicago	419,537	399	120	+ 3.33
Dade County, Florida	254,235	270	66	+ 4.09
Philadelphia	194,698	251	166	+ 1.51
Hawaii	165,455	139	92	+ 1.51
Montgomery County, Maryland	96,271	115	34	+ 3.38
Palm Beach, Florida	90,235	359	25	+14.36
New Orleans	83,188	127	9	+14.41
Jefferson County, Colorado	75,337	140	13	+10.77
Charlotte–Mecklenburg, North Carolina	74,146	99	25	+ 3.96
Cleveland	72,639	258	12	+21.50
Atlanta	65,458	160	60	+ 2.67
El Paso, Texas	61,857	118	42	+ 2.81
Tucson	56,475	45	24	+ 1.88
St. Louis	50,000	84	159	+ 0.53

SOURCE: Allan C. Ornstein, "Centralization and Decentralization of Large Public School Districts," *Urban Education*, 24 (1989), p. 234. Used by permission.

tion might look at these two districts because their commitment to decentralization seems more evident because of their administrative assignments. (See Administrative Advice 11-1.) Nevertheless, the concept of decentralization seems to be on the decline for two reasons: (1) the drop in percentage of decentralized school districts, from 67 percent (forty-two out of sixty-six) in 1980 to 31 percent (sixteen out of fifty-one) in 1988, and (2) the majority of districts currently claiming to be decentralized seems more committed to centralization.

Other data also suggest that, despite apparent decentralization, the large, urban school districts in fact remain highly centralized. Decisions regarding curriculum, instruction, staff-

ADMINISTRATIVE ADVICE 11-1

QUESTIONS TO CONSIDER WHEN YOUR SCHOOL DISTRICT CONSIDERS CONSOLIDATION OR DECENTRALIZATION

Both school consolidation and decentralization often involve emotional issues—where some groups are perceived "winners" and others are "losers." Often the issues become highly vocalized at school meetings and in the local press, and so-called solutions are often slogans rather than carefully worked-out concepts understood and accounted for in the rhetoric or press. We assume the "community voice" is the most visible or vocal, and yet we sometimes fail to consider the silent parents who have their own views of reform for their children's education. Thus, there is good reason to proceed with caution. As an administrator, ask yourself the questions below. Be candid and analytic in your answers.

- Who are the advocates?
- What are their motivations? What are their political–economic reasons? Do they have hidden agendas?
- Does the majority of the community want to consolidate (decentralize)? Or is a small, well-organized group behind the plan?
- Do students, parents, teachers, community residents gain under the plan? How?
- Which parents or community residents lose, or feel they lose, under the plan?
- How do various interest groups feel about the plan? Is there considerable conflict or emotion? Is it really worthwhile to proceed, given the conflict or emotion? Why?
- How do the various interest groups want to be represented under the plan? Are there differences among groups based on race, ethnicity, social class, or residents with and without children?
- How do community agencies and local business groups fit into the plan? Have their concerns or interests been considered?
- As a result of the plan, will teaching jobs or administrative positions be affected? Is there current concern among the professional staff?
- What administrative levels (central office, decentralized or field office) should be consolidated (decentralized)? Why?
- How does the plan affect student performance? Are there data to indicate the plan will have a positive impact on student performance?
- What unit size is most effective? Most efficient? Is there past history in adjacent (or similar) communities or school districts to verify these assumptions?
- When does bigness lead to increased bureaucracy? When does smallness lead to reduced range of educational services?
- What is the projected cost of the plan? Is it realistic? Is it worthwhile in terms of assumed outcomes?
- Does the plan consider future population growth? Student enrollments? School construction sites? School integration?
- Who really benefits by the plan? Do students? (Remember, they are the real consumers and the reason for the schools.)

ing and teacher evaluation, student testing, graduation requirements, and budgeting are still made at the central level, or at what is sometimes referred to as the "downtown" office. Furthermore, the central office is increasingly involved in negotiations with teachers' unions, compliance with court-ordered busing requirements, affirmative action, and allocation of state monies and special programs for the local district. All these trends tend to expand the authority of the main district office and reduce the effect of decentralization.[20]

LOCAL SCHOOL BOARDS

The local school boards of education have been delegated powers and duties by the state for the purpose of ensuring that their schools are operated properly. Despite the fact that their prerogatives are limited by the state, school boards have assumed significant decision-making responsibility. School boards have the power for the most part to raise money through taxes. They exercise power over personnel and school property. Some states leave curriculum and student policy in the hands of the school board, but others, by law, impose specific requirements. In general, the school board must conform to state guidelines to qualify for state aid, as well as conform to federal guidelines where federal monies are involved.

Methods of selecting board members are prescribed by state law. The two basic methods are election and appointment. Election is thought to make for greater accountability to the public, but some people argue that appointment leads to greater competence and less politics. (See the PRO/CON Debate.) Election is the most common practice. In 1989 91 percent of school board members nationwide were elected in nonpartisan elections, 4 percent were elected in partisan elections (as members of a political party), and only 5 percent were appointed.[21]

Appointment is more common in large urban districts than in suburban or small-town districts; 11 percent of urban board members in 1987 were appointed. A few states specify a standard number of board members, still others specify a permissible range, and a few have no requirements. Most school boards (80 percent) comprise a seven- to nine-member range, with the largest school board having nineteen members; the average size is seven members.[22]

A recent nationwide survey of school board members indicates that the number of women on school boards has increased, from 25 to 28 percent in the early 1980s to 34 to 39 percent in the late 1980s. Minority representation has remained stable at 7 percent. (Southern states show a higher minority representation on school boards: 14 percent black and 4 percent Hispanic.)[23] School board members tend to be older than the general population (79 percent are over age forty); more educated (68 percent have had four or more years of college); wealthier (31 percent have family incomes of $70,000 or more, and 15.4 percent earn more than $100,000 annually); and more likely to be professionals or managers (50 percent) or owners of their own businesses (12 percent). Interestingly, 40 percent have no children in school right now, and 60 percent are relative neophytes, having served on the boards for five or fewer years.[24]

The largest school systems (those enrolling 50,000 or more students) tend to have more heterogeneous boards. A recent survey indicates that minority members constitute 29 percent of the school board in these systems; women make

[20]Jack Frymier, *One Hundred Good Schools* (West Lafayette, IN: Kappa Delta Pi, 1984); Frymier, "Bureaucracy and the Neutering of Teachers," *Phi Delta Kappan,* 69 (1987), pp. 9–14; and David Rogers and Norman H. Chung, *110 Livingston Street Revisited,* rev. ed. (New York: New York University Press, 1983). Also see "Community Control Decentralization Models," proceedings of a conference on urban education, *Educational Reform: Promises and Pitfalls* (Chicago: Chicago Urban League, 1988), pp. 34–36.

[21]"Twelfth Annual Survey of School Board Members: Here's Looking at You," *American School Board Journal,* 177 (1990), p. 34.

[22]Nellie C. Weil, "The Significance of Being a School Board Member," *American School Board Journal,* 175 (1987), pp. 1–4; "Tenth Annual Survey of School Board Members," *American School Board Journal,* 175 (1988), pp. 17–19.

[23]"The Typical School Board Member," *American School Board Journal,* 176 (1989), pp. 21–24; "School Board Survey: Happily Ever After," *American School Board Journal,* 177 (1990), pp. 28–33.

[24]"Twelfth Annual Survey: Here's Looking at You."

PRO/CON DEBATE

■

THE POLITICS OF SCHOOL ELECTIONS

Although people in the United States value the democratic process, for many people the term *politics* carries a negative connotation. *Politics* implies trade-off, compromise, less-than-perfect solutions, and, perhaps, secret deals that benefit those in power. Given this perception, the practice of electing to office those who set policy for schools is debatable.

QUESTION Considering the political ramifications of elections, should school board members be elected?

ARGUMENTS PRO

1 Service on the school board requires little political experience. Concerned citizens can assume office and contribute to the general welfare in important and meaningful ways without major changes in their personal or professional lives. They need not be or become career politicians.

2 Election is effective and sacred. The electoral process guarantees that issues are discussed in an open forum. Voters choose candidates who are most conversant with the issues and most able to act upon them.

3 Single-issue candidates are rarely elected to office because their constituents are a small portion of the community. If elected, their perspective broadens as they learn about other issues and the board's responsibilites.

4 An appointed board vests power in the person making the appointments. It leads to rule by an elite or specific pressure group rather than rule by the people.

5 As chief executive officers, school superintendents are accountable to the community for the state of the schools. It is right and proper for local citizens to express their concerns to their elected board members and for board members to carry these concerns to the superintendent. Board members protect superintendents from capricious expectations.

ARGUMENTS CON

1 A seat on the school board is sometimes an entry-level political office. Board members who are striving for more prestigious offices use the board seat to attract the attention of the media and the public, thereby bringing undue stress to the superintendent and the school district.

2 Election is inefficient. For example, many school board members are elected to three-year terms. It takes them at least two years to learn boardsmanship. Then they begin running for re-election.

3 Single-issue candidates may be elected to the board. Their narrow focus prevails, regardless of the needs of the community or the schools.

4 Appointed board members are selected on the basis of their unique skills at policy development. Those making appointments ensure that a board is balanced so that all interests are represented.

5 Some of the most competent school superintendents lose their positions because they are unable or unwilling to appease elected board members. This is especially apparent in small towns where local citizens often want to run the schools. They are more concerned about administrative details than large policy issues.

TABLE 11 ▪ 3   Current Problems Facing Schools: Boards versus Public

AS SEEN BY THE SCHOOL BOARD	TOTALS* Percent	AS SEEN BY THE PUBLIC	TOTALS Percent
Lack of financial support	45	Drug abuse	34
State mandates	36	Lack of discipline	19
Facilities	33	Lack of proper financial support	13
Curriculum development	27	Poor curriculum/poor standards	8
Drug abuse	21	Large schools/overcrowding	8
Management/leadership	21	Difficulty getting good teachers	7
Collective bargaining	20	Parents' lack of interest	6
Declining enrollment	17	Drinking/alcoholism	4
Parents' lack of interest	15	Low teacher pay	4
Personnel relations	11	Integration/busing	4
Large schools/overcrowding	10	Teachers' lack of interest	4
Finding good teachers	6	Crime/vandalism	4
Pupils' lack of interest/truancy	6	Pupils' lack of interest/truancy	3
Disrespect for other students/ teachers	4	Disrespect for teachers/other students	3
Integration/busing	3	Moral standards	3
Poor curriculum/poor standards	3	Facilities	1
Crime/vandalism	1	Mismanagement of funds/ programs	1

SOURCE: "Current Priorities: Boards vs. Public," *American School Board Journal,* 177 (1990), p. 35. Copyright 1990 the National School Board Association. Used by permission.

*Respondents to the school board survey were asked to indicate their top three concerns from those listed. The totals represent the percentage of respondents who checked that concern as one of their top three. Respondents to the public poll, on the other hand, were asked to name the biggest problems facing their public schools; they were *not* given answers from which to choose. In both surveys, percentages total more than 100 because of multiple responses.

up 36 percent, but family income and educational levels are more diversified.[25]

School Board–Public Problems

The top five problems of school board members focus on lack of financial support, state mandates, facilities, curriculum development, and drug abuse (Table 11-3). Financial concerns has been the number-one problem between 1982 and 1989.[26] On the other hand, the public has ranked finances consistently lower: number three or four since 1982.[27] The second and fourth concerns of school board members reflect state and local pressures to improve what goes on in schools and classrooms. The third-ranked problem reflects the growing age of school buildings and the related problem of infrastructure costs. Drug abuse has consistently moved up the boards' ranking order.

By comparison, the public has considered drug abuse as the biggest worry or school problem between 1986 and 1989. In the eyes of the public, drug abuse and lack of discipline have consistently ranked as the two most important

[25]Allan C. Ornstein, "Composition of Boards of Education of Public School Systems Enrolling 50,000 or More Students," *Urban Education,* 16 (1981), pp. 232–234.
[26]"Money and Other Worries," *American School Board Journal,* 177 (1990), pp. 34–35.

[27]The annual Gallup poll of the public's attitude toward the public schools is published in the September and/ or October issues of *Phi Delta Kappan.*

problems throughout the 1980s.[28] These two rankings are related to a perceived breakdown of student behavior, including moral standards, pupils' lack of interest and truancy, drinking and alcoholism, crime and vandalism, disrespect for teachers, and fighting. As Table 11-3 shows, school board members do not have such strong feelings about the breakdown of school discipline, moral standards, or the law. Interestingly, both school boards and the public are not too concerned about school integration or busing, which was one of the most controversial issues about ten years ago.

School Board Meetings

There are three general types of board meeting: regular, special, and executive. The first two are usually open meetings, and the public is invited. The third type is usually closed to the public and deals with managerial issues or serious problems. Open or **public board meetings** obviously enhance school–community relations and allow parents to understand the problems of education as well as air their concerns; however, they can also degenerate into gripe sessions or conflict if someone in charge is not skilled in guiding large-group discussions and building consensus.[29] If a skilled leader is not available, it is best to limit the number of public meetings.

Holding closed or **executive board meetings** to reach major policy decisions is generally discouraged, but school boards occasionally use this tactic if conflict and tension arise.[30] Many school districts, however, have mandated open meetings except under certain specified and rather limited conditions. However, the executive meeting, if properly organized, produces the best results in terms of time management and outcomes.

School board meetings are actually control systems that bring school resources into line with school policies. One way to ensure that organizational work is directed toward the appropriate mission statements or goals is to make school board meetings more focused in terms of resources and policies.

School board meetings, just as with meetings involving school administrators, are rarely one-time events; they are usually part of an ongoing cycle. Writes one researcher, "People prepare for them, attend them, then follow up on them. Most often, any one meeting is really part of a meeting system, a series of meetings called to address a specific problem or issue."[31] What this suggests is that events outside the meeting room affect what goes on in the meeting room.

Managers in private industry contend they spend 25 to 60 percent of their time in meeting rooms, and much of that time is wasted. "Meetings are where you keep the minutes and throw away the hours,"[32] Thousands of school administrators would most likely nod in agreement—school meetings are places where participants learn to doodle, look attentive, nod politely, and pinch themselves to keep awake. Most people agree that school meetings, including board meetings and staff meetings, should be trimmed, and that shorter meetings (no more than one to one and one-half hours) are more productive than longer meetings.[33] (See Administrative Advice 11-2.) Board meetings (or meetings in general) with too many people—or people from too many bureaucratic layers—with many different interests or agendas will cause bogdown. However, data suggest that strong superintendents conduct longer meetings (two to

[28]Ibid.

[29]Michael Boone, "Make Sure Your New Superintendent Measures Up to Constituent Expectations," *American School Board Journal*, 176 (1989), pp. 31–32.

[30]*School Boards Strengthening Grass Roots Leadership* (Washington, D.C.: Institute for Educational Leadership, 1987); Jay Scribner and David O'Shea, "Political Developments in the Urban School Districts," in C. W. Gordon (ed.), *Uses of the Sociology of Education*, Seventy-Third Yearbook of the National Society for the Study of Education, Part II (Chicago: University of Chicago Press, 1974), pp. 380–408.

[31]Lynn Oppenheim, "Why Meetings Sometimes Fail," *Executive Educator*, 11 (1989), pp. 21–22.

[32]Ibid, p. 21.

[33]Raj K. Chopra, "How We Trimmed Meeting Time," *Executive Educator*, 11 (1989), p. 23; and "Make Your Meetings Matter," *Executive Educator*, 11 (1989), p. 22.

ADMINISTRATIVE ADVICE 11-2

MAKING MEETINGS MORE MEANINGFUL

Most administrators spend too much time at meetings and are unable to devote sufficient time to important policy and leadership issues. The need is to trim meeting time while making the most of meetings. Here are some guidelines, from one school superintendent, to make meetings more productive.

- *Purpose.* The first question to ask is whether the meeting is needed or can the task be accomplished without a meeting—say, in a memo or phone call.
- *Punctuality.* The chairperson should be on time to set an example and begin promptly. Others will get the message.
- *Focus.* The purpose of the meeting should be stated in advance in the form of a written handout or stated earlier at a previous meeting.
- *Participants.* Smaller is better. How small? Groups of more than ten are likely to become nonproductive; meetings with five to seven participants are likely to be most productive.
- *Subgroups.* Subgroups or task-force groups should be organized when the original group exceeds ten members. Subgroups should be or-

ganized according to the talents and interests of the people involved and how well they work together.
- *Follow-Up.* Meetings are not only endings but also are beginnings. Minutes should be kept and published to ensure follow-up, monitor progress, and used as a reference.
- *Teamwork.* Although it is best to seek consensus, it cannot always be achieved, and it should not be sought to avoid a decision or to avoid accountability. Ideally, trust, free exchange of ideas through analysis of the issues, and freedom to disagree are important characteristics of a productive meeting.

Source: Adapted from Raj K. Chopra, "Make Your Meetings Matter," *Executive Educator,* 11 (1989), p. 23.

---

three hours per session), more meetings, and more board functions than do weak superintendents.[34] In school districts controlled by the board, members make quick decisions and board meetings average less than one hour, with the superintendent simply carrying out board mandates.

School Board Responsibilities

The administration and management of schools is big business, and school board members must

have or acquire knowledge of good business practices. Overall, school boards have fiscal responsibility of approximately $200 billion each year and employ nearly 4 million individuals; this makes them the largest nationwide employer.[35] Board members must also be fair and mindful of the law when dealing with students, teachers, administrators, parents, and other community residents. Board members are public servants and represent the community and are expected to govern the school system without encroaching on the authority of the super-

---

[34]Vincent T. Beni, Bruce S. Cooper, and Rodney Muth, "Boards and Superintendents: Balance the Power," *American School Board Journal,* 175 (1988), pp. 24–25.

[35]*Estimates of School Statistics 1988–89* (Washington, D.C.: National Education Association, 1989), Table 2, p. 7; "The School Board Story in Numbers," *American School Board Journal,* 174 (1987), p. viii.

intendent. Members, in theory, have no authority except during a board meeting and while acting as a collective group or board.[36] Board members must be politically prudent because someone will eventually ask for a favor—a friend, a friend of a friend, or a special-interest group—and this pressure should be resisted.

According to a recent survey of sixty-six Illinois school superintendents, school boards have become more political and divisive in recent years; board members are less willing to compromise on major issues, and there is a greater tendency among candidates to represent coalitions or special-interest groups when running for election. In short, new board members seem more interested in the views of their electors than in the views of other board members or professional educators.[37]

In districts where the school board is elected, board members are subject to the same laws as other elective officials; in many states, each member must file a statement of ethics. In the final analysis, the quality of the local schools is an important factor in determining the community's reputation, the value of property, and the willingness of businesses to locate in the vicinity. Board members represent more than 26 percent of the adult population who have school-age children; they represent the public at large; and they must be willing to work with businesses, government, and community organizations to promote the community's schools and the students' welfare.[38]

The powers and responsibilities of school boards may be classified into the following categories:

1. *Policy.* School boards set the general rules about what will be done in the schools, who will do it, and how it will be done.
2. *Staffing.* Technically, the board is responsible for hiring all employees of the school district. In practice, however, school boards usually confine themselves to recruitment and selection of the school superintendent (the district's chief executive office) and high-ranking members of the central office staff. Decisions on the hiring and retention of principals and teachers are usually made at lower levels of the hierarchy, after review by professional peers.
3. *Employee Relations.* School board members are responsible for all aspects of employee relations, including collective bargaining with teachers' unions. Large school districts rely on consultants or attorneys to negotiate with teachers; small school districts may use the superintendent or a school board committee to negotiate.
4. *Fiscal Matters.* The board must keep the school district solvent, effect savings when possible, and get the most out of every tax dollar. The school district usually has a larger budget than does any other local public agency; the school superintendent normally makes more money than any other local official, including the mayor, fire chief, and police chief.
5. *Students.* The board addresses questions of student rights and responsibilities, extracurricular activities, attendance, and requirements for promotion and graduation.
6. *Curriculum.* The school board is in charge of developing curriculum—especially as it relates to state law and guidelines—and approving textbooks.
7. *Community Relations.* The school board must be responsive to parents and other members of the community.
8. *Intergovernment Requirements.* Federal and state agencies establish a variety of requirements for local schools, and the school board is responsible for seeing that these mandates are carried out.[39]

[36]Robert S. Ross, "The Local School Board," *American School Board Journal,* 174 (1987), pp. 5–10.

[37]David Elsner, "School Boards More Political," *Chicago Tribune,* 22 January 1990, Section 2, p. 4.

[38]Weil, "The Significance of Being a School Board Member," p. 2.

[39]Eva K. Bascal, "On Being a Board Member," *American School Board Journal,* 174 (1987), pp. 11–16; Ross, "The Local School Board."

In general, the most efficient school boards pull together as a team and get along with the superintendent. They are characterized by effectively using the strengths of each other, having confidence in each other's abilities, giving one another honest feedback about each other's performance in board matters, and generally supporting one another, especially when the "chips are down."[40] Contrary to popular opinion, board members perceive board colleagues who ask many questions as naive or stupid—or even as troublemakers. Open board meetings tend to discourage give-and-take and honest communication; few board members in these sessions ask challenging questions, test ideas, or candidly discuss the issues. In a public meeting, they rarely function as an effective team.

THE SCHOOL SUPERINTENDENT

One of the board's most important responsibilities is to appoint a competent superintendent of schools. The superintendent is the executive officer of the school system, whereas the board is the legislative policy-making body. Because the school board consists of laypeople who are not experts in school affairs, it is their responsibility to see that the work of the school is properly performed by professional personnel. The board of education often delegates many of its own legal powers to the superintendent and her staff, although the superintendent's policies are subject to board approval.

The Superintendent's Job

One of the major functions of the school superintendent is to gather and present data so that school board members can make intelligent policy decisions. Increasing board reliance on the superintendent and staff is evident as school districts grow in size. The superintendent advises the school board and keeps members abreast of problems; generally, the school board will refuse to enact legislation or make policy without the recommendation of the school superintendent. However, it is common knowledge that when there is continued disagreement or a major conflict over policy between the school board and the superintendent, the latter is usually replaced. According to recent survey data, the average tenure of superintendents is approximately six years.[41] Other nationwide data suggest the average tenure for a superintendent is less, about four years; according to school board members, the ideal superintendent's contract should last two to three years (and then be open for renewal). Although it comes as no surprise that the majority of superintendents move around every few years seeking "greener pastures," it is a surprise to learn in a recent (1990) survey that 24 percent of superintendents in the largest 100 school districts were freshmen superintendents.[42]

Although a wealth of data exists on what makes a school principal effective, there is little information on what makes a superintendent effective and to what extent, if any, he contributes to teacher effectiveness or student performance. This dearth of information is probably related to the fact that the superintendent is considered a manager of the entire district, not a direct leader of curriculum, instruction, teaching, or learning.

The superintendent's powers are broad and her duties are many and varied. Besides being an adviser to the board of education, she is usually responsible for certain functions. They include the following:

1. Serves as supervisor and organizer of professional and nonteaching personnel (e.g., janitors and engineers).

---

[40]William J. Banach, "These Eleven Traits Are the Hallmarks of Winning School Board Teams," *American School Board Journal*, 176 (1989), pp. 23–24.

[41]"Highlights of Administrators' Survey," *Education Week*, 20 January 1988, p. 23.
[42]Allan C. Ornstein, "School Superintendents and School Board Members: Who They Are" (unpublished 1991); "School Board Survey: Happily Ever After."

2. Makes recommendations regarding the employment, promotion, and dismissal of personnel.
3. Ensures compliance with directives of higher authority.
4. Prepares the school budget for board review and administers the adopted budget.
5. Serves as leader of long-range planning.
6. Develops and evaluates curriculum and instructional program.
7. Determines internal organization of the school district.
8. Makes recommendations regarding school building needs and maintenance.[43]

In addition, the superintendent is responsible for the day-to-day operation of the schools within the district and serves as the major public spokesperson for the schools.

Superintendents are often under strong pressure from various segments of the community, and much of the superintendent's effectiveness will depend on his ability to deal with such pressure groups. In large, urban school districts, for example, demands may be made for better facilities for students with handicaps or learning disabilities, more bilingual programs, improved vocational education, and school desegregation. In middle-class suburbs, parents may be especially sensitive to student achievement scores, demanding upgraded academic programs if they feel the education is not as superior as their children deserve. Such students are often overprogrammed and overstressed, and a confident school leader is needed to balance the demands and expectations of the parents with the sociopsychological needs of the students. In small or rural districts where enrollments are declining, the superintendent may be pressured, on the one hand, to save money by closing schools and, on the other hand, to keep all schools open to preserve the pride and identity of the community.

Superintendents' Salary and Performance

According to a 1988 *Business Week* survey, the top executives in private industry (768 executives in 354 companies, or the top 2 at each company) earned an average of $1.13 million in salary and bonus; throw in long-term compensation, fringe benefits, and stock options exercised in 1988, and the average pay jumped to $2.03 million per year. Leading the list of top-paying executives was Mike Eisner, the chairman of Walt Disney, with $7.6 million in salary and $32.5 million in stock options. Lawrence Rawl, Exxon's chair, made $1.4 million. Lee Iacocca's salary of $2.1 million was supplemented with $1.6 million in stock options.[44]

The same year, the 173 superintendents in the largest school districts in the nation (25,000 or more students) averaged $90,110 with a range of $60,000 to $150,000,[45] with about an additional $10,000 to $25,000 in extra benefits (not counting sabbaticals and pensions).[46] In 1990, New York City's school superintendent Joe Fernandez had the dual distinction of running the largest school district (940,000 students) and earning the most among top school executives,

---

[43]Edgar L. Morphet, Roe L. Johns, and Theodore L. Reller, *Educational Organization and Administration*, 4th ed. (Englewood Cliffs, NJ: Prentice-Hall, 1982); Allan C. Ornstein, *Education and Social Inquiry* (Itasca, IL: Peacock, 1978); and Paula Silva, *Educational Administration: Theoretical Perspectives on Practice and Research* (New York: Harper & Row, 1987).

[44]"How Much Top Execs Made in '88," *USA Today*, 21 April 1989, p. 2B.
[45]Telephone conversation with Gary Marx, associate executive director, American Association of School Administrators, April 25, 1989. By 1989–90, the average superintendent's salary was $95,735 in districts enrolling 25,000 or more students; it was only $75,425 nationwide. See footnote 47.
[46]Allan C. Ornstein, "How Your Perks Stack Up," *Executive Educator*, 12 (1990), p. 23; personal conversation with Howard Smucker, former superintendent of Lisle (Illinois) School District, professor of educational administration, Loyola University of Chicago, April 26, 1989.

that is $195,000 (some $50,000 more than the New York mayor).[47] In 1988 the top 768 executives' pay increased 17 percent over the previous year; for the 1988 to 1989 school year, the top 173 superintendents' pay increase was 4.4 percent.[48]

Comparing level of responsibility, size of budget, number of personnel, and separate (school) sites that a superintendent oversees in school districts of 25,000 or more students and if she worked in private industry, her pay would be in excess of $350,000 to $400,000. For the 16 largest school districts comprising 100,000 or more students, the salary would be in the range of $500,000 to $750,000.

Corporate boards keep an eye on other firms when deciding on how much to pay top administrators, to avoid being raided. When directors give their chief executives a raise, they tend to lift salaries above the industry average and thus create a new high or yardstick for other companies to match or exceed. When superintendents go before the school board for a raise, they have to contend with board members who frequently earn less money and are under pressure to keep down expenses and resulting property taxes. Because most school superintendents earn more than their local government counterparts—fire chiefs, police chiefs, and mayors—it is difficult to argue before the community or taxpayers' group that higher salaries are warranted. When student performance exceeds projections, the argument can be made that it was the input, not the treatment that made the difference. When student outcomes decline, criticism is often leveled at the teachers and administrators. Hence, it is a no-win situation for leaders in charge of schools.

It must be noted that schools are noncompetitive and do not deal in bottom lines or profit; they are not-for-profit organizations, and the kind of people that are selected to run the schools fill a political need, not an economic need. Often the idea is to hire a "safe" person, someone who will get along with the school board president, or hire a person from a particular minority, ethnic, or religious background. Schools are what Milton Friedman calls a "tampered marketplace," not a "free marketplace." Finally, superintendents are political animals, not necessarily business leaders or people expected to assert positions. Superintendents are expected to report and follow policy. Given a tough-minded school board or a small community with an entrenched power structure, their expectations for leadership are further lessened; the idea is to get along with people, keep one's nose clean, and not embarrass important players on the board or in the community.

The Superintendent and School Board

Today's superintendents must not only work with his staff but must also have a good relationship with a demanding public that is more informed than ever about educational issues and a school board that is increasingly scrutinizing the superintendent's performance and results. Board members, parents, the community, and the professional staff hear a great deal about reform and have their own set of expectations (often high), political agendas (sometimes hidden), and ideas how students should be educated (often pushing a particular program or subject area that will benefit their children, sometimes at the expense of others.) Today's superintendent must deliver the goods, ("accountability" is one of the watchwords in education), withstand public scrutiny, and provide more services without increased funding.[49]

[47]Ornstein, "How Your Perks Stack Up." Los Angeles Superintendent Leonard Britton, head of the nation's second largest system earned $164,500. And in Chicago, the third largest school district, Superintendent Ted Kimbrough was paid $175,000.

[48]Telephone conversation with Gary Marx, April 25, 1989.

[49]Sidney A. Freund, "Superintendent: Here's How I Stay Friends with the Board President," *American School Board Journal,* 175 (1988), pp. 39–40; Allan C. Ornstein, "Superintendents: Gauge Your Performance and Productivity," *Executive Educator,* 12 (1990), pp. 22–25.

Although the public is better educated and has become more demanding in recent years, the superintendent's real sense of anxiety or concern should be with school board members who frequently do not understand how complex systems are managed and who, despite their dedication and hard work, often are politically motivated and sometimes divided themselves on many issues. Sometimes it is healthy to have a diverse school board (with members who have different views on life), but when the board fails to act together or sends mixed messages to the superintendent, it places great stress on the superintendent.

According to observers, when the school board and superintendent are out of sync, the superintendent often gets bogged down in trying to please the board or defending her decisions and is unable to lead. (See Administrative Advice 11-3.) Boards that are divided among themselves or are continuously challenging the superintendent invite the resignation of the superintendent and a succession of short-lived superintendents. It is the schools, staff, and students that often lose when board–superintendent power often tips the same way.[50]

For the most part, however, school board–superintendent relations are better than critics might think. Nationwide school boards (2166 respondents) are happy with their superintendents. Although there may be grumblings among board members, 53 percent are "very satisfied" with their school chiefs, and another 30 percent are "satisfied." Only 12 percent are "dissatisfied" or "very dissatisfied." Board members who were elected or appointed after the superintendent took the reins are more dissatisfied than those who were on the board when the superintendent was hired.[51]

Specifically, with respect to superintendent–school board interactions, the behavior of board members tends to cluster along a continuum from passive acquiescence to proactive-supportive to restive vigilance. *Passive acquiescent* board members tend to rely primarily on the information and interpretations provided by the superintendent (or the administrative staff) and refer to the superintendent for problem resolutions and professional judgment or recommendations. In contrast, *restive vigilant* board members personally visit schools and central offices on a regular basis, cultivate a wide range of information sources, actively participate in local and state education committees, build support for their own goals and objectives, and provide a check for and challenge the superintendent. *Proactive-supportive* board members exhibit similar behaviors to restive vigilants in their degree of active involvement in school affairs, but they are similar to passive acquiescents in that they usually support the superintendent rather than scrutinize or challenge the person's stance.[52]

Based on a sample of twenty-six board members in six Arizona school districts, the variables of board member gender, occupation, and political viewpoint correlate with the three identifiable patterns. Female board members and those who are not employed outside the home (retirees or homemakers) tend to be restive or proactive. Males, nonretirees, and nonhomemakers are more often passive. Proactive and passive board members ascribe to a traditional interpretation of parliamentary democracy and deference to the executive leadership role in government. Restive board members assert the notion of participatory democracy, lay control, and the rights of the people.[53] Under most conditions and with most superintendents, especially the traditional type, restive vigilant board members can be viewed as trouble, and superintendents can pos-

[50]Beni, Cooper, and Muth, "Boards and Superintendents: Balance the Power"; Michael W. Kirst et al., "School Boards: The Forgotten Players on the Education Team," *Phi Delta Kappan,* 69 (1987), pp. 53–59; and Donald E. Langlois, "Where Have All the Leaders Gone?" *Executive Educator,* 11 (1989), pp. 24–26.
[51]"Twelfth Annual Survey: Happily Ever After."

[52]Marilyn Tallerico, "The Dynamics of Superintendent–School Board Relations," *Urban Education,* 24 (1989), pp. 215–232.
[53]Ibid.

ADMINISTRATIVE ADVICE 11-3

■

FORGING A PRODUCTIVE PARTNERSHIP BETWEEN THE SUPERINTENDENT AND BOARD PRESIDENT

Most superintendents can use a little advice on how to keep on the good side of the board president. To be sure, the president can be the superintendent's best ally and the person to trust and turn to for information. The relationship must be nurtured, and the tips below are written by a superintendent and should help other superintendents gain support of the board president (or, for that matter, how other school managers can gain support with those to whom they report).

■ *Communicate Regularly.* The superintendent must be aware of issues and decisions that may result in controversy or a problem, so the board president can be alerted. She should meet regularly with the president.

■ *Plan the Agenda Together.* The superintendent should plan board meetings together with the president. The superintendent may advise at meetings, but they are run by the president.

■ *Conduct "Postgame" Analysis with the President.* Right after board meetings, or the next day, the superintendent and president should review what happened. How could things have been better handled?

■ *Let the President Run Board Meetings.* It's his meeting. The president, not the superintendent, should recognize citizens and board members.

■ *Let the President Handle Arguments or Difficult Board Members.* This is the president's, not the superintendent's job. The superintendent might discuss specific concerns along these lines in private.

■ *Praise the President Publicly.* People like to be recognized or "stroked." Because board members usually don't get paid, they can use some recognition for a job well done. This goes double for the president.

■ *Invite the President to Accompany You on National, State, and Local Events or Meetings of Significance.* Superintendents should let others see and appreciate the president's close support or similar purpose. (This suggestion can be risky and personalities are a factor to consider.)

■ *Call the President First in an Emergency.* No one likes to be surprised or hear something important secondhand. In absence of clear policy or in an emergency, the superintendent may have to take action. But the board president should be consulted, if possible, or as soon as possible.

■ *Let the President Know When You Are Out of the District for More Than One Day.* The board president should know when the superintendent will be out of the office and who is second in command or who to contact in an emergency.

■ *Recognize It Is the Board, Not Only the President, Whom You Serve.* The superintendent serves at the pleasure of the entire board. Although the board president is highly influential and can help ensure the superintendent's success, this person is only one vote. The best way to work with the entire board is to recognize and deal with all members equally.

Source: Adapted from Sidney A. Freund, "Superintendent: Here's How I Stay Friends with the Board President," *American School Board Journal*, 175 (1988), p. 39.

sibly "lock horns" with the board if the membership is predominantly restive.

Superintendents' Problems and Performance

Of the top reasons why superintendents lose their jobs, three can be classified into professional weaknesses:

1. *Lack of Rapport with the Board.* This is the most serious problem, usually related to refusal or failure of the administrator to accept criticism, work with board members, support board policy, or follow the written law, directions, or instructions.
2. *Lack of Staff Support or Respect.* The superintendent needs the backing of the professional staff, especially at the central office. Without support and respect, her days are numbered due to lack of cohesion and the chain of command breaking down.
3. *Poor Top-Down Communication.* Failure to clearly communicate and keep board members, community residents, and/or school personnel informed places the superintendent in a precarious position. When matters go astray or become controversial, critics often claim indignation, surprise, or lack of responsibility because they were not informed.[54]

Whereas these three problems can plague any superintendent, given the inappropriate ingredients, the second problem is more common among new superintendents from the outside who are hired in large school districts, which have an entrenched bureaucracy or centralized

staff from the "old guard." If the superintendent is continuously perceived as an "outsider" or bent on "reforming" or changing the system, rank-and-file administrators are likely to close in ranks against the new person. This was in part the reason for the dismissal or resignation of Calvin Gross and Harvey Scribner in New York City, Ruth Love in Chicago, Mark Shedd (now deceased) in Philadelphia, and Barbara Sizemore in Washington, D.C.

Major reasons why superintendents ultimately come under attack or resign can be classified into ten problem areas:

1. Too many board members who want to run the show, that is, too many people think they are "presidents"
2. Budget cuts, accompanied by a shrinking tax base
3. Increasing amounts of reports and paperwork to meet government or legal requirements
4. Dissension among school board members
5. Declining enrollments matched with increasing expenditures
6. Taxpayers' resistance to supporting education
7. Teacher strikes and militancy
8. Special-interest groups who persistently promote their own causes
9. Student crime and vandalism, as well as discipline problems
10. News media that is erroneous or controversial[55]

Although only two reasons (1 and 4) are directly linked to the school board, two others are related to community factors (2 and 6), which in turn have a ripple effect on board members who represent the community.

Although school boards have stated procedures for evaluating superintendents, too often the procedure is not technically valid, reliable, or useful, and it may result in turning the eval-

---

[54]David A. Fultz, "Eight Ways Superintendents Lose Their Jobs," *American School Board Journal,* 163 (1976), pp. 42, 51; Ornstein, "Superintendents: Gauge Your Performance and Productivity"; and Greta Shepherd, "Survival Strategies and the Superintendency." Paper presented at the annual meeting of the American Educational Research Association, San Francisco, April 1986.

[55]Ronald W. Rebore, *Educational Administration: A Management Approach,* (Englewood Cliffs, NJ: Prentice-Hall, 1985).

uation process into whatever board members decide to make of it. In theory, the superintendent's evaluation is not complicated; it should be based on precise *criteria* (agreed-on behaviors or competencies) and a method of *measurement* (such as a rating scale, observations, letters, or self-appraisal reports).[56]

Board members, working with or independent of the superintendent, can determine the priorities, behaviors, or responsibilities they wish to stress. Table 11-4 shows nine major areas of responsibility, with equal weight, originally adopted by the American Association of School Board Administrators (AASA) in 1980 and are the criteria that it still recommended in 1990. The steps in the evaluation procedure should be clear, too; for example, the Scarsdale, New York, school district abides by following policy to set the boundaries of the evaluation: using job descriptions, setting standards of expectations or achievement, defining effectiveness in terms of expectations or achievement, agreeing on a measuring instrument, conducting the evaluation, discussing the evaluation with the superintendent, and encouraging communication or follow-up conferences or reports.[57]

As Dean Speicher, president of AASA asserts, school superintendents must learn to act as CEOs; they must exhibit courage and take risks "on behalf of students, staff, and community." They must become "visionaries, strategists, and diplomats" as they put their plans in place and organize the key players around their educational goals.[58]

Based on a review of fifty years of research (and including the classic studies of Chester Bernard, Philip Selznick, and James McGregor Burns), Larry Cuban concludes that the superintendent must do the following to accomplish desired results:

1. Imagine what the organization can become; define the mission; set the goals.
2. Motivate peoples' energies toward achieving the organizational goals.
3. Link the mission to organizational routines and behaviors.
4. Promote certain values that give the organization a distinctive character.[59]

Cuban argues that leadership at one level in the school district influences what occurs at the next level below, a top-down model that most superintendents adopt. The superintendent's leadership style filters down from the central office to the school principal, affecting the behavior of lower-ranking administrators.[60] With this top-down model, if the superintendent is business- or task-oriented, then low-ranking administrators pick up these cues and modify their behavior accordingly. But if the superintendent is humanistic or people-oriented, then administrators will modify their behavior in the other direction. Indeed, most school administrators have sufficient common sense not to irritate people on top.

In this connection, John Gardner, the former secretary of Health, Education and Welfare and currently director of Common Cause (a national not-for-profit citizen coalition) has identified six special characteristics of leaders that are appropriate for school superintendents:

1. *Think Long Term.* Think beyond the day's crisis, beyond the next meeting or report. This includes commitment to superior service or a product, encouraging experimentation, willingness to support failure (and the ability to bounce back from failure rather than being stymied by failure).

[56]Allan C. Ornstein, "Research on Teaching: Issues and Trends," *Journal of Teacher Education,* 36 (1985), pp. 24–31; Ornstein, "Research on Evaluation: Measurements and Methods," *Education and Urban Society,* 18 (1986), pp. 176–181.
[57]Frank F. Calzi and Robert W. Heller, "Make Evaluation the Key to Your Superintendent's Success," *American School Board Journal,* 176 (1989), pp. 33–34.
[58]Dean Speicher, "Courage, Risks Essential to Leadership," *School Administrator,* 46 (1989), p. 6.

[59]Larry Cuban, *The Managerial Imperative and the Practice of Leadership in Schools* (Albany: State University of New York Press, 1988).
[60]Ibid.

TABLE 11 ▪ 4   Evaluating the School Superintendent: Responsibility Criteria

Board Relations

1. Preparation of reports and materials for the board
2. Presentation of reports to board
3. Recommendations to the board
4. Responding to requests from the board
5. Keeping the board informed about operations in district
6. Implementation of board actions
7. Other (specify)

Community–Public Relations

1. Contacts with media
2. Interpreting district problems and concerns to community and public
3. Interpreting the educational program to the community
4. Responding to concerns of community
5. Periodic communications (publications, reports, newsletters, etc.) to community
6. Other (specify)

Staff–Personnel Management

1. Employment of personnel
2. Utilization of employed personnel
3. Administration of personnel policies and procedures
4. Administration of salary and benefits program
5. Direction of employee relations program
6. Administration of personnel evaluation programs
7. Other (specify)

Business and Fiscal Management

1. Determination of educational needs of district
2. Forecasting financial requirements
3. Budget preparation
4. Management of budget allocations
5. Cost accounting and cost effectiveness management
6. Procurement of equipment, materials, supplies, etc.
7. Financial reporting
8. Other (specify)

Facilities Management

1. Planning and providing physical facilities
2. Management of maintenance of buildings and grounds

2. *Awareness of the Outside.* Grasp the relationship of the organization with conditions external to the organization. This means setting a course or direction, while being aware of trends impacting on the organization.
3. *Managerial Excellence.* Set priorities and organize around priorities. This also includes keeping the system functioning, making decisions, setting agendas (rather than following the crowd), and focusing on opportunity (as opposed only to problems).
4. *Emphasis on Intangibles.* Be conscious of vision, values, and motivation and understand intuitively the factors involved in the leader–constituent interaction. An essential factor is

---

TABLE 11 ▪ 4   Continued

Facilities Management (continued)

3. Providing for the security and safety of personnel and property
4. Planning for and managing modifications, renovations, expansions, and discontinuation of facilities
5. Directing the utilization of facilities
6. Other (specify)

Curriculum and Instructional Management

1. Keeping current with trends and developments in curriculum and instruction
2. Initiating new programs, modifying existing ones, and discontinuing others
3. Direction of supervision of instruction
4. Monitoring effectiveness of instructional programs
5. Assessment of effectiveness of instructional programs
6. Planning and direction of in-service and staff development
7. Management of state and federal programs and projects
8. Other (specify)

Management of Student Services

1. Providing comprehensive student personnel services
2. Management of enrollment and attendance policies and procedures
3. Management of student behavior and discipline
4. Providing for health and safety of students
5. Liaison with community agencies concerned with student services
6. Other (specify)

Comprehensive Planning

1. Developing and implementing short- and long-range planning
2. Developing management systems (example: MBO)
3. Training administrators and supervisors in planning
4. Accountability procedures
5. Evaluation of planning results
6. Other (specify)

Professional and Personal Development

1. Keeping self current professionally
2. Representing district at local, state, and national meetings of interest to education
3. Contributions to profession by writing and speaking
4. Participation in local, state, and national professional organizations
5. Other (specify)

SOURCE: Adapted from *Evaluating the Superintendent* © 1980, pp. 42–44. Used by permission of American Association of School Administrators, Arlington, VA.

the capacity to inspire others, to organize members of the organization into a team, and to make them feel as winners (and not losers).

5. *Political and Communication Skills.* Develop these skills in order to cope with conflicting requirements of multiple constituencies. This means the ability to deal with employ-ees as well as outside representatives from labor, government, business, and the press (and the school board, community, and parents).

6. *Think in Terms of Renewal.* Revise or change structures and/or processes of the organization. This means aiming high (or going beyond what is safe or easy), and it means

establishing a management or professional team that can run the organization (to hire the best or strongest) because the leader cannot cover all bases, at least not in a complex organization.[61]

The American Association of School Administrators (AASA) and National Association of Secondary School Principals (NASSP) fully endorse these six leadership characteristics and point out how practicing school administrators can implement these characteristics as part of the school environment. They also emphasize that many of the recent education reports on excellence emphasize different notions of leadership that parallel Gardner's six characteristics; moreover, these reports tend to associate strong leadership with effective school districts and schools.[62]

Superintendents' Skill Areas

The AASA, working in conjunction with the University of Texas, conducted a nationwide survey of superintendents who ranked fifty-two skills in the order of their importance for effective performance of superintendents. The ten most important skill areas were (1) leadership, (2) personnel management, (3) fiscal responsibility, (4) school–community relations, (5) teacher evaluation, (6) cost-effective budgeting, (7) motivational techniques, (8) conflict mediation, (9) testing and evaluation of student performance, and (10) curriculum development and instructional planning.[63] These top-ten skill

areas are now considered generic skills for effective superintendents.[64]

John Murphy and colleagues have published a series of research studies associating twelve school districts (ranging in size from 2000 to 19,350 students and five to twenty-nine schools) whose student achievement scores exceeded expectations, as well as the scores of other districts, after controlling for the students' socioeconomic status over a three-year period. Nine superintendents' functions or areas of responsibility were defined and associated with these high-performing school districts:

1. *Selection.* Ten out of twelve districts had administrative internship programs to socialize potential principals. When hiring principals, five superintendents stressed technical skills in curriculum, instruction, and teaching, and four stressed human relation skills and the ability to motivate people.
2. *Supervision.* In ten out of twelve districts, the superintendent was personally responsible for the supervision and evaluation of principals. In the two largest remaining districts, one of the assistant superintendents assumed the responsibility. Superintendents averaged 21 eight-hour days per year at school sites, between 8 to 10 percent of their total work year.
3. *Evaluation.* Principals in all districts were evaluated annually; procedures were clearly defined; the criteria and method of evaluation were known in advance. All principals received formal evaluations that were reviewed in a conference setting.
4. *Staff Development.* Participation in administrative staff development was mandatory in all twelve districts, although it was sometimes voluntary for teachers in many of the same districts. The emphasis was on improving curriculum, instruction, teaching, and

[61]John Gardner, "Leaders and Managers," *NASSP Bulletin,* 72 (1988), p. 143; Gardner, "Leadership: Attributes and Context," *NASSP Bulletin,* 73 (1989), p. 58.
[62]*Challenge for School Leaders,* (Arlington, VA: American Association of School Administrators, 1988).
[63]Telephone conversation with Noland Estes, professor of educational administration, University of Texas—Austin (former superintendent of Dallas school district), May 25, 1989.

[64]Telephone conversation with Gary Marx, Associate Executive Director, American Association of School Administrators, May 25, 1989.

teacher evaluation. All superintendents modeled a strong instructional leadership role for the principals.

5. *Rewards and Sanctions.* None of the twelve districts had a merit-pay program for principals, and salaries were not tied to evaluation results. Only the largest district provided differential salaries based on student enrollments. A number of superintendents reported that they frequently promoted internally when filling a central office position, but the only major formal reward was continued employment.

6. *Goals.* All superintendents reported the district had written goals; eight indicated they had specific objectives at the school level. All twelve superintendents used district goals as influencing budget allocations, and all districts had a comprehensive testing program that coincided with the goals or objectives of the school program.

7. *Resource Allocation.* Resource allocations in all twelve districts were determined by the central office and used to control and constrain school activities and spending. The schools received an extra-small allotment per student; $20 average at the elementary level and $50 average at the high school level. These funds could be used at the principals' discretion and could be transferred among budget items.

8. *Monitoring.* Superintendents relied strongly on the supervision and evaluation of the principals' behaviors. Frequent site visits and regular reviews of progress on school goals were the major monitoring activities used by the superintendents. Test scores were used to monitor school goals or objectives. Principals averaged 3.3 district meetings a month with the superintendent; superintendents spent about two-thirds of the time at these meetings discussing technical issues; the remaining time was devoted to communicating expectations and discussing immediate problems.

9. *Technical Specifications.* All superintendents

attempted to influence technical activities related to curriculum, instruction, and evaluation. Nine of the twelve districts had a preferred method of teaching or instruction, which they expected principals to emphasize in their schools. Superintendents reported a variety of control techniques to ensure the preferred teaching or instructional model was used in the schools, including regular classroom visits by district and site-level administrators, district office reviews of teachers and principals, and staff-development programs that focused on the approved model.[65]

What emerges in the research is a superintendent who establishes the direction and tone of the school system. He has a philosophy or mission, even a preferred teaching or instructional model, which is embedded at the district and school level. The superintendent is a no-nonsense person who controls, coordinates, and communicates the operation to the district and school-level staff. He monitors, reviews, and holds rank-and-file administrators accountable according to prescribed goals and/or procedures. The person is "hip-deep" in school district and school activities—very much aware of what is going on within the system. Emphasis is on school matters dealing with curriculum, instruction, teaching, learning, and evaluation.[66]

Here the reader might raise the question of whether a superintendent in a larger school district, 25,000 or more students, could spend so much time on these technical matters and not

---

[65]Joseph Murphy and Philip Hallinger, "Characteristics of Instructionally Effective School Districts," *Journal of Educational Research,* 81 (1988), pp. 175–180; Murphy et al., "The Administrative Control of Principals in Effective School Districts," *Journal of Educational Administration,* 25 (1987), pp. 161–192.

[66]Joseph Murphy and Philip Hallinger, "The Superintendent as Instructional Leader: Findings from Effective School Districts," *Journal of Educational Administration,* 24 (1986), pp. 213–236; Murphy and Hallinger, "Characteristics of Instructionally Effective School Districts."

have to delegate them to lower-ranking administrators and leave more discretion to the principal in deciding these matters. The reader might also conclude that the site visits and monitoring functions of the superintendent would be more limited in a larger school district.

Indeed, this type of superintendent tends to coincide more with our earlier definition of a manager, and not a leader. It is similar to a military model or task master in which George Patton and Vince Lombardi would feel comfortable. The superintendent seems much more concerned with controlling and coordinating activities, doing things her way—end of discussion— or what James Thompson would refer to as the "technical" aspects of running an organization.[67] (For Thompson, the more the organization maneuvers, modifies, or compromises its behavior, the more disruptive and costly it is, a highly close-ended view of organizations.)

Leadership, according to our earlier definition, is still evidenced by the superintendents in the study; they possess vision and values and are able to establish direction and meaning for members of the district and schools. But the leadership style that emerges is not overwhelmingly humanistic or people-oriented and provides minimal professional autonomy at the school level. The maverick school principal would have trouble lasting in such a school system.

THE CENTRAL STAFF

To fulfill his responsibilities, the superintendent is assisted by a **central office staff**. In large districts of 25,000 or more students, there may be many levels in the staff hierarchy: a deputy superintendent, associate superintendents, assistant superintendents, directors, department heads, and a number of coordinators and supervisors, each with supporting staff members. The picture is further complicated when a large

school district decentralizes its operation into several areas or subdistricts, there may be a "field" superintendent, with her own staff (as well as other administrators), in each area who reports to an associate superintendent in the central office.[68] Although the idea of decentralization is to reform and streamline the system, what often happens is that the school district gets a new bureaucratic layer.

Most large school districts are highly centralized, not decentralized. Central staff matrices are often built on top of other matrices, each with its own functions that are jealously guarded. (See Administrative Advice 11-4.) Decisions, which should take days or weeks, often take months or even years, as each department conducts its own review and adds its own recommendations to be considered by the next level. This phenomenon is not only typical of large school districts but also of large corporations who have had to learn some tough lessons about inefficiency and have recently trimmed and streamlined top layers to save money.[69] In an era of retrenchment, school administrators may have to learn the same lesson.

Large Districts: Increased Centralized Offices

Large, urban districts have tended to expand their centralized staff and activities over recent years in order to administer court-ordered desegregation and state and federal guidelines, programs, and funds and to cope with union-style teacher associations. All these trends, in one recent study, lead to elaborate bureaucratic efforts, in which central office personnel are hired

---

[67]James D. Thompson, *Organizations in Action* (New York: McGraw-Hill, 1967).

[68]Allan C. Ornstein, "Administrative Decentralization and Community Policy," *Urban Review*, 15 (1983), pp. 3–10; Joseph A. Raelin, "Control vs. Autonomy in School Management," *Principal*, 68 (1989), pp. 28–31.
[69]Thomas Moore, "Goodbye, Corporate Staff," *Fortune*, 21 December 1987, pp. 65, 68, 76; Allan C. Ornstein, "School Finance Trends for the Year 2000," *Educational Horizons*, 69 (1990) in print.

ADMINISTRATIVE ADVICE 11-4

■

CONSIDERING A PROMOTION TO THE CENTRAL OFFICE?

Many successful principals are lured into central office positions and view the move as a promotion in terms of status and salary. Before considering the move, especially if one is successful and happy as principal, read between the lines in the job description, visit the central office, and speak to trusted central office colleagues. Some important questions to consider are

- What does the word *coordinate* actually mean?
- Does the word *supervise* ever appear in the job description? What are the ramifications?
- What is the superintendent's perception of these descriptive terms?
- Will I have line authority for decision making or will I be only a facilitator?
- Will I provide a genuine professional service to the educational process, or is the job best defined as a district "gofer"?
- What does the statement "other duties as as-

signed by the superintendent" really mean?
- What is the overall mission or objective of the position? Does it have ongoing tasks and responsibilities included, or are many of them short-term or terminal tasks?
- Are there other benefits beyond those enjoyed by the principalship in the new job?

Source: Adapted from Robert Blaine, "From Principal to Central Office Administrator," *NASSP Bulletin,* 72 (1988), p. 101. Used by permission.

---

to oversee these efforts.[70] In addition, when there is a changing of the "guard" at the top level in large school districts, new managers are sometimes brought in from the outside and/or others are promoted from within. The "old guard" or outgroup often are career administrators with tenure. They are not replaced but reassigned; thus, the central staff continues to grow. Similarly, school principals who are displaced because of community politics or pressures often find refuge at the central office in a new quasi-administrative–clerical position, and their seniority and tenure are protected.[71]

Economics or efficiency is not always the key issue in large, urban districts; rather, school politics and ethnic considerations often affect who gets hired or fired. To support the bloated bureaucracy, school districts sometimes waste money and hire consulting firms to claim that the bureaucracy is needed and that administrator–teacher or administrator–student ratios are within tolerant ranges, by selecting and comparing school districts elsewhere that are just as top heavy or more so at the central level.[72] Only when the money runs out, enrollments are drastically down, and the community is looking to put a lid on spending will school board officials look to topple school administrators or take other

---

[70]Frymier, "Bureaucracy and the Neutering of Teachers."

[71]Priscilla Ahlgren," An Overbundance of Decision Makers?" *Milwaukee Journal,* 30 July 1990, pp. 1, 5; Fritz Hess, "Who'll Replace Retiring School Leaders," *American School Board Journal,* 175 (1988), pp. 43–48.

[72]Leo Gorenstein, "Chicago Board Pays Firm $300,000 for Study That Claims Bureaucracy Shouldn't Be Cut," *Substance,* 7 (1988), p. 5; Rogers and Chung, *110 Livingston Street Revisited.*

saving measures. However, most school districts will consolidate facilities, close down schools, and/or cut teaching positions before they trim down the central office staff.[73]

A centralized authority is characteristic of school districts that have a "tall" hierarchy and where there is increased specialization of professional tasks. In a centralized system, important decisions can be made quickly with few personnel involved. A decentralized authority suggests a "flat" hierarchy and/or several school sites that are considered part of a particular subdistrict or area. Upper management must be willing to work through subordinates in a decentralized system. However, subordinate power is only temporary, as long as the person has the title or until the job or task is completed. Many superintendents (as well as associates or assistants) are turf-conscious and are reluctant to part with their authority.

Small Districts: Understaffed Central Offices

Small school districts, and especially rural ones, face almost the opposite dilemma. They tend to be understaffed at the central level to the extent that superintendents, and whatever assistant superintendents or directors there are, often seem overworked and involved in many areas of responsibilities, which they lack time to adequately perform. As one superintendent (twenty years experience) of a small school district in Pennsylvania stated: "Owing to skimpy staffing in central offices, many school chiefs do the work of several administrators. Eventually, they are unable to distance themselves from day-to-day tasks [and lose sight of] the big picture." The problem of not enough time for small-school superintendents and their central staff "is real,"

and some of these administrators become "isolated and frustrated" by all their chores.[74] As another superintendent of a small school district in Illinois asserted: "Most of my job is hands on, nonmanagerial work. I am involved in almost everything—from helping to select textbooks, visiting teachers in classrooms, and working with parents. Superintendents in large school districts are far removed from the 'nuts and bolts' of [working with individual or small groups of teachers and parents], and serve mainly in an executive capacity."[75]

Some districts are so small (26 percent have fewer than 300 students and another 26 percent have between 300 and 1000 students)[76] that the superintendent is slotted only one or two assistants (sometimes on a part-time level). In still other cases, the superintendent is expected to manage two adjacent districts in an effort for both districts to save money.[77] Obviously, there is no central office to speak about in these small school districts, and the superintendent relies on the school principals (and teachers) to carry out many activities that are otherwise delegated to the central office personnel in large school districts.

It is common for school principals and teachers in large school districts (25,000 or more students) to be sometimes disfranchised from decisions involving specific areas such as curriculum, instruction, teaching, testing, and learning, and they become distant with the top administration.[78] In small school districts (1000 or fewer students), teachers and principals are often overburdened with these types of respon-

---

[73]Allan C. Ornstein, "Trimming the Fat, Stretching the Meat for School Budgets," *School Administrator*, 46 (1989), pp. 20–21; Ornstein, "School Budgets for the 1990s," *Educational Digest*, 55 (1990), pp. 15–16.

[74]Langlois, "Where Have All the Leaders Gone?" pp. 24–26.

[75]Telephone conversation with Ken Kaufman, superintendent of Bensenville, Illinois, School District, April 27, 1990.

[76]*Digest of Education Statistics, 1989* (Washington, D.C.: Government Printing Office, 1989), Table 80, p. 90.

[77]*Reorganization Feasibility Study*.

[78]Frymier, "Bureaucracy and the Neutering of Teachers"; Gene I Maeroff, "Teacher Empowerment: A Step Toward Professionalism," *NASSP Bulletin*, 72 (1988), pp. 52–60.

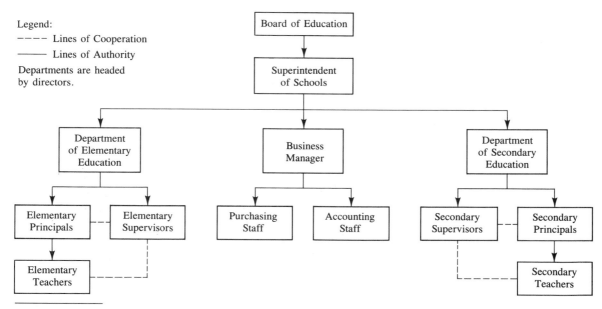

FIGURE 11-3 Typical Small-Sized School District (1,000 to 5,000 Students)
(SOURCE: Allan C. Ornstein and Daniel U. Levine, *Foundations of Education,* 4th ed., © 1989, p. 247. Used by permission of Houghton Mifflin Company, Boston.)

sibilities. In the first situation (large districts), teacher empowerment is the issue; in the second situation (small districts), administrative and teacher overload is the issue.

Organizational Hierarchy

In small school districts, the operation of the central office is less bureaucratic simply because there are fewer layers. Figure 11-3 illustrates a small (and "flat") district of more than 1000 and fewer than 5000 students, which represents 35 percent of all districts. Figure 11-4 shows a larger (and "taller") **organizational chart** of a medium-sized school district with 5000 to 25,000 students; this is representative of almost 10 percent of the school districts nationwide.[79] The organizational hierarchy of

larger school districts would be cumbersome, and those with 100,000 or more students (.01 percent of all school districts) would extend off the page. Most readers would have difficulty understanding these latter charts, not because they are unknowledgeable but because of the nature of bureaucratic and hierarchical complexity in big school districts.

Efficiency Ratios

Just because large school districts have more hierarchical layers at the central office and their organizational charts are taller and more difficult to understand, this does not necessarily mean they have better or worse manager–student ratios or are more or less efficient in running the schools within the district. For example, in a recent survey of fifty-one school districts with 50,000 or more students, the manager–student ratio at the central office averaged

---

[79]*Digest of Education Statistics, 1989,* Table 80, p. 90.

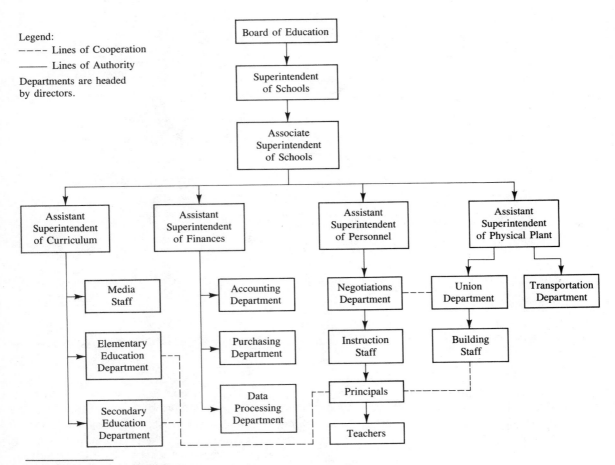

Legend:
---- Lines of Cooperation
—— Lines of Authority
Departments are headed
by directors.

FIGURE 11-4   Typical Medium-Sized School District (5000 to 25,000 Students)
(SOURCE: Allan C. Ornstein and Daniel U. Levine, *Foundations of Education*, 4th ed., © 1989, p. 246. Used by permission of Houghton Mifflin Company, Boston.)

1 manager per 569 students and the median was 578. The ranges were as high or efficient as 1 manager per 1650 students and as low or inefficient as 1 manager per 161 students.[80]

Table 11-5 shows the large school districts with the most efficient central offices, that is, the ones that seem most streamlined in terms of

manager–student ratios. Eleven school districts out of fifty-one have 1 manager per 750 students, or more, ratios. School districts enrolling 100,000 or more students ($n = 16$) average 1 manager per 579 students, whereas those with 50,000 to 99,999 students ($n = 35$) average 561. Thus, size is not a major factor. In fact, small districts (which have flatter organizational charts by virtue of their size) may have lower (or seemingly inefficient) manager–student ratios because 3 or 4 managers at the central office or

[80]Allan C. Ornstein, "Administrator/Student Ratios in Large School Districts," *Phi Delta Kappan*, 70 (1989), pp. 806–808.

TABLE 11 ▪ 5   Most Efficient Large School Districts, Based on Manager–Student Ratios, 1988

	STUDENT ENROLLMENT	STUDENT ADMINISTRATOR RATIO
Granite, Utah	74,278	1650.0:1
Clark County, Nevada	100,039	1539.0:1
Jordan, Utah	61,995	1512.0:1
Mesa, Arizona	59,304	1446.0:1
Indianapolis	50,437	1401.0:1
Los Angeles	592,273	1343.0:1
Nashville–Davidson County, Tennessee	66,325	908.5:1
Jefferson Parish, Louisiana	57,856	890.0:1
Tucson	56,475	818.5:1
Chicago	419,537	808.5:1
Dade County, Florida	254,235	756.5:1

SOURCE: Adapted from Allan C. Ornstein, "Administrative/Student Ratios in Large School Districts," *Phi Delta Kappan,* 70 (1989), p. 807. Used by permission.

even 1 extra manager in say, a district of 5000 or fewer students, will skew the ratios. Thus, the data do not apply in small districts.

In terms of maximum efficiency ratios, one researcher concludes that school districts should aim for 1 central office manager per 1000 to 1200 students. At the present, only six of the fifty-one surveyed school districts achieved this level of efficiency.[81] But as budget-minded school officials look at administrative jobs, there probably will be improved manager–student ratios and more school districts approaching these numbers. In school districts with declining student enrollments, this target will be difficult to achieve without blood spilled at the central administrative level. It will be up to moderate voices and rational groups to prevent this kind of surgery. In school districts with increasing student enrollments, this target is feasible, and what may be needed is to wait for administrative attrition to take its effect.[82]

Finally, we need to ask the following: To what extent do administrator–student ratios represent cost effectiveness and efficiency, and to what extent to do the ratios connote budget restraints and limited education spending? At what point do administrative numbers become costly, laborious, and a drag on decision making? What is the optimal number of school administrators in relation to the number of students? How many associate and assistant superintendents are necessary? How many directors and coordinators are needed? How big should be their support staffs? A reduction program may be directly related to economic factors, but who gets eliminated is a political consideration and can have legal implications.

THE PRINCIPAL AND THE SCHOOL

Usually, each school has a single administrative officer, a principal, who is responsible for the operation of the school. In small schools, the

[81]Ibid.
[82]Ibid.

person may teach part time as well. In large schools, there also may be one or more assistant or vice principals. The administrative hierarchy may also consist of a number of department chairpersons, a discipline officer (e.g., dean of boys, dean of girls), a director of guidance, and so on.

Although functions vary by locality and size, the principal is primarily responsible for administering all aspects of a school's operations. It is common practice for the principal to work with some type of community group for the improvement of the school; this group is often a PTA or an advisory-school community committee. Increased teacher militancy and the movement toward teacher empowerment have also led many principals to share decision-making responsibilities with teachers. This new role for teachers is seen by school authorities, including many principals, as essential if schools are to improve.

Conditions of Employment

On the average, grades K to 8 principals work 51 hours a week on school-related activities, while the number of hours a day ranges from 7 to 9 hours.[83] High school principals average about 53 hours a week, dividing 42 hours on the job and 11 hours in the evening.[84] In theory, the work of high school principals can be categorized into 149 specific tasks in which unscheduled meetings account for 27.5 percent of their time, scheduled meetings for 17.3 percent, desk work 16 percent, personal exchanges (and conversations) 14.1 percent, hallway–classroom tours 7.7 percent, and phone calls 5.8 percent.[85] In total, face-to-face contacts involve 59 percent of the principal's time on the job, and they tend to occur in their offices (usually in meetings);

thus, skill in verbal communication is an important part of the principal's job. Similar percentages are reported in two separate studies of elementary principals' task performance by time.[86]

Two researchers asked principals in the Lake Washington, Washington, school district to specify how they spend time and how they would prefer to spend time. Five general categories of work activities were developed: administrative operations, staff and curriculum development, community relationships, student services, and evaluation (Table 11-6). Detailed logs were kept for several weeks. Discrepancies exist between actual and ideal use of time, where both elementary and secondary level principals would prefer to spend more time on staff–curriculum development and staff evaluation. On the other hand, they would prefer to spend less time on administrative operations (that is, daily tasks, meetings, and paperwork) and student services (primarily discipline and record-keeping functions).

Leadership Role of the Principal

Although there is considerable agreement in the literature on the need to improve the leadership roles of the principal, there is considerable disagreement on what behaviors or practices principals should pursue—and to what extent should principals be a **general manager** or **curriculum–instructional leader**. According to one researcher, seven constraints make the roles and behaviors of the principal unclear:

1. Lack of precise definition of instructional leadership
2. Disparities in the level of competence expected from principals among university training programs

---

[83]James L. Doud, "The K–8 Principal in 1988," *Principal,* 68 (1989), pp. 6–12. Based on a text with the same title; see Table 11-8.

[84]William J. Martin and Donald J. Willower, "The Managerial Behavior of High School Principals," *Educational Administration Quarterly,* 17 (1981), pp. 69–90.

[85]Ibid.

[86]Doud, "The K–8 Principal in 1988"; John T. Kmetz and Donald J. Willower, "Elementary School Principals' Work Behavior," *Educational Administration Quarterly,* 18 (1982), pp. 62–78.

3. Varying criteria for hiring and evaluating principals
4. Variety and fragmentation of the job, as well as unexpected interruptions
5. Disputed notions of what is effective teaching
6. Rewards and incentives that lack a relationship to goal attainment or performance
7. Limitations imposed by collective bargaining and teacher contracts [87]

When given the opportunity to categorize their professional colleagues into one of five leadership roles (principal/teacher, scientific manager, instructional leader, curriculum leader, or general manager), 60 percent of secondary school principals in a North Carolina sample of 370 choose general manager.[88] Female principals and principals with more formal education (doctorate degree), however, prefer the roles of curriculum or instructional leader compared to male principals and principals with less education (masters degree, sixth-year certificate) who prefer the role of general manager.

In a study of 149 successful elementary school principals in Massachusetts, selected on the basis of being strong leaders and because of their schools' student achievement levels, more than 75 percent described themselves as "instructional leaders" who devoted most of their own professional development time and resources to curriculum, instruction, and school improvement.[89]

Other data suggest that elementary school principals spend more time on curriculum and instructional matters than do secondary school principals, but still not enough time given the fact they must still deal with leaking roofs, shrinking budgets, and personnel squabbles. Secondary school principals, especially those in large schools, devote more time to managerial concerns. The latter group of principals rely on their assistant principals and chairpersons in various subject areas to deal with curriculum and instructional activities.[90] On the other hand, elementary schools are smaller than high schools and are often cornerstones of homogeneous neighborhoods, whereas secondary schools often cut across and include many neighborhoods. Because of neighborhood size and homogeneity, elementary principals must be more sensitive to the needs, views, and priorities of parents and community members, which often center around curriculum and instructional leadership.

Managerial Role of the Principal

The role of manager is essential for the principal and is probably the most important aspect of school leadership. In their classic text on organizational behavior, Daniel Katz and Robert Kahn divide management skills into three major areas: *technical,* involving good planning, organizing, coordinating, supervising, and controlling techniques; *human,* dealing with human relations and people skills, good motivating and morale-building skills; and *conceptual,* emphasizing knowledge and technical skills related to the service (or product) of the organization.[91] (For principals, conceptual leadership connotes knowledge or curriculum, instruction, teaching, and learning.) Thomas Sergiovanni has added two other areas of management for school

---

[87]Rick Ginsberg, "Worthy Goal . . . Unlikely Reality: The Principal as Instructional Leader," *NASSP Bulletin,* 72 (1988), pp. 76–82.

[88]Dale L. Brubaker and Lawrence H. Simon, "How Do Principals View Themselves, Others," *NASSP Bulletin,* 71 (1987), pp. 72–78.

[89]Laura A. Cooper, "The Professional Development of Principals: The Principal's Perspective," unpublished doctoral dissertation, Harvard University, 1988; Cooper, "The Principal as Instructional Leader," *Principal,* 68 (1989), pp. 13–16.

[90]William L. Boyd, "What School Administrators Do and Don't Do," *Canadian Administrator,* 22 (1983), pp. 1–4; Doud, "The K–8 Principal in 1988"; Lester Golden, "New York City APs," *NASSP Bulletin,* 72 (1988), pp. 118–120; and Linda Scheive, "New Roles for Administrators in Rochester," *Educational Leadership,* 46 (1988), pp. 53–55.

[91]Daniel Katz and Robert L. Kahn, *The Social Psychology of Organizations* (New York: Wiley, 1966).

TABLE 11 ▪ 6   An Analysis of the Principal's Use of Time

	ACTUAL USE OF TIME (Percent)	IDEAL USE OF TIME (Percent)
Elementary Principals		
Administrative operations	13	09
Staff–curriculum development	24	35
Community relations	16	14
Student services	21	12
Evaluation	26	30
Secondary Principals		
Administrative operations	14	10
Staff-curriculum development	17	27
Community relations	14	15
Student services	40	24
Evaluation	15	24

SOURCE: Adapted from James L. Hager and L. E. Scarr, "Effective Schools—Effective Principals: How to Develop Both," *Educational Leadership,* 40 (1983), p. 39. Copyright © 1983 The Association for Supervision and Curriculum Development. Used by permission.

administrators, including *symbolic leadership,* those actions the principal emphasizes and wishes to model to the staff, and *cultural leadership,* those values and beliefs the principal believes are important.[92] In all five areas of leadership, the principal attempts to organize the school's mission or goals; this is the principal's contribution to the school (reflecting his philosophy of education and psychology of learning), which bonds students, teachers, and parents together as believers in the school.

Similarly, James Lipham and Robb Rankin have developed a "four-factor theory" of leadership for principals. The four factors are structural, facilitative, supportive, and participative leadership (Table 11-7). Note that all these lead-

ership factors emphasize administrative and managerial skills. The authors contend that no one of these leadership styles is best, rather the successful principal is able to modify or adapt the four leadership factors to the demands of the school setting.[93] The persistent use of a single leadership factor renders the principal ineffective. Nonetheless, all of us have particular strengths and weaknesses. A balanced leadership team—say, in which the principal is a strong participative and supportive leader and the assistant principal is strong on the other two dimensions—enhances the effective operation of the school.

---

[92]Thomas J. Sergiovanni, "Leadership and Excellence in Schools," *Educational Leadership,* 41 (1984), pp. 4–13.

[93]James M. Lipham and Robb E. Rankin, *Change, Leadership, and Decision Making in Improving Secondary Schools* (Madison: Wisconsin Center for Educational Research, 1982).

TABLE 11 ▪ 7   Four Leadership Styles for Principals

Structural Leaders

1. Take immediate action on urgent decisions.
2. Exercise clear and decisive delegation to members of the staff.
3. Stress organizational goals and outcomes.
4. Develop a cohesive school philosophy as a basis for decision making.
5. Monitor the implementation of decisions.
6. Establish positive relations with the district office and the community.

Facilitative Leaders

1. Obtain and provide the requisite resources.
2. Establish and reinforce school policies.
3. Minimize bureaucratic paperwork.
4. Offer suggestions for solving job-related problems.
5. Schedule activities.
6. Help get the job done.

Supportive Leaders

1. Express encouragement and appreciation for others' efforts.
2. Demonstrate friendliness and approachability.
3. Show kindness to others.
4. Trust others with delegated responsibilities.
5. Reward individual efforts.
6. Enhance staff and student morale.

Participative Leaders

1. Approach issues open-mindedly.
2. Are willing to modify preconceived positions.
3. Seek decisional input and advice.
4. Foster positional and emergent leadership.
5. Work actively with individuals and groups.
6. Involve others appropriately in decision making.

SOURCE: Adapted from James M. Lipham, Robb E. Rankin, and James A. Hoeh, *The Principalship: Concepts, Competencies, and Cases* © 1985, pp. 61–62. Used by permission of Longman, Inc., New York.

Curriculum–Instructional Role of the Principal

Although there is considerable agreement in the literature on the need for the principal to be a leader in the areas of curriculum and instruction, there is considerable disagreement on what specific roles and behaviors should be exhibited and how much time should be devoted to these twin areas of leadership. When principals are surveyed, they often consider curriculum and instruction aspects of the job as one of the top-priority work areas and that they need to spend more time on the job related to these two technical areas of development.[94]

---

[94]Carol D. Glickman, *Supervision and Instruction: A Developmental Approach,* 2nd ed. (Needham Heights, MA: Allyn and Bacon, 1990); Van Cleve Morris et al., *Principals in Action: The Reality of Managing Schools* (Columbus, OH: Merrill, 1984); and Nancy J. Pitner, *Training of the School Administrator* (Eugene: University of Oregon Press, 1982).

But a significant discrepancy exists between statements and actions. Data suggest that teachers do not view curriculum–instructional leadership as a major responsibility of principals,[95] do not see much evidence of such leadership on the part of principals,[96] are reluctant to accept principals in this leadership capacity,[97] often feel that principals are not capable of providing such leadership, and don't always want the principal's assistance in these technical areas that teachers consider to be more appropriate for peer coaching and collegial staff development.[98]

Principals have historically spent little time coordinating activities in curriculum and instruction, about 15 to 20 percent,[99] and spend much less time (3 to 7 percent) observing teachers in the classroom,[100] complaining that managerial activities take up most of their time. Dealing with the daily operation of the school and attending scheduled and unscheduled meetings tend to take up most of their time. Although the major principal associations (NAEP and NASSP) overwhelmingly envision the principal as a curriculum–instructional leader and this theme continually appears in their respective journals (which principals read), the realities of the job do not permit emphasis in these twin leadership areas.

In this connection, Joseph Murphy has developed six curriculum and instructional roles for the principal:

1. *Promoting Quality Instruction.* Ensuring consistency and coordination of instructional programs and defining recommended methods of instruction.
2. *Supervising and Evaluating Instruction.* Ensuring that school goals are translated into practice at the classroom level and monitoring classroom instruction through numerous classroom observations.
3. *Allocating and Protecting Instructional Time.* Providing teachers with uninterrupted blocks of instructional time and ensuring that basic skills and academic subjects are taught.
4. *Coordinating the Curriculum.* Translating curriculum knowledge into meaningful curricular programs, matching instructional objectives with curriculum materials and standardized tests, and ensuring curriculum continuity vertically and across grade levels.
5. *Promoting Content Coverage.* Ensuring that content of specific courses is covered in class and extended outside of class by developing and enforcing homework policies.
6. *Monitoring Student Progress.* Using both criterion- and standardized-reference tests to diagnose student problems and evaluate their progress, as well as using test results to set or modify school goals.[101]

Based on a review of the research, according to Murphy, the six major dimensions or roles

---

[95]Sharon F. Rallis and Martha Highsmith, "The Myth of the 'Great Principal': Questions of School Management and Instructional Leadership," *Phi Delta Kappan,* 68 (1986), pp. 300–304; Thomas J. Sergiovanni et al., *Educational Governance and Administration,* 2nd ed. (Englewood Cliffs, NJ: Prentice-Hall, 1987).

[96]Thelbert L. Drake and William H. Roe, *The Principalship,* 3rd ed. (New York: Macmillan, 1986); Michael Fullan, *The Meaning of Educational Change* (New York: Teachers College Press, 1982).

[97]Robert J. Garmston, "How Administrators Support Peer Coaching," *Educational Leadership,* 44 (1987), pp. 18–26; Allan A. Glatthorn, "A New Concept of Supervision," *Educational Horizons,* 65 (1987), pp. 78–82.

[98]Garmston, "How Administrators Support Peer Coaching"; Glen Grube, Henry G. Cram, and Timothy M. Melchior, "Taking Risks to Improve Instruction," *Educational Leadership,* 46 (1988), pp. 17–20. Also see Daniel L. Duke, *School Leadership and Instructional Improvement* (New York: Random House, 1987).

[99]Boyd, "What School Administrators Do and Don't Do"; Doud, "The K–8 Principal in 1988"; and Martin and Willower, "The Managerial Behavior of High School Principals."

[100]Duke, *School Leadership and Instructional Improvement;* James M. Lipham, Robb E. Rankin, and James A. Hoeh, *The Principalship* (New York: Longman, 1985); and Morris, *Principals in Action.*

[101]Joseph Murphy, "Principal Instructional Leadership," in P. W. Thurston and L. S. Lotto (eds.), *Advances in Educational Administration,* Vol. 1–B (Greenwich, CT: JAI Press, 1990), pp. 162–200.

TABLE 11 ▪ 8   Elementary School Recognition of Successful Schools and Principals

Effective Elementary Principals Emphasize

1. Knowledge of effective instructional practices
2. Understanding of child growth and development
3. Support of teachers
4. Well-designed and coordinated instructional programs
5. Use of academic time
6. Frequent assessment of student achievement
7. Supervision of instruction
8. Constructive feedback to teachers
9. Ability to communicate—write and speak
10. Ability to apply technology to management—use of spreadsheets, word processors, databases, etc.
11. Understanding of the political process
12. Knowledge of effective school practices
13. Understanding of leadership theories and principles
14. A vision of the future

SOURCE: Adapted from James L. Doud, *The K–8 Principal in 1988* (Alexandria, VA: National Association of Elementary School Principals, 1989); David C. Smith, *Principals for 21st Century Schools* (Alexandria, VA: National Association of Elementary School Principals, 1990).

exemplify an effective principal; moreover, his research supports the assumption that the distinguishing reason for effective schools is a school principal who exhibits strong curriculum–instructional leadership.

Effective Principals

The basis for judging effective schools is somewhat narrow, largely based on student outcomes on standardized tests in basic-skill areas (mainly reading and math). The data usually focus on inner-city elementary schools, and when suburban and secondary schools are included, it is often unclear to what extent the findings apply to different schools by social-class setting or grade level. The findings are only correlational, meaning it is not clear whether the leadership characteristics of the principal produce effective schools or whether effective schools create effective principals. Given all these flaws, nonetheless, the data tend to be highly repetitive.

The U.S. Department of Education has honored three times the nation's outstanding elementary schools. (In the most recent recog-

nition program, in 1990, some 221 schools were selected, ranging in size from 170 to 1,414 students.) Criteria for selection has always included student achievement in reading and math.[102] The behaviors of the principals of the recognized schools have been summarized in two recent publications by the NAEP and are listed in Table 11-8. As illustrated by the table, effective principals are well informed and perform well many technical roles related to supervision, instruction, teaching, learning, and evaluation. Moreover, they are skilled in the areas of communication, human relations, and the political process.

Whereas the broad specific behaviors reviewed in Table 11-8 tend to characterize elementary school principals, another U.S. Department of Education nationwide school recognition program also identified 202 "unusually effective" secondary schools and their principals. As many as fourteen specific behaviors of the principal

---

[102]Louanne M. Wheeler, "The 1989–90 Elementary School Recognition Program," *Principal,* 70 (1990), pp. 11–19.

TABLE 11 ▪ 9   Secondary School Recognition of Successful Schools and Principals

Effective Secondary Principals Emphasize

1. Clear academic goals
2. High expectations for students
3. Order and discipline
4. Rewards and incentives for students
5. Regular and frequent monitoring of student progress
6. Opportunities for meaningful student responsibility and participation
7. Teacher efficacy
8. Rewards and incentives for teachers
9. Concentration on academic learning time
10. Positive school climate
11. Administrative leadership
12. Well-articulated curriculum
13. Evaluation for instructional improvement
14. Community support and involvement

SOURCE: Adapted from John W. Arnn and John N. Mangieri, "Effective Leadership for Effective Schools: A Survey of Principal Attitudes," *NASSP Bulletin,* 72 (1988), p. 3. Used by permission.

were identified and appear in rank order in Table 11-9.

In general, the characteristics of effective principals, as supported by a review of numerous research investigations from 1980 to 1990, describe the effective K to 12 principal as one who evidences strong leadership in the areas of curriculum and instruction and who has implemented

1. High expectations for student achievement (even though the actual achievement of students may not be as high in high SES schools)
2. Well-articulated curricula
3. Well-articulated instructional programs
4. Clearly defined goals, objectives, and/or standards
5. Maximized learning time
6. An emphasis on reading and math skills
7. Staff-development programs (and other avenues for professional growth)
8. A sense of order in the classrooms and school
9. A method for monitoring student progress
10. Incentives or rewards for students and teachers

11. Parent–community involvement
12. Positive school climate[103]

What seems to be paramount in the effective schools literature is the need to change the organizational structure, as well as to put emphasis on the principal's leadership and the process of teaching and learning. These changes don't cost much in dollars, but the dividends can be immense. The message is simple: we can go about improving schools at minimal cost.

SUMMARY

1. There are several plans for organizing school districts. Most districts comprise elementary schools, middle grade or junior high schools, and senior or high schools.
2. Schools are organized into school districts, and there are today over 15,000 public school systems

---

[103]Daniel U. Levine and Allan C. Ornstein, "Effective School Settings," *Urban Review* (1990) in print; Allan C. Ornstein, "In Pursuit of Cost-Effective Schools," *Principal,* 70 (1990), pp. 28–30.

operating under a widely accepted system of laws, regulations, and customs.

3. Whereas most small and rural school districts have consolidated their schools since 1930, decentralization has occurred in large urban areas since the 1960s. However, the number of decentralized school districts has declined since 1980.

4. School board members are agents of the state, chosen locally (and in most cases elected) to run the local schools.

5. Board members are the official link between the public and school administration. Board members reflect the public will and have managerial responsibilities that are crucial to the operation of schools.

6. The relationship between school boards and superintendents deserves continued attention; school board members and superintendents must work together and avoid overt conflict. When differences or tensions exist between board members and the superintendent for too long, most superintendents are forced to resign.

7. Superintendents spend most of their time as managers, not as leaders. The average workday is largely desk work, phone calls, and scheduled meetings. Superintendents interpret school board policy and carry it out in connection with contemporary events; there is little time for them to initiate policy.

8. The central administrative staff, usually consisting of an associate superintendent, a number of assistant superintendents, department heads, and coordinators, are given responsibility by the superintendent to help run the schools. The central staff is usually top heavy in large districts and streamlined in small districts.

9. Principals spend the most time as general managers but would prefer to spend more as curriculum–instructional leaders. The realities of the principal's job often prevent emphasis on the latter two areas of leadership.

KEY TERMS

consolidation

decentralization

public board meeting

executive board meeting

central office staff

organizational chart

general manager

curriculum–instructional leader

DISCUSSION QUESTIONS

1. What is the ideal school district size? Defend your number(s).

2. Why have school districts consolidated? Why have they decentralized? What are the advantages and disadvantages of each trend?

3. What are the advantages and disadvantages of an elected or appointed local board of education?

4. How would you describe an effective superintendent? How do you see the superintendent's role in context with effective schools?

5. How would you describe an effective principal? What differences or emphasis, in terms of leadership behavior, do you envision for an elementary vs. secondary principal?

SUGGESTED READINGS

Arthur Blumberg, *School Administration as a Craft* (Needham Heights, MA: Allyn and Bacon, 1989). An easy-to-read book about the craft of administering schools, with helpful hints.

Challenges for School Leaders (Arlington, VA: American Association of School Administrators, 1988). Based on research findings, an outline of skill areas and strategies for becoming an effective school leader.

Larry Cuban, *The Managerial Imperative and the Practice of Leadership in Schools* (Albany: State University of New York Press, 1988). Stemming from personal experiences, a new way for understanding the nature of school management.

Edward Eaton (ed.), *Shaping the Superintendency* (New York: Teachers College Press, 1990). A criticism of bureaucratic and technocratic forces impacting at the school district and central staff level.

John I. Goodlad, *A Place Called School* (New York: McGraw-Hill, 1984). An influential overview of what takes place in schools and how to improve them.

Thomas B. Gregory and Gerald R. Smith, *High Schools as Communities: The Small School Reconsidered* (Bloomington, IN: Phi Delta Kappa Educational Foundation, 1987). Simply put—small is better.

Gerald C. Ubben and Larry W. Hughes, *The Principal: Creative Leadership for Effective Schools* (Needham Heights, MA: Allyn and Bacon, 1987). A practical analysis of management practices at the school level.

12

LEGAL CONSIDERATIONS AND EDUCATION

In this chapter, we attempt to answer these questions concerning the law as it applies to public schools. We begin our discussion by exploring the legal framework for public education. We examine the legal significance of federal and state constitutions and statutes, the major provisions of the U.S. Constitution affecting education, and the basic structure of the federal and state judicial systems. Then we discuss such personnel-related issues as certification, employment contracts, nonrenewal and dismissal, discrimination in employment, and torts. Next, we examine such student-related issues as school attendance, corporal punishment, suspension and expulsion, search and seizure, freedom of expression, and classification practices. Finally, we discuss such school–state issues as school desegregation, religion in the schools, and challenges to state finance schemes.

We emphasize decisions of the U.S. Supreme Court and those decisions of the highest state courts. The cases cited were selected for their precedent value on substantive legal principles of school law rather than their recency.

LEGAL FRAMEWORK FOR PUBLIC EDUCATION

All three units of government—federal, state, and local—exercise some degree of authority and control over U.S. public education. Educational governance of public schools is the result of constitutional and statutory provisions of the federal government, the fifty state governments, and case law. The degree of authority and control that local school boards have over school operations depends on the constitutional and statutory provisions of their state.

Federal Role in Education

Education is not a function specifically delegated to the federal government. This is recognized in the Tenth Amendment to the U.S. Constitution, which provides that "the powers not delegated to the United States by the Constitution, nor prohibited by it to the States, are reserved to the States respectively, or to the people." Although education is not specifically delegated to the federal government, it has exercised considerable influence in educational matters, primarily through the provisions of the federal Constitution, decisions of the U.S. Supreme Court, and congressional acts.

The Federal Constitution   The Constitution established three separate branches of government: legislative, the Congress (Article I); executive, the president (Article II); and judicial, a Supreme Court and necessary inferior courts (Article III).[1] These three branches of government provide a system of checks and bal-

ances to ensure that the intent of the Constitution is upheld.

The federal Constitution is the supreme law of the land. All statutes passed by Congress, state constitutions and statutes, and policies of local boards of education are subject to the provisions of the U.S. Constitution. The provisions of the Constitution that have had the greatest impact on the operation of public schools are Article I, Section 10, and the First, Fourth, Fifth, and Fourteenth Amendments.

Obligation of Contracts.   Article I, Section 10, provides in part that "no state shall . . . pass any . . . law impairing the obligation of contracts." This article guaranteeing the **obligation of contracts** has been litigated in numerous public school cases. Court decisions have verified that contracts entered into by school districts (including personnel contracts and other contracted services) are fully protected under Article I, Section 10. The provision also applies when a state legislature seeks to alter a teacher tenure or retirement statute in which contractual status prevails under the law.[2]

First Amendment.   The **First Amendment** provides that "Congress shall make no law respecting the establishment of religion, or prohibiting the free exercise thereof; or abridging the freedom of speech, or of press; or of the right of the people peaceably to assemble, and to petition the Government for a redress of grievances." The first part of the amendment dealing with religious freedoms precipitated litigation challenging government aid to parochial schools and public school policies objected to on religious grounds. The *freedom of speech* portion has evoked numerous court cases involving students' and teachers' rights to freedom of expression. The *rights of assembly* part has precipitated litigation involving students' organizations and employees' rights to organize and bargain collectively.

[1]U.S. Constitution, Articles I, II, III, ratified 1789.

[2]Ball v. Board of Trustees of Teachers Retirement Fund, 58 Atl. 111 (N.J. 1904).

Fourth Amendment. The **Fourth Amendment** provides in part that "the right of the people to be secure . . . against unreasonable searches and seizures . . . and no Warrants shall issue, but upon probable cause. . . . " This amendment has been the subject of litigation involving searches of students' lockers and person and, in some cases, teachers' rights to privacy.

Fifth Amendment. The **Fifth Amendment** reads in part that "no person . . . shall be compelled in any criminal case to be a witness against himself, nor deprived of life, liberty, or property without due process of law; nor shall private property be taken for public use, without just compensation." The first clause is relevant to cases where teachers have been questioned by superiors about their alleged activities with subversive organizations. The **due process clause** pertains specifically to acts of the federal government. The last clause is germane in instances where states or school boards acquire property for school building purposes.

Fourteenth Amendment. The **Fourteenth Amendment** provides in part that no state shall "deprive any person of life, liberty or property without due process of law. . . . " Numerous education cases involving this provision have come to the courts. Compulsory school attendance laws give students a property right to attend school. Teachers with **tenure** have a property right to continued employment. Liberty rights include interests in one's reputation and the right to personal privacy.

The Fourteenth Amendment also provides that no state shall "deny to any person within its jurisdiction the equal protection of the law." The **equal protection clause** of the Fourteenth Amendment has been involved in a wide variety of education cases in recent years. Among them are cases involving alleged discrimination based on race, sex, ethnic background, age, and handicaps and state financing of public schools.

Federal Statutes   Article I, Section 8, grants Congress "the power . . . to lay and collect taxes . . .

and provide for the Common Defense and general Welfare of the United States. . . . " This provision is based on the assumption that a high level of education is essential for the civic and economic prosperity of the nation. That is, to improve education is to provide for the general welfare of the United States. Congress acts under the "general welfare" clause when it passes federal statutes and provides federal tax dollars for school programs within the states. Federal statutes have provided extensive education programs in such areas as defense, vocational education, civil rights, elementary and secondary education, bilingual education, sex discrimination, special education, protecting the confidentiality of student records, and pregnancy bias.[3]

State Role in Education

At no point does the federal Constitution refer to education. This, coupled with the language of the Tenth Amendment (" . . . powers not delegated to the United States by the Constitution, nor prohibited by it to the States, are reserved to the States respectively, or to the people"), vested in state government the legal responsibility for the control and direction of public education. Thus, while federal authority is restrictive concerning education, the state has complete authority to provide a public education system.

State Constitutions   The United States is organized into two streams of government activity: a federal legal system and fifty separate state legal systems. Each state has its own constitution that forms its basic laws. The primary function of state constitutions is to restrict the powers of state legislatures to exact laws that are at variance with federal law or the provisions of state constitutions.[4] Generally, state constitutions contain a mandate for the establishment of pub-

---

[3]*Digest of Education Statistics* (Washington, D.C.: Government Printing Office, 1990).

[4]E. Edmund Reutter et al., *The Law of Public Education,* 4th ed. (Mineola, NY: Foundation Press, 1989).

lic education systems. Frequently, state constitutions deal with the same subjects as federal constitutions do, but, on some issues, such as separation of church and state, state constitutions may be more stringent.

State Statutes   Every state legislature enacts, amends, and repeals laws. These laws affecting public schools form the statutes of the fifty U.S. states. Recall that the Tenth Amendment of the U.S. Constitution is a plenary, absolute, power grant to the state legislatures over public education. However, the laws enacted cannot contravene federal law or the state constitution.

For example, over the years, the federal government has limited state authority over public education as school-operation matters have been challenged in the courts. Decisions on such state issues as racial desegregation of public schools, teachers' free speech, students' symbolic protest, students' procedural due process, constitutionality of corporal punishment, search and seizure, and nontort liability of school board members have placed state authority over public school operations within the legal boundaries of the federal Constitution. Courts resolved these conflicts, and those decisions became part of **case law,** that is, principles of law derived from court decisions.

Local Boards of Education   Obviously, state legislatures cannot assume supervisory responsibility for public schools. In keeping with the framework of decentralization of educational operation, the general supervision and administration of each state's public school system is delegated to state and local boards of education who in turn are responsible for hiring school administrators and classroom teachers. These groups have the authority to enforce policies and procedures for the operation and management of public schools. Their actions must be within the legal boundaries of federal and state constitutions and statutes. For example, building principals and classroom teachers rely on this authority in dealing with such issues as administering student punishment, suspensions and

expulsions, searching a student's locker, and the like.

The Courts

The provisions of federal and state constitutions, statutes, and policies of local boards of education do not guarantee proper execution of the law. A mechanism exists in our legal system for allowing an individual or group whose constitutional rights may have been violated to seek adjudication in the courts. Courts, however, do not act on their own initiative. Instead, courts settle only those disputes referred to them for decision.[5]

The U.S. judicial system is complex and multifaceted. As noted earlier, it is organized into one federal court system and fifty state court systems.

Federal Court System   Article III, Section 1, of the U.S. Constitution provides that "(t)he judicial power of the United States shall be vested in one Supreme Court, and in such inferior courts as the Congress may from time to time ordain and establish."[6] These courts have the authority to adjudicate cases dealing with a provision of the federal Constitution or a federal statute. For example, a federal court might decide an alleged breach of contract between a board of education and a private contractor under Article I, Section 10, of the U.S. Constitution or the nonrenewal of a tenured teacher's employment contract under the same article or the due process clause of the Fourteenth Amendment.

The federal court system contains three levels of general jurisdiction: district courts, courts of appeals, and the U.S. Supreme Court. In addition, there are some courts of special jurisdiction such as the claims court, tax court, and court of international trade. Figure 12-1 depicts the federal court system.

---

[5]Ibid.
[6]U.S. Constitution, Art. III, Sec. 1, ratified 1789.

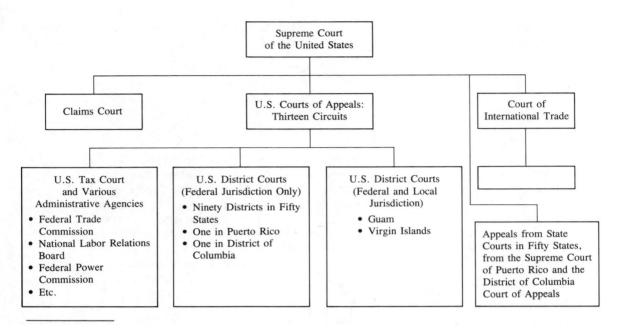

FIGURE 12-1   The Federal Court System (SOURCE: Adapted from *A Guide to the Federal Courts*, rev. ed., Washington, D.C. WANT Publishing, 1984.)

The federal court system contains ninety federal district courts. These are designated as courts of original jurisdiction or trial courts and serve as the first level in the federal court structure. Each state has at least one district court, and many states have between two and four districts. For example, California, New York, and Texas have four district courts each. In addition, separate districts exist with federal jurisdiction only in Puerto Rico and the District of Columbia and with federal and local jurisdictions in Guam and the Virgin Islands.

Appeals from the federal district courts can go to the U.S. Courts of Appeals, the next level in the federal court system. There are twelve federal circuits, with an appeals court for each. A thirteenth federal circuit court has jurisdiction to hear special claims such as customs, patents and copyrights, taxes, and international trade. (See the map in Figure 12-2.) Decisions rendered in each appeals court are binding only in the states within its circuit, but such decisions often influence other federal appeals courts dealing with similar issues.

The U.S. Supreme Court, the highest court in the system, is the court of final appeal on federal law questions. Of the education-related questions that eventually reach the Court, petitioners claim that a state's statutes or the policies of a local board of education have violated their constitutional rights or some provisions of federal law. In cases directly involving educational matters, certain provisions of the U.S. Constitution are involved more often than others. These provisions, noted previously, are Article I, Section 10, and the First, Fourth, Fifth, and Fourteenth Amendments, especially the due process and equal protection clauses of the Fourteenth Amendment.

State Court Systems   Because education is a state function, state courts decide most cases involving educational matters. Each state has its own unique court structure, but similarities exist. Many states have a three-level structure similar to the federal court system. Typically, there are courts of original jurisdiction (trial courts), courts of appeal (appellate courts), and the

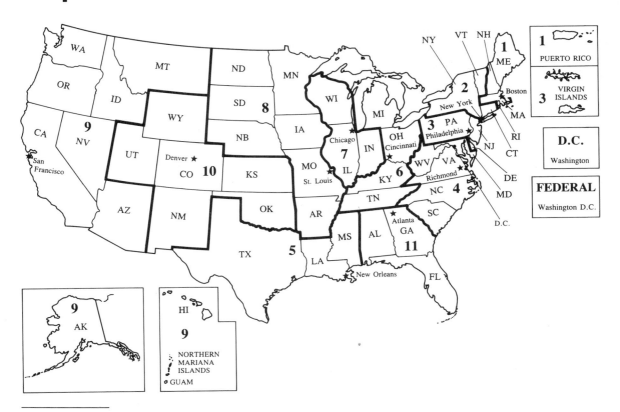

FIGURE 12-2   The Thirteen Federal Judicial Circuits

state's highest court (Supreme Court), often referred to generally as the "court of last resort." Names assigned to these courts at each of the three levels are not uniform among the states. Decisions rendered by the state's highest court can be appealed to the U.S. Supreme Court only if a question of federal law is involved.

THE LAW AND PROFESSIONAL PERSONNEL

The federal Constitution vested in state government the legal responsibility for the control and direction of public education through the fifty state legislatures. However, the actual administration of public school systems is delegated to state boards of education, state departments of education, and local boards of education. These agencies adopt and enforce reasonable rules and regulations emanating from statutes enacted by state legislatures for the operation of public school systems. In this section, we discuss the following issues related to professional personnel: certification, contracts, termination of employment, discrimination in employment, and tort liability.

Certification

The schools employ several categories of professional personnel: superintendents, principals, curriculum specialists, business managers, school psychologists, social workers, counselors, classroom teachers, and the like. To be eligible for employment in a professional position, the individual should possess a valid certificate issued according to statutory provisions of a given state. These statutes, varying from state to state, concern requirements and procedures for obtaining the different certificates. Generally, the legislature delegates the legal authority to issue and process certification to state boards and departments of education. In some states, however, the legislature delegates that authority to a local school district as is the case in New York City and more recently in Chicago.

The preparation standards for each type of certificate are similar from state to state, with only a few exceptions. For example, every state except Nebraska requires applicants to have a college degree with a minimum number of credit hours in a prescribed curriculum. Besides educational requirements, other prerequisites may include evidence of good moral character, a minimum age, U.S. citizenship, and satisfactory performance on a state-administered examination.

The initial certification is usually issued for a specified period of time, including various designations such as temporary, emergency, conditional, standard, life, or permanent. It is the certificate holder's responsibility to keep it renewed. This may require evidence of additional coursework, professional experience in a public school, or passage of a standardized examination such as the National Teachers Examination (NTE). Certificates also include specific endorsements (e.g., superintendent, principal, counselor, teacher), subject areas (e.g., English, social studies, mathematics, sciences), and grade levels (e.g., elementary, middle or junior high school, high school). A school board's failure to assign professional personnel to positions for which they are certified can result in loss of state accreditation and federal funding.[7]

The state also has the power to revoke certification. Certification revocation is different from dismissal from employment by a local board of education. A local school board can legally dismiss a superintendent, principal, teacher, or other professional employee, but the state is generally the only government body that can revoke a certificate. Moreover, state statutes usually specify the grounds and procedures for certification revocation. For example, under the Kentucky statute, it is provided that "any certification . . . may be revoked by the state board of education for elementary or secondary education, on the written recommendation of the superintendent of public instruction, for immorality, misconduct in office, incompetency or willful neglect of duty. . . . Before the certification is revoked the defendant shall be given a copy of the charges against him and given an opportunity, upon not less than ten (10) days' notice, to be heard in person or by counsel."[8]

Contracts

A certificate renders the holder eligible for employment in a state; it does not guarantee employment. Statutory law provides that local boards of education have the legal authority to enter into contracts with professional personnel. The relationship between a school board and its professional employees is contractual. The general legal principles governing contracts—offer and acceptance, competent parties, consideration, legal subject matter, and proper form—apply to this contractual relationship.

Offer and acceptance pertains to the job description, compensation level, and time of performance to which both parties have agreed. In most states, because only the board of education has the power to employ personnel, it must exercise that function itself. It cannot delegate the employment duty to the superintendent of schools or to individual members of the school board. Further, a local board of education is considered to be a legal body only as a corporate unit; therefore, for a board to enter into a valid

[7]Martha M. McCarthy and Nelda H. Cambron-McCabe, *Public School Law,* 2nd ed. (Needham Heights, MA: Allyn and Bacon, 1987).

[8]Kentucky Rev. Stat., Ch. 161.120 (1990).

contract with a teacher or other professional personnel, there must be a meeting of the board.

Competent parties means that, for a valid contract to exist, the parties must be authorized by law to enter into a contractual relationship. By law the school board possesses the legal authority to enter into contracts. A teacher or other professional employee is legally competent to contract providing she possesses the necessary certification and meets other state requirements. An application of this element of contracts is found in a Kentucky case. A teacher lacked a certificate when she began teaching and was ineligible for one because she was under the state's minimum-age requirement for certification. Consequently, the contract between the parties was void, and the teacher was not entitled to receive a salary for the work she performed while a minor.[9]

Consideration pertains to the promises bargained for and exchanged between the parties. Consideration is something of value—usually money or the equivalent. Promises to perform services gratuitously are not contracts because they are not supported by consideration. To have valid consideration, each party must give up something of value. In the case of an employment contract, consideration consists of the exchange of promises between the employee and the school district. The employee promises to perform specified services, and the school board promises to pay a specified salary.

Legal subject matter refers to mutual assurance between the parties that the job and its performance would not be a violation of the law. Finally, *proper form* means that all legal requirements, as stipulated in the state's statutes, must be followed in order for a contract to be valid. The precise form for contracts may vary from one state to another, but in most states, the statute requires that contracts with professional personnel be written.[10]

The policies and procedures of the local board of education, provisions of the state constitution and its statutes, and the collective bargaining agreement, if there is one, are considered part of the contract between the school district and the teacher or other professional employee. It is recommended therefore that the aforementioned inclusions to an employee's contract be referenced either in the body or on the face of the contract; they then become expressly part of the individual employment contract.

Termination of Employment

Local boards of education possess the legal authority to terminate the employment of school personnel. The U.S. Supreme Court bestowed on school boards this authority when it held that " . . . school authorities have the right and the duty to screen the officials, teachers, and employees as to their fitness to maintain the integrity of the schools as part of ordered society. . . . "[11] However, despite the legal authority of a board of education to terminate the employment, it cannot arbitrarily discharge personnel at anytime.

Tenure Law   Tenure statutes protect teachers (and other school district personnel specifically enumerated in state statutes) from arbitrary actions by local boards of education. The courts have sustained the constitutionality of such statutes. Teachers' Tenure Act cases[12] have concluded that tenure exists to protect competent teachers and other members of the teaching profession against unlawful and arbitrary board actions and to provide orderly procedures for the dismissal of unsatisfactory teachers and other professional personnel.

Tenure is attained by complying with specific provisions prescribed by state statutes. The nature of these provisions varies from state to state,

---

[9]Floyd County Bd. of Educ. v. Slone, 307 S.W. 2d 912 (Ky. 1957).

[10]Gordon v. Board of Directors of West Side Area Vocational Tech. School, 347 A.2d 347 (Pa. 1975).

[11]Adler v. Bd. of Educ., 342 U.S. 485 (1952).

[12]Teachers' Tenure Act Cases, 329 Pa. 213, 197 A. 344 (1938).

but certain conditions are included in most legislation. Nearly all statutes require that teachers serve a probationary period before tenure becomes effective. Generally, the probationary period ranges from three to five years, during which time a teacher is employed on a term contract. On completion of the probation period, personnel acquire tenure either automatically or by school board action. Texas law is an exception and permits the local school board to select between adopting continuing contracts or remaining under term contracts, in which case teachers do not have tenure.[13]

Which positions are to be covered under tenure laws is within the prerogative of state legislatures. In some jurisdictions, tenure legislation extends to selected administrative positions, but rarely to superintendents. Others afford tenure only to teachers. For example, in South Carolina, South Dakota, and Missouri, a school administrator possessing a teacher's certificate is a "teacher" within the meaning of tenure laws.[14] In Kentucky, "(t)he term 'administrator' for the purpose of (tenure) shall mean a certified employee, below the rank of superintendent. . . . "[15]

Although principals and certain other supervisory personnel can acquire tenure either as teachers or as principals in states having tenure laws, superintendents are not generally covered by tenure in that position unless the statute specifically indicates such inclusions. For example, the Illinois Supreme Court ruled that, because they are district employees who require certification, superintendents are covered by the tenure law, but that the tenure protection extended only to a teaching position and not to an administrative one.[16] On the other hand, tenure can be acquired by superintendents in New Jersey.[17]

In discussing the termination of employment of teachers and supervisory personnel, the terms *nonrenewal* and *dismissal* are often used interchangeably. There is a substantial difference, however, in the manner in which the termination operates in each case. If not protected by tenure, a school employee may be nonrenewed for no reason or for any reason whatsoever, providing it does not violate an employee's substantive constitutional rights (e.g., free speech, protection against racial discrimination). Courts have reasoned in these cases that the contract has simply terminated and there is no "expectancy of continued employment." Dismissal, on the other hand, whether under tenure status or during an unexpired contract, is permissible only "for cause." Consequently, a dismissal of a tenured employee or a nontenured professional during a contract year is entitled to a due process hearing embodying all the statutory and constitutional safeguards.

Dismissal Procedures   Most tenure laws provide specific procedures for dismissing tenured employees. The procedure typically includes three elements: notice by a specific date, specification of charges against the employee, and a hearing at which the charges are discussed. When state law describes a specific procedure for dismissal, it must be followed exactly to make the action legal.

Besides the procedures required under state law, tenure rights qualify for constitutional procedural protections encompassed within the concepts of **property** and **liberty interests** under the due process clause of the Fourteenth Amendment. The holding of a teaching position qualifies as a property right if the employee has an unexpired contract or has acquired tenure. The aforementioned protections of the Fourteenth Amendment do not normally extend to nontenured employees. The Supreme Court has affirmed the view of the courts that nontenured employees have no property or liberty interests in continued employment.[18] In exceptional situ-

---

[13]White v. South Park I.S.D., 693 F. 2d 1163 (5 Cir. 1983).

[14]Snipes v. McAndrew, 313 S.E. 2d 294 (S.C. 1984); Waltz v. Bd. of Educ., 329 N.W. 2d 131 (S.D. 1983); Fuller v. N. Kansas City S.D., 629 S.W. 2d 404 (Mo. 1982).

[15]Ky. Rev. Stat., Ch. 161.720, Sec. 8 (1990).

[16]Lester v. Bd. of Educ. of S.D. No. 119, 230 N.E. 2d 893 (Ill. 1967).

[17]N.J. Stat. Ann., Sec. 18A: 28–5(4) (1989).

---

[18]Roth v. Bd. of Regents, 408 U.S. 564 (1972).

ations, courts have recognized "de facto tenure" where there was no tenure law, but tenure was acquired by custom and precedent.[19] However, de facto tenure is not possible where there is a well-established statewide tenure system.

A liberty interest would be an issue in dismissal, and due process required, when evidence exists that a charge has been made that places a stigma on an employee's reputation thus foreclosing future employment opportunities or seriously damaging his standing in the community.[20] A liberty interest would not be a constitutional safeguard when school board members and school administrators refrain from making public statements or release information that is derogatory to the employee. Even when statements are made, if they simply describe unsatisfactory performance in general, normally they do not constitute a constitutional violation of the employee's Fourteenth Amendment rights.

Examples of charges against employees not involving stigma include ineffective teaching methods, inability to maintain classroom discipline, and inability to get along with administrators and colleagues. Failure to award tenure does not automatically create a stigma. Examples of stigmas that qualify for constitutional due process protection include the following charges: manifest racism, immoral conduct, serious mental disorder, a drinking or drug problem, willful neglect of duty, and responsibility for the deterioration of a school.[21]

Causes for dismissal are generally specified in state statutes and differ from one state to another; however, there are similarities. For example, in Kentucky tenured employees can be dismissed for insubordination; immoral character or conduct; physical or mental disability; or inefficiency, incompetency, or neglect of duty.[22] In Illinois cause for dismissal is specified as incompetency, cruelty, negligence, immorality or other sufficient cause and whenever in the board's opinion a teacher is not qualified to teach

or the best interests of the school require it.[23] In Connecticut cause is enumerated as inefficiency, incompetency, insubordination, moral misconduct, disability as shown by competent medical evidence, elimination of position, or for other due and sufficient cause.[24] (See Administrative Advice 12-1.)

Discrimination in Employment

Recent federal laws intended to remove discrimination in employment have had a direct impact on school board employment practices. Such legislation includes Title VII of the Civil Rights Act of 1964, Title IX of the Education Amendments of 1972, the Rehabilitation Act of 1973, the Equal Pay Act of 1963, the Age Discrimination Act of 1986, and the Pregnancy Discrimination Act of 1978. In addition, guidelines and policies from such federal agencies as the Equal Employment Opportunities Commission (EEOC), the Office of Economic Opportunity (OEO), and 42 U.S.C. Section 1983, in particular, have been applied in claims of employment discrimination. This section briefly discusses some of the major precedents bearing on race and sex discrimination, emanating from landmark court decisions.

Most litigation involving challenges of discrimination in teacher and administrator employment rely on Title VII of the Civil Rights Act of 1964. Title VII is a broad-based federal civil rights statute that prohibits employers from discriminating against employees on the basis of race, color, religion, sex, or national origin.

Beginning in the early 1970s, the federal courts heard several cases challenging discrimination. In 1971 the U.S. Supreme Court, in *Griggs v. Duke Power Company,* determined that Title VII of the Civil Rights Act of 1964 (pertaining to hiring, promotion, salary, and retention) covered not only overt discrimination but also practices that are discriminatory in operation.[25] The Court held that an employment practice is

[19]Perry v. Sinderman, 408 U.S. 593 (1972).
[20]Roth v. Bd. of Regents.
[21]Reutter et al., *The Law of Public Education.*
[22]Ky. Rev. Stat., Ch. 161.790 (1990).

[23]Ill. Ann. Stat., Ch. 122, Sec. 10–22.4 (1990).
[24]Conn. Gen. Stat. Ann., Tit. 5A, Sec. 10–151 (1989).
[25]Griggs v. Duke Power Co., 401 U.S. 424 (1971).

ADMINISTRATIVE ADVICE 12-1

LEGAL GUIDELINES FOR DISMISSAL

School employees can be dismissed for a variety of reasons ranging from elimination of a position to incompetency. When a tenured school employee challenges her dismissal, the burden of proof is on the school district. The following guidelines, drawn from rulings in actual cases, can help administrators handle employee dismissals properly.

■ *Dismissal for Willful Violation of School District Rules, Regulations, and Policies.* In such cases, the hearing officer will be interested in what you did before the dismissal. Specifically, the officer will want answers to such questions as these: Did you maintain adequate records to justify termination? Did you conduct a fair and objective investigation and provide the employee due process? Did you inform the employee of all reasons behind your decision to dismiss him? Did you clearly communicate school rules and penalties for violations to the employee? Did you enforce the rules and impose discipline fairly and consistently?

■ *Dismissal for Incompetence or Negligence.* Generally, dismissal is considered too harsh a penalty for a single instance of incompetence or negligence. Usually, hearing officers in such cases are especially interested in the staff development opportunities offered to the employee.

To meet substantive and procedural requirements in a case of this kind, you should (1) set reasonable standards of performance, (2) provide specific documentation to prove the employee's incompetence or negligence, (3) establish and follow a progressive staff development program aimed at helping incompetent and negligent employees improve their performance, (4) enforce performance standards consistently and fairly, (5) consider the employee's work record and length of service before deciding on the proper discipline, and (6) conduct a thorough and fair investigation of the employee's incompetence or negligence and provide the employee due process.

■ *Dismissal for Insubordination.* Usually, hearing officers will uphold dismissals for insubordina-

tion as long as the supervisor's directives to the employee have been contractually proper and reasonable and as long as the proper dismissal procedures have been followed.

To protect yourself in such cases, administrators should (1) ensure that work assignments are contractually proper and reasonable; (2) communicate work directives clearly, both orally and in writing; (3) give assignments; (4) follow a progressive staff development program aimed at improving employee performance; (5) give adequate warnings concerning the consequences of insubordinate behavior; (6) consider the employee's work record, length of service, and other extenuating circumstances; (7) tell the employee your reason for dismissing her at the time of dismissal; and (8) conduct a thorough and fair investigation, including due process.

■ *Dismissal for Union Activities.* Most union activities are not considered just cause for dismissal. Generally, however, hearing officers uphold dismissal when there is sufficient proof of the employee's active leadership and participation in an unauthorized strike. In such cases, administrators should (1) review the employment contract to determine what union activities are considered offenses for which an employee can be dismissed and (2) present a high degree of proof to support your charge that the employee played a prominent and responsible role in causing or prolonging an illegal strike.

Source: Adapted from Edward R. Lilly, "What to Do Before (and After) You Say, 'You're Fired'!" *Executive Educator,* 10 (1988), pp. 18–19.

prohibited if the exclusion of minorities cannot be shown to be related to job performance. The case involved requiring job applicants to possess a high school diploma and make a satisfactory score on a general intelligence test as criteria for employment. The practice was shown to discriminate against black applicants. During the same year, the Court, in *Phillips v. Martin Marietta Corporation,* handed down a decision relative to the disparate treatment of the sexes in the workplace. The Court ruled that discriminatory treatment of the sexes, by employment practices not necessary to the efficient and purposeful operation of an organization, is prohibited by the same federal legislation.[26]

The effect of these two landmark decisions was to force employers to remove "artificial, arbitrary, and unnecessary" barriers to employment that discriminate on the basis of race and sex classification. In 1972 the coverage of these provisions of Title VII, which previously had applied only to private employment, were extended to discriminatory employment practices in educational institutions. Subsequent to *Griggs* and *Phillips,* lower courts have applied these same legal standards to Fourteenth Amendment, Section 1983, and Title VII equal protection cases.

To establish a constitutional violation of equal protection, aggrieved individuals must prove that they have been victims of discrimination. In 1981 the Supreme Court set forth the procedural steps to file a Title VII suit.[27] The plaintiff has the initial burden of establishing a prima facia case of discrimination by showing the existence of five factors: (1) member in a protected group (e.g., minorities, women, aged, handicapped), (2) application for the position, (3) qualification for the position, (4) rejection for the position, and (5) employer's continued pursuit of applicants with the plaintiff's qualifications for the position. These factors constitute an initial, or prima facia, case of discrimination in any type

of personnel decision. Once a prima facia case of discrimination is established, the defendant (employer) must articulate a nondiscriminatory reason for the action. If this is accomplished, the plaintiff (employee or applicant) then must prove that the explanation is a pretext for discrimination, the real reason for the personnel decision being based on the consideration of "impermissible factors" in employment.[28] The legal standards emanating from *Griggs* and *Phillips* in claims of discriminatory employment practices under Title VII have been applied also under civil rights legislation barring discrimination based on age and handicaps.

Tort Liability

A **tort** is a civil wrong, not including contracts, for which a court will award damages. The three major categories of torts are intentional interference, strict liability, and negligence. Instances of intentional interference and strict liability in school-related injuries are rare and will not be pursued in this section. Accordingly, we examine the elements of negligence and the defenses against liability. Liability under Section 1983 of the Civil Rights Act is also addressed.

Elements of Negligence   To establish a legal cause for action in tort, four essential elements must exist: The individual has a duty to protect others against unreasonable risks; the individual failed to exercise an appropriate standard of care; the negligent act is the proximate cause of the injury; and a physical or mental injury, resulting in actual loss or damage to the person, exists.[29]

Duty. School employees have a **duty** to protect students entrusted to their care from being injured. Specifically, these duties include adequate supervision and instruction, maintenance

---

[26]Phillips v. Martin Marietta Corp., 400 U.S. 542 (1971).

[27]Texas Department of Community Affairs v. Burdine, 450 U.S. 248 (1981).

[28]McDonnell Douglas Corp. v. Green, 411 U.S. 792 (1973).

[29]William Prosser, *Law of Torts,* 4th ed. (St. Paul: West, 1971).

of premises and equipment, and foreseeability. The test of foreseeability is whether under all circumstances the possibility of injury should have been reasonably foreseen and that supervision likely would have prevented the injury. For example, a teacher was found guilty of negligence when an eighth-grade pupil was injured from pebble-throwing that continued for almost ten minutes during a morning recess.[30] Similarly, in a New Jersey suit, an elementary school principal was held liable for injuries suffered when a pupil was struck by paperclips shot from a rubber band by another child before the classrooms opened. The court found the principal had acted improperly by announcing no rules with respect to the conduct of students before entering classrooms, by not assigning teachers to assist him in supervising the pupils before school, and by engaging in activities other then overseeing the activities of the pupils.[31]

Standard of Care. Failure of a school employee to act in a manner that conforms to an appropriate **standard of care** can render said employee negligent. The standard of care is that which a reasonable and prudent person would have exercised under similar circumstances. For example, the Oregon Supreme Court said "Negligence . . . is . . . the doing of that thing which a reasonably prudent person would not have done, or the failure to do that thing which a reasonably prudent person would have done, in like or similar circumstances. . . . "[32] The model for the reasonable and prudent person has been described as one who possesses "(1) the physical attributes of the defendant himself, (2) normal intelligence, (3) normal perception and memory with a minimum level of information and experience common to the community, and (4) such superior skill and knowledge as the actor has or holds himself out to the public as having."[33]

The standard of care required would depend on such circumstances as the age, maturity, and experience of students; the type of activity; the environment; and the potential for danger. The amount of care owed to children increases with the immaturity of the child. A higher standard of care is required in shop, physical education, and laboratory classes and in situations and environments that pose a greater threat of danger, (e.g., school field trips).

Proximate Cause. There must be a connection between the action of school personnel and the resultant injury sustained by the pupil. Courts will ask, Was the failure to exercise a reasonable standard of care the **proximate cause** of the injury? The cause of the injury first must be established. Then it must be shown that there was some connection between the injury and the employee's failure to exercise a reasonable standard of care.

As in determining whether an appropriate standard of care has been exercised, the test of foreseeability is used in establishing proximate cause. It is not necessary that a particular injury was foreseen for proximate cause to be established. If reasonable precautions are taken and an intervening injury not foreseen occurs, no negligence exists. Such was the case when a student returned to his desk and sat on a sharpened pencil placed there by another student. School authorities were not held liable for the injury.[34]

Injury. There must be proof of actual loss or damage to the plaintiff resulting from the **injury.** If the injury suffered is caused by more than one individual, damages will be apportioned among the defendants.[35] A school district may be required to compensate an injured party for negligent conduct of an officer, agent, or employee of the district. Individual school board members or employees (superintendents, principles, teachers) may also be liable personally for

---

[30]Sheehan v. St. Peter's Catholic School, 291 Minn. 1, 188 N.W. 2d 868 (1971).

[31]Titus v. Lindberg, 49 N.J. 66, A.2d 65 (1967).

[32]Biddle v. Mazzocco, 284 P.2d 364 (Ore. 1955).

[33]Kern Alexander and M. David Alexander, *American Public School Law,* 2nd ed. (St. Paul: West, 1985), p. 457.

[34]Swaitkowski v. Bd. of Educ. of City of Buffalo, 36 A.D. 2d 685 (N.Y. 1971).

[35]McCarthy and Cambron-McCabe, *Public School Law.*

ADMINISTRATIVE ADVICE 12-2

GUIDELINES FOR SAFER PLAYGROUNDS

You risk a lawsuit every time a child sets foot on your school playground. A child falls from a slide or ladder; a child injures himself on the swings or seesaws. To protect students from injury—and schools from liability—the enlightened school administrator learns to identify and eliminate these dangers. To help make your playgrounds better and safer, the following principles of design, maintenance, and supervision are suggested:

- *Avoid Steep Slopes.* Ramps, slides, or climbing nets should not be installed at angles of greater than forty-five degrees and preferably closer to thirty-five degrees. The steeper the slope, the greater the risk a child will suffer injury.
- *Limit Falls to Twenty-Four Inches.* A playground structure should follow a multilevel design—a series of constantly rising platforms. The distance between levels should vary from eighteen to twenty-four inches, depending on the age of the children using the equipment. If a play structure is designed properly, no child should be able to fall more than two feet.
- *Consider Accessibility.* Playground design must take the "flow of play" into account. Injuries often occur when children who are impatient to wait their turn look for unsafe paths to their destination. The principle here: Give children room to play together and avoid waiting in line.
- *Provide Safe Clearances.* Place play equipment at least twenty feet away from trees, fences, or other playground structures.
- *Consider Exposure to the Sun.* Installing playground equipment under the shade of trees or buildings allows children to play longer and

more actively. Shade also reduces the risk of sunburn or burns caused by hot metal slides.
- *Provide Enclosed Spaces.* Providing partially enclosed tube slides or tunnels makes playground equipment more versatile. Enclosures must be large enough for children to move freely through them and to permit teachers to supervise visually.
- *Use Interconnective Play Components.* An interconnective play structure connects ramps, climbing nets, stairs, slides, platforms, and pathways to provide easy movement throughout the play structure.
- *Use Good-Quality Materials.* Safe playground equipment requires strong, durable, and nontoxic material. The equipment must be structurally sound to support the weight of many children and adults at the same time. All edges must be rounded, smooth, and free of splinters.
- *Inspect Equipment Regularly.* Regular inspections are essential to ensure the safety of playground equipment.

Source: Adapted from Louis Bowers, "Follow These Guidelines for Better—and Safer—Playgrounds," *Executive Educator,* 11 (1989), pp. 27–28.

torts that they commit in the course of their duties. (See Administrative Advice 12-2.)

Defenses Against Negligence Several defenses can be invoked by a defendant (school board, superintendent, principal, teacher) in a tort action. These defenses include contributory negligence, assumption of risk, comparative negligence, and government immunity.

Contributory Negligence. If it is shown that a student's own negligence contributed to the injury, the law in many states would charge the student with **contributory negligence.** However, a student cannot be charged with contributory negligence if he is too immature to recognize the risks: "[A] standard of care which is adequate when dealing with adults generally will not be adequate when dealing with children."[36] For example, in states such as Illinois, Michigan, North Carolina, Ohio, and Wisconsin, courts have ruled that students under seven years of age cannot be prohibited from recovery damages because of negligence. In other states, the age has been set at four, five, or six years. And for older children up to the age of fourteen, there is a "rebuttable presumption" that they are incapable of contributory negligence.[37]

Assumption of Risk. Another commonly used defense in tort actions is the doctrine of **assumption of risk.** It is based on the theory that one who knowingly and willingly exposes oneself to a known danger may be denied tort recovery for injuries sustained. An essential requisite to invoking a defense of assumption of risk is that there be knowledge and appreciation of the danger. Thus, it was held that a child who was cut by submerged broken glass while playing in a high school sandpit did not assume the risk of injury because he did not know the glass was in the sandpit.[38] On the other hand, the Oregon Supreme Court found an assumption of risk in the injury of a high school football player when he was injured in a scheduled football game.[39] Like contributory negligence, courts will consider the age and maturity level of students when assessing a defense of assumption of risk in tort.

Comparative Negligence. Where the common law rule of contributory negligence and assumption of risk is followed, plaintiffs whose own negligence contributed to an injury are barred com-

pletely from recovery. This harsh rule has been modified. A number of states have adopted the doctrine of **comparative negligence.** Under the comparative negligence doctrine, a plaintiff can obtain a proportionate recovery for injury depending on the amount of negligence she contributed to the injury. Specific statutory provisions vary from state to state.[40]

Government Immunity. The origin of the doctrine of **government immunity** from tort liability can be traced to two early cases, one in England in 1788 and the other in Massachusetts in 1812.[41] The courts held that the government could not be sued for negligence. Thus, the precedent of the immunity of school districts from tort liability was established and remained in effect until the passage of the Federal Tort Claims Act of 1946. Subsequently, the doctrine of state immunity in tort has been abrogated or modified by state legislatures. However, tort law does extend certain immunity to teachers and administrators in the scope and performance of their duties. One example is administering corporal punishment in schools.[42]

School board members too have some degree of immunity in the scope and performance of their duties. However, Section 1983 of the Civil Rights Act rooted in 1871 changed the status of the immunity of school board members for their activities, which provides that every person who subjects any citizen of the United States to the deprivation of any rights secured by the Constitution be liable to the (injured) party in an action at law.[43] A plethora of court cases have been litigated under this act, primarily dealing with First and Fourteenth Amendment rights. The tort liability of school board members was further extended under Section 1983 to students by the Supreme Court decision in *Wood v. Strick-*

---

[36]Leroy J. Peterson, Richard M. Rossmiller, and Marlin M. Volz, *The Law and Public School Operation,* 2nd ed. (New York: Harper & Row, 1978), p. 253.

[37]Louis Fischer, David Schimmel, and Cynthia Kelly, *Teachers and the Law,* 2nd ed. (New York: Longman, 1987).

[38]Brown v. Oakland, 124 P. 2d 369 (Cal. 1942).

[39]Vandrell v. S.D. No. 26C Malheur Cty., 233 Ore. 1, 376 P. 2d 406 (1962).

[40]William D. Valente, *Law in the Schools,* 2nd ed. (Columbus, OH: Merrill, 1987).

[41]Russell v. Men of Devon, 100 Eng. Rep. 359, 2 T.R. 667 (1788); Mower v. Leicester, 9 Mass. 237 (1812).

[42]Ingraham v. Wright, 430 U.S. 651 (1977).

[43]42 U.S.C., Section 1983 (1871).

land.[44] The Court held that school board members could be sued individually by students whose constitutional rights were denied. The case involved a denial of due process of students in a suspension hearing.

THE LAW AND STUDENTS

Schools exist for the purpose of educating its citizenry. Throughout its history, education has served as the backbone of the U.S. democratic system. This view is based on the premise that the country is best served by an educated, enlightened citizenry. With this mandate, the states have enacted legislation pertaining to the education of the nation's youth. These statutes provide regulations pertaining to school attendance, student discipline, freedom of expression, and classification practices.

School Attendance

All fifty states have some form of compulsory school attendance law. These statutes provide the right of children residing in a district to receive a free public education up to a certain age and exacts penalties for noncompliance on parents or guardians.

Compulsory Attendance Laws   The courts have sustained compulsory attendance laws on the basis of the legal doctrine of **parens patriae.** Under this doctrine, the state has the legal authority to provide for the welfare of its children. In turn, the welfare of the state is served by the development of an enlightened citizenry.

Attendance at a public school is not the only way to satisfy the compulsory attendance law. Over sixty years ago, the U.S. Supreme Court in *Pierce v. Society of Sisters* invalidated an Oregon statute requiring children between the ages of eight and sixteen to attend public schools.[45] The Court concluded that by restricting attendance to public schools, the state violated both the property rights of the school and the liberty interests of parents in choosing the place of education for their children, protected by the Fourteenth Amendment to the Constitution.

Subsequent to *Pierce,* states have expanded the options available to parents (guardians) for meeting the compulsory attendance law. For example, currently in the state of Kentucky, a parent is in compliance with that state's statute by selecting from the following options: enrolling their children, who must regularly attend, in a private, parochial, or church-related day school; enrolling their children, who must regularly attend, in a private, parochial, church- or state-supported program for exceptional children; or providing home, hospital, institutional, or other regularly scheduled, suitable, equivalent instruction that meets standards of the state board of education.[46]

Parents or guardians who select one of the options to public school instruction must obtain equivalent instruction. For example, the Washington Supreme Court held that home instruction did not satisfy that state's compulsory attendance law, for the parents who were teaching the children did not hold a valid teaching certificate.[47] In its decision, the court described four essential elements of a school: a certified teacher, pupils of school age, an institution established to instruct school-age children, and a required program of studies (curriculum) engaged in for the full school term and approved by the state board of education. Subsequently, statutes establishing requirements for equivalent instruction (such as certified teachers, program of studies, time devoted to instruction, school-age children, and place or institution) generally have been sustained by the courts.[48]

---

[44]Wood v. Strickland, 420 U.S. 308 (1975).
[45]Pierce v. Society of Sisters, 268 U.S. 510 (1925).

---

[46]Ky. Rev. Stat., Ch. 159.030 (1990).
[47]State ex. rel. Shoreline S.D. No. 412 v. Superior Court, 55 Wash. 2d 177, 346 P. 2d 999 (1959).
[48]State ex. rel. Douglas v. Faith Baptist Church of Louisville, 454 U.S. 803 (1981).

Exceptions to Compulsory Attendance   The prevailing view of the courts is that religious beliefs cannot abrogate a state's compulsory attendance law. An exception is the U.S. Supreme Court ruling in *Wisconsin v. Yoder*, which prevented that state from requiring Amish children to submit to compulsory formal education requirements beyond the eighth grade.[49] The Court found that this was a violation of the free exercise of religion clause of the First Amendment. However, most other attempts to exempt students from school based on religious beliefs have failed.

It is commonly held that married pupils, regardless of age, are exempt from compulsory attendance laws. The rationale is that married persons assume adult status, and consequently the doctrine of parens patriae no longer applies. The precedent in this area is based on two Louisiana cases in which fifteen and fourteen-year old married women were considered not "children" under the compulsory attendance law.[50] A later New York case followed the rationale of the two Louisiana cases in declaring that the obligations of a married woman were inconsistent with school attendance.[51] It should be noted, however, that a state cannot deny married minors the right to attend school if they wish.

Some parents have used illness as an exemption from compulsory school attendance. In such situations, the school has the right to require proof of illness through medical certification of a physician. For example, in an Illinois case, parents were charged with truancy when their school-age child was absent from school for 339½ days during a two-year period. As a defense, the parents claimed illness of the child as a reason for non-school attendance. The pupil's physician testified that the child suffered from allergies but not sufficient to warrant excessive absence from school. The charge of truancy against the parents was upheld by the Illinois court.[52]

Recent controversy has focused on school attendance of pupils with acquired immune deficiency syndrome (AIDS). The National Centers for Disease Control (CDC) have provided some guidelines to assist schools in developing appropriate policies dealing with the question. The CDC stipulates that students with AIDS who are under medical care may continue regular school attendance unless they have skin eruptions, exhibit inappropriate behavior such as biting, or are unable to control bodily secretions. (See Administrative Advice 12-3.)

Vaccinations   In an effort to protect the health and welfare of all students, states have required students to be vaccinated. The precedents in this area are derived from two U.S. Supreme Court cases decided nearly a century ago.[53] A more recent case struck down a challenge to a state's mandatory vaccination on religious grounds, even though there was no epidemic imminent.[54]

Residency Requirements   Generally, eligibility to attend tuition-free the public schools of a district is extended by statute to school-age children who have a domicile in the district or who are residents of the district. To understand the decision of the courts in this area, it is necessary to define the residence and domicile of pupils and their parents. These terms are legally defined as follows:[55]

- **Domicile** is a place where one intends to remain indefinitely, and each person may have only one domicile. A minor child's legal domi-

---

[49]Wisconsin v. Yoder, 406 U.S. 205 (1972).

[50]State v. Priest, 210 La. 389, 27 So. 2d 173 (1946); in re State, 214 La. 1062, 39 So. 2d 731 (1949).

[51]In re Rogers, 36 Misc. 2d 680, 234 N.Y.S. 2d 179 (1962).

[52]People v. Berger, 65 Ill. Dec. 600, 441 N.E. 2d 915 (1982).

[53]Jacobsen v. Commonwealth of Mass., 197 U.S. 11 (1905); Zucht v. King, 260 U.S. 174 (1922).

[54]Bd. of Educ. of Mt. Lakes v. Maas, 56 N.J. Super. 245, 152 A 2d 394 (1959).

[55]Joseph R. Nolan and Michael J. Connolly, *Black's Law Dictionary*, 5th ed. (St. Paul, West, 1979).

ADMINISTRATIVE ADVICE 12-3

■

G CDC GUIDELINES FOR AIDS EDUCATION PROGRAMS

uidelines for AIDS education have been developed to help school personnel and others plan, implement, and evaluate educational efforts to prevent unnecessary mortality associated with AIDS. The guidelines incorporate principles for AIDS education that were developed by the president's Domestic Policy Council and approved by the president in 1987. You can assess the extent to which your district program measures up with the guidelines by answering each question below:

■ To what extent are parents, teachers, students, and appropriate community representatives involved in developing, implementing, and assessing AIDS education policies and programs?

■ To what extent is the program included as an important part of a more comprehensive school health education program?

■ To what extent is the program taught by regular classroom teachers in elementary grades and by qualified health education teachers or other similarly trained personnel in secondary grades?

■ To what extent is the program designed to help students acquire essential knowledge to prevent HIV infection at each appropriate grade?

■ To what extent does the program describe the benefits of abstinence for young people and mutually monogamous relationships within the context of marriage for adults?

■ To what extent is the program designed to help teenage students avoid specific types of behavior that increase the risk of becoming infected with HIV?

■ To what extent is adequate training about AIDS provided for school administrators, teachers, nurses, and counselors—especially those who teach about AIDS?

■ To what extent are sufficient program development time, classroom time, and educational materials provided for education about AIDS?

■ To what extent are the processes and outcomes of AIDS education being monitored and periodically assessed?

Source: Adapted from Centers for Disease Control, "Halt the AIDS Rampage," *School Administrator*, 10 (1988), pp. 53–55. Used by permission.

---

cile is that of her father except in special circumstances, such as the father's death or parental separation or divorce where custody of the child has been awarded to the mother or another custodial guardian.

■ **Residence** is the place where one is actually, physically living.

Generally, it is held that a child has the right to attend the public school of a district in which he is living—unless the child is living in that district solely for the purpose of attending school

there, in which case the child is not entitled to education without the payment of tuition.[56]

Curriculum   The state legislature has the authority to prescribe the curriculum of the public schools. Such authority is based on the premise that the course of study in the public schools includes those subjects that are essential to

---

[56]Turner v. Bd. of Educ., N. Chicago Community H.S. Dist. 123, 54 Ill. 2d 68, 294 N.E. 2d 264 (1973).

good citizenship. All states require teaching of the federal Constitution, and most mandate instruction in U.S. history. Other subjects commonly required include English, mathematics, science, family life and sex education, drug education, and health and physical education.

All state-mandated courses must be offered, but local school boards have great latitude in supplementing the curriculum required by the state legislature. The precedent-setting case in this area was the landmark 1874 decision of the Michigan Supreme Court, which held that the local board of education had the authority to maintain a high school.[57] This landmark decision and subsequent cases established the implied powers of local school boards in curricular matters. These implied powers apply not only to additions of specific curricular elements, such as sex education, drug education, competitive sports, and vocational education programs, but also the determination of methods of carrying out state-mandated curriculum. Generally, the courts have sustained such local board activities, providing they do not contravene the state constitution and the federal Constitution.

Student Discipline

It is expected that schools will be operated according to the rules and regulations of local boards of education. However, teachers and other school personnel are granted wide discretion in disciplining students. The legal doctrine that defines the relationship of educator to pupil is **in loco parentis** ("in place of the parent"). The doctrine is well stated in a precedent-setting Wisconsin case:

> While the principal or teacher in charge of a public school is subordinate to the school board . . . , and must enforce rules and regulations adopted by the board . . . , he does not derive all his power and authority in the school and over his pupils from affirmative action of the board. He stands for

the time being in loco parentis to his pupils, and because of that relation he must necessarily exercise authority over them in many things concerning which the board may have remained silent.[58]

In this section, we examine students' rights pertaining to corporal punishment, expulsions and suspensions, and search and seizure.

Corporal Punishment   Under common law, teachers and other school personnel have the right to administer reasonable corporal punishment, which is the infliction of physical pain on a student for misconduct. State statutes deal with corporal punishment in different ways. Some states authorize it; others forbid it. Still others are silent on the matter, but by implication allow it.[59] Massachusetts and New Jersey prohibit corporal punishment by statute. In Maryland state board of education policy bans corporal punishment. New York permits corporal punishment unless local boards of education prohibit it. Kentucky allows a teacher to use physical force to maintain reasonable discipline in a school, class, or other group.[60]

In the landmark Supreme Court decision, *Ingraham v. Wright,* the Court held that corporal punishment of students does not violate the Eighth Amendment nor the due process guarantees of the Fourteenth Amendment. The Court said that the Eighth Amendment's prohibition of cruel and unusual punishment applies to criminals only and is not applicable to the disciplining of students in public schools. The Court noted that "at common law a single principle has governed the use of corporal punishment since before the American Revolution: teachers may impose reasonable but not excessive force to discipline a child." Regarding due process, the Court held that a student is not entitled to notice and a hearing prior to the imposition of corporal punishment.[61]

---

[57]Stuart v. S.D. No. 1 of Village of Kalamazoo, 30 Mich. 69 (1874).

[58]State ex. rel. Burpee v. Burton, 45 Wis. 150, 30 Am. Rep. 706 (1878).

[59]H. C. Hudgins and Richard S. Vacca, *Law and Education,* 2nd ed. (Charlottesville, VA: Michie, 1985).

[60]Ky. Rev. Stat., Ch. 503.110 (1990).

[61]Ingraham v. Wright, 430 U.S. 651 (1977).

Expulsions and Suspensions   Expelling and suspending students from school are among the most widely used measures of disciplining students. From a practical standpoint, expulsion is the exclusion of a student from school for a period of time exceeding ten days or more. Under common law, expulsion is vested exclusively in the board of education. Professional personnel may not expel students unless authorized by state statute.

Generally, courts have held that expulsion of students from school jeopardizes a student's property interests in an education. Thus, students are guaranteed at least minimum due process under the Fourteenth Amendment. The following list enumerates suggested elements of recommended procedural due process in such cases:[62]

1. A speedy and full notification of the charges should be given to the accused.
2. The accused should be provided an opportunity to answer the charges and to prepare an adequate defense.
3. The hearing should be conducted by an impartial tribunal.
4. The accused should be given the names of adverse witnesses, access to adverse evidence, and the right to introduce evidence.
5. The decision must be based on the evidence adduced at the hearing.
6. A prompt finding, giving the reasons for the decision and the evidence supporting it, should be delivered at the conclusion of the hearing.
7. The accused (or her counsel) should have the right to cross-examine adverse witnesses and introduce witnesses in her defense.
8. The accused has a right to representation by legal counsel.
9. A written record of the proceedings should be maintained.
10. The accused should have the right to appeal an adverse decision.

Suspensions generally involve exclusion of a student from school for a brief, definite period of time, usually not exceeding ten days. In contrast to detailed procedures related to expulsion, state statutes have been less specific regarding the procedures that should be followed when suspending students from schools. Prior to 1975, procedural due process accorded to suspended students was poorly defined. Lower courts differed widely in their interpretation of the Fourteenth Amendment guarantees in suspension cases. In 1975, in *Goss v. Lopez,* the U.S. Supreme Court prescribed the minimum constitutional requirements in cases involving student suspensions of ten days or less.[63] The Court concluded that oral notice to the student of the reason for short suspensions, followed by an immediate, informal hearing by a local school official, would fulfill the due process requirement in brief suspensions. The Court specifically rejected the usual trial-type format including the involvement of attorneys and the presentation and cross-examination of adverse witnesses typical in criminal cases.

Search and Seizure   The Fourth Amendment provides that "the right of people to be secure in their persons, houses, papers, and effects, against unreasonable searches and seizures shall not be violated, and no warrants shall issue, but upon probable cause. . . . " The clause has been involved in numerous criminal cases. Evidence obtained in violation of the amendment is inadmissible in court.

The introduction of drugs and other contraband in schools has placed school officials in the position of searching students' person or lockers, and students claim that such acts are a violation of their Fourth Amendment guarantees. A student's right to the Fourth Amendment's protection from unreasonable search and seizure must be balanced against the need for school officials to maintain discipline and to provide a safe environment conducive to learning. State and federal courts generally have relied on

[62]Julius Menacher, *School Law* (Englewood Cliffs, NJ: Prentice-Hall, 1987).

[63]Goss v. Lopez, 419 U.S. 565 (1975).

the doctrine of in loco parentis, reasoning that school officials stand in the place of a parent and are not subject to the constraints of the Fourth Amendment. In 1985, in *New Jersey v. T.L.O.,* the U.S. Supreme Court held that searches by school officials in schools come within the constraints of the Fourteenth Amendment.[64] The Court concluded that the special needs of the school environment justified easing the warrant and probable cause requirement imposed in criminal cases, provided that school searches are based on "reasonable suspicion."

Freedom of Expression

Of all the freedoms guaranteed in this country, none is more protected than the right of freedom of speech and the press and the right to peaceable assembly as set forth in the First Amendment. Specifically, it provides that "Congress shall make no law . . . abridging the freedom of speech, or of press; or the right of the people peaceably to assemble. . . . " The gamut of protected expression litigated in state and federal courts includes symbolic expression, dress and grooming, oral and written expression, and group associations and assembly. These categories of expression have received differential treatment in the courts.

Symbolic Expression   Historically, students generally played a submissive role in relation to freedom of expression within the public schools. In 1969 the landmark case of the U.S. Supreme Court, *Tinker v. Des Moines Independent School District,* marked the emergence of a new era in students' protected expression in the public schools.[65] The Court invalidated a rule prohibiting students from wearing black arm bands in school as a protest against the Vietnam War. The Court stated that "undifferentiated fear or apprehension of disturbance is not enough to overcome the right to freedom of expression."

Furthermore, the Court declared that the prohibition of the wearing of symbols can be sustained only if such activity would "materially and substantially disrupt the work and discipline of the school."

Thus, the *Tinker* test of "material and substantial disruption" emerged as a determinant in subsequent student expression litigation. The Court made it clear that school authorities would not be permitted to deny a student her fundamental First Amendment rights simply because of a "mere desire to avoid discomfort and unpleasantness that always accompany an unpopular viewpoint."

Student Appearance   School boards may enact reasonable regulations concerning student appearance in school. Appearance regulations have focused on male hairstyles and pupil attire. Student challenges to these regulations have relied on First Amendment constitutional freedoms to determine one's appearance. The U.S. Supreme Court has consistently refused to review the decisions of lower courts on these matters. In one case involving male hairstyle, Court Justice Hugo Black commented that he did not believe "the federal Constitution imposed on the United States courts the burden of supervising the length of hair that public school students should wear."[66]

Pupil Hairstyle   Five of the federal circuit courts of appeal (third, fifth, sixth, ninth, and tenth) have sustained the authority of public schools to regulate hairstyles of male students. Four federal circuit courts (first, fourth, seventh, and eighth) have overturned such regulations, finding that hair-length regulations impinge student's constitutional rights. Significantly, all circuit courts refused to treat hairstyle as a form of symbolic speech, which would implicate the test of the *Tinker* case.[67]

Pupil Attire. Generally, courts tend to provide less protection to some forms of expression (e.g., pu-

---

[64]New Jersey v. T.L.O., 105 S. Ct. 733 (1985).

[65]Tinker v. Des Moines I.S.D., 393 U.S. 503 (1969).

[66]Karr v. Schmidt, 401 U.S. 1201 (1972).

[67]Valente, *Law in the Schools.*

pil hairstyle and attire) than to others (e.g., symbolic expression and student publications). Nonetheless, awareness of constitutional freedoms place limits on school officials to regulate student dress, excluding special situations (e.g., graduation and physical education classes). Pupil attire can always be regulated to protect student health, safety, and school discipline.[68] In short, the extent to which school officials may control student appearance depends more on different community mores and on "the times" than on strict principles of law.

Freedom of Press   Student publications are a form of expression protected by the First Amendment. However, that right is limited by the obligation of school authorities to maintain order and control in the schools. School authorities can control the time, place, and manner of the distribution of printed material according to the U.S. Supreme Court.[69]

Publications paid for with school funds or produced as part of the curriculum of the school (e.g., journalism class) are subject to more controls than are student school newspapers published off campus. However, the fact that a publication is financed by the school does not give school officials the right to suppress or censor the content of student expression per se.[70]

One question that often arises concerning students' freedom of expression is whether school authorities can exercise prior restraint on material to be included in a school publication. In the seventh circuit, two appellate courts have ruled that prior restraint impairs students' First Amendment rights.[71] In contrast, the second, fourth, fifth, and ninth circuits have held that some prior restraints are legal under certain circumstances.[72] They are libel; obscenity, as defined by the courts; speech directed to producing or inciting imminent lawless action; and speech that causes material and substantial disruption of school activities.[73]

Freedom of Association and Assembly   Under the First Amendment, students have a constitutional right to freedom of association and to peaceable assembly. Public schools are places where student associations and clubs are part of the daily routine of the school, some of which have been formally designated as cocurricular activities. However, most schools prohibit secret societies, associations, clubs, fraternities and sororities, and satanic cults. Courts have reasoned that such organizations have a detrimental influence on schools by tending to perpetuate antidemocratic values such as elitism, discrimination, and divisiveness. Various pleas of an abrogation of students' First and Fourteenth Amendment rights in these situations have not prevailed.[74] An Oregon court ruled that any non–school affiliated organization could associate in any manner it wished.[75]

Classification Practices

The courts have evaluated classification practices to determine their legitimacy under the equal protection clause of the Fourteenth Amendment, state constitutions, and state and federal statutes. In this section, we explore student-classification practices based on gender,

[68]Graber v. Kniola, 52 Mich. App. 269, 216 N.W. 2d 925 (1974); Stromberg v. French, 60 N.D. 750, 236 N.W. 477 (1931); Bannister v. Paradis, 316 F. Supp. 185 (D.N.H. 1970).
[69]Grayned v. City of Rockford, 408 U.S. 104 (1972).
[70]Reutter, *The Law of Public Education.*
[71]Fujishima v. Bd. of Educ., 460 F.2d 1355 (7 Cir. 1973); Jacobs v. Bd. of School Commissioners, 490 F.2d 601 (7 Cir. 1973).

[72]Trachtman v. Anker, 563 F.2d 512 (2 Cir. 1977); Williams v. Spencer, 622 F.2d 1200 (4 Cir. 1980); Shanley v. Northeast I.S.D. Bexar City, Tex., 462 F.2d 960 (5 Cir. 1972); Nicholson v. Bd. of Educ. Torrance U.S.D., 682 F.2d 858 (9 Cir. 1982).
[73]Richard D. Strahan and L. Charles Turner, *The Courts and the Schools* (New York: Longman, 1987).
[74]Passel v. Fort Worth I.S.D., 453 S.W. 2d 888 (Tex. Civ. App. 1970); Robinson v. Sacramento U.S.D., 53 Calif. Reptr. 781, 788–789 (1966).
[75]Burkitt v. S.D. No. 1, Multnomah Cty., 195 Ore. 471, 246 P.2d 566 (1952).

marriage and pregnancy, age, ability, and handicaps.

Gender Litigants claiming sex discrimination can seek relief under the equal protection clause of the Fourteenth Amendment, Title VII of the Civil Rights Act of 1964, Title IX of the Education Amendments of 1972, Section 1983, the Equal Educational Opportunities Act of 1974, equal rights amendments to state constitutions, and new and evolving sex discrimination statutes.

To receive affirmation from the courts, defendants in sex discrimination cases must present a preponderance of evidence that gender-based classifications are completely related to a legitimate government purpose. One public school case to reach the Supreme Court, *Vorchheimer v. School District of Philadelphia,* involved a challenge brought by a female student who had been denied admission to an all-male academic high school. The school district maintained among its high schools two sex-segregated schools for high-achievement students. The Court, equally divided, affirmed an earlier Third Circuit Court of Appeals decision that had ruled in favor of the school district.[76]

On the other hand, sex discrimination was held to violate the equal protection clause in two public school districts in which the schools set higher standards for girls than for boys.[77] In another case, the exclusion of male students from participation in a sex-segregated girls' program in a coeducational public high school was held to violate the state constitution's provision against sex discrimination.[78] In a more recent and famous university case, the Court held that the denial of admission to a male registered nurse to a state-supported university for women

was unconstitutional discrimination based on gender classification.[79]

An area that has received much publicity concerning gender-based classifications is high school athletics. A precedent-setting eighth circuit court case invalidated a school policy that restricted participation to only male athletes on several noncontact sports' teams.[80] Generally, most courts have followed suit. The general proposition that female athletes must be provided the opportunity to participate in contact sports either through single-sex or coeducational teams has been sustained as well in federal district courts in Wisconsin, Missouri, and New York and the Pennsylvania Supreme Court. The converse is not true, however; male athletes can be barred from all-female teams if their participation impedes the athletic opportunities of females.[81]

Marriage and Pregnancy Historically, public school districts have generally discouraged, and in some cases even barred, students from school attendance or participation in school-sponsored activities for reason of marriage or pregnancy. In more recent years, courts have invalidated school district policies for differential treatment of married or pregnant students. Federal district courts in Massachusetts, Mississippi, Montana, Ohio, Tennessee, and Texas have held that exclusion from school attendance and from participation in various school-sponsored activities could not be made solely on the basis of marital status or pregnancy.[82]

It is apparent from federal district court decisions in various states that students within the age limits of statutorily permitted school attendance are entitled to a free public school education. As such, they may not be excluded because of marriage or pregnancy from school activities

[76]Vorchheimer v. S.D. of Philadelphia, 532 F.2d 880 (3 Cir. 1976), aff. 430 U.S. 703 (1977).

[77]Bray v. Lee, 337 F. Supp. 934 (D. Mass. 1972); Berkelman v. San Francisco U.S.D., 501 F.2d 1264 (9 Cir. 1974).

[78]Opinion of the Justices to the Senate, 373 Mass. 883, 366 N.E. 2d 733 (1977).

[79]Mississippi University for Women v. Hogan, 458 U.S. 718 (1982).

[80]Brenden v. Independent School District, 477 F.2d 1292 (8 Cir. 1973).

[81]McCarthy and Cambron-McCabe, *Public School Law.*

[82]Reutter, *The Law of Public Education.*

nor isolated from contact with other students within the school environment.

Age   School boards have used age as a criterion for public school admission, compulsory education, and participation in some cocurricular activities. Courts have generally sustained school board policy and state statutes specifying minimum age requirements used in operating school systems. For example, a Wisconsin court and a federal district court in Maine supported a local school board policy and the state's minimum-age law, respectively, as a valid criterion for admission to its public schools. And a New York court upheld a school board policy restricting entry into a special accelerated junior high school program solely on the basis of an age requirement.[83] The Age Discrimination Act of 1975 has had little effect on public school students.

Ability   Generally, courts have supported ability grouping in theory unless racial or cultural bias is shown. In a famous case, *Hobson v. Hansen,* a federal district court in Washington, D.C., invalidated an ability-grouping plan based on the use of standardized test scores because is was shown to discriminate against minority students.[84] Subsequently, the fifth and ninth circuit courts struck down ability-grouping practices based on the use of standardized achievement tests for the same reason. Later, the eleventh, another fifth circuit court, and an Illinois federal district court upheld grouping as free of cultural bias and contributing to the instruction and achievement of minority students.[85]

The Handicapped   Historically, the attitude that prevailed concerning the education of handicapped students was that retarded, learning disabled, emotionally disturbed, deaf, blind, or otherwise handicapped children were not the responsibility of the public schools. Conse-

quently, many handicapped children were exempted from compulsory school attendance laws either by parental choice or by school district design. Nationally, services for the handicapped were either nonexistent or nonextensive. Very few school districts provided services; where such services existed, they were inadequate to meet even the minimal needs of this vulnerable minority group.

In recent years, substantial changes in the attitude toward the handicapped have occurred. Although handicapped students do not comprise any "protected group" (such as race or sex) that is entitled to constitutional guarantees, federal statutes and state special education statutes were enacted to satisfy their constitutional rights. Lower-court decisions and federal and state legislative enactments of the past two decades have mandated that all children, including the handicapped, are entitled to admission to a school and placement in a program that meets their special needs. As summarized in the landmark Supreme Court school desegregation case, *Brown v. Board of Education of Topeka,* "education . . . is a right which must be made available to all on equal terms."[86] Although the *Brown* decision dealt with the constitutional protections afforded minority children, its consent agreement implied a mandate that all students of legal school age must be provided with appropriate school and classroom placement.

Two key court decisions outlined the legal framework for the constitutional protections of handicapped children. In *Pennsylvania Association for Retarded Children* (PARC) *v. Commonwealth,*[87] a federal district court held that retarded children in Pennsylvania were entitled to a free public education and that, whenever possible, handicapped children must be educated in regular classrooms and not segregated from other students. In *Mills v. Board of Education of the District of Columbia,*[88] another federal

[83] McCarthy and Cambron-McCabe, *Public School Law.*
[84] Hobson v. Hansen, 269 F. Supp. 401 (D.C.C. 1967), aff. Smuck v. Hobson, 408 F.2d 175 (D.C. Cir. 1969).
[85] McCarthy and Cambron-McCabe, *Public School Law.*

[86] Brown v. Bd. of Educ. of Topeka, 349 U.S. 294 (1955).
[87] Pennsylvania Association of Retarded Children v. Commonwealth, 334 F. Supp. 279 (E.D. Pa. 1972).
[88] Mills v. Bd. of Educ., 348 F. Supp. 866 (D.D.C. 1972).

district court expanded the PARC decision to include all school-age handicapped children.

Subsequent to the *PARC* and *Mills* decisions, Congress passed two landmark pieces of legislation that led to the rapid development of comprehensive, nationwide educational programs for the handicapped. Section 504 of the Rehabilitation Act of 1973 is a broad-based federal law that addresses discrimination against the handicapped both in the workplace and schools. The statute stipulates:

> No otherwise qualified handicapped individual . . . shall solely by reason of his handicap, be excluded from participation in, be denied the benefits of, or be subjected to discrimination under any programs or activity receiving Federal financial assistance.[89]

Thus, Section 504 would cut off all federal funds from schools that discriminate against the handicapped. The statute also provides that all newly constructed public facilities be equipped to allow free access by handicapped individuals.

Public Law 94–142, the Education for All Handicapped Children Act of 1975, provides federal funds to school districts that comply with its requirements. The major thrust of the act, however, was to ensure the right of all handicapped children to a public education. Major provisions of the law include a free appropriate public education, an individualized education program, special education services, related services, due process procedures, and the least restrictive learning environment.[90]

According to P.L. 94–142, all handicapped children have the right to a "free appropriate public education." An appropriate education for the handicapped is defined as special education and related services. Special education refers to specially designed instruction at public expense, including a variety of opportunities on a spectrum from regular classroom instruction and special classes to placement in a private facility. Related services include transportation, physical and occupational therapy, recreation, and counseling and medical diagnosis. A written **individualized education program** (IEP) is another key element in a free appropriate public education. An IEP includes an assessment of the child's needs, specification of annual goals, strategies (methods, materials, interventions) to achieve the goals, and periodic evaluations of the child's progress. And, finally, a handicapped child must be educated in the least restrictive environment. That is, the placement must be tailored to the special needs of the handicapped student.

THE LAW AND STATE ISSUES

This section focuses on major legal issues pertaining to school desegregation, church–state relations, and school finance schemes.

School Desegregation

A U.S. Supreme Court decision, *Plessey v. Ferguson,* established the **"separate but equal"** doctrine regarding the use of public railroad facilities by blacks and whites in 1896.[91] Subsequently, this doctrine was used as the basis for public school segregation of black and white students for the next fifty years in many states. Under dual school systems, black students attended all-black schools staffed predominantly by black teachers, and white children attended all-white schools. Such de jure segregation was rendered constitutional because the separate-but-equal rationale served as a national standard satisfying the equal protection clause of the Fourteenth Amendment.

In 1954 the landmark decision of *Brown v. Board of Education of Topeka* repudiated the *Plessey* doctrine.[92] The Court stated that "in the

---

[89]Rehabilitation Act of 1973, Sec. 504, 29 U.S.C.A. Sec. 794.

[90]The Education For All Handicapped Children Act, 20 U.S.C.A. Sec. 1401 (1976).

[91]Plessey v. Ferguson, 163 U.S. 537 (1896).

[92]Brown v. Bd. of Educ. of Topeka, 347 U.S. 483 (1954).

field of public education the doctrine of 'separate but equal' has no place. Separate educational facilities are inherently unequal." Because of the significant impact of this decision, the Court postponed for one year the issuance of an enforcement decree. The decision, known as *Brown II,* directed lower federal courts to enforce remedies "with all deliberate speed."[93]

Following *Brown,* southern school districts attempted numerous strategies to avoid desegregation—including transfer provisions; closing the public schools and maintaining state-supported, private, segregated white schools; integrating schools on a one-grade-a-year plan and freedom-of-choice plans; rezoning school districts; and the like—all of which perpetuated segregated dual school systems. Fourteen years after *Brown II,* the Court discarded the "all deliberate speed" criterion for complying with its desegregation enforcement decree. It stated that " . . . every school district is to terminate dual school systems at once and to operate now and hereafter only unitary schools."[94]

This ultimatum was to impact only those states with **de jure segregation**—segregation that is derived from the influence of law and is unconstitutional. Southern school districts were quick to point out that there was plenty of segregation in the North created by social forces (such as housing patterns), independent of state sponsorship, which is called **de facto segregation** and is not unconstitutional. For de jure segregation to exist, three factors must be present: (1) Segregation must be initiated and supported by government action; (2) the action must have been taken with the intent to segregate; and (3) the action must have created or increased segregation.[95]

After the *Alexander* decision, many types of remedies of de jure segregation were ordered by lower federal courts. The famous *Swann v. Charlotte–Mecklenburg Board of Education* busing

case served as a model remedy for school desegregation. The Court concluded: "In these circumstances, we find no basis for holding that the local school authorities may not be required to employ bus transportation as a tool of school desegregation. Desegregation plans cannot be limited to the walk-in school."[96] This case launched busing as an effective tool to remedy school desegregation.

The courts have used interdistrict desegregation as another remedy for de jure segregation in some situations. In what has become known as the "Detroit case," the Supreme Court affirmed de jure segregation in Detroit because it was shown that racially discriminatory acts of one or more school districts caused racial segregation in an adjacent district and that district lines were deliberately drawn on the basis of race.[97] Three years later, the Detroit case was heard by the Supreme Court once again.[98]

The Court ordered several curriculum programs to eradicate the vestiges of de jure segregation, including remedial reading, teacher inservice training in human relations, expanded counseling and career guidance services for minority students, and a nondiscriminatory testing program. Also ordered was state support of one-half the cost to implement these programs. Subsequent interdistrict remedies were ordered in numerous school districts including Jefferson County, Kentucky, which has served as a model of interdistrict desegregation for many years.[99] (See Administrative Advice 12-4.)

Church–State Relations

Issues concerning church–state relations have provided a steady stream of litigation since World War II. No other area in school law, except school

---

[93]Brown v. Bd. of Educ. of Topeka, 349 U.S. 294 (1955).
[94]Alexander v. Holmes Cty. Bd. of Educ., 396 U.S. 19 (1969).
[95]Strahan and Turner, *The Courts and the Schools.*

[96]Swann v. Charlotte–Mecklenburg Bd. of Educ., 402 U.S. 1 (1971).
[97]Milliken v. Bradley, 418 U.S. 717 (1974).
[98]Milliken v. Bradley, 433 U.S. 267 (1977).
[99]Newburg Area Council, Inc., v. Bd. of Educ. of Jefferson County, Ky., 510 F.2d 1358 (6 Cir. 1974), cert. den. 421 U.S. 931 (1975).

ADMINISTRATIVE ADVICE 12-4

Magnet Schools: A Remedy for Racial Imbalance

Educators, not judges, should take the reins in desegregation. One remedy for correcting racial imbalance is good magnet schools. You can realign school attendance boundaries, consolidate with neighboring school districts, or bus students from one attendance area to another. Magnet schools may be the easiest remedy to sell to your constituency though. And they can work if you consider the following tips for putting a successful program together.

- *Act Before Someone Else Forces You.* It's easier to plan at your own pace than at somebody else's. If you are ordered by a judge to desegregate, there may not be enough time to hire a staff, locate a site, purchase supplies, and do a good public relations job.
- *Draw On All Your Resources to Put Your Magnet School Plan into Action.* Your school district's facilities planners can tell you whether your buildings are suitable for the type of magnet school you propose. Your personnel office will know whether you need more staff.
- *Select an Appropriate Site and Be Prepared to Modify the Building if Necessary.* Look for buildings in hard-to-desegregate areas and then modify the buildings to accommodate the magnet themes.
- *Set Aside Enough Money for Startup Costs.* Typically, magnet school programs cost between 10 and 15 percent more per pupil than traditional programs do.
- *Ask Parents What Themes They'd Be Willing to Support.* Parents are your clients; sell them what they want.
- *Select Your School Staff Carefully.* You want dynamic leaders and vibrant faculty members who are committed to the magnet theme and believe that multiracial, multiethnic education is a good thing.
- *Put Together a Detailed Transportation Plan and Test It.* The biggest complaint parents have about magnet schools is transportation. Work out bus routes, schedules, and pickup points in advance and then do trial runs of the proposed routes.
- *Allocate a Set Number of Seats by Grade, Sex, and Race and Plan to Revise Allocations After a Specific Date.* Some seats won't be claimed; others will become vacant as students transfer or move. You'll have to recruit students year-round.
- *Advertise.* Use every way you can to recruit students: radio, television, newspapers, public presentations, and the like.
- *Keep Close Tabs on How the Program Is Doing.* Is the curriculum going as planned? Do the schools have the supplies they need? Are the facilities adequate? Make someone responsible for overseeing the program.

Source: Adapted from Donald E. Wright, William G. Chance, and Deborah L. Smith, "Educators, Not Judges, Should Take the Reins in Desegregation," *Executive Educator,* 11 (1989), pp. 28–29.

desegregation, has received more attention in the courts than issues involving religion in the public schools. In this section, we examine legal developments concerning church–state–education relationships. Our discussion is limited to school prayer and Bible reading, religion in the curriculum, released time for religious instruction, and use of facilities.

Contained in the U.S. Constitution is a separation of church and state provision, which guarantees religious freedom and forbids the establishment of religion by the government. The

First Amendment provides in part that "Congress shall make no law respecting the establishment of religion, or prohibiting the free exercise thereof." These two religious clauses, the *establishment clause* and the *free exercise clause,* protect a person's religious liberty. The two combined prevent religious indoctrination in the public schools and prohibit the use of public funds to support religion.

It should be noted that this provision restricts only the federal government from making such laws. However, through numerous Supreme Court decisions, justices have incorporated clauses in the U.S. Constitution as applicable to the states by means of the Fourteenth Amendment. This has been effected primarily through two Court cases. The free exercise clause was incorporated in *Cantwell v. Connecticut* and the establishment clause in *Everson v. Board of Education.*[100]

School Prayer and Bible Reading   Historically, many public schools began each day with a prayer and/or Bible reading. Three significant Court decisions established the precedent concerning Bible reading in the public schools. In *Engel v. Vitale,* the Court struck down a New York statute requiring the recitation of a prayer as a violation of the establishment clause of the First Amendment.[101] One year later, in *School District of Abington v. Schempp,* the Court declared unconstitutional a Pennsylvania statute requiring Bible reading and recitation of the Lord's Prayer " . . . when it is part of the school curriculum and conducted under the supervision of teachers employed in the schools."[102] The *Lemon v. Kurtzman* decision established a three-factor test of constitutionality under the establishment clause. The Court declared that to withstand constitutional challenge, the statute must pass three tests: (1) It must have a secular purpose, (2) have a primary effect that neither advances nor inhibits religion, and (3) not foster excessive government entanglement with religion.[103] This three-factor test has been applied in most establishment clause cases.

Persistent litigation concerning prayer and Bible reading in the public schools continued in the lower courts, but it was not until 1985 that a similar challenge reached the Supreme Court in *Wallace v. Jaffree.*[104] In this case, the issue was whether setting aside class time for silent prayer was constitutional. The Court held that such activity was unconstitutional. Although the Court applied the three-factor **Lemon test,** a minority of justices objected to its rigidity in assessing individual situations.

Released Time for Religious Instruction   Two Supreme Court cases have addressed the issue of released time for religious instruction. In the first case, *McCollum v. Board of Education,* the Court invalidated a program in which religion classes were taught in the public schools.[105] The Court declared that the use of tax-supported school facilities to promote religious instruction was clearly a violation of the First Amendment. In the second case, *Zorach v. Clausen,* the Court upheld a program whereby students were permitted to leave the school premises during the school day to receive religious instruction at various religious centers.[106] The significant difference between *Zorach* and *McCollum* was that the latter program did not involve the use of public school buildings or the direct use of public funds. Such released-time religious instruction is used in many school communities throughout the country. The arrangement does not violate the federal Constitution as long as the established program is not held on school grounds and is not conducted by teachers or religion instructors affiliated with the school and as long

---

[100]Cantwell v. Connecticut, 310 U.S. 296 (1940); Everson v. Board of Education, 330 U.S. 1 (1947).
[101]Engel v. Vitale, 370 U.S. 421 (1962).
[102]S.D. of Abington Twp., Pa. v. Schempp, 374 U.S. 203 (1963).

[103]Lemon v. Kurtzman, 403 U.S. 602 (1971).
[104]Wallace v. Jaffree, 472 U.S. , 105 (1985).
[105]McCollum v. Bd. of Educ. of S.D. No. 71, Champaign Cty., 333 U.S. 203 (1948).
[106]Zorach v. Clauson, 343 U.S. 306 (1952).

as these instructors are not paid by the school district.

Religion in the Curriculum   The *Lemon* test was used in two cases to assess the permissibility of offering Bible study courses in the public schools. In earlier decisions dealing with the constitutionality of school-sponsored prayer and Bible reading, the courts noted that the teaching of the Bible and religion as an aspect of our culture and our history and as a nonbiased academic subject is permissible. In *Wiley v. Franklin* and four years later in *Crockett v. Sorenson,* the courts ruled such practices unconstitutional.[107] Study of the Bible in both jurisdictions when scrutinized by the courts failed one or more prongs of the *Lemon* tripartite test. In a related case, a third circuit court held that a course on Transcendental Meditation (TM) violated the First Amendment.[108] In applying the *Lemon* test, the court concluded that the objectives of TM may have been secular but the means used were religious.

A recent development in this area involves state statutes requiring the teaching of creationism in courses that also teach about the theory of evolution. State statutes in Arkansas and Louisiana that required balanced treatment of the two scientific perspectives were struck down as efforts to advance religion and in violation of the First Amendment.[109]

Use of Facilities   It is common practice in public schools to permit student organizations to use school buildings during noninstructional time. Local boards of education have implied powers to regulate such use. In such situations, the question arises concerning the constitutionality of meetings involving religious groups. Can student religious groups use school facilities, and if so is this a violation of the establishment clause of the First Amendment? (See the PRO/CON Debate.) The Equal Access Act of 1984 provides that it is

> unlawful for any public secondary school which receives federal financial assistance and which has a limited open forum to deny equal access or a fair opportunity to, or discriminate against, any student who wishes to conduct a meeting within that limited forum.[110]

A school has complied with the *fair-opportunity* requirement if the meetings are (1) voluntary and student-initiated; (2) involve no school or government sponsorship; (3) allow the presence of school employees only in a nonparticipatory capacity; (4) do not materially and substantially interfere with the orderly conduct of educational activities within the school; and (5) are not directed, controlled, or regularly attended by nonschool persons; and the school cannot limit these groups to a specified size.[111]

The constitutionality of this federal statute is questionable. Three federal circuit courts (second, third, and fifth) have held that such meetings are unconstitutional and a violation of the establishment clause of the First Amendment.[112] The courts' view in these cases is that, if these meetings are sanctioned, students will believe that schools support religious groups and that this violates the posture of avoidance of excessive government entanglement with religion outlined in *Lemon.*

---

[107]Wiley v. Franklin, 474 F. Supp. 525 (Tenn. 1979); Crockett v. Sorenson, 568 F. Supp. 1422 (Va. 1983).
[108]Malnak v. Yogi, 592 F.2d 197 (3 Cir. 1979).
[109]McLean v. Arkansas Board of Education, 529 F. Supp. 1255 (Ak. 1982); Aguillard v. Edwards, 765 F.2d 1251 (5 Cir. 1985).

[110]Equal Access Act, Title VIII of P.L. 98–377, 98 U.S.C.A. 1301, Sec. 801 (1984).
[111]Strahan and Turner, *The Courts and the Schools.*
[112]Brandon v. Bd. of Educ., 635 F.2d 971 (2 Cir. 1980), cert. den., 454 U.S. 1123 (1981); Bender v. Williamsport Area S.D., 741 F.2d 538 (3 Cir. 1984), cert. aff. 1055 S. Ct. 1167, 54 L.W. 4307 (1986); Lubbock Civil Liberties Union v. Lubbock I.S.D., 699 F.2d 1038 (5 Cir. 1982).

PRO/CON DEBATE

■

EQUAL ACCESS

Congress passed the 1984 Equal Access Act in an attempt to clarify the unsettled area of law where the free-speech rights of students compete with the right of schools to control access to schools as a forum for public discourse. Since that time, lawsuits and court decisions have only added to the confusion and uncertainty.

QUESTION Should student religious clubs be allowed to meet in public school facilities?

ARGUMENTS PRO

1   Young people should be encouraged to engage in wide-ranging discussions on any issue. The developmental stage of adolescence is one where young adults are interested in religion.

2   Students do not leave their constitutional rights to freedom of speech at the schoolhouse door. They have the right to express their views in the classroom during class time. Why should they not be allowed to express them in after-school activities that are tied to religious groups?

3   Student religious clubs should have the same access to school facilities as is routinely granted to secular groups. Frequently, religious clubs have church or synagogue sponsors, and adults are present to supervise the students.

4   Under the federal equal access law, it is unlawful for a public secondary school that has created a limited open forum to deny access to student-initiated groups on the basis of the religious, political, or philosophical content of the group's speech.

ARGUMENTS CON

1   The U.S. Constitution provides for the separation of church and state. No religious events of any kind should be allowed in public school buildings.

2   Opening the schools to one student-initiated group opens the doors to all student-initiated groups. School administrators need clear restraints on the use of school buildings so that they do not have to decide on the basis of the desirability of one religious group over another. Without a limitation, students may request that an undesirable club, such as a cult or paramilitary group, meet in the school.

3   The current law restricts the amount of supervision that can be exercised over religious clubs. For purposes of safety, school administrators must have the latitude to supervise any student group that meets in the building.

4   The right way to guarantee freedom of religion is to keep the state out of the religious process altogether. To require the schools to allow access to religious groups is to get the schools involved, not to keep church and state separate.

Financing Education

Throughout the history of public education in the United States the property tax has served as the major source of financing public schools at the local level. The use of the property tax to finance public education has received much attention recently and has led to a steady stream of litigation in state and federal courts. Challenges to the present method of financing public schools have been advanced on the issue of equality of educational opportunity for all people. Dependence on local property tax revenues to support public education has caused wide inequities in interdistrict funding of educational programs in various states. The equal protection clause of the Fourteenth Amendment and specific state statutes have been the primary vehicles under which litigants have sought relief. This section focuses on levying taxes and challenges to state finance schemes.

School Taxes   The Tenth Amendment to the U.S. Constitution provides: "The powers not delegated to the United States by the Constitution nor prohibited by it to the states, are reserved to the states respectively, or to the people." This clause confers on the state not only the authority to regulate and control education but also to devise and implement its own system of taxation. Congress was reminded of the sovereignty of the state over public education in an early Supreme Court case. The Court concluded that "all powers not expressly granted to the United States by the Constitution or reasonably implied therefrom were reserved to the states."[113] This statement provided a case law basis for the state's power to tax and to appropriate funds for public schools.

The authority of school districts to raise and collect taxes for schools is a power that must be conferred on them by the legislature. Furthermore, not all districts have the same taxing power. The legislature can classify school districts and delegate varied financial powers to them dependent on their classification.[114]

Basically, there are two broad classifications of school districts with respect to their power to tax and raise funds for public schools: fiscally independent and fiscally dependent school districts. The vast majority of the more than 15,000 public school districts in the nation are fiscally independent.

Fiscally Independent School Districts. These school districts are granted legal authority by the state legislature to set the tax rate on real property, within state constitutional and legislative limits; to levy and collect taxes for the support of local schools; and to approve the expenditure of the funds collected. States require local school boards to prepare budgets of proposed expenditures. In fiscally independent school districts then, boards of education have a relatively free hand in determining how and where expenditures are to be made, subject to limitations on the total amount by the state's constitution or statute. For example, in Florida local school authorities levy and collect taxes for school purposes, independent of the local county or city governments. However, Florida state law sets a legal limit on the tax rates that can be established by local boards of education.[115] Similarly, in Kentucky state statutes grant local school boards authority to tax property for the support of public schools.[116]

Fiscally Dependent School Districts. In this configuration, the board of education prepares and adopts a budget specifying the anticipated expenditures and projected revenue needs. Then a different municipal government may reduce the total budget or eliminate items not required by state law and apportion the school taxes. For example, in Chicago statutory language authorized the school tax levy to be a cooperative endeavor, joining the board of education and city officials. While the local board performed all the preliminary steps in the budget process—preparation, review, and adoption—no school taxes could be forthcoming without the adoption by the city council of an ordinance levying the tax.[117] In a more recent case in Chicago, a two-year collective bargaining agreement was held

---

[113]U.S. v. Butler, 297 U.S. 1 (1936).

[114]Pirrone v. City of Boston, 364 Mass. 403, N.E. 2d 96 (1973).

[115]Gulesian v. Dade Cty. School Board, 281 So. 2d 325 (Fla. 1973).

[116]Ky. Rev. Stat., Ch. 160.593 (1990).

[117]Latham v. Bd. of Educ. of the City of Chicago, 31 Ill. 2d 178, 201 N.E. 2d 111 (1964).

unenforceable regarding the second year's salary provisions. The state statute stipulated that the local board of education could not incur a contractual liability without an apportionment of funds, and apportionments were made annually by the city council.[118] Similarly in Alaska, Maryland, Massachusetts, New Hampshire, New York, and Pennsylvania, school districts are fiscally dependent on the municipal government to apportion taxes for school purposes.[119]

Challenges to State Finance Schemes   Beginning in the late 1960s and continuing to the present, a steady stream of litigation has addressed the issue of inequality of educational opportunity resulting from public school finance schemes. Rooted in the famous landmark desegregation case, *Brown v. Board of Education of Topeka,* courts initially invoked equal protection rights as a means of forcing redistribution of state funds for public education. A key paragraph of *Brown,* often used by plaintiffs in school finance litigation, recognizes the importance of education in contemporary American society:

> Today, education is perhaps the most important function of state and local governments . . . [and] the great expenditures for education . . . demonstrate our recognition of the importance of education to our democratic society. . . . In these days, it is doubtful that any child may reasonably be expected to succeed in life if he is denied the opportunity of an education.

The Court went on to say, "Such an opportunity, where the state has undertaken to provide it, is a right which must be made available to all on equal terms."[120]

Educational Needs Standard   Two 1968 Supreme Court cases challenged the constitutionality of state finance schemes in Illinois and Virginia under the equal protection clause of the Fourteenth Amendment. The first case, *McInnis v. Shapiro,* was a class-action suit brought in behalf of elementary and secondary public school students and their parents in four Cook County school districts in Illinois.[121] The plaintiffs claimed that the Illinois system of public school finance violated the equal protection guarantees of the Fourteenth Amendment. Additionally, they claimed that there were markedly inequitable per-pupil expenditures among Illinois school districts.

In rejecting their contention, the court cited the following points: (1) The Fourteenth Amendment did not require that public school expenditures be made solely on the basis of "educational needs"; (2) "educational expenses" were not the "exclusive yardstick" for measuring the quality of a child's educational opportunity; and (3) there were no "judicially manageable standards" by which a federal court could determine if and when the equal protection clause is satisfied or violated. The court further stated, "The General Assembly's delegation of authority to school districts appears designed to allow individual localities to determine their own tax burden according to the importance which they place upon public schools." The U.S. Supreme Court affirmed the judgment. In the same year, the Court rejected a second challenge in Virginia, *Burruss v. Wilkerson,* advanced on the **educational needs standard.**[122]

Fiscal Neutrality Standard   In 1971 the California Supreme Court, in *Serrano v. Priest* (Serrano I), contradicted the stance taken by the U.S. Supreme Court two years earlier.[123] In both *McInnis* and *Burruss,* the U.S. Supreme Court

[118]Bd. of Educ. v. Chicago Teachers Union, Local 1, A.F.T., 26 Ill. App. 3d 806 N.E. 2d 158 (1975).

[119]Hudgins and Vacca, *Law and Education.*

[120]Brown v. Bd. of Educ. of Topeka, 347 U.S. 483 (1954).

[121]McInnis v. Shapiro, 293 F. Supp. 327 (N.D. Ill. 1968), aff., McInnis v. Ogilvie, 394 U.S. 322 (1969).

[122]Burruss v. Wilkerson, 301 F. Supp. 1237 (W.D. Va. 1968), 310 F. Supp. 372 (W.D. Va. 1969), aff., 397 U.S. 44 (1970).

[123]Serrano v. Priest, 5 Calif. 3d 584, 96 Calif. Rptr. 601, 487 P. 2d 1241 (1971).

rejected the federal constitutional theory that education is a right under the Constitution. The Court left in the hands of state legislatures the responsibility to remedy any existing inequities in state funding systems. *Serrano v. Priest,* then, represents an evolutionary step in judicial expansion of equal rights protection under the federal Constitution regarding public school finance. This case generated more reaction than any decision rendered in a state court, for it restricted the state's plenary power to devise and implement its own system of funding public schools.

The plaintiffs in *Serrano,* a group of elementary and high school pupils and their parents, brought a class-action suit against the state of California and the county of Los Angeles pertaining to the financing of the public schools. The plaintiffs argued that the California school finance scheme, which relied heavily on local property taxes, caused wide interdistrict disparities in per-pupil expenditures. Such a system was not fiscally neutral, according to the court, because it made the quality of a child's education dependent on the wealth of her school district and therefore invidiously discriminated against the poor in violation of the equal protection clause of the Fourteenth Amendment and similar provisions in the California constitution. The California Supreme Court concluded that under the **fiscal neutrality standard,** the quality of a child's education could not be a function of the wealth of the child's local school district but rather must be based on the wealth of the state as a whole.

The California Supreme Court in *Serrano v. Priest (Serrano II)* reaffirmed its position in *Serrano I* and provided remedies available to the legislature to rectify the wide disparities in the state-funding formula in California. Included among the remedies were the following proposals: full state funding to be supported by a statewide property tax; district consolidation with boundary realignments to equalize assessed valuations of real property among school districts; retention of present school district boundaries with removal of commercial and industrial property from tax-warrant rolls for school purposes and placement on state–tax warrant rolls for school purposes; and implementation of a voucher system.[124] One decade later, *Serrano v. Priest (Serrano III)* held that there had been full compliance with the original *Serrano* order to improve the inequities in state financing of public schools in California.[125]

The *Rodriquez* Case   Another major case that has had significant impact on public school finance was *San Antonio Independent School District v. Rodriquez.* The U.S. Supreme Court altered the *Serrano* attitude that public education is a fundamental right protected by the Constitution. Further, it struck down the fiscal neutrality standard that the quality of public education cannot be a function of wealth, other than the wealth of the state as a whole. *San Antonio v. Rodriquez* marked a return to the view that education is a plenary power grant to the states and not directly a federal matter.

Rodriquez was originally heard by a three-judge federal district court in Texas in which the state's school finance system was challenged. The plaintiffs alleged that the Texas system of financing its public schools, which relied heavily on the local property tax base, tolerated inequitable per-pupil expenditures among local school districts and discriminated against poor families. The rationale of fiscal neutrality and precedents of *Serrano* fashioned their plea. The district court concluded that the Texas system of financing public schools was a violation of the equal protection clause of the Fourteenth Amendment.[126]

Upon appeal of the state of Texas, the U.S. Supreme Court reversed the lower court.[127] The appellees' rationale was rejected on two fundamental points. First, the Court commented that

---

[124]Serrano v. Priest, 18 Calif. 3d 728, 135 Calif. Rptr. 345 (1976), cert. den. 432 U.S. 907 (1977).
[125]Serrano v. Priest, 226 Calif. Rptr. 584 (1986).
[126]Rodriquez v. San Antonio I.S.D., 337 F. Supp. 280 (W.D. Tex. 1971).
[127]San Antonio I.S.D. v. Rodriquez, 411 U.S. 1 (1973).

the evidence did not support the contention that the Texas finance system was discriminatory against the poor. The Court stated that the suit involved "a large, diverse, and amorphous class, unified only by the common factor of residence in districts." Further, the fiscal neutrality standard was struck down by the Court because the Texas school finance system was based on a statewide minimum foundation program financed by state and local revenue. The program was designed to provide at least a basic education to each student in the state. Local school districts contributed a portion to the state's foundation program reflective of the assessed property valuation in the district. The Court concluded that no child was completely deprived of educational opportunity in Texas.

Second, concerning the issue of whether education is a "fundamental" constitutional right under the equal protection clause, the Court concluded that there was no such right "explicitly or implicitly guaranteed by the Constitution." In so ruling, the Court reverted to the traditional attitude of leaving the financing of public schools in the hands of state legislatures. The Court concluded: "The . . . complexity of the problems of financing . . . a state-wide public school system suggests that there will be more than one constitutionally permissible method of solving them, and that, within the limits of rationality, the legislature's efforts should be entitled to respect."[128]

Post-*Rodriquez* Litigation   Subsequent to *Rodriquez,* litigation in school finance issues continued to flourish. The federal courts were abandoned, however, as an arena for such litigation. The Supreme Court's position in *Rodriquez* made it clear that successful challenges to state finance systems be pursued on state constitutional grounds rather than on the provisions of the U.S. Constitution. Plaintiffs continued to pattern their arguments on the *Serrano* and *Rodriquez* cases. Because of individual differences

in each state's constitution, decisions have been inconsistent.

The highest courts in ten states (Arizona, Colorado, Georgia, Idaho, Maryland, Michigan, Oklahoma, New York, Ohio, and Oregon) have upheld the state's system of financing public schools as constitutional. Most of these decisions were rendered by the court using the *Rodriquez* rationale and precedents. On the other hand, decisions by the highest courts in eight states (Arkansas, California, Connecticut, Kentucky, New Jersey, Washington, West Virginia, and Wyoming) have struck down the constitutionality of the state's public school finance system. Most of these decisions were rejected primarily on the legal principles forwarded by the California Supreme Court in *Serrano.*[129]

SUMMARY

1. All three units of government—federal, state, and local—exercise some degree of authority and control over public education.
2. The state has been given plenary power over public education through the Tenth Amendment to the U.S. Constitution.
3. Nevertheless, the federal government has exercised and continues to exercise profound influence in educational matters, primarily through the provisions of the federal Constitution, decisions of the U.S. Supreme Court, and congressional enactments.
4. The provisions of the Constitution that have had the greatest impact on the public schools are Article I, Section 10, and the First, Fourth, Fifth, and Fourteenth Amendments.
5. Litigation has reached both federal and state courts primarily in the areas of school desegregation, religion in the schools, and, more recently, challenges to state school finance schemes.
6. U.S. Supreme Court decisions have been prevalent also in such student-related issues as corporal punishment, search and seizure, freedom of expression, and various classification practices related to sex, marriage and pregnancy, ability grouping, and handicaps.

---

[128]Ibid.

[129]LaMorte, *School Law.*

KEY TERMS

obligation of contracts
First Amendment
Fourth Amendment
Fifth Amendment
due process clause
Fourteenth Amendment
tenure
equal protection clause
case law
property interest
liberty interest
tort
duty
standard of care
proximate cause
injury
contributory negligence

assumption of risk
comparative negligence
government immunity
parens patriae
domicile
residence
in loco parentis
individualized education program
"separate but equal"
de jure segregation
de facto segregation
Lemon test
educational needs standard
fiscal neutrality standard

DISCUSSION QUESTIONS

1. What are the roles the federal, state, and local governments play in the operation of schools?
2. What is the basic structure of the federal and state judicial systems?
3. Which provisions of the U.S. Constitution have had the greatest impact on litigation involving public schools? Discuss the major Supreme Court cases applicable to each provision enumerated, and evaluate the principles of law derived from these court decisions.
4. What can school administrators hope to gain from a knowledge of the sources of law that impact schools?
5. Which case (or cases) has had the greatest impact on your role as a professional educator, or which has changed your attitude toward the operation of schools?

SUGGESTED READINGS

Kern Alexander and M. David Alexander, *American Public School Law,* 2nd ed. (St. Paul: West, 1985). Provides an excellent introduction to school law, including an historical perspective.

H. C. Hudgins and Richard S. Vacca, *Law and Education,* rev. ed. (Charlottesville, VA: Michie, 1985). Provides a good handbook to supplement the more general comments on school law found in other texts.

Michael W. LaMorte, *School Law,* 3rd ed. (Englewood Cliffs, NJ: Prentice-Hall, 1990). Useful to anyone concerned about school law.

Martha M. McCarthy and Nelda H. Cambron-McCabe, *Public School Law,* 2nd ed. (Needham Heights, MA: Allyn and Bacon, 1987). Provides a comprehensive treatment of the evolution and current status of the law governing public schools.

E. Edmond Reutter et al., *The Law of Public Education,* 4th ed. (Mineola, NY: Foundation Press, 1989). Covers principles of law applied to problems of education, including hundreds of cases and judicial decisions.

Richard D. Strahan and L. Charles Turner, *The Courts and the Schools* (New York: Longman, 1987). Meant as a source to generate a basic understanding of legal issues that should guide educational planning and decision making.

William D. Valente, *Law in the Schools,* 2nd ed. (Columbus, OH: Merrill, 1987). Can be used as a basic reference for graduate studies and as a practical desk reference for school administrators and counselors.

IV

ADMINISTRATION OF PROGRAMS AND SERVICES

13

CURRICULUM DEVELOPMENT AND IMPLEMENTATION

FOCUSING QUESTIONS

1 How can we define curriculum? What definition do you prefer?
2 What approach to curriculum do most administrators adopt? Why?
3 What approach to curriculum do you prefer? Why?
4 How do philosophy of education and psychology of learning influence curriculum and instruction?
5 Why are curriculum development models usually behaviorist in nature? Can humanistic educators rely on such models? Why? Why not?
6 What criteria do you use in selecting content and experiences for planning curriculum?
7 How are content, experiences, and environment related in the planning of curriculum?
8 Why is change difficult to implement in schools?
9 What strategies or methods of change do you feel are important for your own school environment?

In this chapter, we attempt to answer these questions about curriculum development and implementation by first defining curriculum and examining the four basic approaches to develop it. Then we list the criteria for and define the administrator's role in planning and implementation. Finally, we look at ways to implement new curriculum and to urge staff to accept the change it may bring about.

Much of the professional literature currently stresses the need for supervisors and administrators to become more involved in curriculum development and implementation. The need to plan effective curricula is obvious because curriculum is often considered "the heart" of the school process. The difficulty, however, is there are various definitions of curriculum development and implementation. Not everyone agrees what curriculum is or what is involved in curriculum development and implementation. We present a definition to allow different views and interpretations to exist—and which permits school administrators to become more involved in curriculum matters.

CURRICULUM DEFINITIONS AND APPROACHES

What is curriculum? What is its purpose? How does it affect students, teachers, and administrators? The way we define curriculum in part reflects our approach to it. A curriculum can be defined as a *plan* for action, or a written document, which includes strategies for achieving desired goals or ends. Most educators agree with this definition, as do most administrators who approach curriculum in terms of a behavioral or managerial outlook.

Curriculum can also be defined broadly, as dealing with the *experiences* of the learner. This view considers almost anything in school, even outside of school (as long as it is planned) as part of the curriculum. It is rooted in John Dewey's definition of experience and education, as well as Hollis Caswell and Doak Campbell's view, from the 1930s, that curriculum was "all the experiences children have under the guidance of the teacher."[1] Humanistic curricularists and elementary school administrators subscribe to this definition, at least more so than traditional curricularists and secondary school administrators.

Curriculum can be viewed as a *field of study*, that is, as an intellectual or an academic subject that attempts to analyze and synthesize major positions, trends, and concepts of curriculum. The approach tends to be historical and philosophical and, to a lesser extent, social and psychological in nature. The discussion of curriculum making is usually scholarly and theoretical, not practical, and concerned with many broad issues of curriculum. Many administrators would reject this approach as lacking in practical value; administrators who might appreciate this approach as providing a worthwhile framework to help explain curriculum are those with advanced degrees and/or with several courses in curriculum. Those who might have faith in curriculum as a field of study would appreciate the functions of theory and theory building. They would also view curriculum as a system with its own definitions, operational constructs, assumptions, postulates, generalizations, laws, and specialists to interpret this knowledge.[2]

Finally, curriculum can be viewed in terms of specific *subject matter* (mathematics, science, English, history, etc.) and *grade levels*. The emphasis from this viewpoint would be on knowledge, concepts, and generalizations of a particular subject or group of subjects (such as the core curriculum, which combines two separate subjects such as history and English, or the broad fields curriculum, which combines many similar subjects into new courses such as social studies, language arts, or general science). All curriculum approaches have elements of this definition—that is, there is recognition of subjects and grades.

Behavioral Approach

Rooted in the University of Chicago school, this is the oldest and most popular approach to curriculum. As a means–ends approach, it is logical and prescriptive. It relies on technical and scientific principles and includes models, principles, and step-by-step strategies for formulating curriculum.[3] Usually based on a plan, sometimes called a "blueprint," goals and objectives are specified, content and experiences are sequenced to coincide with the objectives, and learning outcomes are evaluated in relation to the goals and objectives.

---

[1]John Dewey, *Experience and Education* (New York: Macmillan, 1938); Hollis L. Caswell and Doak S. Campbell, *Curriculum Development* (New York: American Books, 1935), p. 69.

[2]Allan C. Ornstein, "The Theory and Practice of Curriculum," *Kappa Delta Pi Record*, 24 (1987), pp. 15–17; Allan C. Ornstein and Francis P. Hunkins, "Theorizing About Curriculum Theory," *High School Journal*, 72 (1989), pp. 77–82.
[3]Allan C. Ornstein, "The Field of Curriculum: What Approach? What Definition?", *High School Journal*, 70 (1987), pp. 208–216.

This curriculum approach, which has been applied to all subjects for more than two-thirds of this century, constitutes a frame of reference against which other approaches to curriculum are compared and criticized.[4] Other names have been used to identify this approach—including logical/positivist, conceptual/empiricist, experimentalist, rational/scientific, and technocratic.[5]

The behavioral approach started with the idea of efficiency, promoted by business and industry, and the scientific management theories of Frederick Taylor, who analyzed factory efficiency in terms of time-and-motion studies and concluded that each worker should be paid on the basis of his individual output, as measured by the number of units produced in a specified period of time. Efficient operation of the schools (and other social systems), sometimes called **machine theory** by its critics, became a major goal in the 1920s.

Often ensuring efficiency in schools meant eliminating small classes, increasing student–teacher ratios, hiring few administrators, cutting costs in teacher salaries, maintaining or reducing operational costs, and so on and then preparing charts and graphs to show the resultant lower costs. Raymond Callahan later branded this idea the "cult of efficiency."[6] The effects were to make administration in general and curriculum making more scientific, at least more precise, and to reduce teaching and learning to precise behaviors with corresponding activities that could be measured.

Franklin Bobbitt described the problems as he set out to organize a course of studies for the elementary grades. "We need principles of curriculum making. We need not know that we should first determine objectives from a study of social needs . . . [and] we had not learned that [plans] are means, not ends."[7]

Bobbitt further developed his objectives and activities approach in the early 1920s in *How to Make a Curriculum*. He outlined more than 800 objectives and related activities to coincide with student needs. These activities ranged from the "ability to care for [one's] teeth . . . eyes . . . nose, and throat; . . . to keep home appliances in good working condition; . . . to spelling and grammar."[8] Bobbitt's methods were sophisticated for the day; but taken out of context, his list of hundreds of objectives and activities, alongside with the machine or factory analogy that he advocated, were easy to criticize.

It was left to Ralph Tyler, a graduate student of Bobbitt, to recognize the need for behavioral objectives that were not as tiny or lockstep, whereby basic techniques of curriculum, instruction, and evaluation were combined in a simple plan. He outlined four broad questions that he believed should be answered by anyone involved in planning or writing a curriculum for any subject or grade level:

1. What educational purposes should the school seek to attain?
2. What educational experiences can be provided that are likely to attain these purposes?
3. How can these educational experiences be effectively organized?
4. How can we determine whether these principles are being attained?[9]

Although Tyler's questions were not new when he wrote them, rather a condensed version of the Twenty-Sixth Yearbook of the National Society for the Study of Education (NSSE),

[4]Herbert M. Kliebard, *The Struggle of the American Curriculum: 1893–1958* (New York: Routledge & Kegan Paul, 1987); William H. Schubert, *Curriculum Books: The First Eighty Years* (Lanham, MD: University Press of America, 1980).

[5]John McNeil, *Curriculum: A Comprehensive Introduction*, 4th ed. (Glenview, IL: Scott, Foresman, 1990); Schubert, *Curriculum Books*.

[6]Raymond Callahan, *Education and the Cult of Efficiency* (Chicago: University of Chicago Press, 1962).

[7]Franklin Bobbitt, *The Curriculum* (Boston: Houghton Mifflin, 1918), p. 283.

[8]Franklin Bobbitt, *How to Make a Curriculum* (Boston: Houghton Mifflin, 1924), pp. 14, 28.

[9]Ralph W. Tyler, *Basic Principles of Curriculum and Instruction* (Chicago: University of Chicago Press, 1949), p. 1.

he put forth the ideas in easy-to-read and brief form (128 pages). His approach, considered today a classic method and read by curriculum specialists and school administrators, combines behaviorism (objectives are an important consideration) with progressivism (the emphasis is on the needs of the learner); the procedures outlined are still applicable in varying situations today.

Managerial Approach

This approach considers the school as a social system, reminiscent of organizational theory, whereby groups of people such as students, teachers, curriculum specialists, and administrators interact according to certain norms and behaviors. Administrators who rely on this approach plan the curriculum in terms of programs, schedules, space, resources and equipment, and personnel and departments. This approach advocates, among other things, the need for selecting, organizing, communicating with, and supervising people involved in curriculum decisions. Consideration is given to committee and group processes, human relations, leadership styles and methods, and decision making.

An offshoot of the behavioral approach, the managerial approach also relies on a plan, rational principles, and logical steps, but not necessarily behavioral approaches. The managerial aspect tends to zero in on supervisory and administrative aspects of curriculum, especially the organizational and implementation process.[10]

Advocates of this approach are interested in change and innovation and in how curriculum specialists, supervisors, and administrators can facilitate these processes. The curriculum specialist and supervisor is considered to be a practitioner—a change agent, resource person, and facilitator—not a theoretician. She reports to an administrator and follows the mission and goals of the school. If the school does not appreciate change, then the change role of the job is minimized. If the school is progressive, then changes are expected to be progressive. If the school emphasizes the Three Rs, then the curriculum specialist introduces plans accordingly.

The managerial approach is rooted in the organizational and administrative school models of the early 1900s—a period that combined a host of innovative plans involving curriculum and instruction that centered around individualization, departmentalization, nongrading, classroom grouping, homeroom and work–study activities. It was an era when various school district plans were introduced by their respective superintendents in an attempt to modify the horizontal and/or vertical organization of the schools. The names of the plans were usually based on either the school district's name or organizational concept—such as the Batavia (New York) Plan, Denver Plan, Elizabeth (New Jersey) Plan, Pueblo (Colorado) Plan, Platoon (Gary, Indiana) Plan, Portland (Oregon) Plan, Santa Barbara (California) Plan, Study Hall (New York City) Plan, and Winnetka (Illinois) Plan. Superintendents and associate superintendents were very much involved in curriculum leadership, often developing a plan in one school district and being hired by another one to implement the plan there. Hence, there was a good deal of hopscotching around of administrators, based on a combination of their managerial and curriculum skills.

The managerial approach became the dominant curriculum approach in the 1950s and 1960s for various school principals and superintendents. During this era, Midwest school administrators and professors (with administrative backgrounds) dominated the field of curriculum in terms of setting policies and priorities, establishing the direction of change and innovation, and planning and organizing curriculum and instruction.

The pace setters for this era were such school superintendents as Robert Anderson (Park Forest, Illinois), Lesliee Bishop (Livonia, Michigan), William Cornog (New Trier Township,

---

[10]Ornstein, "The Field of Curriculum."

Winnetka, Illinois), Robert Gilchrist (University City, Missouri), Arthur Lewis (Minneapolis), Sidney Marland (Winnetka, Illinois), Lloyd Michael (Evanston, Illinois), Stuart Rankin (Detroit), and J. Lloyd Trump (Waukegan, Illinois). Of course, there were other superintendents (or associate superintendents) from outside the Midwest who were also influential, such as Chester Babcock (Seattle), Muriel Crosby (Wilmington, Delaware), Gerald Firth (Roselyn, New York), and John McNeil (San Diego).[11]

These superintendents were very active politically, both at the local and national levels. They used the professional associations and their respective journals and yearbooks as platforms to publicize their ideas. In particular, they were frequently published by the Association for Supervision and Curriculum Development, American Association of School Administrators, and National Association of Secondary School Principals. Many like Anderson (Harvard), Firth (University of Georgia), Lewis (University of Florida), McNeil (UCLA), and Trump (University of Illinois, Urbana) became professors at major universities; others became active as board directors and executive committee members of professional and administrative organizations that have had major impact on curriculum, supervision, and administration.

Most of these administrators tended to be less concerned about teaching and learning than about organization and implementation. Similarly, they were less concerned about subject matter, methods, or materials than improving curriculum in light of policies, plans, and people on a schoolwide or school district basis. They envisioned curriculum change and innovation as they administered the resources and restructured the schools. Most of their innovative practices can be grouped into five categories— personnel, instructional media, instructional groups, grading, and schools—and how they were to be organized or modified:

1. Personnel changes focused on the way staff was to be used in the classroom, involving team teaching, differential staffing, and teacher aides (or paraprofessionals).
2. Media changes focused on instructional technology, including programmed instruction, language laboratories, educational television, and computer-assisted instruction.
3. Grouping practices involved individualized instruction, independent instruction, small-group instruction, and various homogeneous and heterogeneous groups.
4. Grading practices included nongraded plans, continuous progress plans, and pass-fail.
5. School plans were numerous and included various options such as flexible scheduling and module scheduling, as well as open schools, schools without walls, community schools, street academies, special service schools (for the emotionally disturbed or mentally retarded), and specialized schools (music, art, engineering, science, etc.).[12]

Ironically, most of the curriculum innovations developed during this period are still considered viable today and often discussed in the literature and implemented as new or innovative. Indeed, these administrators had good theoretical insight, and their practices would prove to last; their plans were usually well thought out and developed properly.

Systems Approach

It was not far to leap from organizing people and policies, a managerial view, to organizing curriculum into a system. The systems aspect tends to view various units and subunits of the organization in relation to the whole, and

---

[11]Allan C. Ornstein and Francis P. Hunkins, *Curriculum: Foundations, Principles, and Issues* (Englewood Cliffs, NJ: Prentice-Hall, 1988).

[12]For a discussion of the innovations of this era, see Maurie Hillson and Richard T. Hyman, *Change and Innovation in Elementary and Secondary Organization*, 2nd ed. (New York: Holt, Rinehart & Winston, 1971); Glenys G. Unruh and William A. Alexander, *Innovations in Secondary Education*, 2nd ed. (New York: Holt, Rinehart & Winston, 1974).

organizational units, flowcharts, and committee structures are often diagrammed as the curriculum plan is introduced and monitored.[13]

Sometimes referred to as **curriculum engineering**, the approach includes processes necessary to plan the curriculum by *engineers*—superintendents, directors, coordinators, and principals; *stages*—development, design, implementation, and evaluation; and *structures*—subjects, courses, unit plans, and lesson plans. The systems approach to curriculum was influenced by systems theory, systems analysis, and systems engineering. These principles, originally developed by social scientists in the 1950s and 1960s, are used or at least discussed widely by school managers as part of administrative and organizational theory.

In the systems approach to curriculum, the "parts" of the total school district or school are closely examined in terms of their interrelatedness and influence on each other. Components like departments, personnel, equipment, and schedules are planned to create changes in people's behavior and expectations. In general, information is communicated to administrators who consider alternatives and choices.

One particular application of the systems approach was developed by the Rand Corporation and has rapidly spread from government to business agencies. It is called a planning, programming, budgeting system (PPBS), and it brings together those components with the system's structure, functions, and capabilities. In this case, the system is the curriculum.

Another well-known systems approach is the program evaluation and review technique (PERT), which was introduced by the Department of Defense and subsequently spread to business and industry in the 1960s; like PPBS, it has been introduced into education. Progress and interruptions of various facets of the program, in this case the curriculum, are computed, analyzed, and made available to administrators. Progress reports are continually

updated, reflecting changes in schedule, possible difficulties, and achievement rates. In both systems' approaches, the curriculum is closely monitored by administrators; revisions and corrective action are introduced on a continual basis.

It was George Beauchamp (a former school administrator and professor of curriculum) that developed the first systems theory of curriculum. He divided theories of education into five major theories of equal importance: administrative, counseling, curriculum, instructional, and evaluation.[14] Many school administrators do not accept this notion of equal theories, for they view administration as their major system or field of study and curriculum as a component or subsystem of the major system. In fact, they often delegate supervisors to take care of curriculum matters, especially if they view their leadership role chiefly in terms of management. On the other hand, curriculum specialists usually view curriculum as the major system and related fields such as supervision, teaching, instruction, and evaluation as subsystems, which help implement the curriculum.[15]

However, what Beauchamp was trying to convey is that the five theories of education are *applied* realms of knowledge that draw their ideas from the foundations of education: psychology, sociology, history, philosophy, and so on. Rather than dispute what the major systems or subsystems are, it is more important to design procedures that are applicable to the real world and use whatever theory that can be helpful.

Administrators who value the systems approach take a macro, or broad, view of curriculum and are concerned with curriculum issues and questions that relate to the entire school or school system, not only in terms of subjects or grades. They ask theoretical questions, often re-

---

[13]Ornstein, "The Field of Curriculum."

[14]George A Beauchamp, *Curriculum Theory*, 4th ed. (Itasca, IL: Peacock, 1981).
[15]Allan C. Ornstein, "Curriculum, Instruction, and Supervision—Their Relationship and the Role of the Principal." *NASSP Bulletin*, 70 (1986), pp. 74–81.

TABLE 13 ■ 1   Fundamental Questions of Curriculum

EIGHTEEN QUESTIONS—1930

1. What period of life does schooling primarily contemplate as its end?
2. How can the curriculum prepare one for effective participation in adult life?
3. Are the curriculum-makers of the schools obliged to formulate a point of view concerning the merits or deficiencies of American civilization?
4. Should the school be regarded as a conscious agency for social improvement?
5. How shall the content of the curriculum be conceived and stated?
6. What is the place and function of subject matter in the education process?
7. What portion of education should be classified as "general" and what portions as "specialized" or "vocational" or purely "optional"? To what extent is general education to run parallel with vocational education and to what extent is the latter to follow on the completion of the former?
8. Is the curriculum to be made in advance?
9. To what extent is the "organization" of subject matter a matter of pupil-thinking and construction of, or planning by, the professional curriculum-maker as a result of experimentation?
10. From the point of view of the educator, when has "learning" taken place?
11. To what extent should traits be learned in their "natural" setting (i.e., in a "life-situation")?
12. To what degree should the curriculum provide for individual differences?
13. To what degree is the concept of "minimal essentials" to be used in curriculum-construction?
14. What should be the form of organization of the curriculum? Shall it be one of the following or will you adopt others?
    (a) A flexibly graded series of suggestive activities with reference to subject matter which may be used in connection with the activities? Or,
    (b) A rigidly graded series of activities with subject matter included with each respective activity? Or,
    (c) A graded sequence of subject matter with suggestion for activities to which the subject matter is related? Or,
    (d) A statement of achievements expected for each grade, a list of suggested activities, and an outline of related subject matter, through the use of which the grade object may be achieved? Or,
    (e) A statement of grade objectives in terms of subject matter and textual and reference materials which will provide this subject matter without any specific reference to activities?
15. What, if any, use shall be made of the spontaneous interests of children?

---

ferred to as the "fundamental" or "basic" questions of curriculum, listed in Table 13-1. These questions do not have simple or linear answers, and they evoke philosophical and political debates among respondents.

These types of questions were first raised in 1930, when a famous twelve-person committee on curriculum, headed by Harold Rugg, presented a general statement on curriculum making and raised eighteen "fundamental questions" for the National Society for the Study of Education (see Table 13-1). They were raised again in the 1983

Yearbook of the Association for Supervision and Curriculum Development,[16] and still later on by other curriculum specialists.[17] A more recent

[16]Elizabeth Vallence, "Curriculum as a Field of Practice," in F. W. English (ed.), *Fundamental Curriculum Decisions*, 1983 Yearbook (Washington, D.C.: Association for Supervision and Curriculum Development, 1983), pp. 154–164.

[17]Ornstein and Hunkins, *Curriculum: Foundations, Principles, and Issues*; William H. Schubert, *Curriculum: Perspective, Paradigm, and Possibility* (New York: Macmillan, 1986).

TABLE 13 ■ 1   Fundamental Questions of Curriculum (continued)

16. What types of material (activities, reading, discussion problems and topics, group projects, etc.) should the curriculum-maker analyze for activities in which [students] actually engage?
17. How far shall methods of learning be standardized?
18. Administrative questions of curriculum-making.
   (a) For what time units shall the curriculum be organized?
   (b) For what geographic units shall the curriculum be made [national, state, school district, local school]? What is the optimal form in which to publish the course of study?

FIFTEEN QUESTIONS—1987

1. How is curriculum defined?
2. What philosophies and theories are we communicating, intentionally or not, in our curriculum?
3. What social and political forces influence curriculum? Which ones are most pertinent? Which constrain or impose limitations?
4. How does learning take place? What learning activities are most suitable for meeting the needs of our learners? How can these activities best be organized?
5. What are the domains of curriculum knowledge? What types of curriculum knowledge are essential?
6. What are the essential parts of a curriculum?
7. Why do changes in curriculum take place? How does change affect the curriculum?
8. What are the roles and responsibilities of the curriculum specialist?
9. How is the curriculum best organized?
10. What are the roles and responsibilities of the teacher and student in organizing curriculum?
11. What are our aims and goals? How do we translate them into objectives?
12. How do we define our educational needs? Whose needs? How do we prioritize these needs?
13. What subject matter or content is most worthwhile? What are the best forms of content? How do we organize them?
14. How do we measure or verify what we are trying to achieve? Who is accountable, for what, and to whom?
15. What is the appropriate relationship between curriculum and instruction? Curriculum and supervision? Curriculum and evaluation?

SOURCE: Harold Rugg et al., "List of Fundamental Questions on Curriculum Making," in G. M. Whipple (ed.), *The Foundations of Curriculum-Making*, Twenty-Sixth Yearbook of the National Society for the Study of Education, Part II (Bloomington, IL: Public School Publishing, 1930), p. 8; Allan C. Ornstein, "The Theory and Practice of Curriculum," *Kappa Delta Pi Record*, 24 (1987), p. 16. Used by permission.

set of fifteen fundamental questions (1987) is also presented in Table 13-1.

The posture one takes in answering the questions in Table 13-1 will greatly influence the planning of curriculum: the place and function of subject matter; the type of subjects offered; the methods and materials for facilitating instruction; the role of curriculum specialists and supervisors, as well as teachers; and how the school (or school district) is organized to carry out curricula functions. It will determine in part how curriculum is to be developed and imple-

mented, as well as the policies and processes involved in administrating the curriculum.

Humanistic Approach

Some administrators and curriculum leaders reflect on the field and contend that the above approaches are too technocratic and rigid. They contend that in our attempt to be scientific and rational, administrators (or supervisors) in charge of curriculum miss the personal and social aspects of curriculum and instruction; ignore the artistic, physical, and cultural aspects of subject matter; rarely consider the need for self-reflection and self-actualization among learners; and, finally, overlook the sociopsychological dynamics of classrooms and schools. This view is rooted in progressive philosophy and the child-centered movement of the 1920s and 1930s (which was spearheaded by Teachers College and such people as Hollis Caswell, William Kilpatrick, and Harold Rugg), as well as in humanistic psychology, which deals with valuing, ego identity, psychological health, freedom to learn, and fulfillment, as highlighted by the more recent works of Arthur Coombs, Abraham Maslow, and Carl Rogers.[18]

From this approach, a host of curriculum activities have emerged, mainly at the elementary school level, including lessons based on life experiences, group games, group projects, artistic endeavors, dramatizations, field trips, social enterprises, learning and interest centers, and child and adolescent needs. These activities include creative problem solving and active student participation; they emphasize socialization and life adjustment for students, as well as stronger family and school–community ties. They are representative of Parker, Dewey, and Washburne's (Parker and Washburne were superintendents) ideal school and the kinds of curriculum activities they put into practice and are still practiced in many private and university lab schools and upper-middle-class school districts across the United States.

The humanistic curriculum seems more conducive for middle- and upper-middle-class students, as well as higher achievers. Evidence suggests that these students exhibit high independence in learning and are better off in low-structured situations in which they can exercise their own initiative. Lower-class students often lack inner controls necessary for self-discipline, and low-achieving students often lack cognitive skills necessary for independent learning. These

students need high conforming rules and highly structured activities in class.[19]

This does not necessarily mean that inner-city schools cannot be humanistic. What counts is that teachers and administrators have faith in and high expectations for students, attempt to form meaningful and honest relationships between teachers and students (not coercive or controlling relationships), and that teachers try to foster individuality, self-direction, and self confidence. Without a humanistic principal, a person who is more concerned about people than tasks, it is almost impossible for inner-city schools (or for that matter suburban or rural schools) to exhibit a humanistic atmosphere.[20] Inner-city schools tend to be characterized not only by the regular bureaucratic tasks (which many schools exhibit) but also by basic tasks dealing with classroom discipline, reading and language problems, and lack of parental support for learning. Without involved parents and better childhoods, we will never see lasting reform or humanistic programs that work.

Curriculum leaders who believe in the humanistic approach tend to put faith in cooperative learning, independent learning, small-group learning, and social activities, as opposed to competitive, teacher-dominated, large-group learning, and only cognitive instruction. Each child, according to this approach, has some input in curriculum and shares responsibility with teachers in planning classroom instruction. Administrators tend to permit teachers more input in curriculum decisions. Curriculum committees are "bottom-up" instead of "top-down," and students are often invited into curriculum meetings to express their views on content and experiences related to curriculum development.

The humanistic approach became popular again in the 1970s, as relevancy, radical school

---

[18]Allan C. Ornstein, "Analyzing Curriculum Development," *NASSP Bulletin* (in print 1991).

[19]Carolyn M. Evertson and Regina Weade, "Classroom Management and Teaching Style," *Elementary School Journal*, 89 (1989), pp. 374–393; Richard E. Snow, "Individual Differences and the Design of Educational Programs," *American Psychologist*, 41 (1986), pp. 1029–1039.

[20]Ornstein, "Analyzing Curriculum Development."

reform, open education, and alternative education became part of the reform movement in education. Today, demands for educational excellence and academic productivity have resulted in emphasis on cognition, not humanism, and on subjects such as science and math, not art or music. The humanistic approach has always represented a minority view among administrators, who are usually more concerned with the "nuts and bolts" of curriculum—that is, the Three *R*s in elementary school and the basic academic subjects in secondary school. However, it has now been relegated almost to a fringe view, overshadowed by a return to "back to basics" and tougher academic standards.

CURRICULUM DEVELOPMENT

The need to develop curriculum is obvious; however, there are various ways to define and proceed with **curriculum development**. Ideally, those who are affected by curriculum should be involved in the process of *planning* and then in the process of *implementation* and *evaluation*. Table 13-2 raises important questions pertaining to these three phases of curriculum. Administrators and supervisors involved in curriculum making should be willing to discuss these questions with their respective board members and professional staff. But like many aspects of education, there is some debate about the formula to follow in order to achieve the particular educational goal. Although there are many developmental models of curriculum to choose from, we focus on one representative model for each approach listed here. (See Administrative Advice 13-1.)

Tyler: Behavioral Model

Tyler is often considered the bridge between the first and second half-century of the field of curriculum, whereby he fused the best ideas of curriculum making during the early period and set

---

TABLE 13 ▪ 2   Outlining the Steps in Curriculum Development

Planning a New Curriculum

1. Who determines priorities?
2. Who develops the time line?
3. Who assigns members to curriculum committees?
4. Who coordinates the efforts of curriculum committees?
5. Who devises the curriculum-development process?

Implementing the Curriculum

1. Who decides on the materials and activities for the new curriculum?
2. Who determines how much money will be needed to carry it out?
3. Who decides what staff development will be offered to prepare teachers to use it?

Evaluating the Curriculum

1. Who decides how the curriculum will be evaluated?
2. Who is responsible for carrying out the evaluation?
3. Who is responsible for reporting the results of the evaluation to teachers, administrators, school board members, and the public?

SOURCE: Adapted from Michael Campbell, Judy Carr, and Douglas Harris, "Board Members Needn't Be Experts to Play a Vital Role in Curriculum," *American School Board Journal*, 176 (1989), p. 30. Copyright 1989, the National School Boards Association. Used by permission.

ADMINISTRATIVE ADVICE 13-1

■

GUIDELINES FOR CURRICULUM DEVELOPMENT

Below are some guiding statements to help clarify some of the steps involved in curriculum development. These statements, according to the authors, are based on school practice and apply to all curriculum models.

- The curriculum-design committee should include teachers, parents, and administrators; some schools might include students, too.
- The committee should establish a sense of mission or purpose in the early stages or meetings.
- Needs and priorities should be addressed in relation to students and society.
- School goals and objectives should be reviewed, but they should not serve as the guiding criteria on which to develop the curriculum. Such criteria usually connote a broad educational philosophy to guide curriculum development.
- Alternative curriculum designs should be contrasted in terms of advantages and disadvantages such as cost, scheduling, class size, facilities and personnel required, existing relationship to present programs, and so on.
- To help teachers gain insight into the new or modified design, it should reveal expected cognitive and affective skills, concepts, and outcomes.
- Principals have significant impact on curriculum development through their influence on

school climate and their support of the curriculum process.
- District administrators, especially the superintendent, have only a peripheral impact on curriculum development because their outlook and concerns center on managerial activities. Their curriculum role is minor, but their support and approval are essential.
- State education officials have even less impact on curriculum development, although various departments publish guides, bulletins, and reports that can be informative. However, these educators establish policies, rules, and regulations that affect curriculum and instruction.
- The influence of special-interest groups and local politics should not be underestimated. Polarization or conflict has frequently obscured reasonable efforts for reform and meaningful dialogue between educators and parents in regard to educational matters.

Source: Adapted from Francis P. Hunkins and Allan C. Ornstein, "Designing the Curriculum: A Challenge for Principals," *NASSP Bulletin*, 72 (1988), pp. 58–59. Used by permission.

the stage for the modern period.[21] Tyler proposed a number of steps in planning a curriculum, outlined in Figure 13-1, starting with the goals of the school. These goals would be selected on the basis of what he called **sources of information** about important aspects of contemporary life, subject matter, and the needs and interests of learners. By analyzing changing society, at the local, state, or national level, it

could be determined what goals (and also what subject matter) were most important. By consulting with subject specialists (as well as teachers), helpful decisions could be determined about concepts, skills, and tasks to be taught in the various subjects (reading, math, science, etc.). By identifying the needs and interests of students, a beginning point in content, methods, and materials could be determined. (Hence, Tyler helped popularize the concept of a needs assessment study.)

[21]Tyler, *Basic Principles of Curriculum and Instruction*.

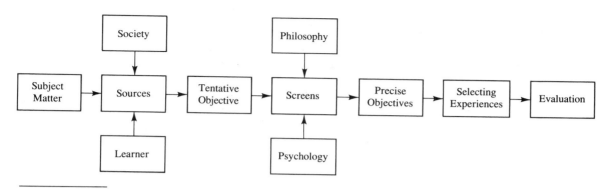

FIGURE 13-1   Organizing the Curriculum

Tyler then suggested that the school staff, possibly organized as a curriculum committee, **screen** the recommended *goals* according to the school's (or school district's) philosophy and beliefs about psychology of learning (or what some might call learning theory). What resulted from this screening process were *instructional objectives*, more specific than the school's goals and designed for classroom use.

Tyler then proceeded to the *selection of learning experiences* that would allow the attainment of objectives. Learning experiences would take into account the developmental stage of the learners, such as their age and abilities, and consider the learners' background (present attainments), external environment (classroom and school), and what the learner did (his behavior) when learning. Tyler next talked about *organizing learning experiences* in a systematic way to produce maximum, positive effect. Here he elaborated on the vertical (recurring subject matter such as social studies from grade to grade) relationship and horizontal (integration of different subjects at the same grade level) relationship of curriculum.

Tyler elaborated on the need for *evaluation* to determine whether the objectives were achieved or the learning experiences actually produced the intended results. Also, it was necessary to determine whether the curriculum was effective or ineffective and whether changes should be made or a new curriculum was warranted.

Although Tyler never introduced his model of curriculum development in a graphic manner, Figure 13-1 helps interpret what he was hoping to achieve. Because Tyler did not clarify at what level his model could be used, school district or school level, or whether it was a top-down (line-staff) model or bottom-up (teacher empowerment) model, it has the possibilities of both orientations. However, at the period of his writings, the top-down model prevailed in schools: Curriculum experts usually presented ideas for teachers to develop, and administrators either supervised or delegated supervision to ensure that the ideas were implemented in the classroom.

Saylor, Alexander, and Lewis: Managerial Model

Galen Saylor and his colleagues are from the behavioral school. However, as former administrators, they were very clear about the lines of authority and the need for supervisors and administrators to be in charge of the curriculum at the state and local district levels, in terms of curriculum guidelines and textbook selection, as well as at the school level, in terms of subjects

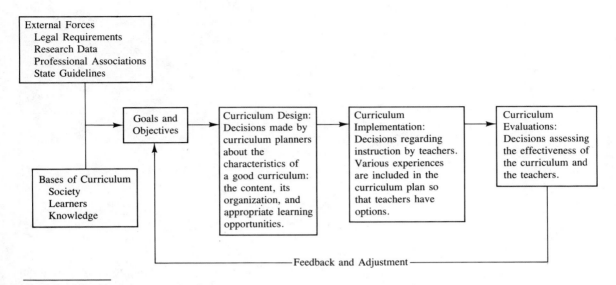

FIGURE 13-2   **Managing the Curriculum**
(Source: Adapted from J. Galen Saylor, William M. Alexander, and Arthur J. Lewis, *Curriculum Planning for Better Teaching and Learning*, 4th ed.; © 1981, pp. 29–30. Used by permission of Holt, Rinehart & Winston, New York.)

for study on the basis of grade levels.[22] Saylor saw curriculum as a general plan, whereby particular plans for individual programs of studies, courses of study, syllabi, unit plans, policy statements, handbooks, and learning packages were being used in different parts of the school and school district by many groups of people and individuals. Curriculum had to be put together or incorporated as a total package, or "curriculum plan," by those in charge of running the schools.

As Figure 13-2 indicates, a number of considerations enter into the development of curriculum. *Goals and objectives* are largely influenced (1) by external forces such as legal requirements, current research, professional knowledge, interest groups, and accreditation agencies and (2) by the bases of curriculum such as society, learners, and knowledge.

(These bases were similar to Tyler's sources, which had originally been elaborated on by Boyd Bode and John Dewey.)

Agreed-on goals and objectives then provide a basis for *curriculum design*, that is, a view of teaching and learning. Five different designs are examined: subject matter/disciplines, competency, human traits and processes, social functions and activities, and individual needs and activities. A subject-matter design emphasizes the role of knowledge and problem-solving activities. Specific competencies emphasize performance objectives, task analysis, and measurable outcomes. Human traits and processes are concerned with the learners' feelings, emotions, and values, as well as the affective domain of learning. A design that focuses on social functions and activities emphasizes the needs of society and, to a lesser extent, the needs of students. The individual needs and interests design is concerned with what is relevant to and motivates learners and what learning experiences lead to their full potential. Depending on the nature of management, the design can be op-

[22]J. Galen Saylor, William M. Alexander, and Arthur J. Lewis, *Curriculum Planning for Better Teaching and Learning*, 4th ed. (New York: Holt, Rinehart & Winston, 1981).

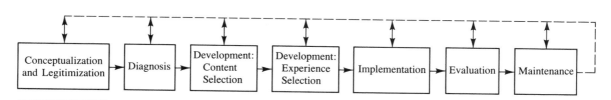

FIGURE 13-3   **Curriculum Systems**
(SOURCE: Adapted from Francis P. Hunkins, "A Systematic Model for Curriculum Development," *NASSP Bulletin*, 69, (1985), p. 24. Used by permission.)

tional and chosen by the classroom teacher, or it can be recommended by a school curriculum committee (administrators, supervisors, and/or teachers) or recommended by the central school district. School authorities, however, rarely require a design because curriculum matters involve teachers as well as possibly students and parents.

Curriculum implementation is mainly concerned with instructional activities that facilitate or put in practice the design. It includes instructional methods, materials, and resources, often listed in courses of study, unit plans, and lesson plans and often observed in classrooms as the teaching and learning process unfolds. Curriculum implementation includes supervision of instruction, teacher–supervisor planning and meetings, as well as staff development programs. The help teachers receive from resource personnel, supervisors, and administrators is the basis of implementation.

Curriculum evaluation involves the procedures for evaluating student outcomes and the curriculum plan. Evaluative data become the basis for decision making and planning among administrators. Administrators rarely engage in this type of evaluation; rather, they often delegate it to supervisors or outside consultants who report their findings to administrators, who in turn have the option to communicate the findings to teachers, parents, or the community.

Hunkins: Systems Model

The curriculum-development model suggested by Francis Hunkins is an example of a systems

approach, sometimes called an engineering approach, and is a little more complicated than the previous two models. As Figure 13-3 shows, it calls for administrative input in all stages and especially in the first two and last three stages.[23] The *conceptualization and legitimization* stage is unique from most curriculum models because it allows philosophical questions, mission statements, and school district goals to be raised and answered and relates those questions and answers to the stages that follow. *Diagnosis* deals with the problems of the school district (or school), the needs of students and possibly staff, and the transformation of goals into instructional objectives.

The next two stages deal with *content* and *experiences* and the basic issues of selection in which instructional leaders and teachers play a major role. The selection process (related to content and experiences) should correspond with the goals of the school and objectives of the subject matter. At this stage, administrators and teachers should assess the needs of the learners, classify objectives into broad themes or domains, and then make decisions about appropriate content and experiences.

Depending on the level of curriculum development, a school superintendent or principal can organize a curriculum committee (whose members are chiefly teachers) for different subjects that recommends the major content and experiences to be taught throughout the school years. Each committee furnishes a tentative syl-

---

[23]Francis P. Hunkins, "A Systematic Model for Curriculum Development," *NASSP Bulletin*, (1985), pp. 15–22.

labus for its subject area, and the syllabus is directed straight into classrooms for teachers to use, review, and modify. These comments are funnelled back to appropriate committees to consider as the full and final syllabus is developed.[24]

Implementation, the fifth stage, involves supervisors of instruction (such as vice principals, chairpersons, and resource personnel) assisting teachers in the classroom; it also includes ongoing assistance such as supervisor—teacher conferences and meetings, teacher participation at professional conferences and inservice meetings, and organized staff development programs.

The *evaluation* component includes both formative (ongoing stage for purpose of modifying the curriculum) evaluation and summative (end of the program or school year) evaluation. Administrators use the data to make decisions about modifying, terminating, or continuing the program. The *maintenance,* or final, stage involves the methods and means by which the program is managed and ensures that the curriculum will continue to function effectively or be replaced by an alternative. This stage also involves a monitoring function, organization of personnel, information flow, and reporting.

Weinstein and Fantini: Humanistic Model

Gerald Weinstein and Mario Fantini link sociopsychological factors with cognition so learners can deal with their problems and concerns. For this reason, these authors consider their model a "curriculum of affect." In viewing the model, some readers might consider it part of the behavioral or managerial approach, but the model shifts from a deductive organization of curriculum to an inductive orientation and from traditional content to relevant content.[25]

The first step, shown in Figure 13-4, is to identify the *learners,* their age, grade level, and common cultural and ethnic characteristics. Weinstein and Fantini are concerned with the group, as opposed to individuals, because most students are taught in groups. Therefore, knowledge of common characteristics and interests is considered prerequisite to differentiate and diagnose individual problems.

In the second and third step, the school determines the learners' *concerns* and assesses the reasons for these concerns. Student concerns include the needs and interests of the learners, self-concept, and self-image. Because concerns center around broad and persistent issues, they give the curriculum some consistency over time. Through *diagnosis,* the teacher attempts to develop strategies for instruction to meet learners' concerns. Emphasis is on how students can gain greater control over their lives and feel more at ease with themselves. In *organizing ideas,* the next step, the teacher should select themes and topics around learners' concerns rather than on the demands of subject matter. The concepts and skills to be taught should help the learner cope with her concerns.

The *content* is organized around three major principles or what Weinstein and Fantini call vehicles: life experiences of the learners, attitudes and feelings of the learners, and the social context in which they live. These three types of content influence the concepts, skills, and values that are taught in the classroom, and they form the basis of the "curriculum of affect."

According to the authors, *learning skills* include the basic skill of learning how to learn which in turn increases learners' coping activity and power over their environment. Learning skills also help students deal with the content vehicles and problem solve in different subject areas. Self-awareness skills and personal skills

---

[24]Roy L. Rummler, "Curriculum Blues? Turn to Teachers," *Executive Educator,* 11 (1989), pp. 30–31, 37.

[25]Gerald Weinstein and Mario D. Fantini, *Toward Humanistic Education* (New York: Praeger, 1970).

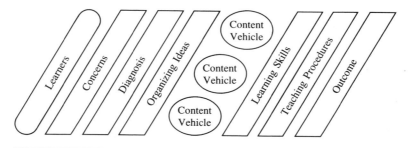

FIGURE 13-4   **Curriculum of Affect**
(SOURCE: Gerald Weinstein and Mario D. Fantini, *Toward Humanistic
Education*, p. 35. Copyright © 1970 by the Ford Foundation. Used by by
permission of Holt, Rinehart & Winston.

are recommended, too, to help students deal
with their own feelings and how they relate to
other people.

Teaching procedures are developed for learning skills, content vehicles, and organizing
ideas. Teaching procedures should match the
learning styles of students, which in turn are
partially based on their common characteristics
and concerns (the first two steps). In the last
step, the teacher evaluates the *outcomes* of the
curriculum: cognitive and affective objectives.
This evaluation component is similar to the evaluation components of the previous models (Tyler, Saylor, and Hunkins); however, there is more
emphasis on the needs, interests, and self-concept of learners—that is, affective outcomes.

COMPONENTS OF CURRICULUM DEVELOPMENT

Curriculum leaders must always be concerned
with *what* should be included and *how* to present
or arrange what is selected. In other words, they
must first deal with content or subject matter
and then learning experiences. Regardless of
the curriculum approach or development model
used, curriculum leaders cannot ignore these
two components.

Groups charged with curriculum planning
have options in selection of **content** and **experiences**—to be determined in part by the
philosophical and psychological views of the
committee members and school. Unquestiona-
bly, there is too much content and too many
learning experiences to include, and committee
members (or those in charge of curriculum)
must make decisions about what content and
experiences to include.

Criteria for Selecting Content

Curriculum planners should apply criteria in
choosing curriculum content. Although the following criteria are neutral and can fit into any
curriculum approach or model, various philosophical camps might place greater emphasis on
particular criteria. For example, Hilda Taba, in a
classic text on curriculum, maintains that content should include the following functions.

1. *Four Levels of Knowledge.* These include specific facts, skills, and processes; basic ideas
   such as generalizations, principles, and
   causal relationships within the subject matter; concepts dealing with abstract ideas,
   complex systems, multiple causations, and
   interdependence; and thought systems or

methods of problem solving, inquiry, and discovery.

2. *New Fundamentals to Master*. The content in many subjects becomes increasingly obsolescent, especially in light of the explosion of knowledge. The curriculum must be periodically updated to include new content to be learned.

3. *Scope*. Scope is the breadth, depth, and variety of the content and includes the coverage or boundaries of the subject.

4. *Sequence*. By sequencing, there is recognition of and need for differentiating levels of knowledge, that learning is based on prior knowledge, and that the curriculum should be cumulative and continuous.[26]

5. *Integration*. Integration emphasizes the relationships among various content themes, topics, or units; it helps explain how content in one subject is related to content in another subject.[27]

A more recent text establishes seven additional criteria to consider when selecting and organizing content. Whereas Taba stresses cognitive learning theory for her five criteria, these particular criteria combine cognitive and humanistic psychology:

1. *Self-Sufficiency*. A guiding principle for content selection is that it helps learners attain learning skills and self-sufficiency in learning (economy of the teacher's effort and time in instruction and economy of students' efforts and time in learning).

2. *Significance*. Content should contribute to learning particular concepts, skills, or values; it should be significant in terms of what knowledge needs to be transmitted to students.

3. *Validity*. As new knowledge is discovered, old knowledge that is less relevant, misleading, or incorrect must be pruned. Only relevant and accurate knowledge should be a part of the curriculum content. The content should also be sound in relation to stated goals and objectives.

4. *Interest*. Content is easier to learn when it is meaningful. The interest criterion is a progressive concept, but all content should be selected in part on the basis of students' interests.

5. *Utility*. Content should be useful in and out of school. What is considered useful will also reflect philosophy.

6. *Learnability*. The content must be within the experiences and understanding of the learner; content should be selected and arranged on the basis that it makes learning easy, at least less difficult, for students.

7. *Feasibility*. The content must be considered in terms of time allotted, personnel and resources available, and sometimes existing legislation, political climate, and money. Although some educators may like to think that they have an entire world of content from which to choose, they do have limitations on their actions. (Consider content related to sex education, race relations, morality, and religion, as starters.)[28]

Criteria for Selecting Learning Experiences

Tyler, in his classic text on curriculum, outlined five general principles in selecting learning experiences. These experiences can take place in the classroom, outside the classroom (say, in the schoolyard, auditorium, or laboratory), or outside the school (on a field trip, in the library or a museum, etc.).

---

[26]This concept is similar to Jerome Bruner's idea of a "spiral curriculum": Previous learning is the basis of subsequent learning; learning should be continuous, and the content (or subject matter) is built on a foundation (from grade to grade).

[27]Hilda Taba, *Curriculum Development: Theory and Practice* (New York: Harcourt, Brace & World, 1962).

[28]Ornstein and Hunkins, *Curriculum: Foundations, Principles, and Issues*.

1. *Learners Must Have Experiences That Give Them Opportunity to Practice the Behavior(s) Implied by the Objective(s)*. If the objective is to develop problem-solving skills, then students must have ample opportunity to solve problems. In other words, there must be experiences for students to practice what they are required to learn.

2. *Students Must Obtain Satisfaction in Carrying Out or Performing the Learning Experiences*. Students need satisfying experiences to develop and maintain interest in learning; unsatisfying experiences hinder learning.

3. *Learning Experiences Must Be Appropriate to the Students' Present Attainments*. This basically means that the teacher must begin where the student is and that prior knowledge is the starting point in learning new knowledge.

4. *Several Experiences Can Attain the Same Objective*. There are many ways for learning the same thing; as long as they are effective and meaningful, a wide range of experiences is better for learning than a limited range. Capitalize on the various interests of students.

5. *The Same Learning Experience Usually Results in Several Outcomes*. While students are acquiring knowledge of one subject or idea, they often develop ideas in other subjects and certain attitudes toward the original subject.[29]

More recently, the criteria for selecting experiences have been stated in the form of a question: Will the learning experience do what we wish it to do in light of the overall aims and goals of the program and specific objectives of the curriculum? The following are specific extensions of this question. Are the experiences

1. Valid in light of the ways in which knowledge and skills will be applied in out-of-school situations?

2. Feasible in terms of time, staff expertise, facilities available within and outside of the school, community expectations?

3. Optimal in terms of students' learning the content?

4. Capable of allowing students to develop their thinking skills and rational powers?

5. Capable of stimulating in students greater understanding of their own existence as individuals and as members of groups?

6. Capable of fostering an openness to new experiences and a tolerance for diversity?

7. Such that they will facilitate learning and motivate students to continue learning?

8. Capable of allowing students to address their needs?

9. Such that students can broaden their interests?

10. Such that they will foster the total development of students in cognitive, affective, psychomotor, social, and spiritual domains?[30]

What educators need to remember is that content and experiences are interrelated. If students are engaged in some experience in classrooms, such as reading a book, they are combining that experience with content. Students cannot engage in learning without experiencing some activity and content. Likewise, students cannot deal with content without being engaged in some experience or some activity. Content and experience comprise curriculum unity.

Educational Environments

As we cannot separate content from experiences in the actual delivery of the curriculum, we also cannot divorce the experiencing of content from the space within which the experience and content occur. Until recently, curriculum leaders

---

[29]Tyler, *Basic Principles of Curriculum and Instruction.*

[30]Ronald C. Doll, *Curriculum Improvement: Decision Making and Process*, 7th ed. (Needham Heights, MA: Allyn and Bacon, 1989); Decker Walker, *Fundamentals of Curriculum* (San Diego: Harcourt Brace Jovanovich, 1990).

have not given much attention to the **curriculum environment** of the school other than to ensure that students had adequate light, heat, chairs, desks, and places to hang their clothes.

Educational space, crucial to meaningful educational experiences, is the place where the curriculum unfolds. "Space," John Holt notes, "creates activity; it allows students to generate places and moods."[31] Students who experience a creative or low-restrictive environment are much more likely to be stimulated, to realize their potential, and to be excited about learning. Students who experience a structured or highly restricted environment are more likely to be passive, conforming, and more dependent on the teacher to provide guidance.

The more an administrator considers curriculum or instruction as his or her chief interest, the more he or she is inclined to consider the classroom environment in terms of learning centers or potential for learning. The more an administrator is involved in managerial decisions, the more he or she is inclined to consider the educational environment in terms of scheduling, budgeting, and legality.

Persons who favor curriculum look at environment in terms of four criteria when they plan the curriculum.

1. *Adequacy*. This refers to environmental controls such as sufficient lighting or heating so that students can learn with ease. It also encompasses appropriate acoustics and equipment that are appropriate for students' learning styles and needs.
2. *Suitability*. The shape and dimension of the environment is a consideration when planning an activity. Is the classroom large enough to accommodate open-seating patterns? Is the classroom designed so that everyone can easily see the chalkboard?
3. *Efficiency*. This involves the characteristics of the classroom space that are likely to im-

prove instructional effectiveness and whether instruction can take place with the least amount of efforts by students and teachers. If students are to have a microcomputer at their desks, are there sufficient electrical outlets? Will students easily see their teacher?
4. *Economy*. This relates to actual cost, and hopefully savings, in terms of capital outlay that is achieved by the design or modification of an existing classroom environment for a particular aspect of curriculum.[32]

Leadership Considerations

Regardless of how one views the relationship between content, experience, and environment, the center of curriculum development continues to be the local school, which in turn is related to the abilities and performance of the school principal and her assistants. The key to curriculum leadership is not the school superintendent, who should be more concerned about managerial decisions; it is the school principal.

The problem is, however, that many school superintendents are not clear about delegating authority over curriculum matters to the school principal. The superintendent is usually much clearer about delegating responsibility at the centralized level—say, to the business manager or director of public information—than about delegating it to the principal. In these cases, it seems that the superintendent is more concerned about business or community affairs—that is, how the school district appears—than curriculum for students the district serves.

Another problem seems to involve a conflict between local school personnel (namely, teachers, chairpersons, and principals) and supervisors from the central office—and that the latter sometimes bypass or ignore the prerogatives of

---

[31]John Holt, "Children Are Sensitive to Space," in T. G. David and B. D. Wright (eds.), *Learning Environments* (Chicago: University of Chicago Press, 1975), p. 83.

[32]Allan C. Ornstein, "Components of Curriculum Development," *Illinois School Research and Development*, 26 (1990), pp. 204–212.

curriculum leaders in their own schools. On the other hand, principals who are zealots are sometimes known to operate their schools as little fiefdoms or empires, ignoring the advice and help of the supervisors from the central office. Certainly, the roles and responsibilities of the various school personnel, as they relate to curriculum matters, need to be clear to avoid conflict.

In large school districts (50,000 or more students), the central office usually houses a curriculum department whose responsibility is to develop curriculum materials and guides while minimizing the role of the teacher and school principal. Curriculum development is centralized and usually rubber-stamped at the school level; what ideas people have at the local level are passed upward but often lost in the paper shuffle at the centralized level.

In small school districts, however, teachers, principals, and even parents are expected to spend substantial time and effort in curriculum making. Under the leadership of the principal, schools are often expected to develop mission statements, a clear understanding of what constitutes learning, the content and experiences to be included in the curriculum, how the curriculum is to be implemented and evaluated, and how the community is to be included.[33] Many teachers and principals become involved in curriculum development as a matter of professional routine; but they are rarely, if ever, paid for their time after 3 P.M.

Differences also exist between elementary and secondary school principals. Most elementary principals devote more time to curriculum and instructional matters than do their secondary counterparts, and they view themselves more often as curriculum or instructional leaders than managers. Secondary school principals usually complain they have little time for curriculum and instruction (although they recognize the importance of such matters) and see them-

selves more often as general managers.[34] Most school principals have been taught to accept some bureaucratic, scientific, or rational model of management, but elementary principals have been forced to throw away their managerial theories and deal with the needs and concerns of the students at the school door, as well as their parents and the community.[35]

Part of the difference is related to school size. Within the same school district, high schools are usually two to four times the size of elementary schools. In high schools that house more than 1000 students (24 percent of U. S. high schools), principals are often engaged with a continual stream of problems in which they have difficulty leaving the office, and they are more concerned about administrative detail and formal structures than people.[36] Another reason for the difference is that in medium-sized secondary schools (750 to 1000 students) and large secondary schools (1000+ students), there are usually chairpersons responsible for particular subject areas who plan with teachers and supervise curriculum and instruction. Elementary schools do not have chairpersons as part of their staff, and the focus is on the Three *R*s (not particular subjects) in which the principal is supposed to provide the curriculum and instructional leadership in this general area of study.

Some balance is needed. In large school districts, curriculum leaders at the central level should make it easier for school personnel to become involved in curriculum opportunities. In small school districts, teachers involved in curriculum should be paid for their services or relieved from other duties, so they can devote time to curriculum. Without being made to feel

---

[33]Donald S. Monroe, "Curriculum Development: The Medium Is the Message and the Message Is Crucial," *NASSP Bulletin*, 72 (1988), pp. 1–7.

[34]Dale L. Brubaker and Lawrence H. Simon, "How Do Principals View Themselves, Others?" *NASSP Bulletin*, 71 (1987), pp. 72–78; Ornstein, "Components of a Curriculum."

[35]Dan Cilo, "Principals: Leave Your Offices, Improve Your Schools," *NASSP Bulletin*, 73 (1989), pp. 111–114; Ornstein, "Components of Curriculum Development."

[36]Allan C. Ornstein, "School Size and Effectiveness: Policy Implications," *Urban Review*, 22 (1990).

guilty, school authorities should recognize that teachers are already performing important responsibilities other than curriculum development and teachers should have the option to reject new responsibilities. (See Administrative Advice 13-2.)

HOW IMPLEMENTATION OCCURS

Whenever the curriculum leader attempts to implement the curriculum, the principles of change come into play. Much that is planned and developed often does not get implemented, much of what is new or innovative rarely gets off the ground, and what gets reported often gathers dust on shelves. Many charged with **curriculum implementation** have neither a good macro view of the change process nor realize that it occurs at different levels or stages and must be monitored on a continuous basis.

Although experienced leaders of curriculum realize that implementation is an essential aspect of curriculum development, only in recent years has implementation become a major concern—largely due to the nature of change and not curriculum. As two authors maintain in their review of change and innovation, "If there is one finding that stands out in our review, it is that effective implementation of . . . innovations

---

ADMINISTRATIVE ADVICE 13-2

■

THE PRINCIPAL AS A CURRICULUM LEADER

Much has been written in recent years about the principal's role in curriculum. Based on a survey of twenty-nine secondary school principals in suburban Cook and Lake Counties, Illinois, three researchers list in rank order the curriculum functions that principals contend they engage in on a frequent (ranking 1–5) to infrequent (ranking 13–17) basis. Some of the functions should help the reader expand his view of the principal's role in curriculum.

- Develops an orientation program for new teachers.
- Develops a clear set of school goals and objectives.
- Involves individual departments in curriculum development.
- Encourages curriculum communication with her school and others in the district.
- Handles controversial issues that involve the curriculum.
- Spends time visiting teachers in the classroom.
- Plans staff development programs.
- Rewards curriculum innovation.
- Encourages use of library and media services by teachers.

- Modifies school plant (environment) to improve instruction.
- Organizes staff for curriculum development.
- Involves teachers in curriculum development.
- Works with curriculum consultants in improving curriculum.
- Serves as a resource for instructional methodology and techniques.
- Plans the curriculum.
- Develops curriculum materials for the classroom.
- Involves the community in curriculum development.

Source: Adapted from Barney M. Berlin, Jack A Kavanagh, and Kathleen Jensen, "The Principal as Curriculum Leader: Expectations vs. Performance," *NASSP Bulletin*, 72 (1988), p. 44.

requires time, personal interaction and contacts, inservice training, and other forms of people-based support." Their research shows that the leadership style, personal relations, and personal contacts of implementers and planners are crucial to effect change and "implement most innovations."[37]

Implementation involves extensive actions by many parties, not just an action group, staff, or administrator; it involves attempts to change peoples' knowledge, attitudes, and actions. This also suggests that implementation, as well as change, is an interaction process between those who create the program and those who deliver it. A high degree of school district and schoolwide implementation involves interacting with and educating individuals about the worth of the program and how it can be carried out. In this connection, social scientists have furnished a definition of total implementation that is useful: (1) the acceptance, (2) over time, (3) of some specific idea or practice, (4) by groups, individuals, or other adopting units, (5) to specific channels of communication, (6) within a social structure, (7) according to a given system of values or culture.[38] Implementation, then, attempts to influence behavioral change in a direction deemed necessary; it occurs in stages and takes time to win people over to change.

Incrementalism

People want to change; yet they are also afraid of change, especially if it comes quickly or if they feel they have little control or influence over it. People become accustomed to the status quo and prefer to make modifications in new behavior in small and gradual steps.

The professional world of the teacher does not allow for much receptivity to change. Many ed-

ucators have described the teacher's daily routine as presenting little opportunity for interaction with colleagues. This isolation results partly from the school's organization into self-contained classrooms and partly from the teaching schedules. According to Seymour Sarason, the reality of the school has made teachers feel that, professionally, they are on their own. It is their responsibility, and theirs alone, to solve their own problems. This posture causes teachers to view change introduced into the program as an individual activity. Viewing their struggles as solitary, teachers often develop a psychological loneliness that results in hostility to administrators and outside change agents who seem insensitive to the teachers' plight.[39] Dan Lortie has noted that, in fact, many factors detrimentally affect teachers' receptivity to change: "Teachers have a built-in resistance to change because they believe that their work environment has never permitted them to show what they can really do." Many proposals for change strike them as "frivolous and wasteful"—not addressing the real issues which deal with student disruptions or discipline, student reading problems, administrative support, etc.[40]

Curriculum leaders must create an environment that encourages openness and trust and gives feedback so that teachers realize that their contributions are appreciated and their talents considered worthwhile. Teachers need time to "try" the new program to be implemented. They need time to reflect on new goals and objectives; to consider new contents, learning experiences, and environments; and to try out new tasks. They need time to map out their tactics for meeting the challenges of the new program, and they need time to talk to their colleagues. Teachers can handle new programs if the changes demanded in their attitudes, be-

[37]Michael Fullan and Alan Pomfret, "Research on Curriculum and Instruction Implementation," *Review of Educational Research*, 47 (1977), pp. 391–392.

[38]Elihu Katz, Martin L. Levin, and Herbert Hamilton, "Tradition of Research on the Diffusion of Innovation," *American Sociological Review*, 28 (1963), pp. 237–252.

[39]Seymour B. Sarason, *The Culture of the School and the Problem of Change*, 2nd ed. (Boston: Allyn and Bacon, 1982); Sarason, *Human Services and Resource Networks* (San Francisco: Jossey-Bass, 1988).

[40]Dan Lortie, *Schoolteacher: A Sociological Study* (Chicago: University of Chicago Press, 1975), p. 235.

haviors, and knowledge are to be attained in manageable increments.

Implementation does not occur all at once with all teachers. Ideally, an implementation process allows sufficient time for certain groups of teachers to try out the new curriculum in "pieces." Two researchers have found that teachers go through levels of use with a new curriculum. First, they orient themselves to the materials and engage in actions that will prepare them to deliver the curriculum. Their beginning use of the new curriculum is mechanical, and they follow the guide with little deviation. Their delivery of the curriculum becomes rather routine, and they take little initiative to make any changes in it. As they become more comfortable with the curriculum, they may begin to modify it, either to adjust it to their own educational philosophies or to better meet students' needs.[41]

Successful implementers appreciate that it takes time for teachers to "buy into" a new curriculum and to become skilled in delivering the new program. Curriculum leaders should anticipate teachers' questions and concerns and plan potential strategies for addressing them.

In planning change or innovation, those who will be affected by it experience various levels of concerns or anxieties: first, concern about self; second, concern about the mechanics or operation of the new program or curriculum; and third, concern about students (and others such as colleagues or the community).[42] These stages of concern are important for school leaders to recognize, especially those in charge of implementation of curriculum change. Effective ad-

ministrators should be prepared first to deal with personal issues, then professional or technical issues, and finally client issues. In this connection, Table 13-3 presents a hierarchical list of stages of concern that should be useful for school leaders involved in planning curriculum change.

Communication

It is almost an axiom that whenever a new program is being designed, communication channels must be kept open so that the new program does not come as a surprise. Frequent discussion about a new program among teachers, principals, and curriculum workers is a key to successful implementation.

But communication is a complex phenomenon. It has been defined as the transmission of facts, ideas, values, feelings, and attitudes from one individual or group to another. Put simply, communication deals with message processing between the sender and the receiver of a message. The curriculum specialist must be sure that the communication network is comprehensive and that avenues for message sending exist in all levels of the school system. An effective system is not rigid but allows different population members input opportunities and vehicles.

If curriculum leaders only want to communicate facts about a new program, they can communicate such facts by means of letters, memos, articles, research reports, or speeches. Sometimes they need to communicate to staff the underlying assumptions, values, and points of view embedded in a new curriculum. If the new program is a major change, then the curriculum leader may wish to use such communication vehicles as workshops, meetings, role playing, and demonstrations.

Despite the various means available for communication, the key to communication is the individual. Communication involves messages among people, not hardware. Thus, the curriculum leader needs to create a climate conducive to effective communication among all members

[41]Susan Loucks and Ann Lieberman, "Curriculum Implementation," in F. W. English (ed.), *Fundamental Curriculum Decision* (Alexandria, VA: Association for Supervision and Curriculum Development, 1983), pp. 126–141. See also Ann Lieberman (ed.), *Schools as Collaborative Cultures* (New York: Falmer Press, 1990).

[42]Philip W. Jackson (ed.), *Contributing to Educational Change* (Berkeley, CA: McCutchan, 1988); Thomas J. Sergiovanni and John H. Moore (eds.), *Schooling for Tomorrow: Directing Reforms* (Needham Heights, MA: Allyn and Bacon, 1989).

TABLE 13 ▪ 3   Stages of Concern in Curriculum Change

1. *Informational.* A general awareness of the innovation and interest in learning more detail about it are evidenced. The person seems unworried about change or innovation, and the discussion is clinical or objective.

2. *Personal.* The individual is uncertain about the demands of the change and his role with it. The person is now beginning to ask questions or deal with issues involving organizational structure, personal considerations, and potential conflicts with existing structures or people.

3. *Management.* Attention focuses on the process and tasks involved in carrying out change. The issues are now organizing, scheduling, time demands, costs, and efficiency.

4. *Consequence.* Attention focuses on the relevance of the change for students, the processes affecting students, and evaluation of student products.

5. *Collaboration.* The focus is on coordination and cooperation with others regarding the change.

6. *Refocusing.* Emphasis is on assessing overall benefits from the change, including the possibility of minor refinements, major modifications, replacement with another alternative, or termination.

SOURCE: Adapted from Gene E. Hall and Susan F. Loucks, "Teacher Concerns as a Basis for Facilitating and Personalizing Staff Development," *Teachers College Record,* 80 (1978), pp. 36–53.

of the educational staff and community (both person to person and mass communication). She needs to inform all persons of the avenues that are established for communication. She also needs to inform all persons that their views are welcome and that they all have a responsibility to participate in sending and processing messages.[43]

Cooperation

Cooperation between all persons who will implement the program must occur if change is to be successful and to become institutionalized. Ample research supports the practice of engaging teachers in new ideas and programs that will find expression in their classrooms. In many ways, teachers are the experts, and so their commitment to the new curriculum is necessary.

Such commitment depends heavily on how active they have been in conceptualizing and developing the new program.

Reviews of research indicate that if teachers actively participate in curriculum development and implementation, the likelihood of successful implementation is increased.[44] This may be partly because emotion as well as rationality is inevitably an element of change. People require the involvement of their total beings—their feelings, sentiments, and values—if they are to accept, tolerate, or support change. Table 13-4 provides a three-phase implementation process for school district reform or innovation. The groups of teachers to be formed can be according to subject areas, grade levels, or a special curriculum project. As participants meet, teachers are encouraged to view the new plan or program as an expansion (or improvement) of what they are already doing.

[43]H. Dickson Corbett and Joseph J. D'Amico, "No More Heroes: Creating Systems to Support Change," *Educational Leadership,* 44 (1986), pp. 70–72; Frank W. Freshour, "Listening Power: Key to Effective Leadership," *Illinois School Research and Development,* 26 (1989), pp. 17–23.

[44]Gordon Cawelti, "Designing High Schools for the Future," *Educational Leadership,* 71 (1989), pp. 30–35; Francis P. Hunkins and Allan C. Ornstein, "Curriculum Innovation and Implementation," *Education and Urban Society,* 22 (1989), pp. 105–114.

TABLE 13 ■ 4   Three-Step Implementation Process Involving Administrators and Teachers

Phase I: Shaping a District Vision to Guide the Reform

In a small group, teachers and principals develop a common vision of the district reform and begin to see themselves as valued members of a team effort.

1. Participants learn about the intent of the reform through cooperative learning techniques in which they read and discuss articles and district and state documents about the reform in general and its impact on specific disciplines.

2. Participants begin to shape a mental image of what they want to accomplish with students and how this might look in the various disciplines.

3. Participants break into subgroups to draft performance expectations for the major segments of schooling. Those from the middle grades describe the type of culminating activity/project appropriate for graduating eighth graders, primary teachers describe one for exiting third graders, and so on.

4. District personnel review the performance expectations for grades 3, 6, 9, and 12 and return them to the group with suggestions for modification. This process is repeated until agreement is reached.

Phase II: Translating the Vision into Operational Plans

Once performance expectations are agreed on for the major segments of schooling, participants begin long-range curriculum plans.

1. The subgroups break down further to familiarize themselves with the design procedure and to modify it for their subjects. Each subgroup outlines one hypothetical year-long plan.

2. After sharing and critiquing those plans, the subgroups break down further. Individual teachers, or small groups teaching the same grade or course, outline benchmark activities/projects within a classroom plan for one of the subjects they teach.

3. These plans, which will be their flexible guides for beginning Phase III, include a brief sketch of the sequence of events during the first unit: how they will introduce and develop content, skills, and concepts leading up to the first benchmark activity/project, and how they will assess learning. (Some principals may elect to leave the sessions in which teachers are developing these detailed plans.)

Both John Goodlad and Charles Silberman noted that many of the reforms of the 1960s and 1970s actually "wrote" the teachers out of the educational process. Innovators designed teacher-proof materials, which meant that basically all teachers had to do was "hand out" the materials and the students would learn.[45] In some cases, teachers were viewed as the "objects" of reform, a somewhat condescending view, and often labeled as the "targets." Teachers viewed the programs as invasions over which they had no control, a key reason why these programs did not reach the intended levels of implementation. In fact, what often occurred was that the teachers closed ranks against the reform packages.

Educators have come to learn, sometimes the hard way, that for change to be effective, teachers must be committed to it and they must see that it has professional value to them. Teachers often judge change by how it will address the immediate needs they encounter in their daily work.

[45]John I. Goodlad et al., *Curriculum Inquiry: The Study of Curriculum Practice* (New York: McGraw-Hill, 1979); Charles E. Silberman, *Crisis in the Classroom* (New York: Random House, 1970).

TABLE 13 ■ 4	Three-Step Implementation Process Involving Administrators and Teachers (continued)

4. Once plans have been outlined and the subgroups have reviewed and critiqued them, the entire group reconvenes to compare a few examples from each subgroup.

5. Participants individually consider what "first steps" they could take to translate their curriculum plans into practice. Principals and teachers from the same school then work together to decide where to begin.

6. The entire group decides on a game plan for how they will work together over the coming months. Ideally, the sessions in Phases I and II have been conducted during the summer. Now they set the schedule for a series of working sessions that will bring them all back together every three weeks or so during the school year. They establish the time and agenda for the first session.

Phase III: Experimenting with the Plans

1. As teachers experiment with ways to modify classroom practices and principals develop ways to support them, the group meets regularly to compare notes and devise new strategies.

2. They may call on specialists on topics such as developing lessons for a particular subject, establishing cooperative learning groups, and observing and giving feedback to teachers in the classroom.

3. The facilitator may present additional information to expand participants' understanding of less obvious factors that may affect teachers and students, such as the effects of teacher expectations, of tracking, and so on.

4. Teachers begin visiting one another's classrooms between working sessions to exchange ideas and provide feedback to one another.

5. Principals exchange school visits to share ideas for school-level strategies for supporting teachers and for giving them feedback in their classrooms.

6. As the group proceeds, members will continuously modify their original plans so that curriculum planning and staff development are being carried out simultaneously.

SOURCE: Janet Kierstead and Sally Mentor, "Translating the Vision into Reality in California Schools," *Educational Leadership,* 46 (1988), p. 37. Copyright © 1988 by the Association for Supervision and Curriculum Development. Used by permission.

To a large extent, then, successful change is more a function of people and organizations than of technology or even money.[46] It appears that even though teachers indicate that they want involvement, what most of them really want is input into the decisions. They want programs that reflect their philosophies and views of education.

Only recently has the educational literature analyzed that much of what goes on in an organization is governed by a culture, including a way of behaving and surviving. The school culture is not opposed to change or innovation; indeed, schools have evolved considerably in policies, programs, and functions and have responded to the changing demands of society.[47]

[46]Linda Lambert, "Staff Development Redesigned," *Phi Delta Kappan*, 69 (1988), pp. 665–668; Edward Pajak and Joseph J. Blase, "The Impact of Teachers' Personal Lives on Professional Role Enactment," *Review of Educational Research*, 59 (1989), pp. 283–310.

[47]Ann Lieberman, *Building a Professional Culture in Schools* (New York: Teachers College Press, 1988); Kenneth A. Sirotnik and John I. Goodlad, *School–University Partnerships in Action* (New York: Teachers College Press, 1988).

But schools also have **survival mechanisms**, or what some social scientists call "maintenance" and "stability" functions, and these survival mechanisms are self-reinforcing and more established than change mechanisms. The culture of school establishes certain restrictions and regularities on teachers and administrators; to effect reform, reformers cannot interfere with or violate the established norms and behaviors of the organization.

Support

Implementation costs in terms of both time and materials. Curriculum designers need to provide the necessary support for their recommended programs or program modifications, to facilitate their rapid implementation. They have to do this to build self-confidence among those affected. Educators often require staff development and in-service training and time to feel comfortable with new programs. Such programs must be designed so that they can be integrated into and supported by the organizations within which they are designed to function. Staff development programs that work have resulted from collaborative staff efforts and have addressed the needs of those who are to be impacted by the new curricula.[48]

Without adequate financial support, efforts to get a program "going" districtwide will fail. When federal monies were flowing, many school districts were innovative, but they failed to add funding for their innovations into their regular school budgets. When the federal monies (which were essentially meant to be start-up monies) ran out, the districts discontinued their new programs, citing lack of necessary funds. If school districts, today, create new programs using federal or state grant money, called "soft money," they need to devise ways to support these programs, once implemented, with "hard money"—money that is part of the regularly allocated school budget.

Money is required for materials and equipment to institutionalize a new program. Money is also necessary to provide often-overlooked human support for the implementation effort. But money alone is not the answer. The field of education is suffused with reforms and new programs that cost millions of dollars, spearheaded by "experts" who knew what was best, and failed. The missing ingredient was faith—faith in people and the support systems they needed to help themselves and to buy into the new program. Experts, outside consultants, and change agents must invest a little more in people, and less money, in order to succeed with their innovations. They must have more faith in the desire and abilities of those in schools to participate as professionals in designing and changing their own workplace; they must understand that the new program must become legitimatized within the system, that people (or professionals) must accept the innovation, and that they have a right to succeed or fail on their own terms.[49]

A trusting relationship must exist among all parties in the school, especially the administration and teachers. The principal is a key guarantor of successful innovation and implementation at the school level, and the superintendent is the key person at the school district level.[50] Disagreement does exist, however, on how principals and superintendents should furnish human support.

Implementation is a collaborative and emotional effort. Peer support is vital if implementation is to be successful. Lortie points out that

[48]Ben M. Harris, *Inservice Education for Staff Development* (Needham Heights, MA: Allyn and Bacon, 1989); Donald C. Orlich, *Staff Development: Enhancing Human Potential* (Needham Heights: MA: Allyn and Bacon, 1989).

[49]John I. Goodlad, *The Dynamics of Educational Change* (New York: McGraw-Hill, 1975); Susan J. Rosenholtz, *Teachers' Workplace: The Social Organization of Schools* (New York: Longman, 1989).

[50]Daniel L. Duke, *School Leadership and Instructional Improvement* (New York: Random House, 1987); William E. Eaton (ed.), *Shaping the Superintendency* (New York: Teachers College Press, 1990).

teachers spend the majority of their working time in individual classrooms with their students; therefore, they have minimal communication with their peers. By and large, they are left on their own with little input or assistance from colleagues or supervisors, unless a crisis develops.[51] Opportunities for teachers to work together, share ideas, jointly solve problems, and cooperatively create materials greatly enhance the probability of successful curriculum implementation. (See Administrative Advice 13-3.)

IMPLEMENTATION AS A CHANGE PROCESS

Implementation, an essential part of curriculum development, brings into reality anticipated changes. Simply put, curriculum activity is change activity.

What is change? What happens when change occurs? Can people predict the consequences of change? Can people control those changes that directly impact them? Administrators can exert some control over the process of change but to do so requires that they understand change. Understanding the concept of change, and the various types of change, allows individuals to determine sources of change. It also helps them realize that even though they cannot really predict the consequences of change, they can make "best-guess" forecasts about its results.

According to the research, for **curriculum change** to be successfully implemented, five principles should be followed to help avoid mistakes of the past.

1. *Innovations Designed to Improve Student Achievement Must Be Technically Sound*. This means that changes should reflect research about what works and what does not work, as opposed to whatever designs for improve-

ment happen to be popular today or tomorrow.
2. *Successful Innovation Requires Change in the Structure of a Traditional School*. By structural change, we mean major modification of the way students and teachers are assigned to classes and interact with each other.
3. *Innovations Must Be Manageable and Feasible for the Average Teacher*. We cannot innovate ideas concerning critical thinking or problem solving when students cannot read or write basic English or refuse to behave in class.
4. *Implementation of Successful Change Efforts Must Be Organic Rather Than Bureaucratic*. Strict compliance, monitoring procedures, and rules are not conducive for change; this bureaucratic approach needs to be replaced by an organic or adaptive approach that permits some deviation from the original plan and recognizes grass-roots problems and conditions of the school.
5. *Avoid the "Do Something, Do Anything" Syndrome*. The need is for a definite curriculum plan, to focus one's efforts, time, and money on content and activities that are sound and rational, not a scam or simplistic idea.[52]

The data indicate that the principles "are systematically interrelated, and that with the possible exception of the [principle] regarding structural change, they apply equally well to all levels of education." Administrators will benefit by "considering their applicability in the particular context of their own schools and school districts."[53]

Change Typologies

Persons charged with curriculum activity, specifically, innovations or implementation, need to

---

[51]Lortie, *Schoolteacher*.

[52]Daniel U. Levine, Rayna F. Levine, and Allan C. Ornstein, "Guidelines for Change and Innovation in the Secondary School Curriculum," *NASSP Bulletin*, 69 (1985), pp. 9–14.

[53]Ibid., p. 14.

ADMINISTRATIVE ADVICE 13-3

■

INFORMATION CHECKLIST FOR IMPLEMENTING CURRICULUM CHANGE AND INNOVATION

Administrators involved in curriculum implementation will have concerns about change and how teachers will react to it. People prefer the status quo when they are familiar and satisfied with it. The checklist below consists of a number of questions that deal with the organization of information that school leaders might wish to include in a presentation to the staff. The emphasis of these questions deals mainly with teachers' personal and technical concerns.

- How will a teacher's personal day be changed by the innovation?
- How much additional preparation time will the innovation require?
- How much paperwork will be involved in implementing and monitoring the innovation?
- How will the innovation "fit in" to the content to which learners have already been exposed?
- What kinds of teacher resource materials will be provided?
- Will resource materials be in each teacher's room, in a separate room in the school, at the central administration building, or at some other location?
- What kinds of new learning materials will be provided for learners?
- Are reading levels and other characteristics of these materials clearly appropriate for learners to be served?
- What patterns of teacher–learner interaction will be demanded?
- Will any required instructional procedures demand teaching techniques teachers have not already mastered?
- What kinds of in-service training will be provided?

- What is the relationship of the innovation to standardized tests learners must take?
- What allowances are there going to be for possible declines in standardized test scores resulting from an instructional program new to teachers and learners alike?
- What are the implications of the new program for classroom management?
- How strong is the central district administration's commitment to the support of the new program?
- To what extent are principals familiar with elements of the new program and able to assist teachers in implementing it?
- Who, specifically, can be called on for help if there are problems regarding implementation of the innovation?
- Will this person be willing to visit individual classrooms?
- What school library and media resources can support the new program?
- To what extent do parents know about and support the new program?

Source: Adapted from David G. Armstrong, *Developing and Documenting the Curriculum* (Needham Heights, MA: Allyn and Bacon, 1989), pp. 213–214.

understand the nature of change. Warren Bennis has identified several useful types of change:

1. *Planned change* is change in which those involved in the change process have equal power and function in a prescribed fashion.

People identify and follow precise procedures for dealing with the activity at hand. Planned change is the ideal.
2. *Coercion* is characterized by one group determining the goals and intentionally excluding others from participating. The group in con-

trol has the major power and works to maintain the unequal power balance.

3. *Interaction change* is characterized by mutual goal setting and a fairly equal power distribution among groups. But those involved often lack a deliberateness of effort; they are uncertain how to follow through with the plans of development and implementation. Few procedures are carefully developed. People are more or less left on their own.[54]

The opposite of planned change is natural or random change. This type of change occurs with no apparent thought and no goal setting on the part of the participants. Natural change is what often occurs in schools. Curricula are adjusted or modified and implemented not as a result of careful analysis, but as a response to unanticipated events. Reactions to demands by legislatures or pressure groups that certain programs be implemented, for example, are inconsistent and based on whim and rhetoric.

We can also consider change according to its complexity. Those involved in investigating the change process have identified five kinds of change using complexity as the organizer:

1. *Substitution*. This depicts alteration in which one element can be substituted for another. For example, a teacher can substitute one textbook for another. By far, this is the easiest and most common type of change.

2. *Alteration*. This type of change exists when someone introduces into existing materials and programs new content, materials, or procedures that appear to be only minor and thus are likely to be adopted readily.

3. *Perturbations*. These changes could at first disrupt a program, but they can then be incorporated into the ongoing program within a short time span. An example of a perturbation is the principal adjusting class schedules, which would affect the time allowed for teaching a particular subject.

4. *Restructuring*. These changes lead to modification of the system itself—that is, the school or school district. New concepts of teaching roles, such as differentiated staffing or team teaching, would be a restructuring type of change.

5. *Value-Orientation Changes*. These are shifts in participants' fundamental philosophies or curriculum orientations. Major power brokers of the school or participants in the curriculum must accept and strive for this level of change for it to occur. However, if teachers do not adjust their value domains, any changes enacted are most likely going to be short-lived.[55]

And, we can consider change in terms of **decision making**. The following model includes four operations: state the goal, generate ideas, prepare a plan, and take action. Each operation requires a decision; in each decision, the administrator or decision maker identifies problems (focus), looks at options (analysis), and makes a decision (synthesis) based on information. Each operation includes three similar steps, making up a twelve-step decision-making and change process. (The examples of problems, options, and selections are ours.)

  I. State the Goal
    1. *Identify Problems in the Situation*. Enrollments are increasing from 1200 to 1300 this year and are projected to be 1800 two years from now. We would like to build a new school, but the power brokers of the community seem to be against it.
    2. *Create Goal Options*. We could hire a consultant to perform a needs assessment study. We can mount a news campaign and hold meetings in the school auditorium to publicize the need for a new school. We can speak quietly to selected board members who may empathize with us.

[54]Warren Bennis, *Changing Organizations* (New York: McGraw-Hill, 1966); Bennis, *On Becoming a Leader* (Reading, MA: Addison-Wesley, 1989).

[55]McNeil, *Curriculum: A Comprehensive Introduction*.

3. *Select the Goal.* Which goal is most practical? Which goal has the least risk? What problems (possibilities) are associated with each option?

II. Generate Ideas

4. *Identify Goal Problems.* We discovered that the consultant fee would need to be approved by the school board. Based on conversations with selected administrators, we think the news campaign would create controversy. If we privately speak to selected board members, there is no guarantee that other members will not learn about our meetings and create a furor.

5. *Create Idea Options.* We might drop our plans for a new school and wait for a new school board to be elected. We might survey how the parents (or taxpayers) feel about the need for a new school.

6. *Select Ideas.* Let's try the second plan.

III. Prepare a Plan

7. *Identify the New Problem Situation.* Some of us are concerned that the survey will split the community. Perhaps we need an open forum or public hearing on the issue. What about an open discussion at the next board meeting?

8. *Create Plan Options.* Perhaps we can try other possibilities. What about a demographic study this year while we wait for new school board elections? Then we might have more information and a more receptive school board.

9. *Select a Plan.* Let's go with a discussion at the next board meeting and see who is on our side, against us, and neutral. Then, we can meet privately with the neutral board members and those on our side. Next year, when elections are required, we will run our own candidates to replace those who oppose us.

IV. Take Action

10. *Identify Plan Problems.* We need to have two people speak at the next board meeting. We will have fifteen minutes.

Who can speak clearly and concisely? Who is influential?

11. *Create Action Options.* John, who can you call? What about Dave Roberts? He has three children attending school, and he is an attorney. There is Sam Kershner. He is a professor of education at the local university. Valerie Dickens is a businesswomen with two children. She is very vocal about the overcrowding.

12. *Select Next Actions.* We have two weeks to make a decision. Marcia will call Dave, Sam, and Valerie and make a decision on which two people are willing to speak.[56]

Although change that occurs in the schools cannot be fit into precise categories, administrators need to realize that model types and methods do exist and that planned change is the ideal. But change is not synonymous with improvement. Education is a normative activity. A person's advocating and then managing change mean, in effect, making a statement about what he thinks is valuable. This is why people can use the same change procedures and generate different curricula. They have different values and different perceptions of what education should be.

Resistance to Change

A curriculum leader who accepts that people are the key to successful curriculum activity and implementation is cognizant of the barriers that people place between themselves and change efforts. Perhaps the biggest barrier is inertia among the staff, the administration, or the community. Many people think it is just easier to keep things as they are. If we think of ourselves as systems, we realize that we like to maintain steady states. We have traditions to which we

---

[56]Charles E. Wales, Anne H. Nardi, and Robert A. Stager, "Decision Making: A Paradigm for Education," *Educational Leadership*, 43 (1986), pp. 37–41.

adhere and institutions that we cherish—and we do not wish to change them. Many people are happy with the current school setup as a bureaucracy.

Wanting to keep things as they are is often mixed with believing that things do not need to be changed or that the change being suggested is unwise and will thus be unproductive in meeting school objectives. Educators themselves argue this point. Some say that the schools are fine and just need to be maintained, whereas others claim that the schools are not responsive to the times and require major modification. The status quo tends to be maintained if those suggesting change have not presented precise goals for the new program being suggested—that is, they have not planned adequately what the new program will look like or indicated ways in which the new program will be superior to the existing one.

Often, teachers have not been able or willing to keep up with scholarly development. They have not stayed abreast of the knowledge explosion that would allow them to feel committed to curriculum change and the implementation of new programs. Teachers frequently view change as just signaling more work—something else to add on to an already overloaded schedule for which little or no time is allotted. Usually, no extra money or reward is earmarked for the extra work either. Often they view new curricular programs as requiring them to learn new teaching skills, develop new competencies in curriculum development and the management of learning resources, or acquire new skills in interpersonal relations. In some instances, even staff development programs fail to develop those competencies necessary for teachers to become active participants in innovation.

Another reason administrators have difficulty getting teachers to accept innovation is, according to Edgar Friedenberg, people who go into teaching tend to be conformist in nature, not innovative. These people have succeeded in the school system as it has existed. They have learned to play it safe and to keep a low profile in a bureaucratic system run by administrators

who do not like "waves" created.[57] They have found success and fulfillment first as students and now as teachers in this system, and for this reason many see no reason to change it. To many beginning teachers, the bureaucracy in place is a welcome and familiar support system, and they are often slow to change it.

Can educators cope with the demand for more change or for assuming change-agent roles? Uncertainty fosters insecurity. Often educators who feel comfortable with the present are reluctant to change for a future they cannot comprehend or see clearly. People often prefer to stay with certain known deficiencies than venture forth to uncertain futures, even if the changes most likely would be improvements. Bringing new students or parents into the curriculum realm or organizing the program in new ways makes many teachers uneasy.

Another factor that causes people to resist change is the rapidity of change. Many people feel that if something is implemented this year, it will most likely be abandoned when another innovation appears and will thus make most of their efforts useless. There have, in fact, been enough bandwagons in education to make educators innovation-shy.

Sometimes people resist innovation and its implementation because they are ignorant. They either do not know about the innovation or they have little information about it. Curriculum leaders must furnish all affected parties— teachers, pupils, parents, community members—with information about the nature of the program and its rationale. Ideally, all affected parties should be informed either directly or indirectly by school representatives of the reasons for the new program.

People often resist change, too, if no financial or time support is given for the effort. A project for which no monies are budgeted is rarely destined to be implemented. School districts often budget monies for materials but fail to allocate

---

[57]Edgar A. Friedenberg, *Coming of Age in America* (New York: Random House, 1965).

funds for the creation of the curriculum plan, its delivery within the classroom, or necessary in-service training. Also, we raise the question whether a person who earns $20,000 to $40,000 is supposed to be a **change agent**. Teachers are not paid enough to innovate; that is the role of a leader, not of a teacher. Teachers are required to implement change, but the school leader (principal) or school district leader (superintendent) should be the one to initiate change and provide the ingredients and processes for constructive change. On the other hand, teachers are virtually an untapped source of energy and insight, capable of profoundly changing the schools if they act as a group and direct their energies to local and state policy matters.

It may seem that administrators face insurmountable problems. But resistance to change is good because it requires change agents to think carefully about the innovations and to consider the human dynamics involved in implementing programs. Having to "fight" for change protects the organization from becoming proponents of just random change and educational "bandwagonism."

Improving Receptivity to Change

Curriculum activity involves people thinking and acting. Leaders of curriculum development, and especially implementation, realize that the human equation is of paramount importance and that they must therefore understand how people react to change. Often people say they are willing to change but act as though they are unwilling to adjust. A successful change agent knows how people react to change and how to encourage them to be receptive to change.[58] A wise administrator understands that teachers often are reluctant to change their own behavior, because of habit, tradition or laziness, but often

feel that their colleagues need changing. A smart administrator understands that people often say they want change, but not for themselves, and she must separate lip service from action. The change agent must listen carefully and move slowly in these types of settings in order to incorporate into the change process those who really prefer no change.

Curriculum innovation and implementation require face-to-face interaction—person-to-person contact. Those persons charged with implementation must understand the interpersonal dimension of leadership. Curriculum innovation and implementation is a group process involving individuals working together. The group not only enables certain actions to occur but also serves to change its individual members.

Of course, if a group is to change individuals, it must be attractive to its members. The ideas and values the group expresses must be acceptable to the individuals within the group. This is why curriculum leaders need to make sure that the members of the group are clear about the platform on which they are to build the curriculum. As groups talk about the need to change and the strategies for implementation, they create a pressure for change within the educational system. Creating a well-formed group, with a clear sense of mission and confidence that it can bring about change, is one way to make individuals receptive to the notion of change.

Analysis of the past decade to improve schools has resulted in a much better understanding of the steps that must be taken to ensure that change and/or innovation efforts have a significant and lasting impact. Among the lessons that can be deduced from past change efforts are the following:

1. *Adaptive Problem Solving*. Change or innovation must be introduced in such a way that the staff can reasonably implement it.
2. *School-Level Focus*. The focus in bringing about change must be at the school level where the problems occur; teaching and learning take place at the school level, not the district level.

---

[58]Bruce R. Joyce, Richard A. Hersh, and Michael McKibbin, *The Structure of School Improvement* (New York: Longman, 1983).

3. *Compatibility.* Successful reform depends on whether changes introduced are implementable, that is, teachers perceive that they can use the reforms.
4. *Principal's Leadership.* Successful implementation requires change in institutional arrangements and structures; the building principal is the key person for making such decisions.
5. *Teacher Involvement.* To fully cooperate, teachers must have a voice in designing and implementing change. They must be given time, resources, and opportunity to collaborate and make decisions.
6. *Top-Down/Bottom-Up Approaches.* Both approaches have been underscored as important for change. The bottom-up approach encourages a sense of "ownership" among teachers. The top-down approach communicates to teachers: "*We* are trying a new approach, *we* are going to implement it, and *we* are going to help each other."
7. *Staff Development.* Staff development in terms of continuous participation, feedback, and support of the staff is essential for school improvement.
8. *School–Business Cooperation.* Some of the most promising reforms and innovations include "partnerships" between schools and business—sort of a revitalization or rediscovery of the old "stewardship" concept of the private sector.[59]

However, in regard to the last item, business involvement in schools can be controversial, as the PRO/CON Debate indicates.

Curriculum leaders can also increase educators' willingness to change by "linking" the needs and expectations of the individuals with those of the organization. Each person has certain needs and interests that she expects to fulfill within the school organization. Every individual who comes into a system plays a mul-

titude of roles; each professional brings to her role her personality as well. Rarely, however, are institutional expectations absolutely compatible with individual needs. Misalignment can cause conflict. Administrators need to recognize that they cannot always avoid this conflict; they must manage it. The way they manage it is reflected in their own personality and leadership behavior.

At the school level, the principal is the key person for matching individual needs and institutional expectations; she is crucial in creating school spirit and receptivity to change by promoting trust and teamwork. However, she can dampen spirit and change by promoting distrust and demoralization. What matters most to principals—values and attitudes—gets articulated (directly and indirectly) to the school staff. At the school district level, the same is true, only then the key person is the superintendent. What he values gets filtered down to the central administration, principals, and school staff.

Guidelines for Change

Much has been written about the nature of change and the best methods to promote change. Based on the research of Fortune 500 companies, ten principles, which are generic in nature, influence most organizations, including schools. Leaders do make a difference, and those who wish to implement change should

1. Move groups of people in the same direction through mostly noncoercive means.
2. Move people in a direction that is genuinely in their own long-term interests.
3. Establish a set of processes or strategies that aligns the needs and values of individuals and groups with the mission and goals of the organization.
4. Develop a set of strategies that will move the organization toward achieving its mission or goals.
5. Instill cooperation and teamwork within the organization, aimed at achieving shared goals.

[59]Allan C. Ornstein and Daniel U. Levine, "School Effectiveness and Reform: Guidelines for Action," *Clearing House*, 64 (1990), pp. 115–118.

PRO/CON DEBATE

■

CORPORATE INFLUENCE

The corporate influence on schools and other public agencies such as government is considerable. The business sector heavily influences the task forces recommending education reform. Corporations inform educational policy groups about the skills needed by high school graduates. Businesses sponsor schools and fund programs. Recently, the issue of corporate influence on the curriculum has focused on the use of corporate-sponsored curriculum materials: books, pamphlets, wall posters, slides, films, audio tapes, videos, and Whittle Communications' Channel One.

QUESTION Is the use of corporate-sponsored instructional materials appropriate in the classroom?

ARGUMENTS PRO

1   A variety of instructional materials should be available in classrooms. These include corporate-sponsored materials. It is the teacher's role to ensure that materials are balanced and all points of view are considered.

2   Corporate-sponsored materials are free or available at a nominal cost. School budgets are limited. Therefore, schools should take advantage of free materials.

3   Corporations have the financial resources and the expertise to develop quality publications or media. They frequently do so in concert with teachers who ensure that materials are well suited to classrooms and students' learning needs.

4   Advertising is prevalent in schools—on soft-drink cups, athletic scoreboards, students' tee shirts, and the pages of educational magazines.

5   This is a consumer society. High school students must be sophisticated consumers. Channel One provides an opportunity for students to practice this skill with teachers' guidance.

6   Channel One is a powerful tool to combat U.S. students' woefully inadequate preparation in current events. It will succeed only if it produces a marketable product that justifies its cost.

ARGUMENTS CON

1   Corporate-sponsored materials should be used with caution or not at all. They are dangerous because they are a means to the corporate end but appear in the guise of "educational materials."

2   Students must attend schools and should not be a captive audience for corporate America while they are in school.

3   The corporation has an unfair fiscal advantage over other individuals or organizations with opposing points of view. Alternate viewpoints are not presented, or their presentation is sometimes unsophisticated.

4   Advertising in the required curriculum compromises the integrity of public education; it should not be permitted.

5   In school, children should be free of commercial influence. By using corporate-sponsored materials, schools signal to students that the traditional values are replaced by commercialism.

6   Channel One is a vehicle for Corporate America to capitalize on a single-age audience and to sell its advertisers' products. It should not be leased with public funds.

6. Allow for input and participation in decision making among participants, as opposed to directing or dictating.
7. Motivate a group of key people who are committed to the mission and goals of the organization.
8. Be consistent and practice what is preached.
9. Deliver what is promised and promise only what is feasible and within one's authority to follow through.
10. Create and maintain professional work conditions, attractive work environment, challenging work opportunities, and opportunity for career development.[60]

Two important characteristics seem to sum up the qualities of the above leader. First, he is viewed as trustworthy and tends to obtain the best work from employees in terms of quantity and quality. When administrators are trusted, workers tend to exhibit more emotional stability, satisfaction in working, improvement in originality, willingness to take risks, and adaptability to change. Second, the leader is more people-oriented than task-oriented. When administrators are concerned about people, people tend to put more effort into achieving the goals of the organization. The bottom line is still important, and it improves because people are willing to extend effort and complete tasks, not because they are being directed or coerced. Positive comments, praise when it is honest, and subtle manipulation by the leader are much more effective than merely delegating tasks and expecting them to be completed on time. The latter is representative of a military and "machine" model that does not work well in a professional organization or a modern era, especially with the growth in rights of labor.

On a more focused basis, when working with teachers who are involved in curriculum innovation or implementation, the human element continues to surface. In this context, Ronald Doll sets forth five basic people-oriented principles for curriculum improvement.

1. Nothing of major significance is likely to happen until teachers' real concerns surface; the climate of the school (or school district) can contribute to the emergence of these concerns.
2. The behavior of educational leaders can either help or hinder initial and ongoing progress.
3. The idea must be conveyed that improvement requires time and persistence.
4. The school environment must be one of working with people rather than requiring people to work.
5. Feelings tend to improve as curriculum groups become "in groups" to which members feel they belong.[61]

SUMMARY

1. Curriculum can be defined in many ways: as a plan, in terms of experiences, as a field of study, and in terms of subject matter and grade levels. Most curriculum leaders in schools are comfortable with three out of four definitions, except the one about a field of study, with which theoreticians and professors tend to feel comfortable.
2. There are four basic approaches to developing curriculum: behavioral, managerial, systems, and humanistic. Most school administrators adhere to the first two approaches. The systems approach is a little more theoretical, and the humanistic approach tends to coincide with progressive thought.
3. The classic method of curriculum development is based on the Tyler model, which is behaviorist in nature.
4. There are a number of fundamental or basic questions in curriculum that help determine the planning and implementation of curriculum, the function of subject matter, and the role of curriculum leaders and specialists.
5. Regardless of definition or approach, curriculum can be organized into three major components:

[60]Dean Speicher, "Leadership with Vision," *School Administrator*, 46 (1989), p. 6.

[61]Doll, *Curriculum Improvement: Decision Making and Process*.

content, experiences, and environment. Content basically answers the *what* of curriculum, and experiences and environment answer the *how*.

6. Curriculum implementation is largely a function of leadership style and involves personal interaction, program development, and organizational structures.

7. In implementing curriculum, administrators need to consider the nature of incrementalism, communication, cooperation, and support.

8. Implementation involves change, and a number of change models depict change from simple modification to complex, major shifts in philosophy and organization.

9. People often resist change, as well as accept it. An effective administrator can work with and convince her staff to be more receptive than resistant to change. A number of leadership characteristics improve receptivity to change among staff participants.

KEY TERMS

machine theory
curriculum engineering
curriculum development
sources of information
screens
content and experiences
curriculum environment

curriculum implementation
survival mechanism
curriculum change
decision making
change agent

DISCUSSION QUESTIONS

1. What definition of curriculum do you prefer? Why?
2. What approach to curriculum do you prefer? Why?
3. In developing curriculum, what criteria for selecting content do you feel are important? What criteria not mentioned in the chapter would you add? In developing curriculum, what criteria for selecting experiences do you feel are important? What criteria not mentioned in the chapter would you add?

4. How can curriculum implementation be improved in your school? As a curriculum leader, how do you involve teachers and students, if at all, in curriculum making?

5. How can the change process in schools be improved? As a curriculum leader, what specific steps would you take to improve the receptivity to change in your school?

SUGGESTED READINGS

Carol D. Glickman, *Supervision and Instruction*, 2nd ed. (Needham Heights, MA: Allyn and Bacon, 1990). A "bottoms-up" administrative approach to supervising and evaluating instruction.

Philip W. Jackson, ed., *Contributing to Educational Change* (Berkeley, CA: McCutchan, 1988). Distinguished scholars discuss a variety of topics dealing with educational change.

John D. McNeil, *Curriculum: A Comprehensive Introduction*, 4th ed. (Glenview, IL: Scott, Foresman, 1990). An easy-to-read text for the beginning curriculum student.

Allan C. Ornstein and Francis P. Hunkins, *Curriculum: Foundations, Principles, and Issues* (Englewood Cliffs, NJ: Prentice-Hall, 1988). A comprehensive text for the sophisticated or experienced curriculum student.

Thomas J. Sergiovanni and John H. Moore (eds.), *Schooling for Tomorrow* (Needham Heights, MA: Allyn and Bacon, 1989). A discussion of the reform movement in education, with emphasis on related change-based and implementation issues.

Ralph W. Tyler, *Basic Principles of Curriculum and Instruction* (Chicago: University of Chicago Press, 1949). A classic curriculum book, largely exemplifying a behavioral approach.

Decker Walker, *Fundamentals of Curriculum* (San Diego: Harcourt Brace Jovanovich, 1990). An up-to-date curriculum text, combining philosophical and historical foundations with technical aspects of curriculum making.

14

SCHOOL FINANCE
AND PRODUCTIVITY

In this chapter, we attempt to answer these questions about financing and productivity by first examining the sources and distribution of funding. Next we explore the methods of school funding and the advantages and disadvantages of each. Then we discuss developing budgets and the correlation between expenditures and student productivity. Finally, we examine how aging school buildings and environmental hazards can affect expenditures.

EDUCATION AND ECONOMICS

Education is big business. The replacement value of the 84,000 public elementary and secondary schools amounts to an estimated $1 trillion (based on about $75 per square foot), and the 1990 operating school budget of grades K to 12 was more than $200 billion, which was equivalent to more than 4 percent of the **gross national product** (the value of all goods and services produced in the United States). Because most school-related costs (including salaries) have increased more rapidly than inflation in recent years, the business of schooling is in deep trouble. Not only has the federal government reduced its commitment to education in terms of real dollars (after inflation is taken into account), but also the majority of state budgets have been plagued by deficit or near-deficit spending since the mid-1980s. In 1989, for example, twenty-seven states were considered fiscally unhealthy, with monetary balances of less than 3 percent, and twenty-nine states ranked budget issues related to education as the number-one concern among all other human services.[1]

The result: There is no guarantee that all the nation's schools will be able to open up on time each September and finish the full school year and still pay all their bills. Each year several school districts are forced to engage in some fuzzy accounting and to move capital expenses to pay operating costs in order to keep the school doors open. Others are required to seek emergency funds from the state government or to pass local emergency bond referendums to pay their bills.

Since the early 1980s, school board members, who are the people closest to the problem of school financing, have consistently ranked "lack of financial support" as their number-one challenge.[2] This ranking should come as no surprise; board members have to watch the bottom line. In an era of reduced, direct federal education spending, increasing state budget constraints, and local taxpayer resistance to higher price tags

for education, the people responsible for financial decisions are very sensitive to expenditures and capital outlays.

The three major sources of revenue or financial support for public schools are the local, state, and federal governments. State and local money remains the basic source of revenue for public education. Table 14-1 shows that although revenues from federal sources steadily increased from 0.4 percent in 1929–1930 to a high of 9.8 percent in 1979–1980; the percentage then began to fall. The relative decrease in the federal contribution is expected to continue for the 1990s. In contrast, contributions by the states have rapidly increased from 16.9 percent in 1929–1930 to 50.2 percent in 1988–1989. Estimates for 1995 put state revenue contributions at approximately 55 percent—making up for federal and local shortfalls in revenues. Local revenue sources have decreased from 82.7 percent in 1929–1930 to 43 percent in the 1980s. It is expected that local revenue contributions will continue slightly downward, especially in large urban areas that are under financial pressure and in some suburban areas where the population contains fewer school-age children.

TAX SOURCES OF SCHOOL REVENUES

The operation of public schools relies primarily on revenues generated from taxes, especially the property tax on the local level and sales and income taxes on the state level. Some kinds of taxes are considered better than others. Most people today accept several criteria for evaluating various types of taxes. Most commonly mentioned are the following four:

1. *A Tax Should Not Cause Unintended Economic Distortions.* It should not alter economic behavior, change consumer-spending patterns in favor of one good or service for another, negatively affect a taxpayer's willingness to

---

[1] *Broken Purse Strings: Congressional Budgeting, 1974–88* (Washington, D.C.: Urban Institute Press, 1988); *Leading Fiscal Issues in the 1989 Legislative Sessions* (Denver: National Conference of State Legislatures, 1989).

[2] "Sixth Annual Survey of School Board Members," *American School Board Journal*, 171 (1984), pp. 24–27, 40; "Money Remains the Root of Your Problems," *American School Board Journal*, 176 (1989), p. 24; and "Money and Other Worries," *American School Board Journal*, 177 (1990), pp. 34–35.

work, or cause the relocation of business, industry, or people.

2. *A Tax Should Be Equitable*. It should be based on the taxpayer's ability to pay. Those with greater incomes or with property worth more money should pay more taxes than those with less income or less desirable property. Taxes that are not equitable and that require lower-income groups to pay a higher proportion of their income than higher-income groups are called **regressive taxes**. In contrast, taxes that require high-income groups to pay higher percentages of their income are called **progressive taxes**.

3. *A Tax Should Be Collected Easily*. This requires that the tax be collected with minimum costs to the taxpayer or government; it also means that it should be difficult to evade and should have no loopholes.

4. *The Tax Should Be Responsive to Changing Economic Conditions*. During inflation (when government costs and expenditures rise), the tax revenue should also rise; in a recession, the tax revenue should decrease. Responsive taxes are **elastic**; those that are not responsive are **inelastic**.[3]

LOCAL FINANCING OF PUBLIC SCHOOLS

Although education is the responsibility of the states, they have traditionally delegated much of this responsibility to local school districts. As indicated earlier, the local contribution to school financing has decreased over the last several decades, whereas the state contribution has increased. Nevertheless, local funding remains a crucial part of public school financing.

---

[3]James Guthrie and Rodney J. Reed, *Education Administration and Policy* (Englewood Cliffs, NJ: Prentice-Hall, 1986); Donald E. Orlosky et al., *Educational Administration Today* (Columbus, OH: Merrill, 1984); and *Interstate Tax Comparisons* (Denver: National Conference of State Legislatures, 1989).

Property Tax

The **property tax** is the main source of revenue for local school districts, accounting for more than 90 percent of local revenues. It is the most important tax supporting education, with a long history in this country. (The property tax has been used since the colonial period.)

Property taxes are determined by first arriving at the **market value** of a property—the amount the property would likely sell for if it were sold. Then the market value is converted to an **assessed value** using a predetermined index or ratio, such as one-fourth or one-third; for example, a property with a market value of $80,000 might have an assessed value of only $20,000. The assessed value is always less than the market value in order to protect the owner and to avoid controversies and appeals. Finally, the local tax rate, expressed in mills, is applied to the assessed value. A **mill** represents one-thousandth of a dollar; thus, a tax rate of 25 mills amounts to $25 for each $1000 of assessed value.

The property tax does not rate well on the criterion for equity. Because of different assessment practices and lack of uniform valuation, people owning equivalent properties may pay different taxes. This results in unequal treatment of equal property. The property tax does not always distribute the tax burden according to the ability to pay. A retired couple may have a home whose market value has increased substantially, along with their taxes, but because they live on a fixed income they cannot afford the increasing taxes. In this respect, it can be argued that the property tax is regressive.

In addition, the property tax is not immediately responsive to changing economic conditions. In some states, properties are reassessed every one to two years; but in others, reassessments occur only every three to four years. Thus, a property's assessed value and actual tax are often based on old market conditions. If property values have risen since the last reassessment, then the municipal government is losing potential tax income; if property values have decreased, property taxes may be overburdensome,

TABLE 14 ■ 1   Revenues of Public School Grades K to 12 by Government Source, 1929–1930 to 1988–1989

SCHOOL YEAR	AMOUNT IN THOUSANDS OF DOLLARS				PERCENTAGE OF TOTAL SCHOOL REVENUES		
	Total	Federal	State	Local	Federal	State	Local
1929–1930	$2,088,557	$7,334	$ 353,670	$1,727,553	0.4	16.9	82.7
1939–1940	2,260,527	39,810	684,354	1,536,363	1.8	30.3	68.0
1949–1950	5,437,044	155,848	2,165,689	3,115,507	2.9	39.8	57.3
1959–1960	14,746,618	651,639	5,768,047	8,326,932	4.4	39.1	56.5
1969–1970	40,266,923	3,219,557	16,062,776	20,984,589	8.0	39.9	52.1
1979–1980	96,880,944	9,503,537	45,348,814	42,028,593	9.8	46.8	43.4
1980–1981	105,904,908	9,808,007	50,207,192	45,809,709	9.3	47.4	43.3
1988–1989	185,121,978	11,645,928	93,937,990	80,528,060	6.3	50.2	43.5

SOURCE: *The Condition of Education, 1987* (Washington, D.C.: Government Printing Office, 1987), Table 1.13, p. 36; *Digest of Education Statistics, 1982* (Washington, D.C.: National Center for Education Statistics, 1982), Table 66, p. 75; *Digest of Education Statistics, 1983–84* (Washington, D.C.: National Center for Education Statistics, 1984), Table 62, p. 77; and *Estimates of School Statistics, 1988–89* (Washington, D.C.: National Education Association, 1989), pp. 6–7.

thereby causing a declining neighborhood to deteriorate further.

The property tax is not always easy to collect. Collection depends on the efficiency of the local tax collection department. Wealthy individuals and businesses that contest their property taxes often receive abatements. Most states specify the basic minimum property tax rate that local school districts can levy. An increase in the tax rate usually requires voter approval at the local level. Since the mid-1970s, local school districts have had difficulty getting voter approval for raising taxes.

User Fees

Besides the property tax, some school districts gather revenues through user fees, special income taxes, and revenue-sharing monies. **User fees**—that is, fees charged specifically to people who use a certain facility or service—are becoming increasingly popular (both with state and local governments) for supporting, partially or wholly, specific services or functions. Usually, income from user fees is earmarked for a particular agency fund supporting the activity that justifies the imposition of the fee. In instances where the fee does not cover the entire cost for the service, and they rarely do, the legislature may pick up the difference by appropriating general revenues.

These fees are attractive because the public helps pay for the service's provision and only people using it are taxed. We should expect greater increases in user fees, especially if state or local revenues fall short, because they can be assessed on almost any government service or function.[4] A few school districts (mostly affluent) already levy user fees on bus service, textbooks, athletic and recreational activities, nursery classes, and after-school centers. To maintain balanced budgets, the schools will probably increase these fees, just as colleges and

[4]Telephone conversation with Chris Pipho, director of the Information Clearing House, Education Commission of the States, Denver, March 15, 1990.

universities are increasing tuition fees. But, just as college and university tuitions are regressive, because they are not determined on an ability-to-pay basis, so are user fees.

Urban/Suburban Disparities

Helpful as state and federal aid is to most school districts (see Table 14-1), the differential ability of school districts to support education still persists. A school district located in a wealthy area or an area with a broad tax base can obviously generate more revenue than can poor school districts. As a result, in the majority of states today, total expenditures per student are frequently two to four times greater in the five wealthiest school districts than in the five poorest school districts.[5] These variations exist among communities in every state, and they tend to be growing wider between urban and suburban areas adjacent to them. This trend is more apparent in the Northeast and Midwest, due to the flight of urban populations and businesses to the suburbs and Sunbelt states.

Most urban property taxes are alarmingly high, about 30 percent higher per capita than taxes in adjacent suburbs. High property taxes make it difficult to attract middle-income residents and new jobs to broaden the tax base. As the cities lose their middle-class population and businesses, their tax base is further undermined. They are forced to cut city services, including education, to balance their budgets; these cuts drive away more middle-class persons and businesses and more tax revenues. The cycle reinforces itself, and this is one reason for the decline of many urban schools. Financing has become the major problem for many city schools, and recommendations for cutting costs and reducing wasteful programs have become

important issues.[6] (See Administrative Advice 14-1.)

Municipal and Educational Overburden

Cities are plagued by what is commonly called **municipal overburden**, or severe financing demands for public functions due to population density and the high proportion of disadvantaged and low-income groups. The result is that the large cities cannot devote as great a percentage of their total tax revenues to the schools as suburban and rural districts can. For example, in the mid-1980s, Cleveland, Detroit, Gary, Indiana, Newark, New Jersey, and New York City spent less than 30/35 percent of all local tax revenues for school purposes whereas the rest of their respective states were able to spend 45 to 50 percent of local taxes for schools.[7]

Then there is the issue of **educational overburden**. A large percentage of the student population in city schools is in technical and vocational programs, which cost more per student than the regular academic high school program. Similarly, there is a greater proportion of special-need students—namely, poor, bilingual, and handicapped students—in the city schools than in suburban or rural schools. These students require remedial programs and services, which cost 50 to 100 percent more per student

---

[5]Harry Hatry et al., *Program Analysis for State and Local Governments*, 2nd ed. (Washington, D.C.: Urban Institute Press, 1988).

[6]Allan Odden, "Sources of Funding for Education Reform," *Phi Delta Kappan*, 66 (1986), pp. 335–340; Allan C. Ornstein, "Urban Education for the 1980s: Trends and Issues," *Phi Delta Kappan*, 62 (1982), pp. 516–518; and Ornstein, "Urban Demographics for the 1980s," *Education and Urban Society*, 16 (1984), pp. 477–496.

[7]Allan C. Ornstein, "Regional Population Shifts: Implications for Educators," *Clearing House*, 59 (1986), pp. 284–290. Also see Isabel V. Sawhill, *Challenge to Leadership* (Washington, D.C.: Urban Institute Press, 1988).

ADMINISTRATIVE ADVICE 14-1

■

BORROWING WITH BONDS

Most states allow the local school district to borrow money from the citizens by floating a bond issue. In this way, the school board raises money for capital projects such as new buildings, remodeling programs, replacement or purchase of expensive equipment (i.e., boilers or buses) and facilities (i.e., pools or parking lots). Subject to state statutes and debt limitations (usually related to the assessed valuation of the district's property), bond issues must be passed in a local election to learn whether the people wish to incur additional debt for the district. If passed, the bonds are prepared, publicized, purchased, and traded. In this connection, school administrators should know the facts about bonds.

■ The amount to be repaid by the school district is the *principal amount*, *face value*, or *par value*, which is printed on the face of the bond.

■ The repayment date is the *maturity date*.

■ The interest rate paid by the school district to the person who owns the bond is the *coupon rate*.*

■ The period of time that the bond is outstanding is the *term*. Municipal bonds usually have a term from one through twenty years.

■ Bond certificates either come with coupons, which are *clipped* from the bond and presented for interest payments; or the bonds are *registered* with the issuing agent who mails the interest payments directly to the bond holder.

■ The *bearer* form is used with most municipal bonds, by which the person who holds the bond is presumed to be the owner.

■ When the bonds are backed up by collateral, such as property, the bonds are referred to as *mortgage bonds*.

■ When the bond is issued on the full faith of the borrower, it is called a *debenture*.

■ *Municipal bonds* are issued by cities, states, and political subdivisions.

■ Municipal bonds differ from corporate bonds in that they are *tax exempt*.

■ There are three basic types of municipal bonds:

■ *General obligation bonds*, which are backed by the faith and taxing authority of the issuer.

■ *Revenue bonds*, which are backed by the earning power of the facility constructed. (A stadium would generate gate receipts that would be used to retire the bonds.)

■ *Special tax bonds*, which are backed by a special tax levied yearly to pay the principal and interest of a maturing series. This is the type generally issued by school districts.

■ Bonds are rated by the following two independent agencies, which measure the probability of a bond issuer being capable of repaying the principal amount at maturity and the interest schedule.

■ Standard and Poor's Corporation uses the first four letters of the alphabet—AAA, AA, A; BBB, BB, B; CCC, CC, C; through D (default)—in rating bonds, with AAA being the most secure.

■ Moody's Investor Service Incorporated also uses the alphabet but stops with C.

Source: Adapted from Jeffrey B. Little and Lucien Rhodes, *Understanding Wall Street* (Cockeysville, MD: Liberty Publishing, 1978), pp.126–128.
*This is still a practice with old bonds, but most new bondholders can register their bonds with the issuing company and checks can be directly forwarded to the bondholder.

than basic programs.[8] Moreover, the need for additional services tends to increase geometrically with the concentration of poverty.[9] City schools, therefore, have to spend more educational resources per student than a similar-size school district or group of school districts comprising middle-class students.

Finally, city schools tend to have a greater proportion of senior teachers at the top of the pay scale than do their suburban counterparts. Many suburban districts have as a matter of policy replaced many experienced teachers to save money. They have also experienced a high turnover of pregnant teachers who did not return to the teaching profession. Cities have higher vandalism costs, lunch costs, desegregation costs, insurance costs, and maintenance costs (their buildings are older than suburban schools) per school than do other districts within the state. Both city and rural school districts spend more than suburban districts on transportation.[10]

STATE FINANCING OF PUBLIC SCHOOLS

Over the years, the states have delegated many powers and responsibilities to local school districts; nevertheless, each state remains legally responsible for educating its children and youth. Because many local school districts now have trouble financing their own schools through property taxes and the federal government is reducing educational spending, the states are expected to assume greater financial responsibility for and control over the schools.

The sales tax and personal income tax are the two major sources of revenue for states. Because states currently pay over 50 percent of the cost of education, these two taxes are important elements in the overall support of public education.

Sales Tax

As of 1988, as many as forty-five states had statewide sales taxes, with such taxes making up approximately 30 percent of state revenues.[11] Although the sales tax is considered a viable means for raising tax money for education, it may cause some economic distortions; for example, the difference in the tax rates may make it worthwhile to travel to the low-tax or no-tax state to purchase expensive items.

Despite this distorting effect, the sales tax meets the criterion of equity if food and medical prescriptions are removed from the tax base. If the tax is placed on all goods, however, low-income groups are penalized because they spend a large portion of their incomes on basic goods such as food and drugs.

The sales tax is elastic because the revenue derived from it tends to parallel the economy. The trouble is, when the state (or nation) is in a recession, sales tax revenues decrease sufficiently to reduce the state's income. The tax is useful because relatively small changes in the rate result in large amounts of revenue, which can reduce or eliminate deficits. In 1988, for example, in Louisiana a sales tax increase of two cents accounted for $320 million, or more than 10 percent of the total state tax revenue.[12]

[8]Roe L. Johns, Kern Alexander, and Edgar L. Morphet, *The Economics and Financing of Education*, 4th ed. (Englewood Cliffs, NJ: Prentice-Hall, 1983); Ann M. Miline and Jay Moskowitz, "State Experiences with Special Needs Students." Paper presented at the annual meeting of the American Educational Research Association, Montreal, April 1983.

[9]Daniel U. Levine and Allan C. Ornstein, "Research on Classroom and School Effectiveness," *Urban Review*, 21 (1989), pp. 81–95; Joseph F. Murphy and Walter E. Hack, "Fiscal Problems of Central-City Schools," *Urban Review*, 4 (1983), pp. 229–244; and Isabel V. Sawhill, "What Happened to the War on Poverty?" *Urban Institute Policy and Research Report*, 19 (1989), pp. 7–9.

[10]Johns, Alexander, and Morphet, *The Economics and Financing of Education*; Murphy and Hack, "Fiscal Problems of Central-City Schools"; and *Report of the State Superintendent on Schools and School Districts in North Carolina* (Raleigh: North Carolina State Department of Public Instruction, 1986).

[11]*State Budget Actions in 1988* (Denver: National Conference on State Legislatures, 1988).
[12]Ibid.

In 1970 the median sales tax was 3 percent, and only one state had a rate as high as 6 percent. By 1987 the median rate was 4.75 percent, and seven states had rates of 6 percent or higher. Since 1985 rate increases were enacted to offset both the erosion of the sales tax base (especially in farm and energy states) and the fact that states have increasingly exempted food (twenty-eight states) and drug (forty-four states) purchases from the tax base.[13]

Personal Income Tax

The personal income tax is the second largest source of tax revenue for the states, representing more than 25 percent of state revenues in 1988. Only ten states do not levy a personal state income tax. Just as the sales tax rate varies among states, from 2 percent to 8 percent, the state income tax (based on a percentage of personal income) also varies.[14]

A properly designed income tax should cause no economic distortions. Assuming no loopholes, it rates very high in terms of equity. In theory, the personal income tax is supposed to reflect the taxpayer's income and ability to pay. The income tax is also more equitable than other taxes because it considers special circumstances of the taxpayer—such as dependents, medical expenses, moving expenses, and the like—and uses tax deductions or credits to take into account these variations among individuals. It becomes less equitable only if the taxpayer has many items that can be deducted to minimize his income tax.

The personal income tax is very elastic; it allows the state government to vary rates (if it wishes) according to the economy. On the other hand, the elasticity of the income tax makes it vulnerable to recession because the revenue derived from it declines at a faster rate than revenue from other tax sources.

As a result of the 1986 Tax Reform Act, personal state taxes have become more progressive than they were formerly, due to decreased property write-offs and increased standard deductions and personal exemptions. By 1987 a total of eleven states that formerly imposed taxes on poor families eliminated them, and several others lightened them on the poor and middle-class families.[15]

Other State Taxes

Other state taxes contribute limited amounts to education. These taxes include excise taxes on liquor and tobacco products; motor vehicle license taxes; estate and gift taxes; real estate transfer taxes; insurance premium taxes; hotel taxes; and severance taxes (on the output of minerals and oils).[16]

There is a growing trend to establish state lotteries to support education in many of the twenty-nine states where lotteries existed in 1989. Although this was a major purpose of the lotteries, funds have been diverted to meet other social priorities such as geriatric care, social welfare agencies, and road construction. The result is that in most states the lottery contributes less than 2 percent of the total revenue for education. In nine states, however, the lottery is used strictly or mainly for education purposes (California, Florida, Illinois, Michigan, Montana, New Hampshire, New Jersey, New York, and Ohio).[17] After money for prizes, marketing, and administration of the program has been subtracted, even in these states the net proceeds to

[13]Allan C. Ornstein, "State Financing of Public Schools: Policies and Prospects," *Urban Education*, 23 (1989), pp. 188–207; *Significant Features of Fiscal Federalism, 1987* (Washington, D.C.: Advisory Commission on Intergovernmental Relations, 1987).

[14]*State Budget Actions in 1988.*

[15]*State Deficit Management Strategies* (Denver: National Conference of State Legislatures, 1987).

[16]Ornstein, "State Financing of Public Education"; *The Unfinished Agenda for State Tax Reform* (Boulder, CO: National Conference of State Legislatures, 1988).

[17]Telephone conversation with Pam Greenberg, senior research analyst, National Conference of State Legislatures, June 15, 1989.

public schools are only 10 to 15 percent of the money generated[18]—a fraction of the so-called billions that were promised to voters. But these taxes are regressive because a higher proportion of low-income people play the lottery and spend larger percentages of their annual income on it. (This is also true with taxes on tobacco and alcoholic beverages.)

The States' Ability to Finance Education

Some students are more fortunate than others, simply by geographic accident. State residence has a lot to do with the quality of education received. In 1988–1989, as Table 14-2 shows, Alaska, Connecticut, New Jersey, and New York spent more than $7000 per student (calculated on the basis of average daily attendance). In contrast, eleven states spent less than half the amount, and Alabama, Arkansas, Idaho, Mississippi, and Utah spent less than $3000 per student. Utah had the distinction of spending the least: $2574.

It is incorrect to assume that, based on dollars only, the education priorities of some states are higher than are the priorities of other states. We must ask what the states can afford, and this has a lot to do with the personal income of the states' inhabitants. Also, we must ask what the states spend on all other services and functions such as social spending, housing, transportation, and medical. In the first case, we are able to get a good idea of the states' financial ability to fund education; in the second case, we can determine the states' priorities.

The ability to finance education (shown in Table 14-2) is also associated with regional attitudes toward education. For example, eleven out of twelve states in the Southeast, and all four

states in the Southwest, spent less money on education per student than the national average ($4509) in 1989. Compounding this fact, the local percentage of school revenues was also below the national average (43.5 percent) in fifteen out of sixteen of these states. Similarly, there was dependence (as historically has been the case) on the federal government to make up some of the local revenue shortfalls, as illustrated by the fact that the federal contribution for education was above the national average (6.3 percent) in fourteen out of sixteen of these states. (These states comprise most of the Sunbelt region, which tends to be more politically conservative and spend less money per capita in human services than the Frostbelt region.)

In contrast, in the Northeast (which represents more than half the Frostbelt), ten out of eleven states locally spent more money per student than the national average, and the local percentage of school revenues was also above average in nine out of eleven states. As one might expect, the federal contribution to education in these eleven states was below the national average in nine cases. Historically, the Northeast and Midwest (or Frostbelt region) have been net losers in the tax burden borne and monies received back from the federal government in terms of programs, contracts, and assistance.[19]

STATE AID TO LOCAL DISTRICTS

State funding of education is largely based on a mixture of **discretionary funding**—that is, subjective criteria based on need or eligibility requirements—and **formula funding**, whereby all recipients are treated equally and the role of the administrator is merely ministerial. Over the years, the states have moved more toward discretionary funding in education, while the federal government (since Chapter II in 1981) has adopted formula funding.

[18]Chris Pipho, "The Lottery Luster," *Phi Delta Kappan*, 68 (1987), pp. 254–255; "State Lotteries: Do They Really Benefit Public Schools?" *School Board News*, 9 July 1986, pp. 1, 14.

[19]Allan C. Ornstein, "Decline of the Frostbelt," *Dissent*, 30 (1983), pp. 366–374.

TABLE 14 ▪ 2   Revenues and Expenditures for Public Education, 1988–1989

	PERCENTAGE OF SCHOOL REVENUES BY SOURCE			TOTAL EXPENDITURES PER PUPIL
	Federal	State	Local	
United States	6.3	50.2	43.5	$4509
Alabama	11.7	71.4	16.9	2915
Alaska	8.9	63.6	27.5	7134
Arizona	3.9	50.7	45.4	3904
Arkansas	9.3	60.9	29.8	2698
California	7.2	69.1	23.5	4075
Colorado	4.8	39.5	56.7	4633
Connecticut	4.0	45.7	50.3	7199
Delaware	8.0	68.1	23.9	5506
District of Columbia	10.5	0.0	89.5	5827
Florida	6.3	53.7	40.0	4487
Georgia	7.1	59.7	33.2	4143
Hawaii	7.8	92.1	0.1	4034
Idaho	7.0	60.2	32.8	2946
Illinois	8.2	36.6	55.2	4513
Indiana	4.1	60.6	35.3	3858
Iowa	5.6	46.2	48.2	4289
Kansas	5.3	43.2	51.5	4404
Kentucky	9.9	70.0	20.1	3655
Lousiana	12.1	55.1	32.8	3352
Maine	6.8	53.5	39.7	4845
Maryland	5.3	39.4	55.4	5391
Massachusetts	4.9	45.1	50.0	5818
Michigan	3.9	36.3	59.8	4576
Minnesota	4.3	56.2	39.5	4577
Mississippi	15.0	54.5	30.5	2846
Missouri	5.5	40.5	54.0	3838
Montana	8.3	48.6	43.1	4259
Nebraska	5.2	24.5	70.3	3732
Nevada	4.3	39.3	56.4	3974
New Hampshire	2.9	7.1	90.0	4334
New Jersey	4.0	43.6	52.4	7571
New Mexico	12.2	76.0	11.8	4034
New York	5.0	44.7	50.3	7738
North Carolina	6.9	60.5	29.6	3872
North Dakota	7.2	51.4	41.4	3447
Ohio	5.0	47.8	47.2	4138
Oklahoma	9.4	62.4	28.2	3212
Oregon	6.3	26.6	67.1	4818
Pennsylvania	4.5	46.5	49.0	5621
Rhode Island	4.1	45.5	50.4	5939
South Carolina	6.9	52.6	37.5	3465
South Dakota	8.8	28.0	63.2	3329
Tennessee	9.6	49.7	40.7	3305
Texas	8.0	43.4	48.6	3842
Utah	6.2	56.6	37.2	2574
Vermont	5.8	41.4	52.8	5057
Virginia	4.7	34.6	60.7	4744
Washington	5.9	72.8	21.3	4339
West Virginia	8.6	63.4	28.0	3879
Wisconsin	4.4	40.2	55.4	5117
Wyoming	4.6	51.8	43.6	5462

SOURCE: Adapted from *Estimates of School Statistics, 1988–89* (Washington, D.C.: National Education Association, 1989), Table 2, p. 7. Federal and state percentages have been calculated by authors.

State Funding Methods

States use five basic methods to finance public education. Some states combine more than one method.

1. *Flat-Grant Model.* This is the oldest, simplest, and most unequal method of financing schools. State aid to local school districts is based on a fixed amount multiplied by the number of students in attendance. It does not consider the special needs of students (bilingual students are more expensive to educate than native English-speaking students), special programs (vocational programs are more expensive than regular programs), or the wealth of the school districts (wealthy school districts have more money to spend on students or schools than do less wealthy school districts).

   In most states, the distribution of education funds is based on some type of equalization plan designed to provide extra money for less wealthy school districts. The remaining four methods each seek to bring about greater equality of educational opportunity by allocating more funds to the school districts in greatest need of assistance.

2. *Foundation Plan.* This is the most common approach, and its purpose is to guarantee a minimum annual expenditure per student for all school districts in the state, irrespective of local taxable wealth. However, the minimum level is usually considered too low by reformers and wealthy school districts far exceed the minimum levels. School districts with a high percentage of low-income students suffer under this plan.

3. *Power-Equalizing Plan.* This is a more recent plan, and many of the states have adopted some form of it. Under this scheme, the state pays a percentage of the local school expenditures in inverse ratio to the wealth of the district. Although the school district has the right to establish its own expenditure levels, wealthier school districts are given fewer matching state dollars. The program is constrained by lower and upper limits, and the matching dollars are insufficient for poor school districts. In the end, the equalization effect is usually insufficient.

4. *Guaranteed–Tax Base Plan.* The guaranteed-tax plan has the same economic philosophy as the power-equalizing plan, that is, equalizing fiscal capacity and expenditures as much as possible. This is accomplished by determining an assessed valuation per student, which the state guarantees to the local school district. State aid becomes the difference between what the district raises per student and what the state guarantees per student.

5. *Weighted-Student Plan.* Students are weighted in proportion to their special characteristics (i.e., handicapped, disadvantaged, etc.) or special programs (e.g., vocational or bilingual) to determine the cost of instruction per student. For example, a state may provide $4000 for each student in a basic program, whereas the state contribution per student may be 1.3 times higher, or $5200, for vocational education and 1.5 times higher, or $6000, for a handicapped student. (See the PRO/CON Debate.)

School Budgeting

Budgeting is both an executive and legislative function. The executive (superintendent and staff at the district level, principal and/or assistant at the school level) proposes and the legislative (board of education) enacts. On formal adoption by the school board, the budget becomes a legal document that serves as the basis for annual expenditures, accounting, and auditing. According to one financial school officer, five major steps are involved in budgeting: preparation, submission, adoption, execution, and evaluation. The third step, adoption, involves the school board whereby it appropriates specific amounts for specific categories. The other four

PRO/CON DEBATE

■

EDUCATION FOUNDATIONS

Foundations are a relatively new alternate revenue source in public education. Local citizens establish and govern a foundation as a nonprofit agency. It solicits private funds, equipment, and services from both individuals and corporations. Since the late 1970s, nearly seventy school districts have developed an educational foundation.

QUESTION Are education foundations that operate as independent third-party agents an appropriate revenue source for schools?

ARGUMENTS PRO

1 Many school districts already receive funds via grants from states, the federal government, corporations, and private foundations. An education foundation is a natural and reasonable extension of this practice. It targets the school as an organization to support by local citizens who wish to give more than is required.

2 Foundation funding circumvents the political process involved in taxation. New initiatives can be supported without the drain of catering to special-interest groups or engaging in turf battles.

3 Those who are concerned about the erosion of financial support for schools can participate in the reversal of this trend through their donations to local schools via a foundation.

4 A foundation is cost-efficient. As a grass-roots organization, it can enlist volunteer management. The local foundation board generally knows where additional resources are and how to access them.

ARGUMENTS CON

1 Public schools are funded in the main through public tax dollars. To radically change this model endangers the public shared ownership of schools and schooling. All adult members of the community should participate in the education of the next generation of the citizenry, according to their ability to participate.

2 The school board is responsible for school funding. It considers all community interests and decides which programs to fund. A foundation that is not accountable to taxpayers threatens the public trust.

3 Declining support for schools is always a concern. The need is to re-evaluate how education is funded so that all children receive an equal and high-quality education. Jumping on the bandwagon of the first idea that appears to have merit is an inappropriate solution to any problem.

4 A foundation is a private organization and has the potential of attracting an elite who, because they are the source of revenue, can unduly influence decisions.

steps involve the superintendent, business manager, and/or principal.[20]

[20]Harry J. Hartley, "Budgeting," in R. A. Gorton, G. T. Schneider, and J. C. Fisher (eds.), *Encyclopedia of School Administration and Supervision* (New York: Oryx Press, 1988), pp. 40–41.

Typically, the annual budget is organized around four major categories: objects (e.g., salaries, supplies, travel), functions (e.g., instruction, transportation, plant), programs (e.g., English, math, gifted education), and location (school, group of schools, or district). The state usually mandates the items for objects and functions, whereas the school district usually develops the items for programs and locations.[21] The budget may also include other features such as a list of goals, objectives, or criteria; projected revenues from all local, state, and federal sources; comparison of expenditures for last year by categories; the amount needed to pay the principle and interest for the school bonds maturing during the fiscal year; and a budget summary.[22] (See Administrative Advice 14-2.)

Although the major responsibility for submitting a budget rests with the superintendent (and her staff), depending on the superintendent's management style the school principal's role in budgeting may be limited or substantial. A superintendent that maintains a highly centralized administration will most likely limit the principal's input in budgeting—filling out requisitions, receipts, and disbursements. A superintendent that believes in a decentralized administration, site budgeting, or school-based management will probably delegate more budget responsibility to the principal.[23]

Regardless of the amount of professional empowerment, the school staff must understand that only 5 to 10 percent of the district's budget is available for modification: 60 to 70 percent is earmarked for salaries and benefits; 15 to 20 percent is for operating expenses such as utilities, water, insurance, repairs and maintenance; and another 5 percent should be committed to reserves and replacement. Although the school principal (and staff) may be permitted to make budget recommendations, the school board establishes the budget.

The principal's budgeting roles can be classified into four major activities: (1) *budget planning*, assisting the superintendent in identifying budget priorities and focusing on school needs at the planning stage; (2) *budget analysis*, dealing with goals, objectives, and evaluative criteria, suggestions for curriculum materials and instructional equipment, and communicating concerns of the students, teachers, parents, and community about specific expenditures or special purposes; (3) *budget requesting*, involving a review of requests by different groups such as teachers or parents, establishing program priorities, submitting a total budget, and negotiating specific items; and (4) *budget controls*, dealing with inventory control expenses, receipts and disbursements, monthly reporting, and balancing the books at the building level.[24] (The fourth activity deals with the regular operation of the school and involves ongoing paperwork and record keeping.)

In large elementary schools, a person (perhaps assistant principal or teacher) representing a program area or grade level, and in secondary schools a department head, is usually asked to list needs in order of priority. If it becomes necessary to reduce school budgets because of cutbacks, the trimming process usually begins with the low-priority programs or items. Ultimately the principal submits the budget to the central office, and it is either approved or modified, sometimes through negotiation with the principal and sometimes without negotiation. Eventually, an approved budget is returned to the principal. Each month a person at the program or department level may be required to fill out requisitions and purchase orders; each month a budget summary to date may be returned by the business manager or financial officer at the district level to the principal and/or department or program level, indicating the amount of money remaining in each account item.

The principal is usually required to submit a monthly budget to the central office, which includes several income and expense categories.

[21]Hartley, "Budgeting"; K. Penney Sanders and Francis C. Thiemann, "Student Costing: An Essential Tool in Site-Based Budgeting," *NASSP Bulletin*, 74 (1990), pp. 95–102.

[22]Ronald W. Rebore, *Educational Administration: A Management Approach* (Englewood Cliffs, NJ: Prentice-Hall, 1985).

[23]Sarah D. Caldwell and Fred H. Wood, "School-Based Improvement—Are We Ready?" *Educational Leadership*, 46 (1988), pp. 50–53; Hartley, "Budgeting."

[24]Gerald C. Ubben and Larry W. Hughes, *The Principal: Creative Leadership for Effective Schools* (Needham Heights, MA: Allyn and Bacon, 1987).

ADMINISTRATIVE ADVICE 14-2

■

CHECKLIST FOR DEVELOPING A SCHOOL BUDGET

A budget reflects the local needs of the school (or school district), its history, and fiscal health. A number of state and local factors such as past practices, state/local codes and regulations, and board policies influence the process, format, and contents. Below is a general checklist for administrators to adapt and use when organizing their budget for their own local situation.

PROCESS: CONDUCTING THE HEARINGS

	Yes	No
1. Roles of board and superintendent clearly defined	☐	☐
2. Board financial policies updated regularly	☐	☐
3. Accuracy and timeliness of all financial data	☐	☐
4. Adequate staff involvement in budget request	☐	☐
5. Adequate public hearings and citizen participation	☐	☐
6. Budget document (or summary) widely distributed	☐	☐
7. Compliance with legal requirements	☐	☐
8. Community/political support generated for budget	☐	☐
9. Contingency strategy for cuts (budget options)	☐	☐
10. Efficient accounting/financial reporting system	☐	☐

FORMAT: ORGANIZING THE DOCUMENT

11. Attractive cover, title page, overall appearance	☐	☐
12. Table of contents or index; numbered pages	☐	☐
13. Names of board members, officers listed	☐	☐
14. Table of organization, administrators listed	☐	☐
15. Budget message or letter of transmittal	☐	☐
16. Graphics—artwork charts, figures, tables	☐	☐
17. Clarity of style; avoidance of technical jargon	☐	☐
18. Manageable size and shape of document	☐	☐

Table 14-3 illustrates some of the budget categories or items that might be included. Depending on the accounting system adopted by the school district, the budget items may be more extensive. In general, the accounting system should include among other procedures required receipts, vouchers, banking all cash received, a method for authorizing expenditures, expenditures paid only by check, a regular audit, and monthly and annual reporting.[25]

---

[25]Edward F. DeRoche, *An Administrator's Guide for Evaluating Programs and Personnel*, 2nd ed. (Needham Heights, MA: Allyn and Bacon, 1987).

Administrative Advice 14-2 (continued)

19. Glossary of key financial terms ☐ ☐
20. Concise executive summary ("budget-in-brief") ☐ ☐

CONTENTS: COMPILING THE DATA

21. Political feasibility of bottom-line request ☐ ☐
22. School system goals and objectives ☐ ☐
23. Budget assumptions, guidelines, or priorities ☐ ☐
24. Object budget summary (e.g., salaries, supplies) ☐ ☐
25. Program budget summary (e.g., reading, math) ☐ ☐
26. Site budget summary (e.g., individual schools) ☐ ☐
27. Budget history (expenditures for past five years) ☐ ☐
28. Unit-cost analysis (per-pupil expenditures) ☐ ☐
29. Summary of estimated revenues (all sources) ☐ ☐
30. Explanation of impact on tax rates ☐ ☐
31. Explanation of major cost factors (contracts, inflation) ☐ ☐
32. Budget coding system explained (chart of accounts) ☐ ☐
33. Performance measures program outcomes; test data ☐ ☐
34. Pupil enrollment projections by grade ☐ ☐
35. Staffing history and projections ☐ ☐
36. Long-range plans (five years) for the school system ☐ ☐
37. Justification for major decisions (layoffs, school closing) ☐ ☐
38. Comparisons with other districts (or with state averages) ☐ ☐
39. Capital budget summary (capital improvement projects) ☐ ☐
40. Budget detail (line-item expenditure data) ☐ ☐

Source: Adapted from Harry J. Hartley, "Checklist for Evaluating Local School Budgets," *American School Board Journal*, 46 (1989), p. 36. Copyright 1989, the National School Boards Association. Used by permission.

A word of caution is needed. Whether the budget is being prepared on a school district or school level, school leaders must be responsible and guard against faddism and wasting money on unproven programs, methods, or other phenomena that have an inadequate research base or limited history of empirical success. Too many programs and concepts in education expand on the basis of testimonial data or on ideas that are considered "innovative" or "reform-oriented" after appearing in the popular educational journals.

Why educational leaders continually jump onto popular bandwagons and spend large sums

TABLE 14 ■ 3   Internal Categories/Accounts for an Annual School Budget

BUDGET ITEM	MONTHLY		YEAR TO DATE		ANNUAL BUDGET	PERCENT YEAR TO DATE (YTD) BUDGET
Income	Actual	Budget	Actual	Budget		Actual Annual Budget
Pictures/yearbook						
Soda machine						
School store						
School newspaper						
Student clubs						
Laboratory fees						
Library fees/rentals						
Student clubs						
Miscellaneous						
Expenses						
Instructional materials						
Workbooks						
Textbooks						
Supplementary books/materials						
Library materials						
Computer software						
Duplicating materials						
Maps, graphs, models						
Instructional Equipment						
Video equipment						
Computer equipment						
Auditory/visual projectors						
Displays, chalkboards						
Organizations						
Teacher club						
Student council						
Student newspaper						
Band/orchestra						
Intramural activities						
Computer club						
Language club						
Ski club						
PTA						
Special purpose						
Field trips						
Hospitality						
School–community dinners						
Professional travel						
TOTAL EXPENSES						
Cash Flow (Deficit)						

of money in the absence of hard data is difficult to answer. One possible explanation, however, involves "popularism" and "pressure" as pendulums soar and take on a life of their own. Robert Slavin maintains that before administrators adopt a program on a large scale, pilot testing is needed and the program must be evaluated in school settings as if the district was thinking about investing money in the program or practice.[26] The emphasis must shift from what's new to *what works*.

SCHOOL EFFECTIVENESS AND PRODUCTIVITY

There are few agreed-on indicators to determine the ideal (or most efficient) size of schools or to determine whether a school is effective. Just what is a productive, or well-run, school? When do decision makers at the local or state level know that they are getting their money's worth in a school? The indicators are extremely fuzzy, but we will take positions to help clarify the data.

Size of Schools

Educators have long debated the optimal size for an individual school in terms of efficiency and student outcomes. Based on a review of research, the average student enrollment for elementary schools is 403, and for secondary schools it is 721. A school is considered too small where underutilization of staff and curriculum occurs and when the operating unit cost per student exceeds the average cost in the state. A school is considered too large when a loss of personal or school identity among students occurs; they are unable to fully participate in social and athletic activities or have difficulty interact-

ing among themselves or feel they do not belong to the student body or school in general.[27] There is a sense of aimlessness, isolation, even despair among a large number of students—which in turn causes other social and psychological problems (such as delinquency, drugs, and cults) which are more overt in nature.

In terms of numbers, 19 percent of public elementary schools are considered too small (fewer than 200 students), and 16.5 percent are too large (over 600 students). As many as 27 percent of the public secondary schools are too small (under 300 students) and as many as 10 percent are too large (over 1500 students); moreover, .46 percent of the secondary schools enroll 3000 or more students.[28]

Conventional wisdom has maintained that large schools were more efficient and offered more diversified opportunities for students. This thinking was derived from Raymond Callahan's "Cult of Efficiency," which associated bigness with growth and productive efficiency and greater opportunity to specialize. It is also based on James Conant's description of the American high school during a period of school consolidation, whereby he promulgated the need for large, "comprehensive" high schools (comprising graduating classes of 100 students or more) and considered small high schools as a problem in terms of lack of special facilities and subjects and economically wasteful.[29] Large schools were considered well organized and offering something for everyone, as well as a means for promoting integration and democratic values among students of varied backgrounds under

---

[26]Robert E. Slavin, "PET and the Pendulum: Faddism in Education and How to Stop It," *Phi Delta Kappan*, 70 (1989), pp. 752–758.

[27]Allan C. Ornstein, "Private and Public School Comparisons," *Education and Urban Society*, 21 (1989), pp. 192–206.

[28]*Digest of Education Statistics, 1989* (Washington, D.C.: Government Printing Office, 1989), Table 85, p. 99; Ornstein, "Private and Public School Comparisons," Table 3, p. 195.

[29]Raymond Callahan, *Education and the Cult of Efficiency* (Chicago: University of Chicago Press, 1962); James B. Conant, *The American High School Today* (New York: McGraw-Hill, 1959).

one roof. Whatever strengths small schools had—a sense of community, minimum bureaucracy, and curriculum offerings that coincided with the "core curriculum" (four years of English and history; three years of science and math; and two or three years of a foreign language)—were overlooked. [30]

Sociological data strongly suggest that small schools (K to 12) are often considered part, even the hub, of a homogeneous neighborhood where parental involvement and school–community relations are high. Parental pressure is often felt on the school, teacher expectations are felt on the home, and people in small, homogeneous communities tend to cooperate in school and civic activities; in fact, social life often centers around school and community activities. [31]

As larger schools are divided into smaller and smaller unit sizes, students have the potential to play an increased role in school–community functions. Students have a better chance to participate in leadership roles and extracurricular activities, especially the high status ones such as student government, student newspaper, school band, and numerous athletics. They also have a better chance for academic recognition, based on the fact that they are competing with fewer students on a school districtwide or schoolwide basis. [32] Moreover, the sociopsychological benefits of recognition and affiliation, and the result in terms of self-concept and motivation for achievement, are well documented in the social and educational literature.

Large schools, according to one author, exclude students, teachers, parents, and community members from curriculum development, and the curriculum becomes centralized and standardized by the administrative hierarchy. Large high schools win state championships in sports and national recognition in academic scholarships, and they also have impressive bands and student papers. [33] Yet, with the exception of a few talented ball players, scholars, and social elites, most students don't participate or receive recognition from their teachers or counselors; thus, the costs for these extra facilities and activities are high per student. No more than 25 percent of the student body, according to classic and current research, consider themselves part of school life, and no more than 10 to 15 percent consider themselves part of the "in" crowd. [34]

In this connection, Thomas Gregory and Gerald Smith argue that school size, school structure, and community life are interrelated and should be seriously considered in the school reform literature. After a review of several studies, they recommend a high school *size* of no more than 250 students because larger enrollments mentally result in a counterproductive preoccupation with control and order and anonymity works against the concept of sharing ideas and working together in cognitive and social learning. As for the *structure*, the authors are concerned with governance and how space, time, and people are organized—in small schools these kinds of arrangements are more supportive and positive to human functioning. By *community*, Gregory and Smith are concerned with the bonding of people—commitment and morale among students, teachers, and parents—and a feeling of a stake in the school and a place to live

[30]Gerald Unks, "Differences in Curriculum Within A School Setting," *Education and Urban Society*, 21 (1989), pp. 175–191.

[31]Allan C. Ornstein, "Controversy Over Size Continues," *School Administrator*, 46 (1989), pp. 42–43; Ornstein, "Size: An Evolving Controversy," *Clearing House*, 63 (1989), pp. 156–158.

[32]Philip A. Cusick, *The Egalitarian Ideal and the American High School* (New York: Longman, 1983); Joyce L. Epstein and Nancy L. Karweitt, *Friendship in Schools* (New York: Academic Press, 1983); and Allan C. Ornstein, "School District and School Size," *PTA Today*, 15 (1989), pp. 16–17.

[33]Unks, "Differences in Curriculum Within a School Setting."

[34]James S. Coleman, *The Adolescent Society* (New York: Free Press, 1961); Philip A. Cusick, *Inside High School* (New York: Holt, Rinehart & Winston, 1973); Eleanor Farrar, Arthur G. Powell, and David K. Cohen, *The Shopping Mall High School* (Boston: Houghton Mifflin 1985); Sara L. Lightfoot, *The Good High School* (New York: Basic Books, 1983); and *Youth Indicators 1988* (Washington, D.C.: Government Printing Office, 1988).

and find meaning in the community. This sense of community is easier obtained in small schools that are located in the small towns and villages of America.[35]

The characteristics of "large" appear to consistently connote negative descriptors, at least a "less satisfying" school experience.[36] Children, even adults, get lost in large organizations; they easily fall into the cracks, unless they are special. Because most students (and adults) are average but still prefer to make the team or excel in front of their peers, they have a better chance of being recognized (and feeling good about themselves) when the numbers are fewer and the surroundings are more familiar. Large schools tend to be more expensive per student than smaller ones because of salaries and extra curriculum and instructional offerings, but student outcomes (even when social class is held constant) appear to be higher in small schools.

Effective Schools

A powerful and long-term commitment is required to bring about substantial, widespread, and enduring gains in the performance of students. Attention must be paid to the school as an institution and, in the final analysis, to the larger context of the school district and the environment in which schools operate. The effectiveness of the school as a whole helps determine what happens in each classroom, In the words of one observer, "School performance is unlikely to be significantly improved by any measure or set of measures that fails to recognize that schools are institutions"—complex organizations composed of interdependent parts, "governed by well-established rules and norms of behavior, and adapted for stability."[37] Money does not seem to be the key or secret ingredient; rather, a number of intangible items that promote school effectiveness and productivity seem to coincide with school climate or culture.

Elementary Schools   Most of the recent research on **effective schools** has focused on elementary education. Authors of various studies generally have identified specific characteristics of effective elementary schools and have usually defined effectiveness at least partly in terms of outstanding student achievement. One of the best-known studies is that of Ronald Edmonds and his colleagues, who defined an effective school as one in which lower-class students score as high as middle-class students on basic-skills tests. Based on analysis of such schools, Edmonds identified an effective school as one in which there is strong leadership, an orderly, humane climate, frequent monitoring of students' progress, high expectations and requirements for all students, and focus on teaching important skills to all students.[38]

Other observers and groups frequently extend this type of list to include one or more additional characteristics. A good example is the analysis used by the Connecticut School Effectiveness Project, which describes an effective school as having the following characteristics:

1. A *safe and orderly environment* that is not oppressive and is conducive to teaching and learning
2. A *clear school mission* through which the staff shares a commitment to instructional goals, priorities, assessment procedures, and accountability
3. *Instructional leadership* by a principal who understands and applies the characteristics of instructional effectiveness

[35]Thomas B. Gregory and Gerald R. Smith, *High Schools as Communities: The Small School Reconsidered* (Bloomington, IN: Phi Delta Kappan Educational Foundation, 1987).

[36]John I. Goodlad, *A Place Called School* (New York: McGraw-Hill, 1984).

[37]John E. Chubb, "Why the Current Wave of School Reform Will Fail," *Public Interest*, 90 (1988), p. 29.

[38]Ronald R. Edmonds, "Programs of School Improvement: An Overview," *Educational Leadership*, 40 (1982), pp. 4–11; Edmonds, "Characteristics of Effective Schools" in U. Neiser (ed.), *The School Achievement of Minority Children* (Hillsdale, NJ: Erlbaum, 1986), pp. 89–111.

4. A climate of *high expectations* in which the staff demonstrates that all students can attain mastery of basic skills
5. High *time on task* brought about when a high percentage of students' time is spent "engaged" in planned activities to master basic skills
6. Frequent *monitoring of student progress*, using the results to improve individual performance and the instructional program
7. Positive *home–school relations* in which parents support the school's basic mission and play an important part in helping to achieve it[39]

Several individuals and agencies have gone even further in refining and modifying research to identify characteristics of unusually effective schools. Besides the characteristics highlighted by earlier studies, Lawrence Stedman's research has emphasized several other key features of effective schools, including (1) attention to goals involving cultural pluralism and multicultural education and (2) emphasis on responding to students' personal problems and developing their social skills.[40] Other educators have stressed cooperation between educators and parents and parental participation in school decision making; their formulation is being used to guide projects in New Haven, Connecticut, Baltimore, and some other school districts.[41]

Secondary Schools   Relatively few studies have concentrated on the characteristics of unusually effective secondary schools, other than those already identified for elementary schools. (Our use of the term *secondary schools* refers to middle schools, which usually include a combination of grades 6 through 8; junior highs, which usually include grades 7 through 9; and senior highs, which include grades 9 or 10 through 12.)

Because the goals and programs of most secondary schools are diverse and complex, it is difficult to conclude that one school is generally more effective than another, particularly when the social class of the student body is taken into account. In addition, hardly any secondary schools enrolling mostly lower-class students stand out as being relatively high in achievement. However, there is a strong support for the conclusion that effective secondary schools have made structural changes to improve the performance of their students. By *structural change*, we mean major modifications in the way students and teachers are assigned to classes, along with the concomitant changes in school schedules, teacher selection, and related policies and practices.[42] These are practices that add minimal or no extra cost.

One of the few senior high schools for which concrete data indicate unusual effectiveness is South Boston High School. Reform of South Boston occurred over several years during a time of continuing turmoil in the Boston school system, but by 1980 impressive data were available on improvement in the performance of students. For example, average reading scores increased in one year from the 16th percentile to the 40th percentile in the ninth grade and from the 18th to the 32nd percentile in the tenth grade. In addition, in four years, the percentage of graduates attending postsecondary education institutions increased from less than 8 percent to 40 percent. Structural and related changes that appear to have been most important in accounting

[39]William J. Gauthier, Raymond L. Pecheone, and Joan Shoemaker, "Schools Can Become More Effective," *Journal of Negro Education*, Summer (1985), pp. 388–408; Daniel U. Levine and Lawrence W. Lezotte, *An Interpretative Review and Analysis of Research and Practice Dealing with Usually Effective Schools* (Okemos, MI: National Center for Effective Schools, 1989).

[40]Lawrence Stedman, "The Effective Schools Formula Still Needs Changing," *Phi Delta Kappan*, 69 (1988), pp. 439–442.

[41]James P. Comer, "Parent Participation in the Schools: How Do We Improve Programs for Parent Involvement?" *Educational Horizons*, 66 (1988), pp. 58–59. Also see Lee Daniels, "An 'Active Partnership' That Spurs Learning," *New York Times*, 20 January 1988, p. B8; Mary Hatwood Futrell, "Home and School: Restoring Trust," *Education Week*, 3 February 1988, p. 4.

[42]*Effective Schooling Practices: A Research Synthesis* (Portland, OR: Northwest Regional Educational Laboratory, 1984).

for these and other improvements at South Boston included the following:

1. A new principal made major changes in traditional organizational patterns and insisted that staff re-examine their instructional methods.
2. More than two-thirds of the faculty were replaced by teachers willing to discard ineffective, traditional methods.
3. Nearly all ninth and tenth graders were placed in reading and writing courses rather than in traditional English classes.
4. Students were placed in mathematics courses rather than "business mathematics," which for the most part repeated beginning arithmetic.
5. A number of in-school and out-of-school alternatives were established. These alternatives included a self-contained school within a school that emphasized academic learning and a minischool that emphasized individual instruction.
6. Work–study programs based on learning opportunities in the community were made available to many students after the ninth grade.
7. Discipline, including strict attendance policies, was introduced.
8. Guidance in personal development was emphasized.
9. School price and spirit were systematically emphasized.[43]

Comparable changes have taken place at George Washington Preparatory High School, located in an inner-city community in Los An-geles. Following the appointment of a new principal (George McKenna) in the late 1970s, student achievement and the percentage of graduates going on to college increased substantially, and the daily absence rate fell from 33 percent to less than 10 percent. Among the actions and changes that appeared to have helped in bringing about these improvements were the following:

1. Parents and students were required to sign a contract in which students promised to obey school rules, adhere to the dress code, and complete all assignments.
2. Approximately 85 percent of the faculty were replaced by teachers willing and able to implement change in organization and instruction.
3. Parents played an active part in monitoring school attendance.
4. Teachers were required to assign homework and visit the homes of absentees.
5. Strict discipline was enforced, frequent "hall sweeps" were undertaken to apprehend students not in class, and antigraffiti squads of students were organized.
6. Remedial and tutoring programs were established in all subject areas; students receiving a D or F were required to attend Saturday sessions.
7. "Magnet centers" in mathematics, science, and communications were established to provide small classes and extra help for students in college-prep courses.[44]

Because no two schools share exactly the same problems and possibilities, one cannot say that other secondary schools should implement exactly the same set of changes as was introduced at South Boston or George Washington. However, some of these changes, such as emphasis on firm but fair discipline, insistence on more rigorous standards, increased stress on reading and math for students below grade level, and activities to build school spirit, have received

[43]Geraldine Kozberg and Jerome Winegar, "The South Boston Story: Implications for Secondary Schools," *Phi Delta Kappan*, 62 (1981), pp. 565–569; Daniel U. Levine and Eugene E. Eubanks, "Organizational Arrangements in Effective Secondary Schools," in J. J. Lane and H. J. Walberg (eds.), *Organizing for Learning* (Reston, VA: National Association of Secondary School Principals, 1988); and Daniel U. Levine, Rayna Levine, and Allan C. Ornstein, "Guidelines for Change and Innovation in the Secondary School Curriculum," *NASSP Bulletin*, 69 (1985), pp. 9–14.

[44]*Schools That Work* (Washington, D.C.: Government Printing Office, 1987).

considerable support in research on effective approaches at high schools with many low achievers. In addition, both schools illustrate the importance of changes in organizational structure and that schools can increase their student output with little extra input.

Effective-School Indicators

Criteria of effectiveness for schools put emphasis on student achievement scores. Some of the indicators commonly assessed include (1) a comparison of expected levels of student achievement with current levels of achievement, (2) analysis of levels of student achievement in a prior grade compared with that in the present grade; (3) a comparison of achievement scores between similar schools, sometimes after controlling for family income or social class; (4) a comparison of subgroups of students by gender, race, and social class; and (5) an analysis of grading inflation and how it skews achievement levels. High schools can also analyze or compare student participation and achievement in advanced placement courses or honor classes, student achievement by programs or courses, high school graduation, and college acceptance.[45]

Other indicators might include attitudes and levels of satisfaction among students, staff, parents, and community residents, as well as a number of previously mentioned characteristics of school effectiveness such as clear academic goals, order and discipline, focus on academic learning time, and remedial and tutoring programs.

Interestingly enough, almost all these criteria involve little or no extra money; rather, they require changes in school climate or school culture that can be induced by school leadership and changes in school structure. Almost any

school that continuously monitors its entire program and how it impacts on students (and other groups such as staff, parents, and community) and continuously seeks to improve teaching and learning, should enhance their effectiveness. (See Administrative Advice 14-3.)

In making comparisons with control and experimental groups or in achievement scores, the following information may be useful in illustrating outcomes of students or changes in their learning growth.

1. The number of students eligible for free or reduced lunch
2. The highest level of formal education completed by the parents, especially the mother
3. The per-capita income of families in the community
4. The cognitive abilities of children in the initial grade (first grade for elementary school, ninth grade for high school) offered by the school
5. The percentage of racial, ethnic, or non-English-speaking students in the school (or families within the community)
6. The per-student expenditures of the school compared with expenditures in other communities in the state[46]
7. The average classroom size
8. The average number of minutes per school day or school year or the average number of minutes per school day or school year in the subjects being assessed
9. The extra amount of money being spent on disadvantaged students, remedial students, handicapped students, gifted and talented students, and/or bilingual students
10. The extra amount of money (or extra cost per student) needed to raise levels (at a specific level) beyond the normal level or beyond the level of a comparative group with normal expenditures[47]

[45]David P. Crandall and Susan F. Loucks, *A Roadmap for School Improvement* (Andover, MA: The Network, 1983); *Documenting Student Gains in the Outcomes Accreditation School* (Boulder, CO: North Central Association, 1988).

[46]*Documenting Student Gains in the Outcomes Accreditation School.*
[47]Allan C. Ornstein, "School Size and Effectiveness: Policy Implications," *Urban Review*, 22 (1990), pp. 239–245.

Judgment or basis for success can be discussed on several levels, that is, the school district, school, or grade level. Site visitors, superintendents, or school principals can use them as a yardstick for their own reporting.

Table 14-4 illustrates indicators at the elementary, junior high school, and high school levels for judging effectiveness. The elementary indicators are based on the North Central Association's guide for self-study and team visits in evaluating successful schools. The junior high and high school indicators are based on the U.S. Department of Education's Secondary School Recognition Program, which identified 202 ef-

---

TABLE 14 ■ 4   Indicators for Judging School Effectiveness

ELEMENTARY SCHOOL INDICATORS	JUNIOR HIGH/MIDDLE SCHOOL INDICATORS	HIGH SCHOOL INDICATORS
1. Scores on norm-reference tests	1. Student performance on standard achievement tests	1. Student performance on standard achievement tests
2. Scores on criterion-reference tests	2. Student performance on minimum-competency tests	2. Student performance on minimum-competency tests
3. Scores on teacher-made tests, writing samples, and other "nonobjective" measures	3. Student success in high school	3. Numbers of students who go on to postsecondary education, enlist in the military, or find employment
4. Valid measures of affective outcomes such as self-concept	4. Daily student and teacher attendance rates	4. Student and teacher attendance rates
5. Teacher (and administrator) opinions of student goal attainment	5. Rates of student suspensions and other exclusions	5. Rates of suspensions and other exclusions
6. Opinions of students, parents, and community residents	6. Awards for outstanding school programs and teaching	6. Student awards in academic or vocational competition
7. Participation of students in extracurricular activities	7. Student awards in academic or vocational competitions	7. Awards for outstanding school programs
8. Student awards and distinctions		
9. Attendance		
10. Amount of material borrowed from media center or library		
11. Quality of student performance in programs such as art, music, and drama		
12. Community support organizations devoted to school programs		

SOURCE: Elementary school indicators adapted from *Assessing Student Outcomes* (Boulder, CO: North Central Association, 1985), p. 10. Secondary school indicators adapted from John W. Arnn and John N. Mangieri, "Effective Leadership for Effective Schools: A Survey of Principal Attitudes," *NASSP Bulletin*, 72 (1988), p. 3.

ADMINISTRATIVE ADVICE 14-3

■

ATTRIBUTES AND RELATED INDICATORS OF EFFECTIVE SCHOOLS

Research indicates several common characteristics or indicators of effective schools. The descriptors below include important characteristics and related indicators, based on interviews, observations, and analysis of self-studies involving 571 successful middle, junior high, and high schools. In the original data, fourteen attributes were documented; we have focused on what we feel are the ten major findings or categories that administrators of grades K to 12 can use in analyzing their own schools or for preparing for a site visitation by an outside evaluative team. Whereas the attributes provide a general framework or starting point, the indicators help establish more precise parameters or yardsticks in establishing your own school profile.

Attributes	Indicators
■ Clear academic goals	Presence of written goals
	Evidence of actions toward goals
	Consistency in statements of principals, teaching staff, and parents
	Evidence of discussion and communication of goals
■ High expectations for students	Academic requirements
	Student reports on homework and work demands in class
	Reports on academic and behavioral standards
	Enrollments in honors or advanced placement classes
■ Order and discipline	Classroom—hallway observations
	Description of climate
	Identification of discipline as a problem area
	Data on suspensions
■ Frequent monitoring of student progress	Descriptions of assessment and evaluation procedures
	Identification of testing procedures

fective secondary schools. Whereas the elementary school indicators tend to mix cognitive and affective outcomes, the secondary school indicators are more achievement- and prosocial-oriented. The elementary school indicators go beyond students and also look at staff, parents, and the community; the secondary school indicators focus on students and their performance.

SCHOOL FINANCE TRENDS

As the 1990s unfold, a number of monetary trends, which have direct meaning for administrators, are impacting on schools. As we examine those trends, we should note that the notions of "equal educational opportunity" and "egalitari-

Administrative Advice 14-3 (continued)

Attributes	Indicators
■ Meaningful student responsibility and participation	Information on student government, extracurricular programs and participation, and community programs Assessments of student autonomy in the school Student perceptions
■ Teacher efficacy and morale	Procedures for staff participation Assessments of teacher autonomy Assessments of teacher influence in the school Assessment of rewards and incentives
■ Academic learning time	Classroom observations Reports on actions to increase instructional time Estimates of homework by students
■ Positive school climate	Attendance data for staff and students; data on discipline Staff and student perceptions Observations on climate, teacher–student relations, facilities, etc.
■ Administrative leadership	Interviews with staff, parents, and administrators Description of administrative roles Assessment of administrative involvement in instruction
■ Community support and involvement	Parents' and teachers' perceptions Parent, community, and business involvement

Source: Adapted from Stewart C. Purkey and Marshall S. Smith, "School Reform: The District Policy Implications of the Effective Schools Literature," *Elementary School Journal*, 85 (1983), pp. 353–388; Purkey and Smith, "Effective Schools: A Review," *Elementary School Journal*, 83 (1983), pp. 427–452. Also see Bruce L. Wilson and Thomas B. Corcoran, *Successful Secondary Schools* (New York: Falmer Press, 1988), pp. 59–65.

anism" are no longer the focus of attention as in the 1970s and early 1980s. Today, the focus is on "excellence," "efficiency," and "productivity." Budgets today are leaner and meaner, and less real money (after accounting for inflation) is earmarked for schools. In part this is because national productivity in the last twenty years has been flat or near flat so that there is less real money to split up among all public groups and sectors of the economy; moreover, the growing elderly population is demanding more of the economic pie—at the expense of children and youth. For example, since 1975 the economic well-being of the elderly has improved while the well-being of children has deteriorated. This is due to increased tax burdens to parents and tax transfers and Social Security benefits to the aging population.[48]

Streamlining Budgets

In an era of taxpayer wariness, demands for school accountability, reduced federal spending for education, and tight state budgets, school boards are being pressed to eliminate needless spending before recommending tax increases. Not only must school outcomes measure up to expected standards, but the budget must stand up to close scrutiny.

Although the taxpayer's resistance toward increased property tax for schools crested in the 1980s, we are still experiencing a demand to prune school budgets and save money. Because of the competing demands for public money, especially from our "graying" population, coupled with the reduced number of households with children in school, we are forced to downsize our school expenditures and do more with less money.[49]

Businesses and corporations have learned to slim down in many ways—by selling off unprofitable enterprises, closing old plants, cutting corporate and regional staff; in some respects, life in the "minimalist" corporation is tougher but simpler. With smaller staffs, decisions can be made more quickly, accountability is clearer, and many people seem to work harder. Not surprisingly, the same principles are being applied to the public schools. Corporate leaders often serve on school boards, and the gospels of "streamlining" and "cost efficiency" have spilled over to

U.S. education. In the 1990s, we should continue to see the following cost-reducing trends:

1. *Classroom Size.* Classroom size, in the interest of economy, has leveled off at 17.2 students per teacher since 1989.[50] The data on classroom size and student achievement are somewhat complex and contradictory, and most studies (about 80 percent) show no significant differences between achievement in small classes and in large classes[51]—that is, other variables are more important, such as tutoring and time on task.

   When differences are found, they are about as likely to favor large classes as small. Some recent reviews of the research have shown that class size is only related to pupil achievement when the size of classes is reduced sufficiently (originally thought to be below fifteen students but in most cases below five students) to result in altered teaching methods.[52] Thus, educators should not be too quick to reduce class size without considering whether money is available or whether teachers can adopt appropriate methods for small classes.

2. *Modernization of Older Buildings.* In the era of declining enrollments, many older school buildings were closed. Often these facilities were rented to other social service agencies such as churches and community centers. In some cases, school buildings were sold to private developers, who converted them into shopping malls, condominiums, and the like.

   Even in times when more schools are clearly needed, the funds to build them may

---

[48]See John L. Palmer, Timothy Smeeding, and Barbara B. Torrey, "America's Young and Old: Comparisons of Well-Being," *Urban Institute Policy and Research Report*, 18 (1988), pp. 4–5.

[49]The proportion of people age sixty-five and over increased from 6 percent in 1950 to 11.3 percent in 1980; it is expected to increase to 20 percent or more by 2030. The number of households made up of married couples with children declined from 40 percent in 1970 to less than 30 percent in 1984; it is expected to be less than 25 percent by 1995.

[50]*Digest of Education Statistics, 1989*, Table 56, p. 69.
[51]Eric A. Hanushek, "The Impact of Differential Expenditures on School Performance," *Educational Researcher*, 18 (1989), pp. 45–51.
[52]Julie Hazzard, "Reducing Class Size—Affordable? Efficient?" *Education Week*, 22 November 1988, p. 21; Allan C. Ornstein, "In Pursuit of Cost-Effective Schools," *Principal*, 70 (1990), pp. 28–30; and Robert E. Slavin, "Class Size and Student Achievement: Small Effects of Small Classes," *Educational Psychologist*, 24 (1989), pp. 99–110.

be hard to find. This is especially true in the major cities of the Frostbelt, where the costs of land and labor and the need to enclose and insulate space makes the total cost of new construction twice what it would be in the rural South or Southwest.[53]

To minimize costs, many districts will choose to maintain and modernize their old buildings, especially in the Northeast and Midwest, in the hope of avoiding extensive new construction. Although proper maintenance of older buildings is expensive, it is often less costly than starting from scratch. Older buildings frequently were better constructed than recent ones; moreover, older buildings per se are not detrimental to student learning.

3. *Smaller Schools*. Emphasis will be placed on smaller schools because they can be cheaper than larger schools, especially if they are well insulated and stress optimal utilization of space. Big and expensive cafeterias, auditoriums, and gymnasiums may become expendable areas due to major fuel, lighting, insurance, and maintenance expenses associated with them. These facilities add to construction costs, remain unoccupied for a large portion of the day and year, and cost a great deal to operate and maintain. Smaller schools usually mean not only more efficient use of space but also fewer administrators, which results in lower costs.[54]

4. *Energy Economies*. Between 1973 and 1980, the total bill for heating schools in the United States tripled, despite reduced fuel consumption.[55] School officials responded

and discovered several ways to reduce energy use. Nevertheless, energy prices continued to rise, doubling again in most parts of the country by 1984.[56] However, after 1984 consumption-cutting techniques paid off when coupled with sharply declining prices. For example, the bill for heating Midwest schools in 1988 returned to 1980 price levels.[57]

The next energy crisis is now! Some schools will be forced to dial down temperatures, delay warming up the school before classes each morning, or reduce heat in the hallways. Still, other schools continue to save money by insulating pipes, walls, and windows and installing energy-saving devices. An increasing number of school districts are bypassing utility companies and buying directly from gas and oil distributors. Future-oriented school officials will invest money by upgrading equipment to more energy-efficient forms and by training personnel to operate in an energy-efficient manner. Those schools that have been slow to take precautionary energy-related steps in the recent past, when time was available, are paying dearly as we progress through the 1990s.

5. *Teacher Layoffs*. Teacher layoffs were common in the 1970s through the mid-1980s as enrollments sagged. Most school districts across the country reduced their teaching force on the basis of seniority or tenure because these quantitative standards were clear. School officials avoided decisions on the basis of merit or evaluations because these standards were unclear and open to more controversy.

Because teacher layoffs threatened careers and provoked strikes, many school districts were reluctant to engage in larger staff reductions and sometimes preferred to opt

[53]William Brubaker, "Building for Tomorrow," *American School Board Journal*, 175 (1988), pp. 31–33, 66; Allan C. Ornstein, "School Budgets in the 1990s," *Education Digest*, 55 (1990), pp. 15–16; and Sally B. Zakariya, "School Construction Is a Hot, New Board Game," *American School Board Journal*, 175 (1988), pp. 27–30.

[54]Allan C. Ornstein, "Trimming the Fat, Stretching the Meat," *School Administrator*, 46 (1989), pp. 20–21.

[55]John Mulholland, "How to Save in School Fuel," *Phi Delta Kappan*, 62 (1980), p. 639; Stephen F. Sloan et al., *Energy in School Costs Too Much* (Albany: New York State Senate Research Service, 1982).

[56]Allan C. Ornstein, "Frostbelt–Sunbelt Energy Policies," *High School Journal*, 67 (1984), pp. 92–103.

[57]*Illinois State Building Energy Expense Study FY 1986 and Projected FY 1987–90* (Springfield: Illinois Department of Energy and Natural Resources, 1987); telephone conversation with Brian Quirke, public affairs specialist, U.S. Department of Energy, June 21, 1989.

for cuts in services and programs or to flatten teacher salaries. Nevertheless, some large school districts such as New York, Chicago, Detroit, Baltimore, and Indianapolis (where enrollment reductions were dramatic) were forced to reduce their teaching force more than 10 percent between 1975 and 1985.[58]

Although the era of large-scale teacher layoffs has passed at least temporarily, layoffs will persist in areas that are experiencing school consolidation and decreasing student enrollments. Whereas school officials are hiring in most parts of Arizona, Florida, and other parts of the Sunbelt, districts in Ohio and Oklahoma are still laying off teachers.[59]

6. *Administrative Layoffs.* The focus of streamlining has begun to shift away from teachers to nonteaching positions. When a school district faces the need to downsize, guidance counselors, curriculum specialists, and other noninstructional personnel make easy targets. At the central level, layoffs of coordinators, directors, managers, and assistant superintendents have occurred recently. When administrators are let go for budget reasons, there is much less outcry than when teachers are cut.

Recent budget cuts in many large school districts suggest that other districts may find it possible, even necessary, to operate with smaller central staffs. We might argue that an overly trimmed central staff office reflects strained budgets and is unable to perform all necessary tasks, but it is just as likely that a fat central office is inefficient and needs to slim down in an age of reform and retrenchment.

Administrators who sit in the central offices away from schools generate their own layers of bureaucracy within their departments—additional supervisors, consultants, and support staff—all of whom, no doubt, are good to have and are useful on frequent occasions. But they do bloat the school district payroll, and in tough times they are unnecessary.

A school district's organizational chart should be something that a parent can understand, yet most of the charts depicting large school districts cannot be understood by many professional educators. In an age of downsizing, the time is coming to clear out the crowd at central offices. Profitable corporations have learned this lesson, in some cases the hard way. Some large companies operate with as few as 1 headquarters manager to 5000 employees.[60] Now is the time for wise decision makers to slowly eliminate staff matrices built on top of other matrices; doing so through attrition will be far less painful than waiting for financial problems to force school officials to perform surgery or spill blood.

Environmental Hazards

The Environmental Protection Agency (EPA) has ordered government and commercial property owners to clean up **asbestos-laden buildings** that have been housing people at work and in school for the last twenty-five to fifty years. Estimated costs to clean up these buildings are hard to come by, although one estimate is $100 billion for government and commercial buildings and $3.1 billion for some 45,000 schools in

[58]James G. Cibulka, "Response to Enrollment Loss and Financial Decline in Urban School Systems," *Peabody Journal of Education*, 61 (1983), pp. 64–78; Ornstein, "Regional Population Shifts: Implications for Educators."

[59]*The Condition of Education, 1987* (Washington, D.C.: Government Printing Office, 1987), Table 1.18, p. 46; *Projections of Education Statistics to 2000* (Washington, D.C.: Government Printing Office, 1989), Figure 44, p. 75; and Allan C. Ornstein, "Teacher Salaries in Social Context," *High School Journal* 73 (1990), pp. 129–132.

[60]Thomas Moore, "Goodbye, Corporate Staff," *Fortune*, 21 December 1987, pp. 65, 68, 76; Allan C. Ornstein, "School Finance in the 90s," *American School Board Journal*, 177 (1990), pp. 36–39.

31,000 school districts.[61] Another nationwide study puts the estimate at $1.2 billion or at $22,858 per school and $31 per student: where the cost exceeds $150 per student in 10 percent of the schools, and where Oklahoma City School District had the dubious distinction in 1990 of having a $65 million bill and $1,688 cost per student.[62] These costs are based on an estimate of $15 to $25 a linear square foot to remove asbestos, based on whether this once acclaimed "wonder fiber" is located in the ceilings, walls, floors, or basements.

Some 15 to 20 million children and 1.5 million school employees are subject to exposure on a daily basis. The estimates of people who will die from direct exposure to asbestos-contained buildings are extremely low (25 a year) compared to those who will die each year due to the workplace (10,000 a year).[63] The ultimate question is, Do we need to spend all this money on asbestos removal? At what level of exposure is asbestos unsafe? If asbestos is intact, not flaking and out of reach of students and employees, should it be removed? Although airborne asbestos can be deadly (more than 1 percent in the air), the dangers of inert asbestos are minimal in most buildings, according to recent data.[64] Nonetheless, children are considered to be especially vulnerable because their longer life expectancy means that a latent asbestos-related disease has more time to develop.

During the 1970s and 1980s, the federal government imposed many environmental requirements and regulations on the schools but did not provide funds for compliance. Many school districts delayed in removing the asbestos, while others used funds from their school maintenance budgets to comply with federal regulations. However, one EPA study reports that as much as 75 percent of all school cleanup work was done improperly up to 1985.[65] Rather than mitigating the problem, it is likely that the problem has been exacerbated in many cases; indeed, the "cure" may be worse than the "disease," especially with a lot of "rip and skip" companies.

All school districts should have already inspected for asbestos, formulated a removal plan for any asbestos found, and removed it by 1990. The new law, Public Law 100–368, amended in 1989, required prompt and detailed plans for abatement of all asbestos in our schools, as efficiently and safely as possible. It should be pointed out that removal is not the only form of abatement, although the great majority of school districts have chosen this option. Encapsulation, if done properly, can last for several years (ten or more years depending on what and how the materials are applied) at an average cost of 10 percent of the removal bill.[66] The savings is obvious, but in some cases when the asbestos is loose or crumbling, removal is the best solution. In still other cases, encapsulation is only a stopgap measure until a school district can raise sufficient money for removal. (See Administrative Advice 14-4.)

School districts that have not met the EPA deadline, in terms of removal (or encapsulation), must explain the reasons to state officials, provide advance notice of public meetings on abatement to all groups concerned—so they can voice their opinions—and document the steps they are taking to comply with the EPA.

And while some schools are just getting over the shock of asbestos, **radon gas** poses a new

[61]Louis S. Richman, "Why Throw Money at Asbestos?" *Fortune*, 6 June 1988, pp. 155–170.

[62]Allan C. Ornstein and Robert C. Cienkus, "The Nation's School Repair Bill," *American School Board Journal*, 177 (1990), pp. 2A–4A.

[63]James J. Florio, "Asbestos in the Schools: New Requirements Take Effect," *PTA Today*, 14 (1988), pp. 31–32; Richman, "Why Throw Money at Asbestos?"

[64]Michael D. Lemonick, "An Overblown Asbestos Scare?" *Time*, 29 January 1990, p. 65; Andrew Trotter, "Reassessing the Asbestos Risk," *Executive Educator*, 12 (1990), pp. 10A–10B.

[65]Telephone conversation with Robert Garratt, staff specialist, Environmental Protection Agency, Region 5, June 7, 1989; Trotter, "Reassessing the Asbestos Risk."

[66]Tom Probst, "Case Study: Asbestos Encapsulation," *Executive Educator*, 12 (1990), pp. 11A–12A.

ADMINISTRATIVE ADVICE 14-4

DEALING WITH ASBESTOS-ABATEMENT CONTRACTORS

Most school districts, especially the larger ones, are still involved in asbestos abatement. Some still need time extensions, some have an abatement plan in place, others are involved with contract bids, and others are in the process of removing or encapsulating this "wonder fiber." Here are some questions that school districts might follow or consider when selecting an asbestos contractor.

- How many companies are bidding for the job? (Permit at least three to bid each job, especially if the cost is more than $3,000.)
- Has the company performed other jobs for your district?
- How long has the company been in business? (There are many new asbestos-abatement companies.)
- What are the company's assets? What jobs has the company performed? For whom? Is the company willing to provide references?
- Has someone in the district called the regional or state EPA and local regulatory agency to ensure that the company has not been cited for health or work violations?
- Are the contractor's workers fully certified? Is the company licensed or certified by the state or local regulatory agency?
- Is the company bonded for performance? Do the workers have adequate liability insurance?
- Does the company carry adequate liability insurance? From an A or A+ rated insurance company? At least a $5 million umbrella policy for each occurrence (not cumulative)?
- Does the company employ a state licensed health (or air-quality) engineer? If not, will an engineer supervise the health aspects of the job?

- Are the health safeguards clearly outlined in the proposal and contract? Will the contaminated areas be properly sealed off?
- Will the company test the air quality before the job, hourly on the job, and after the job? Who will ensure that the readings are accurate? (Preferably an independent or third party should inspect the quality of the air and conduct appropriate tests.)
- Is a timetable clearly established? Are penalties provided for unusual delays?
- Will the public be properly notified when the job is to commence? Will students be in the surrounding area? What about vacation or summer time?
- Besides removal, what other options has the asbestos company suggested? Will guarantees be included with the other options?
- How viable are the options? Have you considered the cost for removal versus the cost for the options?
- Does the district's contract with the company include a save harmless agreement? Does the district have an escape clause (and right to hire another company) in the event that legal, health, or governmental problems arise?

cancer threat in U.S. schools. (It is considered the second leading cause of lung cancer.) Preliminary EPA tests show dangerously high levels of the invisible, odorless gas in 54 percent of the 130 schools randomly checked; homes are also affected. In short, many of our children are exposed to a risk equivalent of smoking $\frac{1}{2}$ to $1\frac{1}{2}$ packs of cigarettes a day.[67]

[67]*Radon in Schools*, Bulletin No. 520 (Washington, D.C.: Government Printing Office, 1989); Hugh Wright, "Radon Gas New Threat in Schools," *USA Today*, 21 April 1989, p. 1A.

The gas seeps into buildings from soil and rock as radium-266 decays. In some cases, well water may be a source of radon. No EPA, federal, or state guidelines exist for containment or abatement of the gas; however, the threat is considered dangerous, and levels are too high in schools to wait for the EPA. Basically, testing procedures include testing (1) all school rooms on and below ground level, (2) in the cold months of the year, (3) for two days to four weeks depending on the type of test. Screening test results over 4 pCi/L (picoCuries/liter, or one trillionth of a unit of radian) are considered concern for a lengthy retest (9 to 12 months); levels over 100 pCi/L are considered sufficiently dangerous to relocate children.[68] Average corrective costs per school run from as low as $1000 if ventilation adjustment works to $10,000 if subventilation is needed.

Infrastructure Costs

The nation's educational infrastructure is in a state of critical disrepair. By **infrastructure**, we mean the basic physical facilities that underpin the school plant (plumbing, heat, electric, roof, carpentry, etc.). Building experts estimate that our schools are deteriorating at a faster rate than they can be repaired, and faster than most other public facilities. Plumbing, electrical wiring, and heating systems in many schools are dangerously out of date; roofing is below code; and exterior materials (brickwork, stone, and wood) are chipped or cracked. The cost of deferred expenditures currently runs over $100 million in Los Angeles, Detroit, Chicago, Seattle, and Miami's Dade County, with an enormous bill of over $600 million for the New York City schools.[69]

The accumulated cost to repair the nation's public schools, according to knowledgeable sources, ranges from as low as $50 billion to $150 billion, including replacement, maintenance, and repairs.[70]

Although experts maintain that schools need to allocate 3 to 5 percent a year for replacement, recent findings suggest that schools allocate less than 3 percent a year. The investment in new school construction is equally insufficient. Whereas colleges and universities allocate 7 percent annually for new construction and other public sectors allocate 8 percent, public schools allocate approximately 3.5 percent.[71]

Schools in cities and in the Frostbelt (Northeast and Midwest) suffer the greatest infrastructure problems because they are the oldest and the most decayed. As many as 42 percent of the schools in the older industrial cities of the Midwest and 34 percent in the Northeast were built before 1930; a large number were constructed before 1900. For example, nearly half of Chicago's 597 school buildings were built before 1930, and as many as 83 schools still in existence in 1989 were built before 1900. In St. Louis and Minneapolis, half of the schools are sixty years old or older.[72] (See Table 14-5.) Although one might argue that these school districts are more efficient, because they don't demolish old buildings, another observer might argue that these districts suffer from old, deteriorated buildings.

A building has five stages. It has lived its normal life the first twenty years, especially in the Sunbelt where construction is cheaper. When it is twenty to thirty years old, frequent replacement of equipment is needed. When it is

---

[68]*Radon in Schools*. Also see Donna Harrington-Lueker, "Are Pesticides the Latest Peril Facing Your Schools?" *Executive Educator*, 12 (1990), pp. 21–23.

[69]*The Maintenance Gap: Deferred Repair and Renovation in the Nation's Elementary and Secondary Schools* (a joint report by the American Association of School Administrators, Council of Great City Schools, and National School Boards Association, Washington, D.C., 1983); Ornstein and Cienkus, "The Nation's School Repair Bill."

[70]Telephone conversation with Paul Abramson, director, Intelligence for Education, May 13, 1988; telephone conversation with Michael Spring, publisher, *American School and University Magazine*, May 13, 1988.

[71]Ann Lewis, *Wolves at the Schoolhouse Door: An Investigation of the Condition of Public School Buildings* (Washington, D.C.: Education Writers Association, 1989).

[72]Ornstein and Cienkus, "The Nation's School Repair Bill"; telephone conversation with Carol Heinrich, staff specialist, Bureau of Management Information, Chicago Public Schools, March 5, 1990.

TABLE 14 ▪ 5   School Districts with the Newest and Oldest Schools

RANKING	SCHOOL DISTRICT	NUMBER OF SCHOOLS	NUMBER OF NEW SCHOOLS*	PERCENTAGE OF NEW SCHOOLS
1	Gwinnett, GA	60	32	53.3
2	Jordan, UT	70	36	51.4
3	Cumberland, NC	68	30	44.1
4	Broward County, FL	157	60	38.2
5	San Antonio, TX	50	18	36.0
6.5	Chesterfield, VA	48	17	35.4
6.5	Arlington, VA	48	17	35.4
8	Mt. Diablo, CA	54	19	35.2
9	Cobb County, GA	77	25	32.5
10	Virginia Beach, VA	69	22	31.8

RANKING	SCHOOL DISTRICT	NUMBER OF SCHOOLS	NUMBER OF OLD SCHOOLS†	PERCENTAGE OF OLD SCHOOLS
65	Chicago	597	264	44.2
66	Detroit	287	130	45.3
67	St. Louis	134	65	48.5
68	Minneapolis	57	28	49.1
69	Houston	233	116	49.8
70	Portland	108	54	50.0
71	Akron, OH	59	30	50.8
72	Prince William County, GA	82	47	57.3
73	Buffalo, NY	75	45	60.0
74	Kansas City, MO	79	48	60.8

SOURCE: Allan C. Ornstein and Robert C. Cienkus, "The Nation's School Repair Bill," *American School Board Journal,* 177 (1990), p. 4A. Copyright 1990, the National School Boards Association. Used by permission.

*Fifteen-years-old or less.

†Sixty-years-old or more.

NOTE: School districts with the highest ratio of new schools (one to fifteen years old) are located in the South and West and suburban areas; school districts with the highest ratio of old schools (sixty years or more) are (with the exception of two) located in the Northeast and Midwest and (with the exception of one) big cities.

thirty to forty years old, most of the original equipment and materials should have been replaced, especially roofs, lighting fixtures, and heating equipment. Accelerated deterioration takes place when it is forty to fifty years old because neighborhoods and needs often change. A fifty-year-old building is sometimes too new to abandon, especially in the Frostbelt where there is usually good construction; but, after sixty years, a number of buildings are usually abandoned, reconstructed, or replaced.[73]

Nationwide, 25 percent of school buildings are considered in "inadequate" condition, 33 percent are "adequate," and 42 percent are

[73]Lewis, *Wolves at the Schoolhouse Door; The Maintenance Gap: Deferred Repair and Renovation in the Nation's Elementary and Secondary Schools.*

"good." Leading the list of inadequate building are Connecticut (60 percent), California (55 percent), Washington, D.C. (50 percent), Illinois (50 percent), and Rhode Island (40 percent). Of the buildings that are inadequate, 61 percent need major repairs, 43 percent are obsolete, 42 percent have environmental hazards, 25 percent are overcrowded, and 13 percent are structurally unsound.[74] Many, of course, have multiple problems.

In comparison with other public sectors, the construction and repair needs for schools rank among the most serious in the nation. Yet it is doubtful if the public is willing to spend sufficient money to meet these needs. A nationwide survey of the largest 100 school districts (74 percent responded) identified in rank order the top three repair items that schools are spending: (1) roofs, averaging $21,555 per school and $29 per student; (2) heating and air conditioning at $17,652 per school and $24 per student; (3) painting at $15,101 per school and $22 per student. Other costly repair items in descending order were plumbing and sewer repairs, electric repairs, carpentry, brick and mortar, carpet and tile, and insulation.[75]

For the most part, educators and the public alike are unaware of the time bomb that is ticking in U.S. schools. What catches our attention is the need to improve curriculum and instruction; the safety and operating efficiency of schools, although essential, are not on the minds of the public.

Many school officials are aware of the problem but have left it for the next generation of school people. But ignoring our inadequate school facilities has enormous implications for future educational costs and potentially inadequate schools. The longer we wait, the greater the cost for future educational services and the more difficult it becomes to sustain long-term educational (and economic) growth. Either we devote, today, a greater share of local and state revenues

to the repair and renovation of our educational facilities, or we burden our children and grandchildren with crippling educational expenses.

School Closings/Openings

One of the great financial and management decisions facing school officials from the 1970s to the mid-1980s was declining student enrollments. This decline in total enrollments started in the grade schools in 1972 and completed the cycle in the high schools by 1987. The educational system was ill equipped to manage this slowdown and smallness, given several past generations of growth in almost all social and economic aspects of life. We were forced to trim the fat, conserve, and think small to survive. School boards were not only forced to cut spending and lower tax rates during this period but were also inclined to close schools.[76]

Many of us may have forgotten that this era of retrenchment—of closing down schools—led to a great deal of conflict and emotionalism between parents, community residents, and school board members as decisions had to be made about which schools were to be closed and whose children were to be bused to another school. One option was to mothball schools, leaving them subject to vandalism and standing as a blight on their neighborhoods, and to spend money on maintaining nonproductive pieces of real estate. Although some school districts opted to lease out schools for a lengthy period of time—say, ten years or so—most districts sold their schools to various social agencies (churches, private schools, community centers, elderly centers, etc.) and private investors often for less than fifty cents on a dollar.[77] A rough guess is that

[74]Lewis, *Wolves at the Schoolhouse Door.*
[75]Ornstein and Cienkus, "The Nation's School Repair Bill."

[76]Allan C. Ornstein, "Thinking Small for the Future," *School and Community*, 68 (1982), pp. 6–7.
[77]William L. Boyd and Dennis R. Wheaton, "Conflict Management in Declining School Districts," *Peabody Journal of Education*, 61 (1983), pp. 25–36; Allan C. Ornstein, "Thinking Small for the 1980s," *Clearing House*, 55 (1982), pp. 279–280.

during this fifteen-year period (1970 to 1985) 200 to 500 schools a year nationwide were closed and sold.

School closings and retrenchment decisions were characterized by avoidance and delay because of the delegation of parents superintendents encountered in their offices and political storms board members encountered at their meetings every time a district proposed a school closing. It was common for many school districts to create a lag of about five years or more in responding to the problem. The reluctance of school officials to close schools during this period is especially evident in Los Angeles, which lost 92,000 students in nine years but did not close down a single school, as it was in Baltimore, which lost 55,000 students and only closed three schools.[78]

A totally different tactic involved school districts that lost students and suffered financial burden. For example, the Tulsa, Oklahoma, school district lost more than 26,000 students in the 1970s and more than 14,000 in the 1980s (a 50 percent drop in total number of students from 1969 to 1989). This resulted in forty-three school closings between 1971 and 1989 (a net loss of 28 percent of the total number of schools).[79] As many as fourteen schools were sold, from a low of $110,000 to a high of $3.3 million; fourteen were leased (and are still owned, bringing in a total annual revenue of $1.1 million); and the remaining were either replaced or merged into another school.[80]

From 1981 to 1988, student population trends and school closings varied according to city–county location and geographic location. Hardest hit overall were city school systems, especially those in the Northeast and Midwest. The city systems responding to a nationwide survey in 1989 lost a net 86,678 students in this period. County systems, by contrast, had a net gain of 95,298 students. These overall population trends correlated with school closings: Cities closed a net 212 schools during the seven years; county systems closed a net 6 schools.[81]

A half-dozen Frostbelt city systems experienced truly massive net losses during the seven years, both in total student population (each losing between 10,000 and 40,000 students) and in school buildings. Chicago and Detroit each closed a net of 38 schools, Indianapolis 24, Philadelphia 23, Baltimore 18, and Cleveland 15 (Table 14-6). Interestingly, the only county systems to face really large losses were also in the Northeast: Prince George's County, Maryland, closed a net 44 schools, and Montgomery County closed a net 32 schools. Overall, of the school districts surveyed, those in the Northeast had 129 net school closings, and those in the Midwest had 136 net closings.

The Sunbelt region, on the other hand, evidenced net gains in students and schools in the large systems surveyed. The South had 26 net openings in nineteen systems reporting; the Southwest, 35 net openings in nine systems; and the West, 14 net openings in seven systems. The Southwest experienced the most uniform gain in schools, with eight of nine of the systems surveyed evidencing net school openings.

The big gainers in net school openings were in Florida: Hillsborough County (15), Palm Beach County (12), Dade County (6), Orange County (6) Pinellas County (4), and Duval County (3). The big loser was Maryland, with a combined net loss of 104 schools in just four large systems: Prince George's County, Montgomery County, Baltimore City, and Baltimore County.

Table 14-6 shows the school districts with the greatest net closings and openings during the

[78]James G. Cibulka, "The Politics of School Closing in the Ten U.S. Cities." Paper presented at the annual meeting of the American Educational Research Association, New York, March 1982.

[79]Telephone conversation with Lyle Young, associate superintendent of instructional support services, Tulsa School District, June 7, 1989.

[80]Larry L. Zenke, School Consolidation Recommendations—1988 (Tulsa, OK: Tulsa Public Schools, February 1988), Attachments 1, 3, pp. 14–16, 18–20.

[81]Allan C. Ornstein, "Opening New Schools Depends on More Than Enrollment," American School Board Journal, 176 (1989), pp. 40–41.

TABLE 14 ■ 6   School Closings and Openings in Large School Districts, 1981–1988

SCHOOL DISTRICT	STUDENT POPULATION GAIN/LOSS	CLOSINGS (−)	OPENINGS (+)	NET SCHOOL CLOSINGS/ OPENINGS (−/+)
Districts with most net closings				
Prince George's County, Maryland	− 18,568	− 45	+ 01	− 44
Chicago	− 38,960	− 38	00	− 38
Detroit	− 29,787	− 41	+ 03	− 38
Montgomery County, Maryland	− 2,572	− 40	+ 08	− 32
Indianapolis	− 15,600	− 27	+ 03	− 24
Philadelphia	− 29,641	− 23	00	− 23
Los Angeles	+ 53,677	− 22	00	− 22
Baltimore	− 19,719	− 30	+ 12	− 18
Cleveland	− 10,850	− 16	+ 01	− 15
San Diego	+ 5,686	− 19	+ 05	− 14
Districts with most net openings				
Cobb County, Georgia	+ 13,847	− 01	+ 08	+ 07
El Paso, Texas	+ 1,214	00	+ 07	+ 07
Mesa, Arizona	+ 23,653	00	+ 08	+ 08
Palm Beach County, Florida	+ 19,074	− 01	+ 13	+ 12
Jefferson County, Colorado	− 2,801	− 01	+ 14	+ 13
Clark County, Nevada	+ 13,828	00	+ 14	+ 14
Hillsborough County, Florida	+ 4,878	00	+ 15	+ 15
Jordan, Utah	+ 13,847	00	+ 18	+ 18

SOURCE: Allan C. Ornstein, "Opening New Schools Depends on More Than Enrollment," *American School Board Journal,* 176 (1989), p. 41. Copyright 1989, the National School Boards Association. Used by permission.

1980s. With the exception of two systems (Los Angeles and San Diego), the largest net school closings were in Frostbelt systems with declining student populations. Los Angeles and San Diego had historical reasons for closing more schools than they opened, even though their student populations were growing. Between 1971 and 1980, each had experienced major declines in student enrollment without closing a single

school. So in the 1980s, these two systems had to make up for their previous enrollment losses by closing schools.

As the table indicates, county and suburban schools located in the Sunbelt and experiencing significant enrollment increases account for the largest net openings. Jefferson County, Colorado, is the only district that lost student enrollment while it opened more schools than it closed because schools were growing at a rapid pace in the district's outer fringes, even as student enrollment declined in the older section of the district.[82]

For most Sunbelt school districts, 1985 was a turning point in which school openings exceeded school closings, coinciding with a shift in student enrollments. 1987 to 1988 was the turning point for many Frostbelt states, when school districts stopped closing schools. Nationwide school enrollments are in the middle of the growth cycle, and school openings are in the beginning of the cycle. Enrollment increases are expected to continue until 1992 and building beyond 2000 in thirty-three states—mostly Sunbelt and Plain states.[83] The result is, the public school investment in new schools will be significant in the near future to house the "new baby boom" that will appear on the doorsteps of schools.

Financing the Building Boom

Public school investment in new schools, compared to other public sectors, has been minimal in the last 15 or 20 years because of previous taxpayers resistance and student-enrollment declines. Nationwide, 61 percent of the schools were constructed during the 1950s and 1960s, and only 6 percent were built in the 1980s; more than 20 percent are more than fifty years old, and the percentage is growing each year.[84]

Where will the money come from to build new schools? Although the states fund about 50 percent of the revenues for the operation of schools, they only contribute about 23 percent for construction. Estimates are that combined state and local money will only finance 39 percent of the need from 1990 to 1992.[85] According to one study, twenty-seven states use grant programs (equalized, flat, or matching) to finance new schools, twelve states rely on state or local bonds, two states use fully funded capital programs, but sixteen states provide no state financial assistance.[86] (Based on these numbers, some states use more than one program.)

Building a new school is no simple task. The rules are complex, the stakes are high, and the considerations are political.[87] Try these questions, for example: How many students will the school accommodate? Where will the building site be located? How will attendance boundaries be drawn? Have environmental concerns been fully addressed? How will the cost be funded? How will voters react? Which companies will get the contracts? How many minority contractors will be hired? The list of questions, with the potential for vague answers, is endless.

School board members must always consider costs. Here are some issues that impact on costs and to which people involved in decisions should have answers:

1. *Climate*. Is the climate mild enough for children to eat and play outdoors? Or, must most or all school facilities be indoors?
2. *Energy*. Because energy costs will continue to rise, the need for energy-efficient buildings is obvious. What is the difference between the cost and projected savings for a heat pump or solar-energy collectors?
3. *Setting*. Is there ample land for a horizontal, single-story building, or will the building need to be multistory? Can we afford additional land to build parking spaces? How many?
4. *Government Regulations*. Just to name a few regulations, how does the law affect space requirements, environmental codes, building materials, and provisions for minority contractors?
5. *Labor/Materials*. Is there a pool of available and qualified laborers to build the schools?

[82]Ibid.

[83]*Projection of Population by States, 1988–2010* (Washington, D.C.: National Association of State Directors of Education Plant Services, 1989); *Projection of Education Statistics to 2000.*

[84]Lewis, *Wolves at the Schoolhouse Door.*

[85]*Projection of Population by States, 1988–2010.*

[86]Ibid.

[87]Zakariya, "School Construction Is a Hot, New Board Game."

Must labor be brought in from another state? Must materials be shipped in from out of state? What is the politics of hiring an out-of-town contractor for less money than the local vender who is less efficient? Should we hire only union workers?

6. *Supply/Demand*. Must we compete with other types of construction projects for labor and materials, or is it a buyers' market for goods and services? Should we wait until next year, when interest rates are high (low) and local construction is down (heated)?

7. *Financial Capacity*. Does the community have sufficient bonding power, or does the community usually reject bond issues? Which bank should be used for financing what portion of the construction?

8. *Land Costs*. What are comparable land values in the area? Should we sell off parts that we own because of demand? Should we buy for future construction, in what area of the city (town)?

9. *Population Demographics*. Where is the best place to build to keep our middle-class tax base? What about new schools for our lower-class or minority population? How about school integration? How do we weigh the cost of construction in relation to building new schools to attract business?

10. *Uses*. Will the school have a single, traditional use? Will it be a multipurpose building, whereby we make use of the plant before and after school hours? Should we build a year-round school for the purpose of maximizing its use?[88]

Is it possible for one school serving the same number of students to be three or four times more expensive than the other? You bet. Consider different building requirements (construction codes, insulation factors, space requirements), building designs (open-air or enclosed, horizontal or vertical), land prices, professional fees, labor and material expenses, and so on. A large portion of a school in warm climates can use open spaces, compared to colder climates. A New York City or Chicago attorney charges $175 to $250 an hour compared to $100 to $125 for an attorney in New Orleans or Tampa, Florida. A union carpenter costs more than $20 an hour in the Northeast or Midwest urban areas; the cost is half in southern urban areas, and in rural areas, it is even cheaper. The cost of land can be twice to ten times as high in one city (New York, Chicago, or Los Angeles), compared to another city (Baton Rouge, Louisiana, or El Paso, Texas, or Jacksonville, Florida). In short, where you build is important. The cost of school building can run from approximately $50 to $60 per square foot in rural southern areas to $100 to $125 per square foot in the major cities (and adjacent metropolitan areas).[89]

Another factor to consider is square footage. High schools need more square footage per student, about one and one-half times more, than do elementary schools to adequately serve their clientele. The reason is related to specialization and additional facilities for older students—larger auditoriums, pools, theaters, cafeterias, indoor gyms, outdoor ball fields, student parking lots, and so on. Also schools in cold climates cannot use outdoor areas as effectively as schools in warm climates. A typical high school serving 1000 students might comprise 100 square feet per student (at $50 per square foot) in the rural South. Another high school serving the same number of students might comprise 200 square feet per student (at $100 per square foot) in the urban Northeast or Midwest. The school's total cost in the urban Northeast or Midwest can run three to four times as high as in the rural sites: one school cost $5000 per student, and the other cost $20,000 per student. To be sure, these differences in school construction costs have ramifications for property tax assessments.

Schools in the future will cost more than current prices because the designs will be

---

[88]William Brubaker, "No Two Building Projects Are Really Comparable," *American School Board Journal*, 175 (1988), p. 33; Allan C. Ornstein, "Building New Schools," *Education and Urban Society* (in print 1992).

[89]Brubaker, "No Two Building Projects Are Really Comparable"; Ornstein, "School Finance in the 90s."

more complex and built for varied functions using more sophisticated components and materials. There will probably be more (1) technological equipment, such as computers, videos, and satellite dishes; (2) school laboratories; (3) places for small-group and independent study; (4) flexible spaces, module classrooms, and adaptable walls; (5) contrasting or great spaces such as common rooms, atria, and open courtyards; (6) innovative spaces and materials such as underground structures and new plastic and prefabricated materials; (7) expensive lighting, heating, and communication equipment; (8) energy-conservation controls and solar features; (9) earth bermings and high clerestory windows; (10) curved corners and curved furniture; (11) pitched roofs and arches; and (12) centers or wings to house child-care, elderly, and community services.[90] Yesterday's "boxy" classrooms and rectangular buildings will increasingly be replaced by flexible spaces and a variety of exterior designs.

SUMMARY

1. Schools are supported by the local, state, and federal revenues, with the greatest share derived from state sources and the smallest share from federal sources. Since the early twentieth century, state port has increased dramatically, and local support has been reduced; federal support grew until the early 1980s and then began to decline.
2. School finance is based on the principle of equality of opportunity; nevertheless, there is wide variation in the financial ability among states and within states (at the local school district level) to support education. Not all states or school districts can finance education equally well.
3. Poorer school districts tend to receive more money from their respective states than do wealthier

school districts. Poorer states, especially those in the South and Southwest, tend to receive more money from the federal government than do wealthier states and states in the Northeast and Midwest. The additional amount of revenue received, however, rarely makes up for the total difference in expenditures.

4. There are five basic methods the states use to finance public education. The flat-grant model is the oldest and most unequal method because it is based on a fixed amount multiplied by the number of students in attendance. The most common methods of finance are based on some type of equalization plan to supplement less wealthy school districts. The power-equalizing plan (which deals with inverse ratios of wealth) and weighted-student plan (which deals with special characteristics of students and special programs) are the most common methods.
5. Most school budgets are organized around four major categories: objects such as salaries and supplies; functions such as instruction and staff development; programs such as English or special education; and location, whereby the school or group of schools is considered.
6. Developing a budget can be classified into four major activities: planning or identifying priorities; analysis, dealing with goals or evaluative criteria; requesting, that is, establishing priorities and negotiating; and controls, dealing with inventory, receipts, and disbursements.
7. Education costs per student tend to be higher in smaller and larger schools.
8. Most research indicates that specific items related to school effectiveness are not cost-related; rather, they deal with organizational climate and culture.
9. Although the demand to lower property taxes for school spending declined in the 1980s, there is still significant pressure to trim school budgets and save money. Competing demands for public revenues, especially from the aging population, and the fact there are fewer households with children attending school, are part of the reasons why taxpayers are not interested in spending more money for schools.
10. Controversy over school infrastructure costs and environmental hazards such as asbestos and radon gas are likely to affect school expenditures in the 1990s.

---

[90]Brubaker, "Building for Tomorrow"; Ornstein, "Building New Schools"; and Marlee C. Rist, "Schools by Design," *American School Board Journal*, 176 (1989), pp. 42–43, 48.

KEY TERMS

gross national product
regressive taxes
progressive taxes
elastic taxes
inelastic taxes
property tax
market value
assessed value
mill

user fees
municipal overburden
educational overburden
discretionary funding
formula funding
effective schools
asbestos-laden building
radon gas
infrastructure

DISCUSSION QUESTIONS

1. Why do city schools have more fiscal problems than suburban or rural schools?
2. What state taxes are used to provide school revenues? Which ones are progressive? Regressive?
3. Why is it important to look at each budget item in terms of the percent year spent to date and the annual projected budget?
4. What are the primary reasons for closing schools? What options do school administrators have when they must close down schools?
5. What factors or financial considerations must school administrators deal with when building schools?

SUGGESTED READINGS

Robert Gilchrist. *Effective Schools: Three Case Studies of Excellence* (Bloomington, IN: National Educational Service, 1989) A detailed description of three excellent schools honored by Phi Delta Kappa and the U.S. Department of Education.

James Guthrie, Walter I Garmes, and Lawrence C. Pierce. *School Finance: Educational Equality, Efficiency, and Choice* (Englewood Cliffs, NJ: Prentice-Hall, 1988). How school dollars are distributed and what reform alternatives are available.

Stephen Jacobson and James A. Conway. *Educational Leadership in an Age of Reform* (New York: Longman, 1990). The politics of school leadership and school finance in an era of school reform.

Michael Katz. *The Undeserving Poor* (New York: Pantheon, 1990). About 33 million people, considered poor by Katz's definition, who pay more for schools in terms of what they can afford.

Leading Fiscal Issues in the 1990 Legislative Sessions (Denver: National Conference of State Legislatures, 1990). A summary of the leading fiscal issues, from child-care credit on personal income tax to increasing teacher salaries.

Ann Lewis. *Wolves at the Schoolhouse Door: An Investigation of The Condition of Public School Buildings* (Washington, D.C.: Education Writers Association, 1989). An eye-opener about the condition of U.S. schools.

The Unfinished Agenda for State Tax Reform (Denver: National conference of State Legislatures, 1988). Summary of major tax actions, with implications for education.

15

PERSONNEL ADMINISTRATION

In this chapter, we attempt to answer these questions concerning personnel administration in school organizations. We begin our discussion with an overview of the personnel process. Then we look at recruiting, selecting, and training and development of personnel. Performance appraisal and compensation are discussed next, and last we explore union–management relations, including the negotiation and administration of the collective bargaining agreement.

THE PERSONNEL MANAGEMENT PROCESS

The personnel management process comprises six programs: human resource planning, recruitment, selection, training and development,

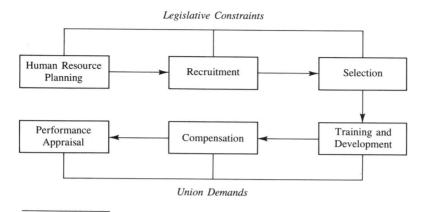

Union Demands

FIGURE 15-1   The Personnel Management Process

performance appraisal, and compensation.[1] Figure 15-1 outlines the personnel management steps, which are affected by legislative constraints and union demands.

1. *Human Resource Planning.* Good **human resource planning** involves meeting current and future personnel needs. The school administrator ensures that personnel needs are met through ongoing analysis of performance objectives, job requirements, and available personnel, coupled with a knowledge of employment laws.
2. *Recruitment.* Once personnel needs have been identified, **recruitment** involves locating qualified applicants to satisfy the organization's personnel plans.
3. *Selection.* After carefully evaluating applicants in the recruiting pool, the organization makes a **selection** of candidates who meet the job requirements.
4. *Training and Development.* **Training** involves improving employees' present skills; **development** concerns preparing personnel for

additional responsibilities or advancement in the organization.
5. *Performance Appraisal.* **Performance appraisal** involves rating personnel performance in relationship to the organization's standards and goals. Features of this step involve rewarding personnel, providing feedback, and maintaining communications between administrators and subordinates.
6. *Compensation.* **Compensation** involves decisions concerning salary, fringe benefits, and merit.

HUMAN RESOURCE PLANNING

School organizations typically plan their future needs for supplies, equipment, building capacity, and financing. School organizations must also plan to ensure that their human resource needs are satisfied. Human resource planning involves identifying staffing needs, forecasting available personnel, and determining what additions or replacements are required to maintain a staff of the desired quantity and quality to achieve the organization's mission.

[1]Michael R. Carrell et al., *Personnel: Human Resource Management*, 3rd ed. (Columbus, OH: Merrill, 1990); Terry L. Leap and Michael D. Crino, *Personnel/Human Resource Management* (New York: Macmillan, 1989).

The human resource planning function involves at least three different elements: job analysis, forecasting demand and supply, and legal constraints.

Job Analysis

Superintendent, assistant superintendent, director of personnel, curriculum coordinator, legal counsel, labor relations specialist, principal, assistant principal, college president, dean, and professor are all jobs. To recruit and select the appropriate personnel for specific jobs, it is necessary to know what the job entails. **Job analysis** is the process of obtaining information about jobs through a systematic examination of job content.[2] A job analysis usually consists of two parts: a job description and a job specification. The **job description** is a written statement that outlines the duties and responsibilities expected of a job incumbent. It usually includes a job title, the title of the incumbent's immediate supervisor, a brief statement of the job goal, and a list of duties and responsibilities (Table 15-1).[3] The **job specification** is a written document that outlines the qualifications—education, skills, and experience—that a person needs to accomplish the duties and responsibilities set forth in the job description.

Job analysis provides valuable information for forecasting future staffing needs and other personnel management functions. For example, the data produced by the job analysis can be used to develop appropriate recruitment and selection methods, to determine dimensions on which personnel should be evaluated, to determine the worth of jobs for compensation purposes, and to develop training programs for personnel.

Job-Analysis Techniques   A variety of techniques are available for conducting a job analysis. The technique most appropriate for a given situation depends on a number of factors, such as the type of job being analyzed, the resources available for doing a job analysis, the scope of the job, and the size of the organization. Some of the most commonly used techniques for conducting a job analysis include the following: observation, work sampling, critical incidents, interviews, and questionnaires.[4]

Observation. The most straightforward method of job analysis is **observation** of people performing the job. Observation can be a good way of examining jobs that consist mainly of observable physical activity. Jobs such as school custodian, groundskeeper, and machine operator are examples. Analyzing a job through observation is not appropriate where the job requires much abstract thinking, planning, or decision making (e.g., superintendent, labor relations specialist, college dean).

Work Sampling. A variation of the observation technique is the **work-sampling** approach. The job analyst periodically samples employees' activities and behavior on jobs that have long cycles, that have irregular patterns of activity, or that require a variety of different tasks. For example, research on the administrative demands of school principals consistently shows that they are fragmented and rapid-fire.[5]

A personnel administrator could examine the job activities of twenty-five or thirty high school principals on a given day or randomly select twenty-five or thirty days of the school year and observe the job activities of one or two principals during those days. This approach is similar to the one used by Henry Mintzberg in his analysis of a school superintendent and that of Harry Wolcott in his study of school principals.[6] Both researchers, however, went well beyond the

---

[2]U.S. Department of Labor, *Handbook for Job Analysis* (Washington, D.C.: Government Printing Office, 1990).

[3]The sample job description was provided by the New Orleans Public Schools.

[4]U.S. Department of Labor, *Handbook for Job Analysis.*

[5]Suzanne E. Estler, "Decision Making," in N. J. Boyan (ed.), *Handbook of Research on Educational Administration* (New York: Longman, 1988), pp. 305–320.

[6]Henry Mintzberg, *The Nature of Managerial Work* (New York: Harper & Row, 1973); Harry Wolcott, *The Man in the Principal's Office* (New York: Holt, Rinehart & Winston, 1973).

TABLE 15 ▪ 1   Job Description

Job Title:	School Principal
Job Goal:	To administer and supervise all activities and personnel within an assigned school, toward the fullest possible development of the skills and motivations of each pupil for fulfillment as a responsible and significant human being.
Reports To:	District Superintendent
Supervises:	All professional and nonprofessional staff assigned.

Job Responsibilities:

1. Supervises the school's instructional and extracurricular programs and all activities within the school.
2. Works toward the improvement of the instructional program within the school through faculty study groups and other evaluation processes.
3. Implements all board policies and administrative rules and regulations.
4. Develops and encourages programs of orientation and self-improvement of teachers and others within the school.
5. Determines the work assignment of all professional personnel assigned to the school.
6. Plans and conducts faculty meetings.
7. Observes and reviews the performance of all personnel to provide a basis for effective counseling and for encouraging optimum performance.
8. Assists in the selection of teaching personnel and recommends to the assistant superintendent for personnel candidates for positions.
9. Provides for the health, safety, and welfare of students and staff within the school.
10. Maintains standards of student discipline designed to command the respect of students and parents and to minimize school and classroom interruptions.
11. Coordinates the use of student transportation services provided for the school.
12. Develops working relationships among school staff and school system resource personnel available to the school.
13. Makes regular and thorough inspections of the school plant and school properties.
14. Supervises the preparation of all school reports, student records, and the school's internal accounts, and maintains a record-keeping system.
15. Approves or initiates requisitions for supplies, equipment, and materials necessary for the operation of the school.
16. Interprets activities and policies of the school to the community and encourages community participation in school life.
17. Makes recommendations to the district superintendent and the superintendent concerning policy, practice, or personnel for the purposes of improving the quality of the school system.

work-sampling approach in their analysis of school principals and superintendents. They used a combination of ethnographic techniques including observation, interviews, document analysis, and structured questionnaires to obtain their data.[7]

[7]Harry F. Wolcott, "Ethnographic Research in Education," in R. M. Jaeger (ed.), *Complementary Methods for Research in Education* (Washington, D. C.: American Educational Research Association, 1988), pp. 187–249.

Critical Incidents. Another variation of the observation technique, known as **critical incidents**, examines only those job activities leading to successful or unsuccessful performance. This approach is similar to the trait approach used to identify effective and ineffective leaders. An outside consultant, an immediate supervisor, or a job incumbent can conduct this technique. Direct observation and the two variations thereof are frequently used in conjunction with interviewing.

Interviews. Probably the most widely used technique for determining what a job entails is the **interview** technique, and its wide use attests to its advantages. Observation of a school district's labor relations specialist, for example, would only reveal that the district's chief negotiator conducts research, prepares proposals and counterproposals, confers with management's bargaining team, and negotiates at the bargaining table. This method fails to identify other important aspects of the job, such as analytic thinking and problem solving. Interviewing the labor relations specialist allows that person to describe important activities of the job that might not be revealed through direct observation.

Questionnaires. Many organizations use job-analysis **questionnaires** to elicit information concerning what a job entails. Such questionnaires have at least two advantages. First, they can pool the responses of numerous job incumbents and compare job activities across many jobs, using a standard set of common dimensions. Second, questionnaires can generate much information quickly and inexpensively. For example, a job analyst could administer a questionnaire to 100 job incumbents in less time than it would take to observe a single job or interview one job occupant.

The U.S. Air Force has developed the Comprehensive Occupational Data Analysis Program (CODAP).[8] It elicits data about hundreds of job tasks. Another popular, structured job-analysis questionnaire is the Position Analysis Questionnaire (PAQ) developed at Purdue University. It consists of 194 items designed to assess six broad categories of work activity: information input, mental processes, work output, relationships with others, job context, and other job

characteristics such as working irregular hours.[9] The PAQ is inadequate for analyzing upper-level administrative or professional jobs (superintendent, college dean) because it fails to address higher-level cognitive processes such as abstract thinking and strategic planning. Well-known instruments designed to elicit information about upper-level administrative jobs include the Management Position Description Questionnaire (MPDQ) and the Professional and Managerial Position Questionnaire (PMPQ).[10]

Forecasting Demand and Supply

The second phase of human resource planning, **forecasting** demand and supply, involves using any number of sophisticated statistical procedures based on analysis and projections. Such forecasting techniques are beyond the scope of this discussion.

At a more practical level, forecasting demand involves determining the numbers and kinds of personnel that the organization will need at some point in the future. Most school administrators consider several factors when forecasting future personnel needs. The demand for the organization's product or service is paramount. Thus, in a school district, student enrollments are projected first. Then the personnel needed to service the projected enrollment is estimated. Other factors typically considered when fore-

[8]Raymond E. Christal and John J. Weissmuller, "New Comprehensive Data Analysis Programs (CODAP) for Analyzing Task Factor Information," *JSAS Catalog of Selected Documents in Psychology*, 7, (1977), pp. 24–25.

[9]Ernest J. McCormick, Robert C. Mecham, and Paul R. Jeanneret, *Technical Manual for the Position Analysis Questionnaire* (PAQ) (West Lafayette, IN: Department of Psychological Sciences, Purdue University, 1972).
[10]Walter W. Tornow and Patrick R. Pinto, "The Development of a Managerial Job Taxonomy: A System for Describing, Classifying, and Evaluating Executive Positions," *Journal of Applied Psychology*, 61 (1976), pp. 410–418; John L. Mitchell and Ernest J. McCormick, *Development of PMPQ: A Structured Job Analysis Questionnaire for the Study of Professional and Managerial Positions* (West Lafayette, IN: Department of Psychological Sciences, Purdue University, 1979).

casting the demand for personnel include:[11] budget constraints; turnover due to resignations, terminations, transfers, and retirement; new technology in the field; decisions to upgrade the quality of services provided; and minority hiring goals.

Forecasting supply involves determining what personnel will be available. The two sources are internal and external: people already employed by the organization and those outside the organization. Factors school administrators typically consider when forecasting the supply of personnel include:[12] promoting employees from within the organization; identifying employees willing and able to be trained; availability of required talent in local, regional, and national labor markets; competition for talent within the field; population trends (such as movement of families in the United States from the Northeast to the Southwest); and college and university enrollment trends in the needed field.

Internal sources of employees to fill projected vacancies must be monitored. This is facilitated by the use of the human resource audit, or the systematic inventory of the qualifications of existing personnel. A **human resource audit** is simply an organizational chart of a unit or entire organization with all positions (usually administrative) indicated and keyed as to the promotability of each role incumbent.

Figure 15-2 depicts a human resource audit, or inventory, chart for a hypothetical school district. As Figure 15-2 shows, the superintendent can see where she stands with respect to future staff actions. The superintendent's successor is probably the assistant superintendent for instruction. This person has a successor, the director of elementary education, ready for promotion. Subordinates to the director of elementary education are two principals who are promotable now, three who will be ready for pro-

motion in one or two years, two who are not promotable, and one who should be dismissed.

The other subordinate to the assistant superintendent of instruction, the director of secondary education, is satisfactory but not promotable. That person has two principals who are promotable now, one who will be promotable with further training, and one who is satisfactory but not promotable.

The assistant superintendent of business requires further training before being ready for promotion. Here is a person who knows the job of business management extremely well but lacks training in other aspects of the superintendency, such as curriculum development, personnel administration, public relations, and the like. Some of the accountants reporting to the assistant superintendent of business are promotable now, while others are either nonpromotable or require additional training before being ready for promotion.

The assistant superintendent of personnel, while occupying a very specialized function, is promotable now. Subordinates to that person occupy such specialized jobs that, although performing these roles satisfactorily, they require additional training before being ready for promotion to assistant superintendent of personnel.

The assistant superintendent of research and development was a newly created position in this hypothetical school district. Because of the specialized nature of the position, that person requires considerable training before being ready for promotion. Subordinates to that position are designated similarly.

The analysis provided in Figure 15-2 is very valuable to the school administrator. Future needs and the potential of the existing administrative staff have been identified, and weaknesses have been uncovered. These data can help administrators plan immediate promotions for personnel from within the organization who are promotable, plan for appropriate training and development of others, or dismiss those who are unsatisfactory. If there are an insufficient number of candidates inside the organization to fill

---

[11]Robert Kreitner, *Management*, 4th ed. (Boston: Houghton Mifflin, 1988).
[12]Ibid.

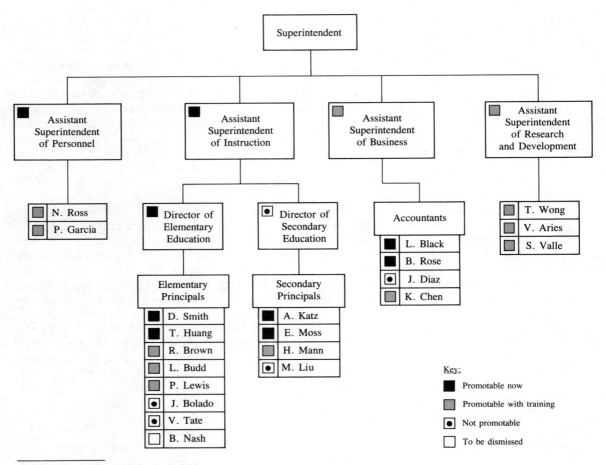

FIGURE 15-2   Human Resource Audit for Administrative Personnel

vacancies, staffing specialists typically analyze labor markets.

Legal Constraints

Legislation designed to regulate hiring practices affects nearly every aspect of employment—from human resource planning to compensation. Our intent is not to make school administrators into attorneys but to examine the basic laws that relate to employment decisions. School administrators must avoid possible charges of discrimination on the basis of race, color, gender, national origin, age, or disability.[13] Table 15-2 summarizes some of the major laws pertaining to the personnel process.

Women and Minorities   The landmark legislation designed to ensure equal employment opportunity is the Civil Rights Act of 1964. In 1965 President Lyndon B. Johnson issued Executive

[13]James Ledvinka, *Federal Regulation of Personnel and Human Resource Management*, 2nd ed. (Northridge, CA: Kent, 1990).

Order 11246 (amended by Executive Order 11375 in 1967). One feature of these executive orders was that they obligated employers to go beyond the provisions of nondiscrimination of the Civil Rights Act and to actively seek out women and minorities and hire, train, develop, and promote them. In 1972 Congress established the **Equal Employment Opportunity Commission (EEOC)** and passed the Equal Employment Opportunity Act. This amendment to the Civil Rights Act of 1964 extended the jurisdiction of the EEOC and gave it the power to initiate court action against noncomplying organizations.

Older Workers   Congress passed the Age Discrimination in Employment Act in 1967. The act originally prohibited discrimination in employment of those people forty to sixty-five years of age; the act was amended in 1978 to move the top age from sixty-five to seventy years; and in 1986 the upper age limit was removed. In essence, the law prohibits discrimination in hiring, firing, compensating, or any other conditions of work of any person forty years of age or over. Exceptions to the legislation include tenured faculty and some high-salaried executives or for documented health- or performance-related reasons.

The Handicapped   The Vocational Rehabilitation Act was passed in 1973 and amended in 1978. The act requires employers who have a contract with the federal government worth $2500 or more to take affirmative action to hire and promote qualified handicapped persons. A handicapped person is defined as any individual with a physical or mental disability that limits normal activities such as walking, seeing, speaking, or learning. The law stipulates that the handi-

TABLE 15 ▪ 2   Major Laws Affecting Hiring Practices

LAW	BASIC REQUIREMENTS
Title VII of the Civil Rights Act of 1964 (as amended)	Prohibits discrimination in employment on the basis of race, color, religion, gender, or national origin.
Age Discrimination in Employment Act of 1968 (as amended)	Prohibits discrimination in employment against any person forty years of age or over.
Equal Pay Act of 1963	Prohibits wage discrimination on the basis of gender; requires equal pay for equal work regardless of gender.
Rehabilitation Act of 1973	Requires employers to take affirmative action to employ and promote qualified handicapped persons.
Pregnancy Discrimination Act of 1978	Requires employees to treat pregnant women and new mothers the same as other employees for all employment-related purposes.
Vietnam Era Veterans Readjustment Act of 1974	Requires employees to take affirmative action to employ disabled Vietnam War veterans.
Occupational Safety and Health Act (OSHA) of 1970	Establishes mandatory safety and health standards in organizations

capped individual must be capable of performing the particular job for which she is being considered.

Veterans   The Vietnam Era Veteran's Readjustment Act of 1974 requires employers with federal contracts to take affirmative action to employ disabled veterans. The act also provides job assistance for Vietnam-era veterans in the form of job counseling, training, and placement.

Equal Employment Opportunity   **Equal employment opportunity** (EEO) is the right of all persons to work and to advance on the basis of merit, ability, and potential without regard to race, color, religion, gender, or national origin. Table 15-2 summarizes the primary legal base for EEO and supporting legal activities. The provisions of these acts generally apply to all public and private organizations employing fifteen or more people. The EEOC administers and federally enforces the various equal employment opportunity acts. The EEOC provides assistance to employers in developing affirmative action programs and in resolving discrimination complaints brought against employers.

Affirmative Action Programs

Whereas EEO legislation prohibits discrimination in recruitment, hiring, promotion, compensation, and discharge, **affirmative action programs** are designed to increase employment opportunities for women and other minorities including veterans, the aged, and the handicapped. Based on two executive orders, originally issued by President Johnson, affirmative action requirements apply to public and private employers and educational institutions who either have contracts with or receive monies from the federal government. The intent of the program is to ensure that women and other minorities are represented in the organization in percentages similar to their percentage in the labor market from which the organization draws personnel. For example, if the labor pool in a community is 15 percent black and 5 percent Hispanic, then 15 percent and 5 percent of the labor force of an organization operating in that community should be black and Hispanic, respectively.

In general, affirmative action programs should include the following:[14] (1) making concerted efforts to recruit and promote women, minorities, the handicapped, and veterans, including recruiting through state employment services and at minority and women's colleges; (2) limiting the questions that can be asked in employment applications and interviews; (3) determining available percentages of women, minorities, and the handicapped in the labor market; (4) setting up goals and timetables for recruiting women, minorities, the handicapped, and veterans; and (5) avoiding testing unless it meets established guidelines.

RECRUITMENT

Whether recruitment of personnel should precede or follow selection is an interesting question. College athletics is a case in point. Coaches in major universities who run successful athletic programs determine their staffing needs (players), scan selected high schools and junior colleges, select the players they want, and then recruit them.

The University of Louisville basketball program has become one of the most successful in the country. For example, the team won two NCAA Championships in the 1980s (1980 and 1986), and the team made it to the final four playoffs in the NCAA tournament in six of the eleven years between 1980 and 1990. To what can this success be attributed? Obviously, Louisville has an outstanding coaching staff. However, part of the explanation lies in the method of recruiting personnel (players) for the team.

---

[14]Leon C. Megginson, Donald C. Mosley, and Paul H. Pietri, *Management: Concepts and Practices*, 3rd ed. (New York: Harper & Row, 1989).

Denny Crum, the University of Louisville's men's basketball coach, has computerized information on the qualifications of basketball players from across the country. This procedure facilitates identifying, tracking, and screening personnel (players) for his basketball program. The plotting is done in what he refers to as "the War Room."[15] Crum selects his personnel (basketball players) first, monitors their progress in high schools or junior colleges, and then recruits them. School organizations typically work in reverse order. Recruiting potential employees first, they then select the personnel they want from among the pool of recruits. Using this method, there is no guarantee that the pool of recruits from which selections are ultimately made are competent.

School districts can take lessons from the top college athletic coaches, who consistently acquire talented personnel to fill strategic slots in their organization. Just as a weak-to-mediocre athlete cannot be miraculously transformed into an All American, neither can weak faculty members and administrators be "trained and developed" out of their mediocrity. The key to the quality of an instructional program is the competency of its professional staff. Thus, recruitment and selection of competent personnel is an extremely important function of school administrators.

All school organizations, at one time or another, engage in recruiting to replace or expand their supply of personnel. Some organizations recruit better personnel than others, which is later reflected in the quality of their instructional programs. Recruitment refers to the process of generating a pool of competent applicants needed to fill the available positions in an organization. Emphasis on the word *competent* is important. No matter how personnel are later selected, developed, and compensated, it is important to begin with a group of high-caliber job applicants. Overall, sources of personnel available to fill vacant positions can be categorized as sources inside the organization and sources outside the organization.

Internal Sources

The existing pool of employees presently within the school system is one source of recruiting personnel. Individuals already employed by the district might possess excellent qualifications for a vacant position. There are some advantages to using **internal recruitment.** First, it allows administrators to observe an employee over a period of time and to evaluate that person's potential and job behavior. These factors cannot be easily observed off the job. Second, when employees see that competence is rewarded with promotion, their morale and performance will likely be enhanced. Third, employees are likely to identify their long-term interests with an organization that provides them with a chance for promotion and hence are less likely to leave the organization. Fourth, employees can be better qualified: Even positions that do not appear unique require familiarity with the people, policies, procedures, and special characteristics of the organization. Finally, when carefully planned, promoting from within can act as a training device for developing middle- and top-level administrators such as principals, central office administrators, and superintendents.[16]

Internal recruiting sources include the following: inventory charts, informal search, talent search, and job posting.[17]

Inventory Chart   In filling administrative vacancies, a human resource audit of the type discussed earlier is helpful (see Figure 15-2). Many

[15]Billy Reid, *Born to Coach: How Denny Crum Built the University of Louisville into a Basketball Powerhouse* (Louisville, KY: Courier Journal and Louisville Times, 1986).

[16]David A. DeCenzo and Stephen P. Robbins, *Personnel: The Management of Human Resources*, 3rd ed. (Englewood Cliffs, NJ: Prentice-Hall, 1988).

[17]John B. Miner and Mary Green Miner, *Personnel and Industrial Relations,* 4th ed. (New York: Macmillan, 1985).

large school districts have computerized information on their administrators' qualifications and promotability. When a vacancy occurs at the administrative level, the computer can search the list of administrators having the qualifications that match the requirements of the position.

Informal Search   In large school districts having a personnel department, the administrator of the division or school having a vacancy consults the personnel director, and together they consider one or more possible candidates for the position. The administrator or the director may interview one or more employees who appear to have the necessary qualifications for the position. After the interview, the position may be offered to one of the candidates.

While the informal search was commonly used in the past, it represents a **closed recruitment system;** that is, it tends to exclude most employees who might be interested in the position from applying. Legislation to ensure equal employment opportunity and affirmative action (see Table 15-2) has resulted in a more **open recruitment system.** That is, there has been an increase in the in-house advertisement of all job vacancies.

Talent Search   A closely related procedure that represents an **open recruitment system** is the talent search. The school district uses this method when it anticipates vacancies at the administrative level and wishes to promote from within the system. Contrary to the informal search, a talent search is widely advertised throughout the school district. Training programs are offered that will qualify personnel for promotion. Employees are asked to notify the personnel department or their building or division administrator if they are interested in participating in the training program. Some training programs are administered independently by the school district or collaboratively with a local university or consulting firm. Those who indicate an interest are administered a

battery of cognitive or psychological tests and assessed in other ways. Employees who are selected are given appropriate training and then placed in a talent pool. They continue in their current jobs until an appropriate position for which they are qualified becomes vacant.

Job Posting   Another procedure to facilitate implementation of a promotion-from-within policy is job posting. A job-posting system gives every employee an opportunity to apply for a vacant position within the school district. The posting notification may be communicated on bulletin boards throughout the district, in the weekly or monthly school district newsletter, or in a special posting sheet from the personnel department, outlining all positions currently available. The job posting usually contains information regarding job title, a brief job description, salary range, and school or division location. Collective bargaining agreements may contain a provision for job posting. In such instances, job posting can be formal. Unions generally prefer that promotions be based on seniority, whereas administration prefers that decisions be based on merit.

Internal sources of recruitment, involving talent searches and job posting, have received attention recently due to equal employment opportunity and affirmative action programs. Government agencies monitoring employment practices frequently require school districts that previously did not practice open recruitment and solicit inside candidates to do so. The ultimate goal of such procedures is to prevent women and minorities from being kept in lower-paying, entry-level jobs.

External Sources

Internal sources do not always produce enough qualified applicants to fill vacant positions in the school district. Several **external recruitment** sources are available and include educational institutions, employment agencies, executive-search firms, temporary-help agencies, advertising, and unsolicited applicants.[18]

Educational Institutions Universities, colleges, vocational schools, technical schools, and high schools are all important sources of recruits for most school districts. High schools or vocational schools can provide blue-collar applicants such as plant-maintenance workers; business or secretarial schools can provide white-collar staff such as bookkeepers and clerical personnel; colleges and universities can provide professional staff such as teachers, counselors, social workers, and school psychologists; and graduate schools can often provide administrative personnel such as superintendents and principals.

Most universities and colleges operate placement services. Potential employers can review credentials submitted by applicants. For professional positions in great demand, school districts may send recruiters to campuses for the purpose of interviewing job applicants. On-campus recruiting can be an expensive and time-consuming process. However, because there is a great deal of competition for the top graduating students in professional-type jobs, the recruiting visit may be worth the time and expense if a high-quality applicant is hired. Like the top business firms and athletic programs, school organizations need to do more active recruiting of top students graduating from universities and colleges.

Employment Agencies Every state in the United States operates a state employment agency under the umbrella of the U.S. Training and Employment Service (USTES) of the U.S. Department of Labor. There are 2400 such offices, which are staffed by state employees and funded by the federal government.[19] The service is free to all job applicants. These agencies have a poor image, which is no reflection on their competence or service. State employment agencies are perceived by job applicants as having few high-skilled jobs, and employers tend to view such agencies as having few high-quality applicants.

There are thousands of private employment agencies in the United States. Private agencies provide more services to an employer and are perceived to offer employers higher-quality applicants than public agencies do. For example, some private employment agencies advertise the position sought, screen applicants, and sometimes even provide a guarantee of satisfactory service to the hiring organization. For these services, a fee is charged, which is absorbed by the organization, the employee, or shared between the two. Such fees are usually set by state law. Private agencies can be sources of clerical, white-collar, and administrative personnel.

Executive-Search Firms Many major corporations, hospitals, universities, and large school districts now use executive-search firms (or "headhunters," as they are commonly called) to recruit middle-level and top-level executives. (See the PRO/CON Debate.) In searching for a superintendent of schools, for example, whose compensation package may be in excess of $125,000 a year, the school district is often willing to pay a very high fee to locate precisely the right person to fill the vacant position. A fee of 25 to 35 percent of the superintendent's first year's salary, plus $500 a day for expenses is not uncommon. These firms have contacts throughout the United States and are especially well trained in contacting highly qualified candidates who are already employed. In fact, executive-search firms will not accept unsolicited applications from persons seeking employment. This procedure, often referred to as "pirating," is a common practice today among the larger, more successful organizations.

Temporary-Help Agencies Organizations such as Kelly Services and Manpower can provide school organizations with temporary help. Traditionally

[18]Ibid.

[19]U.S. Department of Labor, *Employment and Training Report of the President* (Washington, D.C.: Government Printing Office, 1990).

■

SUPERINTENDENT SEARCHES

One of the most important decisions a school board can make is the appointment of a superintendent of schools. Some boards conduct a search on their own. Some work with their local intermediate unit or district superintendent. Minimal expense is incurred with either of these options. Other boards employ executive-search firms or superintendent-search consultants (generally, educational administration professors who specialize in this service). Search firms and search consultants charge large fees.

QUESTION Does the involvement of an executive-search firm or a superintendent-search consultant justify the expense?

ARGUMENTS PRO

1 Boards rarely have the expertise to conduct a legal search. Candidates' civil rights are protected by law and regulation. Without the guidance of experts, boards have been known to make serious errors in these areas.

2 Consultants and search firms can get inside information about candidates because they know the network and have the credibility to tap into the network. They are more likely to learn sensitive information about candidates from references and other sources.

3 Consultants and search firms are constantly on the alert for good candidates. They follow the careers of promising administrators and share perceptions with each other. They have an expert's knowledge of the candidates.

4 Aspiring superintendents know who the search consultants are and can strive to attract their attention.

5 The intermediate unit heads or district superintendents are expert at conducting searches. However, because the superintendent works in a dependent relationship to them, the intermediate unit or district superintendent has a vested interest in the identification of candidates who fit their profile, not the school district boards' profile.

6 The use of professional searchers depoliticizes the process of identifying a superintendent. The consultant is an outside person without ties in the district who can be disinterested about the identification of candidates.

ARGUMENTS CON

1 Boards can learn how to conduct an appropriate search by consulting the state school board association and reviewing the literature.

2 Board members can learn what they need to know about candidates from a careful reading of résumés, telephone contact with references, thoughtful interviews, and site visits to candidates' workplaces.

3 Consultants and search firms are notorious for nurturing and recommending white males whom they perceive to be the best candidates in their network. Their network is the "old-boy" network.

4 The search experts become king-makers. They gain power because aspiring administrators must stay in their good graces. Candidates call search consultants' interviews at national conferences "meat markets."

5 Intermediate unit heads or district superintendents are as expert at search consulting as the firms that charge for the service. In addition, they know the school district well and therefore can help the board find a candidate who will meet its unique needs.

6 The school board makes the final selection of the superintendent whether or not a search consultant is involved.

developed to supply secretarial, clerical, and semiskilled labor, the temporary-help agencies have expanded to include skilled and technical areas. One such agency is Account Temps, which provides temporary help in the accounting and computer fields. School districts can rent on a day-rate basis people with a broad range of skills, such as engineers, computer technicians, or accountants. Employing temporary help may be more efficient than employing permanent staff during peak periods. Temporary employees do not receive the fringe-benefit package required of permanent employees; and costly layoffs (paying unemployment compensation) during less active periods can be avoided.

Advertising Advertising in newspapers, trade magazines, and professional journals is a widely used method of external recruiting. A local newspaper can be a good source of blue-collar workers, clerical staff, and lower-level administrative personnel. Trade and professional journals enable school organizations to aim at more specialized employees. For example, the *Chronicle of Higher Education* is a major source used to recruit personnel in higher education. Administrative positions in the public schools can be advertised in the *School Administrator, Executive Educator, NASSP Bulletin, Principal, Educational Leadership, Educational Researcher,* or *Phi Delta Kappan.*

In contrast to print advertising in publications such as newspapers and trade and professional journals, other forms of recruitment advertising are used less frequently. These include television, radio, and billboards. Advertising usually generates a large pool of applicants who then must be screened carefully to determine those who are qualified.

Unsolicited Applicants Another source of prospective job applicants is the file, maintained at the school district office, of unsolicited candidates. Unsolicited applicants communicate with the school district by letter, by telephone, or in person. The qualifications of unsolicited appli-

cants depend on several factors: the condition of the labor market, the school district's reputation, and the types of jobs available. Regardless of these factors, there will always be some unsolicited applicants in most school districts—people entering the labor force for the first time, women returning to work after a period of child rearing, or individuals improving their employment situation. Generally, the use of unsolicited applicants is prevalent in staffing clerical and plant-maintenance jobs. A school district with a good reputation can also rely on this source in filling professional positions including teachers and other support personnel.

Internal Versus External Recruitment

Both internal recruitment and external recruitment have advantages and disadvantages to the school district (Figure 15-3).

Promoting from within can work to the school district's advantage. Applicants are already familiar with the organization, have a known performance record within the district that can be examined, and may be less expensive to recruit than external candidates. As indicated previously, internal recruitment also improves morale and loyalty among employees because they believe that competence is rewarded with promotion. However, there are at least two disadvantages of internal recruitment: organizational inbreeding—a "but we've always done it that way" mentality and increased political behavior if it is perceived that such behavior may result in a promotion.

External recruiting, on the other hand, infuses the organization with "new blood," which may broaden present ideas and knowledge and question traditional ways of doing things. The abundance of external sources almost guarantees that the school district will find an adequate number of candidates from which to choose. Promoting from outside the organization also provides an opportunity to recruit women and minorities at all levels in the school district. Ex-

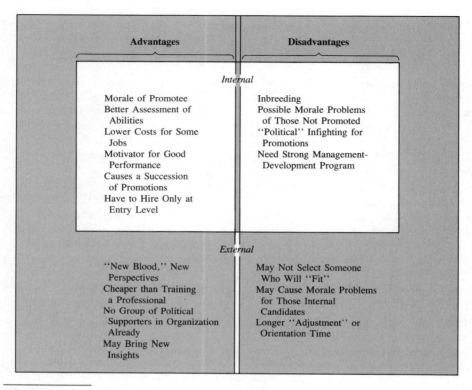

FIGURE 15-3   Internal and External Recruitment
(SOURCE: Adapted from Robert L. Mathis and John H. Jackson, *Personnel: Human Resource Management*, 5th ed., p. 229). Copyright © 1988 by West Publishing Company. Used by permission.

clusive reliance on promotions from within may further inhibit the entry of these groups into higher-level positions in the school district, assuming that past underrepresentation of these groups currently exists. On the negative side, using external sources can be quite costly, particularly the hiring of middle-level and top executives. In general, most school districts use a mixture of internal and external sources of recruitment.

As discussed earlier, one of the most important instructional decisions a principal or superintendent makes is hiring his teaching personnel. School administrators share one of the same concerns faced by top-level managers everywhere: how to find great employees and keep them productive and satisfied while they're at work. (See Administrative Advice 15-1.)

SELECTION

Once applicants have been recruited, the school district must select the most qualified persons to fill existing vacancies. A comprehensive discussion of selection techniques can be found in personnel administration texts. The most common procedure involves a series of steps including biographical information, reference

ADMINISTRATIVE ADVICE 15-1

TIPS TO FIND AND KEEP GOOD TEACHERS

Here are several tips to help school administrators find and keep good teachers.

- Never hire a first-year teacher at full salary. Offer a first-year teacher an internship at 60 to 70 percent of a second-year teacher's salary. Each intern should be directly supervised by an experienced teacher who can serve as a mentor.
- Pay the mentor teacher $5000 a year for each intern she supervises. Offer this mentorship to the best teacher on your faculty. The mentor teacher should supervise only one intern per school year.
- Use interns and aides to monitor halls, restrooms, cafeterias, recess, and bus boardings. Do not give these duties to experienced teachers.
- At least two master teachers and an administrator should observe and unanimously approve teachers with two or more years of intern or classroom experience, who are under consideration for full-time employment.
- Do not award teachers lifetime tenure. Instead, contract with them for one, two, or five years.
- Any teacher who, at the end of the first five-year contract period, is going to be invited to sign a second five-year contract should be offered a half-year sabbatical. Any teacher who, at the end of the second five-year contract period, is

going to be invited to sign a third five-year contract should be offered a full-year sabbatical.
- Advertise widely for teachers at colleges and universities with high-quality education programs.
- Recruit qualified, former teachers who are still certified to teach part-time.
- Don't expect teachers to grade, counsel, or coach more than eighty students within a school semester.
- Provide all teachers with their own desk and telephone, as well as access to secretarial services.
- Provide each department with a booster club—doing for that department what booster clubs do for athletic coaches. For example, the business department booster club would ensure that needed equipment such as computers or calculators was available for student training.
- Hold a semiannual banquet to honor all teachers who have been selected by student representatives from each grade and school in the district.

Source: Adapted from Cynthia Parsons, "Twelve Tips to Find and Keep Good Teachers," *School Administrator*, 46 (1989), p. 30. Used by permission.

checks, interviews, tests, and assessment centers[20] (Figure 15-4).

Biographical Information

The first step in the selection process is searching for evidence of past performance in a candidate's record. This information can be secured

from an application blank, a résumé, a letter of application, writing samples, school records or college transcripts, and similar biographical data. Research shows that **biographical information** can predict future job performance because a person's behavior is consistent over time.[21] The use of such information in making

---

[20]Robert Gatewood and Hubert Feild, *Human Resource Selection*, 2nd ed. (Hinsdale, IL: Dryden Press, 1989).

[21]Terry W. Mitchell and Richard J. Klomoski, "Is It Rational to Be Empirical—A Test of Methods for Scoring Biographical Data," *Journal of Applied Psychology*, 67 (1982) pp. 411–418.

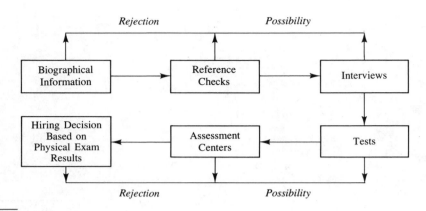

Rejection   *Possibility*

FIGURE 15-4   Steps in the Selection Process

selection decisions is based on the idea that an effective predictor of future performance is past performance.

An approach that can be used to analyze biographical data is the *weighted method*. Statistically weighted biographical data can further enhance the predictability of job performance. The weighting procedure consists of identifying background factors on which high-performing employees tend to differ from low-performing employees. Differential weights are then assigned to these background factors. The weightings are based on a statistical analysis that has shown, over time, that there is a high correlation between some background factors or categories of information and high or low performance.[22] Each candidate for a job receives a final score based on this analysis. The administrator then hires personnel who obtain a high score when their biographical information is weighted using this method. Thus, school employers increase the likelihood of employing high-performing personnel.

In practice, most school districts use different background factors, depending on the job level. For professional and administrative

personnel, for example, biographical data may include an application blank, a letter of application, a résumé, a writing sample, and undergraduate and graduate transcripts. For building-maintenance, clerical, and other noncertificated staff, background factors might consist of a different application blank, school records, military records, and other biographical sources.

Reference Checks

Reference checks fall into two categories: letters of recommendation and subsequent telephone follow-up inquiries of the final candidates for a position. Letters of recommendation can be considered part of the biographical information or screening process and usually precedes the interview. Telephone follow-up inquiries typically are made after all other steps in the selection process are completed and just prior to making the hiring decision. For example, the administrator may wish to contact by telephone the present employer or student-teaching supervisor of each of the three leading candidates for a teaching position. Some school organizations mistakenly omit this vital step.

Letters of recommendation are generally of little value in the selection process, for at least four reasons. First, job applicants usually ask for

---

[22]James J. Asher, "The Biographical Item: Can It Be Improved?" *Personnel Psychology*, 25 (1972), pp. 251–269.

references from persons who are likely to write complimentary letters. As a result, letters of recommendation are biased in the applicant's favor. Second, the recommender may possess only limited knowledge of the applicant. Third, under the Privacy Act of 1974, people have the right to examine letters of reference concerning them unless they waive that right. Due to this privacy legislation, recommenders are reluctant to provide negative information about an applicant in writing for fear of being sued. Fourth, occasionally, recommenders will write a favorable letter of recommendation for an incompetent applicant in order to facilitate their leaving their current employment. In one actual situation, the board of education of a suburban school district dismissed a teacher on the recommendation of the superintendent of schools. Later, the teacher sued the board and superintendent for damages. To avoid the legal costs of a trial, the superintendent was instructed by his board of education, at the urging of the dismissed teacher's attorney, to write a favorable letter of recommendation for the alleged incompetent teacher. The superintendent did so, and the lawsuit was dropped.

Despite their questionable value, school organizations typically require letters of recommendation as part of the selection process. There are ways to improve the validity of reference checks. First, telephone the references and ask for an oral recommendation. Most people are more likely to provide complete and frank statements orally than they would in writing. Second, contact people other than those referred by the job applicant. This increases the pool of information available about the candidate. Third, allow more credence to references provided by previous employers than those provided by other nonemployment sources such as colleagues, friends, ministers, and the like. Fourth, give more weight to references of those candidates who have waived their right to view their letters of recommendation. Fifth, contact the applicant's two previous employers. This provides wider coverage of previous employment. These techniques will strengthen the validity of reference checks. The rationale underlying reference checks, like biographical information, is that past performance will to a great extent predict future performance.

Interviews

The interview is perhaps the most widely used personnel technique in the selection process. It serves as a two-way exchange that allows both the school district and the applicant to gather information that would otherwise be difficult to secure. Unfortunately, despite its widespread use, the interview is a poor predictor of job performance.

Interviewing Problems   Six major interviewing problems should be avoided:[23]

1. *Unfamiliarity with the Job.* Interviewers frequently are unfamiliar with the job. When interviewers do not know what the job entails, the following conditions result: Interviewers do not ask the right questions, interpret the obtained information differently, have faulty impressions of the information supplied, and spend time discussing matters irrelevant to the job.
2. *Premature Decisions.* Interviewers tend to make a decision about an applicant in the first few minutes of the interview before all relevant information has been gathered. Then they spend the rest of the interview seeking information that confirms their initial impression.
3. *Emphasis on Negative Information.* Interviewers tend to weight negative information supplied by the applicant more heavily than positive information. On occasion, the interviewer may change his mind, but the change tends to be from positive to negative rather than vice versa. In fact, in most cases, interviews tend to be a search for negative information.
4. *Personal Biases.* Some interviewers tend to have preconceptions and prejudices about

---

[23]Gary Dessler, *Personnel Management*, 4th ed. (Englewood Cliffs, NJ: Prentice-Hall, 1988).

people. Some examples follow: "fat people are lazy"; "people from the East are unfriendly and arrogant"; "people from the South are slow"; "people with low foreheads are stupid." Other biases may reflect negatively against some minority groups or in favor of those candidates who have backgrounds similar to the interviewer(s). As ridiculous as these prejudices may seem, many of these personal biases still exist today. Furthermore, some interviewers are overly impressed with surface signs of composure, manner of speech, and physical appearance.

5. *Applicant Order.* Interviewer's ratings of an applicant are influenced by the order in which candidates are interviewed. For example, when an average applicant is interviewed immediately following one or more below-average applicants, the average applicant tends to be evaluated well above average. A similar process works in reverse. If an average applicant follows an outstanding applicant, the former is rated below average.

6. *Hiring Quotas.* Interviewers who have been given hiring quotas tend to rate applicants higher than interviewers who have not been given quotas. Thus, pressure to hire influences the interviewer's judgments of the applicant and thereby diminishes the usefulness of the interview as a selection technique.

Improving the Interview Process   School organizations will continue to use interviews regardless of the problems. Thus, researchers have identified several techniques for improving the interview process:[24]

1. *Use a Structured Interview Format.* Interviews should be more structured. In a structured interview, questions are written in advance,

scaled on a standardized rating scale, and asked of all job applicants. The structured interview has three major advantages. It brings consistency to the interview process; it provides an opportunity to develop questions that are relevant to the job; and it allows screening and refinement of questions that may be discriminatory. In addition, the structured interview is more defensible in court. A less-structured method can be used when interviewing administrative personnel. That is, the interview is still carefully planned in terms of content areas covered, but it allows more flexibility by the interviewer.

2. *Train Interviewers.* One way to improve the validity and reliability of the interview is to train interviewers. Effective interviewing requires specific skills including asking questions, probing, listening, observing, recording unbiased information, rating, and the like. Specifically designed workshops can teach these skills. A cadre of trained interviewers can then interview job applicants.

3. *Keep a Written Record of Each Interview.* Keeping a written record of each interview facilitates a comparison of the applicants interviewed. To make accurate comparisons among the candidates, maintain and preserve the details of their responses and impressions. Without such information, later deliberations and decision making will be less accurate and valid.

4. *Use Multiple Interviewers.* Using multiple interviewers facilitates a comparison of evaluations and perceptions. Specifically, it allows the school district to place greater confidence in areas where consensus of opinion exists. And it opens up discussion in specific areas where disagreement occurs, with the purpose of arriving at an equitable hiring decision. Personnel who have specific knowledge of the job and the candidate's immediate supervisor-to-be would provide a well-balanced interview team. Or the district may wish to use a cadre of trained interviewers in every interview situation.

---

[24]Martin J. Yate, *Hiring the Best: A Manager's Guide to Effective Interviewing*, 2nd ed. (Cambridge, MA: Adams House, 1988).

5. *Get the Applicant to Talk.* The main purpose of an interview is to learn as much as possible about a job applicant. This can be accomplished by getting the applicant to talk. Establish a friendly, open rapport with the applicant early in the interview, with some brief comments about the organization and the job. Then shift to a preplanned question format. Listen carefully to content. Probe for answers to all questions and check for inconsistencies. Relate responses given to questions during the interview to written biographical information supplied earlier. Pay attention to nonverbal cues such as tone of voice, general personality, and emotional characteristics of the applicant. For example, failure of a candidate to maintain eye contact may be a danger sign. Thus, observation during an interview is as important as listening.

6. *Use the Interview as One Aspect of the Selection Process.* Avoid using the interview as the sole criteria for selecting applicants. By the same token, the interviewer(s) should not be the sole decision makers concerning who is or is not hired. Supplement the interview with data from other sources, including biographical information, results of tests, written references, and telephone inquiries. Interviewers may not be privy to the telephone reference checks, which may rest exclusively in the hands of the top-executive officer. When the aforementioned suggestions are implemented, the interview can be a useful source of information in the selection process.

Today's candidates for teaching positions are skilled in the techniques of making a good impression during an interview. This makes the school administrator's task of asking the right questions during the interview more difficult. A recommended interview technique that is more effective involves asking specific, probing questions about candidates' past experiences, such as how they handled a discipline problem or taught a difficult lesson. This intensive grilling of teacher candidates should provide greater insight into their abilities. (See Administrative Advice 15-2.)

Tests

A comprehensive survey of 2500 corporations revealed that 64.5 percent use **testing** as a device in hiring and promotion decisions.[25] Most U.S. firms give an hour-long test for entry level, blue-collar workers, and applicants for top-management positions take personality tests requiring a day or less. In contrast, the Toyota Motor Corporation in Georgetown, Kentucky, puts candidates for entry-level, shop-floor jobs through fourteen hours of testing.[26] School districts, however, infrequently use tests as an employment device. Perhaps school organizations should change that practice based on the evidence from business firms.

Many human resource experts believe that testing is the single best-selection device. Tests yield more information about an applicant than do biographical information and letters of recommendations, and they are less subject to bias than are interviews. The primary advantages of testing include finding the right person for the job, obtaining a high degree of job satisfaction for the applicant because of a good "fit" between the organization and the person, and reducing absenteeism and turnover.[27]

Although there are many kinds of tests available for school district use, they can be classified into four major groups: achievement and performance tests, aptitude tests, personality tests, and interest tests.[28]

---

[25]Irving E. Alexander, *Personology: Method and Content of Personality-Assessment and Psychobiography* (Durham, NC: Duke University Press, 1990).

[26]Fred Luthans and Richard M. Hodgetts, *Business* (New York: Dryden Press, 1989).

[27]Ramon J. Aldag and Timothy M. Stearns, *Management* (Cincinnati: South-Western, 1987).

[28]James V. Mitchell (ed.), *The Ninth Mental Measurements Yearbook*, Vols. I and II (Lincoln: The Buros Institute of Mental Measurements, University of Nebraska Press, 1985).

ADMINISTRATIVE ADVICE 15-2

■

INTERVIEWS: GRILL TEACHERS ABOUT THEIR EXPERIENCES

School administrators who interview candidates for school positions frequently allow their questions to become vague and theoretical. Instead, ask specific questions that force teacher candidates to tell you how they have performed in the past. Below are a few sample questions, together with what you want to learn from the response.

■ *"Describe a Lesson Plan During Your Career (or Student-Teaching Experience) That Went Extremely Well."* Good teachers are creative, and they use unusual and imaginative approaches to keep students interested in learning. For example, top candidates will tell you about taking students to a football field for a mathematics lesson involving measurements or describe introducing Shakespeare's *Julius Caesar* while wearing a bedsheet toga.

■ *"Tell Me About a Time When You Helped Someone Achieve Success."* Good teachers will tell you stories about the boy labeled a poor speller who the teacher helped earn an *A* on a spelling test or about the girl who was helped to overcome her shyness and later went on to campaign for student council. A good teacher's face lights up when describing a student's success.

■ *"Tell Me About a Time When a Student or Class Taught You Something."* The best teachers recognize that learning is continuous and mutual—with the line between teacher and student often blurred. For example, a winning candidate will tell you about studying up on the stars because a class of fifth graders was passionately

interested in astronomy or recall researching the publishing industry because a high school senior was eager to publish her short stories. The talented candidate welcomes the chance to research a topic on someone else's behalf.

■ *"Tell Me About a Situation That You Realize Now You Probably Mishandled."* Good teachers learn from their mistakes. If a job candidate never struggled with a discipline problem or cannot analyze the reasons for failing to identify a student with a learning disorder, then you should be wary. The talented teacher admits mistakes and then moves on.

■ *"Describe Your Own Most Memorable Teacher."* A good teacher will probably carry the memory of one special role model. For example, a talented teacher will tell you stories about the model teacher's kindness, individual attention, or incredible motivation. Note these traits. The teacher candidate will probably try to emulate the model teacher.

Source: Adapted from Coleen Armstrong, "Interview Advice: Grill Teachers About Their Track Records," *Executive Educator*, 10 (1988), p. 29. Copyright 1988, the National School Boards Association. Used by permission.

Achievement and Performance Tests   These tests measure the applicant's ability to perform the tasks required in a job. Examples include typing and dictaphone tests for secretaries, speed and accuracy tests for computer operators, and a driving test for driver education teachers. The National Teacher Examinations (NTE) is an

achievement test. Candidates for administrative positions are often given "in-basket tests," designed to examine their judgment. The applicant is given an in-basket of letters, memoranda, telephone messages, and the like dealing with various school situations that might arise on the job and asked what she would do under the circumstances. (This is one of several exercises typically used in assessment centers, discussed later.)

Aptitude Tests   These tests measure the potential of an applicant to perform some task. They are diversified in that some measure cognitive aptitudes, while others measure special aptitudes such as mechanical, clerical, or creativity. The Graduate Record Exam (GRE) and Miller Analogies Test (MAT), used by colleges and universities as a criterion for graduate school admission, are examples of cognitive aptitude tests. The Wechsler Adult Intelligence Scale is an aptitude test that measures general intelligence.

Personality Tests   These tests attempt to measure personality characteristics that might be important on the job, such as emotional stability, introversion and extroversion, self-confidence, aggressiveness or submissiveness, neurotic tendencies, and many other characteristics and traits. Proponents claim that projective-type tests, such as the Rorschach (ink blot) test, Thematic Apperception Test (TAT), and the Sentence Completion Test are less subject to "faking" than other personality tests.

Interest Tests   These tests attempt to measure an applicant's interest in performing various kinds of activities. The notion underlying the administration of interest tests to job applicants is that certain people perform jobs well because the job activities are interesting. The purpose of this type of test is to create a better "fit" between the applicant and the specific job. Two popular interest tests are the Kuder Preference Record and the Strong–Campbell Interest Inventory.

The three major problems with using tests as an employment-selection device are that they are time-consuming to administer, some require training to administer and score, and tests discriminate against minorities. Ethnic minorities, such as blacks and Mexican-Americans, may score lower on certain paper-and-pencil tests because of cultural bias. EEOC guidelines and amendments to the Civil Rights Act prohibit employment practices that artificially discriminate against individuals on the basis of test scores.[29] That is, the test must relate to actual performance on the job, the test must be valid (measures what it purports to measure), and the test must be reliable (scores of the test taker are repeatable over time).

Assessment Centers

The National Association of Secondary School Principals (NASSP) Assessment Center is an approach to the selection of school principals that is rapidly gaining in popularity.[30] It is particularly good for selecting present school district employees for promotion to principal or assistant principal positions. A typical NASSP Assessment Center lasts two days, with groups of six to twelve assessees participating in a variety of administrative exercises. Most **assessment centers** include two in-basket tests, two leaderless-group exercises, a fact-finding exercise, and a personal interview. A panel of NAASP-trained assessors assess candidates individually on a number of dimensions, using a standardized scale. Later by consensus, a profile of each candidate is devised.

Assessment centers are valid predictors of administrative success, and some business firms now use them for hiring technical workers. Assessment centers are also used to help design training and development programs for the purpose of improving the leadership skills of pre-service principals and in-service principals.[31]

[29]*EEO Policies and Programs*, rev. ed. (Washington, D.C.: BNA Books, 1990).

[30]Paul W. Hersey, *How NASSP Helps Identify, Develop Superior Principals* (Reston, VA: National Association of Secondary School Principals, 1987).

[31]Paul W. Hersey and Donald E. Beers, *Springfield: Skill Development for School Leaders* (Reston, VA: National Association of Secondary School Principals, 1989); Hersey and Beers, *Leaders 123: A Program to Improve Instructional Leadership Skills* (Reston, VA: National Association of Secondary School Principals, 1989).

Some universities use the assessment center to pinpoint areas of strengths and weaknesses on which graduate students can then focus during their doctoral studies in educational administration. For example, the University of Louisville puts each of its doctoral candidates in educational administration through a standardized NASSP Assessment Center during their first semester of study. Faculty and students then work together to develop the latters' skills based on the results of their assessment profile.

Hiring Decision

The final step in the selection process is the hiring decision. The person who has successfully passed through the steps in the process is offered employment. The offer may be subject to the successful completion of a physical examination.

There is no perfect selection procedure. As Figure 15-5 indicates, each step in the selection process can have a potentially adverse effect on one or more protected minorities. Discriminatory practices in the past were the catalyst for much of the recent legislation prohibiting discrimination against minority groups. Most school organizations make an effort not to discriminate in their hiring practices.

TRAINING AND DEVELOPMENT

After recruiting and selecting new personnel, the next step is training and development. Some authors distinguish between the two forms of intervention as follows: Training typically refers to teaching lower-level or technical employees how to perform their present jobs; development refers to teaching administrators and professionals the skills needed for both present and future positions.[32] For simplicity sake, both interven-

tions will be referred to as training. That is, school administrators need to help all personnel to fulfill their potential by learning new skills and developing their abilities to the fullest. The three basic steps or phases in any training program are assessment, training, and evaluation.

Assessment of Training Needs

A *needs analysis* should precede the planning and execution of a training program. In a needs analysis, the school administrator or personnel department determines exactly what the staff-training needs are before designing a program to meet them. A needs analysis typically has a threefold focus: *organizational analysis* (analyzing the needs of the entire school district now and in the future), *operational analysis* (analyzing the needs of a specific group of jobs or positions), and *individual analysis* (analyzing the needs of the specific individual).[33] A needs analysis helps specify training objectives, the criteria for training activities, and the criteria against which the programs will be evaluated.

There are several methods of determining which needs to focus on in the training programs. The first method is to evaluate the school district's output variables (see Figure 1-2). Such variables include performance levels and growth levels of students and employees, student-dropout rates, employee turnover, student and employee absenteeism, school–community relations, employee–management relations, student attitudes toward school, employee job satisfaction, and the like. Another method for determining training needs is direct feedback from school district employees regarding what they feel are the organization's development needs. A final method of determining training needs involves projecting. If new programs, procedures, or equipment are predicted, some type of corresponding training will be needed.

---

[32]Dessler, *Personnel Management*.

[33]Andrew D. Szilagyi, *Management and Performance*, 3rd ed. (Glenview, IL: Scott, Foresman, 1988).

	Blacks	Females	Elderly	Handicapped
Intelligence and Verbal Tests	✓✓	+	✓	?
Work-Sampling Tests	+	NE	NE	NE
Interview	+	✓✓	✓	✓
Educational Requirements	✓✓	+	✓	?
Physical Tests (Height, Weight, etc.)	+	✓✓	?	✓✓

Key:

✓✓ Fairly established evidence of adverse impact
✓   Some evidence of adverse impact
?   No data that bears direct evidence of adverse impact but seem likely depending on type of handicap or type of test
NE No or little evidence to indicate one way or the other
+   Evidence indicates that particular minority group does as well as or even better than majority members

FIGURE 15-5   Adverse Effect of Selection Devices on Minorities
(SOURCE: Adapted from Richard D. Arvey and Robert H. Faley, *Fairness in Selecting Employees*, 2nd ed., © 1988. Used by permission of Addison-Wesley Publishing Co., Reading, MA.)

Training Techniques

Numerous techniques used for training and development are available. Table 15-3 presents the most common training and development techniques. The key is to match the technique with the objectives of the training and development program. For example, if the objective is for employees to learn school district policies and procedures, assigned readings, lecture, and programmed learning might be an effective approach. If the objective is developing better human relations, group decision making, or communications, case discussion, conference, role playing, and sensitivity training might work well. If the objective is to teach a skill, behavior modeling, on-the-job training, and vestibule training might be the most appropriate techniques. Other considerations in selecting a staff

development technique include cost, time constraints, number of employees, type of employee (maintenance, clerical, professional, or administrative), and who will do the training.

Evaluating the Training Program

Evaluating the effectiveness of a training program is the final phase of a training and development effort. Evaluation generally occurs during four stages: before training and development begins, during training and development, immediately after the training and development experience, and after a length of time on the job.[34]

_____

[34]Ibid.

TABLE 15 ▪ 3   Common Training and Development Techniques

METHODS	COMMENTS
Assigned readings	Readings may or may not be specially prepared for training purposes.
Behavior modeling	Use of a videotaped model displaying the correct behavior, then trainee role playing and discussion of the correct behavior. Used extensively for supervisor training in human relations.
Simulation	Both paper simulations (such as in-basket exercises) and computer-based games teach management skills.
Case discussion	Small-group discussion of real or fictitious cases or incidents.
Conference	Small-group discussion of selected topics, usually with the trainer as leader.
Lecture	Oral presentation by the trainer, with limited audience participation.
On the job	Ranges from no instruction, to casual coaching by more experienced employees, to carefully structured explanation, demonstration, and supervised practice by a qualified trainer.
Programmed instruction	Self-paced method using text followed by questions and answers; expensive to develop.
Role playing	Trainees act out roles with other trainees, such as "boss giving performance appraisal" and "subordinate reacting to appraisal" to gain experience in human relations.
Sensitivity training	Called T-group and laboratory training, this is an intensive experience in a small group; individuals try new behaviors and give feedback; promotes trust, open communication, and understanding of group dynamics.
Vestibule training	Supervised practice on manual tasks in a separate work area with emphasis on safety, learning, and feedback.

SOURCE: Adapted from Ricky W. Griffin, *Management,* 3rd ed., p. 363. Copyright © 1990 by Houghton Mifflin Company. Used by permission.

Ideally, the best method to use in evaluating the effectiveness of training is the controlled experiment. In a controlled experiment, one or more groups that receive training (experimental groups) and a group that does not receive training (control group) are used. Secure relevant data [e.g., some output variable(s)] before and after the training in both the experimental group(s) and the control group. Then make a comparison of the performance of the groups to determine to what extent any change in the relevant variable(s) occurred as a result of training.

One study, which used a quasi-experimental design, found no change in principals' leadership effectiveness before and immediately following situational leadership training but did discover a change in their effectiveness three years after training.[35]

---

[35]Salvatore V. Pascarella and Fred C. Lunenburg, "A Field Test of Hersey and Blanchard's Situational Leadership Theory in a School Setting," *College Student Journal,* 21 (1988), pp. 33–37.

PERFORMANCE APPRAISAL

Once employees are trained and in place in their jobs, school administrators usually begin to appraise their performance. There are many reasons to appraise how well employees are performing. First, the school district needs a check on the effectiveness of its personnel-selection procedures, by comparing scores on various selection devices used with later performance on the job. Second, administrators use the evaluations to make decisions about compensation, promotions, transfers, and sometimes demotions or terminations. Third, performance appraisals show the school district where training-and-development programs are needed and later gauge whether these have been effective. Finally, if employees are to perform their jobs better in the future, they need to know how well they have performed them in the past. School administrators also use feedback about employees' performance to recognize them for a job well done and to motivate them.[36]

Don't let teacher performance appraisal become an empty ritual. According to a survey of forty-two school systems in eastern Pennsylvania, two researchers found that the vast majority of teachers earned top ratings. Was this the evolution of a new excellence in teaching, or were there other ways of interpreting the data? (See Administrative Advice 15-3.)

Performance-Appraisal Methods

Organizations currently use several methods to appraise performance. For the sake of simplicity, we can group them into three categories: the judgmental approach, the absolute-standards approach, and the results-oriented approach.

Judgmental Approach Under this approach, a school administrator or performance appraiser is asked to compare an employee with other employees and rate the person on a number of traits or behavioral dimensions. These appraisal systems are based on the exercise of judgment by the superior. Four widely used judgmental approaches are graphic rating scales, ranking, paired comparison, and forced distribution.[37]

Graphic Rating Scales. A popular, simple technique for evaluating employees is to use a **graphic rating scale.** Table 15-4 shows a typical rating scale for a school administrator. Note that the scale lists a number of important work dimensions (such as leadership and management) and a performance range for each one. For each work dimension, the evaluator circles the numerical value that best describes the employee's performance. A 5-point evaluation scheme is typically used to assess the important work dimensions: (1) unacceptable, (2) needs improvement, (3) acceptable, (4) commendable, and (5) outstanding. The assigned values for each dimension are then added up and totaled.

Ranking. An alternative method to graphic rating scales involves having administrators rank their subordinates in order of their performance effectiveness from best to worst. The usual procedure requires the rater to write the name of the best subordinate on the top of a list, then the name of the worst at the bottom and continue this sequential procedure until all subordinates are listed. **Ranking** is most frequently used for making personnel decisions such as promotions or the merit salary increase each employee will receive.

Paired Comparison. A modification of the ranking procedure is the **paired-comparison** technique. The method overcomes the problem associated with differentiating between subordinates in the middle range of the distribution, that is, the average employees. Under paired compar-

---

[36]Allan M. Mohrman et al., *Designing Performance Appraisal Systems: Aligning Appraisals and Organizational Realities* (San Francisco: Jossey-Bass, 1989).

[37]John Ivancevich and William F. Glueck, *Foundations of Personnel–Human Resource Management*, 4th ed. (Homewood, IL: Irwin, 1989).

ADMINISTRATIVE ADVICE 15-3

■

SUGGESTIONS FOR IMPROVING PERFORMANCE APPRAISALS

School administrators often fail to effectively observe and evaluate the teachers they do evaluate. The result: Performance appraisal becomes an empty ritual. Are any of these well-known characteristics involved in teacher performance appraisal in your schools?

■ The principal who, after counting up the number of observations yet to complete, goes on an annual "observation blitz" in May
■ The usually somnolent teacher who, when being observed, wakes up enough to put on a live performance
■ The rookie administrator who doesn't know (but is about to learn) that he is supposed to accept or ignore the marginal members of the faculty's "Old Guard"
■ Panicky teachers' union leaders who go into orbit at the idea of more classroom observations
■ Building principals who lobby in September to set "humane" (low) evaluation standards
■ Favorite principal ploys:
  1. *The Double Play.* The principal sits in the back corner of the classroom, one eye on the teacher's performance and the other on some budget requisitions
  2. *The Passing Stranger.* The harried principal spends a few minutes in a class and then— with a whispered and placating, "You certainly know what you're doing"—disappears.
  3. *The Shrinking Violet.* The principal meekly makes some tentative suggestions for improvement during a postobservation confer-

ence but quickly retreats when greeted with a barrage of excuses ranging from illness to poor teaching conditions and unsympathetic bosses.

Here are four suggestions for improving the process:

■ Institute a team approach to performance appraisal, including department heads, assistant principals, and central office administrators— not just principals.
■ Put teacher performance appraisal at the top of a principal's many responsibilities.
■ Free up time for principals to spend in teacher evaluations by conducting tighter meetings, screening work before passing it on to them, and doing business by telephone.
■ Train principals how to observe, take notes, and analyze teaching and how to present the results in a tactful but useful way to teachers.

Source: Adapted from Donald E. Langois and Mary Rita Colarusso, "Don't Let Teacher Evaluation Become an Empty Ritual," *Executive Educator*, 10 (1989), pp. 32–33. Copyright 1989, the National School Boards Association. Used by permission.

---

isons, raters compare only two subordinates at a time until all two-way comparisons have been made among all employees. After rating all pairs, the administrator can put the subordinates into a rank order by counting up the number of times each employee has been judged superior.

Forced Distribution. "Grading on a curve" is a good example of the **forced-distribution** meth-

od of performance appraisal. With this technique, the rater places a predetermined percentage of ratees into four or five performance categories. For example, if a 5-point scale is used, the school administrator might decide to distribute employees as follows: 5 percent in the "unacceptable category," 25 percent in the "needs improvement category," 40 percent in the "acceptable category," 25 percent in the

TABLE 15 ▪ 4   Abbreviated Graphic Rating Scale for School Administrators

WORK DIMENSION	RATING				
	Unacceptable	Needs Improvement	Acceptable	Commendable	Outstanding
Leadership	1	2	③	4	5
Management	1	2	3	4	⑤
Personnel administration	1	2	③	4	5
Administrative teaming	1	②	3	4	5
Budgeting	1	2	③	4	5
TOTAL: 16					

SOURCE: Fred C. Lunenburg, "One Method of Determining Administrative Salaries," *New York State School Board Association Journal*, January (1986), p. 20. Used by permission.

"commendable category," and 5 percent in the "outstanding category." The usual procedure for accomplishing such a distribution is to record each employee's name on a separate index card. Then, for each dimension being appraised (leadership, management, etc.), place the employee's index card in one of the five categories.

Absolute-Standards Approach Most appraisal measures that employ an absolute-standards approach are based on job analysis. As discussed earlier, this type of analysis can provide a more detailed description of the actual behavior necessary for effective performance. School adminstrators compare the performance of each employee to a certain standard instead of the performance of other employees; thus, they rate the degree to which performance meets the standard. The most common performance-appraisal processes in this group are checklists, essays, critical incidents, and behaviorally anchored rating scales.[38]

---

[38]Leap and Crino, *Personnel/Human Resource Management*.

Checklists. The most common technique in the absolute-standards group is some sort of **checklist.** Checklists tend to be more behaviorally based than either graphic rating scales or other employee-comparison methods. Table 15-5 presents a somewhat humorous example of a checklist that might be used to appraise school administrators' performance. More elaborate procedures such as weighted and forced-choice checklists are also available. Specific weights are assigned to a list of work behaviors in the *weighted checklist*. A *forced-choice checklist* consists of job-behavior statements with two to five response items in each set that correlate with high- and low-performing employees. The end result is a single numerical rating that is useful for personnel decisions such as salary, promotion, and the like.

Essays. The **essay** method requires the rater to describe in writing each employee's strengths and weaknesses, along with suggestions for ways to improve performance. Some school districts require every rater to respond to specific open-ended essay-type questions, whereas others allow considerably more flexibility. Com-

TABLE 15 ▪ 5　A Guide to Appraising School Administrators' Performance

PERFORMANCE FACTOR	OUTSTANDING	HIGH SATISFACTORY	SATISFACTORY	LOW SATISFACTORY	UNSATISFACTORY
Quality	Leaps tall buildings with a single bound	Needs running start to jump tall buildings	Can only leap small buildings	Crashes into buildings	Cannot recognize buildings
Timeliness	Is faster than a speeding bullet	Only as fast as a speeding bullet	Somewhat slower than a bullet	Can only shoot bullets	Wounds self with bullets
Initiative	Is stronger than a locomotive	Is stronger than a bull elephant	Is stronger than a bull	Shoots the bull	Smells like a bull
Adaptability	Walks on water consistently	Walks on water in emergencies	Washes with water	Drinks water	Passes water in emergencies
Communication	Talks with God	Talks with angels	Talks to himself	Argues with himself	Loses those arguments
Relationship	Belongs in general management	Belongs in executive ranks	Belongs in rank and file	Belongs behind a broom	Belongs with competitor
Planning	Too bright to worry	Worries about future	Worries about present	Worries about past	Too dumb to worry

SOURCE: Anonymous.

pared to employee-comparison methods, the essay method is time-consuming and difficult to quantify. Variations in the writing skills of raters is another limitation. Some school districts have combined the graphic and essay methods by providing space for comments on the graphic rating scale.

Critical Incidents. The **critical-incidents** technique begins by identifying job requirements for successful performance. Job requirements are those behaviors that determine whether the job is being done effectively or ineffectively. The school administrator keeps a log, for each subordinate, of both effective and ineffective "incidents" of on-the-job behaviors. The incidents are then analyzed and refined into a composite picture of the required essentials in a particular job. From this a checklist is developed, which constitutes the framework against which the

subordinate is evaluated. During the evaluation conference, the administrator can refer to the critical incidents to correct work deficiencies, identify training needs, or praise successful performance.

Behaviorally Anchored Rating Scales. A newer and somewhat related approach to the critical-incident technique is the **behaviorally anchored rating scale** (BARS). It was developed to cope with the problem of identifying scale anchor points. Specifically, the scale points such as unacceptable, needs improvement, acceptable, commendable, and outstanding (as shown in Table 15-4) may be difficult to define and may lead to unreliable or invalid appraisal results. Hence, the BARS defines scale points with specific behavior statements that describe varying degrees of performance. The form for a BARS generally covers six to eight specifically defined perfor-

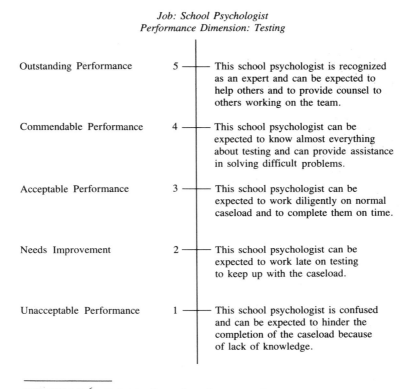

Job: School Psychologist
Performance Dimension: Testing

Outstanding Performance	5	This school psychologist is recognized as an expert and can be expected to help others and to provide counsel to others working on the team.
Commendable Performance	4	This school psychologist can be expected to know almost everything about testing and can provide assistance in solving difficult problems.
Acceptable Performance	3	This school psychologist can be expected to work diligently on normal caseload and to complete them on time.
Needs Improvement	2	This school psychologist can be expected to work late on testing to keep up with the caseload.
Unacceptable Performance	1	This school psychologist is confused and can be expected to hinder the completion of the caseload because of lack of knowledge.

FIGURE 15-6   Behaviorally Anchored Rating Scale

mance dimensions. A BARS should be developed for each dimension.

Figure 15-6 shows an example of a BARS for the testing competence-performance dimension for school psychologists. The scale anchors define the particular response categories for the evaluator. The response made by the evaluator is specific enough to be used as feedback in an appraisal interview with the school psychologists and is meaningful to the subordinate. For example, if the school psychologist were given a 3 on this dimension, the subordinate would be given the specific performance indicators that led to the evaluator's rating.

Results-Oriented Approaches   In recent years, results-oriented approaches to performance appraisal have been suggested as an alternative to

the judgmental and absolute-standards approaches. As the name implies, the emphasis of results-oriented approaches is on the evaluation of results—both quantitative and qualitative. Put another way, the focus is on what the subordinate is supposed to accomplish on the job rather than a consideration of the subordinate's traits or on-the-job behaviors.

Management by Objectives. One popular results-oriented approach is management by objectives (MBO). We discussed MBO in Chapter 4 as an application of goal-setting theory[39] and, more specifically, as a motivational technique. MBO

[39]Edwin E. Locke and Gary P. Latham, *A Theory of Goal Setting and Task Performance*, (Englewood Cliffs, NJ: Prentice-Hall, 1989).

can also serve as the foundation for a school district's performance-appraisal system. It is particularly well suited to high-level administrative positions for which methods such as BARS may be inappropriate.

Briefly, this program typically includes two major elements. First, at some point in the appraisal process, the supervisor and the subordinate meet to discuss goals, which are established by the supervisor alone or jointly by the supervisor and the subordinate. Second, the supervisor and the subordinate meet to appraise the subordinate's performance in relation to the previously established goals. For example, suppose a high school principal sets a goal of increasing average daily attendance (ADA) in her building next year by 15 percent. At the end of the school year, this goal provides a framework for performance appraisal. If attendance has increased by 15 percent or more, a positive performance appraisal is likely. However, if ADA has increased by only 5 percent and if the principal is directly responsible for the results, a more negative evaluation may be in order. Then suggestions for improvement can be specified.

Other Results-Oriented Measures. Besides MBO, school administrators can use a variety of other results-oriented measures to assess subordinate performance. Some suggestions include measures of quantity of output, such as number of articles published, words typed, or items produced; measures of quality, such as reputation of the journal, typographical errors, or items rejected; measures of lost time, such as absenteeism or tardiness; or measures involving education, training, or experience, such as time in the field or time in a particular position. Although these measures tend to be nonjudgmental, they measure only one dimension of job performance. Such measures can also be tied to an MBO program.

Rating Errors

In conducting performance appraisals, school administrators must be careful to avoid making rating errors. Four of the more common rating errors are strictness or leniency, central tendency, halo effect, and recency of events.[40]

Strictness or Leniency   Some supervisors tend to rate all their subordinates consistently low or high. These are referred to as **strictness** or **leniency errors.** The strict rater gives ratings lower than the subordinate deserves. This strictness error penalizes superior subordinates. The lenient rater tends to give higher ratings than the subordinate deserves. Just as the strictness error punishes exceptional subordinates, so does the leniency error. Strictness–leniency bias presents less of a problem when absolute standards and results-oriented approaches to performance appraisal are used.

Central Tendency   Some raters are reluctant to rate subordinates as very high or very low. They dislike being too strict with anyone by giving them an extremely low rating, and they may believe that no one ever deserves to get the highest possible rating. The result of this type of attitude is that everyone is rated around average. Figure 15-7 depicts examples of strictness, leniency, and **central-tendency** biases. The distribution of ratings on the left of the figure indicates a strictness error; those in the middle indicate a central-tendency error; and the cluster on the right indicates a leniency error.

Halo Effect   When a single positive or negative dimension of a subordinate's performance is allowed to influence the supervisor's rating of that subordinate on other dimensions, a **halo effect** is operating. For example, the supervisor likes Tom because he is so cooperative. The halo effect leads Tom's supervisor to automatically rate him high on all appraisal dimensions, including leadership, management, personnel administration, administrative teaming, and even budgeting. The result is that subordinates are rated

---

[40]Joe Baker, *Causes of Failure in Performance Appraisal and Supervision: A Guide to Analysis and Evaluation for Human Resources Professionals* (Westport, CT: Greenwood, 1988).

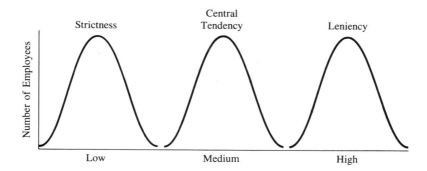

FIGURE 15-7   Strictness, Central-Tendency, and Leniency Performance Ratings

consistently high, medium, or low on all performance-appraisal dimensions.

Recency of Events   Ideally, performance appraisals should be based on data collected about a subordinate's performance over an entire evaluation period (usually six months to a year). However, as is often the case, the supervisor is likely to consider recent performance more strongly than performance behaviors that occurred earlier. This is called the **recency-of-events error.** Failure to include all performance behaviors in the performance appraisal of a subordinate can bias the ratings.

Strictness or leniency, central tendency, halo effect, and recency of events are all errors that result in inaccurate performance appraisals of employees. The absolute-standards and results-oriented approaches to performance appraisal, particularly BARS and MBO, attempt to minimize such rating errors.

COMPENSATION

The compensation of employees is another important component of the personnel process.[41] A sound compensation program can help organizations attract qualified applicants, retain desir-

able employees, and motivate and reward high employee performance. The formal compensation system takes the form of wages and salaries and fringe benefits.

Wages and Salaries

Because wages and salaries affect every member of the organization, it is one of the most important parts of a compensation program. A successful compensation program involves three major decisions: wage-level decisions, wage-structure decisions, and individual-wage decisions.

Wage-Level Decisions   To develop an equitable compensation program, personnel administrators determine wage and salary levels that are comparable for the industry and geographic area. "Wage leaders" are those organizations that pay employees more than the average paid for similar jobs in the industry and geographic area. One example of a wage leader is the Rochester (New York) Public Schools, known as the Rochester Experiment, which pays its teachers among the highest salaries in the nation—some at $70,000 a year.[42]

[41]Charles Fay and Richard Beatty, *The Compensation Sourcebook* (Amherst, MA: Human Resource Development Press, 1988).

[42]Jerry Buckley, "The Rochester Experiment: A Blueprint for Better Schools," *U.S. News and World Report*, 104, 2 (1988), pp. 60–65; Buckley, "The Rochester Experiment: School Reform, School Reality," *U.S. News and World Report*, 104, 24 (1988), pp. 58–63.

"Wage followers" pay less than the average for the industry and area. Most organizations make an effort to pay what the competition is paying. A **wage survey** can be used to determine what other organizations pay employees. Then personnel administrators can adjust wage levels to meet or exceed the comparable rates.

The salaries that a school district pays its certified employees vary by geographic area. Table 15-6 shows the survey information for 12 school district jobs in eight geographic regions. For example, school districts in the Far West paid the highest average salaries for all the jobs surveyed, ranging from $83,529 for superintendents and $62,440 for high school principals to $35,310 for teachers and $38,975 for school librarians according to a national survey of salaries in public schools conducted by the Educational Research Service.

In addition, there is published information on nonsupervisory jobs on which school organizations can draw. The Bureau of Labor Statistics has conducted a number of surveys covering various blue-collar and white-collar jobs in different regions of the country. Many professional associations also conduct surveys focused on specific jobs. For example, the National Association of Elementary School Principals (NAESP), National Association of Secondary School Principals (NASSP), American Association of School Administrators (AASA), and Association for School Business Officials (ASBO) survey wage levels, respectively, for elementary, middle, and high school principals, school superintendents, and school business officials. The American Association of University Professors (AAUP) annually surveys wage levels for college and university professors.

Wage-Structure Decisions   Whereas wage level involves the comparison of wages and salaries paid in comparable organizations, wage structure describes the relative worth of particular jobs within the organization. To determine what jobs are worth, many organizations use a technique called **job evaluation.** The basic information necessary for a job evaluation is obtained during job analyses, discussed earlier. The results of job analyses describing such items as responsibilities, education, skill requirements, and physical requirements of the job are used to evaluate the job. The higher the evaluation, the higher the wages or salaries associated with the job.

The four principal systems of job evaluation are job ranking, the classification system, the point system, and the factor-comparison method.[43]

Job Ranking.   **Job ranking** is the simplest form of job evaluation. Responsibilities and other characteristics associated with each job are examined, and the jobs are ranked from the most demanding to least demanding. To facilitate this ranking, benchmark jobs are selected, and others are inserted between them. For example, the most highly skilled nonsupervisory job in a school district is a computer programmer, and the lowest is that of maintenance worker. In between are numerous gradations of jobs. When a few of these nonsupervisory jobs are analyzed and placed on the scale, the remaining jobs can be ranked by comparing them with those already on the scale.

Classification System.   A **classification system** places jobs and salaries in levels. The U.S. Civil Service has eighteen classification levels (L1 through L18) that are used to determine salary ranges for its employees. These classification levels are assigned to jobs from most to least difficult and important. For example, school organizations typically have classification levels for clerical employees: Receptionists may be classified as level 1 (L1), secretaries L2, private secretaries L3, and office managers L4, and the like. If such a job evaluation is districtwide, it ensures that there is some internal equity in the ranking of jobs based on hierarchical positions.

Point System.   One of the most widely used methods of job evaluation used today is the **point**

---

[43]Ernest Dale, *Management: Theory and Practice*, 4th ed. (New York: McGraw-Hill, 1978).

TABLE 15 ▪ 6   Average School Salaries By Region, 1989–1990

POSITION	NEW ENGLAND	MIDEAST	SOUTHEAST	GREAT LAKES	PLAINS	SOUTHWEST	ROCKY MTS.	FAR WEST	ALL REGIONS
Superintendents (contract salary)	$69,337	$78,516	$75,043	$72,448	$69,888	$79,603	$64,905	$83,529	$75,425
Deputy/assoc. supts.	72,191	73,358	65,856	72,032	64,730	65,531	61,849	77,071	69,623
Assistant superintendents	60,981	66,222	57,319	62,951	59,477	60,815	56,847	69,872	62,698
Directors, managers, coordinators, and supervisors for:									
Finance and business	50,398	54,393	47,346	53,512	49,771	49,236	48,336	58,866	52,354
Instructional services	52,780	58,907	51,053	58,678	51,376	52,529	50,873	63,410	56,359
Public relations/ information	48,565	45,465	42,780	47,613	41,171	43,089	40,641	50,874	44,926
Staff personnel services	56,019	58,486	52,011	60,682	54,230	51,836	51,773	61,178	56,344
Other areas*	48,430	50,066	45,849	48,953	44,078	44,302	43,168	53,589	47,890
Subject area supervisors	46,716	51,834	42,822	48,191	42,027	40,895	41,340	49,910	45,929
Other administrative staff†	43,047	39,556	37,131	41,385	37,309	35,580	35,000	43,734	39,428
Principals									
Elementary	50,307	53,099	44,397	48,224	44,522	44,677	43,395	54,813	48,431
Jr. high/ middle	53,936	57,317	47,793	52,855	49,416	48,886	45,717	57,775	52,163
Sr. high	56,864	59,638	51,759	56,250	52,978	52,079	49,071	62,440	55,722
Assistant principals									
Elementary	44,301	46,467	36,570	43,029	38,976	35,974	39,665	47,014	40,916
Jr. high/ middle	48,850	50,224	39,007	45,879	42,393	38,365	40,813	49,312	44,570
Sr. high	48,285	50,529	40,647	48,001	43,825	41,440	42,201	53,401	46,486
Classroom teachers	33,964	34,689	26,883	33,425	27,874	26,355	27,542	35,310	31,278
Counselors	37,156	38,662	31,558	38,184	32,561	33,000	31,836	40,847	35,979
Librarians	34,330	35,593	29,730	36,029	29,823	30,099	29,307	38,975	33,469
School nurses	22,293	29,204	20,825	27,144	20,962	23,412	23,520	33,870	26,090

SOURCE: Educational Research Service, © 1990. Used by permission.
*Includes pupil personnel, research, food services, health, transportation, federal programs, media services, plant operations, etc.
†Includes all central office administrative and professional staff not specified above.

system. Under the point system, various factors are designated—for example, mental requirements, skill requirements, physical requirements, responsibilities, and supervision—and the maximum number of points allowable for each is determined. A computer programmer will then receive the maximum number of points for mental requirements, and other jobs proportionately less according to the amount of mental requirements they require. Wage rates are then linked to the number of points assigned to the job.

Factor-Comparison Method. As with the point system, the **factor-comparison method** also makes use of job factors. However, the factor-comparison method creates a key scale for measuring jobs. This is the basic difference between it and the point system. Typically, twenty or thirty jobs in the organization are analyzed to form the key comparison scale. Each job is ranked by each factor in turn, and the portion of the total salary paid for this factor is determined. This in turn determines the weight to be given to each factor in arriving at a final ranking. Table 15-7 presents the factors used in a hypothetical school district's job-evaluation system and the percentage of total wages that determines each one.

The major advantage of the factor-comparison method over the point system is that higher-level jobs can be added to an original system. The point system, for example, requires developing separate systems to handle maintenance, professional, and administrative tasks, whereas the factor-comparison method can take care of each of these levels within a single system.

Individual-Wage Decisions

Once wage ranges are developed for jobs, how does an administrator determine what to pay an employee? The easiest decision is to pay a single rate for each wage classification. More typically, decisions about individual wages generally are based on a combination of factors. Employees are paid according to qualification level, that is, their prior work experience and their skill level. For example, a

TABLE 15-7   Key Comparison Scale

FACTOR	PERCENTAGE
Mental requirements	20
Skill requirements	30
Physical requirements	5
Responsibilities	20
Supervision requirements	25
TOTAL:	100

secretary (L2) with five years of experience is likely to earn more than a beginner, due to superior skill development. Employees are also paid based on **seniority,** that is, the length of time they have worked for an organization or in their current job. For instance, most school districts use a lock-step salary schedule for determining pay increases for teachers based solely on job seniority. Finally, employees may be paid for their performance on the job, that is, their **merit.**

Benefits

Wages and salaries make up the major part of an organization's compensation package. Equally important are the benefits paid to employees. A recent survey reveals that benefits comprise nearly 40 percent of the cash compensation paid to employees, and in some industries, employee benefits represent two-thirds of its payroll costs.[44] Some of these benefits are legally required. For example, the Social Security Act requires retirement pay, disability pay, and survivor's benefits. Unemployment compensation, also required by the act, provides subsistence payments to employees who have been laid off. All states have workers' compensation laws, which provide for those who suffer job-related illnesses and injuries. Other voluntary benefits

---

[44]U.S. Chamber of Commerce, *Employee Benefits 1990* (Washington, D.C.: U.S. Chamber of Commerce, 1991).

include health and dental insurance, life insurance, retirement benefits, paid vacations and holidays, sick-leave pay, credit unions, recreational programs, and payment for graduate courses completed.

UNION–MANAGEMENT RELATIONS

A **union** is an organization of employees formed for the purpose of influencing an employer's decisions concerning conditions of employment. **Union–management relations** is the ongoing relationship between a group of employees represented by a union and management in the employing organization. The basis for any union–management relationship is **collective bargaining,** the process of negotiating and administering a collective bargaining agreement or negotiated contract between a union and the employing organization. Collective bargaining agreements specify the rights and duties of employees and management with respect to wages, hours, working conditions, and other terms of employment. They constitute a major influence on the day-to-day operation of a school as well as the long-term administrative activities of the school district.[45]

Union Membership

The labor union movement in the United States began in response to undesirable management practices in industry. It has spread to include employees in the public sector, such as teachers and government workers. Teachers represent the largest group of employees in an educational institution. Today, all but nine states have enacted statutes specifically establishing some rights of employees in public schools to bargain collectively with boards of education. Over 80 percent of the nation's teachers belong to either the National Education Association (NEA), which has over 1.5 million members, or the American Federation of Teachers (AFT), which has about .5 million members.[46]

Collective Bargaining

Collective bargaining is the process of negotiating between management and employees on the terms and conditions of employment. It is collective in the sense that the employees, as a unit, select representatives from its membership to meet with management to discuss issues that need to be resolved. The union bargains on items that represent the concerns of its membership. Management tries to advance the interests of the organization.

Bargaining Issues Collect bargaining agreements are complex and often lengthy, written contracts that are legally binding on both management and the union(s) representing its employees. A recent agreement between the Jefferson County (Kentucky) Board of Education and the Jefferson County Teachers' Association is over sixty pages long.[47] It is more streamlined than most. Although the specific provisions of collective bargaining agreements vary from one school district to another, the collective bargaining process and negotiated agreement generally address the following issues.[48] (Because teachers make up the largest group of employees in schools, we will limit our discussion to teachers' collective bargaining agreements. It should be noted, however, that school administrators collectively bargain with other employee unions as well.)

---

[45]John R. Schermerhorn and James G. Hunt, *Management for Productivity* (New York: Wiley, 1989).

[46]U.S. Department of Labor, Bureau of Labor Statistics, *Employment and Earnings* (Washington, DC: Government Printing Office, 1990).

[47]Jefferson County Board of Education, *JCBE–JCTE Agreement, 1988–1992* (Louisville, KY: Jefferson County Board of Education, 1988).

[48]Peggy Odell Gonder, *Collective Bargaining* (Arlington, VA: American Association of School Administrators, 1981).

Management Rights. During collective bargaining, unions strive to increase wages, protect job security, and improve the work conditions of employees. On the other hand, management tries to protect and clarify its rights as employer. Any rights not given to the union in the collective agreement are assumed to belong to management. These are called **management rights.** A strong management rights clause in the contract reinforces statutory rights of the board of education and aids in limiting the authority of an arbitrator in the grievance process. A common management rights clause is a lengthy list of specific management prerogatives, such as the right to supervise all operations; control all property and equipment; determine the size of the work force; assign work to be done; introduce new methods, programs, or procedures; hire and fire employees; promote, demote, and transfer employees; and in general maintain an orderly, effective, and efficient operation.

Narrow-Grievance Definition. A grievance procedure is a formal system by which contract disputes are expressed, processed, and judged. The definition of a grievance in a written collective bargaining agreement determines which employee complaints are subject to binding grievance arbitration. A **narrow-grievance definition** that limits employee complaints to the specific written agreement is recommended. Such an approach does not preclude other complaint procedures. It does limit what a grievance arbitrator can decide during the written terms of the negotiated agreement in force.

No-Strike Provision. Federal law prohibits strikes by teachers. Most states have passed similar laws. Because teacher strikes occur despite the laws against them, additional protection can be gained through a **no-strike provision** in the collective bargaining agreement. Such a provision puts the union on record against strikes and involves the union in the enforcement of the laws prohibiting them. In addition, a no-strike provision usually permits management to impose monetary damages on teachers who engage in an illegal strike.

Zipper Clause. A **zipper clause,** or waiver provision, stipulates that the written agreement is the complete and full contract between the parties and that neither party is required to bargain on other items during the term of the agreement. The purpose of such a provision is to avoid continuing negotiations after the contract has been ratified; when coupled with a strong management rights clause, it limits the role of past practice used by grievance arbitrators.

Such a provision, however, does not preclude the parties from negotiating further if both agree. New bargaining strategies, including collaborative or win–win bargaining would be an exception to the use of a zipper clause. The idea of collaborative bargaining is that union and management negotiate continually during the year as problems arise.

Maintenance of Standards. Management should avoid a **maintenance-of-standards** provision. Such a provision is routinely included in most union proposals and incorporates the school district's current practices on a wide range of items, many of which are not mandatory subjects of bargaining. Furthermore, a maintenance-of-standards provision leaves the district vulnerable to the role of past practice used by grievance arbitrators in settling contract disputes. It is the antithesis of a management rights provision and a zipper clause.

An example of a maintenance-of-standards provision is the following:

> All conditions of employment, including teaching hours, extra compensation for work outside regular teaching hours, relief periods, leaves and general working conditions shall be maintained at not less than the highest minimum standards, provided that such conditions shall be improved for the benefit of teachers, as required by the express provisions of this agreement. The agreement shall not be interpreted or applied to deprive teachers of professional advantages heretofore enjoyed, unless expressly stated herein.[49]

Management should avoid such a provision.

---

[49]Ibid., p. 22.

Just Cause. The term **just cause** is found in numerous collective bargaining agreements in public education and is routinely included in most union proposals. There is a danger in using such a term, from management's standpoint, because *just cause* has no clear definition. If a collective bargaining agreement has binding arbitration as the last step in the grievance procedure, then an arbitrator will decide what the term means. The arbitrator's interpretation of the term may be different from what management had intended. For example, suppose a collective bargaining agreement contained the following provision: "No teacher will be disciplined without *just cause*." What does *just cause* mean in this case? It will likely mean something different to management than to employees. The point is that the meaning of *just cause* must be spelled out clearly somewhere in the contract or eliminated entirely.

Reduction in Force. Most all collective bargaining agreements have some form of **reduction-in-force** (RIF) provision. Seniority, or length of continuous service within a certificated field, is the key factor used in employee layoff and recall. Some agreements allow for **bumping,** which means that teachers laid off in one certificated field may replace another teacher in another certificated area who has less seniority in that field than the bumping teacher. A few RIF provisions stress other factors such as affirmative action and teacher merit. Such provisions are more favorable to management but are opposed by most teachers' unions.

Wages and Benefits. Much time at the bargaining table is devoted to wage increases and fringe-benefit improvements. Wage and salary increases are often stated as across-the-board salary increases for steps on a lock-step salary schedule and **cost-of-living adjustments** (COLA) based on the Consumer Price Index in a designated geographic area. Besides salary increases, unions often demand improvements in various fringe benefits such as insurance programs (life, health, and dental); pension plans; merit pay; and sick leave, personal days, and paid religious holidays. Compensation costs in today's school districts often range from 75 to 85 percent of the total budget.

Other Issues. Among other important bargaining issues are grievance arbitration, teacher evaluation, class size, school calendar, and the like. Binding grievance arbitration is not a problem providing the rest of the agreement protects management prerogatives. Likewise, teacher evaluation, class size, and school calendar should not be overly restrictive on the school district.

The Bargaining Process To bargain these issues, management and the union each selects a negotiating team. Opinions vary widely on who should conduct management negotiations. In small school districts, the superintendent or a board member often conducts negotiations with the teachers' union. Experts advise against this practice, however.[50] In large districts, a full-time administrator (director of employee relations, assistant superintendent, or director of personnel) usually serves as chief negotiator. Still other districts employ an outside negotiator—an attorney or labor relations specialist.

One of a superintendent's basic personnel decisions concerning collective bargaining is whether to have a labor relations specialist at the bargaining table to advise the school district or perhaps even represent the district during negotiations. When hiring a labor relations specialist, the superintendent must decide how much authority to give him or her. (See Administrative Advice 15-4.)

One or more building administrators often are included on management's negotiating team. These people live with the contract day-to-day; they know its weak and strong points; they will administer the new agreement; and they will likely give the contract greater support if they can participate in the changes made in it. The union team generally consists of the local union

---

[50]Michael Pennella and Stephen Philips, "Help Your Board Negotiate: Stay Off the Bargaining Team," *Executive Educator*, 9 (1987), pp. 28–29.

ADMINISTRATIVE ADVICE 15-4

GUIDELINES FOR USING A LABOR RELATIONS SPECIALIST

If you have selected your labor relations specialist well, you probably have little reason to worry about the outcome. Nevertheless, you can help make the best use of the specialist by using the following techniques.

■ *Set Ground Rules.* To use your labor specialist well, the school board, superintendent, labor specialist, and other members of the bargaining team must agree on what goals and timetables are realistic. Discuss the fiscal and managerial limits on what you might be willing to give up. But do not stifle the specialist with procedural rules. Give your labor specialist room to innovate. Avoid second-guessing him or her as the process unfolds.

■ *Build a Bargaining Team.* The delicate verbal and nonverbal confrontation that bargaining entails places great demands on participants and makes the selection of the bargaining team crucial. A poorly chosen team can handicap the labor specialist and threaten negotiations. Select team members who are compatible with each other.

■ *Monitor the Bargaining Process.* The superintendent should meet periodically with the entire bargaining team to promote harmony and to

hear the views of all team members. In addition, the superintendent should have private discussions with the labor specialist to critique him or her and suggest midcourse corrections in strategy.

■ *Take Advantage of the Labor Specialist "Outsider" Role.* Benefit from the labor specialist's ability to evaluate proposals on the basis of the amount of experience in negotiating numerous contracts. When a new proposal appears at the bargaining table, let the specialist ask questions about it and discuss it with him or her later.

■ *Evaluate Results.* After negotiations are over and the contract is ratified, evaluate the labor specialist. How good was the performance? Did he or she achieve realistic goals? Was the process handled skillfully? Was it too confrontational?

Source: Adapted from Larry Nyland and Robert Schwerdtfeger, "Help Your Hired Gun Shoot Straight," *Executive Educator*, 11 (1989), p. 30. Copyright 1989, the National School Boards Association. Used by permission.

president and other members of the local membership. Its team may also include an attorney or a labor relations specialist from a regional unit who negotiates for other teachers' unions in the region.

Once each side has selected its negotiating teams, the bargaining process begins. The bargaining takes place in face-to-face meetings between management and union representatives during which numerous proposals and counterproposals are exchanged. Several rounds of negotiations may be needed to reach agreement on

all issues. When the two parties agree on the issues, a new negotiated contract is presented to the union membership and the board for a **ratification vote.** If both parties approve the agreement, it goes into effect. If they reject the agreement, each goes back to the bargaining table for another round of negotiations.

An **impasse** is said to exist when both parties are unable to reach agreement on a contract. State procedures vary when the union and the school board are deadlocked in negotiations. Most states have some provision for resolving impasses. Some states, like Wisconsin, have developed a procedure for resolving impasses. The procedure involves the following three steps:

1. *Mediation.* The two contending parties meet with a neutral third person who attempts to persuade them to settle the remaining issues through discussion and by proposing compromise provisions to the contract. The mediator acts as a facilitator, however, and has no legal authority to force the parties to accept the suggestions offered.
2. *Fact Finding.* The state appoints a group or committee to investigate and report the facts that are presented by each party. The fact-finding committee's recommendations are generally made public, which places additional pressure on the parties to come to agreement.
3. *Arbitration.* If the parties are still at an impasse, state law may require the union and the school board to submit to arbitration or binding arbitration. Guidelines for teachers' contracts in Wisconsin, for example, stipulate that arbitrators must choose the proposal of either the school board or the teachers' union, but not a compromise solution. This forces the two contending parties to bring their contract proposals closer together. The result has been a decrease in teacher strikes in Wisconsin.[51]

Bargaining Tactics   Negotiators use a number of tactics to improve their bargaining. Four tactics that are typically used are counterproposals, trade-offs, the caucus, and costing proposals.[52]

Counterproposals. Collective bargaining consists of the exchange of proposals and counterproposals in an effort to reach settlement between the

[51]Randall B. Dunham and Jon L. Pierce, *Management* (Glenview, IL: Scott, Foresman, 1989).
[52]Richard G. Neal, *Bargaining Tactics* (Manassas, VA: Richard Neal Associates, 1982); William G. Weber, *Effective Collective Bargaining in Public Education* (Ames: Iowa State University Press, 1988).

negotiating parties. A proposal is an offer presented by one party in negotiations for consideration by the other party. A **counterproposal,** which is designed to bring the parties closer together on an issue, is an offer suggested as an alternative to the previous proposal by the other party. Because it is the union that is seeking improved conditions of employment, it introduces the majority of proposals. Generally, management responds to the union's demands through counterproposals. Actually, there are at least two advantages to this approach for management: (1) The party that moves first on an issue is usually at a disadvantage, for he invariably reveals some information helpful to the other negotiator; and (2) the union, as the initiating party, is forced to work for every concession it gets.

Trade-offs. Another bargaining tactic is the **trade-off,** which is giving one issue in return for another. For example, the trade-off process works as follows: A teachers' union will make a number of proposals, such as (1) fair share, (2) salary increase, (3) increased sick leave, (4) increased personal days, (5) extra holiday(s), (6) hospitalization, (7) life insurance, (8) dental insurance, (9) maternity leave, (10) binding arbitration of grievances, (11) past-practice provision, (12) reduction-in-force procedures, (13) teacher evaluations, (14) class size, (15) school calendar, and the like. Management then responds by stating that it will grant a 5 percent salary increase if the union withdraws its proposals for increased sick leave and personal days, hospitalization, life insurance, and dental insurance. Further, management will grant the past-practice clause if the union drops its request for binding arbitration of grievances. All proposals are "packaged" in this manner until the teachers' union and the school board reach a settlement. While neither party wants to give up its item, each may perceive the exchange as a reasonable compromise.

Caucus. A basic principle of negotiating is that only one person speaks at the bargaining table—

the chief negotiator. The other members of the bargaining team must remain quiet. Remaining quiet at the bargaining table can be a frustrating demand for the other members of the bargaining team. A **caucus** is a private meeting of a bargaining team to decide what action to take on a particular phase of negotiations. It provides an opportunity to get needed input from other team members and to release built-up tensions that arise during stressful negotiations.

Costing Proposals. All proposals in collective bargaining have direct, hidden, and administrative costs. Management must know the cost of all union proposals. Therefore, **costing proposals** is another important bargaining tactic.

Preparation for this phase of bargaining should be a continual process throughout the school year. Such an approach will avoid errors made in costing proposals hastily during the heat of negotiations. The logical department in a school district to maintain a data bank and generate data for costing proposals is the business office. This office can then provide a database to the board's negotiating team at the beginning of the bargaining process.

The following guidelines for costing proposals are recommended:[53]

1. *Cost Proposals Accurately.* Typically, the union will request copies of all cost data that management prepares. Management can expect distribution of part or all of the data supplied. Therefore, prepare cost data carefully. All calculations must withstand the scrutiny of the public, a mediator, fact-finding committee, or arbitrator.

2. *Cost Proposals Separately.* Cost each union proposal separately. For example, the estimated cost of increasing the number of personal leave days must be costed independently of a proposal for increasing the number of sick days. Each must be based on historical data and cost projections.

3. *Cost Proposals from Management's Viewpoint.* Prepare costings from management's point of view. For example, proposals to reduce services must consider either the cost of replacing those services or the economic loss resulting from not having those services performed. In one school district in a midwestern state, a teachers' collective bargaining agreement stipulated that high school English teachers were required to teach only four classes a day (not exceeding twenty-five students in a class) in order to alleviate the heavy load of correcting daily written assignments. All other high school teachers in the district taught five classes a day. Because there were twenty-four high school English teachers in the district at an average salary of $30,000 a year, this provision in the contract cost the school district $144,000 a year ($6000 × 24).

4. *Cost Proposals as of a Common Date.* Base all costings on data gathered as of a common date. The usual cycle used in school districts is the fiscal year beginning July 1.

5. *Analyze Comparable Data from Neighboring Organizations.* The board's chief negotiator must be able to analyze comparable data from other neighboring school districts. For instance, cost data from neighboring school districts must not be considered in isolation. Public school financing is tricky business and comprises numerous factors. The personnel practices and curriculum of each situation are different. While the salary schedule in one district may be better than another, the work load in the latter district may be less demanding (e.g., see number 3). Or the salaries in the neighboring district may be distributed differently—higher at the top of the scale but lower at the bottom, for example. Therefore, the board's chief negotiator must be thoroughly familiar with the collective bargaining agreements in neighboring districts. It is a natural tendency for the teachers' union to seek the best of both worlds.

---

[53]Neal, *Bargaining Tactics*, pp. 77–81.

TABLE 15 • 8   Salary Schedule Scattergram for a Hypothetical School District

STEP	B.A.	NO. OF STAFF	COST	STEP	M.A.	NO. OF STAFF	COST	STEP	PH.D.	NO. OF STAFF	COST
1	$20,000	2	$40,000	1	$21,000	1	$21,000	1	$22,500		
2	20,500			2	22,000	2	44,000	2	24,000		
3	21,000			3	23,000	2	46,000	3	25,500		
4	21,500	2	43,000	4	24,000	4	96,000	4	27,000		
5	22,000			5	25,000	2	50,000	5	28,500		
6	22,500			6	26,000	3	78,000	6	30,000	1	$30,000
7	23,000	2	46,000	7	27,000			7	31,500		
8	23,500	3	70,500	8	28,000	2	56,000	8	33,000		
9	24,000	1	24,000	9	29,000	1	29,000	9	34,500		
10	24,500	2	49,000	10	30,000			10	36,000		
11	25,000			11	31,000	3	93,000	11	37,500		
12	25,500	2	51,000	12	32,000	8	256,000	12	39,000		
13	26,000	1	26,000	13	33,000	1	33,000	13	40,500		
14	26,500	2	53,000	14	34,000	5	170,000	14	42,000	1	42,000
15	27,000	5	135,000	15	35,000	3	105,000	15	43,500	—	
TOTALS		22	$537,500			37	$1,077,000			2	$72,000

Total number of teachers: 61
Total of teachers' salaries: $1,686,500
Average teacher salary: $27,647

6. *Supply Specifically Requested Information Only.* Cost data should be pertinent to each proposal. Only management's chief negotiator should be provided with the raw data that was used to prepare summaries. Related data may suggest counterproposals. Never distribute raw data to the union and supply only specifically requested information.

7. *Provide Management's Negotiating Team with a Budget Projection.* Provide management's negotiating team with a budget projection at the start of bargaining. The document can be used to set the tentative limits on the chief negotiator. The budget projections must provide a minimum and several alternatives, including factors that might influence the final budget.

The following are some important factors that influence a school district's final budget.[54] This information should be part of a school district's data bank. Such cost data can assist management's bargaining team in costing proposals.

■ *Salary:*
  Salary schedules and placement of teachers (Table 15-8)
  Average salary of newly hired teachers
  Average base salary of teachers, by school, level, department
  Contract salaries distribution
  Past record of salary schedule improvements (dollar amount and percentage)
  Total cost of past schedule improvements
  Past record of changes in the salary schedule (steps and lanes)
  Projected cost—normal increment, $100 on base schedule, 1 percent schedule increase

■ *Fringe Benefits:*
  Fringe benefits as percentage of salaries paid
  Cost of fringe benefits per new position

[54]Ibid., pp. 79–81.

Leave history—policy and record

Separation pay—number of individuals, per-diem rate, annual rate, average pay

Sabbatical leave—granted, denials, costs, subsequent separations

Retirements—mandatory versus actual, reason for retirement

■ *Staffing:*

Number of employees

Staffing ratios by school, level, department

Recruitment history—applicants, offers, acceptances

Separation history—number, reason, scale placement, turnover experience

General statistics—age, gender, race, marital status of employees

Scale placement—academic advancement record, payment for graduate credits, merit pay

■ *Administration:*

Cost of recruitment

Cost of selection

Cost of training and development

Cost of basic supplies and equipment for new employees

Cost of negotiations

Budget history/forecasting

Expenditure history

Enrollment history and projections

Per-pupil cost history

Reserve trends/forecasting

Building factors affecting conditions of employment

New Bargaining Strategies   Currently, forty-one of the fifty states permit teachers to bargain collectively with school boards. Where such bargaining is allowed, almost all school districts employ traditional or adversarial bargaining. In recent years, collaborative bargaining (also known as win–win bargaining) has emerged. A number of models offer guidelines for this approach.[55]

---

[55]Demetri Liontos, "Collaborative Bargaining in Schools: Case Studies and Recommendations," *OSSC Bulletin*, 31 (1987), pp. 1–28.

Typically, collaborative bargaining focuses on ongoing problem solving rather than dealing with a buildup of issues presented at the bargaining table. Both management and union keep a "tickler file" of problems encountered in administering the current contract. Joint committees deal with the problems encountered. Then when contract language is finally discussed, each party presents specific notes to support their positions. Both parties establish agreed-on groundrules and specific time limits for negotiations, and write trust agreements and memoranda of understanding, and carefully select respected, credible members of negotiating teams. These procedures can help establish trust and a sense of collaboration to solve mutual problems throughout the school year and at the bargaining table.

SUMMARY

1. The personnel process consists of the following steps: human resource planning, recruitment, selection, training and development, performance appraisal, and compensation. Of particular concern for today's administrators is the growing body of laws regulating the personnel process.

2. Human resource planning begins with a forecast of the number and types of employees needed to achieve the organization's objectives. Planning also includes preparation of job descriptions and specifications.

3. Recruitment involves the initial screening of prospective employees. Sources of prospective employees can be located inside or outside the organization.

4. Selection involves choosing an individual to hire from among the pool of applicants who have been recruited. Biographical information, testing, interviews, reference checks, assessment centers are often used as aids in the selection process.

5. Training and development helps employees perform their jobs better and prepares them for future jobs. The training and development process involves determining training needs, designing and implementing the training program, and evaluating the training program.

6. Performance appraisal is the systematic observation and evaluation of employee behavior. Some of the most commonly used methods of appraisal include the judgmental approach, the absolute-standards approach, and the results-oriented approach.
7. Compensation includes wages and salaries and fringe benefits. Wage and salary levels are usually tied to what other organizations in the field pay. Legally required benefits are Social Security, workers' compensation, and unemployment insurance. Other benefits include pension plans, insurance programs, leaves, educational benefits, and the like.
8. Most states permit teachers to bargain collectively with boards of education. Labor relations refers to dealing with employees when they are organized into a union. Management must engage in collective bargaining with the union in an effort to reach agreement on a contract.

Key Terms

human resource planning

recruitment

selection

training and development

performance appraisal

compensation

job analysis

job description

job specification

observation

work sampling

critical incidents

interviews

questionnaires

forecasting

human resource audit

Equal Employment Opportunity Commission

equal employment opportunity

affirmative action program

internal recruitment

closed recruitment system

open recruitment system

external recruitment

biographical information

reference checks

testing

assessment centers

graphic rating scale

ranking

paired comparison

forced distribution

checklist

essay

behaviorally anchored rating scale

management by objectives

strictness error

leniency error

central tendency

halo effect

recency of events error

wage survey

job evaluation

job ranking

classification system

point system

factor-comparison method

seniority

merit

union

union–management relations

collective bargaining

management rights

narrow-grievance definition

no-strike provision

zipper clause

maintenance of standards

just cause

reduction in force

bumping

cost-of-living adjustments

ratification vote

impasse

mediation

fact finding

arbitration

counterproposals

trade-offs

caucus

costing proposals

Discussion Questions

1. List and describe the six major steps in the personnel process.
2. Discuss the advantages and disadvantages of internal and external recruiting. What techniques can administrators use to improve their recruiting and selection practices?
3. What are some of the federal laws and agencies that affect recruitment and selection of personnel?
4. Describe the procedure used to develop a wage and salary structure for a school district.
5. What are the major issues that are negotiated at the bargaining table between the board of education and the teachers' union? Discuss some bargaining tactics that management can use to improve its position in the collective bargaining process.

Suggested Readings

Michael R. Carrell et al., *Personnel: Human Resource Management*, 3rd ed. (Columbus, OH: Merrill, 1990). Provides an up-to-date guide to all facets of personnel administration.

William B. Castetter, *The Personnel Function in Educational Administration*, 4th ed. (New York: Macmillan, 1986). Specifically geared toward personnel management in educational administration.

David A. DeCenzo and Steven J. Holovich, *Employee Benefits* (Englewood Cliffs, NJ: Prentice-Hall, 1990). Provides a thorough overview of compensation and employee benefits as a dimension of human resource management.

William C. Donaghy, *Interview: Skills and Applications* (Salem, WI: Sheffield Publishing, 1991). Provides a systematic examination of the interview process.

James Ledvinka, *Federal Regulation of Personnel and Human Resource Management*, 2nd ed. (Northridge, CA: Kent, 1990). Provides a thorough examination of federal laws affecting the personnel function in organizations.

Robert L. Mathis and John H. Jackson, *Personnel: Human Resource Management*, 5th ed. (St. Paul: West, 1988). Provides an excellent introduction to the basics of personnel administration.

Randall S. Schuler and Vandra L. Huber, *Personnel and Human Resource Management*, 4th ed. (St. Paul: West, 1989). Describes the whole process of personnel administration from human resource planning to performance appraisal.

16

CAREERS IN EDUCATIONAL ADMINISTRATION

In this chapter, we attempt to answer these questions concerning careers in educational administration. We begin our discussion by exploring the concept of a career. Then we discuss career stages in the context of an administrative career. Next, we examine the role stress plays in educational administration, including causes, symptoms, and effects. We also examine individual and organizational strategies for coping with stress and discuss career development in terms of individual and organizational processes. Finally, we examine the potential administrative career opportunities for women and minorities, including barriers to career ascendance and specific programs for overcoming these barriers.

THE CONCEPT OF CAREER

Long hours at an unremitting pace, varied and fragmented tasks, and heavy reliance on verbal communication are all part of a career in educational administration. Good pay and benefits, status, prestige, power, and challenging and interesting work are also characteristic of an administrative career in education. Does this profile appeal to you? If so, then a career in school administration may be for you.

What is a career? To some people, a career means moving upward in an organization, making more money, having more responsibility, and acquiring more status and power. Others view a career as a specific line of work or a profession. Still others believe that a career is more than movement in an organization or a specific line of work. To them a career means psychological involvement in one's work regardless of the salary, responsibility, or status.[1]

A more formal definition of a **career** is a lifelong sequence of work-related positions integrated with the attitudes and motives of the person as she engages in these positions.[2] This definition emphasizes that the concept of career does not imply success or failure, that a career consists of both behaviors and attitudes, and that it is a lifelong sequence of work-related experiences. As such, careers are important to people and to the organization. Careers inevitably integrate the needs of people and organization. Noted management theorists on careers suggest that organizations are dependent on people to perform jobs, and people are dependent on organizations to provide jobs and career opportunities.[3] Thus, school administrators should consider career related issues (e.g., salary schedules and merit pay, job opportunities, and

chances for promotion) in establishing administrative policies and procedures.

CAREER STAGES

It is important for school administrators to understand how careers evolve over time. That information will help administrators to better plan their own careers and help organizations to better understand employees' concerns as they move through **career stages**. Most careers evolve through several stages during a person's working life.

Among the numerous career-stage models that have been proposed, one framework, which is particularly applicable to school administrators, has been developed by Gene Dalton and Paul Thompson. Based on their study of 550 professionally trained people, they propose that careers evolve through four distinct stages. According to Dalton and Thompson, their model applies to people they call "knowledge workers," or people in such professions as engineering, accounting, business management, and science. The principles apply to other employees as well, particularly those who climb the organizational ladder, such as school administrators who must rise through the teaching ranks.

Dalton and Thompson propose that the four distinct career stages differ in terms of the activities employees are expected to perform, the relationships they are expected to develop, and the psychological adjustments they are expected to make.[4]

Stage 1: Apprentice

Stage 1, the **apprentice stage**, begins at the outset of a person's career. During this stage,

[1]Robert Kreitner, *Management*, 4th ed. (Boston: Houghton Mifflin, 1988).

[2]Douglas T. Hall et al. *Career Development in Organizations* (San Francisco: Jossey-Bass, 1986).

[3]Michael B. Arthur et al. (eds.), *Handbook of Career Theory* (New York: Cambridge University Press, 1989).

[4]Gene Dalton and Paul F. Thompson, *Novations: Strategies for Career Management* (Glenview, IL: Scott, Foresman, 1986).

beginning professionals must work closely with more experienced persons. The relationship that develops between beginning professionals and their supervisors is an apprenticeship. The major activities in which beginning professionals are to show competence include learning and following directions. To move successfully and effectively through the apprentice stage, beginning professionals must be able to accept the psychological state of dependence. The apprentice stage continues through the first, or entry-level, job, which is usually nonadministrative, even for those who have an administrative career in mind. For example, in most states several years of teaching experience is required before a person is eligible for certification as a principal.

Activities   Stage 1 involves three types of learning. First, the beginning professional must learn to perform at least some of the organization's tasks competently and determine which tasks are crucial and which require less emphasis. For example, a teacher must learn to prepare lessons, present information, diagnose learning, reinforce and correct students, and evaluate learning. Second, the teacher must learn how to get tasks done, using both formal and informal channels of communication. Finally, the new teacher must perform these tasks while being closely observed for competence and future potential by one or more supervisors. First-year teachers in Kentucky, for example, are called "intern teachers" and are assigned a committee of three supervisors: the building principal, a resource teacher, and a university educator who act as mentors to the novice teacher. A similar procedure exists in the same state for first-year principals, except that the three-member committee consists of the superintendent or designee, an experienced principal, and a university educator.

Relationships   The primary relationship a beginning teacher experiences in Stage 1 is that of subordinate. Ideally, the beginning teacher is assigned a mentor who knows the school, is a successful teacher, and has been trained to work with novice teachers. A mentor is a person who provides support and guidance to a beginning professional.[5] The mentor helps with the learning necessary to develop skills for advancement and tenure in the organization.

Psychological Adjustments   Some professionals cannot cope with being placed in a subordinate state. They feel that they are still being directed and guided by a supervisor, somewhat similar to the professor–student relationship in college. They had anticipated that their first job would provide them with considerably more autonomy. Beginning professionals often find this situation frustrating. However, effectively handling the subordinate–supervisor relationship and the tasks assigned may be crucial to advancement, achieving tenure, and ultimately in building a successful career.

Stage 2: Independent Contributor

Once through the dependent relationship characteristic of Stage 1, the teacher moves into Stage 2, the **independent-contributor stage**, which is characterized by greater independence. The teacher has demonstrated technical competence in the field and can work independently to produce results. These people understand the requirements for success in their profession and need less direction, support, and guidance. The first real administrative position is usually acquired during this stage.

Activities   The focus of activities during Stage 2 is on gaining exposure within the organization and the profession and on continued competent performance. Because many school districts practice hiring their administrative personnel

[5]William A. Gray and Marilynne M. Gray (eds.), *Mentoring: Aid to Excellence in Career Development, Business, and the Professions*, Vol. II (Toronto: IAM, 1986).

from the outside, some aspiring administrators may hold several administrative positions during this period, while learning more about the occupational choices available to them. In fact, many professionals find that they can move up faster and earn more money by moving from one administrative position to another. Typically, the aspiring administrator might begin as a counselor in one school district and then secure several successively higher-level administrative positions in other school districts, including assistant principal, principal, director of instruction, and the like.

Relationships   The primary relationship in this stage is with peers. In fact, some refer to this period as the colleague stage. As mentor relationships begin to diminish, networking becomes important. **Networking** can be seen as an alternative to **mentoring**. It is a process by which employees gain peer support through a network of collegial associations.[6] Collectively, these associations form a broad pool of resources. For women, both networking and mentoring relationships are more important than they are for men. Many women are unable to move into administrative positions because of culture, "the good old-boys network," or other barriers.[7] (These barriers are discussed later in this chapter.) Networking and mentoring relationships can provide professionals with insights concerning how the organization works and exposure to top-level school executives.

Psychological Adjustments   During Stage 2, the professional is expected to rely on much less direction from supervisors. This psychological state of independence may pose some problems for the independent contributor because it is an extreme contrast to the state of dependence required in apprenticeship. The independent-con-

tributor stage is extremely important for the professional's career advancement. Those who fail at this stage do so because they lack the technical administrative skills to perform independently or because they lack the necessary self-confidence to project the proper image of an administrator.

Dalton and Thompson note that many professionals remain in Stage 2 throughout their careers. For example, a principal is able to make a substantial contribution and experience a great deal of personal satisfaction through the administration of a single school building. Many have no desire to move up the organizational ladder to higher-level administrative positions. However, the authors also note that high-performance appraisals tend to diminish with time for those who remain in Stage 2 too long. For others, thoughts focus on the next career stage.

Stage 3: Mentor

During Stage 3, the **mentor stage**, professionals turn their energies to mentoring less-experienced professionals. They broaden their interests and work increasingly more with people outside the organization. Mentoring professionals assume the work of others, and this activity can cause psychological stress.

Activities   Stage 3 professionals perform three roles, which tend to be somewhat overlapping. First, people who enter Stage 3 are expected to become mentors of those in Stage 1. To accomplish this added responsibility, they secure help from those in Stage 2. For example, in a school setting, the assistant superintendent of instruction or director of secondary education will seek the help of the principal in mentoring a beginning teacher or a newly appointed assistant principal.

The second role performed by Stage 3 professionals is that of an "idea person." Mentoring professionals may act as consultants for small groups both inside and outside the organization. From their past experience and success in Stage

[6]Anne Boe and Bettie B. Youngs, *Is Your "Net" Working? A Complete Guide to Building Contacts and Career Visibility* (Oil City, PA: Park Avenue Press, 1990).
[7]Deborah J. Marnell, *Career Warfare: Rising Above the Trenches* (Fountain Hills, AZ: Platinum Career, 1990).

2, they have the ability to pull together the information and resources needed to solve problems. For example, the assistant superintendent may work with various school and community committees to revamp the curriculum, plan new bus routes, or develop a districtwide testing program.

The third role, that of manager, is the most common role found in the mentoring stage. A professional in Stage 2 is typically one or two levels away from the work itself. For example, a principal of an elementary school is probably the teacher's direct supervisor. In a high school, there may be one or two levels (department head and assistant principal) between the teacher and the principal. A mentoring professional, on the other hand, is more distant from the work and, consequently, administers at a more conceptual level. She deals more with concepts than with technical activities. Nevertheless, she assumes responsibility for the technical work done by others. Note the similarity here to Robert Katz's three-skill model.[8]

Relationships   The administrator in Stage 3 has taken on more responsibility. Relationships include not only directional activities but also mentorship and the training of others. The professional in this stage needs to demonstrate a high level of human skills in setting objectives, coordinating, delegating, supervising, and making decisions. The Stage 3 professional must satisfy many people above him in the organization's hierarchy. An assistant superintendent, for example, must have an influence on the superintendent in order to obtain the necessary resources for principals to perform their roles effectively.

Psychological Adjustments   As mentioned previously, Stage 3 professionals assume responsibility for the work of others. This role can result in considerable psychological adjustment. In previous stages, the professional was responsible for

her own work, but now she is concerned with the work of others. Professionals who are not capable of accepting this requirement may move back to Stage 2. For example, many central office administrators miss the autonomy and sense of satisfaction derived from being responsible for their own building when they were principals. However, those who derive satisfaction from seeing others move ahead may remain in Stage 3 for the remainder of their careers. Others move on to the next career stage.

Stage 4: Sponsor

Not all professionals experience Stage 4, the **sponsor stage**. Those who enter this stage are involved in shaping the organization itself. This influence is manifested by interfacing with key people inside and outside the organization; by developing new ways of achieving the goals of the organization; and by directing people, material, and financial resources toward specific organizational goals. Because these activities are so critical to the success and continued growth of an organization, people who perform them are highly valued. For example, public school superintendents and university presidents are paid salaries many times higher than their subordinates.

Activities   Stage 4 professionals direct their attention to long-range strategic planning. To fulfil this function, they perform three roles: manager, entrepreneur, and idea innovator. Managers formulate policy and initiate and implement broad programs. Entrepreneurs have a strong sense of direction for the future. It is what one author refers to as the visionary leader.[9] Idea innovators are people with new ideas for accomplishing the organization's goals. These people

---

[8]Robert L. Katz, "Skills of an Effective Administrator," *Harvard Business Review*, 52 (1974), pp. 90–102.

[9]Marshall Sashkin, "The Visionary Leader: A New Theory of Organizational Leadership," in J. A. Conger and R. N. Kanunga (eds.), *Charismatic Leadership in Management* (San Francisco: Jossey-Bass, 1988).

have gained a reputation outside their organization through professional achievements and publications. This outside reputation enhances their credibility and allows them to play key roles in organizational development. Although we generally think of such activities as being performed by one person—the organization's chief executive—they may be performed by others. For example, in a school setting, key administrators in the divisions of instruction, finance, personnel, and research and development may be sponsors depending on the amount of authority and responsibility that has been delegated to them.

Relationships Stage 4 professionals find themselves involved in two major relationships. First, these professionals are responsible for setting the direction of the organization. Thus, they have a high degree of control over important organizational resources. Selection and development of key people is one of the basic ways of shaping the direction of the organization. The second major responsibility is contact with people and organizations outside their own. This relationship is critical because it brings current information about events and trends into an organization. Such a relationship can be seen in public schools and universities as sponsor professionals interact with federal, state, and local governments.

Psychological Adjustments Depending on the size of the organization, Stage 4 professionals are at least three or more levels removed from the technical work. Because of this distance from the "firing line," they must resist second-guessing their subordinates on operating decisions. Sponsors must learn to influence others through more indirect means such as idea planting, personnel selection, program evaluation, resource allocation, changes in organizational design, and the like. These shifts in leadership style can be a difficult psychological adjustment for Stage 4 professionals who may have used a more direct leadership style in the past.

MANAGING CAREER STRESS

Earlier we characterized the school administrator's work as varied, fragmented, and continuous. In previous chapters, we have seen that school administrators are responsible for organizing the work force, motivating subordinates, making decisions, communicating with others, facilitating change, deploying resources, and leading the organization. School administrators are responsible for high performance. Considering the nature of the school administrator's work, stress is part of the job.

Stress is the physiological and psychological response of an individual to demands, constraints, or opportunities involving uncertainty and important outcomes.[10] Prolonged exposure to stress can produce dysfunctional effects that may affect job performance. In this section, we examine the sources of stress, effects of stress, and techniques for coping with stress.

Sources of Stress

Stressors are environmental conditions that have the potential to cause stress. It is important for a school administrator to recognize stressors because they induce job-related stress, which may influence work attitudes, behavior, and performance.

Figure 16-1 depicts three categories of stressors: organizational, personal, and nonorganizational factors. Of the three, organizational factors have the greatest potential to induce job-related stress. Factors such as excessively high or low job demands, role conflicts and ambiguities, and poor interpersonal relations can influence the stress level school administrators experience. Administrators also feel stress in the transition from one career stage to the next, which is due to the uncertainty often associated

[10]Jenni Adams, *Stress: A New Positive Approach* (New York: Sterling, 1990).

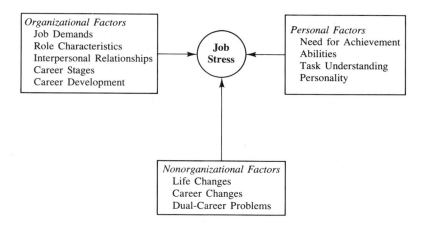

FIGURE 16-1   Sources of Job Stress

with new job experiences and expectations. A somewhat related factor is career development. An administrator can feel stress from underpromotions (failure to advance as rapidly as one desires) or overpromotion (being placed in a job that exceeds one's capabilities). These organizational factors, independently or in concert, can induce job stress.

Several personal factors are sources of stress for administrators in the workplace. Such individual characteristics as need for achievement, aptitudes and skills, task understanding, and personality can influence how individuals experience and react to stress and stressors. For example, personality traits such as authoritarianism, introversion/extroversion, tolerance for ambiguity, locus of control, and self-esteem have been found to be related to job stress.[11] Attention has focused, however, on the **Type A personality**, which seems to relate to the ways in which individuals experience stress. Characteristics of this personality structure include:

- A chronic sense of time urgency
- A constant involvement in multiple projects subject to deadlines
- A neglect of all aspects of life except work
- A highly competitive, aggressive, almost hostile orientation
- An impatience with barriers to goal achievement
- A tendency to measure success by quantity[12]

The time urgency, competitiveness and hostility, multiphasic behavior, and achievement orientation characteristic of Type A personalities predispose these individuals to certain physical disorders such as heart attacks. Much of the stress they feel is of their own making rather than products of their environment.

Finally, nonorganizational factors can also impact the stress a school administrator experiences in the work setting. Such things as life changes (the birth of a child, death of a spouse, divorce), career changes (loss of extra income),

[11]Robert F. Allen, *A Program for Personal Change on Stress Resolution* (Burlington, VT: Human Resources Institute, 1990).

[12]James Quick et al. *Stress and Challenge at the Top: The Paradox of the Successful Executive* (New York: Wiley, 1990).

ADMINISTRATIVE ADVICE 16-1
■

MANAGING STRESS IN THE PRINCIPALSHIP

Here are the major sources of stress that school principals face in performing their duties and techniques to manage stress.

■ *Role Conflict*. Principals serve as members of the superintendent's administrative team and are expected to accomplish district goals. Simultaneously, they serve as leader of the school instructional team and its staff. Frequently, the goals, policies, and directives from the central office are in conflict with the goals, wishes, and expectations of staff members. When such conflicts occur, principals may experience stress.

■ *Instructional Leadership*. Most principals know they are expected to be instructional leaders in their schools. However, most secondary principals find that the administrative role tends to dominate the instructional leadership role. The inability to devote sufficient attention to the instructional leadership role is a source of stress.

■ *Problem-Solving Role*. The principal's office is frequently a collection point for problems. The overall effectiveness of the principal hinges on his ability to resolve these conflicts. Resolving these problems carries a price. The process is time-consuming and stressful.

■ *High Activity Level*. The principal's day is busy, rapid-fire, and fragmented with numerous interruptions. There is little time for careful thought, reflection, and long-range planning. The "on-the-spot" interactions require "on-the-spot" answers and decisions. This causes stress.

■ *External Politics*. Increased accountability resulting from national and state reform mandates, recent Supreme Court decisions, and issues such as AIDS, special education, sex education, drug education, and vocational education have added to the workload and stress level of principals.

Some suggestions for managing the level of stress follow:

1. Do not allow work problems brought to you to become your problem.
2. Learn to delegate responsibilities and duties.
3. Give careful attention to your role as supervisor.
4. Find and maintain a network of trusted professional and personal friends.
5. Develop some activities that can reduce your anxieties and stress.

Source: Adapted from James E. Lyons, "Managing Stress in the Principalship," *NASSP Bulletin*, 74 (1990), pp. 42–49. Used by permission.

and dual careers can influence a person's health and job performance. Dual-career problems typically arise when a married couple attempts to balance two individual careers. Major concerns for couples with dual careers include sharing household chores, child care, and job relocation. Nonorganizational factors can result in a "spillover" of stress, which may influence attitudes, behavior, and job performance.

As noted, schools, by their very nature, are fertile grounds for conflict. The conflicts that occur frequently result in stress for principals, particularly secondary principals. Research on stress in the principalship indicates that much of it is caused by such sources as role conflict, instructional leadership demands, problem-solving role, high activity level, time-management demand, and external politics. (See Administrative Advice 16-1.)

Time Management   School administrators feel more job pressures and time constraints than ever before according to a recent survey.[13] Typically, administrators log in between fifty-one and sixty hours a week, and additional weekend work is not unusual.

School administrators report that they do not have sufficient time to do everything that needs to be done. The variety of problems administrators face and the large spans of control found in most school organizations make it difficult for them to give all aspects of the school program sufficient attention. Not being able to do all that they would like to do in the time available is a continuing source of stress.

According to one management consultant, proper time management is more than a tidy desk and an orderly schedule: It is a career strategy that can help turn any school executive into a high achiever. Furthermore, she asserts that when school administrators allow time to control them, it can result in the kind of stress linked with high blood pressure, heart attacks, excessive irritability, and general anxiety.[14]

The reason some school administrators accomplish so much each day while others struggle just to survive is that achievers view time as a scarce but controllable resource, and they apply useful time-management strategies to their daily lives. (See Administrative Advice 16-2.)

Stress and Performance Stress can either help or hinder job performance, depending on the amount of it.[15] Figure 16-2 shows the relationship between stress and job performance. The vertical axis represents the level of performance from low to high. The horizontal axis represents the amount of stress experienced. At very low levels of stress, job challenges are absent, and performance tends to be low. As stress increases, performance tends to increase because stress helps an individual activate physiological and

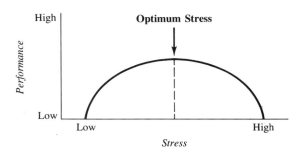

FIGURE 16-2   Relationship of Stress and Performance

psychological resources to meet job requirements. Eventually, stress reaches a point—the optimum-stress level—that corresponds roughly with a person's maximum daily performance capability. Past this point, performance begins to decline. Excessive levels and extended periods of stress can be dysfunctional to the organization because stress interferes with performance. Employees manifest erratic behavior, lose the ability to cope, and cannot make decisions. The key is to balance stress so that an optimum level is reached for each individual.

Effects of Stress

As noted previously, stress is not all bad. In fact, low-level stress can enhance job performance. High-level, prolonged stress, on the other hand, can be dysfunctional to both the individual's health and organizational performance. The effects of job stress can be manifested physiologically, psychologically, and behaviorally by the individual.

On the physiological level, all types of stress produce a chemical reaction in the body. These include changes in metabolism, increased heart and breathing rates, increased blood pressure, and increased perspiration, skin temperature, blood glucose level, and blood clotting. If stress persists and is accompanied by these physiological changes, certain annoying and serious health conditions can result. Among them are heart disease, hypertension, increased blood cholesterol levels, ulcers, arthritis, allergies,

[13]Robert W. Heller et al., "Nationwide Survey: You're Overworked, Underpaid but Reasonably Happy Anyway," *Executive Educator*, 11 (1989), pp. 18–21.

[14]Helen T. Oliver, "Winners Use These Beat-the-Clock Tips," *Executive Educator*, 12 (1990), pp. 21 and 25.

[15]Don Hellriegel, John W. Slocum, and Richard W. Woodman, *Organizational Behavior*, 5th ed. (St. Paul: West, 1989).

ADMINISTRATIVE ADVICE 16-2

■

TIME-MANAGEMENT STRATEGIES

Developing a system to get organized is not only possible but also necessary if you want to be a high achiever. Here are some time-saving strategies to help you manage your time better:

- *Goal Setting*. Set measurable objectives for your career, family, finances, fitness, or social life. Written goals provide a framework to help you assess your use of time. What gets measured gets done.
- *Setting Priorities*. List all pending activities in priority order. Assign the letter *A* to tasks that must be done, *B* to those that should be done, and *C* to those that might be done. Tackle the items on your *A* list first.
- *Brevity*. Stress concise communications. Limit business calls to five minutes. Write one-page memos. Conduct twenty-minute meetings. Prepare executive summaries of lengthy reports.
- *Bunching*. Cluster similar activities together. Schedule blocks of time for returning telephone calls, dictating letters or reports, reading the mail, holding routine meetings, and doing desk work.
- *Chunking*. Break down complex or unpleasant tasks into smaller, more manageable parts. Complete one chunk first (a one-page outline of a lengthy report, for example) and another chunk (maybe the introduction) later.
- *Closure*. Condition yourself to complete each task the first time you start it. Example: Ask a drop-in visitor to wait outside until you finish the memorandum on which you are working. Emphasize completion.
- *Deadlines*. Set personal due dates that precede the stated deadlines, or create deadlines when none is given. Submit reports, budgets, and forms before due dates.
- *Delegation*. Achieve results through others by assigning routine activities (reports, business trips, memorandums, meetings, research) to appropriate subordinates. Share the credit.

- *Elimination*. Get rid of time wasters—long lunches, going-nowhere committees, long telephone calls, trips—anything that distracts you from your goals. Purge files (when in doubt, toss it out).
- *Planning*. Anticipate future events. Planning time saves operating time, so prepare strategic plans, weekly plans, and daily to-do lists. Each morning, review your game plan for the day.
- *Prime Time*. To make the most of your energies, try to get your time clock and your biological clock in sync. Schedule important activities when your energy level is highest.
- *Saying No*. Avoid overcommitting yourself. Success depends on knowing what *not* to do. Be firm but gracious in rejecting tasks unrelated to your goals, and reject time wasters whenever possible.
- *Single Handling*. Finish items in one session. Try to handle each memorandum, folder, letter, or telephone call only once. Avoid multiple handling of items.
- *Hiding Out*. Schedule quiet time. Take a walk, use retreats, close the door, smell the roses, reflect. You need time for thinking and relaxing each day.
- *Fitness*. Jocks have known this for years: Exercise increases energy. To charge your battery, schedule time to jog, golf, play racquetball, or simply walk.

Source: Adapted from Harry J. Hartley, "Make Time to Manage Your Time More Effectively," *Executive Educator*, 12 (1990), pp. 19–20.

gastrointestinal problems, and even cancer.[16] It should be noted, however, that stress is not the only cause of these ailments. The genetic predisposition, diet, and lifestyle of an individual can also contribute to various health conditions.

While not as much attention has been given to the impact of stress on mental health as on physical health, psychological problems at work can be equally dysfunctional to job performance. Among the more common psychological outcomes of stress are anxiety, tension, depression, boredom, and mental fatigue. The effects of these psychological states on employee job performance are lowered self-esteem and poorer intellectual functioning, including the inability to concentrate and make decisions, irritability, forgetfulness, negativism, apathy, and job dissatisfaction. These outcomes of stress can be costly to an organization. For example, there have been an increasing number of workers' compensation awards granted to employees based on job-related psychological stress.[17]

The physiological and psychological effects of stress relate to how employees feel, whereas the behavioral effects indicate what employees actually do under stress. Consequently, an analysis of the behavioral effects of job stress may be most helpful to the school administrator. Any sudden change in behavioral patterns may suggest that an employee is experiencing a high-level stress. Among the more common indicators are extremes in appetite, increased smoking and use of alcohol, drug abuse, impulsive behavior, speech difficulties, accident proneness, higher tardiness and absenteeism, and decreased performance.[18]

Coping with Stress

As noted earlier, school administrators, in particular, are prone to high levels of job stress. Although stress cannot be completely eliminated from their work environments, it can be managed. That is, steps can be taken to minimize its harmful effects not only for themselves but for their employees as well. Several techniques for coping with stress have been proposed. Most fall into two categories: strategies that individuals can apply themselves and procedures that the organization can provide to minimize the onset of stress for employees.

Some specific techniques that individuals can use to manage stress are the following:[19]

- *Exercise*. A growing body of research indicates that individuals who exercise regularly are much less prone to heart disease and hypertension than those who do not exercise regularly. Exercise produces chemical responses within the body that diminish many of the physiological symptoms of stress discussed earlier (e.g., heart rate, breathing rate, blood pressure).
- *Lifestyle Changes*. The best way to reduce and prevent stress is to lead a better life. The individual who has a proper diet, gets adequate sleep, exercises regularly, and avoids smoking, alcohol, and illegal drugs is likely to minimize the harmful effects of stress.
- *Meditation*. Some research findings suggest that **meditation** affects basic bodily functions in a manner equivalent to deep rest. This state has been described as one of four major states of consciousness; the other three are wakefulness, dreaming, and deep sleep. Such relaxation techniques can reduce the symptoms of stress.
- *Biofeedback*. People under medical guidance can learn through electronic machines how to develop an awareness of muscle sensations

[16]Earl Giller (ed.), *Biological Assessment and Treatment of Posttraumatic Stress Disorder* (Washington, D.C.: American Psychiatric Press, 1990).

[17]Charles D. Spielberger and Irwin G. Sarason (eds.), *Stress and Anxiety* (New York: Hemisphere Publishing, 1990).

[18]Joseph D. Noshpitz and R. Dean Coddington, *Stressors and the Adjustment Disorders* (New York: Wiley, 1990).

[19]Dorothy H. Cotton, *Stress Management: An Integrated Approach to Therapy* (New York: Bruner-Mazel, 1990).

throughout the body. With this knowledge comes the ability to exercise control over their involuntary nervous system, which in turn controls internal processes such as heartbeat, breathing, brain waves, and the like. Thus, **biofeedback** may be helpful in reducing some undesirable effects of stress.
- *Networking.* One means of coping with job stress is through a network of social support. This would involve building close associations with sympathetic others, especially coworkers and colleagues, who are good listeners and can build confidence.

Organizational programs to help employees cope with stress are extremely popular. Such programs often include one or more of the following:[20]

- Job redesign (Chapters 2 and 4)
- Supportive organizational climate (Chapter 3)
- Goal setting and management by objectives (Chapter 4)
- Leadership styles (Chapter 5)
- Decision-making skills (Chapter 6)
- Communication skills (Chapter 7)
- Management of change and organizational development (Chapter 8)
- Workshops dealing with role clarity and role analysis (Chapter 8)
- Career development

Career development, which helps employees plan and manage their careers, has become increasingly popular.

CAREER DEVELOPMENT

Career development refers to the methods and procedures used to plan and implement a career by means of education, training, job search, and work experiences.[21] Career development consists of two important elements: career planning and career management. **Career planning** is the personal process of planning an individual's career path. **Career management** focuses on plans and activities performed by the organization to enhance its employees' careers. Because the organization's ability to help meet the needs of its employees influences organizational effectiveness, effective career development requires a long-term fit between the individual and the organization. Figure 16-3 depicts the content of career planning and career management and shows both the interrelationship of these two processes and their relationship to career development.

Career Planning

The steps in the career planning process include self-appraisal, exploring opportunities, setting goals, preparing plans, and implementing plans.[22]

Self-Appraisal   The first step in the career-planning process is to gather data about one's self What skills do I possess? What are my aptitudes? What are my values and interests? What are my internal strengths and weaknesses? What do I enjoy doing? What do I dislike doing?

Books and various tests are available to help people assess themselves.[23] Various tests—such as the FIRO–B; Myers–Briggs Type Indicator; Allport, Vernon, Lindsey Study of Values—measure one's behaviors, interests, and values. Table 16-1 provides a number of the more common paper-and-pencil tests.

---

[20]Patricia Carrington, *Stopping to Gain Perspective: A Skills Training Program for the Management of Stress* (Kendall Park, NJ: Pace Educational Systems, 1990).

[21]Monica E. Breidenbach, *Career Development: Taking Charge of Your Career* (Englewood Cliffs, NJ: Prentice-Hall, 1989).
[22]Thomas G. Gutteridge, *Career Planning and Management* (Boston: Little, Brown, 1987).
[23]Arthur F. Miller and Ralph T. Mattson, *The Truth About You* (Berkeley, CA: Ten Speed Press, 1989).

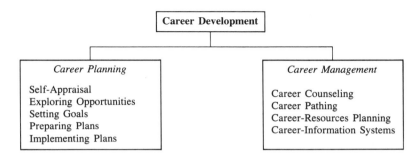

FIGURE 16-3   Career Planning and Career Management as Elements of Career Development

Exploring Opportunities   The next step involves gathering data concerning one's job opportunities both within and outside the organization. In large school districts, the personnel department typically publishes information regarding jobs within the organization, together with qualifications for each job. Opportunities within one's organization are influenced by such factors as student enrollments, separations of various kinds, district policy regarding promotions from within, and internal politics. Economic conditions, the labor market, occupational choices outside the organization, and training and development programs offered by the organization should be evaluated as well.

Setting Goals   After one has assessed herself and determined job opportunities, the next step is to establish long-term and short-term career goals. A goal is a statement of an outcome to be accomplished. A goal may involve salary, position, or other factors. For example, a long-term career goal might include the position of superintendent of schools by age forty-five and an annual salary of $100,000 or higher by the same age. These long-term targets can serve as useful guidelines. They specify minimum standards to achieve within a definite time line. However, shorter-range goals should be established. A person developing a career plan at age twenty-five should set some short-term targets in order to move to the long-range career objectives. For

example, the twenty-five-year-old might set the following targets for age thirty-five: (1) completion of a doctorate degree in educational administration, (2) the position of high school principal, and (3) an annual salary of $60,000. In short, career plans involve many goals, which include long-range and short-range objectives.

Preparing Plans   When preparing plans, each individual should take into account his own skills, abilities, characteristics, and experiences. That is, goals are planned individually. Specifically, preparing plans involves setting time lines, defining resources needed, and constructing procedures to avert barriers to goal achievement. For example, if a principal is unable to secure a promotion within his own school district, he should seek the desired position in another school district.

Implementing Plans   Noted personnel theorists John Ivancevich and William Glueck recommend several guidelines that can increase the success of achieving one's career goals:[24]

1. *Maintain the Greatest Number of Job Options Possible*. Avoid getting stereotyped in one role.

---

[24]John Ivancevich and William F. Glueck, *Foundations of Personnel-Human Resource Management*, 4th ed. (Homewood, IL: Irwin, 1989).

TABLE 16 ▪ 1   Profile of Self-Assessment Instruments

INSTRUMENT	DESCRIPTION
FIRO–B	Available through Consulting Psychologists Press (CPP), this hand-scored instrument measures an individual's characteristic behavior toward other people along the dimensions of inclusion, control, and affection (openness).
Myers–Briggs Type Indicator	The MBTI provides a measure of personality dispositions and interests based on Jung's theory of types. These personality types can be reported according to four bipolar scales: introversion–extroversion, sensing–intuition, thinking–feeling and judging–perceptive. This instrument can be hand-scored.
Allport, Vernon Lindsey Study of Values	The values indexed are theoretical, economic, aesthetic, social, political, and religious.
Test of Imagination	Based on the TAT approach developed by David McClelland, this instrument uses a series of pictures to measure an individual's behavioral motivations in terms of need for achievement, affiliation, and power. Participants respond to each picture by writing a brief, imaginative story indicating what they think is happening, who the people are, what has led up to the situation being portrayed, what is being thought by whom in the picture, what will happen, etc. This instrument must be scored by a trained psychologist, and the sample organizations that use this approach have all retained McBer and Company for this service.
Work Analysis Questionnaire	This is another McBer instrument whereby individuals respond to a series of structured statements about the characteristics of their day-to-day work experience:

My job requires skills on which I have to practice and improve	**Example**	My job does not require skills on which I have to practice and improve
	├───┼───┼───┼───┼───┼───┤	

While staff experience may be necessary when climbing the organizational ladder, line experience is also important for future career success.

2. *Don't Waste Your Time in a Dead-End Job*. Evaluate the school district's promotion policy. Are administrator's promoted from within, or are they hired from outside the school district? If there is no upward mobility in the organization, begin looking outside the school district.

3. *Become a Crucial Subordinate to Your Direct Supervisor*. A crucial subordinate is a person who your supervisor needs as much as you need her. Then you will move when your supervisor moves.

4. *Make Yourself Visible to Your Superiors*. Visibility is how often you are seen by your superiors. Some writers rank visibility as the most critical component for career advancement. The thinking here is that because excellent job performance is commonplace, advance-

TABLE 16 ▪ 1   Profile of Self-Assessment Instruments (continued)

	For each pair of statements, individuals decide which is more appropriate and indicate the point on the scale that shows their relative agreement with each. Following this assessment of the characteristics of their current job situation, individuals respond to each pair of statements in terms of the characteristics of an "ideal" work situation. This instrument must be returned to McBer for scoring and profiling.
Self-Directed Search	This is a self-administered, self-scored instrument that individuals can use to explore their occupational interests. It is available through CPP.
Strong–Campbell Interest Inventory	This is a machine-scored instrument, available through CPP, that evaluates an individual's career interests. One unique feature of this instrument is that it allows for comparisons with persons happily employed in a wide variety of occupations.
Skill Search	This instrument, developed by Richard Gopen, helps individuals rate their social, language, math, clerical, scientific, creative, mechanical/manual, and abstract-reasoning skills along a scale from 0 (no experience, no interest) to X (no experience but interest) through F (fair) and G (good) to VG (very good). Individuals then circle those skills they would most like to use on an ideal job and categorize them according to whether they represent data, people, things, or personal experience.

SOURCE: Adapted from Thomas G. Gutteridge and Fred L. Otto, *Organizational Career Development* (Washington, D.C.: ASTD Press, 1983), pp. 41–42.

ment depends more on how many people know you and how important they are in the organization's hierarchy.

5. *Nominate Yourself for Jobs.* Let your superiors know when you want a promotion. Don't wait for your superiors to determine your job options.

6. *If You Decide to Leave a Job, Do It at Your Convenience.* Don't wait for a situation to get bad or for a dismissal to occur. Quit while you're ahead.

7. *Rehearse Before Leaving a Job.* Write your letter of resignation and wait a week. Think the decision through carefully. Discuss the matter with your family. Take a vacation. Bring your vita up to date. After one week, decide whether or not to leave the job. Once you decide, act.

8. *Don't Let Success in a Job Pre-Empt Your Career Plans.* Take charge of your career. Consider alternative careers. Movement from a career path in public school administration to a professorship in educational administration is an example.

These guidelines are easier to follow if you have made a good self-appraisal, know about job opportunities, have prepared alternative career plans, and have set clear and concise career goals to pursue.

According to one writer, school administrators are made, not born. He claims that achieving eminence is a careful step-by-step process. It's a campaign that can be planned. (See Administrative Advice 16-3.)

ADMINISTRATIVE ADVICE 16-3

■

PLAN YOUR STRATEGY TO GET THAT DESIRED POSITION

If you're just starting the campaign, here is a strategy that can help you land an attractive job offer.

■ *Getting the Knowledge.* Here are must-do's for anyone with eyes on the superintendency:
Learn all you can about instruction and school improvement; get a solid grounding in strategic planning; familiarize yourself with reliable employee-evaluation systems and methods of supervision; study group dynamics and ways of helping people work together; learn about the research on change in organizations; look into ways of giving responsibility and power to others while maintaining accountability; study what's meant by school culture and school climate and find out how to improve them; and learn about curriculum and management at both the elementary and secondary levels.

■ *Climbing the Ladder.* Hitch your wagon to a star. Look for a job in a school system led by an outstanding school chief. Observe everything this superintendent does and offer your help whenever appropriate. Assuming the two of you hit it off well, ask the superintendent to be your mentor. This arrangement will put you in an excellent position of landing a superintendency.

■ *Beginning the Search.* Use your resources including friends and acquaintances, national and state search consultants with whom you are ac-

quainted, professors who know you and the job market well, administrators and board members in other systems, commercial search firms, professional journals and newspapers, and specific school systems in preferred areas.

■ *Getting the Interview.* Once you've found a vacancy, the next challenge is to get the interview. Here are some tips: Make sure your credentials and vita are up to date; write an impressive letter of application; proofread your letter and all other materials carefully; ask somebody who works in the school system to which you are applying to nominate you.

■ *Getting Ready for the Interview.* Here are some suggestions: Gather all information you can about the school system; get out and talk with local citizens; formulate questions you might be asked in the interview and prepare your answers; if possible, get photographs and background information about the board members before the interview.

Source: Adapted from Jerry J. Herman, "Craft a Canny Strategy in Your Battle for the Superintendency," *Executive Educator*, 11 (1989) pp. 16–17, 31. Copyright 1989, the National School Boards Association. Used by permission.

Career Management

Career management refers to organizational activities designed to promote employees' career development. A career-management system consists of coordinating various personnel functions, such as recruitment, selection, performance appraisal, and training and development, with programs designed specifically for em-

ployee-career development. The key components of career management include career counseling, career pathing, career-resources planning, and career-information systems.[25]

---

[25]Richard L. Daft, *Management* (New York: Dryden Press, 1988).

Career Counseling   **Career counseling** can be informal or formal. The most widely used informal counseling approaches are services provided by the school district's personnel department and career counseling provided by supervisors. More formal career counseling includes workshops, seminars, assessment centers, and professional-development academies.

The personnel departments of large school districts often include counseling services for personnel who want to assess their skills, abilities, values, and interests. Career counseling by supervisors occurs during the employment interview, during performance-appraisal conferences, and as part of the day-to-day supervisor–subordinate relationship. Career counseling may also occur prior to horizontal and downward transfers of personnel within the organization.

Workshops, seminars, assessment centers, and professional-development academies are being used increasingly in school districts. Administrators and personnel with administrative potential have received most of the attention to date. Recently, women and minorities have been given attention. Efforts by school districts to train, develop, and promote women and minorities is a sign of the organization's commitment to affirmative action.

Career Pathing   An important aspect of career management is **career pathing**, or a coherent progression of jobs, tracks, or routes that can be expected to lead to career goals and the ways of preparing for and moving into those jobs.[26] For example, in a university, the job sequence involves movement from instructor to assistant professor to associate professor to professor. In many public school districts, the progression toward becoming a superintendent is from counselor to assistant principal to principal to assistant superintendent to superintendent. Certainly, there are variations to this model.

Career Success in the Superintendency. A recent study of the career experiences and career paths of district-level school superintendents reveals marked differences that distinguish the most outstanding superintendents from the rest. The most significant findings that distinguish the career experiences and career paths of the most outstanding superintendents from typical superintendents are the following:[27]

- *Formal Graduate Preparation.* Sixty-two percent of the effective superintendents had completed a doctorate, whereas only 34 percent of the typical superintendents had achieved this degree. Seventy-eight percent of the effective superintendents held multiple supervisory certificates, as compared with 54 percent of the typical superintendents.

- *Career Paths.* The traditional short route in which service as a teacher and principal leads directly to the superintendency was more associated with the typical superintendents. A career path, including time as a high-level central office administrator, was more likely to be followed by effective superintendents.

- *Positions Held.* Whereas only 30 percent of the typical superintendents served in a high-level instructional position (e.g., assistant superintendent of elementary education, director of instruction), 43 percent of the effective superintendents served in one or more positions. Furthermore, 13 percent of the typical superintendents versus 31 percent of the effective superintendents had served in noninstructional high-level positions (e.g., associate superintendent of personnel, director of business operations).

- *Tenure.* Typical superintendents spent an average of 8.4 years in the classroom, whereas the effective superintendents averaged only 5.3 years. Moreover, typical superintendents served an average of 9.6 years as principals, compared with 4.2 years for the effective superintendents.

[26]Leon C. Megginson, Donald C. Mosley, and Paul H. Pietri, *Management*, 3rd ed. (New York: Harper & Row, 1989).

[27]Joan Gibson Burnham, "Superintendents on the Fast Track," *School Administrator*, 46 (1989), pp. 18–19.

In short, success predictors for effective school superintendents include more graduate study and certification, more involvement in professional activities, more experience as a high-level central office administrator, and less experience as a classroom teacher and principal.

Career pathing is useful for planning purposes but should not be administered inflexibly. For example, in the past, most school administrators progressed to the top of the school district by working in only one organization. Today many administrators have worked in several organizations before reaching the top. Furthermore, the increase in the number of women and minorities in administrative positions and an organization's commitment to affirmative action requires changes in traditional career pathing. A system that is not flexible enough to permit this will prevent talented people from progressing to high positions in the organization.[28]

Regardless of the chosen career path, the basic concepts of educational administration presented in this book should be helpful. Administrative success depends, to a great extent, on mastering these concepts. School administrators should have the necessary information concerning the following areas:

- *Development of theory*: The social sciences—psychology, social psychology, sociology, anthropology, and economics, and the relationship between theory and practice
- *Management*: Organizational structure; culture; relations with federal, state, and local governments; and public relations
- *Administrative processes*: Knowledge of motivation, leadership, decision making, communications, and organizational change
- *Personnel administration*: Recruitment, selection, training and development, performance appraisal, compensation, and collective bargaining
- *Legal*: Tort liability, contract liability, certification and contracts of faculty, discharge and retirement, and student personnel

---

[28]David D. Van Fleet, *Contemporary Management* (Boston: Houghton Mifflin, 1988).

- *Finance*: Federal, state, and local relationships; sources of school revenue; apportionment of state school funds; budgetary procedures; and fiscal responsibilities of school administrators
- *Curriculum*: Instructional leadership, curriculum theories and models, curriculum development, implementation, evaluation, and change

Career-Resources Planning   Effective career-management systems depend on data, which usually come from a human resource audit or inventory, job analysis, and forecasts of personnel needs. An analysis of the projected needs (demand) and supply of personnel in the field then follows. **Career-resources planning** develops programs to meet human resource needs. These programs include training and development programs of various kinds and experience through work assignments. An attempt is made to match existing employees with career opportunities within the organization.

Career-Information Systems   Job postings within the organization and formal career counseling are examples of **career-information systems**. Some organizations maintain a career-information center for its employees. Career-information systems can motivate and develop talented personnel within the organization.

ADMINISTRATOR-PREPARATION PROGRAMS

Every educational reform report of the past decade has concluded that schools are only as good as their administrators. The prospect of inadequately trained school leaders is serious when one considers the public schools' struggle with such problems as drug abuse, school violence and vandalism, at-risk youngsters, and AIDS. It is not surprising therefore that calls for reform of university programs for the preparation of school administrators have resounded throughout the nation.

Criticism of administrator-preparation programs has been going on for some time. In 1987 the National Commission on Excellence in Educational Administration made eight specific recommendations for the improvement of university programs for the preparation of school administrators, including the establishment of a National Policy Board for Educational Administration, abolishment of educational administration programs at 300 institutions offering such programs, and reformation of state licensure programs for school administrators.[29]

The latest criticism came in a report released by the National Policy Board for Educational Administration, a coalition of ten national educational organizations including the American Association of School Administrators, National School Boards Association, and University Council for Educational Administration. The National Policy Board for Educational Administration asserted its commitment to the improvement of the preparation of administrators who will lead our nation's elementary and secondary schools and school districts in the future.

An Agenda for Reform

The National Policy Board for Educational Administration recommends a nine-item agenda for reform in the preparation of school administrators. These nine items include the following:[30]

1. Mount vigorous recruitment strategies to attract the brightest and most capable candidates of diverse race, ethnicity, and gender,

including a minority enrollment at least comparable to the region's minority public school enrollment.

2. Dramatically raise entrance standards to administrator preparation programs to ensure that all candidates possess strong analytic ability (assessed by a standardized national test, with admission to preparation programs limited to individuals scoring in the top quartile), high administrative potential, and demonstrated success in teaching, including a master's degree.

3. Ensure the quality of faculty in administrator preparation programs by strengthening faculty recruitment, selection, and staff development; maintaining at least five full-time faculty members who do the bulk of teaching, advising, and mentoring; and ensuring a student–faculty ratio comparable to other graduate programs.

4. Make the doctorate in educational administration (Ed.D.) a prerequisite to national certification and state licensure for full-time administrators who are in charge of a school or school system and abolish specialist and master's degree programs in educational administration altogether.

5. Include one full-time year of academic residency and one full-time year of field residency in the Ed.D. preparation program. Permit modifications in the type or duration of the clinical residency for candidates with full-time administrative experience·in education.

6. Develop the elements of the curriculum to transmit a common core of knowledge and skills, grounded in the problems of practice, including societal and cultural influences, teaching and learning processes, organizational theory, methodologies of organizational studies, leadership and management processes, policy studies, and moral and ethical dimensions of schooling.

7. Establish long-term, formal relationships between universities and school districts to create partnership sites for clinical study, field residency, and applied research.

---

[29]National Commission on Excellence in Educational Administration, *Leaders for America's Schools* (Tempe, AZ: University Council for Educational Administration, 1987).

[30]National Policy Board for Educational Administration, "Improving the Preparation of School Administrators: An Agenda for Reform," May 1989.

8. Establish a national professional standards board to develop and administer a national certification examination and encourage states to require candidates for licensure to pass this examination.

9. Withhold national accreditation of administrator preparation programs unless programs meet the standards specified in the National Policy Board's report and require that criteria for state accreditation and program approval include these standards.

The reform proposals of the National Policy Board include some controversial ideas, such as the recommendations that prospective school administrators be required to complete two years of full-time study (including one full-time year of fieldwork), obtain a doctorate degree before being permitted to administer a school or school district, and pass a national certification examination. These three recommendations, in particular, may need to be modified somewhat in order to be more acceptable to university officials, legislators, state school officers, and practitioners.

Restructuring Efforts Underway

Several efforts are underway across the United States to restructure preparation programs for school administrators. Universities, school districts, and state boards of education are at work revamping curricula, forging stronger relationships between universities and local school systems, and insisting on practical exercises, fieldwork, and internships for prospective school administrators.[31]

One aggressive approach to restructuring is taking place in the Department of Educational Administration at Hofstra University under the direction of Charol Shakeshaft, department chair. For several years now, the faculty has been working to overhaul their preparation program for school administrators. The new program includes meaningful full-year internships in local schools, role-playing and problem-solving exercises, staff development of faculty including allocation of time spent in local schools, and aggressive recruiting of women and minorities into the program, followed by placement of degree recipients into administrative positions in the local schools. Other components of the program involve faculty and practitioners' review of the curriculum annually, student surveys of coursework completed, and exit interviews of graduating students with a panel of professors.

The American Association of School Administrators (AASA) has entered the restructuring movement with its award program for outstanding achievement in leadership preparation. AASA annually recognizes universities for substantive achievement in the preparation of school administrators. Two universities received the AASA Recognition Award for Outstanding Achievement in Leadership Preparation in 1990: Boston University and East Texas State University.[32]

A program coordinated by the School of Management and the School of Education at Boston University relies on the case-study method to provide training in educational administration in an urban setting. Curriculum modules include site-based management with limited financial resources, conflict resolution, observing and analyzing teaching, school-site planning, computer technology, and curriculum planning and development.

The Department of Educational Administration at East Texas State University provides carefully selected, experienced teachers in Texas with the leadership skills needed to become instruction-oriented principals. The program has

---

[31]Del Stover, "Education Is Getting Serious About Administrator Preparation," *Executive Educator*, 12 (1990), pp. 18–20.

[32]AASA Leadership Preparation Awards, "Preparing the Best Educational Leaders," *School Administrator*, 4 (1990), p. 32.

a fifteen-month preservice component, beginning in June and continuing through August of the following year. Coursework during the first summer prepares participants to fill an intern administrator's role on a full-time basis during the following academic year. Each student serves an internship under a selected principal acting as both supervisor and mentor.

While an intern, the student continues coursework toward principal certification in Texas and participates in a colloquium series emphasizing the instructional role of the principal. At the conclusion of the internship, the student returns to East Texas State University to complete certification requirements. Students receive specialized study in conflict resolution, problem identification, problem solving, solution planning, data analysis, team building, and consensus building.

Some states, like Kentucky, have mandated reform of administrator-preparation programs. On July 1, 1988, the Kentucky education department implemented a two-tier administrator-preparation program, which in effect doubled the number of credits required for principal and supervisor certification.[33] The new mandated reform calls for tougher admission standards into administrator-certification programs, including assessment of administrative aptitude measured by a standardized national test, a master's degree in teaching, and a standard teaching certificate. Candidates for certification must pass a state-certified examination in school administration. In addition, a one-year, full-time internship under the supervision and mentorship of a three-member, state-appointed committee consisting of a district superintendent or designee, a principal mentor, and a university educator is required for initial certification. Completion of the first tier of the program allows graduates to administer schools for up to five years. During this time, the principal is serving a probationary period. The final tier of the program allows permanent certification when participants complete the remainder of the courses while holding an administrative position.

WOMEN AND MINORITIES

Concerns about career development for women and minorities is a direct outgrowth of equal employment opportunity and affirmative action legislation. Although women and minorities are advancing within the private sector, they are still underrepresented in educational administration. When the pool of leadership talent is artificially and arbitrarily reduced, it deprives society of unrealized potential. The inequity of influence based on gender and race in our school systems is the focus of this section.

Administrative Careers for Woman

It is unusual to find women running our nation's school systems. Less than 4 percent of America's school districts have women superintendents. This is surprising when one considers that the education field since the beginning of the twentieth century has been predominantly female. At present, women constitute 66 percent of the nation's teachers—82 percent elementary and 47 percent secondary.[34]

The AASA conducted a national survey of the representation of women and racial minorities in school administration. AASA's Office of Minority Affairs determined the number of women and minorities in the superintendency, the assistant superintendency, and the principalship. Results indicated that 3.7 percent of the superintendents, 22 percent of the assistant superintendents, and 24 percent of the principals were women.[35]

Several studies have suggested that there are career differences between male and female school administrators. Women have more years of teaching experience than men (fifteen years

---

[33]Kentucky Revised Statutes, Ch. 161.027 (1988).

[34]*Digest of Educational Statistics* (Washington, D.C.: Government Printing Office, 1990).

[35]Effie H. Jones and Xenia P. Montenegro, *Women and Minorities in School Administration* (Arlington, VA: American Association of School Administrators, 1988).

versus five years) and are older when appointed to administrative positions (median age forty for women, thirty-two for men). Hence, women are deprived of equal access to administrative positions. In addition, one study found that both groups worked approximately fifty-five hours per week, although the women earned substantially less than men.[36]

Discrimination continues to plague women, not only in terms of salary but also in terms of access into administrative positions and sexual harassment once they make their way into the administrative hierarchy. In fact, by the mid-1980s, women were dropping out of administrative positions more frequently than men. Dissatisfaction with institutional decisions, decision-making processes, current leadership, limited upward mobility, lack of mentoring or sponsorship, sexual harassment, and feelings of isolation were cited as contributing factors.[37]

Numerous frameworks for explaining the underrepresentation of women in educational administration have been proposed.[38] These are typically placed within the domains of internal and external barriers.

Internal Barriers   Internal barriers include long-established beliefs that are frequently referred to as stereotypes or myths. These barriers include socialization patterns and background experiences that typify many women and gender-role stereotypes about the abilities of women, their motivations, and their career aspirations.

The concept of socialization focuses on the idea that women have been trained to fill nurturing roles rather than leadership roles in society.

Traditional cultural definitions of femininity emphasize attributes such as sensitivity, conformity, lack of assertiveness, and dependency. However, school administrators are expected to be aggressive, assertive, and competitive; but, at the same time, these traits manifested in women are perceived as negative.

For this reason, society conditions both men and women to believe that women are not as capable of holding leadership positions as men. This notion is not supported by research. Studies by W. W. Charters and Thomas Jovick and the National Association of Secondary School Principals substantiate the superior performance of female school administrators.[39] In addition, Neal Gross and Anne Trask examined the association of gender and competence of elementary school principals in forty-one U.S. cities. Results indicated that the performance of teachers and student achievement was higher in schools headed by female principals than those administered by male principals.[40]

Perhaps partly as a function of their socialization and role conflict is the myth that women tend to have lower career aspirations than men do. Flora Ida Ortiz and Catherine Marshall conclude from their research that, contrary to popular belief, women *do* aspire to administrative careers. These authors suggest that although women have the same career ambitions as men, they do not have the same opportunities. Furthermore, women are denied access to the administration hierarchy, not because of lack of aspirations, but because of "faulty characteristics" unintentionally or intentionally ascribed to them—characteristics that assume

[36]Diana G. Pounder, "The Male/Female Salary Differential for School Administrators: Implications for Career Patterns and Placement of Women," *Educational Administration Quarterly*, 24 (1988), pp. 5–19.

[37]Linda J. Reisser and Linda A. Zurfluh, "Female Administrators: Moving Up, or Moving Out?" *Journal of NAWAC*, 50 (1987), pp. 22–29.

[38]For a comprehensive treatment of women in educational administration, see Charol Shakeshaft, *Women in Educational Administration*, updated edition (Newbury Park, CA: Sage, 1989).

[39]W. W. Charters and Thomas D. Jovick, "The Gender of Principals and Principal–Teacher Relationships in Elementary Schools," in P. A. Schmuck, W. W. Charters, and R. O. Carlson (eds.), *Educational Policy Management: Sex Differentials* (New York: Academic Press, 1981), pp. 307–331; National Association of Secondary School Principals, *Concerns: From the Council of Chief State School Officers Resource Center on Sex Equity* (Alexandria, VA: NASSP, 1983).

[40]Neal Gross and Anne E. Trask, *The Sex Factor in the Management of Schools* (New York: Wiley, 1976).

their inability to perform effectively as school administrators.[41]

External Barriers   External barriers are inherent in the employing organizations. School districts are often designed in ways that help preserve the existing structure. These structures are created either unconsciously or consciously, to ensure the continued participation of the dominant group—that is, white males—and restrict entry and career advancement of other groups—for example, women and minorities. External barriers include such factors as recruitment and selection strategies, evaluation and reward systems, power and authority systems, and other norms and expectations of the organization.[42]

Probably the most far-reaching barrier denying women entrance and advancement in public school administration is role discrimination. These are societal perceptions of traditional and appropriate female and male roles. Society views administration as a predominantly male job. As nurturers and caregivers, women are supposed to be content in instructional roles. That is, men are supposed to be the leaders, and women are supposed to be the followers.[43]

As a result, those who hire school administrators, the majority of whom are male, expect hirees to be male as well. Artificial and arbitrary nonjob-related limitations are placed on women when a position is filled. Examples are failure to recruit; the use of criteria that favor men, such as administrative experience in finance, physical facilities, and contract negotiations; encouragement and sponsorship of male applicants; and excluding females from the power and authority structures of the organization. One author notes that sponsors or mentors encourage

TABLE 16-2   Distribution of School Administration, 1988

RACE/ETHNICITY	NUMBER	PERCENTAGE
Native American	227	0.3
Asian/Pacific Islander	533	0.7
Black	7,585	10.0
Hispanic	4,060	5.4
White	63,665	83.6
TOTAL	76,211	

SOURCE: Adapted from Effie H. Jones and Xenia P. Montenegro, *Women and Minorities in School Administration,* © 1988, p. 27. Used by permission of American Association of School Administrators, Arlington, VA.

and select their protégés and these protégés are selected in the likeness of the mentors. Because men are in the dominant position in most administrative positions, women are less likely to be selected because they do not share the "white male norms" of male mentors.[44] What results, in essence, is a circular socialization process. Men ensure the continued perpetuation of the dominant group, that is, white males. (See the PRO/CON Debate.)

Administrative Careers for Racial Minorities

Members of minority groups are even rarer than women in public school administration. Table 16-2 shows the distribution of school administrators by race. As shown, 16.4 percent of school administrators belong to racial minority groups. Specifically, 10 percent are black, 5.4 percent are Hispanic, 0.7 percent are Asian/Pacific Islanders, and 0.3 percent are Native American.

[41]Flora Ida Ortiz and Catherine Marshall, "Women in Educational Administration," in N. J. Boyan (ed.), *Handbook of Research on Educational Administration* (New York: Longman, 1988), pp. 123–142.

[42]Jeff Hearn et al. (eds.), *The Sexuality of Organization* (Newbury Park, CA: Sage, 1990).

[43]Sylvia Walley, *Women, Theory and Society: From Private to Public Patriarchy* (Cambridge, MA: Basil Blackwell, 1990).

[44]Leonard A. Valverde, "Promotion Socialization: The Informal Process in Large Urban Districts and Its Adverse Affect on Non-Whites and Women," *Journal of Educational Equity and Leadership*, 1 (1980), pp. 36–46.

PRO/CON DEBATE

■

OLD-BOY NETWORK

Women and minorities are underrepresented in administrative ranks. For women, the problem is related to placement. Since the mid-1970s, at least 50 percent of the students in educational administration programs have been women. The pool of female administrative candidates is available, but it is only moderately tapped. For minorities, the problem is recruitment and placement. Minority enrollment in certification programs is insufficient to meet projected needs. Like women, many ethnic minorities are stalled in low- and middle-management posts. Why do these situations persist?

QUESTION Does the existence of an old-boy network prevent able women and minorities from assuming administrative positions?

ARGUMENTS PRO

1 Power brokers limit the upward mobility of women and minorities. Few people make it to the top without the imprimatur of the handful of men who open doors and smooth the path.

2 Those in power mentor protégés with promise. The criteria mentors use are the same that were used to identify them. Their personal prejudices do not allow them to envision women and minorities as the next generation of leaders. They select white protégés who look and act as they do.

3 The establishment decides how to portray school leadership and develops the strategies to ensure that their profile of a good leader is accepted as the norm. The people who name the top educational leaders of the year perpetuate their profile of white male leadership.

4 Boards routinely consult experts in the educational establishment to guide them as they make decisions. Boards are influenced by the "old boys" who seek to maintain the status quo because it is the source of their power.

5 Able women and minorities have always been in the pipeline. Their careers are unsupported by the power brokers, so they remain in secondary positions.

ARGUMENTS CON

1 Upward mobility is the result of many factors: individuals' dispositions and talents, the needs of a particular school or district, the boards' willingness to consider atypical candidates, timing, and luck.

2 Today, many current administrators try to mentor capable women and minorities. However, internal barriers inhibit women and minorities from assuming important roles. They lack a sense of career, fear power, and do not know how to play the system.

3 Administrators chosen for top positions are selected on the basis of their ability to transmit the culture of the organization. They are symbolic leaders. Many communities and organizations are not ready yet for women and minority leaders.

4 Search consultants have encouraged boards to consider protected-class candidates with little success. For example, until recently female board members usually appointed male superintendents.

5 Women and minorities do not have the prerequisite career experience for top administration. There are promising candidates in the pipeline.

About eight out of every ten school administrators (83.6 percent) are white.

At the three surveyed levels—superintendent, assistant superintendent, and principal—the breakdown is as follows: Three percent of the superintendents, 12 percent of the assistant superintendents, and 15 percent of the principals are individuals from racial or ethnic minority groups.

These results closely parallel the findings of another study that profiled superintendents and principals nationwide, based on a random sample of 1704 public school superintendents, 1349 public school principals, and 524 principals in private schools.[45] The only difference in the results from the two studies was the percentage of racial minorities in the principalship. This study reported that 90 percent of the public school principals were white. The AASA survey found that 84 percent of the principals were white, while 16 percent belonged to racial minorities.

Analyzing black representation in school administration separately, both studies found that 1 percent of the nation's superintendents are black, as are 6 percent of the principals. This compares with 13 percent of blacks in the U.S. population, 11 percent of all employed persons, 6 percent of all college graduates, 7 percent of workers in professional occupations, 5 percent of executives and managers in the private sector, and 6 percent of the nation's teachers.[46] These statistics reveal that racial minorities—especially blacks—are still disproportionately represented in school administration.

We speculate that many of the same internal and external barriers cited with respect to the restricted access of women into educational administration apply to minorities as well. One additional concern is the number of blacks in teaching. Unless there is a sudden increase in the number of black teachers, the number of black school administrators in the United States could begin to decline during the 1990s.

Every time a talented minority or female student opts for a "job" rather than a "career," society loses. School districts need the brightest and best people—whatever their race or gender—in leadership positions. (See Administrative Advice 16-4.)

Programs for Women and Minorities

Programs exist in a variety of forms to help women and racial minorities who are interested in careers in educational administration. The programs are designed specifically to address their problems: socialization patterns, low aspirational levels, discrimination, and limited access of both groups into positions in educational administration. Some programs still exist; others have been discontinued. The following are highlights of these programs.[47]

Lyman T. Johnson Fellows Minority Leadership Development Program   In 1989 the University of Louisville and the Jefferson County (Kentucky) Public Schools developed the Lyman T. Johnson Fellows Leadership Development Program. Its purpose is twofold: to identify specific needs of minority candidates for the principalship and to provide developmental preparation activities that maximize each participant's potential. The program focuses on the individual through collegial support groups, mentoring activities, simulations, field experiences, and course offerings in educational administration at the University of Louisville. It is funded by the University of Louisville's Center for Excellence.

[45]Emily Feistritzer, *Profile of School Administrators in the United States* (Washington, D.C.: The National Center for Education Information, 1988).

[46]*Current Population Reports* (Washington, D.C.: Government Printing Office, 1990); *1989 Status Report on Minorities in Higher Education* (Washington, D.C.: Government Printing Office, 1990).

[47]S. Tonnsen et al., *Programs for Preparing Minorities and Women in Educational Administration* (Research Triangle Park, NC: Southeastern Educational Improvement Laboratory, 1989).

ADMINISTRATIVE ADVICE 16-4

■

POSITIVE ROLE MODELS CAN COMBAT STEREOTYPING

Helping students encounter positive role models is one way to diminish career stereotyping. Another way is to provide bias-free programs and curriculum materials. Here are some steps school administrators and teachers can take:

- *Use Unbiased Materials*. Select textbooks and other classroom resources that fairly represent all kinds of people.
- *Offer Career-Awareness Programs*. Career awareness should begin in the early elementary school years. Such programs should introduce students to a wide range of appealing role models; at higher grade levels, the programs could introduce the idea of building a long-term career plan that allows for flexibility and mobility.
- *Give Academic Guidance*. Students need to know why rigorous study and high-level courses are important to their future careers. This academic guidance should begin at an early age because many people commit to a field as early as middle school.
- *Counsel Students on Higher Education*. All students, even those who don't expect to go to college, can benefit from guidance on continuing

their education after high school. Consider, also, the possibility of women's colleges: Some believe that such institutions can give young women a healthy self-image and a head start in the work world.
- *Use Role Models*. Invite women and minority community members to school to "model" specific careers, especially those in which women and minorities are underrepresented. School–business partnerships can be a source of such role models. Or you might use videotapes and films that present images of women and minorities doing successful, satisfying work in the middle and upper levels in their fields.

Source: Adapted from Dianne Pevonka, Sharon Griffin, and Joan L. Curcio, "Positive Role Models Combat Race and Sex Stereotypes," *Executive Educator*, 10 (1988), pp. 26–28. Copyright 1988, the National School Boards Association. Used by permission.

Leadership Opportunity Experience for Teachers (LEO-T) In 1986 the Dade County (Florida) schools instituted a program that offers qualified teachers an opportunity to become assistant principals and principals. Dade County places special emphasis on recruiting from groups that traditionally have been underrepresented in the principalship: ethnic and language minorities and women. Each year, after carefully screening applicants, twenty-six candidates participate in two nine-week school assignments supervised and mentored by carefully selected, experienced principals. The LEO-T program has been re-

markably successful. Approximately three-quarters of the teachers who have completed the program are now assistant principals or principals in the Dade County schools.

Minority Administrator's Program (MAP) Begun in 1986, the University of South Carolina's MAP is designed specifically for prospective black minority school administrators. Its purpose is threefold: to identify a cadre of minority educators to serve as public school administrators, to enhance the problem-solving skills of prospective black school administrators, and to place black minorities in administrative positions.

Administrative Intern Program (AIP) Since 1980 the Duval County (Jacksonville, Florida) School District has been operating AIP for women and racial minorities. Its purpose is threefold: to address the need for securing a balance of women and racial minority staff within each of the district's seven divisions that approximates the general composition of the relevant external labor market, to broaden the base from which female and racial minority future administrators might be identified, and to render the women and racial minorities more competitive with respect to the hiring process.

Internships, Certification Equity/Leadership and Support (ICES) Developed in Kansas, ICES awards scholarships to allow women to attend university summer sessions and ICES workshops on topics such as conflict management, finance, and the politics of education. ICES interns spend ten months in structured school district experiences. ICES is funded by the Women's Educational Equity Act Program (WEEAP).

Women in School Administration (WISA) The program provides field-based courses in an effort to recruit women in rural areas and provide a statewide recruitment and selection policy. It offers workshops in conflict management, power and leadership, time management, and assertiveness training. WISA interns train for ten months in rural school districts across the United States. WISA is also funded by WEEAP.

Assisting Women to Advance through Resources and Encouragement (AWARE) Sponsored by AASA, AWARE provides workshops at six project sites and hosts annual AASA meetings on topics such as networking, self-concept, enlisting sponsors, and interviewing techniques. These programs are targeted at female aspirants to positions in educational administration.

Women in Administration Training Project (WATP) Charol Shakeshaft initiated the program at Hofstra University ten years ago. To date, over 300 female administrative aspirants have participated in the program. In addition to receiving coursework in educational administration at Hofstra, they have been provided with a resource book containing information dealing with strategies for increasing women's access to administrative positions, and annual reunions have been scheduled on a regular basis. Numerous female graduates from the program have been placed in administrative positions in Long Island (New York) schools.

Sex Equity in Educational Leadership (SEEL) Developed in Oregon, this program identifies female teachers and graduate students with administrative potential and provides them with training dealing with entry strategies into school administration.

Female Leaders for Administration and Management in Education (FLAME) This national program sponsors interns who take leaves of absence to pursue full-time graduate studies in educational administration.

Women and Administration Institute (WAI) The program was developed at the University of Southern Florida and is funded by the WEEAP.

Other programs for women and minorities include the Northwest Women in Educational Administration (NWEA), the Oregon Network, the New England Coalition of Educational Leadership (NECEL), the Women's Caucus of the Pennsylvania School Administrator's Association (PASA), the Institute for Administrative Advancement at the University of Wisconsin–Madison, the San Diego Minority and Women Administrators' Training Project at San Diego State University, and the Leadership Skills for Women Administrators at the University of South Carolina.

SUMMARY

1. A career can be defined as a series of movements in an organization, a profession, or a sequence of work-related experiences during a person's lifetime.
2. Careers in educational administration follow predictable stages that include apprenticeship, independent contributor, mentor, and sponsor.
3. School administrators are subject to high levels of personal and job-related stress.
4. Stress is the physiological and psychological response of an individual to demands, constraints, and opportunities involving uncertainty and important outcomes.
5. Stress comes from many sources including organizational, personal, and nonorganizational factors. Organizational factors are excessively high or low job demands, role conflicts and ambiguities, poor interpersonal relations, transition from one career stage to another, and overpromotion or underpromotion. Personal factors include need for achievement, capabilities, and personality. Nonorganizational factors are life and career changes and dual-career problems.
6. Career development is another important responsibility of school administrators. School administrators must take charge of their own careers in order to maximize their success. Because school administrators supervise others, they will also be involved in assisting subordinates in their career development.
7. Career development from both the individual's and the organization's standpoint involves several techniques. Individual strategies include self-appraisal, exploring opportunities, setting goals, preparing plans, and implementing plans. Organizational techniques include career counseling, career pathing, career-resources planning, and career-information systems.
8. Career development for women and minorities is extremely important. In the past, these groups have been subjected to reduced career opportunities in educational administration. This situation is changing as a result of programs designed specifically to help women and minorities to become more integrated into educational administration.

KEY TERMS

career
career stage
apprentice stage
independent-contributor stage
networking
mentoring
mentor stage
sponsor stage
stress
stressors
Type A personality

meditation
biofeedback
career development
career planning
career management
career counseling
career pathing
career-resources planning
career-information systems

DISCUSSION QUESTIONS

1. What is a career? How does it differ from a job?
2. What are the stages identified in Dalton and Thompson's career stages framework? What things can individuals and organizations do that might enhance the development of individuals at various stages in their careers?
3. What are the sources, symptoms, and effects of administrative stress?
4. What are some individual and organizational strategies for coping with administrative stress.
5. What are the special problems women and minorities face in their careers in educational administration. What programs exist to help them overcome these problems?

SUGGESTED READINGS

Michael B. Arthur et al. (eds.), *Handbook of Career Theory* (New York: Cambridge University Press, 1990). A cross-disciplinary text designed to appeal to a diversity of social science scholars.

Anne Boe and Bettie B. Youngs, *Is Your "Net" Working? A Complete Guide to Building Contacts and Career Visibility* (Oil City, PA: Park Avenue Press, 1990). Deals with advice for women on how to network their way to career and job success.

Lynn Davies, *Equity and Efficiency* (New York: Falmer Press, 1990). Examines the reasons why, in practice, the hormonization of equity and efficiency has not proved feasible.

George B. Graen, *Unwritten Rules for Your Career: The 15 Secrets for Fast Track Success* (New York: Wiley, 1989). A useful text for anyone interested in the secrets of career success.

Jeanne Gregory, *Sex, Race, and the Law: Legislating for Equality* (Newbury Park, CA: Sage, 1988). No-

table for its emphasis on the links between race and sex-discrimination law and the very different "structure of disadvantage" revealed through the analyses of case law.

Jeff Hearn et al. (eds.), *The Sexuality of Organization* (Newbury Park, CA: Sage, 1990). Reminds us that the sexual regime, as much as unequal jobs and salary, keeps women down at work.

Charol Shakeshaft, *Women in Educational Administration*, updated edition (Newbury Park, CA: Sage, 1989). By the recipient of the Women Educators' Research Award and the Jack A. Culbertson Award, a comprehensive treatment of women's issues in educational administration.

Name Index

Subject Index